Market Institutions in Sub-Saharan Africa

Comparative Institutional Analysis (CIA) Series
Series Editors: Masahiko Aoki, Avner Greif, and Paul Milgrom

Market Institutions in Sub-Saharan Africa
Theory and Evidence

Marcel Fafchamps

The MIT Press
Cambridge, Massachusetts
London, England

This book was set in Times New Roman on 3B2 by Asco Typesetters, Hong Kong, and was printed and bound in the United States of America.

Library of Congress Cataloging-in-Publication Data

Fafchamps, Marcel.
  Market institutions in sub-Saharan Africa : theory and evidence / Marcel Fafchamps.
    p.   cm. — (Comparative institutional analysis)
  Includes bibliographical references and index.
  ISBN 0-262-06236-4 (hc. : alk. paper)
  1. Africa, sub-Saharan—Economic policy. 2. Capitalism—Africa, sub-Saharan. 3. Free enterprise—Africa, sub-Saharan. 4. Africa, sub-Saharan—Commerce. I. Title. II. Series.
HC800.F33   2004
330.967—dc21   2003052775

10 9 8 7 6 5 4 3 2 1

To Abby, Lionel, and Yvan

Contents

Preface

This book presents ten years of personal research on market institutions in sub-Saharan Africa. Evidence from surveys undertaken in twelve African countries is presented. Although the emphasis of this book is empirical, models are presented that clarify the assumptions underlying the research and sharpen the insights gained from empirical work.

The overarching goal of the book is to develop a better understanding of market institutions in sub-Saharan Africa. Ultimately it should help develop appropriate policy for improving both economic growth and income distribution in Africa. The book is primarily addressed to research economists interested in Africa. However, except for the six theoretical chapters (2, 8, 11, 12, 14, and 17), the material presented here is accessible to researchers in a number of fields as well as policy practitioners. The book can be used for economics courses focusing on Africa.

The history behind this book project is a long one. It starts in Africa itself where I worked for several years before getting a PhD and turning to academe. As associate expert in the Addis Ababa office of the International Labour Organization, I had an opportunity to travel to many parts of sub-Saharan Africa. This is the time when I made my first casual observations about contractual issues. I noted that it was frequent for contractual promises to be ignored or renegotiated but also that people often formed personal bonds stronger than contracts. Since I have a law degree, I was intrigued by these observations because they forced me to challenge the legalistic and formal view of contracts that I had inherited from my training. Living in a difficult and uncertain environment (this was at the height of the military dictatorship), I had many opportunities to reflect that, in an unpredictable world, contracts were difficult to respect. Trust was needed for trade to take place, and trust originated primarily in interpersonal relationships. The organization of African markets in the form of networks had been described by many, regardless of their position on the political spectrum (e.g., Bauer 1954; Jones 1959; Amselle 1977; Cohen 1969; Meillassoux 1971; Staatz 1979).

I then left Africa for California, got a PhD at UC Berkeley, went to work for Stanford University, and forgot about contracts. I thought the issue was important, but I did not see how trust and interpersonal relationships could be modeled using economic theory. This changed in 1990 when Dilip Abreu came to Stanford to teach a course on repeated games. An assistant professor at the time, I audited the course and realized how the formal framework could be used to model long-term relationships. This rekindled my interest in contractual issues. Following the literature of the time (e.g., Kimball 1988; Coate and Ravallion 1993; Kocherlakota 1996; Ligon et al. 2001), my first applications of repeated games went to risk sharing. I published a thought piece in EDCC (Fafchamps 1992), a theoretical exercise on informal credit

(Fafchamps 1999a), and launched empirical work on risk-sharing networks that came to full fruition much later (e.g., Fafchamps and Lund 2002; Fafchamps and Gubert 2002).

While teaching at Stanford in the early 1990s, I came in contact with Paul Milgrom, Masa Aoki, Barry Weingast, and Avner Greif, and became aware of their work on markets and institutions. I met with Douglas North, a frequent visitor to Stanford, and benefited greatly from discussions with him and the rest of the comparative institutions group. Jean-Philippe Platteau also visited Stanford around this time, and we discussed his ideas on markets, subsequently published in a two-part article (Platteau 1994a, b). Coming across the work of sociologists on networks and markets (e.g., Mitchell 1969; Granovetter 1995b), I became interested in graph theory as a way to model networks. I formalized my ideas in two unpublished papers written in 1992, one on the formation of trust—which forms the basis for chapter 8—and another on networks—which is at the core of chapter 17. Based on my understanding of the theoretical literature at the time, I formulated a series of conjectures on traders and markets that are revisited in chapter 1.

In 1992 I was thus ready to envisage empirical work on markets. The opportunity arose when I was asked to collaborate with the Regional Program for Enterprise Development run by the Africa Division of the World Bank. Tyler Biggs, a former HIID hand, was heading the program. Its purpose was to conduct panel surveys on manufacturing firms in Africa. From his earlier years in Taiwan, Tyler was seriously interested in supplier credit as an alternative credit channel for small manufacturers. The strong emphasis on trade credit that he imparted to the early RPED research turned out to provide me with a perfect vantage point from which to examine the respect of contracts.

I was commissioned with others to undertake a study of enterprise finance in African manufacturing. The study was to be based on detailed interviews with subsets of RPED panel firms in different African countries, plus a number of suppliers and clients. We started with Ghana. Following a first visit in September 1992 during which I participated to the RPED survey itself, the small enterprise finance survey took place in January 1993. The small format of the survey enabled me to participate personally at half of the interviews. Under the direction of Carlos Cuevas, the report from this survey was co-authored by Rebecca Hanson, Peter Moll, Pradeep Srivastava, and myself (Cuevas et al. 1993). An unabridged version of my contribution to this report was subsequently published in World Development (Fafchamps 1996). The theoretical model presented in chapter 2 borrows heavily from this article while chapters 4 and 9 build on the empirical results presented there.

Kenya was the next country studied as part of the RPED research on enterprise finance. Survey work took place in September 1993. I coordinated the writing of the

report, which was finalized in June 1994 with contributions from Tyler Biggs, Joha-
than Conning, and Pradeep Srivastava (Fafchamps et al. 1994). By then I was getting
a better handle on the subject and the report was more ambitious, with detailed
coverage of screening practices, socialization, contract enforcement, and the like. The
results confirmed earlier results from Ghana and generated new insights. Empirical
results from this report form the basis for chapters 4, 9, and 21.

The Kenya report was followed by another small survey in Zimbabwe in August
1994. The survey was conducted in Harare with the assistance of John Pender and
Elisabeth Robinson. Again, I was present at more than half of the interviews. The
report was released by the World Bank in April 1995 (Fafchamps et al. 1995). It
revisited some of the issues studied in Ghana and Kenya but expanded coverage to
other issues such as equity financing and loan monitoring. Using the small survey
data, I published an article on trade credit in Zimbabwe (Fafchamps 1997c). Data
from Kenya and Zimbabwe were subsequently combined to produce an article on
ethnicity and credit (Fafchamps 2000). Chapters 4, 9, 13, and 21 borrow from the
Zimbabwe report while chapter 19 is based on the later article.

The initial intention had been to combine the evidence from the small surveys and
the panel surveys into a World Bank sponsored book on enterprise finance in Africa.
Unfortunately, by 1995 nearly all RPED survey teams had fallen out with Tyler, and
the project was abandoned. The consequence was that I failed to gain the access I
had been promised to the panel data.

During this period of RPED research, I came into contact with a number of
people working on related issues, notably Rachel Kranton, Chris Woodruff, Debraj
Ray, and Alessandra Casella. I came to realize that the issues I had been studying in
Africa were of general interest to the economic profession. I also noticed that we
were all gravitating toward similar issues of contract enforcement, trust, search, and
networks. Drawing inspiration from the work of other researchers as well as from my
own fieldwork experience, I wrote theoretical material on market emergence, reputation, and ethnicity. This work, which summarizes the main insights from my three
years of fieldwork, was initially written in 1995 and partly published electronically in
2002 (Fafchamps 2002b). This material forms the basis of chapters 11, 12, and 17.

In January 1996, I was fortunate to begin collaboration with the Industrial Surveys
in Africa (ISA) group led by Paul Collier, Jan Willem Gunning, and Arne Bigsten.
The ISA group was an unusual collaboration in economics as it brought together
a dozen of researchers from diverse backgrounds working together on the RPED
panel data. Individuals or groups of researchers took responsibility for preparing
drafts of specific papers that were then discussed by the group and published jointly.
In collaboration with the group, I wrote an article on contract enforcement using
data from six RPED study countries. This paper, which I co-authored with Bigsten,

Collier, Dercon, Gauthier, Gunning, Isaksson, Oduro, Oostendorp, Patillo, Soderbom, Teal, and Zeufack (Bigsten et al. 2000a), forms the basis for chapter 5, albeit
with an expanded data set. Many other papers were produced by the ISA group
(Bigsten et al. 1999a, b, 2000, 2002). Participation to ISA work indirectly contributed
to the present volume by reinforcing my familiarity with the African manufacturing
sector.

Around the same period, I co-authored a paper on inventories and contractual risk
in Zimbabwe together with Jan Willem Gunning and Remco Oostendorp (Fafchamps et al. 2000). For chapter 7, I reran part of that analysis using data from nine
African countries instead of Zimbabwe alone.

At this point my work on manufacturing firms was reaching an end. With the exception of Ghana where, under the direction of Francis Teal, Oxford University kept
the manufacturing panel alive, data collection on manufacturing firms in Africa was
at a standstill.[1] Furthermore it was time to investigate market institutions in economic activities other than manufacturing.

While spending a summer at the International Food Policy Research Institute
(IFPRI) in 1995, I had discussed my research interests with Ousmane Badiane,
then in the markets division. IFPRI was actively collecting data from agricultural
traders in a number of African countries, and Ousmane immediately showed a deep
interest in the research topic. But funding was a problem. After several efforts, we
were finally successful in securing funds for a survey on contract enforcement among
agricultural traders in Madagascar. We obtained funding in late August 1997 and,
literally overnight, I wrote a questionnaire and hopped on a plane for Antananarivo
to launch the survey.

In Madagascar, I linked up with Bart Minten, whom I had met before at IFPRI.
This was to be the beginning of a long and fruitful collaboration. The Madagascar
survey was conducted from September to December 1997. It led to numerous publications and a book chapter (e.g., Fafchamps and Minten 1999, 2001a, 2002b, c).

Having clarified the operation of agricultural markets in Madagascar, it was vital
to validate our results in other African countries. Once again, the collaboration of
IFPRI was sought. With funding from the World Bank and the assistance of Mylene
Kherallah and Nick Minot at IFPRI, we managed to secure funds for a repeat of the
Madagascar survey in Benin and Malawi. A former student of mine with a lot of
experience surveying traders, Eleni Gabre-Madhin, joined the team and in mid-1999,

---

1. This work was subsequently revived by Oxford University with funding from UNIDO, and new panel
surveys were undertaken in Kenya, Tanzania, and Nigeria. The World Bank itself has now rekindled its
interest in manufacturing surveys in Africa.

agricultural trader surveys were launched in the two countries. Data from these surveys were used for two papers on transactions costs that are not used in this volume (e.g., Fafchamps and Gabre-Madhin 2001; Fafchamps et al. 2002). The data from Benin and Malawi were combined with those from Madagascar to produce a paper on returns to social capital (Fafchamps and Minten 2001b).

The papers written on the basis of the agricultural trader survey data form the basis for chapters 6, 10, part of 13, and 16. In 2001 a survey of Madagascar traders was retaken with funding from USAID and the Pew Charitable Trust. To date, this survey has resulted in a single-authored paper on ethnicity and networks that was presented at PEW conference in 2002 (Fafchamps 2002a). This paper uses data from the 2001 Madagascar survey as well as the 1999 surveys in Benin and Malawi. It is the inspiration for chapter 20.

My research on market institutions continues. Following on my work on property rights with Bart Minten, I have begun examining crime and law enforcement using a national census of communes that Bart and I conducted in Madagascar in 2001, as well as a follow-up survey that Bart managed to organize in the middle of the presidential election crisis of 2002. To date, two papers have been written on these issues. One shows that crime is more prevalent in rural areas, the other that a poverty shock increases some forms of property crime but has no effect on organized crime.

Together with Mans Soderbom, I have begun looking at moral hazard within firms. In this spirit we recently wrote a paper on worker supervision in African manufacturing (Fafchamps and Soderbom 2002). This paper combines matched employer-employee data from the RPED surveys with a 2000 World Bank manufacturing survey I helped organize in Morocco. Analysis of the agricultural data from Benin, Malawi, and Madagascar (2001) is not completed. A detailed analysis of transactions costs has been completed. It suggests that increasing returns to scale are absent or very weak in African agricultural trade. Further work on entry and exit of traders is underway. At of the time of writing, a survey of coffee producers and traders in Uganda is at the planning stage, with possible extensions to other countries. Other opportunities for fruitful work along these lines will no doubt materialize in the future.

In this book the presence of firms of various sizes is taken as given. We simply seek to understand how existing firms deal with each other. As we will see, this is not a trivial question. But the answers we come up with may ultimately depend on the size distribution of firms. As I noted in Fafchamps (1997a), sub-Saharan Africa is characterized by the presence of many small firms and few large ones. Although the methodology used in this book controls for firm size, the suspicion remains that market institutions may look different if firms were fewer and larger. To the extent that market institutions help shape the size distribution of firms, they may have a profound effect on average firm size and hence on aggregate productivity if increasing returns are present. This is a point I already discussed in Fafchamps (1994). I revisit it again in the concluding chapter.

An endeavor as far-reaching as this one can only be the result of a collective effort. Fieldwork on manufacturing firms would not have been possible without the help of Tyler Biggs, Jonathan Conning, Carlos Cuevas, Rebecca Hanson, Peter Moll, John Pender, Elizabeth Robinson, and Pradeep Srivastava. Additional assistance in the field was provided by the members of the economics departments of the universities in Accra, Nairobi, and Harare. Fieldwork on agricultural traders was made possible by the help of Eleni Gabre-Madhin, Mylene Kherallah, Nick Minot, and Bart Minten. Data collection on agricultural traders would not have taken place without the participation of FOFIFA in Madagascar, LARES in Benin, and APRU in Malawi. I particularly wish to thank Jean-Claude Randrianarisoa (FOFIFA), Soulé Bio Goura (LARES), and Richard Kachule (APRU) for their essential contribution to this project. Ousmane Badiane, Chris Barrett, and Gershon Feder were instrumental in securing funding for survey work.

I thank the Industrial Survey in Africa (ISA) team—Arne Bigsten, Paul Collier, Stefan Dercon, Bernard Gauthier, Jan Willem Gunning, Abena Oduro, Remco Oostendorp, Cathy Patillo, Mans Soderbom, Francis Teal, and Albert Zeufack—for accepting me in their ranks and granting me access to the RPED panel data. Their help with the research is gratefully acknowledged.

Manju Kedia assisted with the early data work for the RPED enterprise finance project. Jo van Biesebroeck assisted in merging the RPED data from nine different countries and three different survey rounds. Eliane Ralison and Lalaina Randrianarison helped enter and clean the data from the agricultural survey in Madagascar and produced a number of useful descriptive tables.

Over the years I have received financial support from the World Bank (three small surveys on enterprise finance and supplementary funding for the trader surveys in Benin and Malawi), USAID (1997 agricultural trader survey in Madagascar), GTZ (agricultural survey in Benin and Malawi), and the Pew Charitable Foundation (2001 agricultural trader survey in Madagascar).

Many people have provided comments on various facets of this work. Since it is impossible to do justice to them all, let me thank them collectively. I also would like to thank two anonymous referees who reviewed the book manuscript for The MIT Press and provided many insightful suggestions. All remaining errors are mine.

I ISSUES AND DATA

1 Markets and Traders

The 1980s and 1990s were a period of renewed faith in the virtues of the market. Liberalization, market reform, and privatization constituted the backbone of much policy in the developed world, former socialist economies, and developing countries alike. Paradoxically, little is known about the institutions that support market exchange and how markets can be expected to structure themselves over time. The objective of this book is to throw new light on these issues.

Since the seminal work of North (1973) on the development of capitalism in Europe, the fundamental role that market institutions play in economic growth has become increasingly recognized. In particular, North argued that individual property rights need to be protected from theft and embezzlement as well as from arbitrary expropriation by agents of the state (Cooter 1997). Institutions such as lawyers and courts must exist that ensure compliance with contractual obligations and deter opportunistic breach of contract (Posner 1998).[1] These ideas have largely shaped the research and policy agenda for transition economies and developing countries alike (e.g., Merryman 1977; Eggertsson 1990; Benson 1990; Landa 1994; Baer and Gray 1995; McMillan 1996; Hendley et al. 1998; McMillan and Woodruff 2001). They have also spawn new and insightful research on the various forms that market institutions have taken over the course of human history (e.g., Milgrom et al. 1991; Ensminger 1992; Greif 1993; Greif 1994; Greif 2000).

While most economists now acknowledge that ownership rights must be clearly defined for markets to exist, few go beyond the idea that an efficient court system is necessary and sufficient for market transactions to take place. Much of economics continues to rest on the assumption that economic transactions are anonymous and economic agents perfectly interchangeable, even though other social scientists have often insisted on the personalized nature of much market exchange (e.g., Granovetter 1985; Meillassoux 1971; Amselle 1977; Geertz et al. 1979). Their views are echoed in the works of development economists like Basu (1986), Braverman and Stiglitz (1982), and Bardhan (1995). Williamson (1975) additionally recognized the importance of face-to-face exchange and studied it from the point of view of asset specificity and investment in relationships.

Scholars who have studied the actual performance of markets on the African continent know that institutional arrangements and transaction costs shape patterns of trade and partly determine the extent to which allocative efficiency is achieved. This is true not only in markets where the presence of information asymmetries and enforcement problems are widely acknowledged, like credit, insurance, and labor,

---

1. Messick (1999), however, cautions that little hard evidence exists on the relationship between good legal institutions and development.

but also in markets for land, agricultural outputs, and manufactures. The purpose of this book is to invite a new understanding of the nature of markets in sub-Saharan Africa.

The time is not far when Africa was widely thought to escape the rule of the market. Pre-colonial realities were idealized as gift economics or pre-capitalist collectivism, while many postindependence rulers were declaring their attachment to pan-African socialism. As a result the massive development of market activity that accompanied urbanization and (relative) modernization over the last four decades has gone largely unnoticed. Ironically, one could argue that sub-Saharan Africa today is more market oriented than many advanced countries. Unlike in the West where much of the allocation of resources takes place within large firms and public entities, market transactions remain the dominant allocation mechanism. Take grain, for instance. Except where it is consumed in subsistence farming, getting grain from producer to final consumer requires many more individual transactions in Africa than, say, in the United States. This is because the number of intermediaries is larger and the size of each transaction is smaller. African producers and trade intermediaries are indeed, on average, many times smaller than their Western counterparts. The importance of markets in Africa should therefore not be underestimated.

Yet we know little about how markets operate in practice. Perhaps the best measure of this lack of knowledge is our propensity to call "informal" everything that is not of Western inspiration. The truth is that market activity in Africa is not without form; it is only without economic formalization. It may escape our present understanding, but it does not defy explanation. As we will see in the following pages, African market arrangements and institutions take many forms, and it would be misleading to lump them together into a single "informal sector." A proper investigation of the forms that exchange takes is the object of this book. I show that African market realities are much richer than often recognized. When examined with sufficient care, they appear to the Western eye as both very familiar and inherently remote. The problems that indigenous institutions attempt to solve are the usual ones—commitment failure, asymmetric information, and transactions costs—but the solutions often are original. African market realities are nothing but a transformed image of those in advanced countries. Studying markets in Africa forces us to rethink the very nature of markets.

We will learn that decentralized markets do not necessarily reach efficient outcomes. Market fragmentation is frequent, entry in certain activities is restricted, and individual initiative is not always sufficient to ensure efficiency. Collective action, in the form of government intervention or otherwise, is often welcome and sometimes necessary to help markets achieve their full potential. As the empirical findings presented here demonstrate, a proper understanding of the institutions that support exchange is essential to foster a market-enabling environment. My hope is that this book will help clarify the policy debate on markets in sub-Saharan Africa.

The book brings to light yet another reason why African countries qualify as market economies, namely the overwhelming proportion of Africans who are entrepreneurs. The fraction of Africans who are self-employed and head their own firm is much larger than in developed countries. It is even not uncommon for African households to conduct several businesses simultaneously, such as farming, crafts, trade, and services. Except in South Africa, permanent salaried workers represent a small fraction of the total workforce. It is the extent of allocation by markets, instead of within firms, that characterizes the reality of Africa, and not the absence of markets. This observation then raises another puzzle: Why are large firms so conspicuously absent from the African economic landscape? What induces individuals to initiate several businesses instead of concentrating their resources on a single one? Are African public enterprises in difficulty because they belong to the state or because being large is inherently hard under fragmented market conditions? These issues deserve more research. Although I do not examine these questions here, one of the purposes of this book is to the lay the foundations for such work.

This volume combines theoretical and empirical contributions. Empirical contributions are based on a large number of original surveys, in many of which I have participated. The emphasis is on commodity markets of manufacturing firms and agricultural traders. The theory presented here is built around field observations. Models are presented that capture essential features of African markets and sharpen our understanding of their inner organization. The book switches back and forth between empirical analysis and theory so that they build upon each other to create a comprehensive view of markets in sub-Saharan Africa.

1.1 Allocation and Markets

Before we begin exploring African markets, we need to contrast markets with other possible allocation mechanisms. Allocation can be organized in essentially three different ways: via gift exchange, markets, and hierarchies. Gift exchange is the kind of allocation that takes place within households and families and, to some extent, among friends and neighbors. Gift exchange is different from other allocation mechanisms in that it involves no or few explicit obligations. The division of labor among household members, for instance, is based partly on tradition, and partly on quid pro quo and comparative advantage (e.g., Becker 1981; Fafchamps 2001). Although not all members participate equally in household chores (e.g., Brown and Haddad 1995; Fafchamps and Quisumbing 2002b), there is an implicit understanding that parents, children, siblings, and kin members are all obligated to each other. The founding principle behind gift exchange is that participants must reciprocate for what others do for them by contributing to the collective good of the household or the clan (e.g., Posner 1980; Fafchamps 1992; Platteau 1994a, b).[2]

Like gift exchange, market exchange is based on the concept of reciprocity. In a sales contract, for instance, the buyer reciprocates to the seller by giving money. Because trade is voluntary, what the seller receives must be at least as valuable to her as what she gives. Since the same holds for the buyer, market exchange depends on the existence of gains from trade: the seller must have something that is more valuable to the buyer than to himself for voluntary exchange to take place. This sets markets apart from gift exchange where it is common for exchange to be unequal.[3]

Another sharp distinction between gift and market exchange is that in the latter, reciprocity is explicit. Once buyer and seller have agreed to trade at a specific price and quantity, the contributions of each are clearly defined. In gift exchange, a gift is typically expected to be reciprocated in an unspecified manner at some unspecified future date. In contrast, a seller expects the buyer to reciprocate a precise amount at a specific time. This precision may be a source of confusion and frustration when markets penetrates areas of exchange previously ruled by gift exchange. The need to adhere to the terms of the contract as specified is likely to be challenged, and efforts may be made to renegotiate payment or to delay compliance (Fafchamps and Gabre-Madhin 2001). This clash between market-based and gift-based ethics has long been a source of interest among anthropologists (e.g., Gluckman 1955; Cohen 1969; Sahlins 1972; Ensminger 1992; Landa 1994). To minimize problems, many sales transactions are organized such that compensation is immediate. Rural markets and urban micro-retail are examples of markets dominated by instant trade. To support such markets, the only institutions required are money and a police force that protects property rights.

Although money has no intrinsic value, it can be used by the seller to purchase goods from someone else. Thanks to money, market exchange can organize the allocation of goods and services in a decentralized manner, that is, without external intervention to direct exchange. In addition to being decentralized, markets do not require that agents be altruistic or interested in the common good. In fact markets

2. For instance, by looking after children and helping each other in times of trouble.

3. Think of the distribution of household chores between parents and children in most households, for instance (Fafchamps and Quisumbing 2002b).

work best when agents pursue their own self-interest. These features—decentraliz-ability and reliance on self-interest as primary human motivation—stand in sharp contrast with gift exchange, which requires some coordination and dedication to the common good. This explains why, ever since Adam Smith, markets have been a source of endless fascination for economists who have come to regard the market as the optimal and efficient manner to allocate goods and services (e.g., Hayek 1945; World Bank 1981). Of course, for this beautiful system to perform its function correctly, agents must not cheat (e.g., North 1973; Williamson 1975, 1985), but more on this later.

In market exchange the money that agents accumulate represents what they have contributed to the welfare of the community.[4] To guarantee that individuals do not get more from the community than what they contribute, one must ensure that they do not spend more than they earn. Although seemingly simple, this requirement is a source of endless difficulty whenever agents expect to contribute more in the future than they have contributed in the past. It explains, for instance, why children find it difficult to borrow for school fees, and why households struck by famine or run from their homes by war and violence seldom find someone willing to lend to them. Of course, if loans were freely available, these problems could be avoided. But then it would be only too easy for crooks to exceed their budget constraint, that is, to rob the community of the fruits of its labor. This explains why market forces are often depicted as heartless: they do not care for the sick, the old, and the weak. Social insurance and redistributive justice must be addressed by other means.

Hierarchies are the third mechanism by which goods and services can be allocated among individuals. Firms, government agencies, banks, and parastatals are all examples of hierarchies (Williamson 1975). Unlike markets, hierarchies rely on command and control to allocate resources among their members. Command and control includes orders from hierarchical superior, taxes and fees, and automated plants. Internal accounting is used to keep track of each unit's contribution to the common good of the organization. Central planning in socialist economies can be seen as an attempt to organize the whole economy into a single firm or hierarchy. Capitalist economies, although quick to criticize central planning as impractical and inefficient, themselves rely to a very large extent on command and control within their large corporation and government agencies and through government regulation of economic activity.

---

4. Money, however, is not essential for market exchange. Other ways of keeping track of individual contributions can be used, such as credit cards or clearinghouse agreements such as those practiced among stockbrokers.

Unlike markets, hierarchies are complex organizational structures whose purpose is to centralize the allocation of resources. Because mandated allocation often conflicts with the self-interest of agents in charge of implementation, hierarchies require incentive systems to ensure compliance. For instance, a firm manager may order workers to process raw materials into finished products, but following orders is usually against workers' immediate self-interest. Similarly a government agency may instruct its agents to collect customs duties. Whereas collecting the tax is in the agents' interest, transferring the proceeds to the treasury is not. To prevent shirking and embezzlement, the manager has to threaten workers with dismissal (or worse) and spend resources to monitor their actions. Since preventing shirking is costly, one may wonder why hierarchies exist in the first place, that is, why allocation is not organized via markets instead.

This immediately suggests that to survive in a competitive environment, hierarchies must have an advantage over markets. One such advantage is the presence of returns to scale in the production process or ownership of exclusive but nonrival intangible assets such as patents, business licenses, brand name, or know-how. Hierarchies may outperform the market in other dimensions too, such as search costs, enforcement of contractual obligations, and arbitration of conflicts. Alternatively, hierarchies may be ways of internalizing the talent or human capital of particular individuals, such as the business acumen of the entrepreneur or manager.

1.2   Transactions Costs and Markets in Africa

Having observed the three most common ways of organizing the allocation of resources within an economy,[5] we ought to consider which allocation mechanisms are more important in different economies. In the United States and other developed economies, the domain of gift exchange has all but vanished: the range of goods and services produced by the household for its own consumption is very limited, and social protection is provided primarily through a mix of market and taxes. In contrast, African households, especially in rural areas, provide a wide variety of goods and services to themselves, such as food, shelter, fuel, child and elderly care, training, food preparation, and the manufacture of numerous crafts. In addition solidarity

---

5. In practice, one also encounters hybrid allocation mechanisms that borrow from several basic organizational forms. Informal loans among relatives and friends—what Platteau and Abraham (1987), Fafchamps (1999a), and Fafchamps and Lund (2002) call quasi-credit—is an example of a form of allocation process that borrows from gift and market exchange. A franchise and an exclusive dealership contract are examples of hybrids between market and hierarchy. Family businesses and nepotism in promotion are examples of hybrids between hierarchies and gift exchange.

among relatives and kin represents the dominant form of social insurance. Gift exchange thus constitutes a very important allocation mechanism, which explains why economists working on Africa and other similar parts of the world have long sought to understand the forces that determine the distribution of welfare within households and communities (e.g., Haddad and Kanbur 1990; Platteau 1991; Fafchamps 1992; Haddad et al. 1997; Dercon and Krishnan 2000; Fafchamps and Quisumbing 2002a).

After gift exchange, markets play a paramount role in Africa, arguably more so than in developed economies. The reason is the relative absence of large hierarchies, and the weakness of those that are present. For instance, in surveys of light manufacturing firms in eight sub-Saharan countries (e.g., Bigsten et al. 1999, 2000b), the largest surveyed firm only had 6,000 employees,[6] a very small number compared with those of developed economies. The average size of manufacturing firms in the sample was around 150 employees, even though firms of 5 or fewer employees were excluded from the survey. Since very small firms represent the overwhelming majority of businesses in Africa (e.g., Fafchamps 1994; Daniels 1994; Liedholm and Mead 1999), the average firm size computed over all manufacturers in Africa, including microenterprises, is even smaller. What is true for manufacturing is also true for trade: market intermediation in Africa is characterized by a plethora of small traders, seldom exceeding a handful of employees and family helpers (e.g., Fafchamps 1994; Fafchamps and Minten 1999). Although often criticized as overextended (e.g., World Bank 1981; Bates 1983), African civil service is commonly underequipped and underpaid relative to the many functions it is supposed to assume (e.g., Chew 1990; Collier and Gunning 1999). In addition tax collection is notoriously problematic, with the implication that government expenses are financed from a narrow base, primarily export and import customs and duties. To summarize, Africa has few hierarchies, and whatever hierarchies it has are small in size and, in the case of civil service, not very effective in serving their allocative function.

An immediate corollary of the small size of hierarchies is that, controlling for differences in the domain of gift exchange, markets play a much more important allocative role than in developed economies (Fafchamps 1997a). To see how this is possible, consider, for instance, the number of transactions that are required to channel grain from farmers to urban consumers. In a typical Western country, grain is purchased from farmers by a large corporation (e.g., Cargill), processed in the corporation facilities, purchased by supermarkets and agro-businesses, and sold to consumers. There are very few intermediaries between producer and consumer, and

---

6. Ironically this firm went bankrupt before the surveys were over.

the size of each individual market transaction is very large. In contrast, in Africa, grain to be sold to retailers, and finally to micro-retailers, is first purchased from a myriad of small farmers by collecting agents, assembled for shipment by a rural wholesaler, and purchased by an urban wholesaler or processor (e.g., Bauer 1954; Jones 1959; Staatz 1979; Staatz et al. 1989; Morris and Newman 1989; Gabre-Madhin 1997). There are many intermediaries and most transactions are very small. Thus, judging by the number of transactions required to bring grain from producers to consumers, we could say that grain trade in sub-Saharan Africa is much more market intensive than it is in the United States.

The fact that most market transactions are very small and most market participants are either individuals or very small firms has serious implications for the form that markets take. First, small businesses and poor consumers seldom have valuable assets that can be seized to service a debt. Clearly, the threat of court action is not credible where recovery is either impossible or highly problematic.[7] Even if the faulty party could be forced to pay, the size of the transactions would often be too small to justify court action. Agents would still not take small contractual disputes to court because, regardless of court and attorney fees, valuable time would be lost in court. Therefore it would be difficult if not impossible to significantly broaden the reach of courts by reducing their cost.[8] As we will see in chapters 4 to 6, the evidence indicates that African manufacturers and traders seldom use courts to solve contractual disputes and that the likelihood of court action increases with firm size.

Given that most market transactions are beyond the reach of the law, it is not surprising to discover that African traders and manufacturers opt for trading practices that minimize the potential for breach (e.g., Fafchamps 1996; Bigsten et al. 2000a; Fafchamps and Minten 2001a). If one were looking in developed economies for an institutional equivalent of African markets, the closest would be flea markets and garage sales. Sales are made primarily on a cash-and-carry basis, especially when they involve small farmers, microenterprises, and final consumers. The placement of orders, invoicing, supplier credit, and the provision of warranty are limited to larger firms. Although it difficult to quantify the cost of operating on a cash-and-carry

---

7. One could imagine that agents sue judgment-proof debtors to establish a reputation of toughness (e.g., Kreps et al. 1982; see Hendley 1999 for an example in Russia). If all debtors are judgment-proof, however, such a strategy will fail to increase recovery and is thus irrational.

8. Much of the time cost of a court dispute arises from the necessity to hear witnesses and organize legal arguments. One could imagine simplifying legal procedures to speed up the process, but this would undoubtedly result in a lower quality of adjudication. Although a rigorous analysis of the trade-off between legal standards and judgment quality is beyond the scope of this chapter, it should be clear that summary justice is unlikely to raise confidence in the judiciary.

basis, regression analysis presented in Fafchamps and Minten (2002b) and in chapter 16 suggests that this cost to be quite large.

Other features of African markets compound the problem. The quality of agricultural and manufacturing goods produced by small farmers and artisans is very uneven, given the unsophisticated nature of production and transformation processes. This is particularly true in food production for domestic markets. Because the Green Revolution has largely bypassed sub-Saharan Africa, for the most part farmers continue to use local varieties. Thanks to centuries of seed selection by individual farmers, these varieties have an extremely broad gene pool compared with hybrids or other improved varieties. An immediate consequence is that the quality and taste of domestically produced grain and tubers vary significantly across regions, thereby complicating the task of traders (Fafchamps and Minten 2001a). Genetically speaking, the situation is better for export crops where seeds are more homogeneous and the intrinsic quality of output is less variable. But cash crops also tend to be more susceptible to improper cultivation and handling than local food crops. Quality variation thus plagues Africa's export crop sector as well (World Bank 1999). As a result traders often choose to inspect the quality of products at each transaction, adding to the cost of exchange (Fafchamps and Minten 2001a).

Product quality is also an important issue in manufacturing and services. The problem is particularly severe for industrial inputs where a consistent quality of inputs is required to produce a consistent quality output. In the worst case, improper quality can damage the equipment. Quality control is thus a serious concern in manufacturing as well. Yet manufacturing and services do not fare much better than agriculture. Unlike in developed economies, there are few if any government standards that facilitate quality verification.[9] Moreover, in contrast to developed economies where large corporation invest heavily in name recognition through advertisement, the myriads of firms that dot the African economic landscape are most of the time too small to even consider seeking marketwide name recognition.[10] This lack of transparency about product quality complicates the screening of potential suppliers and makes it difficult to distinguish bona fide producers from hit-and-run operators who sell bad products.

The same lack of transparency is reflected in the screening of customers. Bona fide clients are difficult to distinguish from little crooks and fly-by-night traders. More

9. For instance, laws and regulations on consumer safety standards, food additives, product labeling, and improper advertising. Even when such regulations exist, they need not be applied.

10. A few exceptions can be found in franchising (e.g., international hotels) and in internationally known commodities produced by multinationals or under licence (e.g., soft drinks and cars).

sophistiscated con artists may even mimic honest behavior only to cheat better later. Due to the imperfect coverage and dubious quality of personal identification (e.g., an ID card) and business registry systems in many sub-Saharan African countries, it is fairly easy for delinquent clients to blend into the background of poor anonymous microenterprises and customers. This relative impunity is likely to favor lax payment practices, and as we will see, payment delays are frequent (e.g., Fafchamps 1997c; Bigsten et al. 2000a; Fafchamps and Minten 2001a). Screening potential recipients of supplier credit is thus a complicated and risky affair. As a result supplier credit, invoicing, and payment by check are rare (e.g., Fafchamps 1996; Fafchamps and Minten 2001a).

The plethora of market participants also raises search costs, even abstracting from payment issues (e.g., Kranton 1996b; Gabre-Madhin 1997). Unlike in developed economies, agents can seldom rely on printed catalogs and phone calls to locate what they need with any degree of certainty. Finding goods is a complicated and time-consuming process. Moreover the poor quality of infrastructure in general and roads in particular translates into unforeseen transportation delays and storage losses (Fafchamps 1996). All these factors, and others, combine to make market exchange costly, cumbersome, time-consuming, and unpredictable. It is therefore no wonder that trade margins on agricultural products are higher in Africa than elsewhere (e.g., Minten 1995; Jerome and Ogunkola 1999; Minten and Kyle 1999).

1.3   The Role of Traders

Microeconomic theory has devoted a lot of attention to the study and modeling of two categories of economic agents, producers and consumers. But it has failed to identify a separate role for the economic agent par excellence, namely the trader. General equilibrium theory, for instance, gets some help in matching producers' technology with consumers' preferences from the invisible hand of the Walrasian auctioneer but does not receive any assistance from traders, that is, from those very agents whose function in real life is to implement the matching (Arrow and Hahn 1971). Similarly the theory of international trade studies many important issues pertaining to the commerce among nations, but without ever identifying international trading firms as useful categories for scientific inquiry (e.g., Bhagwati and Srinivasan 1983; Krugman 1990).[11] Finally, the theory of industrial organization, which should mostly concern itself with the organizational structure of the economy, has largely

---

11. The recent work of Rauch and Casella is an important exception (e.g., Rauch and Casella 1998; Casella and Rauch 1998).

failed to recognize trade intermediation as an interesting topic of inquiry, and has focused most of its attention on the internal structure of firms as entities in which commodities are being produced (Fudenberg and Tirole 1991).[12]

In all of these important branches of economic theory, traders are treated as redundant actors. The trade intermediation function that they perform is implicitly assumed so trivial that individual producers and/or consumers can easily undertake it at no cost. Why traders have existed in all societies since very ancient times fails, however, to be accounted for.[13]

Another source of dissatisfaction with the current state of economic theory is that market power is studied as if it were restricted to producers or consumers—for example, the standard monopoly and monopsony cases. Traders are implicitly assumed to operate in a transparent manner: they simply pass prices and commodities without affecting them, except for perfectly competitive trade margins. Doing so ignores the considerable market power that certain trading firms seem to enjoy in practice. It also fails to explain why certain forms of trade are very profitable activities and remain so, as historical evidence suggests, for extended periods of time. Long-distance trade, in particular, is typically the most lucrative enterprise in all pre-industrial economies, not only in economies of the past (e.g., Hopkins 1973; Braudel 1986) but also in many places in the Third World today.[14] An illustration is the wealth accumulated by trading classes in sub-Saharan Africa, whether of Indian, Syro-Lebanese, or indigenous extraction (e.g., Meillassoux 1971; Ensminger 1992).

1.4   Trust and Relationships

This book contends with the existence of traders—and their relative economic prosperity. The starting point is as follows: Markets are normally thought of as decentralized allocation mechanisms, and much has been written on the benefits to be derived from decentralization. Markets, however, cannot exist without coordinated action, if only to define and protect property rights. Whenever these services are not

---

12. Recent theoretical work on networks is a noted exception (e.g., Bala and Goyal 1998, 2000; Kranton and Minehart 2000a, b, 2001; Goyal and Vega-Redondo 2000).

13. Not surprisingly, economic historians constitute an important exception in that they have long recognized the economic role of traders and often made the study of traders their main topic of enquiry (e.g., North 1973; Braudel 1986; Greif 1993).

14. Its profitability is possibly surpassed only by "political entrepreneurship," that is, seeking preferential access to private rents generated by public authorities (e.g., Krueger 1974; Bayart 1989; Murphy et al. 1991; see also Braudel 1986 on tax farming). Of course, maximum rates of profit are achieved when private market power is actively promoted by the state (e.g., chartered companies in eighteenth-century Europe, if privately diverted profits are taken into account; import licencing in most Third World countries today).

provided by the state, mafias and other private armies arise that thrive on protection money—and occasionally have ambition to replace the state itself (North 1990).

Even if property rights are properly defined and protected, market transactions leave much room for cheating (Fafchamps 1996). Economists typically focus on two important aspects of exchange: price and quantity. In real life there are many other contractual dimensions that are equally, if not more, important to the parties, such as the quality of the product, the form and method of payment, and the provision of credit. Any economy is characterized by the presence of information asymmetries (Hayek 1945). As is well known, information asymmetries generate moral hazard and adverse selection. More important, however, information asymmetries generate contract enforcement problems because they make compliance of contractual obligations hard to verify by agents not party to the contract, including courts (Hart and Holmstrom 1987). Consequently contract enforcement through courts and police is necessarily imperfect and requires the support of other enforcement mechanisms (Fafchamps 1996).

In the absence of suitable mechanisms to deter cheating, exchange can only take a rudimentary form, which elsewhere (Fafchamps and Minten 2001a) I have called a flea market economy: no placement of order, no invoicing or payment by check, no credit, and no warranty. Protection against opportunistic behavior enables agents to do business more easily, for instance, by placing orders ahead of delivery, by securing product warranty, and by paying by check upon receipt of a monthly invoice.[15]

In everyday business, personal trust often is an effective substitute for the security provided by costless legal enforcement. In fact, when businessmen and women operating in poor countries are asked how they prevent opportunistic breaches of contract, they typically respond that they conduct businesslike transactions only with individuals they can trust (e.g., Fafchamps et al. 1994, 1995; Fafchamps 1996; McMillan and Woodruff 1999b; Johnson et al. 2000). With strangers, they revert to a cash-and-carry form of exchange: goods are inspected on the spot, and delivery takes place against instant payment in cash (e.g., Bigsten et al. 2000a; Fafchamps and Minten 2001a).

The question then arises as to where trust comes from. In practice, it results primarily from a history of successful exchanges (e.g., Lorenz 1988; Fafchamps et al. 1994, 1995; Fafchamps 1996; Johnson et al. 2002). As we discuss in detail later in this book, relational contracting is the norm between African manufacturers and their suppliers: the length of the relationship exceeds seven years on average, and

---

15. There are commodities such as electricity for which exchange would be extremely cumbersome, if not impossible, if parties could not resort to periodic invoicing.

most supplies of a particular input come from a single supplier. The great majority of manufacturing firms places regular (e.g., monthly) orders from their main suppliers. This is particularly true in manufacturing where firms have been shown to be extremely loyal to their main suppliers even when they have a choice among various sources of supply (Bigsten et al. 2000a). One reason is that a manufacturer's equipment and production plans are typically optimized around very specific inputs and delivery systems. If input specificity were the only reason for long-term relationships, one would not expect relational contracting to be prevalent in agricultural markets. Evidence to the contrary can be found in Gabre-Madhin (1997) and Fafchamps and Minten (1999, 2001a). The role of trust and relationships is examined in detail in part II.

Repeated exchange can be seen as a way of economizing on the costs of establishing personal trust. In certain markets—labor and credit, for example—repeated interaction is so prevalent that it has become the norm. These are typically markets for which the potential for abuse is greatest and the screening costs are largest. Relationship-based networks are therefore expected to arise in markets where screening costs are high and personal trust is a substitute for external enforcement through lawyers and courts (e.g., Hayami and Kikuchi 1981; Ghosh and Ray 1996; Fafchamps 2002b).

1.5 Reputation

Another mechanism for enforcing contracts is reputation—what Greif (1993) calls multilateral punishment strategy. In a reputation enforcement mechanism, cheaters —namely agents who have failed to respect their contractual obligations—are subjected to a coordinated punishment by all (or a subgroup of) other agents. The form taken by the punishment may vary, but it typically involves the threat of exclusion from economic exchange and, possibly, from other forms of social interaction (Spagnolo 1999). The effectiveness of the reputation mechanism depends on the speed with which information about cheaters is disseminated, and on the extent to which it circulates among all agents or remains circumscribed to a small number of them (e.g., Kandori 1992; Raub and Weesie 1990).

The reputation mechanism itself, however, is affected by the difficulty for strangers to assess what exactly went on between parties to a disputed contract. Information provided by one agent about the reliability of another can be false and must be treated with caution. The reputation mechanism is thus vulnerable to the possibility of deliberate disinformation. As a consequence a reputation mechanism alone is likely to be insufficient for enforcing contracts.

Trust-based exchange is a simpler way of bypassing shortcomings in the legal enforcement of contracts. Trust, if one brushes aside the ethical considerations associated with the term, can be seen as the result of an information-gathering process (e.g., Datta 1996; Ramey and Watson 1999; Watson 1999). This issue is explored in detail in chapter 8. The basic intuition is that by interacting with each other, individuals learn something about each other. In particular, they learn about the other party's capability and willingness to comply with an agreed-upon transaction, about his or her ability to dissimulate information or emotions, and about his or her readiness to assume responsibility or display flexibility in case of accident or mishap. The accumulation of such information over time allows individuals to better assess each other's characteristics: in payoffs, technology, preferences, sense of ethics, and so on. It enables them to evaluate more precisely the likelihood that certain transactions will be complied with, and it facilitates trade among people who have identified each other as trustworthy partners. Trust-based exchange thus emphasizes interpersonal relationships—what North (2001) calls "personal exchange" to distinguish it from more impersonal forms of exchange that economists typically associate with the concept of market. Whenever trust plays a crucial role in facilitating transactions and enforcing contracts, the anonymous exchange of economic textbooks tends to be superseded in importance by personalized exchange. This in itself casts a new light on the role of traders as the agents in the economy who specialize in building trust relationships across social groups or entities with different tastes and technologies (Durlauf and Fafchamps 2002).

Contract enforcement difficulties are not the only consequence of information asymmetries. Whenever information about possible sources of demand or supply is not widespread, economic exchange also involves search costs. The existence of search costs in turn confers economic value to information per se. Interestingly, in order for trust to be established, parties to economic exchange typically collect information on each other's technology and preferences. In the presence of search costs, this type of information is thus doubly valuable: not only is it essential for trust, but it also identifies potential sources of supply or demand. To the extent that such information is concentrated in the hands of a few trade specialists, it undoubtedly reinforces their market power and generates informational rents. We revisit this issue in chapter 14.

In the following pages, we speculate about the likely implications that trust has on the shape of economic exchange. In particular, we contrast trust-based exchange with reputation-based exchange, and we derive tentative propositions about the relationship between industrialization, contract enforcement mechanisms, and the place of traders in the economy. We revisit these concepts in more detail in part III.

1.6   Social Network Based Exchange

Personal acquaintance is an information-gathering process, a learning process. Therefore not only does it take time, but it accumulates over time. This leads to the fundamental observation that mutual trust is a self-reinforcing mechanism: as people successfully do business together and learn more about each other, they tend to trust each other more and thus are more likely to conduct business again in the future. This general observation leads to the following conjecture:

CONJECTURE 1.1   Whenever contracts are not perfectly enforceable and therefore mutual trust is an essential condition for economic exchange, the probability for two parties to trade increases with previous economic exchange between them. Consequently a larger share of economic exchange takes place among acquaintances than predicted by random matching.

Conjecture 1.1 derives from the fact that once economic agents have established a certain level of mutual trust, they will often find it convenient and attractive to continue conducting business with the same partners for extended periods of time, instead of relying solely on market competition. In other words, once economic agents have come to know each other well, the relation-specific knowledge they have accumulated locks them into an interpersonal relationship. We formalize this point in chapter 8.

The literature has defined a (multilateral) reputation mechanism as a third-party contract enforcement mechanism whereby information about noncompliance by one individual with some of his contractual obligations is transmitted to other potential or current partners of the offender and used to trigger community or group retaliation. In other words, jointly available information about economic agents—their reputation—is used to coordinate joint punishments (Kandori 1992).[16] Let us define a social network based exchange as a form of economic exchange in which contracts are primarily or exclusively enforced via first- and second-party punishments.[17] If third-party enforcement, whether by courts or reputation, is inexistent or of negligible importance, we have the following conjecture:

CONJECTURE 1.2   Whenever contracts are not perfectly enforceable and a reputation mechanism is inexistent, no economic exchange can take place among unacquainted parties and all exchange is social network based.

---

16. Information need not be instantaneously and costlessly transmitted to all members of the group (e.g., Raub and Weesie 1990; Arthur and Lane 1991). Of course, the more slowly information is transmitted and the higher the cost of information gathering, the weaker is the reputation mechanism for contract enforcement.

17. Second-party punishments of course require repeated interaction between the parties.

When a strong reputation mechanism is present, the information gain procured through personal acquaintance is likely to be small compared to the depth of information conveyed in someone's reputation. Consequently relation-specific knowledge is relatively unimportant and interpersonal relationships can easily be broken as a result of changing opportunities for exchange. On the other hand, when the reputation mechanism is weak or nonexistent (e.g., because of slow transmission of information or because of high costs of information gathering), trust can only result from personal acquaintance. This is another way of saying that, in this case, self-enforcement of contracts can only rely on second-party punishment—what Greif (1993) calls a bilateral punishment strategy. In such an economy, lock-in is very strong and all economic exchange takes place in a segmented fashion along network lines, hence conjecture 1.2. The next conjecture is a direct consequence of the above:

CONJECTURE 1.3   Economic exchange is more likely to be based on reputation in industrialized economies, and on social networks in pre-industrial societies.

Conjecture 1.3 results from the following observations: Information-processing costs determine the effectiveness and viability of a reputation mechanism. The costs increase exponentially with the number of economic agents whose reputation must be monitored, since information about the agents' actions must be channeled to all agents. Economic exchange in pre-industrial societies typically involves a large number of very small firms, while the opposite is true in industrial economies. Industrial economies differ from pre-industrial economies in the way their large firms are organized around mechanized production for a mass market. The large size of industrial firms is a consequence of increasing returns in production, organization, and marketing. In the absence of such increasing returns, firms in pre-industrial societies usually remain small in order to avoid incentive problems and information-processing costs (e.g., Geertz 1963; Fafchamps 1994).

The difficulty of transmitting information about all firms in an accurate and speedy manner precludes the effective operation of a reputation mechanism as a contract enforcement device and as a support to trade in pre-industrial economies (Geertz et al. 1979). In contrast, in industrialized economies, economic agents typically need to keep track of the reputation of only a limited number of large firms. This tends to free economic exchange more from interpersonal relations. Furthermore, even in businesses for which increasing returns to size are absent, industrialized economies have often found ways of establishing a reputation mechanism by standardizing customer services (e.g., franchising in hotels and restaurants).

CONJECTURE 1.4   In social network based exchange, prices are established through mutual bargaining.

Conjecture 1.4 is a direct consequence of the fact that parties to a social network of exchange have accumulated relation-specific knowledge and thus face each other in a bilateral monopoly situation. Of course, to the extent that parties have other alternatives open to them, namely other interpersonal links by which they may secure similar goods and services, bargaining will remain confined within the price band for which exchange is mutually beneficial (e.g., Geertz et al. 1979; Fafchamps 2002b). We discuss this issue in some detail in chapter 14.

CONJECTURE 1.5   The number of intermediaries between consumer and producer is larger in social network based exchange than in reputation based exchange.

Conjecture 1.5 is a consequence of the idea that trust can only exist among people who know each other, and that people can only know a finite (and probably small) number of people. The resulting need for many layers of intermediaries in social network based exchange is best illustrated by an example. Say A lives in village 1 and D lives in village 2. They have different initial endowments and would clearly benefit from trade. They do not know each other, however, and thus cannot trade directly. Fortunately, A knows B who knows C who knows D. Through them, trade can be organized on the basis of mutual trust, and some of the gains from trade can therefore be achieved. Evidence from pre-industrial economies confirms that the number of trade intermediaries is large and indeed often judged excessive from an efficiency point of view (e.g., Geertz et al. 1979; Staatz et al. 1989; Morris and Newman 1989; Berg 1989; Fafchamps et al. 2002).

CONJECTURE 1.6   In social network based exchange, a large share of gains from trade is appropriated by trade intermediaries.

Conjecture 1.6 results from the fact that in the absence of a reputation mechanism, producers and consumers find it difficult to deal with each other directly and often prefer to rely on intermediaries. The intermediaries are thus able, as a group, to extract a significant share of the gains from trade as a return on their relation-specific investment.

CONJECTURE 1.7   In social network based exchange, trade relationships tend to remain nonspecialized unless the development of commodity or activity-specific skills is important and the volume of trade in a particular commodity is large enough for traders to specialize in a particular commodity and/or activity.

Conjecture 1.7 follows from the mutually reinforcing nature of social network based exchange. Once a person has invested in building mutual trust with another person, he has gained a slight competitive advantage in all transactions with that person. Consequently existing networks of exchange are expected to absorb all arbitrage possibilities among their members and to remain nonspecialized. In this case economic exchange tends to be multiplex (Gluckman 1955), and transactions tend to be implicitly or explicitly interconnected (Braverman and Stiglitz 1982).

The competitive advantage of multipurpose intermediaries may, however, be overcome whenever a large volume of trade in a particular commodity makes it profitable for specialized traders to accumulate commodity or activity-specific skills. For instance, cattle trading requires specific skills in order to assess the health and value of an animal on the hoof. Consequently specialized cattle traders are likely to turn up even in social network based exchange (Staatz 1979). The same is likely to be true for long-distance trade. Economic exchanges across towns and villages imply a number of distinct operations, from collection to warehousing, transportation, wholesaling, and retailing. At some links of this chain of operations, the volume of trade in a particular commodity may be sufficient to warrant specialization, while at others it may not. For instance, the collection, transport, and retailing of cereals may be accomplished by multipurpose intermediaries and transporters, leaving the storage and wholesaling to specialized grain merchants. Even when specialization is present, economic exchange may still require interpersonal networks.

CONJECTURE 1.8   In stable pre-industrial economies, exchange may be influenced by culturally inherited economic roles.

Conjecture 1.8 is also a consequence of positive feedbacks in social network exchange. Whenever opportunities for economic transactions do not change over time, as in stable pre-industrial economies, social networks tend to fix the direction and magnitude of exchange flows. The same patterns of exchange will reproduce themselves over generations, and thus become internalized as culturally hereditary economic roles. Examples of such hereditary roles abound and often are hierarchical in character (castes not only in South Asia but also in Africa and Yemen; serfdom, slavery, and other forms of bonded labor; e.g., see Platteau 1995; Genicot 2002). More benign examples concern the concentration of specific economic activities in the hands of a specific ethnic group. We revisit this issue in part VI.

The objective of this book is to formalize and verify these conjectures using survey data from sub-Saharan Africa. We proceed as follows. Chapter 2 sets up a general conceptual framework in which market transactions are viewed as contracts. The various data sources used in this book are presented in chapter 3. Part II examines the evidence regarding contract enforcement in African manufacturing and agricultural trade. The effect of imperfect contract compliance on inventories is illustrated in chapter 7.

Part III focuses on relationships and the formation of trust. A model of trust building is presented in chapter 8. Evidence regarding relational contracting is discussed in the remainder of part III. In part IV we turn to information sharing and reputation. A detailed modeling framework is presented in chapters 11 and 12 to illustrate the various ways in which information sharing can affect contract enforcement. Evidence regarding information sharing is summarized in chapter 13. Part V focuses on networks. Chapter 14 introduces a general conceptual framework to formalize markets as networks. Evidence regarding business networks is discussed in chapters 15 and 16. Part VI is devoted to ethnicity and discrimination. A conceptual framework is presented in chapter 17 that contrasts the effects of networks and statistical discrimination. Evidence of ethnicity effects in market exchange and firm performance is examined in the rest of part VI. Conclusions and policy implications are presented in part VII.

The less technically minded reader may want to skip the theoretical chapters (2, 8, 11, 12, 14, and 17) and focus instead on the empirical and discussion chapters. The reader should nevertheless find comfort in knowing that the work presented in these chapters is built on—and informs—a rigorous conceptual framework.

2 Market Transactions as Contracts

In the 1980s and 1990s there was renewed faith worldwide in the capacity of market forces to allocate resources efficiently. Governments were advised to stop meddling in the allocation process and to let the "free market" reign. Very little, however, is known as to how a free market actually operates. Indeed, we know precious little about how firms deal with each other. For instance, it is unclear how firms that otherwise compete with each other and have opposed interests manage to prevent the opportunistic breach of contract. Yet, if the market is to do a better resource allocation job than the government, then surely it must deter or at least minimize cheating among economic agents.

To analyze market institutions, we first need to recognize market transactions as contracts—for example, sales contracts, credit contracts, and employment contracts. A contract is a set of mutual obligations. For a contract to exist, parties must believe that these obligations will be respected. Given the opportunistic nature of *homo economicus*, a contract is devoid of any interest unless these obligations can be enforced in one way or another.[1] This point, which at the heart of the works of North (1990), Williamson (1985), and their followers, is the starting point and organizing principle of our analysis. Most information asymmetries and transaction cost issues that arise in practice can be shown to revert around contract enforcement. Bringing contracts to center stage bridges law and economics. This bridge helps couch policy recommendations that emerge from the economic analysis of institutions in terms of legal procedures.

2.1 The Enforcement of Contracts

We begin by drawing a typology of how economic agents can be induced to comply with contractual obligations. Willingness to comply is assured only if an enforcement mechanism exists that penalizes breach of contract. Several such mechanisms have been discussed in the literature (e.g., Charny 1990; Ellickson 1991; McMillan 1996; McMillan and Woodruff 1999a, 2000). Enforcement measures within business communities include guilt and shame (Platteau 1994b), recourse to legal institutions (e.g., North 1973; Benson 1990), strong-arm tactics (e.g., Gambetta 1993; Braguinsky 1999), cessations of long-term relationships between agents (e.g., Greif 1993; Winn 1994; Ghosh and Ray 1996; Fafchamps 2002b), and joint punishments for insider information sharing (e.g., Bernstein 1992; Kandori 1992; Greif 1993; Posner 1996; Fafchamps 2002b).

---

1. What McKinnon (1973) calls "strategic default" and lawyers refer to as "opportunistic breach of contract."

Guilt is internal to the individual. The ability to feel guilty in failing to respect business promises varies among individuals. Honesty is largely the by-product of upbringing, what psychologists call "secondary socialization" (e.g., Platteau 1994a, b). It is largely influenced by cultural values and religious beliefs. Shame is another emotion that can be harnessed to enforce behavior. Shame is distinct from guilt in that shame requires some information sharing whereas guilt is internal (Barr 2002a). One can feel guilty for an action even if no one knows about it. Shame, in contrast, comes from disapproval by others. The two emotions are often related because guilt is internalized as one perceives disapproval by one's kin (Platteau 1994b). Guilt and shame are not amenable to economic modeling. Consequently we will have little more to say about guilt and shame in this book, except to recognize that they exist and can be powerful motivations for human behavior.

Enforcement mechanisms that rely on coercion are of two types: legitimate and illegitimate. The legal enforcement of contracts through courts ultimately relies on the state's monopoly over legitimate force (e.g., Benson 1990; McMillan and Woodruff 2000). It is the state's backing that allows creditors to seize a debtor's assets and thus grants collateral value to unmovable property. Illegitimate force can also be used to enforce contractual obligations (Gambetta 1993). Parties may resort to insults and violence directly, hire thugs, or bribe policemen to intervene. In the majority of cases the use of actual physical force is not required; implicit or explicit threats are sufficient. Threats, however, are not always believed. Indeed, whether legitimate or illegitimate, the use of coercion to enforce contracts is costly. For small transactions, legal costs are typically too high to justify court action. Whenever the threat of coercion is not believable, it fails to induce compliance unless the offending party can be persuaded that the aggrieved party will go to court or resort to violence at any cost to preserve a reputation of toughness (Kreps et al. 1982) or out of a moral sense of duty.

The third type of enforcement mechanism is based on quid pro quo: "I behave if you behave" (e.g., Axelrod 1984). It is the threat of retaliation that induces compliance with contractual obligations. For such a mechanism to work, parties must interact repeatedly over time. The simplest form of retaliation is the refusal to further transact—what Greif (1993) calls bilateral punishment strategy. This form of punishment was first studied in the sovereign debt literature (e.g., Kletzer 1984; Eaton et al. 1986; Grossman and Van Huyck 1988). For this punishment to deter breach, the relationship must be worth preserving.

Retaliation may also be inflicted by a group of people who are not party to the contract—what Greif (1993) calls multilateral punishment strategy. Any group punishment requires a coordination mechanism and the circulation of information about contract compliance within the group (e.g., Raub and Weesie 1990; Kandori 1992). Reputation is that coordination and information-sharing device. Enforcement mechanisms based on reputation are vulnerable to disinformation: they do not operate well unless a complementary mechanism ensures the accuracy and veracity of the shared information.

2.2 A Formal Model of Contract Enforcement

The concepts introduced in the previous section are now illustrated formally. Consider a contract by which an economic agent—called the debtor—promises to deliver a quantity f at time 1 to another agent—called the creditor—in exchange for a quantity k at time 0. This definition includes pure credit (k and f money), trade credit (k good, f money), and advance payment (k money, f good). Placing an order with a supplier fits in this general form as well: k then represents the inventory cost saved by the supplier thanks to a better organization of production, and f is the inventory cost saved by the buyer thanks to timely availability of raw materials. Insurance and warranty can be accommodated by letting payment f be contingent on a commonly observable event. Parties value k and f differently so that potential gains from trade exist: the debtor likes to receive k more than paying or delivering f, and vice versa.

The set of subgame perfect contracting equilibria—of contractual promises backed by credible threats—is derived by backward induction. At time 1, the debtor decides whether or not to comply with the contract. The cost of complying in general varies with the debtor's type and unanticipated shocks. For instance, a highly competent craftsman (good type) will find it easier to deliver on time than an inexperienced craftsman (bad type). Similarly a client may not pay because of cash flow problems (bad shock). The cost to the debtor of delivering f can thus be written as $\pi(f, \tau, \varepsilon)$, where τ denotes the debtor's type and ε denotes the state of nature at time 1. Type $\tau \in \Delta$ is any characteristic of the debtor that is relevant to the contracting situation, like his or her professional experience, technology, preferences, and honesty. The state of nature $\varepsilon \in \Sigma$ is any condition exogenous to the parties that was unknown at time 0 and makes contract compliance harder or easier. If compliance is totally impossible, we say that $\pi(f, \tau, \varepsilon) = \infty$. How severely shocks affect debtors' ability to fulfill the contract, in general, depends on their type: those who are less competent or ill prepared have a high cost of compliance $\pi(f, \tau, \varepsilon)$ for many states of nature. The function $\pi(f, \tau, \varepsilon)$ allows for these effects as well. We assume that the sets of possible types Δ and states of nature Σ are common knowledge but that only the debtor knows his or her type τ. Some shocks are observable ex post by both parties; others are known only to the debtor. As a result the debtor has better information about ε than the creditor.

In case of breach of contract, the debtor receives a payoff of 0 but incurs punishment. We consider four types of punishments that correspond to the categories discussed above: guilt, whose utility cost to the debtor is denoted $G(\tau, \varepsilon)$; various forms of coercive action including harassment, threats, and court action, whose cost to the debtor is denoted $P(\tau, \varepsilon, C)$; and two types of punishments based on repeated interaction: the suspension of future trade with the creditor resulting in the loss $EV(\varepsilon, \tau)$; and damage to the debtor's reputation with other potential trading partners leading to a loss $EW(\varepsilon, \tau)$. The term $EV(\varepsilon, \tau)$ represents the value of the relationship, that is, the expected discounted value of future transactions with the creditor; $EW(\varepsilon, \tau)$ is the value of lost reputation, that is, the expected discounted value of future transactions with all those who will refuse to transact with the debtor after a breach has occurred. A rational debtor fulfills the contract if the cost of complying is smaller than all penalties combined:

$$\pi(f, \tau, \varepsilon) \leq G(\tau, \varepsilon) + P(\tau, \varepsilon, C) + EV(\tau, \varepsilon) + EW(\tau, \varepsilon). \tag{2.1}$$

Whenever $\pi(f, \tau, \varepsilon) = \infty$, the debtor is unable to comply, and the contract is breached. There are also situations where the debtor could in theory comply, that is, $\pi(f, \tau, \varepsilon) < \infty$, but equation (2.1) is not satisfied. The debtor is then said able but unwilling to pay.[2] By definition, a debtor who is unable to pay is also unwilling to pay. Penalties, in general, depend on the debtor's type τ and on the realized state of nature ε. For instance, some agents are unscrupulous and have a low $G(\tau, \varepsilon)$. Others are hard to harass and coerce into paying their debts through legal (or illegal) means and have a low $P(\tau, \varepsilon, C)$. Others yet, like fly-by-night operators or firms on the verge of bankruptcy, have a short horizon and little interest in preserving their reputation—low $EW(\varepsilon, \tau)$—and their relationship with the creditor—low $EV(\varepsilon, \tau)$. All these effects are accounted for in equation (2.1). The strength of harassment and threats also depends on the form of the contract C, such as on whether formal guarantees were provided or whether contractual obligations were put down in writing to ease the burden of proof.

Now consider time 0. The creditor is asked to part with k in exchange for a future promise of f. Let $\Pi(k)$ and $\Pi(f)$ be the value of k and f to the creditor. By

---

2. The distinction between inability and unwillingness to repay is blurred in practice. For equity reasons, debtors often are regarded as unable to repay when compliance would be unduly costly, that is, when $\pi(-f, \tau, \varepsilon)$ falls below a socially unacceptable level $B < \infty$.

assumption, there are gains from trade: $\Pi(k) > \Pi(f)$. In forming beliefs about the likelihood of receiving f, a rational creditor evaluates the chances of being paid; that is, the probability that equation (2.1) will be satisfied. In evaluating this probability, the creditor uses all the information, denoted Ω, available at time 0: prior knowledge about the distribution of potential debtor types, information gathered over time through direct interaction with the debtor, and information conveyed by others about the debtor. Formally, let $F(\tau, \varepsilon \,|\, \Omega)$ be the joint cumulative distribution over τ and ε that captures the creditor's beliefs given information Ω. Rank states of the world so that, for any debtor type τ, $\pi(f, \tau, \varepsilon)$ is decreasing in ε: it is easier to comply in good states. Further assume that each of the four penalties listed in equation (2.1) is nondecreasing in ε, meaning that the debtor has more to lose in good than in bad states. We can then define the function $h(\tau)$ as the level of shock ε at which equation (2.1) is exactly satisfied and a debtor of type τ is just indifferent between compliance and breach; that is, $h(\tau) = \varepsilon^*$ such that

$$\pi(f, \tau, \varepsilon^*) = G(\tau, \varepsilon^*) + P(\tau, \varepsilon^*, C) + EV(\tau, \varepsilon^*) + EW(\tau, \varepsilon^*). \tag{2.2}$$

For notational simplicity, let us ignore the possibility of partial payment. Then, for any shock ε above $h(\tau)$, the debtor pays; for any shock below $h(\tau)$, no payment is made. Let $(\underline{\tau}, \bar{\tau})$ and $(\underline{\varepsilon}, \bar{\varepsilon})$ be the lowest and highest values that τ and ε can take. A rational creditor agrees to a contract (k, f) if and only if what he or she expects to receive is greater than what is given:

$$\Pi(k) \le E(\Pi(f) \,|\, \Omega) = \Pi(f) \Pr(payment) = \Pi(f) \int_{\underline{\tau}}^{\bar{\tau}} \int_{h(\tau)}^{\bar{\varepsilon}} dF(\tau, \varepsilon \,|\, \Omega). \tag{2.3}$$

Equation (2.3) can be understood as follows. If the debtor's type were known to be, say, τ, the probability of being paid would be equal to the probability that the exogenous shock ε is greater than $h(\tau)$, that is, to $\int_{h(\tau')}^{\bar{\varepsilon}} dF(\varepsilon, \tau \,|\, \Omega)$. Since the creditor does not know the debtor's type, the probability of being paid must be computed over all possible types, hence the double integral in equation (2.3).

The creditor may be able to affect the probability of repayment by affecting the form C of the contract. For instance, the creditor may request that the debtor mortgage real assets to service the debt in case the debtor goes bankrupt. Arranging legal security is costly and time-consuming, however. Say there are N possible forms the contract C_n can take, each with its own cost B_n. The creditor then must choose a contractual form C_n such that the value of the transaction net of transaction cost $E(\Pi(f) \,|\, \Omega) - \Pi(k) - B_n$ is maximized. The solution to this optimization problem may be to bypass formal guarantees if contract enforcement mechanisms other than

$P(\tau, \varepsilon, C)$ are sufficient. If commercial transactions can be enforced through repeated interaction alone, namely through $EV(\varepsilon, \tau)$ and $EW(\varepsilon, \tau)$, one expects them to make little or no use of formal guarantees and of the court system. Similarly one expects legal institutions providing a lot of security at a high cost B_n to be most relevant for large anonymous transactions. There may also be situations where, for all possible contractual forms C_n, the net value of the transaction is negative. In those cases the creditor refuses to trade. Imperfect enforcement then results in rationing. Small transactions, for instance, are difficult to enforce through courts and, if they are anonymous, cannot rely much on expected future trade. As a result one expects small anonymous transactions to be self-liquidating, with immediate cash payment and no delayed obligations.

The debtor also must agree with the contract ex ante. A rational debtor will do so if and only if he or she expects to derive a benefit from the contract. The debtor knows his or her type, say, τ'. Let then $\pi(k, \tau')$ denote the value of receiving k for the debtor and, again for notational simplicity, ignore partial payments. In period 1, either the debtor pays and incurs a cost $\pi(f, \tau', \varepsilon)$ or does not pay and incurs the punishments listed in equation (2.1). Given the debtor's type, payment occurs with probability $\int_{h(\tau')}^{\bar{\varepsilon}} dF(\varepsilon \mid \tau')$. The debtor therefore agrees to the contract if and only if

$$
\pi(k, \tau') \geq \int_{h(\tau')}^{\bar{\varepsilon}} \pi(f, \tau', \varepsilon)\, dF(\varepsilon \mid \tau')
$$

$$
+ \int_{\underline{\varepsilon}}^{h(\tau')} [G(\tau', \varepsilon) + P(\tau', \varepsilon, C) + EV(\tau', \varepsilon) + EW(\tau', \varepsilon)]\, dF(\varepsilon \mid \tau'). \qquad (2.4)
$$

Equation (2.4) states that the debtor's gain from the contract (first term) must be greater than the expected cost of complying when compliance occurs (second term) plus the expected cost of punishment when compliance does not occur (third term).

Equations (2.3) and (2.4) illustrate the tension inherent to any contract. If enforcement is too lenient, debtors will promise anything knowing that they will not be penalized if they breach their promise. At the limit, if enforcement is zero, $h(\tau) = \bar{\varepsilon}$, the creditor expects no payment at all, and no contract is concluded. Similarly, if enforcement is very harsh, say infinite, and even the best debtors are occasionally unable to comply, then the expected cost of punishment ∞ is larger than the gain from any contract. As a result the debtor refuses to promise something he or she is not sure to deliver. In both cases no contract is concluded, even though there may be significant gains from trade. For trade to occur, enforcement must be sufficiently strong to deter opportunistic breaches but not so strong that it scares away all potential debtors (see Zame 1993 for a similar argument applied to insurance contracts).

2.3 Recourse to Legal Institutions

To see how legal institutions might suffice to protect property rights and prevent opportunistic breach of contract, we must first understand what leads individuals to use these institution to obtain remedy for malfeasance (e.g., Becker 1968; Cooter and Ulen 1988; Johnson et al. 2002). Formal legal institutions are powerless to deter malfeasance unless victims voluntarily seek their protection by reporting crime to authorities and by bringing legal suit against opportunistic breach of contract. If victims fail to seek redress from the law, the threat of formal sanction is not credible and legal deterrence is void (Becker and Stigler 1974).[3]

For a victim to involve legal institutions in the resolution of crimes and contractual disputes, the anticipated benefits from legal action must outweigh the costs. At least four economic factors affect the net expected utility gain from legal recourse: (1) the full cost of legal action, including lawyer's fees, bribes to agents of authority, and the opportunity cost of the plaintiff's time; (2) the expected time delay before compensation is received, which in turn depends on the speed with which legal institutions handle their case load; (3) the uncertainty surrounding expected compensation, which is a function of the ease with which perpetrators can be brought to justice, the complexity of the case, the availability of evidence, the impartiality of judges and police officers, and the imprecision of the law and jurisprudence; and (4) the fear of reprisal from the other party, which itself depends on the effectiveness of the incarceration system and the state's zeal in punishing reprisal. Other important but perhaps less rational motivations for legal action include emotions such as the anger or shame that victims may experience as a result of malfeasance and that may induce or refrain them from seeking legal redress.

It should be clear that no actual legal system, even the most efficient, can ever be exempt of all these problems. Adjudicating justice takes time and effort as outsiders have to be informed of the circumstances of the case and strict procedures have to be followed to ensure that both parties are treated fairly. There will therefore always be situations where victims of malfeasance choose not to call upon the law. Consequently it is illusory to expect legal institutions to ever perfectly deter all opportunistic behavior.[4]

---

3. Except for its possible effect on ethical standards and social norms.

4. Ignoring other information issues relative to detection and collection of evidence. In the United States the legal doctrine of efficient contractual penalties argues that victims of a contractual breach should be awarded compensation high enough to ensure that the other party has just enough incentive not to behave opportunistically (Craswell 1995).

Keeping these caveats in mind, the state of legal institutions often appears unsatisfactory in sub-Saharan Africa. For instance, a recent attitudinal survey conducted under the auspices of the Ministry of Justice of Madagascar shows that Malagasy people have little confidence in their justice system (Ministère de la Justice 1999). They are also have little understanding of how courts operate, which may lead them to blame the respect of legal procedures on corruption and incompetence. Moreover the report notes the existence of sizable side payments required by police to pursue thieves and by court clerks to issue copies of court judgment (e.g., La Lettre de l'Ocean Indien 31/07/1999; see Ministère de la Justice 1999). Other documented forms of corruption include that of judges, although the frequency of occurrence remains unclear. In addition the justice system is slow, and the outcome of legal action uncertain due to conflicting laws and occasional interference from public authorities.

To summarize, the existing literature unanimously finds African legal institutions wanting. Much of the available evidence, however, is in the form of anecdotes and horror stories, so on this basis it is notoriously dangerous to generalize. For instance, the attitudinal survey results presented for Madagascar in Ministère de la Justice (1999) tell a dismal tale of distrust in the legal system, but they only report popular beliefs, not actual fact. Hard evidence on recourse to legal institutions by victims of malfeasance is missing. One purpose of this book is to fill this lacuna.

The ineffectiveness of legal institutions, if true, is likely to have two effects: preventive action, and recourse to alternative contract enforcement institutions. Alternative contract enforcement mechanisms are discussed below. Prevention can take many forms—guarding goods against theft, avoiding contractual practices that leave room for opportunistic breach, building up inventories—but it is costly. Costs can be direct—a guardian's wage—or indirect—inconvenient business practices. A rational agent would engage in preventive action only if the expected utility loss from malfeasance exceeds the costs of prevention. The actual cost of preventive action thus provides a lower bound estimate of the expected utility loss from malfeasance.[5] In other words, if we observe that economic agents go to great lengths to reduce their exposure to opportunistic behavior, this constitutes prima facie evidence that the risk of malfeasance is high.[6] This is true even if prevention keeps the actual frequency of malfeasance low. These issues are discussed in detail in part II.

---

5. Ignoring possible negative externalities, namely prevention by one agent diverts malfeasance toward other agents.

6. Whenever the risk of malfeasance is very high and/or the cost of prevention is prohibitive, particular activities may not take place at all—the corner solution. Traders, for instance, may refrain from buying and selling in insecure regions altogether, and farming in remote areas may be totally discouraged if farmers are incapable of protecting crops in the field. Fear of theft has been suggested to account for lack

2.4 Adverse Selection, Statistical Discrimination, and Moral Hazard

Equations (2.1), (2.3), and (2.4) raise a wide range of information and incentive issues, many of which are analyzed in the economics literature on contracts.[7] We briefly discuss a few relevant results from that literature, beginning with adverse selection. Potential debtors differ in how likely they are to comply with a particular contract. Whenever their characteristics cannot be readily assessed, the potential for adverse selection arises: debtors of the wrong type may enter into a contract knowing that they are unlikely to satisfy their obligations but cannot be forced to comply. As a result creditors may refuse to contract even at terms (trade credit, delivery date, promised quality) that appear very favorable because they fear attracting bad types. Transactions then typically become rationed (Stiglitz and Weiss 1981). Evidence of rationing is expected to take various forms: clients turned down for supplier credit and other payment facilities, clients unable to place orders without paying a deposit, clients not allowed to pay by check, and payment made only after the goods have been thoroughly inspected. Rationing can occur even in the absence of asymmetric information: firms may refuse to contract, not because they do not know the other party's type but because they know too well that the other party is not reliable.

Rationing is not the only possible response to the dangers of adverse selection: investigating the other party's type is another. Here our framework comes particularly useful because it makes predictions as to the type of information economic agents will collect on each other. Firms will want to know whether trade partners are competent in their business, an indicator that they will be able to repay. Firms will want to know whether trade partners are committed to their business and interested in establishing a long-term relationship. This can be achieved, for instance, by observing the other firm's pattern of purchases or sales over a period of time. They

---

of trade, the poor maintenance of plantations, and the early harvesting of coffee in certain regions of Madagascar (e.g., Minten et al. 1998; World Bank 1999).

7. Readers unfamiliar with the literature on contracts may refer to Hart and Holmstrom (1987) and Kreps (1990) for a survey. Moral hazard refers to a situation in which one party to a contract, called the principal, cannot observe the action of the other party, called the agent. As a result the agent is tempted to cheat the principal and must be given incentives to exert proper care. Adverse selection refers to a different situation in which the agent is a type that is not observable by the principal. An undifferentiated contract may then attract the wrong types of agents. A possible solution is for the principal to offer a menu of contracts and hope that agents of different types select themselves into different contracts. Alternatively, the principal may elect to ration supply and refuse to transact at certain terms. Singh (1989) presents two simple models of sharecropping, one with moral hazard and the other with adverse selection. These concepts have been extended in a variety of directions, generating an enormous literature that it would be too fastidious to list here.

may also ask around if the other party has been in business for long and, if yes, whether other firms have encountered problems with that party. They will want to find out if trade partners are honest, for example, by selling small amounts on credit or placing small orders to test them. Firms may wish to know if the other party has a house or a permanent workshop, if it can easily be traced, if their spouse has a steady job, and other ways by which harassment and legal pressure can be brought to bear. They may even socialize with each other to get to know the other party better and keep abreast of how their business is doing.

Collecting information on potential trading partners is costly. To economize on screening costs, firms may simply infer each other's type from easily observable characteristics like sex, race, or ethnicity. Small differences in average type across populations with different observable characteristics can then lead to discrimination (Coate and Loury 1993). To see why, say that many members of a particular group are familiar with a certain trade. Now suppose that a member of that group is offered the choice to do business with an unknown member of the group or with an outsider. The transaction is small, so it is not worthwhile to spend resources investigating the other party. But because of differences in population averages, chances are the insider knows more about the trade than the outsider. It is then safer to deal with the insider. Statistical discrimination can, in the long run, induce the monopoly of a group over a particular sector of activity (e.g., Macharia 1988). We revisit these issues in part VI.

In anticipation of statistical discrimination, debtors may even seek to artificially differentiate themselves by acquiring a costly signal that is correlated with their true type τ. For instance, they may join a religious groups simply to persuade creditors that they have a heightened moral sense and business probity (e.g., Cohen 1969; Geertz et al. 1979). Although it is perilous to interpret people's religious motives, there is some evidence that Islam penetrated Africa in this manner (e.g., Hopkins 1973; Shillington 1989; Ensminger 1992).

Moral hazard is another type of incentive problem that is likely to occur in commercial contracts. Success in business is influenced by the diligence and care with which firms conduct their operations. A debtor's ability to pay or deliver f typically depends on what the debtor does after having received k. Moral hazard can arise even if the creditor perfectly observes the actions of the debtor; the fact that a contract is not perfectly and costlessly enforceable is sufficient. Moral hazard can be formally captured by making the realized state of nature ε depend on an action a taken by the debtor between time 0 and time 1, and by making the debtor's payoff depend negatively on a. In this situation the debtor must be given incentives to apply proper care and effort (Stiglitz 1974). In commercial contracts, the most common form of incentive is the implicit promise of continued transactions as long as performance is satisfactory and foul play is not suspected (Laffont and Tirole 1988). From the point of view of the creditor, it is hard to disentangle (and largely irrelevant) whether breach of contract occurs because the other party is basically incompetent or does not apply enough care. As we will see, in practice, moral hazard gets mingled with the other party's type.

Whether or not the creditor should spend resources monitoring the debtor's actions depends on details of the transaction that are not formally captured in equations (2.1) to (2.4). Our framework nevertheless provides insights as to when monitoring may be useful. For instance, realizing early on that a debtor is facing difficulties often enables the creditor to take conservative measures that increase expected repayment. This is particularly true for large loans secured by assets that could be dilapidated should the debtor go bankrupt, or when acting early enables one creditor to get ahead of others. Given the costs involved, however, continuous monitoring is probably not profitable for small, repeated commercial transactions; ex post monitoring is more likely. To this issue we now turn.

2.5 Excusable Breach, Risk Sharing, and Implicit Contracts

Because of moral hazard and adverse selection, the boundary between inability and unwillingness to comply with contractual obligations, while somewhat precise ex post, is blurred ex ante: a debtor may be unable to comply because she promised something she could not deliver or was careless in executing the contract. Using harsh punishments can deter bad types from making empty promises and provide debtors with incentives to exert proper care and effort. But, as we argued earlier, punishments that are too harsh also discourage bona fide parties who cannot be totally sure they can honor the contract. Extreme sanctions get rid of moral hazard and adverse selection altogether, but they also eliminate bona fide trade.

To discourage opportunistic behavior while allowing enough flexibility for bona fide trade, creditors should assess whether breach of contract was due to unanticipated events or to carelessness and incompetence. If it appears the debtor was at fault (insufficient effort) or incompetent (bad type) the creditor may decide to terminate the relationship and seek reparation. On the other hand, if breach was due to events beyond the control of the debtor, the creditor may prefer to renegotiate the contract and continue the relationship. Making punishment depend on the cause of breach improves efficiency because it deters opportunistic behavior but allows excusable default.

Businesses around the world, but particularly in Africa, are subject to shocks (e.g., Little et al. 1987; Cortes et al. 1987; Steel and Webster 1991). Circumstances arise in which firms are unable to comply with a contract: a power outage may delay production, civil strife may interfere with delivery, or the central bank may not release the foreign exchange on time. Cash flows too vary in unpredictable ways, and firms with insufficient access to insurance and credit from other sources often find themselves unable to honor precise deadlines for payment and delivery (Stone et al. 1992). If these circumstances are purely temporary, it would be silly to abandon the relationship simply because one of the partners is temporarily unable to perform. Intuitively, it is in the interest of the two parties to work things out until the difficulty is over. Empirical evidence indeed suggests that market transactions, far from being rigid contracts, exhibit an unexpected degree of flexibility (e.g., Lorenz 1988 for France and Bigsten et al. 2000a for Africa).

To fully understand how markets operate in practice, we need to conceptually understand what flexibility means and why it exists. Flexibility arises when contractual performance is made explicitly or implicitly contingent upon external events affecting one of the parties. The idea is that a supplier who cannot deliver or a client who cannot pay is allowed to renegotiate the contract and default from his or her original obligations. Theory suggests that it is optimal in this case for the parties to recognize that exogenous circumstances may prevent them from honoring their obligations and to build flexibility into the contract. When exchange is relational, flexibility is facilitated by the implicit agreement that binds the parties: if one party feels cheated, it can decide to break the relationship and force the other party to look for another supplier or client. In addition the aggrieved party may seek reparation by enlisting the help of an external contract enforcement agency. The existence of an implicit threat to seek outside reparation *only* if trust has been broken helps the parties to economize on writing the contract. There is no need to write all contingencies down; all that is required is that parties apply the contract in good faith, that is, to the best of their capacity. These theoretical arguments are clear and have been formalized elsewhere (Hart and Holmstrom 1987). What is unclear is whether they are relevant in practice. Too strict a stance on contract enforcement is particularly counterproductive when all bona fide firms have recurrent difficulties fulfilling their contractual obligations. One would therefore expect a lot of contractual flexibility in high-risk environments. Allowing excusable default is then a way of sharing risk among firms.

From a theoretical point of view, there are several ways in which risk sharing can be incorporated in business transactions. One way is to assume that parties write explicit state-contingent contracts in which payment varies with the state of the world ε

(e.g., Kletzer 1984; Eaton et al. 1986; Grossman and Van Huyck 1988; Udry 1990). In practice, such contracts are too cumbersome to be practical. Furthermore ε is seldom observed perfectly by the creditor and is rarely observable by judges. Parties are therefore likely to opt for other solutions. One is to leave the contract deliberately "incomplete" in the sense of Hart and Holmstrom (1987), for instance, by stating that the debtor will pay "when he can." Enforcement then relies on the force of the relationship: as long as payment delays are reasonable, parties continue their relationship; when the creditor suspects foul play, the relationship ends (Fafchamps and Gubert 2002). Another way to share risk is to specify fully the respective obligations of the parties but implicitly agree that these obligations can be renegotiated in good faith should one party find compliance unexpectedly difficult and costly. The advantage of the third approach over the second is that contracts with clearly specified obligations are easier to argue in court. Explicit contractual obligations can then be seen as a way to influence the bargaining power of each party during the renegotiation process, and thus the functioning of the underlying implicit contract.

To distinguish between excusable and nonexcusable default, creditors must be able to infer ε; otherwise, any recalcitrant debtor could falsely pretend to be unable to pay. Costly monitoring of ε and a is often required for risk sharing to take place (Townsend 1979). Relative performance can also be used to assess the likelihood that the debtor is telling the truth and worked hard enough (Radner 1985). If ε and a are observed indirectly or with a delay, misrepresentation and carelessness can be deterred by increasing the severity of the punishment once cheating is suspected. Finally, false claims and insufficient effort can be discouraged by limiting the number of times the creditor is prepared to be patient. The debtor is like the shepherd boy of the story who he cries "wolf" too many times; when the wolf is really there, no one comes to help.

If recourse to legal institutions is entirely irrelevant, an alternative interpretation of flexibility arises, resulting from the fact that disputes need not be resolved according to legal principles at all. Contract law typically calls for one party to compensate the other in case of breach. In other words, breach of contract is regarded as a fault that requires reparation. Parties to a long-term relationship may find such approach incompatible with the need to maintain goodwill and friendship because assigning fault to one party and calling for compensation is antagonistic and may endanger the relationship. Consequently cases of contractual breach resolved through informal enforcement are expected to yield different outcomes from those enforced by courts. For one thing, parties will probably show more understanding for each other's difficulties and be more willing to implicitly insure each other for unanticipated contingencies. By the same token, cases of breach among acquaintances are more likely to be resolved to the satisfaction of the parties and less likely to sever the relationship. If this is correct, the flexibility made possible by long-term relationships might lead to the apparent contradiction that breach of contract is more frequent among parties who know each other well. The reason is that parties to such relationships lower their guard, hence making more room for breach while at the same time ensuring that most cases of breach are handled in a flexible and relation-preserving manner. In such cases noncompliance with contract terms should not be regarded as evidence of opportunistic behavior but rather as a manifestation of flexibility and complicity between trusting partners. We revisit these issues in part II.

2.6   Trust and Reputation

Not only is the promise of future transactions an important incentive for contract compliance, repeated interaction plays an important role in screening and monitoring. As economic agents learn about each other and revise their prior knowledge Ω, they come to trust each other (Gambetta 1988). Trust can thus be thought of as a form of social capital: it accumulates through "good" actions and dissipates through "bad" actions (e.g., Granovetter 1985; Coleman 1988). The importance of trust in business leads to personalized transactions. To see why, consider a risk-averse firm that has identified a few reliable business partners. The information Ω the firm has begun accumulating on its partners is more precise than Δ, the information it has on the general population of potential trading partners. Reliable partners are also probably better than the average population Δ because they are the result of a selection process. Therefore Ω stochastically dominates Δ: because the firm is risk averse, it prefers to deal with known partners than with unknown firms (Arrow 1971). As the firm continues to trade with the same partners, it collects more information about them, which makes it even more likely to deal with them in the future.

In this regard recent theoretical developments provide a fertile source of inspiration. Kranton (1996a) and Ghosh and Ray (1996) formally show that a decentralized market can discipline itself if cheating is interpreted as a sign of incompetence. The mechanism by which opportunism is deterred, however, leads to markets that differ significantly from those described in economic textbooks. For one thing, exchange is not anonymous but relational: firms economize on screening incompetent partners by establishing long-term relationships with other firms they have learned to trust. As in the Shapiro and Stiglitz (1984) model of unemployment as a disciplining device, cheating by competent agents is deterred by the fear of having to search for a new partner.

Trust-based exchange is thus self-reinforcing and favors the establishment of fairly rigid business networks (Meillassoux 1971). Relational contracting can therefore become an impediment to fully efficient exchange because it makes it costly for firms to switch partners. This may be all right in stable economic environments in which patterns of exchange are constant over time. But, if firms must respond to rapidly changing economic conditions by constantly seeking new partners, being stuck with the same partner forever is not optimal. The reluctance to deal with new-comers in the same way (trade credit, checks, orders) as old partners stifles firm entry and competition (Lorenz 1988). In this case Greif (1993) has shown that information sharing can theoretically increase the fluidity of exchange by reducing the penalty for switching partner.[8]

There exist two types of contract enforcement mechanisms that eliminate the need for personalized relationships: legal enforcement and reputation. Both enable firms to operate within a large group and to rapidly establish business relations with new partners. Thanks to legal institutions, security can be found in unmovable collateral and other formal guarantees without prior acquaintance. Collateral-based enforcement is particularly important for large transactions like bank loans. Even banks, however, seldom rely exclusively on collateral and often seek to assess the trustworthiness of potential borrowers. Reputation is a form of social collateral that can guarantee contract performance without prior acquaintance. Economic agents who belong to an information-sharing group may rely each on other's reputation when initiating business contacts. Reputable firms have a high $EW(\varepsilon, \tau)$ with all the firms in that group, regardless of whether they have dealt with them in the past or not. Concern for one's reputation may be sufficient to ensure compliance and to enable firms to offer credit or take large orders without knowing each other personally (e.g., Milgrom et al. 1991; Greif 1993). Firms within an information-sharing group are at an advantage relative to firms who are outside of it because they can reach further, expand faster, and spread risk more easily. The larger the group among which reputation is shared, the larger is the group of potential business partners, and the more access firms have to a safe business environment.

2.7 Empirical Relevance

Despite its generality the conceptual framework we developed in this chapter generates a number of qualitative predictions that serve as a starting point for our

---

8. To achieve this purpose, however, the stigmatization of cheaters may be necessary; see Milgrom et al. (1991) and Fafchamps (2002b) for details. Firms may also seek to economize on screening costs by relying on statistical discrimination or by refusing to deal with firms outside their network. Empirical evidence on these issues is presented in Greif (1994) and Fafchamps (2000). These issues are discussed in detail in the remainder of this book.

empirical work. The model predicts that contract flexibility is required for exchange to take place. To test this proposition, we investigate in part II whether contractual obligations in commercial transactions are ever breached and what happens if they are. Breach is expected to be excusable only if compliance is made unexpectedly costly by an external shock. To verify this proposition, we identify the reasons why breaches occur. The conceptual framework predicts that enforcement should be more flexible if the environment is more risky. We therefore examine whether contractual flexibility varies in a systematic fashion according to the types of transaction firms are involved in. Finally, the model suggests that harassment may be resorted to as a form of debt collection and ex post monitoring device. To investigate this prediction, we examine how firms deal with breach of contract and what procedures they follow to get paid.

In the presence of imperfect information, the conceptual framework stipulates that creditors will screen potential debtors. What they screen for is expected to depend on the type of enforcement mechanism they ultimately intend to rely on. Parties that rely on courts and legal securities should screen for collateral. Parties to relational transactions primarily should assess whether the debtor is a bona fide firm and is committed to maintaining a business relationship. To do so, they may test potential debtors over a period of time and visit their shop or factory. We explore these issues as well by investigating how firms screen suppliers and clients and what specific information they seek to acquire. The theory predicts that groups of firms or individuals that are able to organize the truthful dissemination of contractual information may be at an advantage relative to other firms or individuals. In the absence of reputation mechanism, business transactions are expected to become heavily personalized; mutual trust must be established before contractual obligations are accepted. To investigate these predictions, in part III we examine the extent to which business relations are personalized. In part IV we look for evidence of reputation mechanisms and information-sharing devices. The model says that without enforcement at all, creditors should refuse to contract: there should be rationing. Small, anonymous transactions are expected to be self-liquidating, with instantaneous payment and no delayed obligations. To verify these propositions, we examine whether firms are willing to grant credit or place orders from anyone, and whether some assurances must be provided first. Finally, the model predicts that repeated commercial interactions can enforce contracts with little or no recourse to formal guarantees and the court system. Legal institutions are expected to be most useful for large anonymous transactions. To address these issues, we study whether firms grant credit to regular customers and place orders from regular suppliers only, and what use firms make of formal legal institutions.

3 The Data

We use data from three sources: (1) a series of panel surveys of manufacturing firms in several African countries, (2) complementary case studies of manufacturing and trading firms in Ghana, Kenya, and Zimbabwe, and (3) surveys of agricultural traders in Benin, Madagascar, and Malawi.

3.1 The Manufacturing Panel Surveys

Industrial data used in this book come from surveys of manufacturing firms. Surveys were conducted in nine countries of sub-Saharan Africa: Burundi, Cameroon, Côte d'Ivoire, Ghana, Ethiopia, Kenya, Tanzania, Zambia, and Zimbabwe. Except for Ethiopia, the surveys were conducted by a variety of national teams coordinated by the Regional Program of Enterprise Development (RPED) of the World Bank. Although the data are generally comparable, occasional discrepancies occur and some data are not available for certain countries.

In each of the nine countries, random samples were drawn among manufacturing firms in four sectors of economic activity: food processing, textile and garments, woodworking and furniture making, and metalworking. These sectors were chosen because these light industries are present throughout the continent and are potential candidates for export growth. Most survey teams sought to divide the sample equally between the four industries. Survey teams in Zimbabwe and Ethiopia, however, simply drew a random sample of manufacturing firms in the four covered sectors.[1] This is reflected in the sectoral composition of the sample, as shown in table 3.1. Country data without stratified sampling tend to be dominated by textile and garment firms.

Sampling frames were typically constructed on the basis of an existing census of manufacturing enterprises, occasionally supplemented by a census of small firms. Samples sizes vary from 120 firms in Burundi to 264 firms in Cameroon. Firms with fewer than 5 employees were, in general, excluded from the sample. Daniels (1994), for instance, reports that, in Zimbabwe, enterprises of less than 5 employees represent around 95 percent of all enterprises of 50 employees or less; the corresponding ratio is 44 percent in the RPED Zimbabwe sample. The data thus represent the small to large-scale manufacturing sector in Africa; microenterprises are ignored.

In most countries sample firms were visited three times at one-year interval: in 1993, 1994, and 1995.[2] Questions were asked on a wide variety of issues. In addition

---

1. The sample design for Zimbabwe is discussed in detail in Bade and Gunning (1994).

2. Ghana and Côte d'Ivoire did not follow this timing: Ghana was surveyed in 1992, 1993, and 1994; Côte d'Ivoire was surveyed in 1995 and 1996. Plans to conduct an additional round of survey in Côte d'Ivoire fell through due to lack of funding. Subsequent rounds in Burundi were canceled due to the rapid deterioration of the political situation in the country and neighboring Rwanda. Two more rounds exist for Ethiopia, but we were not granted access to the data.

Table 3.1
Composition of the RPED samples

	All	Burundi	Cameroon	Côte d'Ivoire	Ethiopia	Ghana	Kenya	Tanzania	Zambia	Zimbabwe
Sectoral composition										
Food processing	23%	33%	27%	25%	15%	25%	22%	16%	28%	24%
Textile and garments	30%	26%	20%	25%	52%	25%	26%	24%	31%	45%
Woodworking and furniture	22%	21%	24%	26%	18%	26%	26%	29%	19%	12%
Metalworking	24%	20%	30%	24%	16%	25%	25%	31%	22%	18%
Firm's characteristics										
Total employment	140	90	162	116	149	43	117	122	109	324
Age of firm	17	11	12	16	17	15	19	16	18	24
Legal status										
Limited liability	54%	38%	62%	55%	19%	45%	51%	66%	72%	74%
Sole proprietor	39%	48%	37%	45%	76%	46%	34%	23%	23%	22%
Partnership	7%	13%	1%	0%	5%	10%	15%	11%	5%	4%
Ownership										
Partial or complete foreign ownership	22%	30%	32%	45%	3%	18%	18%	12%	13%	23%
Partial or complete state ownership	10%	19%	10%	16%	13%	8%	2%	16%	8%	5%
Ethnicity										
African	66%	82%	81%	60%	83%	91%	42%	73%	59%	33%
Asian	14%	3%	2%	0%	0%	0%	51%	24%	26%	13%
European	13%	6%	14%	23%	1%	1%	4%	0%	13%	47%
Mideastern	2%	0%	1%	7%	0%	8%	2%	2%	2%	0%
Other	5%	1%	3%	10%	15%	0%	2%	1%	0%	7%
Number of observations in round 1	1,866	120	240	264	214	200	223	217	215	203
Number of rounds available		1	3	2	1	3	3	3	3	3

Note: Computed using wave 1 data only. The actual number of observations varies depending on missing values.

to standard information on finance, employment, capital stock, investment and sales, data were collected on relationships with clients and suppliers, contractual disputes, and contractual risk (e.g., late deliveries, deliveries of deficient quality deliveries, and late and nonpayment). The latter questions, however, were only asked in the first survey round.

Efforts to design a questionnaire that would work in many different countries and would apply to large and small firms alike led to some compromises. In particular, the questionnaire had to be understood by all respondents, including those with little formal education, no accounting, and unsophisticated business practices. This led to the elimination of questions that required proper accounts or a thorough understanding of standard business practices such as invoicing, payment date, and finance charges. As a result the data collected are at time a bit fuzzy as they involve value judgments by respondents, such as on what constitutes a "late payment."

Despite these shortcomings the RPED data are probably the best available source of information on manufacturing in sub-Saharan Africa today. They also contain an unusual amount of information on relationships among firms and their clients and suppliers.

The main characteristics of sample firms are summarized in table 3.1. The average number of employees for the nine country sample is 140; sample firms are largest in Zimbabwe (324 workers on average), and smallest in Ghana (43). The largest sample firm is in Cameroon with 13,500 employees in 1993. The average age of sample firms is 17 years. The Zimbabwe sample is made of older firms with an average age of 24 years; younger firms are found in Burundi and Cameroon. Most surveyed firms—54 percent—have a limited liability status; other firms are held either in sole proprietorship or in partnership. Some 22 percent of surveyed firms operate under partial or complete foreign ownership, with a high of 45 percent in Côte d'Ivoire and a low of 3 percent in Ethiopia. Partial or complete state ownership occurs in 10 percent of sample firms.

The ethnic makeup of the sample firms varies dramatically among countries. In two of the nine countries, less than half of the sample firms have ethnic Africans as owners. Ethnic Europeans are predominant in Zimbabwe and maintain a strong presence in Cameroon, Zambia, and Côte d'Ivoire. Asians occupy a dominant position in Kenyan manufacturing and are present in Zambia, Tanzania, and Zimbabwe as well (Himbara 1994).[3] In the other countries, entrepreneurs in the manufacturing sector are predominantly of African origin.

---

3. Recent evidence of the role of ethnicity in African manufacturing is provided, for instance, by Fafchamps (2000), Fisman (2002), and Raturi and Swamy (1999).

3.2   The Case Study Surveys

The RPED surveys were complemented with case study surveys of enterprise finance and dispute resolution methods. Surveys were conducted in Ghana, Kenya, and Zimbabwe under the auspices of the World Bank. They too were coordinated by the Regional Program for Enterprise Development. These surveys cover a small number of firms in great depth. Questionnaires and survey design vary somewhat for the three countries, especially for Ghana, on one hand, and Kenya and Zimbabwe, on the other.

Ghanaian firms were interviewed in January 1993 by a team of Ghanaian and World Bank researchers (see Cuevas et al. 1993 for details). The Kenya case study survey was undertaken in September 1993 in Nairobi, Kenya (see Fafchamps et al. 1994 for details). The Zimbabwe survey took place in August 1994 in Harare, Zimbabwe (see Fafchamps et al. 1995 for details). Close to 60 firms were interviewed in each country, two-thirds of which were randomly selected from the first wave RPED panel. In Ghana, 58 firms were interviewed, 39 of which were randomly selected from the RPED 1992 sample—around ten firms in each of the four sectors. In Zimbabwe, 40 firms were randomly selected among the 114 RPED panel firms located in Harare. Of the initial 40 firms, 16 declined to be interviewed and 15 replacements were interviewed in their stead, resulting in a sample of 39 manufacturing firms.

To get a sense of how manufacturing firms interact with traders, a number of suppliers and clients of manufacturing firms were also interviewed. The purpose of this sampling design was to investigate whether traders play a buffer role between various manufacturers or between manufacturers and consumers, and to check whether their views and experiences regarding contract enforcement differ from those of manufacturers. Trading firms were selected among wholesalers and retailers operating in the same four sectors of activity—food processing, textile and garments, wood products, and metal products—as the manufacturing firms. Some were active in several sectors at the same time. Most surveyed traders are primarily in the retail business; the others are involved in wholesaling.

In the absence of a readily available census of trading enterprises, these firms were not randomly selected from an existing census or sample of firms. The sample selection approach was essentially ad hoc and the (small) sample of traders who were interviewed is probably not representative of the population of trading firms in each country. An effort was nevertheless made to include trading firms of all sizes and ethnic origin. How successful the case study surveys were in this endeavor varies across the three countries. In Ghana the trader sample covers primarily small traders in and around markets. The Kenya trader sample is composed partly of shops and wholesalers in the commercial district, partly of stalls on the main market. In Zimbabwe the trader sample is dominated by chains of retail outlets. The differences in the three samples reflect differences in the domestic organization of trade in the three countries and their capital city.

Data were collected on a variety of issues pertaining to enterprise finance and trade credit. Questions were also asked about the problems and difficulties firms encounter with suppliers and clients. The questionnaire included many qualitative questions as well as open-ended questions intended to stimulate discussion and explore issues that could not be anticipated. Respondent were quizzed, for instance, on how they screen customers before granting trade credit, how they respond to late payment by clients, and how they seek enforcement of contractual obligations. Their responses were later coded into consistent categories. The section of the questionnaire dealing with contracts was mostly used as a conversational guide. Respondents were quizzed on their motivations and beliefs regarding suppliers and clients. Past contractual problems were discussed in detail. To avoid biases resulting from firms' reluctance to speak about contractual problems in which they were at fault, questions were limited to nondelivery or late delivery by suppliers, deficient quality of supplied goods, and nonpayment or late payment by customers. Given the nature of the issues raised, body language was an important part of respondents' answers. Several laughed or shrugged, for instance, when asked why some of their clients had not paid them, thereby implying a suspicion of carelessness even if their verbal answer did not mention it. In the discussion of the results in the remainder of this book, we build upon the rich body of qualitative information gathered during interviews.

The data suffer from a number of shortcomings: the coverage and wording of individual questions vary somewhat in the three surveys, many observations are missing, and certain important pieces of information were not collected. Given the small size and partially nonrandom nature of the case study samples, results should be viewed as suggestive rather than definitive. The strength of a case study approach, however, lies not as much in the ability to draw statistically significant or fully generalizable findings as in the ability to gain a deeper insight into the phenomena being studied. The imperfect coverage of the data is compensated by the detailed qualitative information gathered during interviews. Albeit tentative, findings based on these surveys provide a useful assessment, given the near total absence of data in this area.

In the three countries, all sample firms are urban. In Ghana, a dozen firms are from Kumasi. The rest comes from the capital city, Accra, and its industrial satellite,

Table 3.2
Composition of the case study samples

	Ghana	Kenya	Zimbabwe
Manufacturers and traders			
Share of traders in sample	33%	38%	32%
Sectoral composition			
Food processing	26%	17%	29%
Textile and garments	26%	38%	38%
Woodworking and furniture	26%	22%	16%
Metalworking	23%	22%	18%
Firm characteristics			
Total employment	82	77	474
Age of firm	15	19	28
Ethnicity			
African	na	42%	23%
Asian	na	46%	5%
European	na	5%	61%
Other	na	7%	11%
Number of observations	58	58	57

Tema. In Kenya and Zimbabwe, all firms come from the capital city. Sample characteristics are summarized in table 3.2. The samples include firms of all sizes. Trading firms account for roughly one-third of the sample. Many surveyed firms are in the textile and garments sector—a reflection of the important of the sector in African manufacturing.

The average number of employees is larger in the Zimbabwean sample—474 compared to 82 and 77. Trading firms in the sample tend to be smaller than manufacturing firms. The largest sample firm has 5,505 workers. A handful of sample firms are parastatals or government agencies. Most of the smaller firms would typically be considered part of the higher echelons of the informal sector: they all have a stable place of work and they have at least one or two employees. The smallest and most ephemeral microenterprises are not captured in the sample.[4] The average age of surveyed firms varies between 15 years in Ghana and 28 years in Zimbabwe. Trading firms tend to be older than manufacturing firms.

The ethnic composition of the Kenya and Zimbabwe samples is also given in table 3.2.[5] In both countries owners and managers of medium to large firm predominantly

4. See Hart (1988) for a discussion of contractual issues among very small firms.
5. Similar data were not collected in Ghana.

belong to a minority ethnic group. The ethnicity of the dominant business group, however, varies between the two countries. In Kenya, the bulk of surveyed firms are in the hands of ethnic Asians; in Zimbabwe, they are mostly managed by whites.[6] In both cases these communities represent around 1 percent of the country's population. Such degree of ethnic concentration in medium- to large-scale enterprises is not unusual in Africa, although dominant business communities are not always of foreign origin (Bigsten et al. 2000a). In contrast, the overwhelming majority of microenterprises in Kenya and Zimbabwe are in the hands of ethnic Africans (Daniels 1994). These issues are revisited in part VI.

3.3 The Agricultural Trader Surveys

The RPED surveys cover manufacturing firms and, to a small extent, the traders who sell trade with them. The picture of market institutions that they present is thus primarily urban. It largely ignores rural markets. To complement it, data were also collected on traders of agricultural products. Three countries are covered: Benin, Malawi, and Madagascar.

The first survey of agricultural traders was conducted in Madagascar in a joint project between IFPRI (the International Food Policy Research Institute) and the local Ministry of Scientific Research (FOFIFA). The survey consisted of two visits (for a detailed description, see Fafchamps and Minten 1999). The first visit took place between May and August 1997. The questionnaire on the first visit contained mainly questions dealing with the individual characteristics of the traders and with the structure, conduct, and performance of the trading sector. The second visit was conducted between September and November 1997. The same traders were asked about the nature of their relationships with other traders, clients, and suppliers. A total number of 850 traders were surveyed in the first round, 739 of whom were surveyed again in the second round. To facilitate comparison, the analysis presented here is based on traders that could be located in the two rounds.[7]

Similar surveys were subsequently conducted in Malawi and Benin in collaboration between the World Bank, Oxford University, and IFPRI. The main difference is

6. Why it is Asians who dominate in Kenya and whites in Zimbabwe is undoubtedly the result of past policies that favored these two groups. These policies, however, have been discontinued since independence (1964 for Kenya, and 1979 for Zimbabwe after 15 years under Ian Smith's white government).

7. Not surprisingly, the category of traders that was hardest to trace during the second survey round was that of traders who are least formal and have the least permanent form of operation. As a result small itinerant traders tend to be underrepresented in the results reported for Madagascar.

that information was collected in a single visit. Samples of 663 and 738 traders were interviewed in Benin and Malawi, respectively. Data collection took place between August and September 1999 for Benin and between August 1999 and February 2000 for Malawi.

The sample design was constructed so as to be as representative as possible of all the traders involved in the whole food marketing chain from producer to consumer, wherever located. In all three countries the survey sites are market towns where agricultural traders are active. These market towns were selected on the basis of their importance in the agricultural economy of the country, in terms of flows and volumes of the three types of products: major food crops, cash crops, and agricultural inputs.

Due to the absence of reliable census information on the population of traders in both countries, the first step in drawing a random sample was to conduct a census of traders in the selected markets. For Madagascar, traders were surveyed in three different types of location: traders operating in big and small urban markets (these are mostly wholesalers, semi-wholesalers, and retailers), urban traders located outside regular markets (bigger traders, processors, and wholesalers), and traders operating on rural markets (assemblers and itinerant traders). Rural firaisanas were selected through stratified sampling based on agro-ecological characteristics so as to be representative of the various kind of marketed products and marketing seasons. For Benin, lists of traders were first obtained from ONASA (Office National d'Appui à la Sécurité Alimentaire), and the regional bureaus of Ministry of Commerce. In addition to these lists, the survey team undertook a count of traders present on the market day, and used these three sources of information to construct a census from which a sample was randomly draw. In Malawi, a reconnaissance survey of traders was conducted in July through August 1999 in order to count and identify traders according to their status (independent, buying agent, or selling agent), their level (retail or wholesale), and the types of products they traded. Information on the name, type, and location of traders from the reconnaissance survey was then used to draw a random sample of traders.

The survey focused on traders who market locally consumed staples such as cereals, roots and tubers, legumes, and oilseeds. The different forms in which these products are marketed were taken into consideration (paddy and milled rice, maize and maize flour, etc.). Traders involved primarily in fruits, vegetables, and minor crops were excluded. In Malawi, a small number of tobacco buyers are included in the survey. Most surveyed traders focus on main staple foods such as rice (in Madagascar) or maize (in Benin and Malawi).

Table 3.3
Composition of agricultural traders samples

	Benin	Malawi	Madagascar
Total employment (including trader)	2.2	1.5	4.3
Age of firm	15	7	6
Working capital in $	1,471	560	2,061
Storage capacity in MT	7	12	26
Equipment value in $	3,391	501	399
Number of observations	663	738	739

Note: MT = metric tons.

The Benin and Malawi used the same questionnaire, but the questionnaire used in Madagascar was slightly different. In all three cases the coverage of the survey instrument was not only very broad but also innovative in the type of information gathered. The questionnaires covered the following main areas: (1) defining the trading enterprise, (2) trader characteristics, (3) factors of productions and operating costs, (4) trading activities and marketing costs, and (5) relationships and coordination costs. Data were collected on search behavior and costs, quality inspection, contract enforcement and dispute settlement, information, and property rights enforcement.

The main characteristics of surveyed traders are summarized in table 3.3. Surveyed businesses are fairly small and unsophisticated. Few of the traders possess their own means of transport, and for the overwhelming majority of traders, investment in equipment is low compared to working capital. For most traders, working capital is tied up in the product itself. A small number of surveyed traders nevertheless possess large fleets of vehicles, resulting in a large average value of equipment. The size distribution of firms is quite large. In Madagascar, for instance, Fafchamps and Minten (1999) show that traders in the upper tercile of the firm size distribution use fifteen times more working capital and two times more labor, but they obtain almost fifty times more value added than traders in the lower tercile. Hence large traders have much higher total factor productivity than the small ones. Women represent the majority of sampled traders—46 percent of the sample in Madagascar, 36 percent in Malawi, and 81 percent in Benin. Retailers constitute the bulk of the samples.

3.4 Conclusion

The empirical evidence used in this book comes from a wide variety of surveys taken in twelve sub-Saharan African countries. Despite some shortcomings the data are roughly comparable across countries and provide a unique comparative perspective. The author was directly involved in many of the surveys and has interpreted the collected data with an eye on local custom. By covering manufacturers as well as traders, the data generate a more complete picture of market institutions than what could be obtained by looking at firms or traders alone. Armed with these data, we are now ready to delve into the data analysis.

II CONTRACT ENFORCEMENT

We saw in chapter 2 that there are many mechanisms economic agents can potentially use to enforce mutually beneficial agreements. This part examines the evidence on the mechanisms used in practice in sub-Saharan Africa.

We begin in chapter 4 with detailed evidence collected from a series of case studies in Ghana, Kenya, and Zimbabwe. The few samples are complemented by informal discussions between the author and some 175 African firms, and thus these data constitute a useful starting point. Results show that courts and lawyers are not the primary contract enforcement mechanism on which African firms rely.

Chapter 5 combines quantitative evidence from manufacturing surveys conducted in nine countries. Results show that reliance on legal institutions is infrequent and that contracts are flexible. Evidence from surveys of agricultural traders is presented next in chapter 6. Results confirms previous studies and further stresses the importance of risk avoidance as a rational firm response to imperfect contract enforcement. The effect of imperfect contract enforcement on firm behavior is illustrated in chapter 7. We show that firms facing more delivery problems tend to build up larger inventories.

Many of the findings reported here are similar to those described in other parts of the world. This is particularly true of the importance of relational contracting, which has been described in very similar terms in transitional economies where legal institutions to support market are embryonic (e.g., McMillan and Woodruff 1999b; Johnson et al. 2000, 2002). Relational contracting—or personal exchange as North (2001) calls it—appears related with the underdevelopment of markets. This is a point that we explore in detail in the remainder of the book.

4 Evidence from Case Studies in Ghana, Kenya, and Zimbabwe

This chapter investigates the contractual practices of African manufacturing firms and examines whether economic agents use long-term relationships to make contractual performance contingent upon external shocks. Evidence to this effect has already been uncovered in credit transactions among villagers (e.g., Udry 1990, 1994; Fafchamps and Lund 2002) and fishermen (Platteau and Abraham 1987). In contrast to these earlier works that focused on small individual transactions in a rural setting, in this chapter we analyze the extent of contractual flexibility among large manufacturing firms.

Very little is known about how African markets operate in practice. Although some modicum of contractual flexibility is prevalent the world over, casual observation and anthropological accounts (e.g., Cohen 1969; Meillassoux 1971; Amselle 1977; Geertz et al. 1979) suggest that African firms have a more elastic definition of flexibility—to the point where it may have become a source of misunderstanding and cultural prejudice. In their dealings with Africans, for instance, foreigners are often taken by surprise by contractual delays and calls for contractual renegotiation, from which they are quick to conclude that African firms (and Africans in general) are unreliable and opportunistic. This is true not only of the occasional traveler but also of Western firms wishing to source products from Africa (Biggs et al. 1994). This may explain why foreign firms find it difficult to deal with Africans and why African manufacturers have a hard time breaking into export markets. If confirmed by rigorous analysis, this interpretation opens avenues for export promotion other than structural adjustment and devaluation.

This chapter answers some of these questions using the case study data set described in chapter 3. We show that contracts between African manufacturers and their suppliers and clients often are renegotiated: supplies occasionally arrive late or their quality is different from what was ordered, and clients sometimes pay late. Prevention in the form of risk avoidance plays an important role in reducing the occurrence of opportunistic breach. We first discuss evidence from three case studies of manufacturers and traders in Ghana, Kenya, and Zimbabwe. In the next chapter we use panel data on manufacturing firms in nine African countries to examine contract enforcement practices among suppliers and clients. In chapter 6, we report evidence based on cross-sectional surveys of agricultural traders in Benin, Madagascar, and Malawi. Throughout these three chapters we follow two main themes: incidence (frequency of problems) and remedy (action taken).

4.1 Case Studies in Ghana and Kenya

Given the lack of prior information on contractual issues in sub-Saharan Africa, a case study approach was initially adopted. Contract enforcement was studied in two countries, Ghana and Kenya. The small size of the samples (58 firms each) is compensated by the richness of the data collected during in-depth discussions with respondents. Interviews were guided by the conceptual framework outlined in chapter 2. We present survey results in sufficient detail for the reader to realize that the correspondence between our theory and the facts is not superficial but deep-seated. Contractual relations between firms and their clients are reviewed first. Relations with suppliers come next. Strategies used to prevent problems are then discussed. The use of legal institutions is presented at the end. Although the small size and diversity of the sample makes it difficult to draw statistically significant inferences, a detailed even if preliminary picture of contract enforcement in African manufacturing is obtained.

4.1.1 Payment Problems

Firms were asked about nonpayment and late payment problems encountered with clients. Their answers are summarized in table 4.1. Firms were also asked to com-

Table 4.1
Payment problems with clients

	Nonpayment		Late payment	
	Ghana	Kenya	Ghana	Kenya
Percentage of respondents citing problems	58%	60%	82%	81%
Average number of cases per month	0.2	0.7	5.2	1.3
Time elapsed since last case, in months	14.2	20	na	11
Average duration of payment delay, in days			72	142
Percentage of cases that occurred after full delivery	87%	90%	90%	84%
Percentage of cases with partial payment	47%	63%	14%	56%
Percentage of cases involving bounced checks	na	30%	19%	11%
Reason given for nonpayment:				
Client faced financial difficulties	23%	32%	69%	25%
Client was unable to collect payment from own customer	17%	4%	3%	12%
Client had to travel or left the business	14%	11%	7%	14%
Client was dishonest	27%	32%	2%	14%
Mistake or oversight by client	0%	7%	10%	6%
Other	20%	14%	9%	20%
Action taken by respondent:				
Wait, do very little	23%	43%	21%	45%
Harass client	63%	46%	38%	45%
Negotiate a rescheduling of payment	13%	11%	40%	11%

Source: Ghana and Kenya case studies.

ment on the most recent problem they had experienced with a client; answers are these questions presented in table 4.2.

More than half of the firms had ever experienced nonpayment by a client; all were familiar with late payment. In line with the theory, all credit sales seem to implicitly allow late payment: delays of a few days are so common that they are not mentioned by respondents unless specifically prompted. In one-fifth of all Ghanaian credit sales, no specific term is even set for payment: the contract is incomplete. For those instances when respondents considered clients had paid late, the average delay in Ghana ranges from 6 weeks for manufacturing firms up to 20 weeks for traders. This compares to an average payment term of 3 to 4 weeks for those contracts where a payment term is specified. The allowed delay in Kenya similarly goes up to 4 months. In three-fourths of the late payment cases, the transaction with the problematic client was not the first: on average, parties had been doing business for an average of 4 to 6 years (table 4.2). The percentage of firms with nonpayment is higher among large firms, probably because they sell more and are therefore more likely to ever have experienced nonpayment.

Late payment or nonpayment can only occur when an element of credit has entered the transaction. Credit often is voluntary, but it is occasionally forced upon the respondent. Payment problems are often associated with a bounced check, for instance. In a number of nonpayment cases, respondents said they were "conned" by

Table 4.2
Most recent payment problem with clients

	Ghana	Kenya
Percentage of respondents citing problems	76%	100%
Most recent problem was:		
Nonpayment	18%	36%
Late payment	82%	64%
Client was:		
Individual	25%	39%
Firm	62%	46%
Government agency	7%	13%
Other	5%	1%
First sale to client	27%	22%
Years of business with client	4.1	6.3
Direct bargaining was used	82%	72%
Case was settled	63%	na
Respondent is satisfied of outcome	69%	84%
Respondent resumed business with client	67%	43%

Source: Ghana and Kenya case studies.

customers into delivering the goods on the promise of prompt payment. The circumstances of each case vary, but the result is the same: firms were reluctantly, but somewhat knowingly, dragged into a situation of extending credit to a customer. In half of the cases, partial or advance payment was made so that the loss from nonpayment was limited to part of the sale. In Kenya where the information was collected, the percentage of problems occurring with people from the same ethnic group is not significantly different from the proportion of trade credit recipients from the same ethnic group.

Reasons for nonpayment fall into two broad categories: upstream transfer of risk (excusable default), and dishonesty (table 4.1). Half of the respondents mention business difficulties as the major reason for the client's nonpayment. In one case out of five, firms specifically state that clients were unable to sell the goods supplied by or made from goods supplied by the respondent, or that they were unable to collect payment for such goods. Clients thus share commercial risk with their supplier. In a third of the cases, respondents blame dishonesty as the reason for nonpayment. Spurious reasons, such as "the client made a mistake," "the client had to travel," or "the client left that line of business" are also advanced by respondents, often with suspicion, if not of dishonesty, at least of carelessness.

Late payment, on the other hand, is mostly a way of sharing commercial risk with the supplier. It is overwhelmingly blamed on temporary business difficulties experienced by clients. In one-fourth to one-fifth of the cases, these financial difficulties are specifically associated with the client's inability to sell goods supplied by, or manufactured with goods supplied by, the respondent. Firms' answers suggest that in some cases the seller is implicitly providing a warranty that the good will resell well. Family events are also invoked by clients to excuse late payment. Deliberate dishonesty is cited by a few firms, most of them in Kenya. Mistakes and oversights are cited in a few cases, particularly in connection with bounced checks. Whether these were genuine mistakes remains questionable, as a few smiles and shrugs reminded us. But respondents readily accept the excuse in exchange for prompt payment.

Contractual flexibility varies with the risk faced by parties. Nonpayment, for instance, is more prevalent among textile and garment manufacturers, a likely reflection of the economic hardship the industry is facing as a result of trade liberalization. Discussions with respondents indicate that late payment by public firms or agencies is the rule; it is blamed on the financial difficulties experienced by the government. Late payment and nonpayment are also more common the closer firms get to the final consumer: downstream firms, traders, and manufacturing firms dealing directly with customers are more affected than firms dealing mostly with other firms or traders. Half of the payment problems, for instance, happen with an individual consumer or a small firm and in a third of the cases with a trader—often a small retailer or itinerant peddler. Payment problems are thus influenced by what happens at the end of the manufacturing–wholesale–retail chain, probably because flexibility is most needed by poor consumers and microenterprises starved of working capital.

4.1.2 Response to Payment Delays

Firms take different attitudes toward problems that arise. Some, mostly manufacturers, insist they must show flexibility and understanding toward payment difficulties, an attitude that is consistent with the idea of excusable default and the implicit sharing of risk. Others, mostly traders, suspend credit to bad payers and insist on the settlement of old debt before granting new credit, thereby inflicting penalty. Few respondents insisted they actively maintain a reputation of being strict about payment deadlines. The nature of the dilemma faced by an unpaid supplier is best illustrated by the following example, coming from one of the respondents: A woman wholesaler had sold cloth to a retailer. The cloth, however, did not retail well and the retailer was unable to pay the supplier. Refusing the retailer further credit meant that she would remain stuck with slow-selling textiles, her business would go down, and the wholesaler may never recover her money. If, on the other hand, the retailer was given new, hot-selling textiles, her business may regain impetus. In the process, the slow-moving textiles may find buyers and the wholesaler may recoup her money. This example is illustration of the classical creditor's dilemma: throwing good money after bad may be the only way to get both back (Gale and Hellwig 1985). Sharing business risk may be required to recover a commercial debt.

The most likely course of action taken by respondents when faced with nonpayment is to wait for some time then start harassing the client. Discussions with respondents indicate that they initially display understanding when clients invoke plausible excuses to delay payment. As the delay lengthens, however, they become more suspicious and increase their pressure: state contingent monitoring thus appears to be the rule. Direct bargaining is the favored method of conflict resolution (table 4.2) with a steady progression in the pressure applied by the creditor: letters are sent, repeated visits are made to the workplace or the home, strong words are exchanged between respondent and client, screams are heard, and third parties and messengers are involved, and in a few cases, court action is initiated. As a result of these renegotiations, a large proportion of firms, particularly among traders, agree to reschedule payments and to let the client pay in installments. But the boundary between voluntary rescheduling and coerced delay in collection is hard to draw precisely.

Harassment and repeated visits, respondents argue, serve several purposes. First, they are annoying and make the debtor want to find the money. Second, they increase the likelihood that the respondent is there when the debtor gets money. For that reason, visits are mostly made on pay day or market day, or when the debtor collects from its own customers. Third, they enable the creditor to evaluate whether or not the client was hit by a shock. This information can be used to infer the client's type and riskiness, and decide whether to continue the relationship or not. This is akin to state-contingent monitoring. Respondents only give up trying to get their money back either when they have physically lost track of a recalcitrant client and no longer know where to find him or her, or when it has become clear that they are unable to force the client to pay. The ability to impose repayment depends both on the clients' financial ability to repay and on their continued practice of business: respondents appear at a loss trying to recoup from clients who have left their line of business and thus lost interest in the relationship and their reputation, even if they hold other assets, like a home. Those who hold the client's goods as guarantee (e.g., tailors who receive material from their client) eventually sell them.

Harassment methods are adapted to circumstances. One Kenyan respondent, for instance, reported sending his collection agent to debtors at opening time because, in the Hindu tradition, it is bad omen to be asked for money first thing in the morning. More detailed information was collected in Kenya. There, half of the firms also stop credit and deliveries upon payment delay. Most firms declare that their willingness to wait depends on the situation of the debtor. A quarter of the firms use their past experience with the debtor as a basis for evaluation. Some visit their client or observe his consumption pattern. Half of the firms are informed by others or know the client intimately because he or she has a neighboring business or is a family member. Kenyan respondents seem to find out more about their customers than they think their suppliers know about them. A third of them cannot, however, judge whether the excuse made by the client is founded or not. This is particularly true with "up-country" clients whose business is located too far to allow a visual assessment of their situation. It is therefore little surprise that the bad repayment record of up-country customers is a frequent object of complaint among Kenyan respondents.

Payment collection appears effective: in two-thirds of the cases the dispute is resolved satisfactorily and business is resumed. This implies that the ability to re-negotiate the contract in case of excusable default is implicitly present in most credit sales. But it imposes a serious debt collection burden on firms. Those who deal mostly with public agencies, the worst payer of all according to respondents, even have a full-time staff member entirely devoted to that task. Respondents who either have collected a substantial advance or have not yet delivered a custom-made good constitute an important exception: they simply hang onto their output until the customer comes to pick it up and pay.

Exports are a special case because parties rely much more on legal institutions, the letter of credit in particular. Exporters who receive an irrevocable letter of credit from their foreign buyer are seldom paid late since payment is automatic after presentation of transport documents. Banks, however, are accused of delaying the transfer of international funds so as to benefit from the accruing interest. In the case of standard letters of credit, the situation is different, since payment can be delayed if the client challenges the quality of the delivery. The few exporting firms in the sample invariably run into such problems. The absence of SGS-like inspection for goods leaving Ghana, for instance, makes it easy for foreign clients to reject goods after delivery and to extort discounts from Ghanaian exporters. Exports to neighboring African countries are also a source of difficulty. Respondents indicate that red tape is pervasive despite regional trade agreements, and that border duties are an opportunity for custom officers and other officials to extract rents. For those who try to follow legal procedures, the extra cost of paying taxes and bribes and of getting the required paperwork jeopardizes the profitability of the transaction and makes payment to the exporter less likely. As a result trade across African borders is mostly informal and bypasses the institutional setup—of letter of credit and bill of lading, for example—that governs international trade with the developed world. This deprives firms of legal protection against bad payers and poor quality supplies. Most respondents declare avoiding direct import or export with neighboring countries.

4.1.3 Delivery Problems

To contrast how payment issues compare with the placement of orders and the quality of deliveries, firms were asked about late and nondelivery by suppliers and deficient quality of inputs. Their answers are summarized in table 4.3. Results indicate that delivery and quality problems with suppliers are less of a concern than payment problems with clients. We first look at delivery problems, and then at quality deficiencies.

There are more cases of late delivery than of nondelivery in both countries. In Ghana, the frequency of reported late delivery cases is five times higher than cases of nondelivery. The frequency of nondelivery cases in higher in Kenya, but this is driven by outliers; the median number of nondeliveries is 0.2—once every five months. The

Table 4.3
Problems with suppliers

	Nondelivery		Late delivery		Deficient quality	
	Ghana	Kenya	Ghana	Kenya	Ghana	Kenya
Percentage of respondents citing problems	25%	52%	51%	67%	57%	82%
Average number of cases per month	0.1	7.1	0.6	3.8	0.3	1.6
Time elapsed since last occurrence, in months	2.5	6.7	na	4.1	na	na
Duration of the delay, in days			19	20		
Percentage of cases involving imports	29%	8%	29%	7%	13%	2%
Percentage of cases involving government enterprises	7%	32%	18%	7%	11%	11%
Percentage of cases with full or partial prepayment	43%	17%	30%	20%	57%	40%
Percentage of cases with partial delivery	29%	67%	na	17%	na	na
Reason						
Normal manufacturing, storage, or handling defect	na	na	na	na	54%	50%
Supplier was unable to find inputs	29%	52%	25%	47%	32%	0%
Supplier faced equipment breakdown or transport delay	35%	8%	14%	10%	0%	8%
Transport or bureaucratic problem	7%	0%	32%	20%	6%	0%
Supplier could not satisfy all customers	7%	26%	25%	13%	0%	0%
Mistake or oversight	7%	0%	0%	10%	10%	16%
Supplier's costs changed dramatically	14%	13%	0%	0%	0%	0%
Supplier was dishonest	0%	0%	4%	0%	16%	21%

Source: Ghana and Kenya case studies.

average delivery delay is 20 days. Late delivery afflicts large firms more than small firms. In a fifth to half of the cases, partial or total payment was made before delivery, which indicates that respondents may have incurred a loss beyond the inconvenience of a failed order. In Kenya, trading firms and non–Kenyan-African firms are more likely to place orders and to incur failed delivery than manufacturing and Kenyan-African firms.

As with trade credit, contractual flexibility varies with the risk faced by parties. In Ghana, delivery problems are most frequent in the wood sectors, for instance. Competition with exports for good quality timber, we were told, is a major explanation for these difficulties. Before trade liberalization, lumber was implicitly subsidized as a result of the overvalued exchange rate. The devaluation of the Ghanaian currency has led to an increase in the domestic price for timber. To remain competitive, domestic wood industries now rely on low-quality timber, either rejects from exports or timber harvested by small operators with inferior equipment. The supply of this lumber category is particularly erratic. The food sector is also affected by late delivery problems, but the average delay is comparatively short. In other sectors the failure of foreign firms to satisfy orders is the major reason for nondelivery. In Ghana, imports also account for a large proportion of late deliveries with an average delay of 6 to 15 weeks. Kenyan case study firms, being located far from the ocean port of Mombasa, seldom import directly and are thus less likely to incur problems with foreign suppliers. Public firms are notable for late delivery, especially in Kenya, but the delays involved are usually very short.

In all cases, delivery problems are blamed on shocks affecting suppliers and are treated by respondents as cases of excusable default. First on the list of reasons for failed and late delivery are transportation hazards and the inability of suppliers to satisfy all demand. In Kenya, the most common reasons for delivery problems is that the supplier was unable to find suitable inputs, had insufficient capacity to satisfy all, or was delayed by transportation problems. In a few cases, orders were not satisfied by suppliers when cost conditions changed dramatically and prices went up. Equipment breakdown and the supplier's inability to secure essential inputs come next and are most frequently blamed in the wood and metal sectors. Given frequent and unpredictable delays in production, suppliers are unable to guarantee delivery on a given date without holding inventories of finished products. Delays in delivery are thus a way of shifting production risk and a part of commercial risk to the buyer. Discussions with respondents indicate that certain suppliers, particularly public firms, sell at a low price with the implicit understanding that late deliveries are frequent and that the burden of production risk and the cost of holding inventories are transferred onto buyers. Sufficiently low prices induce buyers to put up with late delivery.

The action taken by respondent firms depends whether advance payment has been made or not. When no advance payment was made, firms initially react by waiting or sending an occasional reminder. If delays get too long, they cancel the order. When payment has already been made, firms typically complain and harass the supplier. In a handful of cases, nondelivery was attributed to a drastic change in the supplier's opportunity cost. When only a small portion of the order has not been supplied, firms typically carry over the unfulfilled portion of the contract onto their subsequent order. While traders prefer to wait or cancel their order if the delay gets too long, manufacturing firms are more likely to pursue suppliers and insist on timely delivery. The reason is that manufacturing firms require inputs to operate. Traders told us they have alternative ways of using their funds and can afford to wait.

Firms facing frequent delivery problems indicated during interviews that they minimize the impact on their production activities by overordering, ordering early, building up inventories, or securing supplies from other sources. Although effective, these strategies impose a cost on the firm. We revisit this issue in chapter 14. Furthermore these strategies are not available to firms with insufficient working capital, particularly microenterprises. Firms unable to stockpile inputs must stop production when deliveries are delayed. Traders appear to serve as buffer between manufacturers and suppliers of raw materials: those who operate in industries where nondelivery is frequent face more such cases per year than do manufacturing firms.

4.1.4 Input Quality Problems

Defective quality is a common occurrence, particularly in the wood and food sectors. But it rarely affects more than a small portion of the quantities delivered. The median frequency of occurrence in Kenya is once every five months. Defective quality afflicts large firms 70 percent more than small firms. An advantage of supplier credit is that it enables the client to verify the goods before payment. The credit relationship thus helps enforce quality because the client can threaten to hold up payment until the problem is solved. In 40 percent of the cases, however, payment was made before discovering the defect.

Imports in Ghana are responsible for a large percentage of non- and late deliveries, but they account for few defective quality cases. Respondents attribute this achievement to the inspection of every shipment to Ghana by SGS, an independent Swiss company, at the port of origin. Yet, despite inspection, a number of foreign firms manage to deliver deficient goods. One can only wonder at what might occur without inspection.

Most cases of defective quality are treated by respondents as excusable default and are solved through bilateral negotiations. Half of the respondents attributed the deficient quality to normal manufacturing or handling defect. Occurrences are usually blamed on suppliers' inadequate equipment or on their inability to find inputs of good quality. More than one-third of the firms, however, estimated that the supplier had made a mistake or had been careless or dishonest. A few respondents felt cheated by a supplier who had willfully misrepresented the quality of the good delivered.

The most frequent action taken in case of deficient quality is to return or exchange the goods. The second most frequent action is to negotiate a discount on the next consignment. Two-thirds of the Kenyan respondent were able to exchange the goods; a few got a refund. A fifth of Kenyan firms, however, had to take a loss. These often were small, cash buying firms. A few traders mention that insurance against defective quality is built into the contract, either through an explicit insurance policy against transportation damages, or by supplying a few extra items to compensate for defi-

Table 4.4
Most recent problem with suppliers

	Ghana	Kenya
Percentage of respondents citing problems	67%	100%
Most recent problem was:		
Nondelivery	11%	0%
Late delivery	38%	43%
Deficient quality	51%	57%
Client was:		
Individual	0%	15%
Firm	72%	71%
Government agency	10%	7%
Other	18%	7%
First purchase from supplier	5%	6%
Years of business with supplier	6.1	9.9
Direct bargaining was used	74%	65%
Case was settled	87%	67%
Respondent is satisfied of outcome	83%	86%
Respondent resumed business with client	92%	87%

Source: Ghana and Kenya case studies.

ciencies. To summarize, the risk of defective quality is mostly borne by the supplier. Buyers, however, assume part of the cost of quality screening.

4.1.5 Dealing with Problematic Suppliers

Respondents were asked about their most recent problem with a supplier (table 4.4). Deficient quality is most frequently cited, followed by late delivery; nondelivery comes last. Traders complain most of deficient quality and manufacturers of late delivery. Manufacturing firms have problems mostly with traders, and traders mostly with manufacturers. This is consistent with the role of traders as intermediaries between manufacturing firms, and between domestic firms and foreign suppliers.

The problematic supplier was mostly a large manufacturer, seldom the sole source of supply, never a friend or relative, and (in Kenya) a third of the time from the same ethnic group. In the overwhelming majority of the cases, the respondent had dealt with that supplier before, on average for 6.1 years in Ghana and 9.9 years in Kenya. Sample sizes are too small, however, to conclude whether the difference is significant. As respondents emphasized throughout the interview and as is clear from the next section, few problems are recorded with casual suppliers because firms do not take the chance of a problem happening: such transactions often are of the "inspect-then-pay-cash-and-carry" type and do not involve delayed obligations that make breach of contract possible.

In two-thirds to three-fourths of the cases, direct bargaining with suppliers is used to solve the problem. In the remaining cases, the problem essentially resolves itself. The difficulty is nearly always settled to the satisfaction of the respondent and business continues as before, a feature that is consistent with the idea of excusable default. Exceptions involve distant foreign firms who have failed to supply or have delivered grossly inadequate products. Firms dealing with chronically late suppliers constitute a special case. They rarely find it useful to pester the supplier and prefer to wait. Eventually supplies are delivered and a new order is placed. But the entire situation could hardly be described as satisfactory. Late and erratic deliveries place a strain on the receiving firm, forcing it to build up inventories or wait in line at the factory gate. They may also delay the firm's production and damage its reputation vis-à-vis its own customers. As argued earlier, lower prices often are what induce respondents to put up with poor contractual performance. In a few cases low contractual discipline is attributable to monopolistic firms abusing their position.

4.1.6 Payment to Suppliers (Kenya Only)

Kenyan case study firms were also interviewed about payments to suppliers. Ninety percent of the surveyed firms have ever experienced difficulties repaying suppliers. They estimate that they can delay payment for one month without incurring sanctions. On average, they can stretch repayment to suppliers about three times a year. More than half of the firms seek a direct contact with their supplier whenever they are unable to make one of their payments on time. A fourth of the surveyed firms decide unilaterally when to repay and wait for their supplier to call them up. Those few firms that have given postdated checks or bills of exchange to their suppliers must plead with them to delay presenting them for payment. This is particularly delicate with bills because they can be discounted and are normally collected by banks.

Probit analysis indicates that there are no noticeable differences in repayment difficulties between firm categories. The only exception is that textile and garment firms are significantly more likely to experience problems, a possible reflection of the difficulties encountered in that sector as a result of trade liberalization and competition from imported secondhand clothing.

The great majority of Kenyan suppliers do not attempt to verify the excuse the respondents gives them to delay payment. The most suppliers do is to use their knowledge of general business conditions to assess whether delayed payment is out of line or not with the general situation faced by other firms. Suppliers thus use relative performance evaluation: to assess the difficulties faced by their client, they rely on common knowledge information that is correlated with the hidden shock affecting their client. A few respondents volunteer evidence to their suppliers whenever available—like a bounced check from one of their customers, for instance.

There is a clear implicit understanding that repeated delays hurt the relationship with the supplier. A firm's past payment history influences how compassionate and responsive suppliers are to a firm's payment problems. If past payments have been regular, an occasional delay is accepted without question. If several payments suffer unusual delays, however, the firm is less likely to be given the benefit of the doubt. The supplier's trust is eroded and the firm's reputation will suffer. In most cases the fear of loosing the supplier-creditor's trust and of damaging one's reputation in the community is sufficient to guarantee repayment. Repeated interaction thus substitutes for gathering costly information on the idiosyncratic shocks affecting the debtor.

In the majority of cases there is no explicit guarantee for repayment. The primary punishment is to reduce or cut trade credit; that is, the usual sanction firms incur if they delay beyond reason is suspension of credit or deliveries. Only a few firms cited penalties and legal sanctions as likely sanctions. A couple mentioned debt forgiveness. Detailed discussions with respondents indicate that suppliers' sanctions are subtle and progressive. Suppliers appear to have a preference ordering of their clients that gets revised on the basis of the performance of each. Best deals—such as timely deliveries and preferential access to hard-to-get items—are offered to those clients highest in the ranking. Bad payers have lower priority and won't get anything if the firm has insufficient stock to satisfy the market. A client who has completely fallen out of favor will not be able to place an order and will be politely be turned down, usually on the pretext that the supplier is out of stock. We could not help thinking that certain suppliers, particularly those with market power, deliberately set their selling price just low enough so as to ration their output, then use rationing to discipline their clients.

The overwhelming majority of Kenyan firms said that the supplier's willingness to wait depends on the respondent's situation. Half of the suppliers, however, have no way of verifying what they are told. Some use their knowledge of general business conditions, others observe the respondent's business by themselves, a few exchange information with other businesses. The attitude of respondents during this part of the interview—giggles, smiles, rolling eyes—suggests that most respondents actually play games with their suppliers and use delayed payment as an easy access to cheap credit. The more outspoken respondents actually told us so quite plainly. Everybody

Table 4.5
Recourse to legal institutions

	Ghana	Kenya
Following a dispute with a supplier:		
Ever saw a lawyer	13%	6%
Ever went to court	2%	0%
Ever used arbitration	4%	0%
Threatened to call the police	5%	2%
Ever called the police	5%	0%
Following a dispute with a client:		
Ever saw a lawyer	8%	38%
Ever went to court	6%	21%
Ever used arbitration	4%	6%
Threatened to call the police	14%	4%
Ever called the police	5%	4%

Source: Ghana and Kenya case studies.

knows the nature of the game and no one takes payment delays seriously unless they go beyond what is considered acceptable.

4.1.7 Recourse to Legal Institutions

To help ascertain the role that legal institutions play in the enforcement of contracts, surveyed firms were asked about their use of lawyers and courts. Answers, summarized in table 4.5, indicate that Ghanaian and Kenyan firms make little use of legal procedures. Only a handful of Ghanaian case study firms ever consulted a lawyer. The propensity to consult lawyers is much higher in Kenya, however, especially regarding clients. Virtually no Kenyan firm had ever consulted a lawyer regarding one of their suppliers; none of them had brought a supplier to court. Large firms are much more likely to call upon lawyers than small firms, probably because the size of the transactions would not justify the lawyer's fee. Kenyan-African firms hardly ever use lawyers; nearly half of the non–Kenyan-African ones do.

Most respondents find the assistance of a lawyer useful and effective. One, however, emphasized that sending a lawyer's letter to his most important customers had destroyed the relationship and led the firm to bankruptcy. We also find a sharp difference between the two countries in the propensity to go to court. In Ghana, only four respondents ever went to court with clients or suppliers, one of them several times. Two of the cases were still pending in court at the time of the survey, one of them in a foreign country. For the two firms that got judgment, the outcome was favorable, but the plaintiffs chose not to execute the judgment: a textile wholesaler had second thoughts about throwing an elderly couple out of their home, and a large trading firm hesitated to foreclose because it would have meant putting 500 people out of work and raising political turmoil during an election year. Although Kenyan firms also complain about the unpredictability of court proceedings, the reliance on legal institutions appears more widespread. Although the sample is too small to be conclusive, the use of lawyers and legal institutions appears to be a function of firm size and transaction size. Informality did not seem to be a problem, at least among surveyed firms: no respondent stated that they did not use the legal system because they did not have access to it on account of their lack of legal status.

In Ghana a few respondents expressed concerns that in cases involving the state, courts and tribunals are occasionally subject to political pressure, but not in commercial disputes. Several Kenyan respondents say they have not taken legal action because they perceive the legal system as being both expensive and subject to manipulation—courts, they say, can be bribed by both sides. They claim that the settlements amount to little more than a rescheduling of payments, which does not compensate them for their trouble. Some add that court rulings are not enforceable against "judgment-proof" debtors, that is, debtors without any asset that can be seized. Several respondents also expressed anxiety at having their name muddied by the publicity of a contractual dispute and did not want to acquire a reputation for undue toughness. Private resolution of contractual matters is deemed preferable.

A few surveyed firms made use of arbitration, mostly through a common friend. In one case, independent auditors resolved a dispute between supplier and client by checking both firms' accounts. In another, a lumber trader sought the mediation of the Loggers' Association. In one case in Ghana the respondent obtained the mediation of local Committees for the Defense of the Revolution (CDR) in resolving disputes with suppliers. He nevertheless expressed regrets for involving politically charged paramilitary groups in business matters. As these examples illustrate, reported cases of arbitration are largely informal.

A handful of respondents, many of them traders, involved the police in a dispute with a supplier or client. A few more threatened to do so, principally in Ghana. But, by their own account, they would have refrained if the client had called their bluff. Only a couple of Kenyan firms involved the police or used harsh language with a client. They were not boisterous about it. Involving the police in business problems is a tricky process. The police do not investigate contractual matters; evidence has to be provided by the plaintiff. Moreover the police provides its services in exchange for a bribe. Who gives the highest bribe may gather the most support for his cause. Most respondents expressed a profound dislike for involving the police in contractual disputes.

4.1.8   Responses to Contractual Risk

Despite the survey's limited character, the results we have just presented provide evidence that the lack of contractual discipline is real: Ghanaian and Kenyan firms face regular delivery and payment delays. Imperfect compliance with contractual obligations does not, however, appear to spring from a cultural failure to recognize the need for business predictability: all interviewed firms are quite aware of the economic costs and disruptions caused by delays in payment and delivery, but they recognize that perfect compliance is an ideal out of the reach of their clients and suppliers as well as themselves. Lack of contractual discipline is thus largely a corollary of the prevailing level of economic development. Contract enforcement considerations have profound effects on the way firms deal with each other and with final consumers.

Contract Enforcement and Repeated Interaction
The method most firms use to avoid or minimize problems with suppliers is to inspect goods at delivery and give precise orders well in advance. Firms prefer to deal with suppliers they have had no problem with in the past, or to place their orders on the basis of reputation or brand name. Firms also cultivate good relationships with their suppliers through business lunches and visits, and by paying them on time. Formal proofs and procedures were hardly ever cited as a way of avoiding contractual problems. Kenyan-African firms are much more numerous in citing repeated interaction, reputation, and good relations as ways of avoiding problems. Non–Kenyan-African firms, on the other hand, privilege repeated interaction and attribute more weight to reputation and good relations. Large firms seem to rely more on legal proofs than small firms.

The most effective way of avoiding problems with clients is to insist on complete payment upon delivery. Case study interviews indeed indicate that when firms feel uncertain about the reliability of a client or supplier, they fall back on a flea market mode of transacting: inspect the good on the spot, pay cash, and walk away with it. This way of conducting business is unwieldy for all but the smallest of firms. Better still, one could ask for an advance or down payment when placing the order.

To operate with any degree of predictability, firms must be able to take and place orders, arrange the future delivery of goods and services, dissociate payment from the physical delivery of goods, and seek and provide warranty. In Ghana and Kenya this is achieved mainly through the establishment of long term, personalized relationships. On average, surveyed firms have bought from their credit suppliers for 8 to 9 years, and sold to their credit clients for 6 years. Firms express an overwhelming preference to do business with people they already know, even if it means dealing with a few people only. Showing flexibility and avoiding misunderstanding also help smooth things out.

The main motivation behind contract performance is the desire to preserve profitable, long-term relationships and to maintain sources of supply and demand: firms pay their suppliers because they need more goods in the future; they deliver on time to keep their customers. The business relation itself is the creditor's best collateral. Other forms of contract enforcement are secondary. Harassment is the major form of debt collection strategy, but it is costly to pursue and some debtors appear able to hide from their creditors or to discourage them through delaying tactics.

With the exception of a few Muslim traders, respondents place no emphasis on ethics and religion. Little effort is made to assess the honesty of potential clients or suppliers independently from their interest in establishing a business relationship. The threat of court action is seldom credible because of the costs and long delays involved. Even if court action is successful, respondents hesitate to implement judgments, especially in Ghana. Reputation mechanisms are weak, especially in Ghana. Information about bad payers or unreliable suppliers is not shared among firms. Business transactions are seldom initiated on the sole basis of reputation. Several respondents, when asked whether they pay any attention to their clients' reputation among the business community, indicated that gossip seldom is reliable. A number of firms, principally in Kenya, cited credit checks as a way of assessing potential customers. In Ghana personal recommendation is the only way by which economic agents can capitalize on their good behavior with others. Few firms, however, offer credit to clients on this sole basis.

The value of the relationship to the other party is also what firms focus on when they screen customers and suppliers. One of their main concerns is to establish the other party's business horizon. They know that if the debtor is a fly-by-night concern, the likelihood of breach of contract is high. Firms therefore focus on establishing that a prospective business partner is a bona fide enterprise. They visit their customer's workshop or ask questions about other firms. A few respondents even extend credit on this sole basis. The horizon and degree of commitment of other parties are also assessed indirectly by observing their pattern of cash purchases over time.

Losses due to nonpayment by customers or nondelivery by suppliers are part of a constant learning process. Discussions with respondents suggest that inexperienced firms are more prone to credit recovery problems. Even experienced firms may endure painful consequences when they explore new markets and sources of supply. One of the costs of firm expansion and reorganization of activities is the identification of new reliable business partners through careful screening and trial and error. In the absence of a mechanism to circulate information about firms' contract performance record, experimentation is necessarily slow and perilous. We suspect that it constitutes a hindrance to the restructuring of the Ghanaian and Kenyan economies.

Flexible Contracts, Risk Sharing, and Opportunistic Behavior

The need for contractual flexibility is shared by businesses around the world. But it is probably accentuated in Africa by the low level of economic development. All respondents indicate that the respect of contractual terms regarding consistent quality, rapid delivery, and timely payment is difficult. Final consumers are mostly poor, vulnerable to economic shocks, and consequently bad payers. Markets for raw materials, intermediate goods, specialized services, and capital equipment are thin or nonexistent. Alternative sources of supply often do not exist. Whenever technical difficulties or shortages of imported goods arise, they cannot easily be circumvented and tend to ripple through downstream economic activities.

These factors combine to create delivery, payment, and quality problems. Surveyed businesses adapt to the situation by displaying a high degree of contractual flexibility. Indeed, most of the reasons invoked for contract noncompliance involve the sharing of risk. The fact that parties agree to reschedule deliveries and payments and to continue business suggests that risk sharing is implicitly built into most commercial transactions.

The genuine need for contract flexibility nevertheless opens avenues for opportunistic behavior. Debtors can delay payment by claiming they were hit by a large negative shock. Firms can delay delivery by claiming they could not find suitable inputs. Because such claims are hard to verify, respondents express the concern that contractual flexibility may be abused. They are suspicious of excuses given and attempt to verify them whenever possible and convenient. The most widely used strategy to discourage opportunistic claims is to harass recalcitrant debtors and suppliers. Harassment is a way of penalizing false claims; it also enables creditors to observe the business activities and consumption pattern of their debtors for evidence on their ability to pay.

Several reported cases of nonpayment involve clients who left the business. These cases can be interpreted as situations where the debtor initially had an interest in the business relationship and behaved accordingly for some time. But eventually that interest was lost: business conditions changed; other opportunities arose and interest in the relationship was reduced. Although these experiences could be construed as risk sharing, they were typically not perceived as such by respondents. The following anecdote is a good illustration. A Ghanaian fish trader purchased a quantity of fish on credit with the intent of selling it in villages. Later she discovered that the fish was not selling because farmers were having a bad year. She therefore decided to leave the fish business altogether and to reorient her trading activities to textiles. To start a textile operation she needed funds. She was currently unknown to textile suppliers and could only purchase goods on a cash-and-carry basis. All of her working capital was tied up in fish, which she did not sell well. So the only way for her to get started in textiles was to not pay for the fish she had bought on credit. The sum she owed was not large enough to justify court action. Since she was not intending to reenter the fish business, she did not mind angering fishmongers. She thus carried on with her plan, hoping never to be found. Cases like these are hard to prevent when the main incentive for contract compliance is the preservation of personal relationships and when information about contractual performance does not circulate. The only protection respondent firms have is to make sure they know where to find debtors in case they need to harass them.

Relational Contracting and Trade Intermediation

The institutional response surveyed firms have found to enforcement problems is to deal with a handful of suppliers and clients that they have known for years. This response, although effective in enabling business to develop and firms to gain access to trade credit, leads to the fragmentation of the economy into networks. It limits the range of commercial partners a firm may possibly deal with in a businesslike fashion. Because the economic reach of firms is reduced, one expects specialization and firm growth to be restricted.

Local and foreign institutions have emerged that partly redress the loss of efficiency due to fragmentation. Trade intermediation appears to be one of them. The function of traders, it seems, is essentially to transcend barriers to exchange and to build links between firms that would not otherwise be able to do business with each other. An Accra carpenter who needs wood, for instance, cannot, like his American counterpart, send a fax to a distant lumber company and reasonably expect the wood to show up. He must rely on a trader who has developed a personal relationship with that lumber company. The plethora of commercial intermediaries that characterizes Africa as well as many developing countries can thus be interpreted as a consequence of the high level of contract enforcement difficulties in an undeveloped economy. The replacement of telephones, telexes, and faxes by the ubiquitous trader, however, may represent an additional cost of doing business in Africa because the time and capital traders spend cajoling and policing suppliers and clients must be compensated (Geertz et al. 1979). Efforts to reduce the cost of trade intermediation could therefore be directed at improving the enforcement of commercial contracts.

When trading with the developed world, African importers and exporters rely on a different set of institutions (letter of credit, bill or lading, transport insurance) and intermediaries (banks, insurance companies, SGS), all of foreign origin or inspiration. The main function of these institutions and intermediaries is to ensure the respect of contractual obligations. International banks, in particular, are used to ensure that payment is made upon delivery. These institutions and intermediaries owe their existence to the high cost of inspecting goods at the port of departure and of collecting payment in an alien country. The fact that disputes occur despite their presence is the best illustration of the universal prevalence of contract enforcement problems. Their effectiveness nevertheless indicates that putting in place institutions for the enforcement of contracts can make a difference: thanks to these institutions, African firms can deal with foreign firms they know little about and with whom the enforcement mechanisms on which they rely locally would fail because of the cost of monitoring each other.

4.2   Case Study in Zimbabwe

These issues were revisited during the case study survey of manufacturing firms in Zimbabwe. The survey was devised along the same lines as the Ghana and Kenya case study surveys but focused on a slightly different set of issues. Many results are similar to those for Ghana and Kenya and need not be repeated. More detailed information was collected on what happens in practice when people do not pay.

4.2.1   Contract Compliance

Contracts compliance is no more perfect in Zimbabwe than it was in Ghana and Kenya. Most firms experience problems of late and nonpayment by customers. Large firms are more likely to run into such problems and face a larger number of problematic cases than small firms, a possible reflection of the larger number of clients that large firms have. As one would expect, cases of late payment are much more frequent than cases of nonpayment.

Firms were first asked to imagine what would happen should they or their clients fail to pay. In contrast with Ghana and Kenya, legal action is the most often cited response. Rescheduling is often cited in connection with clients. The interruption of deliveries is seen as a possible sanction against nonpayment in commercial transactions. This finding is consistent with the idea that the threat to discontinue the trade relationship is part of the enforcement mechanism. Firm behavior when faced with an actual contractual problem is somewhat different, however. Firms' initial response when faced with a payment problem is to seek an amiable resolution

Table 4.6
Repayment of supplier credit

	All	African	White	Other
Pay after term?				
Normally	33%	40%	30%	38%
Ever	82%	73%	79%	100%
When payment to supplier was delayed:				
Penalties charged	59%	33%	64%	67%
Penalties paid	42%	13%	50%	44%
Delay > 30 days	27%	0%	30%	33%

Source: Zimbabwe case study.

through direct negotiation. Should these negotiations fail, firms hire a lawyer and threaten to go to court, more frequently so if the client is not paying at all. Private arbitration is rare. Few firms ever threaten clients to call upon the police. The majority of late payment disputes are settled and business resumed. Nonpayment is more likely to sever the commercial relationship, a finding in line with what intuition would suggest. Except for the emphasis on courts and lawyers, these results are similar to those for Ghana and Kenya.

4.2.2 Payment Delays

Interviews further indicate that it is common for firms to delay payment beyond the agreed term. One-third of the sample firms stated that they normally pay after the term, in most cases within a month of the due date. Over 80 percent of the case study firms have delayed payment at least once (table 4.6). Contrary to the idea that contractual behavior is a matter of "culture," we find no significant difference between ethnic groups in their propensity to delay payment to supplier. A somewhat smaller fraction of white firms report paying normally after the term, but a larger fraction of white firms report having delayed payment at least once. Few microenterprises pay after term, partly because they often do not receive trade credit, and when they do, they are afraid to lose it. African firms and microenterprises are less likely to delay for more than one month when they do delay, and are less likely to be charged interest penalties for late payment.

In order to disentangle the effects of race, firm size, and other factors, we ran a probit analysis of whether firms normally or ever pay late. Results shows that food and wood sector firms are less likely to pay late (table 4.7); other firm characteristics are not significant. These results have limited statistical power due to the small number of observations, but they do *not* support the hypothesis that African firms

Table 4.7
Probit regression on whether the firm pays suppliers late

	Normally pays late		Ever pays late	
	Coefficient	p-value	Coefficient	p-value
Firm's characteristics				
Age of firm, in years	−0.02	0.227	−0.01	0.459
Number of employees, in log	0.50	0.144	0.28	0.524
Subsidiary dummy	0.36	0.516	−0.97	0.160
Manufacturer dummy	0.30	0.625	−1.37	0.108
Ethnicity (white is omitted category)				
African owner dummy	0.87	0.119	−0.13	0.832
Other owner dummy	0.78	0.241	4.85	0.926
Sector (metal sector is omitted category)				
Food processing sector dummy	−1.49	0.022	−1.83	0.039
Textile and garments sector dummy	−0.91	0.112	−0.89	0.274
Wood sector dummy	−1.44	0.085	−3.23	0.007
Intercept	−0.66	0.509	3.47	0.023
Number of observations	49		52	

Source: Zimbabwe case study.

and microenterprises receive less trade credit because they are less reliable in repaying loans.

Similarly over 40 percent of the case study firms report that their customers normally pay late, and nearly all firms have had customers pay late at least once (table 4.8). Microenterprises are less likely to have customers pay late and to charge interest penalties; when customers delay payment to microenterprises, they also are less likely to pay more than 30 days late. The reason for these findings undoubtedly is that microenterprises are typically so liquidity constrained that they could not afford having their customers pay late. Whenever they give credit, which tends to be less frequent, it is for a shorter duration and delays are kept short. Interviews with respondents indicated that microentrepreneurs take the time necessary to harass their client until they get their money. They could not survive otherwise. Firms owned by Africans and other non-white ethnic groups also appear less likely to have customers pay late or delay for a long time. A probit regression shows no statistically significant coefficients, however.

4.2.3   Penalties for Late Payment

Next we investigate whether there are significant differences among firms in the incidence of financial penalties for late payment. Probit regressions show that larger

Table 4.8
Repayment of credit by clients

	All	African	White	Other
Pay after term?				
Normally	44%	25%	53%	25%
Ever	96%	82%	100%	100%
When payment by client was delayed:				
Penalties charged	55%	56%	63%	25%
Delay > 30 days	36%	14%	46%	20%

Source: Zimbabwe case study.

Table 4.9
Probit regression on whether financial penalties are charged

	By suppliers		To clients	
	Coefficient	p-value	Coefficient	p-value
Firm's characteristics				
Age of firm, in years	−0.01	0.599	−0.01	0.310
Number of employees, in log	0.62	0.095	0.94	0.030
Manufacturer dummy	−0.92	0.136	0.62	0.498
Ethnicity (white is omitted category)				
African owner dummy	−0.29	0.623	0.66	−1.294
Other owner dummy	0.41	0.498	−1.29	0.030
Sector (metal sector is omitted category)				
Food processing sector dummy	−0.34	0.610	0.43	0.520
Textile and garments sector dummy	−0.22	0.711	−0.39	0.510
Wood sector dummy	−0.11	0.896	0.13	0.860
Intercept	0.11	0.905	−0.98	0.290
Number of observations	43		47	

Source: Zimbabwe case study.

firms are both more likely to be charged financial penalties by their suppliers and to charge financial penalties to their customers (table 4.9). Penalties are thus more standard for larger firms that operate with their suppliers and customers in a less personalized manner. Asian-owned firms, on the other hand, are less likely to charge financial penalties than other firms, indicating that they rely more on informal means of enforcing credit terms. This is consistent with the way Asian firms were found to operate in Kenya (Fafchamps et al. 1994) and stresses the importance of relation-specific capital (i.e., trust) in enforcing trade credit transactions. Several firms, however, indicated that they do not pay financial penalties. Large firms, for instance,

Table 4.10
Repayment of credit by clients

	All	African	White	Other
When delay payment to suppliers, eventually:				
Deliveries are stopped	74%	83%	75%	67%
Legal action is taken	72%	100%	67%	67%
When a client delays payment, firm eventually:				
Stops deliveries	88%	71%	93%	88%
Takes legal action	82%	75%	85%	67%

Source: Zimbabwe case study.

though more likely to be charged interest for late payment, are no more likely than other firms to pay financial penalties.

Respondents were also quizzed on what happens when they pay suppliers late or when their clients delay payment to them (table 4.10). Most firms view repayment delays of less than one month as part of doing business. It is understood that customers sometimes face temporary cash flow problems that prevent them from paying on time. Such delays are not cause for major concern, especially if the customer has a good track record. Firms get more annoyed, and begin taking action beyond 30 days. Many firms nevertheless indicate that what action they take depends on their relationship with the customer and on the extent of communication between the two. Firms repeatedly stated that if a customer comes forward saying he is facing a short-term problem, and then demonstrates a good faith effort to pay, no action is taken beyond, perhaps, the imposition of interest penalties. If the suppliers feels that the customer is not behaving responsibly, however, or if the customer is not valued, the supplier may stop deliveries and, in extreme cases, take the client to court. Firms typically have a hierarchy or sequence of responses when a client fails to pay, beginning with contacting the debtor to find out what the problem is, then using repeated requests, perhaps coupled with threats to stop supplying the customer, then stopping supplies, then sending the customer a final notice, and finally turning the matter over to an attorney. There is some variation among firms, as large, monopolistic firms are quicker to stop deliveries, while others appear at a loss to prevent payment delays on the part of large or monopsonistic buyers, including government agencies. Conversations with respondents indicate that flexibility appears to have diminished in recent years as inflation and tighter monetary conditions have led to much higher nominal interest rates, increasing incentives to pay late and making default more likely. Firms are now more anxious to receive payment on time and willing to impose penalties for late payment than they used to. In many cases they even have reduced the repayment period or stopped providing trade credit altogether.

Most sample firms expect that their suppliers will eventually stop supplying them if they delay payment very long (table 4.10); nearly all of them feel that this would occur within 90 days. Most also feel that suppliers would eventually initiate legal action, though they expect this to take up to 180 days. African and microenterprises appear more likely to expect such actions than other firms, and they expect supply cutoffs to occur sooner than other firms, a possible reflection of their weak economic position. That microenterprises fear legal action more than larger firms is contrary to our initial expectations. We had indeed thought that microenterprises would feel sheltered from judicial action by the high cost of suing them relative to the debts they may have. It may be that microenterprises have wrong expectations and that the threat of court action is not credible. Discussions with attorneys and credit recovery agencies, however, suggest otherwise: Zimbabwean courts seem to deal with uncontested delinquent debts expeditiously, to the point that debt recovery has become routinized and that transaction costs are lower than we had anticipated (see Fafchamps et al. 1995, ch. 3). As a result summons are filed for relatively moderate sums: the threat of court action is, indeed, real. Irrespective of whether debtors' expectations are "rational" or not, the fact remains that they expect to be punished, and this is sufficient inducement not to delay beyond reason.

The great majority of case study firms stop deliveries if their customers are 90 days late in their payments. They also are very likely to take legal action if payments are 180 days late. Among microenterprises, however, only one stated it would stop deliveries if payments were delayed very long. The others said the question was not applicable to their situation because they do not make regular deliveries. Probit analysis further indicates that larger firms are more likely to stop deliveries to their clients (table 4.11). It also confirm that larger firms are less likely to fear interrupted deliveries or legal action should they delay payment for long. Older firms also are less likely to perceive legal action as a potential threat. These findings suggest that relationships and market power are important factors in the enforcement of trade credit contracts: older firms are likely have well established relationships with suppliers, and suppliers have more to lose by attempting to punish a larger firm.

4.3   Conclusion

Using small qualitative surveys with in-depth interviews by the researchers, we have identified many of the processes discussed in chapter 2. For most of the surveyed

Table 4.11
Probit regression on action taken in case of delayed payment

	Suppliers stop deliveries		Suppliers take legal action		Stop deliveries to clients		Take legal action against client	
	Coefficient	p-value	Coefficient	p-value	Coefficient	p-value	Coefficient	p-value
Firm's characteristics								
Age of firm, in years	−0.02	0.185	−0.08	0.068	−0.03	0.439	0.02	0.495
Number of employees, in log	−1.16	0.032	−1.20	0.074	5.03	0.043	−0.08	0.876
Manufacturer dummy	0.64	0.320	−3.11	0.093	6.97	0.474	−6.73	1.000
Ethnicity (white is omitted category)								
African owner dummy	−0.39	0.723	7.73	1.000	4.99	0.141	−0.59	0.400
Other owner dummy	0.16	0.805	1.71	0.148	1.77	0.279	−1.31	0.156
Sector (metal sector is omitted category)								
Food processing sector dummy	1.56	0.123	1.47	0.269	7.07	1.000	−0.87	0.424
Textile and garments sector dummy	1.52	0.055	−1.60	0.255	−5.14	0.158	−0.95	0.274
Wood sector dummy	0.27	0.753	−5.20	0.069	−5.51	0.126	5.58	1.000
Intercept	2.37	0.054	8.31	0.022	−4.88	0.071	8.14	1.000
Number of observations	41		35		41		44	

Source: Zimbabwe case study.

firms, legal institutions are a secondary instrument. Contract enforcement is organized primarily around relationships and reputation—what Greif (1993) calls bilateral and multilateral enforcement strategies. Exchange is largely personalized and trust is the dominant concept in respondents' view of contractual issues. Screening clients and suppliers is an important concern for entrepreneurs. Harassment is the dominant form of debt collection.

In adopting a qualitative approach at the onset of this research agenda, we had the advantage of hearing respondents explain what they see as important. As a result we did not impose on the data a conceptual framework that was too restrictive.

Having clarified the issues surrounding contract enforcement in Africa, we are now ready for a broader but more quantitative approach comparing contract enforcement in several countries. To this we next turn.

5 Evidence from African Manufacturers

A more ambitious exercise was conducted using a panel of African manufacturers. Because of the nature of the panel surveys, less detailed information was collected on contract enforcement practices. Nevertheless, the large number of countries represented and the large number of observations facilitated economic analysis. The empirical analysis presented in this chapter tests simple theoretical predictions regarding the incidence of contractual problems and the way contractual disputes are resolved. The results provide good evidence on the extent of contractual nonperformance in African manufacturing and the local remedies.

5.1 Descriptive Analysis of Relationships with Suppliers and Clients

The way African manufacturers deal with clients and suppliers is depicted in table 5.1. Most surveyed firms sell at least part of their output to end-users of their products such as manufacturers and consumers; the rest is sold primarily to wholesalers and retailers. About a quarter of surveyed firms do at least some of their business with publicly owned entities. On average, sample firms export 8 percent of their output; this proportion is highest in Côte d'Ivoire and lowest in Ethiopia. Some form of written agreement—such as a signed invoice—is used in less than half the sales to clients. The explanation lies in the length of the relationship that binds firms with their clients. Data on the number of years firms have dealt with their clients are not available but the data show that firms have, on average, dealt for seven years with their problematic customers, that is, those that recently failed to pay or paid late. Problematic customers are primarily individual consumers. Roughly one-tenth of late and nonpayment cases occur with relatives or kin.[1]

More detailed information is available on firms' suppliers (see the second part of table 5.1). A quarter of the firms deals with at least one monopolist among their major suppliers, that is, a firm that is the sole available source of a particular input. Monopolies appear more commonplace in Zimbabwe, a feature already noted by Gunning and Mumbengegwi (1995) and a possible heritage of the Unilateral Declaration of Independence (UDI) period during which an international embargo forced the country to be self-sufficient. At the time of the RPED surveys, firms in Ethiopia

---

1. Respondents were asked to mention whether the problematic client was (1) a relative or family member, (2) a member of the same tribe or ethnic group, or (3) none of the above. They seem to have interpreted the question of ethnicity in the narrower sense of kinship. For instance, even in a country such as Burundi where 82 percent of respondents are Africans and where Hutus constitute close to 90 percent of the population, only 7 percent of the respondents said that the problematic client was from the same ethnic group. This could not have occurred if respondents had interpreted ethnicity as a broad categorization into Hutu, Tutsi, or white, for instance.

Table 5.1
Relationships with clients and suppliers

	Total sample		Burundi		Cameroon		Côte d'Ivoire	
	Number of obser-vations	Mean	Number of obser-vations	Mean	Number of obser-vations	Mean	Number of obser-vations	Mean
With clients:								
Type of client:								
Sells to end-users	1,528	77%	119	92%	185	73%	191	70%
Sells to public firms	1,528	27%	119	46%	185	14%	191	17%
Share of exported output	1,771	8%	119	4%	202	10%	224	22%
Formalism:								
Written agreement/invoice	1,528	41%	119	50%	185	53%	191	34%
Characteristics of problematic clients:								
Length of relation (years)	803	7.0	70	2.7	135	3.9	109	19.5
Individual consumer	843	41%	78	71%	149	38%	110	58%
Public firm	843	13%	78	13%	149	15%	110	13%
Relative or kin	690	11%	70	7%	132	14%	93	8%
With suppliers:								
Market power:								
One supplier monopolistic	1,754	24%	113	30%	204	15%	204	28%
One supplier public firm	1,744	29%	110	21%	204	24%	199	18%
Share of imported inputs	1,696	27%	115	42%	189	46%	203	22%
Loyalty to supplier:								
% inputs from one supplier	1,453	73%	79	77%	198	70%	173	78%
Length of relationship (years)	1,551	9.1	88	7.0	188	7.5	204	7.9
Orders infrequent	1,546	23%	113	37%	201	21%	201	22%
Social network capital:								
One supplier friend or family	1,754	5%	113	6%	204	7%	204	3%
One supplier same ethnicity	1,298	10%	0		196	14%	201	4%
Credit terms:								
Receives supplier credit	1,754	33%	113	28%	204	45%	204	33%
Payment terms (days)	1,754	17.0	113	15.3	204	28.5	204	21.6
Gives advance payment	1,754	5%	113	3%	204	12%	204	4%
Characteristics of problematic suppliers:								
First-time supplier	605	10%	41	22%	103	10%	59	8%
Length of relationship (years)	592	8.9	34	2.7	98	5.3	67	11.4
Individual consumer	611	10%	44	0%	101	2%	61	3%
Public firm	611	14%	44	23%	101	9%	61	33%

Source: RPED panel surveys.
Note: Percentages refer to the proportion of responding firms in the category. Otherwise, the mean response is reported.

Ethiopia		Ghana		Kenya		Tanzania		Zambia		Zimbabwe	
Number of observations	Mean	Number of observations	Mean	Number of observations	Mean	Number of observations	Mean	Number of observations	Mean	Number of observations	Mean
181	71%	0		221	77%	217	88%	213	83%	201	68%
181	29%	0		221	17%	217	46%	213	31%	201	24%
214	1%	171	3%	222	7%	215	4%	214	6%	190	12%
181	26%	0		221	45%	217	30%	213	44%	201	52%
0		0		138	5.0	58	6.6	152	7.3	141	4.5
0		0		142	39%	59	32%	156	35%	149	25%
0		0		142	11%	59	42%	156	13%	149	3%
0		0		117	20%	33	9%	136	4%	109	14%
201	19%	197	8%	212	18%	213	25%	213	32%	197	40%
201	46%	196	15%	212	15%	212	49%	213	38%	197	29%
194	48%	171	15%	218	21%	208	13%	213	23%	185	16%
196	81%	0		213	61%	193	78%	211	65%	190	78%
180	8.3	120	7.3	201	9.3	203	8.6	176	9.5	191	14.6
199	27%	0		211	17%	212	33%	212	16%	197	15%
201	4%	197	6%	212	10%	213	3%	213	5%	197	6%
182	4%	0		179	20%	208	7%	211	7%	121	18%
201	11%	197	47%	212	44%	213	11%	213	20%	197	55%
201	5.5	197	20.2	212	22.1	213	4.4	213	9.7	197	26.0
201	6%	197	7%	212	5%	213	5%	213	4%	197	2%
0		0		120	5%	47	23%	117	8%	118	8%
0		0		118	7.1	47	6.9	116	9.2	112	14.9
0		0		121	8%	47	43%	117	9%	120	12%
0		0		121	15%	47	28%	117	11%	120	3%

and Tanzania were much more likely to obtain their inputs from public firms. A quarter of surveyed firms' inputs are imported; the rest is bought locally, possibly from importers. Firms in Burundi, Cameroon, and Ethiopia are more likely to import their inputs than firms in the other six countries.

Firms are extremely loyal to their suppliers. They purchase, on average, close to three-quarters of their most important inputs from the same suppliers, whom they have known for 9.1 years, on average. Only one-quarter of the firms place infrequent orders; others have regular relationships with suppliers. These relationships, however, are primarily based on business acquaintances, and not on family or ethnicity. Only 5 percent of the surveyed firms mention that one of their regular suppliers is a relative or personal friend; only 10 percent have a supplier who is from the same "ethnic group."

Only one-third of the surveyed firms receive credit from their suppliers; this proportion is highest in Zimbabwe and lowest in Ethiopia and Tanzania (the two countries where firms purchase inputs largely from public firms). The average payment term for all sample firms is two and a half weeks; it is of course higher for those who receive supplier credit. Trade credit among African manufacturing firms is discussed in detail in Cuevas et al. (1993), Fafchamps et al. (1994, 1995), and Fafchamps (1997c). In contrast, only 5 percent of the surveyed firms resort to advance payment, often because the supplier insists on it.

Table 5.1 also reports the characteristics of problematic suppliers, that is, those who fail to deliver on time or who deliver deficient quality.[2] Around 10 percent of all cases of breach occur with first-time suppliers, possibly because firms do little business with unfamiliar suppliers.[3] On average, firms have known problematic suppliers for 8.9 years—only marginally less than the length of time they have known their suppliers in general. Problematic suppliers are primarily other firms; some 14 percent of recent cases of contract nonperformance were with public firms.

Next we turn to the incidence of contractual disputes with clients (table 5.2). The data show that some 56 percent of the sample firms experienced cases of late pay-

2. In the RPED surveys the definition of what constitutes late delivery or deficient quality was de facto left to individual respondents. Surveyed firms were simply asked whether they experienced cases of late delivery and deficient quality over the 12 months preceding the survey, and if yes, how many times this occurred. Attempts to collect data on the number of days elapsed between promised delivery date and actual delivery failed: most respondents simply do not remember. Besides, the concept of promised delivery date is an ambiguous one in a world where firms do not truly expect contractual dates to be complied with. Respondents' response should thus be understood as referring to cases in which delivery occurred later than they expected.

3. Another possibility is that first-time suppliers make more effort if they wish to establish a relationship.

ment by clients during the twelve months preceding the survey; over one-third faced cases of nonpayment.[4] With 16.2 occurrences of late payment per year, the annual average of late payment cases is about eight times the average number of nonpayment cases: as could be expected, late payment is a more common phenomenon than nonpayment.

In the great majority of cases of late and nonpayment, firms attempt to resolve the problem through direct negotiations with the client. This proportion is highest in Cameroon and Zambia, lowest in Zimbabwe and Tanzania. A small number of firms resort to private arbitration loosely defined.[5] Some 9 percent of sampled firms ever called the police for help, or threatened to do so. In one-fourth of the problematic cases, the dispute was either brought to the attention of lawyers, and ended up in court, or the threat of legal action was resorted to by the parties. Sharp differences exist among countries: Zimbabwean firms were much more likely to go (or threaten to go) to court than those in Burundi—a possible reflection on the relative reliability of their court systems and the size of surveyed firms in each country. Nearly one-half the cases of late and nonpayment had been settled at the time of the survey. Most of the respondents were satisfied with the terms of the settlement, with little difference across countries. Parties continued to trade in 48 percent of the cases—more in Tanzania, Zambia, and Burundi, less in Zimbabwe—suggesting that dispute resolution methods are moderately successful in solving disputes and bringing parties back together.

Contractual disputes with suppliers are less frequent and less dramatic (see second part of table 5.2). A third of the surveyed firms experienced a late delivery in the year preceding the survey. Untimely delivery was complained about most often in Zimbabwe and least often in Tanzania. The number of reported cases is also much higher in Zimbabwe than elsewhere, suggesting that input delivery risk is particularly problematic in Zimbabwe. Cases of deficient quality are also reported by one-third of the surveyed firms. As with clients, the most commonly used dispute resolution method

4. As in the case of late delivery, the definition of what constitutes a late payment was left to respondents. The reason for doing so is the same: most respondents do not keep track of the length of time elapsed between due date and actual payment date. Besides, given that African banks take several days to clear checks, and that many checks bounce, the actual payment date is a blurred concept. A late payment is thus a payment that is considered delinquent by the respondent, meaning the payment occurred after the date at which the respondent expected payment to be made.

5. Strictly defined, private arbitration is a process by which parties to a contract agree to grant authority to a third party to legally resolve a dispute between them. The arbitrator has the power to adjudicate the dispute and his or her judgment is, in many developed countries, granted the full protection of the law, at par with other judgments. It unlikely that all respondents were acquainted with this legal definition; their answers probably lump together formal arbitrators and informal mediators with no power of adjudication.

Table 5.2
Contractual disputes with clients and suppliers

	Total sample		Burundi		Cameroon		Côte d'Ivoire	
	Number of obser-vations	Mean	Number of obser-vations	Mean	Number of obser-vations	Mean	Number of obser-vations	Mean
With clients:								
Incidence of disputes:								
Late payment	1,828	56%	119	53%	208	72%	234	42%
Number of cases per year	1,512	16.2	107	3.1	0		234	2.4
Nonpayment	1,819	37%	118	41%	202	63%	234	33%
Number of cases per year	1,387	2.0	114	1.5	0		234	1.5
Conflict resolution method:[1]								
Direct bargaining	839	78%	78	86%	149	91%	108	85%
Private arbitration	836	7%	78	5%	147	12%	108	9%
Police	826	9%	78	14%	141	13%	104	13%
Lawyer	837	24%	78	4%	147	24%	108	15%
Courts	837	26%	78	15%	147	22%	108	18%
Outcome of dispute:[1]								
Dispute settled	834	50%	76	39%	145	34%	108	44%
Satisfied with outcome[2]	411	82%	30	80%	50	84%	48	77%
Continue to trade	820	48%	73	59%	142	44%	104	46%
With suppliers:								
Incidence of disputes:								
Late delivery	1,824	30%	118	19%	207	38%	234	22%
Number of cases per year	1,563	4.4	113	0.3	0		234	1.4
Deficient quality	1,820	34%	118	28%	206	44%	234	17%
Number of cases per year	1,369	2.9	115	0.9	0		234	0.4
Conflict resolution method:[1]								
Direct bargaining	486	73%	44	80%	102	84%	59	81%
Private arbitration	591	4%	43	5%	101	2%	56	9%
Police	597	1%	44	2%	96	1%	57	2%
Lawyer	598	4%	44	0%	99	5%	58	3%
Courts	595	3%	44	0%	99	5%	57	0%
Outcome of dispute:[1]								
Dispute settled	471	72%	43	86%	99	78%	57	75%
Satisfied with outcome[2]	332	80%	36	64%	75	85%	41	85%
Continue to trade	495	81%	41	78%	0		59	90%

Notes: (1) Conditional on a dispute having occurred; (2) conditional on the dispute being settled. na: data not available.

Ethiopia		Ghana		Kenya		Tanzania		Zambia		Zimbabwe	
Number of observations	Mean	Number of observations	Mean	Number of observations	Mean	Number of observations	Mean	Number of observations	Mean	Number of observations	Mean
214	43%	197	59%	222	60%	217	25%	215	68%	202	81%
154	0.5	191	7.7	220	5.9	215	3.1	213	18.7	178	90.5
214	23%	195	36%	222	36%	217	12%	214	40%	203	59%
0		193	1.9	221	1.3	216	0.6	213	1.4	196	5.8
0		0		142	73%	58	64%	157	89%	147	54%
0		0		141	4%	59	7%	157	6%	146	5%
0		0		141	4%	59	7%	157	7%	146	5%
0		0		141	30%	59	15%	157	18%	147	48%
0		0		141	28%	59	32%	157	20%	147	44%
0		0		141	50%	59	61%	158	64%	147	54%
0		0		69	88%	36	89%	100	82%	78	73%
0		0		140	43%	59	63%	158	60%	144	35%
214	37%	194	21%	222	38%	217	15%	215	27%	203	52%
176	0.9	188	1.0	221	6.8	215	0.7	213	2.9	203	19.3
214	33%	192	24%	222	42%	217	14%	215	48%	202	54%
0		185	1.5	218	4.0	214	0.5	210	5.4	193	7.5
0		0		0		47	68%	116	77%	118	57%
0		0		112	10%	47	0%	116	3%	116	2%
0		0		120	3%	47	0%	116	1%	117	0%
0		0		121	5%	47	0%	116	4%	113	3%
0		0		119	3%	47	2%	116	4%	113	4%
0		0		0		46	78%	116	61%	110	66%
0		0		0		36	81%	71	85%	73	77%
0		0		119	67%	47	87%	117	79%	112	91%

is direct bargaining. Recourse to other dispute resolution methods is extremely rare: only 4 percent of the surveyed firms went to see a lawyer following disputes regarding late delivery or deficient quality. Most disputes with suppliers are settled and firms continue to trade, even if they are not fully satisfied with the outcome.

To summarize, the surveyed firms have long-term, and quite loyal, relationships with their clients and suppliers. These relationships are primarily grounded in business acquaintances; family, friendships, and ethnicity have little influence in fostering business practices. The data indicate that contractual disputes occur frequently and that most firms experience them. Without equivalent data from other parts of the world, however, we cannot say whether contractual disputes are more frequent in Africa than elsewhere. The majority of contractual disputes are resolved amicably and trade is often resumed. Direct negotiation is the preferred dispute resolution strategy. Detailed examination of the data reveals that outside parties such as arbitrators, lawyers, or the police are called upon only in more serious instances of contractual breach mainly involving nonpayment. Taken together, these results are consistent with the importance of contractual flexibility in helping firms deal with risk, and with the role of long-term relationships is helping firms resolve contractual disputes through face-to-face negotiation. The results are very similar to those of the case study discussed in the first part of this chapter.

5.2 An Econometric Analysis of the Frequency of Contractual Breach

We have seen that countries differ in the frequency of reported cases of breach of contract and in the outcome of contractual disputes. These intercountry differences could, however, arise simply because firms located in separate countries are different. To investigate whether there exist firm characteristics that systematically affect dispute resolution and can account for some of the intercountry differences, we turn to a multivariate econometric analysis of the pooled data. Given the total absence of previous work on these issues in sub-Saharan Africa and elsewhere, we proceed with caution and refrain from imposing too much structure on the estimation. We seek to identify possible determinants of three basic processes: (1) the incidence and frequency of contractual disputes, (2) the choice of dispute resolution method, given that a dispute has arisen, and (3) the outcome of the dispute. We examine these three issues in turn.

We begin with an investigation of the determinants of the frequency of contractual breach. To this effect, we estimate logit regressions on whether or not a firm has experienced at least one case of breach with a supplier or a client over the twelve months preceding the survey. Regressions are run for the pooled sample of nine countries. Country dummies are included.[6]

Theory suggests a variety of forces that may influence the incidence of noncompliance and, hence, the kind of regressors that have to be included in the right-hand side of the regressions. Following our discussion of the theoretical literature in chapter 3, we first expect noncompliance to reflect the environment in which firms operate: enterprises that buy and sell in countries or sectors in which breach of contract is frequent should face more problems than firms that operate in a more disciplined environment. Three sets of variables are used to control for market environment effects: country dummies, sectoral dummies, and the average frequency of contractual disputes and threat of court action faced by firms similar to the respondent.[7] Country and sectoral dummies control for a variety of forces that operate at the local or sectoral level. Their expected effect is as follows.

As we discussed in chapter 2, theory predicts that dispute resolution methods play an important deterrence role. If this understanding is correct, contractual breach should be less prevalent in countries with good legal institutions. Given that Zimbabwe has (or at least had at the time of the survey) a more developed manufacturing sector and legal institutions generally responsive to business needs (Fafchamps et al. 1995), we would expect Zimbabwean manufacturers to encounter fewer cases of breach.

There is, however, another possibility, namely that good legal institutions encourage firms to take more risk because they can obtain reparation from courts. In this case we would expect contractual breach to be more prevalent in countries offering better legal protection. Either way, the presence of good institutions would raise economic efficiency by facilitating exchange, but the source of efficiency gains would be different. In the standard case, efficiency is increased because fewer cases of breach occur; in the alternative case, efficiency rises because trade takes place between parties that would otherwise not trade—or trade differently (e.g., without granting supplier credit or without placing orders). Which efficiency gains are larger is an empirical issue.

6. Bigsten et al. (2000a) reports country-level regressions as well. They are omitted here for lack of space.

7. These averages are constructed by country and sector; that is, a textile firm in Kenya has a different average from a metal firm in Kenya or a textile firm in Cameroon. In addition each observation is omitted from its own average to avoid endogeneity bias. Because of high multicollinearity across average frequency measures, a single frequency measure is used in the regression analysis: the frequency of late payment in regressions involving clients, and the frequency of late deliveries in regressions involving suppliers. In all regressions, the average frequency of threat of court action refers to payment disputes with clients—the type of contractual breach that is most likely to result in legal proceedings.

Food processing is the omitted sector and sector dummy coefficients are relative to the food sector. Given that food products are perishable and their quality variable, we expect more delivery and quality problems in the food sector. Finally, to the extent that business environment affects the incidence of contractual disputes, we expect the average frequency of noncompliance to have a positive and significant effect on the incidence of breach as firms adjust their expectations.

The incidence of contractual noncompliance is also likely to vary with characteristics of the firm. Larger firms, for instance, conduct more transactions and are thus expected to encounter more problems than small firms.[8] Older firms may have identified more reliable clients and suppliers and thus face fewer problems with unreliable firms.[9] The trust they have in their clients and suppliers, however, may induce them to accept delayed deliveries and payment because they believe contractual obligations will eventually be satisfied. The net effect of firm age is thus ambiguous. Firms with a limited liability status may be more willing to take risk with clients and suppliers and are thus expected to face more cases of noncompliance. Regressors for firm size, age, and legal status are included in the regression to control for these possible influences.

Given the existence of business network effects in African manufacturing, as shown by Fafchamps (2000), Barr (2000, 2002b), and Fisman (2002), one also expects better connected firm managers to screen clients and suppliers more easily and thus experience fewer cases of breach. Although RPED surveys did not, as a rule, ask questions on membership in business networks, Fafchamps (2000) and Raturi and Swamy (1999) have shown that the ethnicity of the owner/manager is an important predictor of network membership (see also Fisman 2002). The available evidence suggests that ethnic African manufacturers are, in general, less well connected and, as a result, disadvantaged in access to supplier credit—see part VI for a detailed analysis. We also suspect that foreign- or state-owned firms are better connected to other manufacturers, either through their mother company or through the state. We therefore include a dummy for ethnic African and ethnic European management; Asian management is the omitted category. For the same reason we include dummies for firms that have some foreign or state ownership. If business networks mitigate noncompliance, we expect better connected firms—typically foreign firms, state

---

8. The number of transactions in which a firm is engaged over a set period of time is not proportional to size, however, since larger firms typically engage in larger transactions. Moreover firms may differ in what they mean by a transaction. For a small firm selling purely on a cash basis, a transaction is a single sale or purchase; for a large firm, a transaction can be an order or an invoice, depending on the context. These differences complicate the collection of data across firms of different sizes.

9. Bade and Chifamba (1994) and Fafchamps (1997c, 2000), for instance, provide evidence to this effect.

firms, and respondents of Asian or European ascent—to encounter fewer cases of noncompliance.

It is also possible that the attitude of firms vis-à-vis contracts reflects cultural values that are shaped by ethnic identification, as argued by Greif (1993, 1994) in the case of medieval traders. Certain groups may have higher standards of contractual compliance and thus be quicker to classify an incident as breach. In the African case this may be relevant for foreign owned firms or managers of European ascent. If cultural expectations are important, we would expect these firms to report more cases of breach. Note that the network and culture effects operate in opposite directions in the case of European and foreign owned firms.

The nature of the relationships that firms maintain with clients and suppliers could also affect the incidence of contractual problems. Here we are constrained by the nature of the information collected in the surveys. For clients, we include the share of exports in total sales, as well as dummies for whether the firm sells to individual end-users and whether it sells to public entities. Although payment delays in export markets are longer (Fafchamps 1997c), the institutional mechanism of the letter of credit should reduce the incidence of nonpayment in exports since payment by the buyer's bank is automatic upon presentation of the transport documents. Selling to traders (the omitted category) is generally perceived to be safer than selling to individual end-users such as manufacturers and final consumers. The reason is that traders are in general more liquid and have a faster cash turn-around (Fafchamps and Minten 2002b). Selling to public entities is expected to raise the incidence of payment problems because governments everywhere, but particularly in Africa, are notorious for paying late.

For suppliers, more information is available. We include indicators of market power (share of imported inputs plus dummies for whether the firm faces a monopolistic supplier or a public supplier for at least one of its inputs), indicators of social capital (length of relationship with suppliers, percentage of purchases from main suppliers, and dummies whether firm buys from family and friends and whether firm only makes infrequent purchases), and indicators of credit terms (dummies for whether the firm receives supplier credit and whether it gives advance payment). We expect market power to raise the incidence of contractual problems since monopolists can more easily get away with breach. In contrast, we anticipate stronger relationships with suppliers to reduce the frequency of problems. Finally, we expect that contracts involving credit open more room for breach and thus should raise the frequency of noncompliance. Because the nature of the relationships that firms maintain with clients and suppliers is potentially endogenous, results should only be interpreted as indicative of empirical regularities.

We now investigate whether the data support the above conjectures. Logit regressions on the incidence of contractual noncompliance by clients and suppliers are presented in tables 5.3 and 5.4. Two sets of results are presented. The first set includes fewer regressors but all nine countries; the second set includes more regressors but fewer countries due to missing information. Coefficients are reported in the form of odds ratio to improve readability: an odds ratio greater (smaller) than one means that the regressor raises (reduces) the probability of a contractual problem.[10]

Results indicate that there are significant differences across countries and sectors but also that these differences are not well captured by contract environment variables.[11] After controlling for firm characteristics and sector dummies, Zimbabwe still has the highest incidence of problems with clients and suppliers. Since Zimbabwe also is the country in our sample with the most advanced manufacturing sector and the most developed legal system, these results cast doubt on the idea that a high incidence of contractual breach is synonymous with lack of market sophistication. If anything, contract noncompliance appears more likely in better developed economies where contracts are more complex and the potential for disputes larger. For instance, the likelihood of late payment is higher if an element of credit has entered the contract; similarly late delivery is more likely if the client firm has placed an order for future delivery.

As expected, the incidence of late payment is highest among large firms; for nonpayment, firm size is not significant. Large firms also incur a lot more problems with suppliers. Older firms appear to face more nonpayment problems, not less, but they face fewer problems with suppliers. African-managed firms face more cases of nonpayment than other firms. They are also more likely to complain about deficient quality. These findings are inconsistent with the hypothesis that entrepreneurs of foreign origin operating in Africa cultivate higher standards of contractual behavior than indigenous entrepreneurs.

Regarding the effect of relation-specific variables, we find that selling to or buying from public firms raises the probability of disputes; the effect is significant only for late payment, however. In contrast, selling in export markets reduces the incidence of

---

10. More specifically, an odds ratio measures the effect of a one unit change in a regressor on the probability of experiencing at least a dispute per year, computed at the average value of all regressors. For instance, an odds ratio coefficient of 1.41 for Cameroon (table 5.4) means that manufacturers in Cameroon are 41 percent times more likely than manufacturers in Burundi (the omitted category) to experience at least one late payment problem in the survey year.

11. Unreported regression results show that when country and sectoral dummies are omitted, environment variables are very significant. Once country and sector dummies are included, however, they are no longer significant. This may be due to multicollinearity, given the way environment variables are constructed. This issue deserves more research.

Table 5.3
Logit regression on the incidence of contractual noncompliance by clients

	Late payment				Nonpayment			
	Odds ratio	z-statistic	Odds ratio	z-statistic	Odds ratio	z-statistic	Odds ratio	z-statistic
Country dummies:[1]								
Cameroon	1.41	2.17	2.29	2.43	2.15	2.58	3.61	3.41
Côte d'Ivoire	0.64	−2.27	0.78	−0.94	0.78	−1.28	0.73	−1.52
Ethiopia	0.65	−2.45			0.43	−2.85		
Ghana	1.06	1.29			1.04	0.28		
Kenya	0.99	−0.18	1.34	1.62	0.87	−0.78	0.79	−1.41
Tanzania	0.27	−3.55	0.23	−3.27	0.19	−3.02	0.11	−3.96
Zambia	1.10	0.82	1.49	1.58	0.80	−1.25	0.80	−1.23
Zimbabwe	1.68	3.02	3.09	2.14	2.31	2.02	1.75	1.11
Sectoral dummies:								
Textile	1.81	2.58	2.05	3.94	1.58	1.67	2.00	2.39
Metal	1.81	1.92	1.77	1.70	1.52	1.32	1.72	1.24
Wood	1.65	1.88	1.86	1.96	1.40	1.22	1.86	2.20
Contractual environment:								
Incidence of payment problems	3.35	1.30	1.64	0.34	2.21	0.53	0.34	−0.65
Recourse to legal system			0.55	−0.80			0.78	−0.31
Firm's characteristics:								
Size[2]	1.17	2.81	1.15	1.78	1.07	0.76	1.10	0.89
Age[3]	1.14	1.29	1.18	1.29	1.14	1.32	1.21	2.42
Limited liability status	1.41	2.24	1.32	1.86	1.05	0.22	1.02	0.09
Some state ownership	0.60	−2.70	0.82	−0.75	0.97	−0.15	1.22	1.25
Some foreign ownership	1.01	0.06	0.95	−0.24	1.04	0.21	1.09	0.49
African owner/manager	1.29	1.36	1.14	0.64	1.40	3.08	1.23	2.34
European owner/manager	1.17	1.11	1.14	0.64	1.37	1.01	1.25	0.70
Relationship with clients:								
Sell to manufacturers/consumers			1.08	0.42			1.16	1.38
Sell to public firms			2.10	2.48			1.23	1.55
Share of exports in sales	0.67	−0.72	0.74	−1.01	0.34	−3.69	0.34	−3.58
Number of observations	1,564		1,200		1,554		1,193	
Pseudo R-squared	0.1126		0.1450		0.1018		0.1157	
Correctly classified observations	66%		68%		67%		68%	

Notes: Robust standard errors reported using country-level clustering. (1) Burundi is the omitted country; (2) firm's size = log(number of employees + 1); (3) firm's age = log(survey year − year of inception).

Table 5.4
Logit regression on the incidence of contractual noncompliance by suppliers

	Late delivery				Deficient quality			
	Odds ratio	z-statistic	Odds ratio	z-statistic	Odds ratio	z-statistic	Odds ratio	z-statistic
Country dummies:[1]								
Cameroon	2.58	4.44	3.40	3.73	1.90	2.25	1.71	0.90
Côte d'Ivoire	1.61	4.74	1.47	2.38	0.59	−1.62	0.57	−1.13
Ethiopia	4.36	4.28			1.23	0.80		
Ghana	1.16	0.94			0.64	−1.95		
Kenya	3.15	3.80	4.18	3.68	2.33	4.55	2.13	1.78
Tanzania	0.79	−0.71	0.74	−0.65	0.39	−2.31	0.42	−1.54
Zambia	1.48	1.13	1.47	1.25	2.58	2.63	2.60	1.72
Zimbabwe	3.38	5.72	4.50	3.12	2.35	2.17	2.78	0.93
Sectoral dummies:								
Textile	0.85	−0.45	0.61	−1.26	0.74	−1.04	0.62	−1.30
Metal	0.96	−0.17	0.72	−1.46	0.60	−1.23	0.46	−1.40
Wood	0.79	−0.76	0.53	−1.53	0.84	−0.55	0.67	−1.06
Contractual environment:								
Incidence of supplier problems	0.86	−0.10	0.25	−0.60	0.60	−0.26	0.55	−0.19
Recourse to legal system			0.45	−0.84			0.55	−0.43
Firm's characteristics:								
Size[2]	1.41	6.51	1.45	6.18	1.27	6.03	1.29	6.33
Age[3]	0.83	−1.66	0.85	−1.01	0.84	−2.35	0.81	−1.74
Limited liability status	1.43	1.41	1.32	1.55	1.16	1.22	1.17	1.18
Some state ownership	0.57	−2.22	0.61	−1.29	0.75	−1.19	0.65	−1.64
Some foreign ownership	0.95	−0.29	1.06	0.36	0.71	−1.43	0.75	−1.17
African owner/manager	0.81	−0.60	0.73	−0.77	1.37	1.67	1.53	2.00
European owner/manager	1.11	0.64	0.99	−0.08	1.46	1.18	1.38	1.10
Relationship with suppliers:								
One supplier monopolistic	1.28	1.16	1.29	1.27	0.97	−0.15	0.97	−0.22
One supplier public firm	1.24	1.18	1.14	0.54	1.13	0.75	1.21	1.29
Share of imported inputs	1.34	1.49	1.83	3.30	0.83	−0.57	0.87	−0.47
% purchases from main supplier	0.87		0.87	−0.33			0.53	−1.72
Average length of relationship[4]	1.02	0.21	0.99	−0.12	0.96	−0.55	1.01	0.06

One supplier friend or family	1.86	2.54	2.05	3.39	1.08	0.43	1.12	0.57
Dummy for infrequent purchases			0.77	-1.07			0.71	-1.98
Receives supplier credit	1.44	1.83	1.27	1.03	1.36	1.71	1.52	2.55
Gives advance payment	1.35	1.08	1.20	0.78	1.69	1.70	1.97	1.92
Number of observations	1,289		1,010		1,286		1,009	
Pseudo R-squared	0.1428		0.1683		0.0946		0.1169	
Correctly classified observations	73%		74%		69%		68%	

Notes: Robust standard errors reported using country-level clustering. (1) Burundi is the omitted country; (2) firm's size = log(number of employees + 1); (3) firm's age = log(survey year – year of inception); (4) log of average length of relationship with suppliers in years + 1.

payment problems. The effect is large: a firm that exports all its output is 1.5 (2.9) times less likely to experience a late (non) payment problem than a firm that exports nothing. This may be due to increased reliance on institutional mechanisms such as the letter of credit rather than exemplary behavior on the part of international buyers.[12] On the supplier side, late delivery is more frequent among firms that import their raw materials, a likely reflection of the vagaries of African transportation and port systems. There is much variation across individual countries, however. We revisit this issue in chapter 7 when we discuss the relationship between inventories and contractual risk.

On the supplier side, we find that monopolistic suppliers do not, in general, take advantage of market power to lower contract performance: the coefficient is not significant.[13] Surprisingly, firms that make infrequent purchases encounter fewer problems. One likely explanation is that these firms are very small and operate on a cash-and-carry basis only—what Fafchamps and Minten (2001a) call the flea market economy. Another surprising result is that firms that buy from family and friends encounter many more late delivery problems. One possible interpretation is that it is harder to put pressure on family and friends than on regular suppliers. Finally, as expected, problems are much more frequent among firms that receive or give credit to their suppliers, a result consistent with the idea that contractual breach is more likely in more complex contracts.

So far we have only a single piece of information, namely whether respondent firms reported having experience contractual noncompliance. We now examine the reported number of cases of noncompliance using a simple tobit regression.[14] Results are presented sections 5.5 and 5.6. They confirm that the incidence of payment problems is much larger in Zimbabwe than in the other surveyed countries, and that large firms unmistakably face more contractual problems than smaller firms—hardly a surprise since they are involved in more transactions. Payment problems are more frequent in the textile, garment, and wood sectors. For textile and garments, this

12. The survey did not collect data on recourse to the letter of credit system, but informal discussions with respondents in Ghana, Kenya, and Zimbabwe indicate that letters of credit are used in most imports and exports from outside of Africa. Because of the informal nature of much intra-African trade, respondents seldom export or import within Africa themselves and prefer to rely on intermediaries. The only possible exception is trade with South Africa.

13. To recall, firms with monopolistic suppliers are defined as those who report that at least one of their main suppliers is the sole available source of a particular input.

14. Tobit regression is the appropriate estimator in this case because it corrects for the fact that the dependent variable is censored at zero, namely that a large proportion of firms report zero problems with clients or suppliers. Data on the number of breaches were not collected in Cameroon; this country is dropped from the tobit regressions.

Table 5.5
Tobit regression on the incidence of contractual breach by clients

	Late payment		Nonpayment	
	Coefficient	t-statistic	Coefficient	t-statistic
Country dummies:[1]				
Côte d'Ivoire	−0.75	−2.26	−0.17	−0.60
Kenya	0.66	2.10	−0.01	−0.05
Tanzania	−1.32	−2.87	−1.68	−3.41
Zambia	0.92	2.81	0.06	0.24
Zimbabwe	1.66	3.06	0.99	2.12
Sectoral dummies:				
Textile	0.79	3.25	0.41	1.99
Metal	0.44	1.64	0.17	0.82
Wood	0.43	1.73	0.36	1.66
Contractual environment:				
Incidence of payment problems	0.43	0.41	0.69	−0.55
Recourse to legal system	−0.32	−0.41	−0.61	−0.88
Firm's characteristics:				
Size[2]	0.23	3.64	0.14	2.46
Age[3]	0.16	1.63	0.15	1.68
Limited liability status	0.24	1.22	−0.16	−0.93
Some state ownership	−0.45	−1.35	0.27	0.97
Some foreign ownership	0.08	0.41	0.30	1.70
African owner/manager	0.19	0.98	0.19	1.08
European owner/manager	0.38	1.54	0.11	0.49
Relationship with clients:				
Sell to manufacturers/consumers	0.25	1.24	0.19	1.06
Sell to public firms	0.62	3.48	0.18	1.13
Share of exports in sales	−0.06	−0.29	−0.89	−2.49
Intercept	−2.38	−3.35	−1.38	−2.16
Number of observations	1,000		1,011	
of which are zero	498		655	
Pseudo R-squared	0.1014		0.0672	

Notes: Dependent variable is the log of the number of problems per year + 1. (1) Burundi is the omitted country; (2) firm's size = log(number of employees + 1); (3) firm's age = log(survey year − year of inception).

Table 5.6
Tobit regression on the incidence of contractual breach by suppliers

	Late delivery		Deficient quality	
	Coefficient	t-statistic	Coefficient	t-statistic
Country dummies:[1]				
Côte d'Ivoire	−0.07	−0.12	−1.02	−2.32
Kenya	2.14	3.13	0.92	2.00
Tanzania	0.26	0.37	−0.84	−1.62
Zambia	1.13	1.77	1.54	2.90
Zimbabwe	2.67	3.64	1.05	1.54
Sectoral dummies:				
Textile	−0.63	−1.74	−0.82	−2.66
Metal	−0.25	−0.72	−1.18	−3.04
Wood	−0.32	−0.85	−0.50	−1.71
Contractual environment:				
Incidence of supplier problems	−0.34	−0.15	−1.17	−0.78
Recourse to legal system	−1.25	−1.13	0.03	0.04
Firm's characteristics:				
Size[2]	0.47	4.78	0.27	3.70
Age[3]	−0.22	−1.33	−0.27	−2.24
Limited liability status	0.29	0.99	−0.05	−0.23
Some state ownership	0.08	0.17	0.01	0.02
Some foreign ownership	0.01	0.05	−0.09	−0.38
African owner/manager	−0.43	−1.53	0.15	0.69
European owner/manager	0.14	0.44	0.61	2.37
Relationship with suppliers:				
One supplier monopolistic	0.33	1.33	−0.04	−0.22
One supplier public firm	−0.01	−0.06	0.12	0.62
Share of imported inputs	0.97	2.60	−0.38	−1.30
% purchases from main supplier	0.04	0.09	−0.41	−1.33
Average length of relationship[4]	0.01	0.05	0.04	0.43
One supplier friend or family	1.15	3.01	0.02	0.07
Dummy for infrequent purchases	−0.61	−2.10	−0.16	−0.77
Receives supplier credit	0.31	1.28	0.52	2.85
Gives advance payment	−0.20	−0.34	0.47	1.14
Intercept	−3.18	−3.02	−0.32	−0.36
Number of observations	844		843	
of which are zero	605		551	
Pseudo R-squared	0.1314		0.1028	

Notes: Dependent variable is the log of the number of problems per year + 1. (1) Burundi is the omitted country; (2) firm's size = log(number of employees + 1); (3) firm's age = log(survey year − year of inception); (4) log of average length of relationship with suppliers in years + 1.

probably reflects the difficulties of the industry in the wake of trade liberalization. Older firms seem to do better with suppliers, a result in agreement with the idea that there are returns to experience in choosing and dealing with suppliers. Tobit regression results also confirm that exporters experience fewer payment problems, probably thanks to the letter of credit system. Other characteristics are, in general, not significant, possibly because of endogeneity or omitted variable bias. A thorough investigation of the causality between these various factors requires instruments that are not available in these data and is left fur future research.

5.3 An Econometric Analysis of Dispute Resolution Methods

According to our current understanding of market institutions (e.g., North 1990; Greif 1993; Platteau 1994a, b), the fear of sanction is what induces agents to comply with contractual obligations. These sanctions can take several forms, as were discussed in chapter 2: guilt, harassment, loss of relationship and reputation, legal action involving courts and lawyers, private arbitration, and, more commonly, enlisting the police. We focus here on legal recourse and loss of relationship as these are important sanctions in practice.[15]

Simple theoretical models of relationships, such as the models presented by Kandori (1992), Greif (1993), Ghosh and Ray (1996), Kranton (1996a), Kali (1999), and Fafchamps (2002b), predict that sanctions are applied as soon as breach of contract occurs.[16] Which type of sanction is chosen depends on its relative cost and effectiveness. Given the existence of fixed costs in legal proceedings, the threat of legal action is seldom credible for small size transactions. Suing a poor individual with no assets is rarely cost effective: the chance of recovering anything by legal means is slim so that it is not worth incurring lawyers and court fees. Suing may also be unattractive if the contractual dispute is complex and the evidence hard to verify, so that the outcome of the court process is uncertain. In contrast, breaking a relationship is likely to be counterproductive if the other party is sole buyer or seller. Legal sanctions may not work either; harassment may be the only viable alternative.

---

15. Evidence of reputational sanctions in developed economies is presented, for instance, by Fukuyama (1995), Lorenz (1988), and Bernstein (1992, 1996). Hart (1988), Banerjee and Duflo (2000), McMillan and Woodruff (1999a), McMillan and Naughton (1996), Banerjee and Munshi (1999), Fafchamps and Minten (2002b), and Fafchamps (1996, 1997c, 2000) present evidence for Africa and Asia. Historical evidence is provided, for instance, by Ensminger (1992) and Greif (1993, 1994).

16. This is but an application of the optimal penal code principle of Abreu (1988): gradual sanctions are unnecessary; optimal deterrence is obtained when harsh sanctions are used to punish all deviations from cooperation.

Whenever there exists uncertainty regarding the cause of contract noncompliance, immediate sanctions may not be optimal; a more gradual approach may be needed. To see why, suppose that agents can be hit by two types of shocks, one temporary and the other permanent. In a temporary shock the agents cannot comply with their contractual obligations for a single period; a permanent shock would make the agents forever unable to comply (e.g., bankruptcy). Intuitively, applying harsh sanctions is appropriate only when the other party has been hit by a permanent shock. If the shock is temporary, both parties are better off renegotiating the contract and preserving their relationship. In these circumstances the natural response to a breach of contract is for both parties to negotiate until it becomes clear that the shock is permanent, at which point hard sanctions are applied.

The negotiation subgame is itself fraught with problems, however. Waiting for too long before suing may enable the breaching party to hide assets and evade legal sanctions. The negotiation process is thus likely to be limited in time. The possibility of renegotiation introduces an insurance dimension that can be abused. By analogy with the benefits agents can obtain by filing false insurance claims, parties may profit by calling for undue renegotiation, thereby abusing the other party's willingness to renegotiate contract terms. Agents unable to monitor the situation of the other party may optimally refuse to renegotiate for fear of abuse and may opt for hard sanctions instead.

Although, as argued by Benson (1990), market exchange would become impossible in the total absence of sanctions for breach of contract, punishment of all breach of contract is not required; it is sufficient that breach of contract be punished with a sufficiently high probability. Consequently some agents may be able to free-ride the system by doing nothing in case of breach. In so doing, they do not incur any of the costs associated with dispute resolution and yet they may expect a low probability of breach. By the same token, agents may choose to randomize, namely to punish only a certain percentage of breach they incur. In these cases, or when it is clear that pursuing the breaching party is futile, doing nothing may be the optimal strategy.

This brief, heuristic discussion leads us to expect firms to differ in the way they seek to resolve breach of contract. First, we expect to observe across countries and sectors some differences in reliance on legal institutions that reflect the cost and predictability of legal action. We control for such effects via country and sectoral dummies and the average incidence of contractual disputes. Second, large firms are more likely to engage in large transactions and thus more likely to find legal action cost effective. Third, older firms may have acquired better negotiation and monitoring skills, and may be more familiar with legal institutions. We therefore expect them to be less likely to do nothing when faced with contractual problems. To the extent that limited liability status creates a moral hazard problem and weakens incentives, we expect such firms to be more casual about contractual breach and hence to be more likely to do nothing. Firms may also use their business contacts to monitor contract renegotiation; as a result we expect ethnic Africans to be more likely to either do nothing or use legal recourses given that they have fewer business connections in several of the countries we study, such as Ghana, Kenya, and Zimbabwe (e.g., Fafchamps 2000; Barr 2002b; Fisman 2002). We also include dummy variables indicating whether the firm has some foreign or state ownership. Next firms that value relationships ought to put more emphasis on direct bargaining once problems occur. In contrast, firms that face monopolistic sellers may find it difficult to seek legal reparation. Finally, firms receiving or granting credit to their suppliers ought not to remain inactive when faced with contractual problems. We control for all these factors with the variables listed in the previous subsection. Again, some of these variables are potentially subject to endogeneity bias, a bias we cannot correct for because we do not have good instruments for relationships and network capital. Results should thus be interpreted as suggestive only.

We first examine the probability with which firms seek to negotiate and threaten court action conditional on having encountered a contractual breach. For clients we divide respondents' actions into four categories: (1) do nothing, (2) only negotiate, (3) only use legal institutions, and (4) use both bargaining and legal institutions.[17] For suppliers, the third and fourth categories are merged given the small number of observations in each of them. Since the frequency of late delivery and deficient quality is much lower than that of recovery problems, there are much fewer observations on the supplier side.

Since firms' actions are divided into more than two categories—four for disputes with clients, three for disputes with suppliers—logit is no longer adequate and a multinomial regression approach is required. In the interest of simplicity, we opt for multinomial logit estimation.[18] By construction, the analysis is confined to the firms that experienced contractual breach. Given the small sample size, we limit ourselves to pooled sample regressions. Results are presented in tables 5.7 and 5.8 for clients

17. In practice, the former typically precedes the latter, but we have no data on the sequence of firms' actions.

18. Multinomial logit has been criticized for imposing certain restrictions on agents' choices—the so-called independence of irrelevant alternatives assumption. Given the exploratory nature of our analysis, the substantial extra cost of estimating a more general model is not justified. Qualitatively similar results are obtained using logit regressions on each action separately.

Table 5.7
Multinomial logit regression on conflict resolution method with clients

	Doing nothing		Legal institutions only[6]		Bargaining + legal institutions	
	Coefficient	z-statistic	Coefficient	z-statistic	Coefficient	z-statistic
Country dummies:[1]						
Cameroon	−0.33	−0.37	0.62	0.38	1.03	1.54
Côte d'Ivoire	−0.06	−0.09	−0.34	−0.22	−0.17	−0.27
Kenya	0.74	1.18	1.38	1.12	0.57	1.03
Tanzania	2.23	1.80	1.23	0.58	0.09	0.08
Zambia	0.02	0.03	−0.21	−0.17	−0.22	−0.43
Zimbabwe	1.57	1.57	2.51	1.49	0.72	0.88
Sectoral dummies:						
Textile	−0.52	−1.09	0.18	0.29	−0.34	−0.86
Metal	−0.15	−0.29	−0.09	−0.13	0.28	0.68
Wood	−1.01	−1.94	−0.61	−0.93	−0.37	−0.92
Average incidence of problems:	0.86	0.29	−2.71	−0.52	−0.19	−0.08
Firm's characteristics:						
Size[2]	0.11	0.68	0.53	2.93	0.46	3.89
Age[3]	−0.07	−0.36	0.61	2.01	0.44	2.49
Limited liability status	−0.37	−0.86	1.01	1.64	0.54	1.60
Some state ownership	−0.70	−0.63	−1.82	−1.45	0.21	0.44
Some foreign ownership	−0.51	−1.09	0.03	0.06	−0.56	−1.79
African owner/manager	−0.78	−1.75	−0.39	−0.68	−0.05	−0.15
European owner/manager	−0.43	−0.69	−1.16	−1.77	−0.32	−0.72
Relationship with clients:						
Sell to manufacturers/consumers	0.29	0.56	0.08	0.16	0.06	0.19
Sell to public firms	−0.60	−1.35	−0.27	−0.52	0.02	0.08
Share of exports in sales	−0.79	−0.71	−2.59	−1.75	−1.09	−1.45
Characteristics of problematic clients:						
Individual	1.06	2.51	0.47	0.99	0.35	1.20
Relative or same ethnicity	−0.55	−1.10	−0.36	−0.59	−0.37	−0.97
Length of relationship[4]	−0.18	−1.06	−0.47	−2.27	−0.35	−2.74
Dispute is about nonpayment:[5]	0.22	0.69	1.69	3.89	0.89	3.57
Intercept	−1.71	−1.06	−5.94	−2.25	−3.83	−3.18
Number of observations	528					
Pseudo R-squared	0.2094					

Notes: Direct bargaining only is the omitted category. (1) Burundi is the omitted country; (2) firm's size = log(number of employees + 1); (3) firm's age = log(survey year − year of inception); (4) length of relationship = log(years of acquaintance with problematic client + 1); (5) as opposed to late payment; (6) recourse to one or more of the following: private arbitration, police, lawyers, courts. Threats of recourse to police and courts are included.

Table 5.8
Multinomial logit regression on conflict resolution method with suppliers

	Doing nothing		Some use of legal institutions[7]	
	Coefficient	z-statistic	Coefficient	z-statistic
Country dummies:[1]				
Cameroon	0.66	0.68	1.61	1.03
Côte d'Ivoire	−0.52	−0.59	1.48	1.11
Tanzania	−0.94	−0.86	−37.19	0.00
Zambia	−0.64	−0.64	0.85	0.54
Zimbabwe	1.16	1.35	0.01	0.01
Sectoral dummies:				
Textile	−0.82	−1.55	−1.77	−1.86
Metal	−0.39	−0.78	−1.28	−1.70
Wood	−1.32	−2.03	−1.35	−1.26
Average incidence of problems:	−2.60	−0.83	−5.74	−1.18
Firm's characteristics:				
Size[2]	0.04	0.23	0.61	2.51
Age[3]	0.44	1.81	0.16	0.39
Limited liability status	−0.52	−1.33	−0.11	−0.14
Some state ownership	−0.21	−0.33	−0.30	−0.34
Some foreign ownership	−0.30	−0.64	−0.05	−0.07
African owner/manager	−0.43	−1.05	0.81	1.11
European owner/manager	−0.70	−1.57	−0.37	−0.42
Relationship with suppliers:				
One supplier monopolistic	−0.55	−1.45	−0.35	−0.51
One supplier public firm	0.37	1.05	−0.80	−1.24
Share of imported inputs	−0.87	−1.56	0.83	0.97
% purchases from main supplier	1.92	2.64	−0.08	−0.07
Average length of relationship[4]	−0.36	−1.52	−0.34	−1.01
One supplier friend or family	0.61	1.16	−0.43	−0.38
Dummy for infrequent purchases	0.37	0.90	0.17	0.26
Receives supplier credit	0.01	0.03	0.33	0.56
Gives advance payment	−0.63	−0.76	−0.07	−0.08
Characteristics of problematic supplier:				
Length of relationship[5]	−0.18	−0.82	0.15	0.50
Dummy if public firm	1.39	2.32	2.53	2.29
Dummy if individual consumer	0.94	1.61	0.04	0.03
Dispute about deficient quality:[6]	−1.25	−1.68	1.53	1.59
Intercept	−0.29	−0.19	−3.34	−1.55
Number of observations	325			
Pseudo R-squared	0.1704			

Notes: Direct bargaining only is the omitted category. (1) Burundi is the omitted country; (2) firm's size = log(number of employees + 1); (3) firm's age = log(survey year − year of inception); (4) log of average length of relationship with suppliers in years + 1; (5) length of relationship = log(years of acquaintance with problematic supplier + 1); (6) as opposed to late or nondelivery; (7) some recourse to one of the following: private arbitration, police, lawyers, courts. Threats of recourse to police and courts are included.

and suppliers, respectively. In both tables, bargaining with the delinquent client or supplier is the omitted choice category, Estimated coefficients must therefore be interpreted as differences relative to "bargaining only."[19]

By far the strongest result emanating from table 5.7 is that large firms are more likely to threaten court action against delinquent clients or suppliers. The effect is large and significant in both tables. Large firms probably have easier access to courts given that the costs of legal proceedings are easier to amortize on larger transactions. Results from tables 5.7 and 5.8 therefore suggest that firms with better access to courts make more use of them.

This conclusion only takes all its meaning if it is combined with the finding that large manufacturers face more cases of contract breach. Indeed, these two findings combined imply that better access to legal institutions raises both usage of legal institutions and the frequency of breach. This flies in the face of the commonly held view that strong legal institutions serve to deter contractual opportunism. Our preferred interpretation is that firms operating under the protection of an effective legal system take more risk with clients and suppliers and thus face more problems that they handle through legal channels. The outcome is the same—legal institutions favor exchange—but the channel through which this occurs is not that usually surmised: exchange expands not so much because breach is deterred directly but because firms become more daring in their choice of clients and suppliers.

Among smaller firms, direct negotiation in delinquent payment cases seems to be the method of choice, especially for African owners. This may reflect a cultural preference for nonconfrontational methods of dispute resolution. The length of the relationship between parties is seen to reduce the likelihood of going to court, but the effect is significant only in payment cases. This result is consistent with the idea that valuable relationships serve to discipline contractual behavior without recourse to external enforcement mechanisms. This issue is revisited in part III. The severity of the conflict also influences the dispute resolution method: disputes about nonpayment are less likely to be dealt with via bargaining, and more likely to trigger threats of court action. In contrast, disputes about deficient quality are more likely to be dealt with by negotiating with the supplier.

---

19. For instance, a significantly positive coefficient for Tanzania in the "doing nothing" column of table 5.8 means that Tanzanian manufacturers are much more likely than Burundian to respond to late payment by doing nothing. Since the coefficient of the Tanzania dummy is nonsignificant in the other two columns, it means that Tanzanian manufacturers are less likely than other manufacturers to deal with delinquent clients through negotiations only—the omitted category. The reason is that since probabilities sum to one (manufacturers must take one of the four possible actions), an increase in the probability of undertaking one action—doing nothing—must translate into a decrease in the probability of taking another—here the omitted category, bargaining.

Contrary to expectations, loyalty to suppliers as measured by the percentage of purchases made from main suppliers increases the likelihood of taking no action: loyalty implies trust and hence should facilitate negotiations. Discussions with respondents nevertheless suggest that when parties are extremely well acquainted with each other, minor contractual problems such as late deliveries and quality problems are handled so easily and expeditiously that respondents do not perceive negotiation as taking place at all: "problems take care of themselves," as many respondents put it. Whenever the problematic supplier is a public firm, direct bargaining is less frequent, possibly because it is unlikely to be successful: public agencies are notorious for being unreliable suppliers so that negotiating with them for late deliveries and poor quality is probably seen as a waste of time.

5.4   Outcome of Contractual Dispute

We conclude with an analysis of the outcome of contractual disputes. What happens after a dispute has arisen does shape firms' expectations regarding the outcome of disputes: if all disputes end with sour grapes and broken relationships, it would be optimal for firms to minimize the incidence of disputes. If, in contrast, problems with clients and suppliers are successfully resolved through bargaining or any other means, firms might be more inclined to take chances and less likely to insist on rigorous performance of contracts.

To throw light on these issues, survey respondents were asked to comment on "the most recent case" of contractual breach they had encountered. Responses are therefore subject to truncation since some of the most recent contractual disputes have not been settled yet. We do not, however, have information on when the dispute began, so that we cannot correct for differences in the duration of disputes. The data nevertheless enable us to examine two issues: first, whether the contractual dispute was settled at the time of the interview and, in particular, whether the respondent was satisfied with the outcome,[20] and second, whether the trade relationship continued after the dispute. Regressors are the same as in previous regressions, except that we also control for the method of dispute resolution used by respondents.[21] Results must be interpreted with caution because both the outcome of the dispute and the choice of dispute resolution method are likely to be correlated with the severity of

---

20. The small number of disputes with suppliers that are *not* settled satisfactorily prevented the estimation of the satisfactory settlement regression in the supplier case.

21. Small sample size prevented the inclusion of dispute resolution methods in the trade continuation regression for supplier disputes.

the dispute, which is unobserved. For instance, respondents are unlikely to call upon the police unless they feel that it is their only hope of getting satisfaction. The coefficients of dispute resolution methods are thus subject to omitted variable bias and should be interpreted in this light.

With these words of warning, results are presented in tables 5.9 and 5.10 for clients and suppliers respectively. They indicate that direct bargaining is strongly associated with the settlement of disputes and the resumption of trade. In contrast, recourse to legal institutions such as lawyers, courts, and police result in a much higher probability of severed business relationship. The use of lawyers and threats of court action is also associated with less satisfactory resolution of those disputes that are settled (the effect is only marginally significant, however). This is consistent with the idea that firms seek the protection of legal institutions only when they lose confidence in the other party. Conversations with respondents indeed suggest that lawyers and legal threats are not set in motion as long as firms believe the other party is acting in good faith, trying to comply but is prevented from doing so due to circumstances beyond its control.

Among other results of interest, we note that African-managed firms are more likely to settle payment disputes and to do so satisfactorily after controlling for firm size, age, country, and sector of activity. Combined with evidence that shared ethnicity has a positive effect on the settlement of disputes (the positive and significant coefficient of the "relative or same ethnicity" dummy variable), this can be interpreted as limited evidence of a more lenient attitudes toward payment disputes and a deeper emphasis on flexibility and negotiation among African entrepreneurs. This issue deserves more research.

5.5   Conclusion

We have presented evidence that African manufacturers operate in an environment characterized by contractual nonperformance risk. Results are consistent with the idea that contractual flexibility is a rational response to risk. Expectations regarding contractual performance are thus likely to reflect the environment in which firms operate: the riskier the environment, the higher the need for flexibility, the higher the incidence of contract nonperformance, and the higher the expectation of renegotiation. Large firms face more cases of noncompliance across the board, possibly because they conduct more transactions.

Of the nine countries studied, incidence of contractual breach is much larger in Zimbabwe despite the fact that this country is also the one with the most developed

Table 5.9
Logit regressions on settlement of contractual disputes with clients

	Dispute settled		Settlement satisfactory[6]		Trade relation continues	
	Odds ratio	z-statistic	Odds ratio	z-statistic	Odds ratio	z-statistic
Country dummies:[1]						
Cameroon	0.38	−2.29	2.76	1.07	0.36	−3.37
Côte d'Ivoire	1.31	1.35	4.62	2.91	0.34	−11.39
Kenya	1.74	2.49	14.04	7.56	0.35	−4.71
Tanzania	16.04	4.26	17.01	2.76	0.85	−0.59
Zambia	2.86	5.23	5.31	5.42	0.70	−1.63
Zimbabwe	5.23	4.62	36.64	3.61	0.53	−2.78
Sectoral dummies:						
Textile	0.51	−2.24	0.50	−1.38	0.82	−0.63
Metal	0.25	−10.57	0.52	−1.53	0.76	−3.23
Wood	0.60	−2.89	0.57	−0.92	0.73	−0.97
Average incidence of problems:	21.71	1.72	133.08	1.25	2.44	1.08
Firm's characteristics:						
Size[2]	1.12	1.85	0.65	−2.78	1.06	0.89
Age[3]	1.31	1.38	1.18	1.48	1.11	0.75
Limited liability status	1.04	0.12	2.78	1.11	0.64	−1.52
Some state ownership	0.93	−0.12	4.47	2.65	0.92	−0.16
Some foreign ownership	0.89	−0.60	2.68	3.71	1.39	0.81
African owner/manager	1.96	2.23	2.21	1.76	0.98	−0.05
European owner/manager	1.70	1.26	0.47	−1.70	0.95	−0.12
Relationship with clients:						
Sell to manufacturers/consumers	1.44	1.09	0.88	−0.36	2.00	3.84
Sell to public firms	0.69	−1.46	1.76	0.88	0.97	−0.12
Share of exports in sales	1.13	0.46	1.65	0.67	1.09	0.61
Characteristics of problematic clients:						
Individual	0.63	−1.09	1.07	0.10	0.61	−1.00
Relative or same ethnicity	2.15	3.32	0.57	−0.91	1.09	0.41
Length of relationship[4]	1.17	1.54	0.78	−1.51	1.37	2.58
Dispute is about nonpayment:[5]	0.20	−7.68	0.17	−3.77	0.20	−9.90
Conflict resolution method:						
Direct negotiations	2.11	5.33	0.88	−0.21	1.54	1.68
Private arbitration	1.73	1.15	1.31	0.17	1.82	0.84
Police	0.39	−2.02	0.67	−0.38	0.27	−7.64
Lawyers and courts	0.73	−0.95	0.62	−1.63	0.35	−16.24
Number of observations	525		253		519	
Pseudo R-squared	0.2271		0.2217		0.2395	
Correctly classified	74%		85%		76%	

Notes: Robust standard errors reported using country-level clustering. (1) Burundi is the omitted country; (2) firm's size = log(number of employees + 1); (3) firm's age = log(survey year − year of inception); (4) length of relationship = log(years of acquaintance with problematic client + 1); (5) as opposed to late payment; (6) conditional on the dispute being settled.

Table 5.10
Logit regressions on settlement of contractual disputes with suppliers

	Dispute settled		Trade relationship continues	
	Odds ratio	z-statistic	Odds ratio	z-statistic
Country dummies:[1]				
Cameroon	0.63	−1.07	na	na
Côte d'Ivoire	0.86	−0.33	0.72	−0.86
Kenya	na	na	0.24	−2.07
Tanzania	4.30	1.86	0.33	−1.61
Zambia	0.78	−0.34	0.31	−2.57
Zimbabwe	0.77	−0.45	0.93	−0.15
Sectoral dummies:				
Textile	2.27	2.35	0.89	−0.29
Metal	1.48	1.94	0.79	−0.66
Wood	1.53	0.75	0.57	−0.96
Average incidence of problems:	22.71	2.19	0.02	−1.23
Firm's characteristics:				
Size[2]	1.01	0.03	1.12	1.29
Age[3]	0.85	−0.61	1.36	1.93
Limited liability status	1.03	0.05	1.14	0.21
Some state ownership	1.80	0.75	0.71	−0.29
Some foreign ownership	1.03	0.04	1.15	0.47
African owner/manager	0.77	−0.29	0.83	−0.67
European owner/manager	0.92	−0.12	0.59	−1.25
Relationship with suppliers:				
One supplier monopolistic	0.89	−0.64	1.05	0.09
One supplier public firm	1.31	1.05	1.94	1.73
Share of imported inputs	1.36	0.47	0.69	−1.38
% purchases from main supplier	1.06	0.08	1.36	0.62
Average length of relationship[4]	1.42	1.46	0.93	−0.60
One supplier friend or family	0.61	−0.74	0.54	−1.06
Dummy for infrequent purchases	0.48	−3.46	0.77	−0.95
Receives supplier credit	0.75	−0.55	1.38	0.71
Gives advance payment	1.58	0.80	1.99	0.72
Characteristics of problematic supplier:				
Dummy if first time supplier	0.92	−0.14	0.25	−2.47
Length of relationship[5]	0.93	−0.37	0.95	−0.13
Dummy if public firm	0.26	−5.97	0.61	−1.14
Dummy if individual	1.67	1.31	1.64	0.83
Conflict resolution method:				
Direct negociations	3.57	7.43	Not included[6]	
Use of legal institutions	2.17	1.13	Not included[6]	
Number of observations	320		360	
Pseudo R-squared	0.1343		0.1366	
Correctly classified	75%		83%	

Notes: Robust standard errors reported using country-level clustering. (1) Burundi is the omitted country; (2) firm's size = log(number of employees + 1); (3) firm's age = log(survey year − year of inception); (4) log of average length of relationship with suppliers in years + 1; (5) length of relationship = log(years of acquaintance with problematic supplier + 1); (6) these variables could not be included in the regression due to insufficient number of observations.

manufacturing sector as well as a good legal and court system. Since Zimbabwe is probably the country in the sample where legal institutions best support business (Fafchamps et al. 1995), this finding contradicts the idea that a high frequency of contract noncompliance is a sign of imperfect legal institutions and unsophisticated business practices. We similarly find that large firms are both more likely to encounter contract noncompliance and to make use of lawyers and courts. Taken together, these results suggest that access to supportive legal institutions incite firms to take more chances with suppliers and clients, thereby encouraging trade while at the same time resulting in more cases of breach and more recourse to courts and lawyers. In contrast, firms that have little or no access to courts must rely on alternative institutions such as business relationships and social networks, and adopt cruder business practices to minimize their exposure to contractual risk.

A corollary of the above is that, unless firms feel sufficiently protected, they choose to avoid situations in which problems may arise. As a result the incidence of problems is lower when legal institutions are less developed and the manufacturing sector unsophisticated. This may also explain why large firms, which are more likely to call upon the legal system, are also those who face more problems. Similar conclusions are reached in the next chapter regarding agricultural traders in Madagascar. The role of institutions is further brought to light by the fact that exporting firms face fewer payment problems, despite having to collect payment from firms located in other countries. We interpreted this result as a consequence of the letter of credit mechanism whereby banks located abroad collect payment in the name of the exporting firm. In contrast, importing firms face more late deliveries, probably because of transport and customs delays.

Our results are in line with the idea that African manufacturers expect supply contracts to be flexible. Our findings indicate that contract nonperformance is handled primarily through direct negotiation. Only if negotiation is unsuccessful do firms turn to outsiders such as lawyers and courts and, in certain cases, the police. When this happens, the parties are extremely unlikely to resume their relationship. The existence of long-term relationships with clients and suppliers appears to serve as a facilitator in these disputes, raising the probability that the dispute is settled and that the outcome is judged satisfactory. Relations based on family, friendship, or ethnicity/kinship make it easier for firms to solve disputes but also raises the incidence of contract nonperformance, the two issues being possibly linked.

The chapter contributes to the literature in two ways. First, it demonstrates that regarding contracts as rigid is not only inaccurate, it also fails to recognize that contractual flexibility is necessary for market exchange to take place. This finding is essential for a proper understanding of how markets operate in practice. Second, although the data did not allow us to ascertain the direction of causality between participation in international markets and contractual practices, the evidence presented nevertheless suggest that the relation between the two is strong and deserves further study. What this chapter was able to show is that African manufacturers operate in an environment where contractual disputes are frequent but are mostly dealt with through direct negotiation. The great majority of disputes regarding late deliveries are resolved to the satisfaction of the parties and trade is resumed thereafter. The same is true for many disputes regarding late payment. More work is needed to assess whether African firms exposed to outside influences through trade adopt Western-style contractual practices in their local operations or rather take advantage of local tolerance for late payment and delivery to meet their stricter obligations towards international suppliers and clients.

Taken together with evidence that entrepreneurs who are ethnic Africans seek the resolution of disputes primarily through nonconfrontational means, these results suggests that there may be reasons other than rent seeking and erroneous policies for why Africa trades so little with the rest of the world, namely that foreign firms find it difficult to deal with African firms and find them generally unreliable. In particular, attempts by African entrepreneurs to renegotiate delivery and payment terms ex post—a relatively common practice in local transactions according to the data presented here—are likely to be misinterpreted as opportunistic. While it would be ill advised to overplay the idea—other obstacles to trade remain formidable—it nevertheless opens the door to another way of conceiving and, hence, promoting relations between African and foreign firms, namely trust and network building. This issue deserves further investigation.

6 Evidence from Agricultural Traders

Having looked at manufacturing, we now turn to agricultural trade. Three countries were surveyed: Madagascar, Benin, and Malawi. All three are particularly suitable places to study market institutions at early stages of development because, until recently, their agricultural trade was subject to various forms of government control (e.g., Berg 1989; Dorosh and Bernier 1994; Barrett 1997a, b). All three countries have kept much of the French or English legal code and judicial system they inherited from colonization. Their commercial law may be a little dated, not having been overhauled since independence (e.g., Root 1993; World Bank 1995). But it is likely to be superior to the legal environment that prevails in most transitional economies. Liberalized grain trade in sub-Saharan Africa thus constitutes an interesting test case of the role of law in the development of efficient markets, and it provides a unique window on the early development of markets when laws were not entirely inadequate[1] but their implementation left much to be desired. The analysis presented here should supply useful insights on the likely effect of legal reform in transition economies at a similar level of development.

Using data from three trader surveys, we show that the incidence of theft and breach of contract is low among agricultural traders and that the losses resulting from such instances are small. Prima facie these results suggest that market institutions work well. A closer look at the evidence, however, reveals that low incidence of theft and contractual breach is achieved essentially through low exposure. Theft is rare because many traders do not stock the goods they sell, and if they do, they go to great length in ensuring that their stocks are protected—such as by sleeping in their store. Econometric analysis confirms that overnight storage is a significant risk factor in theft incidence in Madagascar. Among those who transport grain from town to town, payment of protection money and travel in convoy are common—presumably against the risk of ambush that is endemic in certain parts of Africa. A number of surveyed traders even declare refraining from hiring additional workers for fear of employee-related theft. This is particularly true in Madagascar.

The situation regarding contract compliance is similar. Traders limit their exposure to potential breach of contract by adopting commercial practices that leave little room for abuse. Most transactions take a simple cash-and-carry form. Supplier credit is infrequent, and the placement of orders is uncommon. Payment by check and invoicing are virtually unheard of. Traders personally inspect the quality of goods purchased in nearly all transactions. Econometric analysis indicates that exposure is a dominant risk factor in all cases of contractual breach.

---

1. Even if somewhat outdated and contradictory.

Survey results from Madagascar further show that recourse to legal institutions is rare, but that it increases with the severity of the dispute. The use of police and courts is indeed highest in theft cases and lowest in late delivery and deficient quality cases, with nonpayment by clients in between. Direct negotiation with the other party is the dominant conflict resolution method in contractual disputes. Traders' propensity to solve disputes and to resume trade with each other is shown to depend critically on the use of direct negotiations with the other party. Recourse to negotiations in turn depends on the strength of the relationship between trading partners. These results are broadly similar to those reported in the previous chapter. They also resemble the findings of Bernstein (1996) about grain traders in the United States, albeit with even less reliance of formal institutions.

6.1 Incidence of Theft and Breach of Contract

Table 6.1 summarizes the incidence of theft and breach of contract in the twelve months preceding the survey. The proportion of traders who were victim of theft in the previous twelve months varies from 8 percent in Madagascar to 33 percent in Malawi. The total value of stolen goods is small: it accounts for between 0.3 to 0.6 percent of total annual sales. Incidence appears much higher for a handful of respondents, but we cannot rule out the possibility of error in data collection. Of 56 instances of thefts reported in Madagascar, 23 took place at the trader's store during the day, 23 took place at night, 7 during transport, and 3 while the goods were in the hands of third parties (table 6.2). Not all thefts are equally costly, however: the average value of stolen goods is on average nine times higher for thefts at night or during transport. In a third to three-quarters of theft cases, respondents are confident that employees were not responsible; in the rest of the cases, respondents either suspected employees or are unsure. Suspicion toward employees is much higher in Madagascar, where the security situation is known to be bad (e.g., Root 1993; Ministere de la Justice 1999; Fafchamps and Minten 2001a). Not surprisingly, Malagasy traders who suspect employees are those with more employees—7.7 as opposed to 3.4 among respondents who do not suspect their workforce. Theft by employees (or with their assistance) is thus is a concern of surveyed traders, especially large ones located in Madagascar.

Breaches of contract are somewhat more prevalent, but they affect a minority of survey respondents (table 6.2). Except for quality problems, the proportion of sales and purchases affected by breach of contract is less than 5 percent on average. It is much higher for some traders, though. In Benin and Malawi, information is also

Table 6.1
Incidence of theft and breach of contract

	Madagascar	Benin	Malawi
Theft			
Traders who experienced theft in last 12 months	7.7%	16.4%	33.2%
Value of stolen goods relative to annual sales	0.3%	0.6%	0.3%
Maximum value of stolen goods relative to annual sales	93.0%	70.5%	42.1%
Late delivery by suppliers			
Traders who experienced late delivery in last 12 months	8.8%	1.4%	16.4%
Proportion of late deliveries in total transactions	1.6%	0.2%	0.1%
Deficient quality of deliveries by suppliers			
Traders who experienced deficient quality in last 12 months	20.6%	2.7%	40.8%
Proportion of deficient quality deliveries in total transactions[1]	4.4%	6.3%	9.6%
Attempt to renegotiate the agreed-upon price with suppliers			
Traders who experienced an attempt to renegotiate the price	na	12.3%	24.8%
Proportion of such purchases in total transactions[1]	na	10.5%	8.5%
Late payment by clients			
Traders who experienced late payment in last 12 months	30.8%	24.4%	42.1%
Proportion of late payments in total transactions	1.9%	2.0%	2.2%
Nonpayment by clients			
Traders who experienced non payment in last 12 months	6.8%	19.9%	25.1%
Proportion of non payments in total transactions	0.0%	0.6%	0.6%
Attempt to renegotiate the agreed-upon price with clients			
Traders who experienced an attempt to renegotiate the price	na	5.7%	20.2%
Proportion of such sales in total transactions[1]	na	0.1%	4.4%
Number of observations	733	640	731

Notes: The exact number of valid observations varies somewhat from question to question. (1) For Benin, this figure is only available for traders who place orders with suppliers.

available on whether the supplier or client tried to renegotiate the agreed-upon price after the deal. Depending on the circumstances, this can also be conceived as breach of contract. Survey responses suggest that renegotiation occurs fairly often, especially with suppliers, and that it affects a significant volume of purchases. The typical situation is one in which a trader scouts a village in search of produce. A seller is found and a price agreed. The trader then arranges transport and comes back a few hours or days later to pick up and pay. Farmers occasionally take advantage of the situation to raise the price. This is akin to a standard holdup problem.

Deficient quality and late payment are the most often cited problems. But their implied cost is only a fraction of the value of the transaction—such as loss in value due to inferior quality and opportunity cost of capital in case of late payment. The same is true for late delivery. Nonpayment, a much more severe form of

Table 6.2
Exposure to theft and prevention

	Madagascar	Benin	Malawi
Traders who experienced a theft in last 12 months	8%	16%	33%
Of those who experienced a theft:			
% who experienced theft at store during the day	42%	na	na
% who experienced theft from storage at night	40%	na	na
% who experienced theft during transport/consignment	18%	na	na
Of those who experienced a theft:			
% who think theft was not due to employee	32%	61%	72%
% who suspect an employee	37%	5%	9%
% who do not know	26%	33%	18%
Traders who refrain from hiring workers for fear of theft	37%	2%	11%
Traders who stock overnight	72%	86%	95%
Of those who stock overnight:			
% with lock on storage location	99%	75%	87%
% who sleep on premices	64%	18%	48%
% who hire a guard	52%	40%	27%
% who either sleep on premices or hire a guard	95%	55%	64%
Traders who transport goods from one town to another	41%	84%	73%
Of those who transport:			
% who avoid certain locations for fear of theft during transport	4%	8%	17%
% who pay someone for protecting goods in transport	14%	4%	17%
% who travel in convoy	30%	10%	19%
% who either pay for protection or travel in convoy	43%	14%	34%

breach of contract, is quite rare and affects only 0.1 to 0.6 percent of all transactions. These findings are similar, though more pronounced, to those reported in earlier chapters.

Judging from these numbers, the direct costs of theft and breach of contract are quite small—less than one or two percents of annual sales on average.[2] Some traders occasionally suffer more severe losses, however, especially when goods are stolen at night or during transport. On the basis of these numbers, one may be tempted to conclude that the rule of law prevails in rural Africa and that malfeasance is adequately deterred by existing legal institutions. This is in apparent contradiction with

2. Estimated from table 6.2 assuming that losses from late delivery and late payment account for at most 10 percent of the value of sales and that losses from deficient quality account for at most 5 percent of sales value. With these generous assumptions, total losses amount to 0.89 percent of total sales—0.28 percent from theft, 0.04 percent from nonpayment, 0.16 percent from late delivery, 0.22 percent from deficient quality, and 0.19 percent from late payment. Recovered goods are not subtracted from loss from theft.

the fact that 64 percent of the 364 individuals interviewed in Madagascar by the Ministère de la Justice (1999) listed theft as their number one public safety concern, and that the majority of them did not trust police and courts to provide sufficient protection. A closer inspection of the evidence suggests, however, a possible reconciliation: the low incidence of malfeasance owes more to prevention by traders than to legal deterrence. Surveyed traders indeed go to great lengths to minimize the risk of theft and breach of contract.

Table 6.2 lists some of the measures surveyed traders take to minimize theft. Over a third of Malagasy respondents declared refraining from hiring additional workers for fear of employee theft. The magnitude of this figure—and its likely welfare cost in an economy where underemployment is rampant and trade is a major source of employment—perfectly illustrates the idea that the indirect costs of malfeasance are potentially much larger than its direct costs (see Hart 1988 for a similar observation). Table 6.2 also shows that among traders who stock agricultural products, a large proportion sleep on the premises, especially in Malawi and Madagascar. Most overnight storage is both locked and guarded. Of those traders who transport goods from one town to another, a significant minority either pay for protection or travel in convoy.[3] In addition a number of traders declare avoiding certain routes for fear of bandits. Finally, we note that a much smaller proportion of surveyed traders transport agricultural products in Madagascar where the safety situation is the least satisfactory.

A similar picture of limited exposure emerges for quality control. Table 6.3 indicates that, in Madagascar, the price differential between the two most traded rice qualities oscillate between 8 and 9 percent in the capital city. Some of this quality variation is due to differences in traditional crop varieties across regions.[4] This source of quality variation can presumably be controlled by traders simply by verifying the geographical origin of the goods they buy. Some of the variation in quality, however, does not come from regional differences but from improper handling[5] and from natural variation in traditional seed material, thereby making it harder to ascertain. Taken together, the evidence indicates that price varies with quality and that quality cannot be perfectly inferred by a product's region of origin.

---

3. Interestingly, only two traders report doing both.

4. Unlike in advanced economies where most food is produced from a handful of highly homogeneous improved seeds, farmers in Madagascar as well as in much of the tropics rely on their own output for seeds. This process results in widespread dispersion in genetic traits and output characteristics across regions and even villages.

5. For instance, high moisture content, fungus and pest damage, brokens (jargon for grain trader), and presence of stones and sand.

Table 6.3
Variation of quality and inspection by trader

	Madagascar
Traders' assessment of quality variation	
Whether prices vary with product quality:	
A lot	33%
A little bit	61%
Not at all	7%
Whether product quality varies by region of origin	
A lot	37%
A little bit	57%
Not at all	6%
Whether product quality varies within region of origin:	
Always	5%
Often	14%
Sometimes	37%
Seldom	36%
Never	7%
Average price differential between C1 and C2 quality rice[1]	
Retail price	9%
Wholesale price	8%
Verification of quality before purchase	
Trader verifies quality:	
Always	84%
Often	13%
Sometimes	2%
Never	1%
The person who verifies quality is:	
Trader himself/herself	93%
Family helper	4%
Employee or collecting agent	2%
Nobody	1%
Client verifies quality:	
Always	85%
Often	11%
Sometimes	2%
Never	2%

Note: (1) The market price data on rice was collected by the IFPRI-FOFIFA project in Antananarivo (1997).

Table 6.4
Assessment of type and quality

	Benin	Malawi
Traders reporting the existence of different types or varieties	79%	76%
Method used to assess type or variety:		
Direct inspection by trader	99%	100%
Rely on supplier/other	1%	0%
Traders reporting the existence of different qualities	67%	62%
Method used to assess quality:		
Direct inspection by trader	99%	99%
Rely on supplier/other	1%	1%
Price variation due to quality:		
Coefficient of variation of price	14%	10%
Price gap between high and low price as % of mean price	27%	18%

As table 6.3 shows, the overwhelming majority of surveyed Malagasy traders and their clients respond to quality risk by inspecting each and every purchase. The importance of quality inspection is further underscored by the fact that the task is virtually never delegated to family helpers, employees, or collecting agents. Although we did not attempt to measure the time actually spent on quality verification by Malagasy traders, casual observation suggests that the process can be very time-consuming. Furthermore it requires that the trader be present at each purchase, thereby complicating the conduct of business and requiring extensive travel on the part of the trader.

Slightly different information was collected in Benin and Malawi. It is summarized in table 6.4. We see that virtually all respondents assess the type and quality of what they purchase via direct inspection. Only a handful of traders rely on what the supplier tells them. Prices vary significantly with quality, particularly in wetter Benin where humid grain an tubers spoil rapidly.

Reduced exposure is also observed with respect to other sources of breach of contract. Most surveyed traders never place orders from suppliers (85 percent in Madagascar, 94 percent in Benin, and 68 percent in Malawi). Most never give credit to customers (54 percent in Madagascar, 75 percent in Benin, and 64 percent in Malawi). In addition payment by check is unheard of; all transactions are strictly cash.[6] Although such practices presumably reduce contractual risk, they complicate transactions and the planning of business.

---

6. The use of check is absent even of credit transactions, presumably because Malagasy banks are notoriously slow in processing payments and transfers. At the time of the survey, it allegedly took two to three weeks for banks to transfer funds from agencies of the same bank located in two different towns.

6.2 Risk and Limited Exposure

However costly, efforts at minimizing the incidence of malfeasance are in general effective. As indicated by table 6.5, simple t-tests indicate that not storing overnight virtually eliminates the risk of theft in Madagascar. In the other two countries, storage in not significant, probably because the risk of theft is lower. Not placing orders cancels the risk of late delivery, and not giving credit to clients dramatically reduces the risks of late and nonpayment. The results reported in table 6.5 may, however, be unreliable because they ignore the effects of other possible determinants of malfeasance, such as differences in firm size, managerial quality, and regional differences in incidence. They also fail to control for the possibility that prevention is endogenous.

We therefore complement the bivariate analysis reported in table 6.5 with a multivariate regression analysis that controls for possible endogeneity. Results regarding theft are presented in table 6.6. The dependent variable is a binary variable equal to one if the respondent has incurred a theft in the previous twelve months. Explanatory variables include total sales (to control for size), human capital (measured by years of schooling and the log of years of trade experience), and location dummies. Presumably larger firms may experience more theft because they process a larger volume of goods and find it harder to control their employees. Total sales are instrumented to control for the possible feedback effect that theft may have on sales.[7] Human capital is included to control for the possibility that smarter, more experienced traders might be better able to prevent theft. Location variables control for general crime environment and other spatial effects.

Risk factors such as overnight storage and storage capacity are included as regressors as well, to assess their effect on risk (model 1). As expected, results show that Malagasy traders who store overnight are more at risk. The magnitude of the coefficient is very large. Storage capacity has the expected sign, but its t value is below standard levels of significance. The risk of theft is also highest in regions where insecurity is generally perceived to be highest. In Benin, storage appears to reduce the risk of theft, perhaps because the much better security situation induces some traders to keep their goods in unprotected areas, with some increase in the risk of theft. A similar effect is observed in Malawi, but it is not significant.

To control for possible endogeneity of risk factors, we then instrument risky behavior variables and replace them by their predicted value.[8] Results with instrumented

---

7. Instruments include various measures of physical and working capital, labor and management, social network capital, and family background.

8. Instruments include personal wealth, age, and sex of the owner, social network capital, personal traits, and family background.

Table 6.5
Exposure and incidence

	Madagascar	Benin	Malawi
Theft and storage			
Value of stolen goods relative to annual sales:			
Trader does not stock overnight	0.00%	1.46%	0.23%
Trader stocks overnight	0.38%	0.51%	0.29%
t-test	−1.9016	1.0542	−0.5020
p-value	0.0578	0.2946	0.6170
Theft and transport			
Value of stolen goods relative to annual sales:			
Trader does not transport	0.28%	1.89%	0.20%
Trader transports goods	0.28%	0.40%	0.32%
t-test	−0.0268	1.5741	−1.1019
p-value	0.9786	0.1186	0.2709
Late delivery by suppliers			
Proportion of transactions with late delivery:			
Trader does not place orders with suppliers	0.00%	0.00%	0.00%
Trader places orders with suppliers	10.55%	3.53%	0.29%
t-test	−5.8100	−2.1748	−4.7968
p-value	0.0000	0.0365	0.0000
Deficient quality of deliveries by suppliers			
Proportion of transactions with deficient quality:			
Trader does not always inspect the quality of supplies	5.76%	na	na
Trader always inspects quality of supplies	4.19%	na	na
t-test	0.9070		
p-value	0.3660		
Late payment by clients			
Proportion of transactions with late payment:			
Trader does not grant credit to clients	0.33%	0.00%	1.29%
Trader grants credit to at least some clients	3.77%	3.30%	2.66%
t-test	−4.3800	−2.4724	−1.6694
p-value	0.0000	0.0149	0.0956
Nonpayment by clients			
Proportion of transactions with nonpayment:			
Trader does not grant credit to clients	0.00%	0.01%	0.01%
Trader grants credit to at least some clients	0.08%	0.96%	0.88%
t-test	−3.1191	−1.0807	−2.6071
p-value	0.0200	0.2822	0.0094

Note: Test of equality of variance rejected in all cases. All *t*-tests conducted without assuming equality of variance. For Benin, tests for late payment and nonpayment are based on a small number of observations because few traders stated how many transactions they undertake per month.

Table 6.6
Determinants of the incidence of theft

		Madagascar			
		Model 1		Model 2	
		Coefficient	t-statistic	Coefficient	t-statistic
Exposure factors					
Night storage at sales location	Yes = 1	22.612	12.46	4.968	2.83
Storage capacity	Log($x + 1$)	0.156	1.01	0.504	2.60
Trader's characteristics					
Total sales (predicted)	Value	0.151	0.81	0.237	1.57
Years of schooling	Number	−0.041	−0.74	−0.077	−1.43
Years of experience	Log($x + 1$)	−0.220	−0.81	−0.418	−1.60
Location dummies					
Intercept		−25.905		−9.211	−4.60
Number of observations		674		674	
Pseudo R-squared		0.210		0.111	

Note: Logit estimates reported. Model 1: actual value of exposure factors. Model 2: predicted values of exposure factors.

exposure factors are presented under the column model 2 of table 6.6. They confirm that storage raises the incidence of theft in Madagascar but reduces it in Benin.

We run similar regressions for various forms of breach of contract. To control for relationships, we include additional regressors such as the (log of the) number of close relatives in agricultural trade and the number of suppliers and clients known personally by the respondent. Fafchamps and Minten (2002b) indeed demonstrate that better connected traders not only make more profits but also are more likely to place orders and to give and receive trade credit. Following much of the literature (e.g., North 1990; Greif 1993; Fukuyama 1995; Kranton 1996a), they hypothesize that social connections mitigate opportunism. Regional dummies are included to capture possible differences in road infrastructure, climate, and other location specific factors. To the extent that late delivery is due to problems during transport, we would therefore expect late delivery to more prevalent in isolated regions. Since deficient quality is often related to imperfect drying, we would expect quality to be more problematic in humid regions.

Regression results are presented in tables 6.7 to 6.10. Since late delivery cannot occur unless an order has been placed, late delivery regressions are presented only for model 2 with instrumented exposure factor. Estimated coefficients of exposure factors have the right sign and most are significant. This confirms that risk avoidance explains low-risk incidence in the studied countries.

Benin				Malawi			
Model 1		Model 2		Model 1		Model 2	
Coefficient	t-statistic	Coefficient	t-statistic	Coefficient	t-statistic	Coefficient	t-statistic
−1.388	−4.15	−2.005	−2.94	−0.103	−0.26	−1.103	−1.34
−0.016	−0.50	0.007	0.06	0.008	0.33	0.008	0.10
0.127	1.07	0.148	0.68	0.058	0.78	0.083	0.72
0.040	1.10	0.032	0.86	0.011	0.42	0.009	0.35
0.514	2.33	0.426	1.69	0.050	0.40	0.046	0.32
		Included but not shown					
−2.835	−3.22	−2.298	−2.25	−1.218	−1.72	−0.488	−0.53
551		567		698		712	
0.065		0.040		0.005		0.008	

Other results are worth commenting as well. Traders with more business contacts and family members in agricultural trade appear to face a higher incidence of con tractual breach. The effect is not always significant, however. In a number of cases the pattern is reversed for Malawi where better social ties reduces contractual risk. These contradictory findings probably result from two conflicting forces: reduced risk and increased risk taking. In some cases, risk reduction dominates—and the coefficient is negative. In others, the risk taking effect dominates—and the coefficient is positive. We revisit this issue below. Fafchamps and Minten (2002b) find that respondents with more relatives in agricultural trade get significantly lower profits after controlling for all factors and inputs.

To summarize, we have shown that the incidence of theft and contractual breach is low but also that Malagasy grain traders go to great length to reduce their exposure to malfeasance. Regression analysis demonstrated that prevention is effective in the sense that traders who opt for more risky trading practices face a higher incidence of malfeasance. The question remains of why prevention is the dominant method grain traders use to reduce risk. To answer this question, we now examine what happens when a theft or a breach of contract actually occurs.

6.3   Legal Institutions and Deterrence

Questions regarding legal institutions and deterrence were only asked to Malagasy traders. They are summarized in tables 6.11 to 6.14. We see that recourse to the

Table 6.7
Determinants of the incidence of late delivery by suppliers

		Madagascar Model 2		Benin Model 2		Malawi Model 2	
		Coefficient	t-statistic	Coefficient	t-statistic	Coefficient	t-statistic
Exposure factors							
Respondent places orders	Yes = 1	5.900	4.38	4.155	0.82	1.625	2.06
Trader's characteristics							
Total sales	Value	0.008	0.05	0.414	0.57	0.046	0.47
Years of schooling	Value	0.005	0.09	0.098	0.78	0.029	0.85
Years of experience	Log(x + 1)	−0.178	−0.74	0.384	0.38	−0.276	−1.67
Number of relatives in agricultural trade	Log(x + 1)	0.310	1.07	−0.196	−0.29	−0.343	−1.84
Number of suppliers known personally	Log(x + 1)	−0.087	−0.36	−0.292	−0.80	0.323	2.97
Location dummies				Included but not shown			
Intercept		−2.637	−1.59	−9.109	−1.60	−2.909	−3.49
Number of observations		673		563		717	
Pseudo R-squared		0.219		0.188		0.058	

Note: Logit estimates reported. Model 1: cannot be estimated because late delivery does not occur unless an order has been placed. Model 2: predicted values of exposure factors.

police is relatively frequent in cases of theft: as shown in table 6.11, one-third of theft cases were reported to the police, and respondents went to court—presumably as witnesses—in 10 percent of the theft cases. This finding is consistent with the results from the attitudinal survey reported in Ministère de la Justice (1999), where 31 percent of respondents stated they would contact the police if they were a victim of theft. Calling upon the police had no noticeable effect on the probability of recovering stolen items, however: of those traders who went to the police, 24 percent retrieved all or part of their stolen goods; of those who did not, 34 percent retrieved something. The difference is not statistically significant (t value of 0.81). The small number of observations (57 cases of theft) precludes further analysis.[9]

We have a little more information on contractual disputes with suppliers and clients. Surveyed traders were asked whether they ever called upon an intermediary to mediate their contractual disputes with suppliers or clients, and whether they ever went to the police, a lawyer, or a court in relation with a purchase or sales dispute. Their responses, listed in table 6.11, show that apart from an occasional recourse to the police, the use of legal institutions by Malagasy grain traders is extremely low in contractual disputes with suppliers and clients. These results are consistent with results from an attitudinal survey reported in Ministère de la Justice (1999).

One conceivable interpretation of these numbers is that legal enforcement in Madagascar is so effective and predictable that parties rationally anticipate the outcome and prefer to settle beforehand to avoid litigation costs. Table 6.11 indeed indicates that direct negotiations are the instrument of choice to resolve contractual disputes. Mediators are used occasionally as well. But the data also show that the threat of recourse to the police or to courts is extremely rare. In addition these threats tend to be used only in desperate circumstances. Of the eight cases in which a threat of police action was mentioned, for instance, five were for nonpayment by a client. Finally, surveyed traders hardly ever seek the advice of a lawyer. Taken together, these observations suggest that the threat of court action is not an important deterrent of contractual opportunism in the Malagasy grain market. Yet lack of familiarity with courts and legal institutions does not seem to be the main reason for lack of usage: the fact that one-third of robbed traders went to the police and 11 percent went to court does not suggest reluctance for legal institutions per se. What the data therefore indicates is that contractual obligations are largely seen as outside the purview of the law—with the possible exception of nonpayment.

---

9. With such a small number of observations and no suitable instruments, it is impossible to control for self-selection bias in the sense that traders may only go to the police if they cannot solve the theft on their own. The lack of statistical difference in the resolution of cases brought to the police and those handled by traders themselves does not alone constitute sufficient evidence that the police is ineffective.

Table 6.8
Determinants of the incidence of deficient quality deliveries by suppliers

| | | Madagascar | | | |
| | | Model 1 | | Model 2 | |
		Coefficient	t-statistic	Coefficient	t-statistic
Exposure factors					
Owner never verifies quality	Code[1]	0.061	0.30	0.058	0.30
Number of persons authorized to buy	Log(x)				
Trader's characteristics					
Total sales	Value	−0.029	−0.25	−0.029	−0.24
Years of schooling	Number	−0.023	−0.65	−0.024	−0.67
Years of experience	Log($x+1$)	−0.195	−1.10	−0.196	−1.10
Number of relatives in agricultural trade	Log($x+1$)	0.784	3.71	0.819	3.14
Number of suppliers known personally	Log($x+1$)	0.197	1.19	0.206	1.23
Location dummies					
Intercept		−0.573	−0.47	−0.437	−0.34
Number of observations		670		673	
Pseudo R-squared		0.272		0.273	

Note: Logit estimates reported. Model 1: actual value of exposure factors. Model 2: predicted values of exposure factors. (1) Variable coded from 1 = always verify to 5 = never verify.

Table 6.9
Determinants of the incidence of late payment by clients

| | | Madagascar | | | |
| | | Model 1 | | Model 2 | |
		Coefficient	t-statistic	Coefficient	t-statistic
Exposure factors					
Credit sales in total sales	Share	5.045	8.41	2.394	3.67
Trader's characteristics					
Total sales	Value	0.024	0.23	0.186	1.95
Years of schooling	Number	−0.012	−0.36	−0.037	−1.16
Years of experience	Log($x+1$)	−0.010	−0.06	−0.064	−0.37
Number of relatives in agricultural trade	Log($x+1$)	0.423	2.12	0.379	2.06
Number of clients known personally	Log($x+1$)	0.235	1.85	−0.001	−0.01
Location dummies					
Intercept		−1.572	−1.43	−3.148	−3.19
Number of observations		673		673	
Pseudo R-squared		0.227		0.138	

Note: Logit estimates reported. Model 1: actual value of exposure factors. Model 2: predicted values of exposure factors.

Benin				Malawi			
Model 1		Model 2		Model 1		Model 2	
Coefficient	t-statistic	Coefficient	t-statistic	Coefficient	t-statistic	Coefficient	t-statistic
0.795	1.41	0.110	0.08	0.609	2.98	0.684	1.08
0.164	0.49	0.297	0.86	0.145	1.99	0.133	1.37
0.102	1.45	0.115	1.64	0.011	0.41	0.009	0.36
−0.347	−0.64	−0.259	−0.47	−0.321	−2.62	−0.324	−2.64
0.692	1.78	0.747	1.91	0.000	0.00	0.010	0.07
0.060	0.24	−0.016	−0.07	0.292	3.67	0.268	3.16
		Included but not shown					
−6.526	−2.91	−7.210	−3.17	−2.088	−3.23	−2.014	−2.69
566		568		718		718	
0.133		0.118		0.068		0.060	

Benin				Malawi			
Model 1		Model 2		Model 1		Model 2	
Coefficient	t-statistic	Coefficient	t-statistic	Coefficient	t-statistic	Coefficient	t-statistic
1.378	2.58	5.323	3.40	8.340	9.55	1.351	0.68
0.187	1.43	−0.038	−0.25	0.034	0.45	0.004	0.06
−0.049	−1.36	−0.063	−1.72	0.036	1.30	0.038	1.44
−0.641	−3.05	−0.869	−3.82	0.083	0.64	0.060	0.51
0.721	4.25	0.644	3.74	−0.141	−0.93	−0.266	−1.91
0.112	1.20	0.106	1.14	−0.310	−3.47	−0.293	−3.28
		Included but not shown					
−3.900	−4.28	−1.772	−1.54	−0.780	−1.13	0.302	0.46
563		566		716		716	
0.240		0.252		0.159		0.031	

Table 6.10
Determinants of the incidence of nonpayment by clients

		Madagascar			
		Model 1		Model 2	
		Coefficient	t-statistic	Coefficient	t-statistic
Exposure factors					
Credit sales in total sales	Share	1.818	2.11	0.519	0.45
Trader's characteristics					
Total sales	Value	0.170	0.94	0.294	1.74
Years of schooling	Value	0.108	2.03	0.095	1.82
Years of experience	Log(x + 1)	−0.087	−0.33	−0.072	−0.25
Number of relatives in agricultural trade	Log(x + 1)	0.701	2.39	0.707	2.45
Number of clients known personally	Log(x + 1)	−0.245	−1.18	−0.324	−1.33
Location dummies					
Intercept		−4.238	−2.28	−5.314	−3.02
Number of observations		673		673	
Pseudo R-squared		0.184		0.172	

Note: Logit estimates reported. Model 1: actual value of exposure factors. Model 2: predicted values of exposure factors.

This interpretation begs the question of what is the alternative contract enforcement mechanism: if legal institutions offer little or no protection against opportunistic breach, why do surveyed traders bother to place orders and grant credit at all? One thing that is quite clear from interviews is that coercion is not seen as a common or even correct way of resolving contractual disputes. If anything, recourse to courts and police is low because traders perceive these institutions to be too antagonistic and conflictual. Reference to "trust" is the most common answer when traders are asked why contracts are honored. To understand what "trust" means to Malagasy traders, we investigate what happens in dispute cases. The first striking finding is that most contractual disputes are resolved (85 percent of supplier cases and 79 percent of client cases) and trade is resumed in most cases (91 percent of supplier cases and 78 percent of client cases). In addition dispute resolution and resumption of trade are highly correlated; 79 percent of disputes with suppliers and 73 percent of disputes with clients are resolved and trade resumed. These findings are similar to those reported in the two previous chapters.

This suggests that breach of contract, although unwelcome and costly for respondents, occurs within the context of long-term relationships. A reasonable interpretation, largely confirmed by informal discussions with respondents and casual

Benin				Malawi			
Model 1		Model 2		Model 1		Model 2	
Coefficient	*t*-statistic	Coefficient	*t*-statistic	Coefficient	*t*-statistic	Coefficient	*t*-statistic
1.687	2.95	5.190	3.08	3.609	5.56	6.815	2.94
−0.140	−1.00	−0.315	−1.93	−0.122	−1.49	−0.081	−1.01
−0.040	−1.05	−0.048	−1.27	0.042	1.42	0.017	0.55
0.060	0.26	−0.179	−0.73	0.223	1.61	0.186	1.36
0.440	2.52	0.340	1.93	−0.178	−1.12	−0.249	−1.59
0.198	2.00	0.189	1.92	0.198	2.07	0.250	2.45
	Included but not shown						
−3.425	−3.53	−1.551	−1.26	−1.422	−1.94	−1.639	−2.20
563		566		715		715	
0.254		0.254		0.057		0.027	

observation, is that parties implicitly agree to continue trading with each other as long as contractual breach remains infrequent and provided that, when it occurs, a good faith effort is made to resolve the situation. If these conditions are satisfied, the relationship continues; otherwise, it is severed. In other words, relational contracting as modeled, for instance, by Ghosh and Ray (1996) is the key contract enforcement mechanism. We explore this idea more in detail in the next chapter.

This interpretation is confirmed by regression analysis. Table 6.12, for instance, shows that more personalized relations and longer acquaintance with suppliers and clients is associated with efforts to resolve contractual disputes through direct negotiation and, in the case of clients, through mediators. Regression results also indicate that respondents with relatives in agricultural trade are much less likely to negotiate payment problems with clients. Although a priori surprising, this finding is consistent with the idea that disciplining relatives is difficult: if so, why bother waste time negotiating with them. Tables 6.13 and 6.14 further illustrate that direct negotiations have a strong positive effect on the probability of resolving the dispute and resuming trade. In other words, good faith efforts to iron out difficulties are essential to the preservation of trust and relationships. Results again show that payment problems are less likely to be resolved for respondents who have relatives in agricultural trade—and who presumably buy and sell from them.

Table 6.11
Recourse to legal institutions in Madagascar only

Theft	
Trader sought help of the police	37.5%
Trader went to court	10.7%
Number of observations:	57
Disputes with clients and suppliers	
Traders who ever used the following in a dispute with client or supplier:	
A third party as mediator or arbitrator	14.0%
The police	4.0%
A lawyer	0.6%
A court	0.7%
Number of observations	729
Conflict resolution methods used during the last incidence of:	
1. Breach of contract by supplier:	
Trader negotiated directly with supplier	86.0%
Trader sought help of mediator	3.4%
Trader sought help of lawyer	0.0%
Trader threatened to go to the police	0.0%
Trader threatened to go to court	0.6%
Number of observations:	178
2. Breach of contract by client:	
Trader negotiated directly with client	93.6%
Trader sought help of mediator	9.1%
Trader sought help of lawyer	0.5%
Trader threatened to go to the police	3.6%
Trader threatened to go to court	0.9%
Number of observations:	220

The reader may want to know whether relational contracting as enforcement mechanism is complemented by information sharing on cheaters and by collusion to exclude them from future trade, as suggested, for instance, by Kandori (1992), Greif (1993), and others. Table 6.15 provides some useful information in this respect. We see that of those traders who obtain supplier credit, less than one-fifth come recommended by other traders. The dominant credit screening procedure is to purchase several times from the same trader, thereby establishing mutual trust. The most common action taken in response to nonpayment is to stop deliveries. Similar findings are reported by Fafchamps (1996) for Ghana. Very few respondents expect to involve the police or the courts in debt collection, hence confirming that the trade relationship constitutes its own collateral. There is some information sharing about clients who do not pay, but its reach is limited: a majority of respondents estimate that a client who does not pay is either unlikely or very unlikely to lose credit from

Table 6.12
Determinants of choice of dispute resolution method in Madagascar

Dependent variable	Value	Dispute with supplier Direct negotiation Yes = 1		Dispute with client Direct negotiation Yes = 1		Use of mediator Yes = 1	
		Coefficient	z-statistic	Coefficient	z-statistic	Coefficient	z-statistic
Characteristics of transaction							
Case of deficient quality	Yes = 1	0.196	0.616	na		na	
Length of relationship	Log(x + 1)	0.216	4.418	0.072	1.185	0.738	3.273
Amount paid (supplier)/due (client)	Log(x + 1)	0.055	1.991	0.227	4.974	−0.094	−0.968
Characteristic of trader							
Total sales	Log(x)	−0.118	−0.961	0.132	1.057	0.231	1.991
Number of relatives in agricultural trade	Log(x + 1)	−0.234	−1.058	−0.792	−3.457	−0.505	−1.927
Number of suppliers/clients known personally	Log(x + 1)	0.332	1.729	0.383	1.846	0.104	0.531
Intercept		0.918	0.666	−3.163	−2.147	−7.512	−3.849
Number of observations		180		246		246	
Pseudo R-squared		0.229		0.522		0.215	

Note: Probit estimates reported.

Table 6.13
Determinants of conflict resolution with suppliers

		Dispute is resolved (Yes = 1)				Trade is resumed (Yes = 1)			
		Coefficient	t-statistic	Coefficient	t-statistic	Coefficient	t-statistic	Coefficient	t-statistic
Method of dispute resolution									
Direct negotiations with supplier	Yes = 1			2.805	4.585			0.793	1.887
Characteristics of transaction									
Dispute is about quality	Yes = 1	-0.711	-1.912	-0.538	-1.335	0.191	0.596	0.232	0.706
Days of trade with supplier	Log(x + 1)	0.036	0.751	-0.011	-0.185	-0.021	-0.414	-0.053	-0.962
Amount already paid to supplier	Log(x + 1)	-0.037	-1.454	-0.040	-1.363	-0.025	-0.933	-0.027	-1.022
Characteristics of trader									
Total annual sales	Value	0.299	2.177	0.458	2.747	0.259	1.798	0.304	1.982
Number of relatives in agricultural trade	Log(x + 1)	-0.333	-1.623	-0.326	-1.311	0.054	0.230	0.076	0.328
Number of suppliers known personally	Log(x + 1)	0.364	1.680	0.175	0.663	0.129	0.639	0.060	0.286
Intercept		-2.012	-1.278	-5.879	-2.861	-1.696	-1.068	-2.645	-1.523
Number of observations		167		167		171		171	
Pseudo R-squared		0.177		0.412		0.049		0.081	

Note: Probit estimates reported. Results give the outcome of a contractual dispute conditional on a dispute having occurred.

Table 6.14
Determinants of conflict resolution with clients

		Dispute is resolved (Yes = 1)				Trade is resumed (Yes = 1)			
		Coefficient	t-statistic	Coefficient	t-statistic	Coefficient	t-statistic	Coefficient	t-statistic
Method of dispute resolution									
Direct negotiations with supplier				2.375	3.851			1.680	3.743
Recourse to third-party mediator				−1.042	−2.943			−0.925	−2.650
Recourse to lawyer				−0.536	−0.968			−2.014	−2.805
Characteristics of transaction									
Days of trade with client	Log($x+1$)	−0.028	−0.586	−0.016	−0.299	−0.064	−1.366	−0.065	−1.227
Value of the sales transaction	Log($x+1$)	0.048	0.783	0.052	0.758	−0.056	−1.381	−0.136	−2.864
Characteristics of trader									
Total annual sales	Value	0.040	0.457	0.031	0.313	0.033	0.413	0.079	0.913
Number of relatives in agricultural trade	Log($x+1$)	−0.614	−3.555	−0.571	−2.696	−0.481	−2.937	−0.501	−2.604
Number of clients known personally	Log($x+1$)	0.603	3.697	0.713	3.781	0.397	2.617	0.491	2.810
Intercept		−0.975	−0.923	−3.288	−2.589	0.746	0.792	−0.402	−0.393
Number of observations		223		222		235		231	
Pseudo R-squared		0.122		0.286		0.077		0.244	

Note: Probit estimates reported. Results give the outcome of a contractual dispute conditional on a dispute having occurred.

Table 6.15
Trade credit

Procedure to obtain/grant supplier credit	With suppliers	With clients
Purchase several times	83.0%	72.4%
in which case, how many times	7	9
Be referred by another trader	11.3%	17.1%
Provide a bank guarantee or give a deposit	1.5%	2.4%
Fill in forms	0.5%	1.8%
Action taken in case of nonpayment	Supplier	Client
Stop deliveries	77.7%	88.9%
Go to the police	1.6%	4.4%
Go to court	0.5%	1.8%
Loss of credit with other suppliers	Supplier	Client
Very unlikely	11.3%	20.9%
Unlikely	40.2%	58.7%
Likely	31.4%	15.4%
Very likely	17.0%	4.9%
Number of observations	195	342

Note: Data collected only from respondents who receive or give supplier credit.

other suppliers. Exclusion from future trade credit is thus not the dominant form of contract enforcement, although it plays a secondary role.

These findings are further confirmed by table 6.16. Clients themselves are the main source of information on which suppliers rely before granting credit. For two-thirds of the respondents, this is the only source of information on which they rely for screening trade credit applicants. Only a quarter of the respondents obtain information from other traders; 14 percent obtain information from other sources. There appears to be no systematic effort to share information on clients who do not pay: only 13 percent of credit givers discuss bad clients with other traders once of month or more; one-quarter never discuss bad clients at all.

Why there is not more information sharing is unclear. One may be tempted to assume that the ethnic origin of traders is too heterogeneous to allow a fluid exchange of information (e.g., Cornell and Welch 1996; La Ferrara 1997). This is not borne out by the data, however. First, all surveyed traders—like all inhabitants of Madagascar—speak a single common language. Second, traders operate predominantly in their region of origin: over 85 percent of traders operate in the district (*Fivondronana*) of their birth, and the coefficient of correlation between the postal code of their place of birth and the location of their trading activity is as high as 0.76. Only nine traders in the sample are of foreign origin—mostly from Asia. Finally, the overwhelming majority of respondents (91 percent) share a common religion. The

Table 6.16
Screening of potential trade credit recipients

Source of information on client	
Obtain information from client himself/herself	95.9%
Obtain information from other traders	24.0%
Obtain information from other sources	12.3%
Obtain information from client's bank	1.2%
Information sharing with other traders about bad clients	
Once a day	1.5%
Once a week	1.7%
Once a month	10.1%
Occasionally	62.6%
Never	24.1%
Number of observations	344

Note: Data collected only from respondents who give credit to clients.

idea that linguistic, ethnic, or religious barriers prevent the circulation of information cannot therefore be sustained.

One item of information that is worth pointing out is that riots against traders took place in the late 1980s. According to Lonely Planet (1994), "Indo-Pakistani traders ... bore the brunt of Malagasy violence in the 1987 riots. [T]he Indian premises on either sides [of the main street in Tulear] along with most of the central area were gutted" (p. 220). Blanchy (1995) reports that in five major cities, Asian-owned shops were looted and burned; many Asians feared for their life and fled the country, if only temporarily. Barrett (1997a) reports that Asian traders refused to be interviewed by Malagasy enumerators and writes that "[it] is difficult to overstate the sensitivity of ethnic Asian food marketing intermediaries to the political risks of their trade." Judging from Blanchy's (1995) account of Asian businesses in Madagascar, ethnic Asian business networks prior to the riots resembled their counterparts in Kenya (e.g., Marris 1971; Himbara 1994; Fafchamps et al. 1995; Fafchamps 2000). If, as it is likely, Asian traders have pulled out of grain markets to reduce their exposure to political risk, the resulting disruption in existing business networks could explain the current lack of sophistication of grain trade in the country. Still this does not explain why indigenous networks of information sharing have not formed to replace Asian networks. These issues deserve more research.

6.4 Conclusion

As this chapter has shown, in liberalized grain markets property rights are protected and contracts are enforced among agricultural traders. We found that among traders the incidence of theft and breach of contract is low and that the losses resulting from such instances are small. This, however, does not result from reliance on legal institutions—actual recourse to police and courts is fairly rare, except in cases of theft—but from traders' reluctance to expose themselves to opportunism. Judging from the evidence collected, the indirect costs of malfeasance prevention are likely to be much higher than the direct costs of theft and breach of contract.

Grain trade in the three countries studied has little in common with the sophisticated business world that proponents of market liberalization typically envision. With little or no forward contracting, no brand recognition, and no returns to scale in distribution, it resembles more the occasional flea markets of Californian cities than the organized grain markets of the American midwest. Although the direct costs of theft and contractual breach appear low, the methods that surveyed traders use to minimize risk exposure can but add to transactions costs. The need for traders to personally inspect quality on each delivery, combined with their unwillingness to delegate quality control to subordinates and with their reluctance to hire additional workers for fear of theft, undoubtedly restricts firm size and firm growth. The need to guard stocks in person, the total absence of payment by check (that adds to the risk of theft), the infrequent use of trade credit, and the difficulty of placing orders complicate the conduct of business and make trade very labor and management intensive.

The transactions costs of trade are ultimately paid by producers and consumers in the form of a larger spread between farm-gate and retail price (IFPRI 1998). The welfare cost of imperfect markets is thus not negligible. In addition, judging from the extreme dispersion in firm size (Gini coefficient of total sales around 0.75) and the fact that better connected traders economize on transactions costs and reap higher sales and profits (Fafchamps and Minten 2002b), it is far from clear that competition yields efficiency. Indeed, the finding of Fafchamps and Minten (2002b) that traders with better social network capital make more profits suggest that they do not take advantage of their lower costs to drive out small, unconnected traders. In other words, in a flea market economy, the coexistence of a large number of atomistic firms with a small number of large, well-connected traders should not be taken as an indication that competitive forces are sufficient to eliminate rents (see Barrett 1997a for a similar observation). This is because, among other things, small traders' efforts to protect their property rights and avoid being cheated leads to high transactions costs. This issue is examine in more detail in Fafchamps et al. (2002).

Results indicate that grain traders make very little use of the justice system. For policy purposes it would be important to know whether this situation arises because they lack access to the law (cost issue) or because they wish to avoid legal delays and uncertainties (time and risk issues). Cost issues could in principle be handled through a subsidy or small claims courts system,[10] while reducing judicial delays and legal uncertainty probably requires hiring more judges and changing the law.[11] Existing reports on African justice systems (e.g., Root 1993; World Bank 1995; Ministère de la Justice 1999) fail to identify which types of policy intervention should receive priority.[12] Unfortunately, given the extremely small number of legal recourses recorded in the survey, the data cannot distinguish among issues that really matter for African traders.[13] Based on the available secondary evidence, we suspect that the cost of the justice system is more problematic for grain traders than legal risk and delays, which are likely to be small for simple cases of theft or nonpayment. This interpretation finds additional support in the fact that recourse to the law is much more likely in cases of theft than commercial disputes: criminal proceedings are typically cheaper for plaintiffs than commercial cases because police and public prosecutors bear much if not all of the costs of collecting evidence and arguing the legality of the case. Speculation should not, however, hide the fact that our limited data do not clearly establish what kind of judicial reform Africa needs most.

Finding that legal institutions do not play an important role in the enforcement of contracts begs the question of which alternative mechanism is used by agricultural traders. Our analysis suggest that trust-based relationships are the dominant contract enforcement mechanism among grain traders. Trust is established primarily through repeated interaction with little role for referral by other traders. Information on bad clients does not circulate widely, hence severely limiting group punishments for nonpayment. We revisit this issue in subsequent chapters.

10. Another possibility is to expand the current Malagasy system of itinerant judges called *audiences foraines*, as discussed in the World Bank (1995) and Ministère de la Justice (1999).

11. Thanks to an anonymous referee for pointing this out. Judging by the alleged prevalence of corruption in the Malagasy justice system and police, and the suspicion that much of it is a kind of fee for service, perhaps the simplest subsidy would be to pay judges, legal clerks, and policemen better—a recommendation that is already made by Root (1993) and the World Bank (1995).

12. Ministère de la Justice (1999) reports that 20 and 56 percent of the respondents blamed high costs for not going to court and not hiring lawyers, respectively. Respondents also unanimously praised itinerant *audience foraines* whereby judges travel to market towns to administer justice—a system that singularly reduces travel costs for plaintiffs. But the report also documents respondents' concerns about judicial delays, legal uncertainty, and fear of reprisal.

13. With enough data and with suitable instruments for wealth (cost issue), time preference (delays), and risk preference (uncertainty issue), regression analysis should, in principle, be able disentangle which of the three main issues affect traders' propensity to use the justice system.

7 Inventories and Contractual Risk

In chapter 6 we observed the various ways that agricultural traders aim at reducing their exposure to contractual risk. We now revisit the manufacturing panel surveys and look for similar evidence. The specific exposure-reducing behavior that we investigate is the holding of inventories.

According to economic theory, a good reason for firms to hold inventories and liquid assets is the presence of risk. This idea is best exemplified by stockout inventory models (e.g., Holt et al. 1960; Blinder 1982, 1986; Eichenbaum 1989) whereby firms build up inventories to avoid stocking out when faced with demand shocks or late input delivery. The same reasoning applied to liquid assets predicts that firms will build up cash reserves to deal with market fluctuations and late payment by clients (Tsiang 1969). The stockout motive is but an application of the precautionary savings idea (e.g., Zeldes 1989; Deaton 1991) to inventories and cash reserves. In this chapter we test the stockout motive by investigating whether contractual risk (late payment or inadequate input deliveries) affects the inventories and cash reserves held by African manufacturers.

We find that the risk of delayed deliveries and payments explains much of the inventory and liquidity reserve behavior of manufacturers. Our results therefore support recent efforts to explain inventory accumulation from the stockout motive (e.g., Abel 1985; Kahn 1987; Krane 1994). But while the literature has focused almost exclusively on market fluctuations (see Blinder and Maccini 1991 for references), our results highlight the importance of contractual risk, that is, of imperfect contract compliance by clients and suppliers.

The econometric analysis presented here agrees with qualitative information collected during the case study survey. Conversations with Zimbabwean survey respondents, for instance, indicated that one of the major benefits of the structural adjustment program adopted there in 1991 was to increase the reliability of input deliveries. This has led, according to respondents, to a drastic reduction in inventories of inputs and to the gradual disappearance of the practice of input sharing (e.g., Free University of Amsterdam 1995; Fafchamps et al. 1995).[1] Results also agree with the fears of contractual risk often expressed by respondents who tried or considered exporting their products. Similar concerns were expressed by manufac-

---

1. Prior to the liberalization of foreign exchange and international trade in the early 1990s, Zimbabwean manufacturers used to informally borrow inputs and equipment from each other. This practice seem to have developed during the Unilateral Declaration of Independence period (1965–1979) as a result of the economic embargo imposed on Zimbabwe. The extreme shortages of inputs and the spirit of defiance prevalent at the time helped the emergence of this unusual risk-sharing institution reminiscent of village solidarity mechanisms (e.g., Fafchamps 1992; Coate and Ravallion 1993). The presence of this institution constitutes further confirmation of the role that risk plays in inventory management.

turers in other African countries (e.g., Fafchamps et al. 1994; Fafchamps 1996) and by American and European firms trying to source products from Africa (Biggs et al. 1994). Concerns about contractual risk across national boundaries may thus be a serious hindrance to manufacturing exports from Africa.

7.1 Descriptive Analysis

The literature has basically considered three motives for firms to hold inventories and liquidity reserves: minimization of transactions and switching costs, production smoothing, and stockout risk (e.g., Holt et al. 1960; Blinder and Maccini 1991; Ramey 1991; Bental and Eden 1993). Of these three, only the stockout motive relates to firms holding inventories to protect themselves against the risk of late or deficient deliveries. Similar reasoning would apply to firms that hold financial reserves to protect their liquidity position against the risk of late payment by clients. For a detailed discussion, see Fafchamps et al. (2000).

We investigate these relationships using the RPED data set on manufacturers in nine African countries. We begin by taking a look at the data. The general characteristics of the sample are detailed in table 7.1. On the particular survey waves in table 7.1, for Burundi and Ethiopia, we only have wave 1 data. There were only two survey waves in Côte d'Ivoire. As is apparent from the table, some data were not collected in certain countries during the waves: no information on inventories were collected in Cameroon; information on overdraft ceiling was not collected in the first wave. For most waves and countries, information is available on three categories of inventories—inputs, semifinished products, and finished products. For some countries, however, no information is available on the smallest category of the three—inventories of semifinished products.

Despite these shortcomings the data provide a clear and instructive picture of inventory holdings in African manufacturing. In general, firms hold large inventories relative to sales—21 percent of annual sales on average. These figures are high given that all surveyed industries have a fast production time—inventories of semifinished products account for only 14 percent of all inventories, or the equivalent of ten days of production. Of the three categories, inventories of inputs are by far the largest: 13 percent of the value of annual sales on average. This stands in sharp contrast with developed economies where inventories of finished products tend to dominate. If we assume that inputs represents roughly half of the value of the finished product, African manufacturing firms hold, on average, the equivalent to three months of input needs. This inventory is unusually large and suggests a concern with input availability.

There are large differences among countries. Ethiopian firms carry by far the largest inventories, a possible reflection of the landlocked nature of the economy and uncertainties surrounding supply routes through Eritrea. We also note a tendency for inventory averages to "revert to the mean" in waves 2 and 3, suggesting that data from wave 1 may be of inferior quality.

Turning to liquidity, we construct a measure of financial reserves as the difference between the firm's overdraft ceiling and its current overdraft level. This unused portion of the overdraft line of credit can be used to absorb late payment by clients. Since, during the study period, the interest rate on overdraft credit was quite a bit higher than the return on cash balances, firms were unlikely to hold positive balances on other accounts while at the same time paying interest on their overdrafts. Our measure is thus a reasonable measure of cash reserves, at least for those firms with negative balances.

On average, African manufacturers keep 45 percent of their overdraft facility unused. This does not appear to be an excessive figure, as it falls within usual bank guidelines for setting overdraft ceilings. There is some variation across countries, possibly a result of differences in interest rate or availability of credit. Compared to annual sales, firms hold a relatively small financial reserve: on average, 3.7 percent of annual sales, or the equivalent of two weeks of sales. Tanzanian firms appear to experience a dramatic drop in overdraft ceiling between waves 2 and 3, possibly due to a nationwide credit crunch. As a result their average financial reserves are virtually nonexistent in wave 3.

We also report measures of openness to international trade. African manufacturers import, on average, a quarter of their inputs. Imports are lowest in Tanzania. They are highest in Burundi, Cameroon, and Ethiopia. Strangely, two of these three countries are landlocked. They also are among the poorest countries in Africa with largely undeveloped manufacturing sectors. In terms of exports, we see that African manufacturers export little—7 percent of output on average. Some countries export more—notably Côte d'Ivoire and, to less extent, Zimbabwe and Cameroon. In the other surveyed countries, manufacturing exports are extremely limited.

Table 7.1A also reports three measures of contractual risk: whether the firm experienced a case of late payment, late delivery, and deficient quality in the twelve months preceding the wave 1 interview. Contractual dispute questions were not asked in subsequent waves. Results are similar to those reported in chapter 5, with over half of the surveyed firms experiencing at least one case of late payment, one-quarter experiencing a late delivery, and one-third complaining of deficient quality of purchased inputs.

Table 7.1
Inventories and liquidity

	Burundi		Cameroon		Côte d'Ivoire		Ethiopia	
	Number of obser- vations	Mean	Number of obser- vations	Mean	Number of obser- vations	Mean	Number of obser- vations	Mean
A. Wave 1								
1. Inventories								
Annual sales	117	389,694	225	3,952	213	4,886	174	4,857
Inventory of inputs	111	28,862			203	196	166	1,289
Inventory of semifinished goods								
Inventory of finished products	115	26,962			206	171	175	787
Total inventory	110	57,286			199	373	162	2,061
Inventory of inputs/annual sales		7%				4%		27%
Inventory of semifinished/ annual sales								
Inventory of finished products/ annual sales		7%				4%		16%
Total inventory/annual sales		15%				8%		42%
2. Liquidity								
Overdraft amount	115	8,580	199	87	228	97	193	541
3. Foreign trade								
Mean % of imported inputs	115	42%	225	46%	220	20%	189	47%
Mean % of exported output	119	4%	242	10%	232	21%	209	1%
4. Contractual risk								
% firms experiencing late payment	119	53%	208	72%	234	42%	209	43%
% firms experiencing late delivery	118	19%	207	38%	234	22%	209	37%
% firms experiencing deficient quality	118	28%	206	44%	234	17%	209	33%
B. Wave 2								
1. Inventories								
Annual sales			196	4,483	187	3,814		
Inventory of inputs					158	459		
Inventory of semifinished goods								
Inventory of finished products					169	266		
Total inventory					153	763		
Inventory of inputs/annual sales						12%		
Inventory of semifinished/ annual sales								
Inventory of finished products/ annual sales						7%		
Total inventory/annual sales						20%		

Ghana		Kenya		Tanzania		Zambia		Zimbabwe	
Number of obser-vations	Mean	Number of obser-vations	Mean	Number of obser-vations	Mean	Number of obser-vations	Mean	Number of obser-vations	Mean
191	167,242	215	41,275	201	274,354	205	304,309	202	25,556
		217	5,575	207	30,897	211	30,207	182	4,063
		154	1,148	128	16,815	161	4,438	170	1,083
172	12,225	162	2,184	207	33,193	213	24,653	200	2,296
		152	6,521	128	88,883	161	72,663	167	7,583
			14%		11%		10%		16%
			3%		6%		1%		4%
	7%		5%		12%		8%		9%
			16%		32%		24%		30%
151	0	217	4,083	217	60,323	214	15,467	183	1,881
171	15%	222	19%	211	11%	214	24%	199	17%
209	4%	223	7%	216	4%	214	2%	199	11%
197	59%	222	60%	217	25%	215	68%	202	81%
194	21%	222	38%	217	15%	215	27%	203	17%
192	24%	222	42%	217	14%	215	48%	202	54%
194	209,186	196	47,739	123	507,234	191	442,231	198	30,386
124	36,525	201	10,083	186	22,824	199	55,338	200	4,085
113	6,171	198	1,713	174	14,319	196	5,239	197	1,072
117	11,725	202	2,630	186	24,212	197	24,132	201	1,818
109	46,871	194	12,103	171	51,710	195	86,111	197	6,716
	17%		21%		4%		13%		13%
	3%		4%		3%		1%		4%
	6%		6%		5%		5%		6%
	22%		25%		10%		19%		22%

Table 7.1
(continued)

	Cameroon		Côte d'Ivoire		Ghana	
	Number of observations	Mean	Number of observations	Mean	Number of observations	Mean
2. Liquidity						
Overdraft ceiling	194	126	186	142	187	30,745
Overdraft amount	195	70	194	78	187	15,090
Overdraft reserve (ceiling-level)	191	57	183	83	183	6,197
Reserve/ceiling		45%		59%		20%
Reserve/annual sales		1%		2%		3%
3. Foreign trade						
Mean % of imported inputs	198	49%	196	20%	171	15%
Mean % of exported output	202	10%	200	23%	209	4%
C. Wave 3						
1. Inventories						
Annual sales	183	4,783			182	294,557
Inventory of inputs					125	64,108
Inventory of semifinished goods					116	13,980
Inventory of finished products					118	18,221
Total inventory					112	91,150
Inventory of inputs/annual sales						22%
Inventory of semifinished/ annual sales						5%
Inventory of finished products/ annual sales						6%
Total inventory/annual sales						31%
2. Liquidity						
Overdraft ceiling	187	142			176	28,327
Overdraft amount	191	46			178	15,666
Overdraft reserve (ceiling-level)	184	96			176	12,851
Reserve/ceiling		67%				45%
Reserve/annual sales		2%				4%
3. Foreign trade						
Mean % of imported inputs	184	49%			171	15%
Mean % of exported output	199	12%			209	4%

Note: All values given in thousands of local currency units, except in Cameroon and Côte d'Ivoire where they are given in millions of CFA francs. All inventories given in value. No data on inventories were collected in Cameroon. In wave 1, information on the overdraft ceiling was not collected. For Burundi, Côte d'Ivoire, and Ethiopia, total inventory does not include semi-finished goods on which information was not collected. Contractual risk data were collected only in wave 1.

Kenya		Tanzania		Zambia		Zimbabwe	
Number of obser- vations	Mean	Number of obser- vations	Mean	Number of obser- vations	Mean	Number of obser- vations	Mean
203	5,893	201	73,841	198	23,555	199	3,395
206	3,720	200	20,997	202	15,078	200	1,954
202	2,672	199	53,122	198	8,852	198	1,439
	45%		72%		38%		42%
	6%		10%		2%		5%
214	16%	209	11%	203	24%	199	17%
194	6%	201	4%	173	3%	199	11%
202	76,072	138	527,067	196	759,392	183	39,619
205	8,093	120	46,186	196	63,135	178	4,401
196	1,552	113	14,057	196	12,567	176	820
204	3,174	119	10,150	196	32,759	182	2,330
191	12,081	110	55,907	196	108,461	174	7,084
	11%		9%		8%		11%
	2%		3%		2%		2%
	4%		2%		4%		6%
	16%		11%		14%		18%
211	11,410	145	11,384	196	97,798	188	2,996
211	8,255	145	10,033	197	61,814	188	1,715
211	3,166	145	2,610	195	37,521	187	1,314
	28%		23%		38%		44%
	4%		0%		5%		3%
189	17%	149	10%	167	27%	199	17%
172	7%	152	3%	148	3%	199	11%

7.2 Inventories and Contractual Risk

Having described the data, we now turn to multivariate analysis. We wish to investigate whether firms that are more exposed to the risk of late delivery or deficient quality hold more inventories. Let the inventory of firm i in sector s, country c, and time t be written $H_{i,s,c,t}$. Let input delivery risk be written $R^d_{i,s,c}$ (we omit the time subscript since the data are available only for wave 1).[2] We are interested in the relationship between $H_{i,s,c,t}$ and $R^d_{i,s,c}$:

$$H_{i,s,c,t} = f(R^d_{i,s,c}).$$

To assess this relationship, we need to control for other factors likely to influence inventory holdings. The first is simply total sales $S_{i,s,c,t}$: other things being equal, inventories should be roughly proportional to firm sales. Delivery risk also depends on whether inputs are imported or not. To allow for this possibility, we include the share of imported inputs $I_{i,s,c}$ in the regression.[3] We also need to control for differences in production cycle between sectors and for differences in market environment, and interest rates across countries. Because the effect of macroeconomic conditions might vary across sectors, we cross sectoral dummies with country dummies— resulting in some $4 \times 9 = 36$ fixed effects $u_{s,c,t}$.[4] Finally, to control for differences in economic conditions and in survey design, we estimate the relationship separately for each wave. The estimated regression is thus of the form

$$H_{i,s,c,t} = S^{\alpha_s}_{i,s,c,t} e^{\alpha_0 + \alpha_r R^d_{i,s,c} + \alpha_i I_{i,s,c} + u_{s,c,t} + \varepsilon_{i,s,c,t}}, \tag{7.1}$$

$$\log H_{i,s,c,t} = \alpha_0 + \alpha_s \log S_{i,s,c,t} + \alpha_r R^d_{i,s,c} + \alpha_i I_{i,s,c} + u_{s,c,t} + \varepsilon_{i,s,c,t}.$$

The results are summarized in table 7.2. The first three columns correspond to inventories of inputs, semifinished products, and finished products. In the last column the dependent variable is the total of all three. Fixed effects are significant in all regressions but firm-varying regressors explain a large proportion of the variation in inventories—"within" R^2's oscillate between 0.136 and 0.454.

As expected, inventories increase with firm size. Firms that import a larger proportion of their inputs tend to hold more inventories. The effect is most pronounced

---

2. We cannot do firm-level fixed effects since our main variable of interest—contractual risk—was collected only once.

3. Data on the share of imported inputs in total purchases contain many missing values. To minimize the loss of observations, we use the average share over three waves as the regressor. In case of missing data for one year, the average is computed over the other two waves.

4. The actual number of dummies varies depending on the availabilty of country data.

on inventories of inputs, but it carries through to other inventories as well—probably because firm figure that if they have the inputs, they might as well process them. The magnitude of the effect is very large: compared to a firm that uses only domestic inputs, a firm that imports all its inputs holds 4 to 6 *times* more input inventories. A 1 percent point increase in the imported input share raises total inventories by 3 to 4.7 percent. These large effects constitute initial evidence that delivery risk affect inventory practices. But they may be biased if imported inputs tend to be more expensive than domestic ones.

More direct evidence comes from the estimated coefficient on the two contractual risk variables—late delivery and deficient quality. In 11 of the 12 regressions, the late delivery variable has a significantly positive coefficient. The magnitude of the estimated coefficient is large: compared to a firm who always receives supplies on time, a firm experiencing late deliveries holds, on average, 133 to 198 percent more inventories of inputs and 130 to 147 percent more total inventories. A similar albeit weaker effect is shown for deficient quality risk. The variable is significantly positive in five of the twelve regressions, and the magnitude of the effect remains large—87 percent more input inventories in wave 1, 116 percent more in wave 3. Taken together, these results constitute strong evidence that contractual risk affects inventory practices.

To test for robustness, we re-estimated equation (7.1) using tobit regressions with sector-country dummies (some firms do not hold inventories). The model was also estimated using a Heckman selection regression. The results are very similar and are not reported here for the sake of brevity. Contractual risk remains as significant as in table 7.2, often with a larger coefficient. The reported results are more easily interpretable, since they give the effect of contractual risk on average inventory holdings.

7.3 Liquidity and Contractual Risk

We have seen that African manufacturers hold more inventories if they face delivery risk. We now investigate whether they hold financial reserves if they face late payment risk by clients. The reasoning is the same: late payment by clients may lead firms to "stock out" on liquidity, making it difficult for them to pay banks, workers, and suppliers. To protect themselves against liquidity risk, firms may thus hold excess finance in the form of unused lines of credit. The most common such reserve is unused overdraft facility $L_{i,s,c,t}$.

We follow the same approach as in the previous section and regress the log of $L_{i,s,c,t}$ on the log of total sales, late payment risk, and the share of exported output. The latter variable is included to allow for possible delays in processing international

Table 7.2
Inventories and contractual risk

	Inputs		Semifinished products		Finished products		Total inventories	
	Coefficient	t-statistic	Coefficient	t-statistic	Coefficient	t-statistic	Coefficient	t-statistic
Wave 1								
Annual sales (in logs)	1.437	21.71	0.818	7.11	1.388	17.89	1.429	22.51
Imported inputs (share)	0.041	7.53	0.033	3.28	0.019	3.06	0.030	5.80
Experienced late delivery (yes = 1)	1.327	3.31	1.500	2.25	1.275	2.76	1.303	3.37
Experienced deficient quality (yes = 1)	0.874	2.49	0.424	0.79	-0.254	-0.63	0.657	1.93
Intercept	-14.703	-14.40	-7.159	-4.12	-15.450	-12.83	-12.612	-12.80
Number of observations	1,214		595		1,341		1,017	
R-squared:								
Within	0.422		0.184		0.270		0.454	
Between	0.271		0.211		0.183		0.310	
Overall	0.382		0.082		0.221		0.405	
Fraction of variance due to fixed effects	0.187		0.264		0.145		0.216	
Wave 2								
Annual sales (in logs)	0.890	15.01	0.491	6.74	0.796	11.33	0.829	14.90
Imported inputs (share)	0.057	8.01	0.034	3.95	0.043	5.17	0.047	6.93
Experienced late delivery (yes = 1)	1.614	3.24	1.771	2.90	1.870	3.17	1.379	2.92
Experienced deficient quality (yes = 1)	0.405	0.95	-0.353	-0.71	-0.710	-1.41	0.531	1.32
Intercept	-5.166	-5.43	-2.244	-2.01	-5.637	-5.00	-2.391	-2.68
Number of observations	891		716		895		356	
R-squared:								
Within	0.350		0.136		0.220		0.338	
Between	0.191		0.021		0.018		0.186	
Overall	0.315		0.071		0.172		0.303	
Fraction of variance due to fixed effects	0.156		0.265		0.160		0.136	
Wave 3								
Annual sales (in logs)	0.704	13.07	0.416	6.74	0.448	7.07	0.611	11.63
Imported inputs (share)	0.055	7.73	0.035	4.27	0.053	6.33	0.047	6.77
Experienced late delivery (yes = 1)	1.975	3.84	1.498	2.52	0.821	1.36	1.468	2.90
Experienced deficient quality (yes = 1)	1.158	2.78	-0.065	-0.13	1.282	2.65	0.871	2.13
Intercept	-3.926	-4.62	-1.812	-1.87	-1.460	-1.47	-0.836	-1.01

Number of observations	676	653	575	644
R-squared:				
Within	0.381	0.146	0.191	0.326
Between	0.020	0.020	0.052	0.023
Overall	0.234	0.067	0.101	0.173
Fraction of variance due to fixed effects	0.334	0.291	0.245	0.349

Note: Dependent variable is value of inventories (in logs). Estimator is OLS with country-sector fixed effects. Late delivery and deficient quality variable from wave 1. Imported input share is average of all three waves.

Table 7.3
Liquidity and contractual risk

	Wave 2		Wave 3	
	Coefficient	t-statistic	Coefficient	t-statistic
Annual sales (in logs)	0.798	12.68	0.715	11.55
Exported production (share)	0.016	1.77	0.025	2.04
Experienced late payment (yes = 1)	1.199	2.92	0.261	0.56
Intercept	−9.937	−9.39	−7.690	−7.37
Number of observations	1117		893	
R-squared:				
Within	0.161		0.153	
Between	0.022		0.006	
Overall	0.121		0.106	
Fraction of variance due to fixed effects	0.140		0.162	

Note: Dependent variable is value of overdraft reserve (ceiling-level) (in logs). Estimator is OLS with country-sector fixed effects. Late payment variable from wave 1. Exported production share is average of all three waves.

payments. Since overdraft ceiling information is only available for waves 2 and 3, we cannot estimate the relationship for wave 1. The estimated regression is thus of the form

$$\log L_{i,s,c,t} = \alpha_0 + \alpha_s \log S_{i,s,c,t} + \alpha_r R^p_{i,s,c} + \alpha_x X_{i,s,c} + u_{s,c,t} + \varepsilon_{i,s,c,t}, \qquad (7.2)$$

where $R^p_{i,s,c}$ denotes payment risk and $X_{i,s,c}$ is the share of exported output.

The results are summarized in table 7.3. As before, we find that larger firms hold more financial reserves—albeit the increase is not proportional to firm size. As anticipated, exporters tend to hold larger reserves. The effect is significant in both waves. It is also large in magnitude: a firm that exports all of its output holds, on average, 1.6 to 2.5 times more financial reserves than a firm that exports nothing. Again this suggests that exporting firms hold more of a financial buffer.

Contractual risk has the expected positive effect on financial reserves but the coefficient of the late payment variable is only significant in the wave 2 regression. In the latter case the effect again appears to be large: a firm experiencing late payment problems holds, on average, 1.2 times more reserve than one without problems.

To check for robustness, we re-estimate equation (7.2) using tobit, Heckman selection regression, and conditional logit. We also experiment with a two-limit censored regression, using data on the overdraft ceiling as upper limit on the (measured) reserve and omitting firms without overdraft facility. The results, not reported here for the sake of brevity, are by and large similar to those reported in table 7.3.

7.4   Conclusion

In earlier chapters we saw that contractual risk affects the way African firms conduct business. We saw that the incidence of contractual breach is reduced by preventive action such as firms' reluctance to grant supplier credit or their insistence on direct quality control.

In this chapter we investigated another form of preventive action, namely the holding of inventories and liquidity reserves. We found that African manufacturers hold large inventories, especially of inputs. We found that those firms that import their inputs from abroad tend to keep much larger inventories, a finding consistent with the idea that importing is more risky. More direct evidence that contractual risk matters was also found using data on experiences of late delivery and deficient quality. We found that firms facing delivery problems hold significantly larger inventories. This is particularly true for late delivery, less so for deficient quality (which typically affects only a portion of the supplies). The effect is large in magnitude. Together, regressors explain a large proportion of the variation in inventory holdings across firms after controlling for sectoral and country fixed effects.

A similar analysis was conducted on payment risk and financial reserve. We found that exporting firms hold a much larger liquidity buffer, probably because of the uncertainties surrounding international financial transfers to Africa. Late payment risk also has a positive, albeit weaker, effect on liquidity.

Taken together, these results are consistent with the idea that imperfect market institutions have real costs. Not only do they force firms to operate in a more cumbersome manner but also compel them to pile up inventories and liquidity reserves that they then need to protect from theft.

III TRUST AND RELATIONSHIPS

In part II we saw that legal institutions play only a marginal role in the enforcement of commercial contracts. This is particularly true for small transactions among small firms and agricultural traders. Of the twelve countries studied, only among Zimbabwean manufacturers is reliance on courts and lawyers strong—partly because firms are larger, partly because the legal system is better. Elsewhere the enforcement of contracts is primarily based on trust and relationships.

Part III is devoted to a more detailed analysis of the formation of trust and its various roles in fostering market exchange. In chapter 8 a model of trust is developed in which agents test or screen other agents by tempting them to breach small contracts—such as by offering them a small amount of credit and observing whether they repay. How long it takes to screen out undesirable agents depends on the screening technology and the distribution of agents.

We then turn to data and uncover ample evidence that African firms screen their suppliers and clients before trusting them. The trial period required for an unknown firm to "graduate" into the "trusted" category is fairly long—usually several months. But once a relationship is formed, it lasts for a long period. Much of exchange thus takes the form of relational contracting.

8 The Formation of Trust

Sociologists have long emphasized the crucial role that interpersonal relationships play in the life and professional success of individuals and groups (e.g., Granovetter 1985; Coleman 1988; Putnam et al. 1993). Research by anthropologists, sociologists, historians, political scientists, and economists has brought to light the nearly universal reliance on interpersonal relations at early stages of market development (e.g., Bauer 1954; Jones 1959; Meillassoux 1971; Sahlins 1972; Hopkins 1973; Amselle 1977; North 1990; Greif 1993; Landa 1994). In recent years economists too have begun to recognize that economic exchange is influenced by the level of familiarity and trust that exists between agents (e.g., Gambetta 1988; Fukuyama 1995; Greif 1993, 1994; Platteau 1994b; Tadelis 1999; Horner 2002). Recent work has similarly noted the widespread existence of long-term relationships between manufacturers and their suppliers and clients in developed (e.g., Lorenz 1988; Aoki 1988; Dore 1987; Fukuyama 1995) and developing economies alike (Stone et al. 1992). The prevalence of long-term personalized relationships is also the norm in employment contracts.

In a world characterized by imperfect information and enforcement, it has been shown both theoretically and empirically that personalized relationships can facilitate the circulation of information on new technologies (Barr 2000) and market opportunities (Kranton 1996a), the screening of job and credit applicants (e.g., Montgomery 1991; Cornell and Welch 1996), the sharing of risk (e.g., Fafchamps 1992; Coate and Ravallion 1993; Fafchamps and Lund 2002), and the punishment of cheaters (e.g., Kandori 1992; Fafchamps 2002b). Much of this work remains confined to markets such as credit or labor in which moral hazard issues are severe. Applications to markets for commodities have so far been few (see, however, Bernstein 1996; Kranton 1996b; Gabre-Madhin 1997).

In this chapter we focus on trust. By "trust" we mean the *willingness of two or more individuals to enter in a negotiated agreement with each other, to incur obligations, and to acquire rights that have only imperfect legal protection.* Legal protection may be absent, imperfect, or insufficient for the reasons listed earlier. Certain forms of economic exchange are less demanding in terms of trust in this sense. If legal enforcement of contracts is insufficient and trust is absent, trade can only take simple forms, such as the instantaneous sale or barter of homogeneous commodities—grain, salt, or milk—or of low-quality/low-price goods—second-hand consumer items. Whenever trust is absent, the only types of economic exchange one can reasonably hope for are garage sales, flea markets, and the rural markets of pre-industrial societies. And even these simple forms of economic exchange demand that civil peace be assured and that the property rights of trading partners be protected. There are still places in this world where mutually beneficial trade is made difficult by suspicion and lack of trust between different tribes and ethnic groups (e.g., pastoralists vs. farmers) and where local authorities must use all their skill and patience in order to prevent the resentment generated by sour deals to turn into open feuds and bloodshed.

This chapter formalizes the formation or creation of trust through repeated interaction. The focus is not on the structure of trust-based markets, an issue that we revisit at length in chapter 11, but rather on the gradual process by which trust is built over time. The question we ask here is thus similar to the work of Datta (1996), Rauch and Watson (1999), and Watson (1999). After contrasting different contract enforcement mechanisms, a formal model of trust-based exchange is developed. We investigate the interface between trust and legal institutions and show that the provision of legal protection to private contracts, although imperfect, can help support exchange particularly if parties can simultaneously rely on mutual trust. This point has been made, among others, by Bernstein (1992). The role of a reliable currency in minimizing transaction risks and improving Pareto efficiency is discussed at the end.

8.1   The Origin of Trust

If trust is indeed an essential ingredient for the successful development of economic exchange, where does it come from? What can motivate a person A to trust another person B? The approach adopted in most of the industrial organization literature so far has been to emphasize the role of reputation, namely A trusts B because so far B has been nice to A and others (Kreps et al. 1982). Certainly reputation is important, but there is more to trust than reputation. Thieves are a case in point here: while thieves may be deplored by society at large, the trust among thieves may be sufficient for gangs to form and even organized crime to develop. One could argue that reputation is group specific, and that criminals need only to prove to be trustworthy among their peers. However, it seems unlikely that trust can develop on the sole basis of something as tenuous as reputation among persons who are largely disenfranchised and spend a good part of their lives in jail. Trust must rest on something else. We propose that this something else is personal *acquaintance*.

The importance of personal acquaintance in the matter of trust is often recognized in the way people talk about it: "Only trust someone you know." Granting one's trust without previous acquaintance is referred to as blind trust and often condemned as being foolish. But in what sense is acquaintance a possible source of trust? What is there to be known about others? Essentially four things: (1) the type and quality of goods and services that they are able to provide and willing to accept, (2) their motivations for conducting business, (3) their propensity for self-punishment, and (4) their ability to dissimulate. The first refers to the technology and endowments, the second to preferences and payoffs, the third to morality, and the fourth to hypocrisy.

The importance of a proper understanding of what the other party can provide is illustrated by the common practice of testing a potential supplier with a limited order before placing a complete order (e.g., Arrow 1974; Lorenz 1988). Indeed, the intrinsic qualities of goods and services are often hard to assess accurately from simple observation. Extensive testing is required. Furthermore timeliness of delivery, consistency of products and services, ability of the supplier to modify or improve products to suit the buyer's needs, and many other circumstances surrounding the actual implementation of economic exchange often are of crucial importance to the buyer.

This is particularly true whenever the economic performance of the buyer and his relationship with his own customers are critically dependent on the timeliness and consistent quality of supplies, that is, whenever the buyer is an industrial firm. Indeed, mechanization implies standardized inputs, and mass production requires consumer confidence. Industrialization thus demands a more rigorous organization of supplies of raw materials and intermediate inputs, something many poor countries have difficulties to come to grasp with.

Trust is also reinforced by adequate knowledge of the other party's payoffs and preferences. It is important for parties to an exchange to know what the other's motivations for trading are. Indeed, such understanding is essential in order to assess the risks of opportunistic behavior. Of particular importance is whether or not the other party is genuinely interested in doing business not only today but also in the future, and is therefore keen on establishing a continuing relationship—or whether what is being proposed is just a side deal, a way of unloading unwanted materials, or a suspicious offer by a fly-by-night firm. Only a proper knowledge of the other's payoff function can provide an answer, thus the importance of assessing the other party's exact situation, for instance, by visiting his workshop or warehouse.

The propensity for self-punishment, although not necessarily required for trade to take place, can nevertheless help parties to achieve a higher level of trust and therefore sustain more efficient trade practices. It is remarkable, for example, that members of trading networks in pre-industrial societies often share a common religion or are members of the same sect or fraternity, and that their religious authorities are called upon to condemn opportunistic business practices (e.g., Cohen 1969; Meillassoux 1971; Geertz et al. 1979). In these circumstances, ethical behavior in non-business-related activities may be used to infer someone's religious faith and capacity to live up to his own moral code. Church attendance, womanizing, or professed opinions can be thus used as signal of good or bad ethics and influence one's business opportunities.

Finally, trust is easier to establish if parties are in personal contact. Thus the importance of various forms of socialization with business partners, from golf courses to business lunches. Indeed, human beings are usually endowed with only limited capabilities for deceit, and hypocrisy can seldom withstand the close scrutiny that socialization entails, particularly if "truthtelling devices" are used, like alcohol or the excitement induced by sport. Human beings also have a propensity to betray their emotions and feelings in subtle ways, even when they are trying to suppress them (e.g., blushing). Socialization enables people to learn each others' ways of betraying their feelings and to read in their facial expressions messages that an unacquainted person would fail to recognize. It takes an unusual talent to bypass such scrutiny and mimic sincerity for an extended period of time.

Mutual knowledge is thus essential for the establishment of trust. But where does A's knowledge of B come from? Essentially from three sources: (1) direct observation of B by A, (2) information provided by B himself, and (3) information provided by others. Information provided by B, of course, is subject to suspicion, but it is actively sought, if only to allow crosschecking. Information provided by others is what reputation is all about. Clearly, in the absence of previous personal contact, B's reputation will shape A's expectations about B's technology, motivations, and ethics. Whenever it is clear that (1) B's reputation is good, (2) B's loss of reputation would do him great harm, and (3) A is able to significantly hurt B's reputation, and vice versa, then the level of initial trust may be sufficient to allow economic exchange to take place between A and B. When these conditions are not satisfied, however, direct observation is required and mutual acquaintance is necessary before trade can take place.

8.2   A Model of Trust

We now formalize the gradual process of trust building. Consider a stationary exchange economy with $s \in S$ nonstorable commodities. Each individual i is infinitely lived and is endowed with a vector of goods $[e_i^s]$ that is constant over time. We initially assume that no monetary instrument is available and that all trade takes place through bilateral barter. This assumption will be dispensed with in the next section. We also initially ignore monitoring and search costs.

A transfer of good s from individual i to individual j in period t is denoted $g_{ij}^s(t)$. Only net transfers are considered; thus $g_{ij} \equiv -g_{ji}$ always. What individual i consumes of good s is denoted $y_i^s(t)$. Therefore

$$y_i^s(t) = e_i^s + \sum_j g_{ji}^s(t). \tag{8.1}$$

Each individual is risk neutral and has a time-separable utility function defined over the consumption of all goods. The welfare of each individual at time t is thus given by

$$W_i^t = \sum_{q=t}^{\infty} \delta^q U(y_i^1(q), \ldots, y_i^S(q); \alpha). \tag{8.2}$$

For each agent, a vector of individual characteristics $\gamma_i \in \Gamma$ is constructed that contains endowments, discount factor, and utility parameters:

$$\gamma_i = \{e_i^1, \ldots, e_i^S, \delta, \alpha\}. \tag{8.3}$$

Each agent's characteristics are imperfectly observable by others. Beliefs satisfy the common knowledge assumption required to construct a well-defined Bayesian game: there exist a joint distribution $f(\gamma_1, \ldots, \gamma_N)$ such that $f(\ldots, \gamma_{i-1}, \gamma_{i+1}, \ldots \mid \gamma_i)$ is agent i's initial belief about the distribution of other agents' characteristics. Note that subjective beliefs need not satisfy rational expectations. Agents update their beliefs using a Bayesian rule.

The economy above can be treated as a dynamic Bayesian game. Consider the set of equilibria that can be sustained by trigger strategies: if i cheats j, j will never contract with i again. Given that information about cheating remains local, however, i may still be able to contract (and cheat) other players. To prevent any player i from cheating his or her partner j, the instantaneous gain from cheating must be smaller than the long-term gain from a continuing relationship with j.

8.2.1 A Two-Person Economy

First consider an economy in which $N = 2$. The long-term payoff to any of the two players after cheating is his or her autarchy payoff:[1]

$$V_i^a = \sum_{t=0}^{\infty} \delta^t U(e_i^1, \ldots, e_i^S; \alpha) = \frac{1}{\delta} U(e_i^1, \ldots, e_i^S; \alpha). \tag{8.4}$$

---

1. Of course, with only two players, permanent reversion to autarky is not a renegotiation-proof punishment, since both players would be better off resuming trade. When the game is later extended to a large number of players, however, this shortcoming will be less compelling, at least as long as no player has a monopoly on an essential commodity.

Let $[g_{12}^s(t)]$ be a vector of economic exchange at time t; it is assumed to be feasible: $-e_2^s \leq g_{12}^s \leq e_1^s$. Let $G = \{[g_{12}^s(t)]\}$ be a feasible path of future exchange that realizes at least some of the mutual gains from trade. We want to verify whether this path satisfies individual rationality. To do so, we look for equilibria that would survive in the worst possible circumstances, that is, for the maximum possible short-term gains from cheating. Indeed, if cheating can be prevented when opportunistic gains are large, then surely it can be prevented when they are small. Consequently we assume that if one player cheats the other, he or she gets all the positive transfers but avoids the negative ones. This obviously constitutes an upper limit on the short-term gains from cheating in the sense that more careful sequencing of transactions within each period may, in itself, put a lower limit on the gains from cheating.

Thus let the vector $[\bar{g}_{ji}^s(t)]$ be defined as $[\max\{0, g_{ji}^s(t)\}]$. By construction, $g_{ij}^s(t) = -\bar{g}_{ji}^s(t)$. Then two sets of recursive equations need to be satisfied. The first set, equation (8.5) below, determines whether a player i would decide to cheat on a deal with player j and incur the penalty, or meet his or her obligations to player j. The second, equation (8.6) below, determines whether the corresponding player j would decide to accept a deal with player i in the first place, given updated beliefs regarding player i's characteristics and what they imply in terms of player i's likelihood of cheating.

$$V_i(t; \gamma_i) = \max\{U([e_i^s + \bar{g}_{ij}^s(t)]; \gamma_i) + \delta V_i^a(\gamma_i), U([e_i^s + g_{ij}^s(t)], \gamma_i)$$
$$+ \delta E_i[V_i(t+1; \gamma_i)]\} \tag{8.5}$$

$$V_j(t; \gamma_j) = \max\{V_j^a(\gamma_j), p_{ji}(t)(U([e_j^s + g_{ji}^s(t)]; \gamma_j) + \delta V_j^a(\gamma_j))$$
$$+ (1 - p_{ji}(t))(U([e_j^s + g_{ji}^s(t)], \gamma_j) + \delta E_j[V_i(t+1; \gamma_j)])\}, \tag{8.6}$$

where $p_{ji}(t)$ is the probability, as perceived by j, that player i would fail to perform his or her part of the deal.[2]

Partition the set of characteristics Γ into two subsets. The first subset contains all the parameter vectors for which player i would cheat at time t, that is, such that the first maximand term of equation (8.5) is larger than the second. Denote it as $\Gamma^c(i, t; G)$. The other subset contains all the other parameter vectors: $\Gamma^d(i, t; G) = \Gamma \backslash \Gamma^c(i, t; G)$. These sets are defined with respect to a certain path G. Let $h_{ij}(t)$ be the history of play between players i and j from beginning of play until time t. Define $f_j(\gamma_i | h_t)$ to be the subjective probability distribution that player j has about player

---

2. Note that we have implicitly assumed that if players do not find it in their interest to trade now, they will never do so in the future. The reason is that when players do not trade, they do not collect any information about each other. Consequently their priors do not change. Thus, if it is in one player's interest not to trade now, then it should remain so forever.

i's characteristics after having observed history of play h_t starting from some arbitrary priors and using Bayesian updating. By definition, the updated priors of player j after play $t + 1$ are given by

$$f_j(\gamma_i \,|\, h_{t+1}) = \frac{f_j(\gamma_i \,|\, h_t) f(a_{t+1} \,|\, \gamma_i, h_t)}{\int_{\Gamma_i} f(a_{t+1}, \gamma_i \,|\, h_t)}, \tag{8.7}$$

where a_{t+1} refers to the action of player i at time $t + 1$. Then

$$p_{ji}(t) = \int_{\Gamma^c(i, t; G)} f_j(\gamma_i \,|\, h_t) \, d\gamma_i. \tag{8.8}$$

The information conveyed by a player's action has essentially two related components: what transaction was agreed upon, and whether the player cheated or not on that transaction.

PROPOSITION 8.1 (Folk Theorem)   For the economy depicted in equations (8.5) to (8.8), there exists a discount factor $\bar{\delta} < 1$ such that Pareto efficiency in trade can be sustained by trust-based exchange.

Proof   Similar to other proofs of folk theorem (Fudenberg and Maskin 1986).   ∎

The system of recursive equations (8.5) to (8.8) involves complex analysis. There are nevertheless some general and intuitive comments that can be made. First, players who have successfully traded in the past are more likely to trade in the future. This simply results from the fact that successful exchange conveys flattering information about the characteristics of players. Second, other things being equal, an increase in a transfer $\bar{g}_{ji}^s(t)$ for player i at time t increases that player's incentive to cheat. In other words, being overly trusting creates temptations that self-interested players may find irresistible. Consequently it increases the probability of being cheated.

Third, other things being equal, players are more likely to cheat at the first transaction if (1) they are very impatient and/or if (2) they do not possess sufficient endowments to meet their obligations. This means that simple crooks that are characterized by short horizon and/or insufficient endowments tend to reveal themselves immediately. Fourth, other things being equal, optimal G paths specify increasing transactions over time. This is quite intuitive: players will "test" each other for a certain period of time before trusting each other. Fifth, other things being equal, players are more likely to cheat at a subsequent transaction if (1) they are relatively patient and (2) the path G specifies transactions that increase quickly over time. Thus, whether or not embezzlement and other forms of long-term deception occur depends on how fast mutual exchange increases over time. Finally, depending on the shape of the common knowledge distribution function, embezzlement and other forms of long-term deception cannot, in general, be entirely prevented. Prevention requires a structure of beliefs and information revelation such that "information grows slower than exchange," meaning that trust does not grow too fast.

8.2.2 A Multiple-Player Economy

Let us extend the preceding setup to more than $N > 2$ players. Each player i is now assumed to trade with a subset m_i of other players, with the cardinality of that subset being at most $N - 1$. We leave aside the issue of how these sets m_i are determined.[3] Each player now faces 2^{m_i} decisions of whether to cheat partners in m_i, and similarly 2^{m_i} decisions of whether to accept deals with players in that subset. First consider the decisions to cheat or not. Each decision l consists of a vector of players $i \in M_l$ who are cheated, and a complement vector of players $i \in m_i \backslash M_l$ who are not. By assumption, any cheated players forever suspend trade with the untrustworthy player but do not share information about untrustworthiness with others.[4] Denote by $E_i[V_i^{M_l}(t+1; \gamma_i)]$ the expected future payoff of player i after having cheated the players in M_l. The following recursive equations are the individual rationality constraints corresponding to the decision to cheat others, and to the decision to deal with them, respectively:

$$
V_i(t; \gamma_i) = \max \Bigg\{ U\left(\left[e_i^s + \sum_{i \in m_i} \bar{g}_{ij}^s(t) \right]; \gamma_i \right) + \delta V_i^a(\gamma_i),
$$

$$
\ldots, U\left(\left[e_i^s + \sum_{i \in M_l} \bar{g}_{ij}^s(t) + \sum_{i \in m_i \backslash M_l} g_{ij}^s(t) \right]; \gamma_i \right) + \delta E_i[V_i^{M_l}(t+1; \gamma_i)],
$$

$$
\ldots, U\left(\left[e_i^s + \sum_{i \in m_i} g_{ij}^s(t) \right], \gamma_i \right) + \delta E_i[V_i(t+1; \gamma_i)] \Bigg\}, \tag{8.9}
$$

3. The determination of these subsets raises complicated coordination problem; see chapter 14.

4. Players may still try to infer someone's untrustworthiness in other deals from the commodities he or she is trying to acquire. For instance, suppose that certain types of commodities can only be obtained from certain sources, and consider an economy that has been running for some time. In these circumstances, someone's sudden desire to acquire a particular commodity, even at unfavorable conditions, may signal that a previous deal with the primary source of that commodity has turned sour. In other words the pressing desire to acquire a certain commodity may in itself be sufficient to inspire caution to potential partners. Such complications are left for further research.

$$V_j(t; \gamma_j) = \max\left\{ V_j^a(\gamma_j), \sum_{i \in d_i} p_i(t) \left(U\left(\left[e_j^s + \sum_{i \in D_l} g_{ji}^s(t)\right]; \gamma_j\right) + \delta V_j^a(\gamma_j) \right)\right.$$

$$\left. + (1 - p_i(t))(U([e_j^s + g_{ji}^s(t)], \gamma_j) + \delta E_j[V_i(t + 1; \gamma_j)]) \right\}. \tag{8.10}$$

The updating of priors is defined in a manner similar to equation (8.7):[5]

$$f_j(\gamma_{-j} \mid h_{t+1}) = \frac{f_j(\gamma_{-j} \mid h_t) f(a_{t+1} \mid \gamma_{-j}, h_t)}{\int_{\Gamma_{-j}} f(a_{t+1}, \gamma_{-j} \mid h_t)}, \tag{8.11}$$

where γ_{-j} refers to the vector of characteristics for players other than j.

Equations (8.9) to (8.11) define a system of recursive equations that a path G must satisfy in order to be individually rational. The following proposition is an extension of the folk theorem of repeated games to trust-based exchange.

PROPOSITION 8.2 (Folk Theorem)   For the economy depicted in equations (8.9) to (8.11), there exists a discount factor $\bar{\delta} < 1$ such that Pareto efficiency in trade can be sustained by trust-based exchange.

Proof   Similar to the proof of proposition 8.1.   ∎

The absence of a contract enforcement mechanism based on commonly observable reputation makes economic exchange more perilous, however. As a consequence the level of Pareto efficiency that can be achieved must be lower than the one that could be achieved if information about cheaters were publicly available.

PROPOSITION 8.3   Other things being equal, the level of Pareto efficiency achieved via trust-based exchange is lower than that achieved with the help of a reputation mechanism.

Proof   By extension of the proofs in Kandori (1992) and Raub and Weesie (1990).
                                                                                                  ∎

PROPOSITION 8.4   Other things being equal, the level of Pareto efficiency achieved via trust-based exchange is increased if it is combined with first-party enforcement (guilt, remorse, etc.).

---

5. When the economy contains more than two players, there are many subtle ways in which information is conveyed. For instance, the mere fact that a player proposes to transact at period $t > 0$ may constitute an indication that he or she has already cheated others and is now looking for new targets. For the sake of simplicity, these complications are ignored here.

Proof The penalty for cheating is increased in equations (8.5) and (8.9). Consequently a smaller set of individuals with characteristics γ_i will find it in their interest to cheat. The probability for a noncheater to trade with a cheater decreases in equations (8.6) and (8.10), and thus economic exchange becomes a more attractive to noncheaters. ∎

PROPOSITION 8.5   Other things being equal, the level of Pareto efficiency achieved via trust-based exchange is increased if it is combined with a reputation mechanism, even if the latter is imperfect (e.g., transmission of information that is delayed, noisy, partial, or local).

Proof   Same as that of proposition 8.4. ∎

Propositions 8.4 and 8.5 state that trust-based exchange is naturally reinforced by mechanisms of first-party as well as third-party enforcement. In other words, these various forms of enforcement mechanisms mutually reinforce each other and are complementary. An interesting point to make is that these other forms of enforcement may be crucial in inducing a noncheater to try out a new partner. In other words, in the absence of any specific information, the willingness of economic agents to engage in trade with strangers depends heavily on their priors. These priors, in turns, are likely to be shaped at least partially by the reputation that agents enjoy, either individually or as a group, as well as by the ethical standards in vigor in society at large.

Whenever someone's reputation is hard to assess, for instance, when a person does not belong to the same information sharing network (e.g., Mitchell 1969; Laumann and Pappi 1976), or when someone's ethical code is reputed to disregard certain types of promises, for instance, promises to people belonging to a different ethnic group or religion, then transactions may never be initiated. In these circumstances, priors never get updated and trust never has an opportunity to grow. In other words, whenever the initial reputation is sufficiently bad, communities or individuals become locked into Pareto-inferior equilibria. Interestingly, whenever this happens, exogenously modifying people's expectations, for instance, through actions geared toward building confidence across communities, may increase Pareto efficiency.

8.3   Trust and Incomplete Contracts

We now allow the parties to a trust-based exchange economy to sign legally enforceable contracts. If complete contracts could be negotiated costlessly and could be perfectly and costlessly verifiable and enforceable by perfectly impartial courts, opportunistic behavior would no longer be a problem. As we have argued in the first section, however, this ideal is not likely to be met in practice and the possibility of opportunistic behavior remains a hindrance to economic exchange.

It is important to recognize, however, that the institution of legally enforceable contracts, although in an imperfect fashion, can significantly contribute to reduce opportunistic behavior and to increase the level of Pareto efficiency achieved in the economy. To see why, consider the following example.

Suppose that the parties to the trust-based exchange can conclude private agreements that have legality, in the sense that the agreements can be admitted as a basis for legal proceedings in a court. Call such agreements *legal contracts*. Based on the remarks of section 8.1, legal contracts are assumed to be imperfect: complete specifications of their contents may be difficult and costly to do, their enforcement in court is not entirely predictable, court costs may affect both parties, and there may be restrictions as to what kinds of legal contracts are allowed and verifiable (i.e., involving mutual obligations for which evidence can be brought in court). We will show, however, that despite all of these shortcomings, legal contracts usefully complement trust-based exchange, provided that some reasonable conditions are fulfilled.

Before we do so, it is crucial to make a fundamental distinction between the implicit agreement that the parties have formed and the legal contract they could conclude. This is because, although the two are not the same, legal contracts are useful in a wide variety of situations. Indeed, the best way to view the legal contract is as an instrument that defines the legal battleground on which the parties will have to fight, should they disagree about their implicit agreement. It is their legal contract, not their implicit agreement, that shapes their respective chances of achieving a successful outcome in court. In other words, the legal contract is essentially a way of affecting the probability of various legal outcomes, should the parties decide to litigate.

However, while this may be a proper way of thinking about legal contracts, the fact is that courts hardly ever enforce the legal contract itself. All they can typically do is to specify that damages be paid to the plaintiff. In other words, if a legal contract specified that $1,000 had to be paid on January 1, 2005, and it is not paid on time, the best that courts can offer is delayed payment with interest. In a world where credit constraints are prevalent, the delay in payment may make a tremendous difference to the plaintiff. Similarly, if a legal contract specified that a certain item had to be delivered on a certain date, and it is not, the best that courts can offer is some form of financial reparation. In most cases (with the possible exception of real estate cases) the courts are unable to force the defendant to deliver the said item, and the plaintiff has to be satisfied with some form of financial compensation.

In order to provide useful support to the implicit agreement between parties, the legal contract must satisfy certain conditions, which we formalize below. Let L be the number of parties (usually two) to an implicit trust-based agreement A and to a legal contract C, and let o_i stand for the outcome of the litigation process for individual i. The o_i's are net of litigation costs, $g(o_1, \ldots, o_L | C)$ is the joint probability distribution function of legal outcomes for all parties, and $g_i(o_i | C)$ is the marginal probability distribution for individual i. We define ω_i as the money value of the future expected gain from trade for individual i from $t + 1$ to ∞ if the actual agreement A is carried through at time t. Then we set up the possible outcomes in the form of a proposition:

PROPOSITION 8.6   The maximum Pareto efficiency that can be achieved by parties to the agreement A is increased by any legal contract C that satisfies the following properties:

i. For all $i \in L$ who did not comply with their obligations in A, $E[o_i | C] < 0$.

ii. For all $i \in L$ who did comply with their obligations in A while others did not, $E[o_j | C] > 0$.

iii. For all $i \in L$, $E[o_i | C] \leq \omega_i$ if all complied with their obligations in A.

Proof   Insert $E[o_i | C]$ into equations (8.9) and (8.10). For the sake of clarity of presentation, we show the equations in the case where $L = 2$:

$$V_i(t; \gamma_i) = \max\{U([e_i^s + \bar{g}_{ij}^s(t) + E[o_i | C]]; \gamma_i) + \delta V_i^a(\gamma_i),$$

$$U([e_i^s + g_{ij}^s(t)], \gamma_i) + \delta E_i[V_i(t + 1; \gamma_i)]\}, \tag{8.12}$$

$$V_j(t; \gamma_j) = \max\{V_j^a(\gamma_j), p_{ji}(t)(U([e_j^s + g_{ji}^s(t) + E[o_i | C]]; \gamma_j) + \delta V_j^a(\gamma_j))$$

$$+ (1 - p_{ji}(t))(U([e_j^s + g_{ji}^s(t)], \gamma_j) + \delta E_j[V_i(t + 1; \gamma_j)])\}. \tag{8.13}$$

By condition i, the payoff from cheating (the first element at the left-hand side of equation 8.12) has decreased for all i's, which makes it easier to deter cheating. This means that for any given distribution of population characteristics, and for any terms of the agreement A, cheating is deterred for a larger proportion of the population. Simultaneously the payoff from trusting an untrustworthy partner has increased (the p_i term at the left-hand side of equation 8.13). Furthermore the probability p_i of facing a cheater has also decreased since equation (8.12) has changed. Consequently the minimum level of trust required for transacting is also easier to establish. Thus the effect on both equation (8.12) and equation (8.13) is to expand the frontier of Pareto-efficient transactions that satisfy individual rationality.

Condition ii ensures that it is in the interest of the cheated to initiate legal litigation, while condition iii prevents parties from opportunistically initiating legal litigation. Indeed, as long as the gains from future trade are larger than the short-term expected gain from going to court, opportunistically initiating legal suit is prevented.   ∎

Together these conditions require that there be some conformity between the obligations outlined by agreement A and the outcome of legal litigation. In general, the conformity is achieved by matching as closely as possible the implicit agreement with the legal contract. There are exceptions, of course, as the practice of antedated checks and letters suggests.

PROPOSITION 8.7   Let z_i stand for the expected loss in court to player i if he or she cheats: $-E[o_i|C; i$ has cheated on $A] \equiv z_i > 0$. Then the higher is the vector $[z_i]$, the higher is the maximum Pareto efficiency that can be achieved by parties to agreement A with a legal contract C satisfying the three conditions of proposition 8.4.

Proof   Similar to that of proposition 8.4.   ∎

PROPOSITION 8.8   Let y_i stand for the expected gain in court to player i if he or she is cheated: $E[o_i|C; i$ has cheated on $A] \equiv y_i > 0$. Then the higher is the vector $[y_i]$, the higher is the maximum Pareto efficiency that can be achieved by parties to agreement A with a legal contract C satisfying the three conditions of proposition 8.4.

Proof   Similar to that of proposition 8.4.   ∎

Proposition 8.5 and 8.6 are intuitive corollaries of proposition 8.4. They state that a larger penalty for cheaters z or a more generous indemnization of the cheated y increases efficiency in economic exchange.

It may be of interest to know which of the two, z or y, has the largest effect on efficiency. An examination of equations (8.12) and (8.13) indicates that penalizing the cheater more heavily deters cheating directly (equation 8.12), and thus also affects the probability of being cheated that appears in equation (8.13). On the other hand, compensating the cheated induces more transactions only by reducing the cost of being cheated (equation 8.13). This simple observation suggests that penalizing potential cheaters ought to have a larger effect on efficiency than compensating the cheated. If true, this observation would be in agreement with observed legal practices (penalty clauses in contracts; large legal fees imposed by the legal system and often borne by the defendant, etc.). Proving this rigorously, however, requires imposing more structure on the equations (utility function, probability distribution function, priors, etc.). It is left for further research.

8.4   Instantaneous Exchange and the Usefulness of Money

Finally, we turn to the role that money can fulfill in economies characterized by trust-based exchange. To understand the importance of a reliable currency in minimizing transaction risk, we must first figure what the alternatives are. From a purely conceptual point of view, there are essentially three ways of organizing decentralized exchange without resorting to any form of currency:[6] instantaneous barter, delayed barter, and gift exchange. In instantaneous barter no contractual obligations of exchange are carried forward in time. The resulting trade flows can become quite complex, however, since there is no guarantee that the allocations of pairs of economic agents match their needs at any point in time.

In delayed barter, one part of the exchange is conducted instantaneously in the sense that one of the commodities exchanged is delivered immediately, but the transfer of another commodity in payment is delayed. This potentially allows the parties to better match their allocation of goods over time. A good example of this is when a Third World laborer provides agricultural manpower to a farmer, only to be paid at harvest time.

In a gift economy, goods are transferred unilaterally, without any explicit link to a commensurate payment by the recipient of the gift. Reciprocity is crucial to the functioning of such form of exchange, so, from an economist's point of view, a gift economy operates in a way similar to delayed barter. The only caveat is that, in a gift economy, reciprocity need not be in direct line. In other words, if a gives something to b and b gives something to c, reciprocity can be satisfied by c giving something to a. Reciprocity can also be delayed in time. Thus, in terms of the number of transactions involved, a gift economy is potentially the most efficient way of organizing generalized barter.

In all three cases the usefulness of money is obvious. It reduces the complexity of trade flows in the case of instantaneous barter,[7] it allows delayed barter to be split into separate instantaneous transactions, and it can replace the gift economy with a much more transparent way of enforcing reciprocity, namely via individual budget constraints.

Provided that falsified money be easily recognizable, and that the unit of currency be a reliable temporary store of value, the existence of money also reduces many (although not all) of the risks of noncompliance with contractual obligations that are

---

6. Note that for our purpose using an homogeneous commodity as a general mode of payment, such as grain, is identical to using money.

7. Money flows, however, are added.

associated with barter exchange. First of all, money makes instantaneous transactions much easier to carry through. Indeed, the payment in cash for a commodity
or service delivered can be made literally at the exact time of delivery, and is very
easy to verify. This in itself very significantly reduces the possibilities for cheating.
Furthermore, by reducing the complexity of trade flows that instantaneous barter
would imply, money simplifies the movement of commodities between agents. This
too reduces opportunities for cheating. Last, money transforms delayed barter and
gift exchange from transactions with delayed obligations into instantaneous transactions. In so doing, it tremendously reduces the scope for opportunistic behavior
and thus lessens the need for trust among parties.

The effects of money on economic efficiency can be very easily shown in a stylized
formal way. Let the vector $[\hat{g}_{ji}^{s}(t)]$ be the maximum short-term gain that a cheater can
achieve given that money is used as a medium of exchange. Following the discussion
above, assume that

$$U([e_i^s + \bar{g}_{ij}^s(t)]; \gamma_i) \geq U([e_i^s + \hat{g}_{ij}^s(t)]; \gamma_i) \tag{8.14}$$

with a strict inequality for some i's. These assumptions lead to the following
proposition:

PROPOSITION 8.9   The existence of a reliable currency increases Pareto efficiency in
economic exchange.

Proof   From equation (8.14) the gain from cheating has decreased, which makes it
easier to deter cheating in equations (8.5), (8.9), and (8.12). This reduces the set of
agent types γ_i who would find it in their interest to cheat, and thus decreases that
probability that a well-intentioned party would face cheating. Consequently it also
increases the return to any transaction from the point of view of a noncheater and
makes it easier to support exchange in equations (8.6), (8.10), and (8.13).   ■

Monetization of the economy is thus essential whenever the size and number of
economic transactions increases beyond rudimentary types of exchange that can be
sustained through mutual trust and reciprocal gifts. The reliability of the currency,
however, is essential for monetization to take place. In particular, if the currency is
subject to a high inflation tax, then the use of money for conducting transactions
becomes costly, and this may discourage its use, inducing economic agents to revert
to various forms of barter. That this can indeed happen is suggested, for instance,
by the sad experience of Zaire in recent times, where hyperinflation and rapid ero-
sion of the currency is said to have pushed many rural communities back to "self-
sufficiency." In more developed economies, reversion to barter or gift economy may

be impossible. Yet efforts by economic agents to avoid the inflation tax is likely to induce them to switch to a different transaction technology. This chapter thus formalizes the common idea that the resulting diminished usefulness of money to conduct transactions may entail a very large efficiency cost.

8.5 Conclusion

This chapter has clarified the respective roles played by the legal system, reputation, trust, and ethics in the enforcement of private contracts. It was argued that for a variety of reasons, courts provide an imperfect way of enforcing contracts. As a consequence economic agents resort to reputation and trust as mechanisms to improve compliance with contractual arrangements. Reputation mechanisms have been studied elsewhere (e.g., Kreps et al. 1982; Kandori 1992) and shown to be able to generate Pareto-efficiency gains. Trust-based exchange was discussed at length in section 8.2, and its efficiency compared to that achieved by reputation mechanisms.

We observed that when firms face a multiplicity of potential partners, weeding out bad types is costly. The process by which agents screen out undesirable clients or suppliers can be described as a trust-building process. The work of Watson (1999) and Datta (1996) examines this process in further detail.

The study of reputation mechanism and trust-based exchange shows that a certain level of economic efficiency in trade can be achieved by purely private, decentralized, and informal means. This does not mean, however, that public authorities have no role to play in helping the enforcement of private contracts. For instance, in section 8.3 it was shown that incomplete contracts can be a powerful way of modifying the players' payoffs, should one of them fail to respect commonly agreed but unverifiable obligations. In that event, incomplete contracts may enable parties to sustain unverifiable agreements that in their absence would fail to satisfy the individual rationality constraints of players. Similarly it was shown in section 8.4 how a reliable currency can increase Pareto efficiency, even in the absence of legal enforcement of contracts.

The arguments presented in this chapter suggest that the "market," taken for granted by most economists, is in fact a fragile institution that can benefit from careful nurturing by public authorities. In an age of market transition in sub-Saharan Africa and elsewhere, the framework of this chapter helps cast the thorny issue of market reform in previously socialist or interventionist economies, as the market mechanism is closely related to the problems of commitment and trust in public authorities.

9 Trust and Business

The previous chapter has shown how market exchange can arise out of trust. It has also discussed how the building of trust can be seen as the outcome of a progressive weeding out process in which bad types are induced to reveal themselves, leaving only good types. Part II has already provided ample evidence of relational contracting. Using case study surveys in Kenya and Ghana, this chapter provides evidence on trust in African business. We document how trust and business relationships arise and what role they play in the conduct of business. A special emphasis is put on screening procedures for supplier credit.

9.1 Case Study of Ghanaian and Kenyan Firms

We begin with evidence collected from a series of case studies among Ghanaian and Kenyan manufacturers and traders. To assess where trust comes from, firms were asked what strategies they follow to avoid problems with their clients and suppliers. Multiple answers were encouraged. Discussions often followed. We summarize below the information that was collected. Responses are largely consistent with our theoretical predictions regarding screening and the formation of relationships based on mutual trust. They emphasize the dominant role of mechanisms based on repeated interactions in the enforcement of commercial contracts.

9.1.1 Avoiding Problems with Clients

Responses regarding problems with clients are summarized on table 9.1. The most expedient way of avoiding problems with clients is to insist on cash payment on delivery, respondents say. Credit should be granted only to clients who have demonstrated their ability and willingness to pay. These two fundamental, commonsense principles account for most of the answers given. They also correspond to firms' practices: in Ghana, respondents sell to 34 regular customers on average, but only 6.6 of them receive credit.

Relying on legal sanctions and institutions is not perceived as a practical way of preventing problems. Many firms keep simple records of transactions and ask their clients to sign invoices when they get credit. But these records are used more to minimize discussion on the reality of the debt than to ensure payment through legal recourse. Asking for an advance payment is presented by some manufacturing firms as a way of committing customers and reducing problems. Taking an advance also reduces exposure to default. Some respondents argue that requesting a large advance is a way to make sure that the client can afford the goods. This implies firms suspect that some customers would be glad to increase their well-being but let their supplier

Table 9.1
Methods used to avoid problems with clients

	Ghana	Kenya
Risk avoidance		
Insist on immediate cash payment on delivery	68%	58%
Insist on downpayment, deposit, or advance	13%	32%
Keep as guarantee a good incorporating client's materials	8%	6%
External contract enforcement		
Rely on legal proofs and institutions	17%	11%
Trust and direct screening		
Deal with clients with whom had satisfactory business	47%	40%
Assess clients through repeated interaction	19%	23%
Screen clients carefully	15%	17%
Reputation		
Deal with clients recommended by people you know	23%	8%
Deal with clients who have a good reputation	9%	11%
Deal with clients who are nonbusiness acquaintances	6%	4%
Flexibility/rigidity		
Show flexibility when difficulties arise	25%	19%
Suspend new credit to bad payers	17%	17%
Other		
Keep customer satisfied	15%	15%
Render clients captive of firm	8%	
Maintain a reputation of toughness	4%	
Number of valid answers	53	53

Source: Ghana and Kenya case studies.

worry about how to pay for it. One firm out of six mentions keeping customers satisfied as a way of avoiding problems. Respondents note that clients use small defects as an excuse to delay payment or renegotiate prices. Good product quality is a way of denying clients such excuses.

Granting credit only to clients who have paid in the past works well, on average. But how to identify trustworthy customers? One way is to rely on personal recommendation, an unsophisticated form of the reputation mechanism.[1] Clients recommended by trustworthy people are more likely to be trustworthy themselves, respondents argue. An implicit personal guarantee is often provided with the recommendation as well. Although recommending people does not imply the obligation to cover their debts, the guarantor is sure to be pestered by the creditor and asked to intervene should a problem arise. Furthermore the reputation of the recommender

1. As opposed to a sophisticated form like the computerized files of Dun and Bradstreet.

is tarnished if the new client proves unreliable. For all of these reasons people hesitate to endanger their reputation by recommending someone who they believe will cause problems. The process of personal recommendation, respondents say, is therefore relatively safe. Nonbusiness relationships—with relatives, neighbors, and church mates—play little role in identifying trustworthy clients. Several respondents declared that selling on credit to relatives and neighbors amounts to "signing the death warrant of the firm." Payment problems, they argue, would be frequent as friendship and family ties get in the way of pressurizing clients. Few, if any, credit sales to relatives and family members were recorded in the survey. People prefer to recommend relatives and friends for credit or preferential treatment from suppliers.

Reputation per se, as distinct from interpersonal relations, seems to play little role in identifying reliable clients. In Ghana, there seems to be no mechanism whereby information about clients' trustworthiness is shared among firms other than direct recommendation by common acquaintances. When prompted directly, firms declare that they never bother passing information about untrustworthy customers to other firms. Sharing information would provide competitors with an undue advantage, they say. In fact several respondents appeared to relish the idea that their competitors have to deal with the same deadbeats by whom they had been burnt. The only possible exception concerns Accra's women fishmongers, but their situation is somewhat peculiar. They all belong to a closely knit neighborhood, they share the same ethnic background, their husbands go out to sea together, and they all sell in the same market. These women greet bad payers on the main fish market with screams and shouts, thereby sharing information instantly in a simple but effective fashion. Bad clients find it difficult to remain in the fish business because they get cut from the major source of supply. The situation is different in Kenya, as we will learn in the following section.

Some of the surveyed firms use more elaborate procedures to assess a client's credit worthiness. One-sixth of case study firms actively screen prospective trade credit recipients. The simplest method consists of inspecting the client's workplace. It is important, respondents say, to make sure that the client is what he or she claims to be. Simple inspection of the workplace also reveals whether goods are currently being produced and whether the client's business is prosperous. Similarly, when clients are final consumers or itinerant traders, checking their residence and spouse's workplace provides information about their wealth and ability to pay. More elaborate screening mechanisms are undertaken by a few firms. A couple of respondents boast they could ask friends in the bank to run an informal credit check on their customers, thereby revealing useful information about the existence and magnitude of lines of credit, the frequency of bounced checks, and the regularity of deposits and withdrawals. Whether such procedure was licit remains unclear, but both respondents insisted that their contacts among bank staff were essential. Screening can also be done through customer accreditation. In this process, prospective recipients of trade credit (and people allowed to pay by check) provide information about their real and financial assets and possibly put down a deposit as guarantee for payment. A more gradual approach to screening relies on learning progressively about a client's qualities and business performance through repeated sales. Rare are the Ghanaian respondents who are willing to extend trade credit to first-time buyers. Only the couple respondents who are able, thanks to special relations, to run detailed credit checks indicated their willingness to do so if the results of their investigation are satisfactory. The situation in Kenya is discussed in more detail in the next section.

Despite all their sophistication these screening methods offer little protection against good payers who, due to unforeseen circumstances or from their own volition, become bad payers. There is the fish lady who goes out with a bang, buying large quantities on credit and then disappearing into thin air. There is the respected textile trader who retires, leaving large bills unpaid. There is the customer who dies, leaving behind debts that are disavowed by his heirs. There is the client who goes bankrupt, the client who moves to another city, and the client who decides to take on another business. In all of these cases a good business relationship suddenly turns sour, leaving behind unpaid bills. Several reported cases of nonpayment loosely belong to this category. They provide a contrario evidence of the importance of expected future interaction as enforcement mechanism: when interest in preserving the relationship is lost, so is enforcement. In all of these cases respondents were caught unaware: whatever screening and monitoring mechanisms they had put in place were fooled by their good-turned-mischievous client. When probed further, respondents declared that despite screening and monitoring they still expect some portion of their trade loans to be defaulted as a regular risk of doing business.

9.1.2   Avoiding Problems with Suppliers

Similar questions were asked regarding suppliers. Responses are summarized in table 9.2. Again, risk avoidance dominates. More than a third of all the respondents state that the best way to avoid problems is to inspect goods before payment instead of taking them on faith and having to negotiate afterward if quality is deficient. Traders are less likely to inspect goods than manufacturers, possibly because they do not use the goods to produce something and quality is less of a problem. Several Ghanaian firms mention third-party inspection of goods—in particular, inspection of imports by SGS—as a useful protection against deficient quality. In terms of

Table 9.2
Methods used by Ghanaian firms to avoid problems with suppliers

	Ghana	Kenya
Risk avoidance		
Inspect goods at delivery or before payment	38%	38%
Pay cash for goods delivered on the spot	36%	
Order in advance, hold stocks, switch if problem, buy only what is available		21%
External contract enforcement		
Negotiate well defined contract; give precise specifications	32%	28%
Rely on written proofs or formal accreditation		6%
Rely on third-party inspection	8%	
Trust and direct screening		
Deal with suppliers with whom had satisfactory business	34%	38%
Cultivate good relations through visits and lunches	11%	23%
Rely on accreditation and direct inspection of suppliers	6%	
Reputation		
Deal with suppliers on basis of reputation and brand name	11%	13%
Deal with suppliers recommended by people you know	4%	2%
Deal with suppliers who are nonbusiness acquaintances	4%	
Flexibility		
Show understanding when difficulties arise	25%	17%
Other		
Vertical integration; long-term contracts	9%	
Other	4%	21%
Number of valid answers	53	

Source: Ghana and Kenya case studies.

delivery, one-third of Ghanaian firms prefer to pay cash on delivery, thereby avoiding late delivery problems. One-fifth of Kenyan firms stock up to protect themselves against late delivery.

Trust again requires repeated interaction. One-third to two-fifths of the firms declare that the best way to avoid problems is to deal with suppliers with whom they have had satisfactory business in the past. Ghanaian firms indeed deal with as few as 5.2 regular suppliers on average, 2.9 of whom give them credit. They know suppliers who give them credit for 7.9 years on average. Continuing business with reliable suppliers is thus the dominant way of preventing problems. It is not a total insurance against contractual difficulties, but it guarantees that when problems occur, they are more easily resolved. Respondents cite their willingness to show understanding when difficulties arise as a way of avoiding problems. This comment may, at first glance, appear counterintuitive, but it reflects their desire to maintain a positive business relationship with firms that are their major providers of credit and sources of supply.

In the case of traders this desire is complemented by deliberate efforts to cultivate one's image through personal visits and business lunches.

Firms are most likely to face serious contractual problems when they deal with unknown suppliers. New manufacturing firms and firms reorienting their activities toward new sectors and products, for instance, as a result of structural adjustment and changes in relative prices, are most at risk. Traders run into contractual problems because success in commerce, respondents tell us, is based on the ability to take advantage of ever-changing arbitrage opportunities, making it necessary to transact with unknown firms. Firms screen potential suppliers in various ways. The first consists in relying on the reputation of a supplier or on the brand name of the product sold. This method is cited by one respondent out of ten, mostly in the textile and garment industry. The second consists in dealing with suppliers that one knows personally as a result of nonbusiness relations. The third consists in dealing with suppliers who are recommended by people the respondent knows and trusts. Only a handful of respondents, mostly small firms, cite each of the latter two approaches. A few trading firms screen suppliers in a more systematic fashion, using various techniques to directly assess their reliability—credit check, inspection of their premises, and formal process of accreditation.

9.2 Case Study of Kenyan Firms

More detailed follow-up questions were asked in the case study of Kenyan firms. To abstract from risk avoidance, we focus on supplier credit and the conditions under which firms extend trade credit to their clients and receive it from suppliers. We also investigate whether entrepreneurs socialize with other firms.

9.2.1 Getting Trade Credit from Suppliers

We begin with methods by which respondents obtain trade credit from their suppliers. Results are summarized in table 9.3. As we noted in the previous chapter, the major strategy for establishing trade credit with suppliers is through repeated interaction. Two-fifths of the surveyed case study firms first buy goods on cash for a while before qualifying for trade credit from their suppliers. This process is lengthy and has to be repeated for each individual supplier. Three-fifths of the firms, however, use personal contacts, credit acquaintances, and business reputation to secure trade credit from the start. The ability to secure trade credit from the start significantly facilitates launching a new business. One of the surveyed firms, for instance, was a newly established food wholesale business. Thanks to previous acquaintance with

Table 9.3
Establishment of a trade credit relationship with a supplier in Kenya

How was trade credit from your suppliers initiated?	
First bought cash for a while	38%
Used mutual contacts to establish trust	13%
Knew supplier before as employee/partner of another firm	25%
Salesmen/supplier offered credit right from the start	8%
Firm is (part of) a well-known business with a good reputation	10%
Supplier is a subsidiary	3%
Practice continued from previous owner	5%
Number of observations	40
How is reputation established?	
I establish my reputation by being a good paymaster	76%
Not only do I have to be a good paymaster, I must explain my problems	6%
I establish my reputation by never letting one of my checks bounce	2%
It is not a matter of reputation; to sell suppliers have to give me credit	2%
Since I do not get any credit from suppliers, reputation is not an issue	14%
Number of observations	50
Percent of respondents whose suppliers share information of repayment record	46%

Source: RPED Kenya case study survey.

suppliers, the respondent was able to fill his store with suppliers' goods from the very first day of operation. Similar stories were told by many other respondents.

Immediate access to trade credit enables firms to leverage their initial capital and instantly achieve a viable size. Nearly 80 percent of Kenyan-African businesses had to buy cash for a while before qualifying for trade credit (table 9.4). Only one-fifth of them got credit from the start, and none used mutual contacts. In contrast, one-fourth of non–Kenyan-African businesses had to buy cash for a while. There is no strong relationship between firm size and access to trade credit, except perhaps that very large firms get credit from the start on account of their large size and bureaucratic procedures.

Three-fourths of the respondents state that they established their reputation with suppliers by being good payers. Most specified that a good reputation has to be established with each supplier individually. More than half of the surveyed firms believe their suppliers do not exchange information about their payment record and that delaying payment to one of the suppliers does not affect their reputation with other suppliers. The other half perceive themselves as establishing a track record within their business community. Of the 7 Kenyan-African business persons who answered that question, 6 said their suppliers do not exchange information about them; by contrast, two-thirds of the 15 non–Kenyan-African business persons who

Table 9.4
Establishment of trade credit relationships by ethnicity in Kenya

With suppliers	All firms	African	Non-African
How trade credit was initiated			
Bought cash for a while	38%	78%	26%
Used mutual contacts	15%	0%	19%
Knew supplier before	25%	11%	29%
Credit offered from the start	23%	11%	26%
Number of observations	40	9	31

Source: RPED Kenya case study survey.

answered the question stressed that their suppliers do exchange information about their payment record. Reputation looms larger among non–Kenyan-African than among Kenyan-African businesses.

9.2.2   Granting Trade Credit to Customers

The relationship with clients receiving trade credit from the firm is virtually always business only (table 9.5). Only 8 panel firms cite family and friends, mostly traders, as credit customers. Only 16 percent of clients are from the same ethnic group. The average length of the business relation is 9.7 years. It is slightly shorter with private end users, 6.5 years, than with private traders, 11.5 years. Similarly, of 53 cases of sales with advance payment reported by panel firms, 3 occurred with family and friends. Only 4 transactions were with people of the same ethnic background. In 76 percent of the cases, however, the client was already known to the seller. The average length of this relationship was 3 years.

Two-thirds of the case study firms describe a creditworthy customer as someone with whom they have had a long and successful business relation (table 9.5). One-fourth of the firms associates creditworthiness with a good reputation among others—other suppliers, community members, and so on. One firm out of ten mentions previous acquaintance, but not necessarily as a customer. Firms have various strategies to collect information about potential recipients of trade credit. They can be grouped into four categories: direct observation, asking around, repeated interaction, and previous acquaintance. Direct observation is practiced in various forms. Some respondents physically visit their client's business and, in the course of the conversation, observe how well their client is doing. They note how he or she is dealing with customers and workers, the quality and amount of goods in stock, the rapidity with which inventories circulate, and so on. Others rely on their ability to judge a man through interview. One respondent, for instance, said he could judge a

Table 9.5

Establishment of a trade credit relationship with a client in Kenya

How does respondent assess the creditworthiness of customer?	
A creditworthy debtor is one with whom I have had a long successful relation	60%
A creditworthy debtor is one who has a good reputation with others	26%
A creditworthy debtor is someone I know (friend, business acquaintance)	11%
A creditworthy debtor is one who satisfies my formal requirements	2%
Strategies to collect information about a potential debtor	
I test the debtor by giving small loans first	33%
I assess the debtor on the basis of past cash transactions	22%
I ask around about the potential debtor from other suppliers and customers	33%
I ask the debtor to provide references, preferably among people I know	27%
I ask information from the debtor's bank	20%
I visit the potential debtor and observe his business or place of work	31%
I carefully interview or screen the customer, ask him or her to fill a form	13%
I believe that large firms/institutions/wealthy consumers are better paymasters	9%
I use my knowledge of the debtor's business and consumption pattern	7%
I knew the potential debtor before (friend, family, business acquaintance)	27%
I take the chance	9%
Strategies to verify information about a potential debtor	
I make my own observations	28%
I rely on my ability to judge someone from his/her expression/behavior/attitude	8%
The information must cross-checked	28%
The source of information must be someone I know or from my community	23%
The source of information must be credible/is an institution	15%
I cannot/do not cross-check the information given	25%
The debtor is a family member/friend/churchmate	8%
Guarantees	
Number of cases	5
Ask for advance	80%
Ask for guarantor	40%
Ask for postdated check or bill of exchange	40%
Retain ID card	20%
Can legally repossess	20%
Number of observations	45

Source: RPED Kenya case study survey.
Note: The exact number of valid answers varies slightly from one question to another.

man's creditworthiness by how he bargained. If the customer was willing to settle for too high a price, he would suspect either that the client was not serious about repayment, or that he knew little about the business and was unlikely to sell the items. Either way, the respondent concluded that credit should not be given. A few firms rely on their client's wealth and consumption pattern as indicators of their ability to repay.

Respondents ask information about a potential debtor from various sources. Some firms ask the client to provide the names of people who can recommend them. References must preferably be among people known to the respondent. Most, however, operate in a less direct and inquisitive way. They prefer to accept the client's order and inquire with their friends over the phone after the client has left. If they receive a bad report, they subsequently use some excuse to turn the client down for credit. Of course, no one is a dupe. Calling friends and business contacts is most often practiced to screen "up-country" customers, that is, customers who do not reside in Nairobi and whose business the respondent finds costly to visit. In a few cases we were surprised to hear that respondents exchange client-related information with competing suppliers. In a couple of textile firms, respondents even said they meet regularly with other suppliers and discuss late payers and defaulters, thereby constituting what could be called an information-sharing cartel. That firms that otherwise compete for the same clients can agree to share such strategic information serves as a reminder of the critical importance of information sharing to prevent and discourage contract noncompliance.

One-fifth of the firms seek information from the client's bank as well. Banker's opinions tell how the client is dealing with his or her bank and often state for how much their client is "good," that is, for how much credit they can be reasonably counted on. Their main drawback is that they take a few weeks to come. The client may not accept to wait for that long before finding out whether the respondent accepts his or her order. The contrast between firms again confirms that Kenyan-African businesses have fewer business contacts from which they can obtain information about potential recipients of trade credit (table 9.6). They are much more likely to rely on direct inspection of their client's business. Large firms are also more likely to ask around than small firms.

Repeated interaction with the client is another, more personalized way of establishing a trade credit relationship. The creditworthiness of a potential debtor is assessed through his or her past record with the respondent. The regularity and quantity of purchases, the business attitude, the reliability of check payments are all factors that are taken into consideration. The most pressing concern of the trade creditor is whether the debtor is a genuine going concern or a fly-by-night operator.

Table 9.6
Establishment of trade credit relationships by ethnicity in Kenya

With customers	All firms	African	Non-African
Strategies to collect information from potential trade debtor			
Repeated interaction	56%	33%	67%
Ask around	80%	33%	100%
Visit and interview	73%	100%	53%
Previous acquaintance	13%	20%	10%
Take the chance	9%	7%	10%
Number of observations	45	15	30

Source: RPED Kenya case study survey.

Typically small loans are given first, and the promptitude with which they are repaid is evaluated before larger, more regular trade loans are granted. The whole process takes several months. A quarter of the firms also mention previous acquaintance as a mean of assessing a client. Although family relationship or friendship are cited by a few firms, most others refer to previous business acquaintance. Several respondents, for instance, gave credit to clients who were previously working as employees or partners in businesses they were supplying to. A few firms confessed they had no screening process whatsoever; they just take the chance. Some firms cited taking guarantees as a way of assessing truthfulness. Four firms explicitly saw requesting advances from customers as a way of asserting the seriousness of the client's intent.

The source of the information influences how it is evaluated. Respondents trust more information that was cross-checked, and information that comes from people they know or regard as impartial, like banks. Those who can cross-check the information received usually do, especially if they are unsure about their source. Some respondents are unable to cross-check, however; they must either rely on direct observation or trust their single information source. A few respondents were willing to elaborate further on the credibility of their sources. They see information exchange as a quid pro quo. Information sources who deliberately circulate false information hurt their reputation in the community. Credibility is but another aspect of reputation.

9.3 Case Study of Zimbabwean Firms

Similar issues were investigated among Zimbabwean manufacturers and traders. In particular, questions were asked on how firms screen and monitor credit applicants and the role played by collateral.

Table 9.7
Establishment of a trade credit relationship with a supplier in Zimbabwe

How does the respondent receive credit from supplier?	
Screening:	
Fill forms with references and bank name	54%
Buy cash for a while	23%
Reputation:	
Firm has a good reputation/credit is automatically offered	37%
It's all a matter of relationship/relationship was established first	13%
Firm was recommended by third party (guarantor)	4%
Other:	
Firm is a monopsony/dictates its terms	10%
Returned favor	2%
Does respondent receive supplier credit from first purchase?	
Yes	73%
Sometimes	6%
No	21%
Does the supplier investigate the respondent before granting credit?	
Yes	43%
Sometimes	10%
No	47%
Number of valid responses	52

Source: RPED Zimbabwe case study survey.

Case study firms were asked questions about how they obtain trade credit from suppliers and what procedures they use to decide whom they give credit to. Responses show that the most common procedure to solicit credit is to fill out a credit application form and provide trade and bank references (table 9.7). In many cases the firm's relationship with the supplier or its reputation in the business is important. Reputation is used more by large firms; having a prior relationship with the supplier is more important for micro and small firms. A few microenterprises or small-scale African-headed firms were recommended directly to a supplier by a third party. This in itself suggest that reliance on the formal credit reference system was insufficient to dispel the supplier's doubts. A few large firms used their market power to dictate their own credit terms to their suppliers.

When dealing with their own customers, sample firms operate largely in the same way (table 9.8). Only one respondent claimed that over the years he had developed the ability to judge people and thus relied on his own judgment a great deal. Most others require clients to fill a credit application form and to provide references. Many also indicate that they take on customers on a trial basis to allow them to demonstrate their reliability. Many firms collect information about their clients directly, by

Table 9.8
Establishment of a trade credit relationship with a client in Zimbabwe

Does the respondent assess the client before granting credit or take a chance?	
Assess	96%
Sometimes	2%
Take a chance	2%
How does the respondent grant credit to clients?	
Legal guarantee:	
Demands a deposit or bank guarantee from first-time customers	6%
Request client to sign a personnal guarantee form	4%
Screening:	
Fill forms with references and bank name	74%
Inspect premices when assessing work to client's home/investigate	17%
Rely on one's ability to judge character	2%
Buy cash for a while/trial period	60%
Reputation:	
Prospective clients are screened by credit insurance/Dunn & Bradstreet/agent	25%
Client was recommended	13%
Client had a prior relationship	6%
Rely on the client's reputation/size	6%
Does respondent gives supplier credit from first purchase?	
Yes	61%
Sometimes	4%
No	35%
Do clients who did not get credit from first purchase get credit later?	
Yes	70%
No	30%

Source: RPED Zimbabwe case study survey.

inspecting the client's business premises or home, and by asking friends and others about the client's reliability. They also rely on previous acquaintances, on the reputation of the client, and on any other knowledge they may have acquired of that client over time. Several larger firms even require loan applicants to pass an independent screening by Dun and Bradstreet, a credit insurance company, or by their factor. When suppliers are not satisfied, they may request the credit applicant to provide a deposit, a bank guarantee, or a personal guarantee to secure their line of credit.

We ran probit analyses to test under what conditions firms are subjected to formal screening and whether they obtain credit from the first purchase. The results revealed that African firms are both less likely to be formally screened and less likely to obtain credit from the first purchase (table 9.9). This seems to imply that some screening is done purely on the basis of the ethnicity of the applicant. Larger firms are

Table 9.9
Probit regressions on screening and ease of access to trade credit

	Suppliers				Clients			
	Formal screening		From 1st purchase		Formal screening		From 1st purchase	
	Coefficient	z-statistic	Coefficient	z-statistic	Coefficient	z-statistic	Coefficient	z-statistic
Firm characteristics								
Size of firm	−0.100	0.780	1.534	0.021	1.829	0.007	−0.130	0.697
Age of firm	0.000	0.310	−0.010	0.555	−0.040	0.235	0.001	0.938
Manufacturing firm dummy	0.400	0.430	−0.450	0.623	−5.690	0.932	0.788	0.174
Sudsidiary dummy	−0.400	0.500	−0.440	0.590	4.940	0.945	1.330	0.046
Ethnicity (white is the omitted category)								
African owner	−1.120	0.070	−1.710	0.052	0.639	0.507	−1.230	0.031
Asian/other owner	−0.100	0.810	−0.960	0.214	0.424	0.616	−0.680	0.186
Sectoral dummies (metal sector is the omitted category)								
Food processing dummy	−0.800	0.230	0.729	0.502	−1.030	0.320	1.170	0.098
Textile and garment dummy	−0.100	0.920	−0.390	0.626	−1.570	0.070	0.590	0.339
Wood processiong dummy	−0.200	0.750	−0.700	0.560	−0.210	0.862	0.730	0.326
Intercept	0.950	0.270	−0.920	0.460	3.956	0.953	−0.420	0.636
Number of observations	49		48		51		52	

significantly more likely to receive credit from the first purchase, suggesting the importance of reputation as a screening device. As providers of trade credit, large firms are more likely to use formal screening mechanisms such as credit application forms, and bank and trade references. Discussions with respondents suggest that there may be economies of scale in establishing such formalized systems. Several respondents also pointed out that a formal credit application process minimizes the risk of collusion between employees and clients.

African firms are significantly less likely to provide credit to first-time customers. Many plausible explanations for this result are ruled out by the regressions themselves. It is not because these firms are smaller or newer and thus more vulnerable to risk: the coefficients on age and size are very small and entirely nonsignificant. It is not because African firms do not use formal screening mechanisms: the third regression in table 9.9 shows that African firms, if anything, screen more (the coefficient is not significant, however; only size matters in that regression). The most likely explanation for this result is that it is a reflection of the liquidity constraints African firms face. This interpretation is reinforced by the fact that subsidiaries, which as a group are less credit constrained, on the contrary, are more likely to give credit on the first purchase. Alternatively, it may be that African firms sell mostly to other Africans, who, as a group, are poorer and therefore more risky debtors than non-blacks, while subsidiaries sell mostly to other well-established firms, some of which are within their own group. African firms thus must, on the top of having less access to credit, show extra caution in dealing with their own customers. Both explanations are consistent with the fact that black firms give less credit to their customers.

9.4   Conclusion

This chapter has shown that relationships play an important role in the allocation of supplier credit and the avoidance of problems with clients and suppliers. For firms to let clients take goods on credit, they must trust them. Trust originates primarily from repeated interactions, in a way consistent with the model developed in the previous chapter. The trial period can be understood as a simple way of identifying bona fide clients and suppliers and of weeding out crooks and incompetent clients or suppliers. Direct screening via inspection of the client's or supplier's workplace is also practiced, primarily by smaller firms who can afford the time.

   Reliance on legal institutions is limited, except in certain cases such as letters of credit, SGS inspection of foreign imports, and legal guarantees. Various reputation mechanisms are also used, with sharp differences between the three countries. Reputation issues are discussed in more detail in part IV.

10 Relationships and Agricultural Trade

We have seen that relationships matter for the establishment of trust. In this chapter we broaden our perspective somewhat and examine the role of relationships more in detail. This chapter presents evidence on the extent to which relationships are used by agricultural traders in Madagascar to serve a variety of purposes such as the circulation of information about prices and market conditions, the provision of trade credit, the prevention and handling of contractual difficulties, the regularity of trade flows, and the mitigation of risk. Results show that larger and more prosperous traders are those with better relationships. The fact that larger, more successful traders are better connected will hardly surprise anyone who is familiar with African trade patterns (e.g., Bauer 1954; Jones 1959; Cohen 1969; Meillassoux 1971; Jones 1972; Amselle 1977). It is also in line with the new literature on social capital that identifies networks of relationships as a productive asset from which individuals can derive a return. But it runs somewhat contrary to the expectation of policy makers and international agencies that often implicitly assume that larger traders are more sophisticated and that sophistication is synonymous to arm's-length, anonymous exchange.

This is important because the common observations that large traders cultivate close relationships with each other is often interpreted as evidence of collusion and price rigging. Although we cannot comment directly on whether or not collusion is present in Madagascar grain markets, our results indicate that there are many other reasons why traders maintain a network of personal relations, such as access to information, regular trade flows, trade credit, and risk sharing. Our results also indicate that traders with better networks have higher productivity. By itself, this empirical regularity does not, however, constitute evidence that networks contribute to firm performance: relationships could be correlated with productivity simply because they are an inessential by-product of economic success.[1] To ascertain that relationships help productivity, we investigate whether networks play any practical role in the way firms deal with each other and show that relationships serve a useful purpose. This can be regarded as preliminary evidence that relationships and net-

---

1. This issue is quite distinct from that of relation of causality between network capital and firm performance: regardless of whether network capital is useful, its accumulation is at least partly an outcome of past firm performance; it is similar, in this respect, to physical capital. The usefulness of network capital is also a separate from the role of entrepreneurship in firm performance. If network capital is essential to firm growth, at least in certain institutional environments, then smart entrepreneurs must accumulate it to be successful—just like they need to accumulate machinery and equipment. The fact that network capital is critical to firm performance thus does not subtract from the role that entrepreneurship plays in firm development. Finally, the idea that networks are an irrelevant by-product of good entrepreneurship per se can be dismissed offhand: if networks serve no purpose, it is hard to see why entrepreneurs who are, as a rule, extremely busy would bother investing in the social interaction that is required for the formation of networks.

works are more than an irrelevant by-product of market interaction. Fafchamps and Minten (2002b) complement this approach with a rigorous empirical analysis of the contribution of social (network) capital to firm performance.

10.1   Trade and Relationships

We begin with table 10.1, which illustrates the importance of relationships as perceived by traders themselves. The table shows that relationships are by far the most important factor for the success of a trader. Seventy-one percent of the respondents regard reputation and relationships as very important for the success of their business. This proportion is much higher than that for credit, price, or equipment. Access to credit, which is typically presented as a major constraint by small businesses the world over, ranks much lower than relationships: only 11 percent of the respondents see it as a very important factor in business success; close to 40 percent of the respondents think it is not important at all.

It is sometimes argued that relationships are important among the poor because they need the support of their family and community to deal with the vagaries of life while the rich can afford to behave in a more individualistic fashion (Platteau 1996). This is not the case here. Table 10.1 indeed shows that the importance given to relationships rises with firm size: while 62 percent of small firms think relationships are very important, 77 percent of large traders do. It is therefore not the case that the emphasis on relationships results from the presence in the sample of small, poor traders who live in symbiosis with their community. If anything, larger and richer traders put more emphasis on relationships than the poor, not less.

These results beg the question of why relationships are important. To try to answer this question, we examine six possible roles that relationships may play in trade: (1) business training and start-up support, (2) information sharing, (3) regularity of demand and supply, (4) credit, (5) prevention of contractual breaches, and (6) risk sharing.

10.2   Business Training and Start-up Support

Table 10.2 shows that a quarter of surveyed traders had either a father or a mother in trade. Only 14 percent of respondents say they are in this business because of family traditions, however. Half the traders were helped by family and friends at start-up and close to half learned the business with a relative or a friend. The rest learned business on their own. Larger traders seem to have had parents with more experience

Table 10.1
Factors important for success as perceived by traders

	Small	Medium	Large	Total
Personal reputation and relationships				
Not important	7%	6%	3%	5%
A little important	17%	19%	9%	15%
Important	38%	27%	23%	29%
Very important	100%	100%	100%	100%
Access to credit				
Not important	64%	28%	28%	39%
A little important	84%	63%	65%	70%
Important	96%	89%	83%	89%
Very important	100%	100%	100%	100%
Granting credit				
Not important	63%	46%	40%	50%
A little important	90%	82%	75%	82%
Important	98%	98%	94%	97%
Very important	100%	100%	100%	100%
Purchase price				
Not important	7%	2%	5%	5%
A little important	27%	19%	33%	26%
Important	72%	67%	72%	70%
Very important	100%	100%	100%	100%
Sale price				
Not important	1%	1%	1%	2%
A little important	21%	11%	18%	17%
Important	72%	59%	63%	65%
Very important	100%	100%	100%	100%
Transport equipment				
Not important	37%	31%	27%	32%
A little important	56%	44%	46%	49%
Important	84%	69%	68%	73%
Very important	100%	100%	100%	100%
Number of observations	227	254	243	724

Source: Madagascar trader survey.
Note: To facilitate comparison, cumulative percentages of answers are reported.

Table 10.2
Family and business

	Small	Medium	Large	Total
Family in trade				
% with parent in trade	27.8%	24.0%	26.3%	25.8%
Number of years father in trade	3.4	3.8	5.1	4.1
Number of years mother in trade	4.1	3.3	5.1	4.1
% with parent in agricultural trade	22.9%	14.2%	17.7%	18.0%
Number of years father in agricultural trade	2.2	1.9	4.0	2.6
Number of years mother in agricultural trade	2.7	1.8	4.0	2.8
Help at start-up				
% helped at start-up by family/friends	54.2%	48.8%	56.8%	53.2%
Learned working with parents/relative	39.2%	27.2%	25.1%	30.7%
Learned working with friend/partner	15.4%	15.8%	14.0%	14.8%
Learned as employee of trader	0.9%	1.2%	2.9%	2.2%
Learned alone	44.5%	55.9%	58.0%	52.2%
Contacts				
Number of relatives with wage job	1.8	1.7	2.1	1.9
Number of relatives in trade	0.8	0.9	0.9	0.9
Number of relatives in agricultural trade	0.7	0.7	0.8	0.7
Number of traders known personally	6.3	10.3	10.0	8.8
Number of observations	227	254	243	724

Source: Madagascar trader survey.

in trade but otherwise are similar to their smaller counterparts: if anything, they are more likely to insist they learned the business on their own—a finding hardly consistent with the idea that parents in trade is a condition for success. In addition the bottom of table 10.2 shows that traders have typically outgrown their family base: while on average they have about one relative in trade, they know close to ten traders personally. Taken together, this evidence suggests that while, for some traders, family relationships were important at start-up for capital and experience, they do not seem to be strong determinants of business success. If anything, traders who learned the business from their family appear less likely to be successful. In contrast, non-family types of relationships that are initially unimportant seem to grow over time.

Table 10.2 also suggests that the number of traders that respondents know personally is unlikely to be an important determinant of business success: although the numbers reported by small firms are smaller than those reported by medium and large firms, the differences are far from commensurate with variation in firm performance. Furthermore there is no noticeable difference between the answers given by medium and large firms. If network capital matters, then it must be through a channel more specific than simply knowing other traders personally.

Table 10.3
Sources of information on market conditions

	Small	Medium	Large	Total
Prices				
Other traders	81.1%	60.6%	39.9%	59.9%
Suppliers and clients	15.0%	31.1%	37.4%	28.3%
Messengers	3.5%	7.9%	22.6%	11.5%
Public sources	0.4%	0.4%	0.0%	0.3%
Supply conditions				
Other traders	32.2%	19.7%	18.9%	23.2%
Suppliers and clients	64.8%	76.4%	68.3%	70.2%
Messengers	1.8%	3.5%	12.3%	5.9%
Public sources	1.3%	0.4%	0.4%	0.7%
Demand conditions				
Other traders	30.0%	10.6%	10.3%	16.5%
Suppliers and clients	67.8%	85.8%	79.0%	77.5%
Messengers	0.9%	1.6%	8.6%	3.7%
Public sources	1.3%	2.0%	2.1%	2.3%
Number of observations	227	254	243	724

Source: Madagascar trader survey.
Note: Size categories are based on total sales.

10.3 Information Sharing

In contrast with training and start-up support, nonfamily relationships appear critical for getting access to business-relevant information. Table 10.3 lists the sources of information on prices, supply, and demand conditions used by surveyed traders. The numbers bring to light the paramount importance of relationships as sources of information: other traders and suppliers and clients are the major source of business information. Public sources such as newspapers, radio, and public services play an essentially marginal role. Larger traders rely more than small traders on messengers; that is, individuals who are sent explicitly to collect information, but even among large traders their role is dwarfed by relationships. Another interesting regularity present in the data is that small traders are more likely than large traders to seek information from other traders instead of getting information from suppliers and clients. One explanation is that large traders have a closer relationship with their suppliers and clients and so feel they can rely on the information they provide. Small traders, by contrast, probably fear they will be cheated if they trust what suppliers and clients tell them.

The frequency with which respondents share information with other traders appears fairly low, as shown in table 10.4. While most respondents discuss quality

Table 10.4
Information sharing

	Small	Medium	Large	Total	Number of observations
Discuss product quality with other traders					
At least once a day	2%	2%	2%	2%	725
At least once a week	19%	11%	8%	13%	725
At least once a month	28%	27%	20%	25%	725
At least once a year	87%	73%	73%	78%	725
Never	100%	100%	100%	100%	725
Discuss prices with other traders[1]					
At least once a day	2%	3%	4%	4%	339
At least once a week	40%	16%	14%	18%	339
At least once a month	47%	31%	28%	32%	339
At least once a year	87%	76%	80%	80%	339
Never	100%	100%	100%	100%	339

Source: Madagascar trader survey.
Notes: To facilitate comparison, cumulative percentages of answers are reported. (1) Asked of traders with regular clients only.

and prices with others at least once a year, the great majority of them do not discuss these issues every week.[2] Taken together, the evidence suggests that Malagasy grain traders have not formed strong networks of information sharing based on trust. Interpersonal relationships such as those formed with regular clients and suppliers nevertheless serve as conduits for valuable information. This suggests that to the extent that firms benefit from social capital for information gathering, they do not get it for free; they must create it through business contacts and relationships.

10.4   Regularity of Supply and Demand

Another possible role that relationships play is in ensuring supply and demand. Survey results indicate that finding a supplier or a client is a recurrent problem for respondents: between 40 and 50 percent of them face difficulties, at least occasionally, in identifying potential buyers and sellers. As table 10.5 illustrates, traders who experience lots of difficulties are those who have the smallest numbers of regular

2. Some caution should be used when interpreting the results, however. First, respondents seem to have understood the questions relative to "other traders" as meaning "other traders who operate in a manner similar to yours," hence excluding suppliers and clients even if they are traders. Second, questions relative to bad clients and prices were only asked to respondents who have regular clients, thereby introducing a potential bias.

Table 10.5
Presence of regular partners and ease of search

| | Ever fail to find a supplier | | | |
	Never	Occasionally	Often	Total
Regular suppliers				
% with regular suppliers	49.0%	59.8%	42.9%	51.2%
Number of regular suppliers	4.4	3.3	1.5	3.6
Number of observations	404	241	84	729
Percentage of sample	55.4%	33.1%	11.5%	100.0%
	Ever fail to find a client			
	Never	Occasionally	Often	Total
Regular clients				
% with regular clients	76.0%	75.0%	47.0%	71.2%
Number of regular clients	6.5	5.9	2.8	5.8
Number of observations	451	162	116	729
Percentage of sample	61.9%	22.2%	15.9%	100.0%

Source: Madagascar trader survey.

suppliers and clients. In other words, traders with regular sources of supply and demand are less likely to encounter problems. Relationships thus reduce search costs.

Table 10.6 indicates the existence of a strong relationship between firm size and the emphasis on regular suppliers and clients: while large firms do between 40 and 45 percent of their business with regulars, this proportion is much smaller among small traders. As a result larger traders economize on search costs relative to smaller traders and probably have more secure sources of demand and supply. Results further indicate that the ties respondents have with their regular suppliers and clients are not based on family or ethnicity: the overwhelming majority of them (90 percent) describe their ties as business only. This is not entirely surprising given that Madagascar, unlike other developing countries (Bigsten et al. 2000a), shares a single language and sense of ethnic homogeneity.[3] The emphasis that larger traders place on regular clients and suppliers is consistent with their use of suppliers and clients as sources of information about prices and market conditions: the existence of long-term relationships between them to ensure that the information provided is more accurate than what would be conveyed to an unknown trader.

3. Although Malagasy people do not distinguish themselves according to language or ethnicity, they do pay attention to geographical origin. Unfortunately, no questions were asked about the geographical origin of regular clients and suppliers.

Table 10.6
Regular suppliers and clients

	Small	Medium	Large	Total
Regular suppliers				
% with regular suppliers	33.0%	59.4%	62.6%	51.2%
Number of regular suppliers	1.4	3.4	6.2	3.6
% purchases from regular suppliers	22.8%	42.9%	45.6%	36.7%
Number of years known regular suppliers[1]	3.1	4.1	4.7	4.1
Regular clients				
% with regular clients	52.0%	71.3%	88.9%	71.2%
Number of regular clients	3.0	5.8	8.3	5.8
% purchases to regulars	13.3%	26.1%	39.9%	26.8%
Number of years known regular clients[2]	2.3	4.0	4.2	3.8

Source: Madagascar trader survey.
Notes: (1) Computed for the respondents with regular suppliers only. (2) Computed for the respondents with regular clients only.

10.5   Trade Credit

Another reason why traders might value relationships is because they open access to trade credit in the form of payment facilities with suppliers or advances paid by customers. Results do show that respondents virtually never grant or receive trade credit on the first transaction. Relationships thus play an important role in access to trade credit as well.

Table 10.7 reports the proportion of purchases and sales made in cash, on credit, and with advance payment. The overwhelming majority of transactions are cash only. On average, respondents operate one-sixth of their business with some element of credit. When credit is present, it floats predominantly downstream, that is, from seller to buyer. The ratio of payables and receivables over monthly sales shows that respondents are, on average, net givers of credit, not so much because they sell more on credit than they buy but, on the contrary, because buyers take more time to pay.

10.6   Breaches of Contracts and Conflict Resolution

We saw in chapter 6 that agricultural traders seek minimizing their exposure to contractual risk. Table 10.8 reminds us that the frequency of breach is higher among firms that contract forward. Among firms that place orders, for instance, a problem with supplies occurs, on average, in one-third of the purchases; the proportion is even higher for large traders (table 10.8). Among firms that sell on credit, a case of late or

Table 10.7
Trade credit

	Small	Medium	Large	Total
Credit from and to suppliers				
% purchases cash	90.8%	76.9%	79.4%	82.3%
% purchases on credit	9.1%	21.1%	17.2%	15.8%
% purchases advance payment	0.1%	2.0%	3.3%	1.8%
Ratio payables/monthly sales	2.7%	7.7%	5.7%	6.2%
Credit to and from clients				
% sales cash	94.8%	86.1%	76.4%	85.8%
% sales on credit	5.2%	13.3%	22.4%	13.6%
% sales advance payment	0.0%	0.7%	1.2%	0.6%
Ratio receivables/monthly sales	6.6%	9.8%	16.1%	11.6%
Number of observations	227	254	243	724

Source: Madagascar trader survey.

Table 10.8
Frequency of contractual problems

	Small	Medium	Large	Total
With suppliers				
Number of transactions per month	6.5	5.5	11.5	7.8
Number of cases deficient quality per month	0.07	0.30	0.48	0.28
Number of cases late deliveries per month	0.03	0.08	0.10	0.07
% traders who place orders	7.4%	17.8%	19.2%	14.8%
Average incidence of problems[1]:				
Among firms that place orders	17.8%	28.3%	40.7%	31.7%
Among firms that do not place orders	2.4%	4.4%	3.9%	3.5%
Over all firms	3.6%	8.3%	10.7%	7.7%
With clients				
Number of transactions per month	386	325	261	323
Number of cases of late payment per month	0.14	0.77	1.12	0.68
Number of cases of nonpayment per month	0.00	0.03	0.04	0.02
% sales on credit	5.2%	13.3%	22.4%	13.6%
Average incidence of problems[1]:				
Among firms that sell on credit	2.1%	4.5%	5.4%	4.5%
Among firms that do not sell on credit	0.3%	0.3%	0.5%	0.3%
Over all firms	0.7%	2.3%	3.7%	2.2%

Source: Madagascar trader survey.
Note: (1) Computed as the average of the ratio of problems over number of transactions for each firm.

nonpayment arises in one out of every 20 sales. Since these firms do not sell all their output on credit, this translates into one case of late or nonpayment in 20 percent of the credit sales. Fortunately, only one out of every 35 late payment cases turns into nonpayment. What probably keeps this proportion low is the time traders spend chasing late payers. To summarize, the incidence of contractual problems is especially high whenever traders contract forward, which explains why few of them do.

Traders' desire to avoid the contractual problems created by forward contracting singularly complicates exchange and is achieved at considerable cost. First of all, as table 10.8 shows, most transactions take place without orders and without credit. This means that virtually all trade in agricultural products in the entire island of Madagascar takes the form of cash-and-carry transactions. This can hardly be regarded as an efficient and convenient way of conducting trade. Very little, if any, forward-looking transactions occur, and when they do, they are based on a strong relationship of trust between buyer and seller. Since traders hardly ever pay by check,[4] this implies that search costs are higher than they should be, and that massive amounts of currency constantly circulate in the countryside—an invitation to theft and a perfect target for an inflation tax. Not surprisingly, many surveyed traders identify security as their number one problem (IFPRI 1998).

The prevention of problems also has its costs. Table 10.9 indicates that the overwhelming majority of traders and their clients inspect quality before purchasing. In other words, quality is inspected visually *each* time a product changes hands.[5] Given the multilayered nature of agricultural trade and thus the large number of transactions involved in getting foodstuffs from producers to consumers, we see that inspecting quality alone must account for a significant proportion of the spread between producer and consumer food prices.

Table 10.9 also demonstrates that quality inspection is a task that traders hardly ever delegate: although they employ, on average, 3.3 people to assist with the business, traders nearly always inspect quality themselves, presumably because conducting the task accurately is critical for business. In other words, so few cases of bad deliveries are reported not because suppliers are truthful but because buyers go to great lengths to ensure they are not cheated. Given the amount of energy they spend on checking quality, it is surprising that bad deliveries occur at all. Traders' inability or unwillingness to delegate quality inspection also means that their volume of

4. The fact that Malagasy banks—according to what we have heard—take two to four weeks to clear checks drawn on another town hardly incite traders to pay by check: doing so would tie up their working capital for weeks on end.

5. Similar practices are described in Ethiopia by Gabre-Madhin (1997).

Table 10.9
Verification of quality of products

	Small	Medium	Large	Total
Quality inspection by respondent				
% always inspect quality before purchase	92%	83%	78%	84%
% owner inspects quality	99%	93%	89%	94%
% family helper inspects quality	0%	7%	6%	5%
% employee or agent inspects quality	0%	0%	5%	2%
Quality inspection by clients				
% client always inspect quality	90%	86%	82%	86%
Action taken by respondent if supplies are of bad quality				
None/quality is the buyer's problem	69%	49%	46%	55%
Supplier provides a refund/replacement	18%	31%	36%	28%
Other	13%	21%	19%	17%
Action taken by client if supplies are of bad quality				
None/quality is the buyer's problem	77%	58%	52%	62%
Supplier provides a refund/replacement	13%	25%	26%	21%
Other	10%	17%	22%	17%

Source: Madagascar trader survey.

activity is limited by the quantities that the owner can inspect in person. It also implies numerous trips to supply areas, some of which are for nothing since traders do not use telephones, cannot or will not place or take orders, and must search for buyers or sellers once they are on location. Such a system can be but expensive to run and in such an environment having close relationships with regular clients and suppliers must singularly simplify one's business—hence the emphasis put on relationships as a factor of commercial success.

Similar difficulties arise in the granting of trade credit. Table 10.10 shows that the great majority of respondents check the credibility of clients before granting payment facilities. Apart from information collected from the client directly or from a personal visit to the client's shop, respondents rely primarily on information received from traders and other sources such as friends and family. There too relationships serve a role as facilitator of the screening of trade credit recipients. The relatively small proportion of respondents who cite information collected from traders and other sources, and the fact that this proportion diminishes with firm size, nevertheless suggest that reputation mechanisms in agricultural trade in Madagascar can be described as embryonic at best. This stands in stark contrast with the intense sharing of information—and the much higher incidence of trade credit—that were found in Kenya and Zimbabwe (e.g., Fafchamps et al. 1994, 1995; Fafchamps 1997c, 2000, 2002a). There firms were found to actively share information about bad payers,

Table 10.10
Credibility of clients

	Small	Medium	Large	Total
Respondent verifies credibility of client before sale[1]				
Never	6%	7%	5%	6%
Seldom	8%	9%	9%	9%
Sometimes	38%	24%	30%	29%
Often	72%	37%	46%	47%
Always	100%	100%	100%	100%
Sources of information consulted before granting credit				
% get information from client directly	98%	97%	94%	96%
% visit client's shop	9%	28%	33%	27%
% obtain information from other traders	38%	15%	25%	24%
% get information from client's bank	2%	0%	2%	1%
% get information from other sources	23%	11%	8%	12%

Source: Madagascar trader survey.
Notes: Questions were asked only to respondents who ever grant credit to clients. (1) Cumulative percentages reported to facilitate comparison.

either informally (Kenya) or via a credit reference bureau (Zimbabwe). The vetting of clients was also widely practiced. Agricultural trade in Madagascar more closely resembles the manufacturing sector in Ghana where little information sharing was uncovered (Fafchamps 1996).

10.7   Risk Sharing

Relationships can also serve as an insurance mechanism. Business, in general, and trade, in particular, are subject to all kinds of risks—theft, non- or late payment, adverse price fluctuation, storage loss, and so on—each of which can easily cripple a small trading business. In a world where trade credit is nonexistent or rare, a trader without working capital cannot operate. Consequently a trader whose working capital is either lost or tied up in bad debt and unsold stocks loses his or her income. The capacity to borrow from others therefore serves a crucial insurance purpose. Table 10.11 confirms that the overwhelming majority of respondents are involved in helping and being helped by others. Assisting and being assisted can be interpreted as the two sides of the same coin: people help each other because they expect to be helped in return (e.g., Fafchamps 1992; Coate and Ravallion 1993; Fafchamps and Lund 2002). Interestingly, as the table shows, larger traders are as involved in solidarity networks as their smaller competitors, and they have, in general, more friends they can count on in times of trouble. This contradicts the idea that solidarity mecha-

Table 10.11
Risk sharing and access to financial help

	Small	Medium	Large	Total
% who has ever helped others	72.2%	77.2%	80.2%	76.3%
% who has ever been helped by others	76.2%	75.6%	74.5%	75.0%
Number of people who can help	1.7	2.5	2.7	2.3
Number of observations	227	254	243	724

Source: Madagascar trader survey.

nisms necessarily tax the rich and that, as a result, the rich are more individualistic (Platteau 1996).

10.8 Conclusion on Madagascar

We have investigated the role that relationships play in the conduct of agricultural trading businesses. We found that relationships play a wide variety of roles, such as (1) business training and start-up support, (2) information sharing, (3) regularity of demand and supply, (4) credit, (5) prevention of contractual breaches, and (6) risk sharing. Of these, the regularity of supply and demand and risk sharing appear particularly important, in the sense that large traders enjoy a significantly larger proportion of sales and purchases from regular partners and systematically emphasize values and action consistent with risk sharing. Together with the circulation of information, the capacity and willingness to get and give trade credit, place and take orders, and simplify the inspection of quality are additional benefits traders derive from good relationships. The value of relationships, not legal institutions, appears to be what motivates Malagasy grain traders to honor contracts and seek the resolution of conflicts through negotiation. These findings are consistent with the model presented in chapter 7.

The importance of relationships is partly due to the extreme lack of sophistication in business practices: no payment by check, no invoicing, very little trade credit and placement of orders, visual inspection of quality by the trader or a trusted associate at each transaction, screening of clients through visual inspection of their shop and repeated interaction, and little or no evidence of reputation mechanisms to punish opportunistic breaches of contract. This lack of sophistication is not entirely unexpected, as the Malagasy government has historically repressed grain exchange and continues to provide very little, if any, support to private traders in agricultural products. But more than a decade after the initiation of market reform in Madagascar, these findings are disturbing and serve as a sobering reminder that without development of supporting institutions, the free market remains nothing but a flea market. Clearly, relationships alone do not provide a sufficient basis for the development of an efficient trading system. They help mitigate some problems but certainly not all, and they do not benefit all traders alike.

What precise institutions are required is not immediately clear from this work, but results suggest two possible lines of attack. One approach consists in fostering the faster and more widespread accumulation of social capital. This could, for instance, be achieved by facilitating interaction and trust among traders by establishing a Chamber of Commerce or by developing of informal clubs and other brotherhoods.[6] A second approach would be to limit the need for social capital by reducing market imperfections, for instance, by setting up institutions that facilitate payments (e.g., faster check clearing), expedite inspection of quality (e.g., grading), reduce insecurity (e.g., police), circulate information (e.g., radio programs, credit reference bureau), penalize cheaters (e.g., pursue fraud), and reduce risk (e.g., bank line of credit, futures market).

The results presented here suggest that successful traders owe their success not so much to individualism but rather to relationships. If anything, the evidence indicates that it is those who can create and nurture relationships who prosper as traders. Perhaps this is not original. After all, in the popular psyche, the trader is often portrayed as someone who is jovial and relates well with others. But the role of relationships is often overlooked in standard economic models that emphasize the maximization of profit through the accumulation of capital and the command of labor. There is also a social dimension to success, one that relies on the accumulation of valuable business relationships, of social network capital. Among traders, this accumulation process is one's passport to prosperity because it gives better access to information and risk sharing, and it reduces the costs of search, quality control, and contract enforcement.

10.9 Relational Contracting and Trade

We have seen that in sub-Saharan markets, personal relationships have a variety of valuable functions. We showed in this chapter that relationships facilitate the circulation of information about prices and market conditions, the provision of trade credit, the prevention and handling of contractual difficulties, the regularity of trade

---

6. See, for instance, the description of the role that Muslim brotherhoods play in building up social capital among traders in Geertz et al. (1979). The problem with brotherhoods is that they may restrict entry and favor their members at the expense of outsiders (e.g., Taylor 2000; Fafchamps 2002b).

flows, and the mitigation of risk. Of these, the regularity of supply and demand and the sharing of risk appear to be particularly important.

Relationships can help economize on search costs. Using a stylized model of exchange, Kranton (1996b) illustrates how trade within networks reduces search costs and can drive goods away from market exchange. Montgomery (1991) similarly shows that firms can use employee referral to identify and hire high-quality workers. There is plenty of evidence that networks and relationships perform a matching and screening function in many developed as well as developing countries. Referral is a common hiring procedure in the United States (Granovetter 1995b) as well as in Africa (Velenchik 1995). Reportedly, employee referral is extensively used in the Dacca garment sector (personal communication from Junaid Ahmed). Similar practices are found in commodity markets as well. In their description of livestock markets in West Africa, for instance, Eddy (1979) and Staatz (1979) document the role that personal networks play in matching buyers and sellers. A similar function is attributed to networks in the case of long-distance African trade by Meillassoux (1971) and Amselle (1977). In a recent study of Ethiopian grain traders, Gabre-Madhin (1997) describes in detail the role of brokers in bridging surplus and deficit areas and in assisting traders screen grain quality and identify reliable buyers and sellers.

Networks of personal relationships also serve to circulate information. Barr (2000), for instance, demonstrates that Ghanaian manufacturers with better business contacts perform better than less well connected firms. She interprets the evidence as consistent with the idea that large firms use networks to access information about new technologies and market opportunities while small firms rely on closely knit networks of mutual insurance. In a related paper Barr (2002b) discusses other possible roles of information sharing. One such role that has received much emphasis in the theoretical literature is reputation. Kandori (1992) formalizes the idea that if information about breaches of contract circulates freely among economic agents, breach can be deterred by excluding cheaters from future trade. Milgrom et al. (1991) apply this idea to medieval trade in Europe. They argue that the law merchant of Champagne Fairs served as the repository of information, making coordinated exclusion of cheaters possible even among agents who did not know each other. Using ancient correspondence among traders, Greif (1993, 1994) extends a similar concept to medieval trade in the Mediterranean sea and argues that ethnic and religious networks served in information sharing and helped discipline trading agents residing in distant cities.

Chapter 9 provided evidence regarding the role of reputation in enforcing contracts among African manufacturers. Referral by other firms is used as an important screening mechanism, and clients who can provide reliable references get supplier credit faster and more easily. This is not without consequences: Fisman (2001) shows that African manufacturers who get trade credit have a significantly higher level of capacity utilization. Not all firms are able to use referral to facilitate screening, however, for lack of personal contacts with other firms. This is particularly true among small firms and firms headed by individuals with loose ties to existing businesses.

Long-term relationships facilitate interlinking. Lorenz (1988), for instance, explains how relationship-based subcontracting among French manufacturers enables both buyer and seller to make long-term investments in each other's production process. Hart (1995) generalizes this concept to all incomplete contracts and argues that relationships provide a possible solution to the well-known "hold-up" problem (Williamson 1985). Fafchamps et al. (1994, 1995) illustrate how these principles apply to African manufacturing and enable parties to place orders, pay by check, provide supplier credit, and obtain warranty. The typical supplier-client relationship is one in which clients pay suppliers for fear that supplies will not be delivered, and suppliers deliver for fear that clients will not pay.

Not only do relationships enable agents to enter in multifaceted transactions involving various forms of forward contracting (e.g., order, credit, warranty), they also facilitate insurance and finance. For instance, Barr (2000) argues that small Ghanaian firms rely on their network of contacts to secure insurance against liquidity crises. Similar findings are reported in Fafchamps et al. (1995) and Fafchamps and Oostendorp (2002), who argue that access to quick credit is essential for firms to survive liquidity crises. Fafchamps and Minten (2002b) further demonstrate that the performance of Malagasy grain traders depends critically on the number of people on which they can rely for assistance in financial emergencies. Relationships can also facilitate credit and equity financing. Finally Fafchamps et al. (1995) document the practice of shared inputs and machinery among competitors who belong to the same network.

One form of interlinking that is important in difficult economic environments is contractual flexibility. If penalties for breach of contract are too lenient, opportunistic breach cannot be deterred and contracting cannot take place. At the same time, rational economic agents should refuse to incur contractual obligations if the penalty for breach of contract is too strict (Fafchamps 1996). The reason is that unforeseen, yet unverifiable, events can occur that make compliance either very costly or outright impossible. Consequently, if the cost of contractual compliance is hard to predict, it may be impossible to find penalties that deter cheating without discouraging agents from engaging their contractual responsibility. In this case trade does not occur unless agents can use relationships to provide sufficient contractual flexibility, that is, to insure parties against extreme compliance costs. Bigsten et al. (2000a) provide evidence that contract flexibility is an essential feature of industrial input and output markets in sub-Saharan Africa: most disputes with suppliers and clients are resolved amicably through direct negotiations and trade is resumed between the parties. This finding is in agreement with the inherent riskiness of manufacturing production in poor countries (Collier and Gunning 1999). Fafchamps and Minten (2001a) report similar findings for grain markets in Madagascar. Of course, contract flexibility requires economic agents to anticipate delayed payments and deliveries by building up inventories and liquidity reserves. Fafchamps et al. (2000) show, for instance, that Zimbabwean industries accumulate inventories of inputs in response to late delivery risk.

There are yet other ways by which the coordinated and uncoordinated actions of groups of individuals can affect the development and functioning of markets. They can also help individuals coordinate their actions to generate a variety of public goods such as the provision of common infrastructure and institutions, and the lobbying of government and local authorities for preferential treatment and for supportive laws and institutions.[7]

---

7. As has been amply demonstrated by sociologists, for agents to voluntarily contribute to the action of a group, they need to identify with it. The process of group identification is not, however, central to this chapter, so we will abstract from it and use the terms "group" and "community" interchangeably.

IV INFORMATION SHARING

Part III has shown that trust among firms is based on relationships. Trust builds up over time as firms interact with each other and learn about each other's preferences and technology. Before they trust each other, firms must screen each other.

In most cases this is done via a trial period. In some cases, however, firms manage to bypass the trial period if they can be recommended by another firm. This assumes the sharing of information among firms. This part investigates the role of information sharing in the emergence and development of markets.

We begin with a formal model of relational contracting and derive conditions under which contract enforcement can be based purely on relationships. We then introduce information sharing, distinguishing between information on types and on behavior. We show that different market equilibria emerge depending on the kind of information that is transmitted.

Evidence on information sharing and reputation formation is then presented. We find that better connected firms have an advantage over other firms. The evidence suggests that this advantage comes from the reduction in transaction costs permitted by trust.

11 Markets and Information

Drawing insights from the survey work on enterprise finance reported in earlier chapters, we now investigate the spontaneous emergence of markets in the presence of heterogeneous agents and commitment failure. We ask a simple question: Can markets spontaneously emerge in the absence of external contract enforcement mechanism, and if so, under what conditions and under what form? A defining feature of market transactions is that they open the door to contractual abuse (e.g., nonpayment, deficient quality, late delivery). Unless opportunistic breach is effectively deterred, rational agents should refuse to transact, so exchange does not occur (Fafchamps 1996). In contrast to much of the economic literature that implicitly assumes that breaches of contract are prevented by the threat of court action, we focus here on informal enforcement mechanisms based on trust and reputation, otherwise known as relational contracting.

We show that for a relational contracting equilibrium to be fully decentralizable, agents must be heterogeneous and search costly. We derive precise conditions under which relational contracting can spontaneously emerge and deter opportunistic breach, even in the absence of formal market institutions. Unlike in court-based exchange where anonymous transactions are, in principle, feasible, personalized exchange is the rule and commercial relationships are long lasting. Exchange is not anonymous but based on mutual trust and on the sharing of information among agents; first best is not achieved because of breach is not fully deterred and switching costs reduce market flexibility. Exclusion from trade for cheaters is not required for markets to emerge. We also demonstrate that when the screening of potential commercial partners is costly, newcomers may find themselves excluded from trade. Business then becomes monopolized by a group, possibly sharing the same ethnic identity.[1] The relationship between ethnicity and markets is examined in Fafchamps (2000, 2002a).

This chapter extends previous work by Greif (1993, 1994) and Milgrom, North, and Weingast (1991) on medieval merchants and by Shapiro and Stiglitz (1984) and Montgomery (1991) on labor markets. It complements previous work by Kranton (1996b) who also considers the interaction between a reciprocal exchange market and a monetary market exchange but focuses on the minimization of search costs instead of commitment failure. Our analysis builds on the work of Ghosh and Ray (1996)

---

1. Historians have long noticed that business and trade often are in the hands of specific ethnic groups such as Lombards and Genoese merchants in Western Europe, Jews in the Mediterranean, Armenians in the Middle East; see, for instance, Braudel (1986), Geertz et al. (1979), Greif (1993), and Greif (1994). The same appears to be true of many developing countries today, for example, Chinese in Singapore, Malaysia, and Indonesia; Asians in East Africa (e.g., Marris 1971; Himbara 1994); Lebanese in West Africa; whites in Southern Africa.

and Kranton (1996a) who showed that the presence of heterogeneity among agents and the resulting need to screen agents before contracting can alone discipline market participants.[2] Unlike these papers, which rely on static or steady state models, we offer a thorough treatment of equilibrium dynamics and examine how relational contracting may foster the spontaneous emergence of markets. We also expand on these previous works by allowing for the circulation of information among agents.

The literature on relational contracting is large and growing rapidly. It is impossible to do justice to it all, so we limit ourselves to a few contributions that have influenced our analysis. Granovetter's (1985) and Platteau's (1994a, 1994b) discussions of norms and markets helped define market transactions as personal relationships that are subject to abuse. Reputation mechanisms are discussed in Coleman (1988), Kandori (1992), Ellison (1994), and Raub and Weesie (1990). Some of the concepts used here first appeared in the literature on credit (e.g., McKinnon's 1973 definition of strategic default) and on sovereign debt (e.g., Eaton and Gersovitz 1981; Kletzer 1984; Eaton et al. 1986; Grossman and Van Huyck 1988) and have been discussed in the literature on law and economics (e.g., Cooter and Ulen 1988; Craswell 1995; Bernstein 1992, 1996). Tadelis (1999) offers a treatment of reputation as a tradable asset. The originality of our contribution is in the formalization of market emergence dynamics in a relational contracting setup.

The evidence presented in previous chapters suggests that the main reason why firms enter in long-term trading relationships with their suppliers and clients is to save on screening costs and minimize breaches of contract. Firms indeed realize that suppliers and clients differ in competence and honesty; consequently finding reliable commercial partners is difficult and costly. Empirical results further indicate that firms that are able to share information about clients and suppliers save on screening costs, identify reliable partners more easily, and can more readily switch among potential suppliers and clients. The purpose of this chapter is to further our understanding of these phenomena by carefully analyzing a model that reproduces many of the stylized features of manufacturing and agricultural markets in Africa.

11.1   Informal Contract Enforcement

We begin with a brief review of the literature on market exchange in the absence of perfect contract enforcement. Consider a stylized economy comprised of an infinitely

---

2. A similar insight was already present in Shapiro and Stiglitz (1984) who demonstrated that unemployment deters shirking by workers.

lived, constant population of agents who discount the future with a common factor $\hat{\delta}$. Time is divided into trading periods during which agents either trade or do nothing, in which case their instantaneous payoff is normalized to zero.[3] Agents require one unit of a homogeneous good per period. Gains from obtaining this good, denoted $\hat{\alpha}$, are divided equally among agents so that payoffs are symmetrical.[4] In the absence of external contract enforcement, payoffs from the stage game can be represented by the following matrix:

Payoff matrix A		Comply	Breach
	Comply	$\hat{\alpha}, \hat{\alpha}$	$-1, 1$
	Breach	$1, -1$	$0, 0$

An agent's payoff in case of breach is $+1$; the other agent then incurs a loss of 1. With this normalization, $\hat{\alpha}$ can be thought of as the profit margin agents make on the exchange if they comply with their contractual obligations—for instance, supply their clients, pay their suppliers. As is well known, the contractual situation resembles the familiar Prisoner's Dilemma (Milgrom et al. 1991). The unique Nash equilibrium payoff of the one-period trading game is $\{0, 0\}$: in the absence of an external enforcement mechanism, gains from trade are not realized.

Economies such as this one have been extensively studied in the literature. If the economy comprises only two agents, a standard repeated game argument can be used to show that cooperation can be achieved by the threat of future noncooperation (Fudenberg and Maskin 1986). Trade is self-enforcing if the short-term gain from cheating $1 - \hat{\alpha}$ is smaller than the long-term loss from punishment $\hat{\delta}\hat{\alpha}/(1 - \hat{\delta})$. Trade thus requires that both $\hat{\alpha} \geq 1 - \hat{\delta}$.

The repeated game argument has been extended to groups of randomly matched agents by postulating the existence of a reputation mechanism whereby agents refuse to cooperate with known cheaters (Kandori 1992).[5] The fear to lose one's reputation

3. An alternative interpretation of the model is to regard "trade" as short for "businesslike transaction" involving the placement of an order, monthly invoicing, payment terms, use of checks, quality warranty, and so on, and to regard "no trade" as short for "road-side transaction" involving visual inspection of the goods and instantaneous payment in cash. In this case, gains from trade represent the convenience and cost saving of businesslike transactions.

4. Greif (2000) argues that a one-sided Prisoner's Dilemma game is better at capturing the commitment problem associated with exchange. We will use a one-sided commitment game in chapter 17 to derive results very similar to those obtained with a symmetrical exchange game. Symmetry offers some advantages in terms of presentation, which is why it is used here and in chapter 12.

5. Other forms of group punishment are also possible (e.g., La Ferrara 1997; Spagnolo 1999). Cheaters could, for instance, be banned from social events and, more generally, be excluded from their community. We leave this possibility for future research and abstract from it here.

is then what enforces contracts. Requiring that the complete history of play be public knowledge may appear unattainable in practice, given the massive information-processing capability needed to keep track of the contractual histories of all agents. Fortunately a theorem by Abreu (1988) demonstrates that much of the history of play is irrelevant when punishment strategies are optimal. Using Abreu's result, Kandori (1992) shows that a reputational equilibrium can be sustained by sharing relatively simple information such as whether an agent has deviated in the recent past and for how many periods he or she has voluntarily been punished.

For a reputational equilibria to be self-enforcing, information about cheaters must be made available to the group; trade is not sustainable if information circulates poorly or slowly (Raub and Weesie 1990). Furthermore, since economic agents have an incentive to discredit competitors by falsely accusing them of cheating, a reputational equilibrium cannot exist unless the dissemination of false information is itself punished (e.g., laws against defamation and slander), or unless an impartial agent, such as a law merchant (Milgrom et al. 1991) or a credit reference bureau, ensures that information about cheaters is unbiased. As interviews with African manufacturers clearly demonstrated, gossip cannot form the basis for a reputational equilibrium because it is too unreliable and too easily manipulated. In the absence of an external information verification mechanism, agents must request a personal recommendation from a third party they know and trust before accepting an agent as a noncheater.[6] Because agents are limited in the number of potential informants with whom they maintain close contact, reliance on personal recommendations seriously limits the sharing of information.

Reputational equilibria also implicitly assume that agents who trade with cheaters are themselves punished. In our study of manufacturing firms in Ghana, Kenya, and Zimbabwe, we found little evidence that firms collude to exclude breachers from future trade. The majority of respondents believe that cheating on a supplier would hurt their relationship with that particular supplier but would not make it impossible to trade with others. Theory teaches us that if agents can only trade with each other once, as in Milgrom et al. (1991), the prohibition to deal with cheaters is self-enforcing: in losing their reputation, cheaters have lost their only incentive to respect contracts with anyone. If agents can trade repeatedly over time, however, meta-punishment—that is, punishment for failing to punish—is more problematic. Cheaters can indeed credibly "bribe" their way out of exclusion by entering into a

---

6. The use of personal recommendation is, for instance, well documented in the US labor market (see Montgomery 1991 and the references cited therein).

long-term relationship with one agent in exchange for a smaller share of gains from trade.[7] It is easy to verify that in a reputational equilibrium the participation constraint of a past cheater with whom an agent accepts to trade is the same as that of a noncheater. Consequently, as long as $\hat{\alpha} > 1 - \hat{\delta}$, a cheater can always credibly propose an alternative distribution of gains from trade and find an agent who can be bribed. Since both the cheater and his new partner strictly prefer trade to punishment, it is in their interest to keep the transactions secret. Consequently punishing agents who deal with cheaters is difficult.[8] Reputational equilibria are thus harder to support than is commonly recognized and constitute an unconvincing model for markets at their early state of development. We revisit these issues in the next chapter.

Other mechanisms have been suggested in the literature. Contract enforcement can be achieved through contagious equilibria in which breach of contract by a few weakens trust between communities and threatens economic exchange (e.g., Kandori 1992; Ellison 1994). If agents are sufficiently patient and the number of agents is small, the fear of upsetting trust between communities may be sufficient to deter opportunistic breach of contract. This enforcement mechanism offers the advantage that it is easily decentralized and does not require the sharing of information about cheaters. Like reputational equilibria, however, it is not renegotiation-proof if pairs of agents can trade repeatedly over time. It also unclear how a contagious equilibrium can arise from a no-trade situation. To overcome these shortcomings, some, like Becker and Madrigal (1994), have proposed to regard markets as evolutionary stable equilibria of a game in which certain agents have a marked preference for cooperation because they are irrational, altruistic, or subject to guilt (Platteau 1994b). Conditions are then derived under which the presence of such agents is sufficient to ensure cooperation.

Ghosh and Ray (1996) have demonstrated that neither meta-punishments nor special preferences are required for cheating to be deterred provided that two departures from previous models are introduced. That is, pairs of agents may continue to trade if they wish, so relational contracting is allowed, and the economy contains a constant proportion of myopic agents who always cheat. Although myopic agents can easily be induced to reveal their type during a screening/testing phase, such screening is costly. With these assumptions, Ghosh and Ray (1996) showed the exis-

---

7. This concern is similar to the bilateral rationality criterion proposed by Ghosh and Ray (1996).

8. It is of interest to note that credit reference bureaus such as Dun and Bradstreet report "cheaters" but make no effort to collect information on agents who deal with them.

tence of an equilibrium in which the market disciplines itself, much as involuntary
unemployment prevents shirking by employees in the model of Shapiro and Stiglitz
(1984). In this equilibrium, which they call "social equilibrium," agents form long-
term trading relationships to economize on screening costs. We prefer to call it a
relational equilibrium in reference to the relational nature of exchange. A similar,
though simpler, model is presented in Kranton (1996a). Although a relational equilibrium with an initial testing phase would be subgame perfect even in economies
with homogeneous agents, Ghosh and Ray (1996) argue that it would violate *bilateral rationality*: pairs of players would benefit from a coordinated deviation from the
proposed path by skipping the testing phase. The formation of such coalitions would
eliminate any penalty for opportunistic breach and the equilibrium would unravel.[9]

In the remainder of this chapter, we expand on the model of Ghosh and Ray
(1996) in various ways. First, we work out the dynamic behavior of the relational
equilibrium in detail and study the requirements for relational contracting to emerge
from a no-trade situation.[10] Second, we introduce some new features: finitely lived
agents, occasional reshuffling of relationships, and limited information sharing.
Third, we investigate the conditions under which a reputational equilibrium of the
type suggested by Kandori (1992) would satisfy the bilateral rationality criterion
proposed by Ghosh and Ray (1996).

11.2   A Model of Relational Contracting

We now construct a dynamic model of relational contracting and examine how
relational equilibria unfold over time. We first give a precise description of the economy, the action set of each player, and their payoffs. We then demonstrate the existence of a relational equilibrium and derive laws of motion for the economy. In this
section we reproduce Ghosh and Ray's (1996) result that in the presence of heterogeneous agents, the stigmatization of cheaters is not required for exchange to take
place. We also show that agents benefit from sharing information even if cheaters
are not excluded from future trade. Perfect deterrence of opportunistic breaches of
contract is nevertheless not achieved. At the end of the chapter, we focus on two
special cases: a relational equilibrium with no information sharing and a closed-shop
equilibrium.

---

9. Bilateral rationality is but a special case of the coalition-proofness criterion proposed by Bernheim et al.
(1987).

10. The article by Ghosh and Ray (1996) contains only a very brief discussion of the dynamic behavior of
their model.

As mentioned earlier, we consider an infinitely lived economy with a continuum of agents, indexed from 0 to 1, who trade over time and discount the future with a common discount factor $\hat{\delta}$.[11] The economy combines random matching with relational contracting. There are two types of agents: competent and incompetent.[12] Their proportions G and $B = 1 - G$ in the economy are constant and known to all agents, but an agent's type is not directly observable. Competent agents require one unit of a homogeneous good per period. Incompetent agents can only earn a positive payoff by breaching contracts with competent agents. Agents payoffs are private, nonverifiable information.

The economy consists of an infinitely repeated sequence of trading rounds during which agents trade, screen, or do nothing—in which case their instantaneous payoff is normalized to zero. External contract enforcement is assumed inexistent.[13] Each trading round is divided into three stages: the matching stage, the contracting stage, and the compliance stage. These stages are shown in figure 11.1. All agents are initially unmatched. At the beginning of the matching stage, agents decide either to continue trading together or to find a new partner, in which case they join the pool of unmatched agents. Trade is voluntary; if one agent decides to stop a relationship, his partner becomes unmatched. Unmatched agents are randomly paired; they observe each other's identity but not each other's type.[14] Informal information sharing is represented by the assumption that with probability κ_i, an agent i obtains a costless and accurate report summarizing the past actions of the agent it has been matched with.[15]

11. The assumption of an infinite number of agents not only enables us to abstract from strategic interactions that may arise among a small number of agents. It also implies that the aggregate laws of motion of the economy are deterministic along the equilibrium paths we consider.

12. Incompetence encompasses insufficient or antiquated equipment, lack of technical or marketing skills, fragile financial base, and natural predisposition toward dishonesty.

13. This is obviously a simplifying assumption destined to focus the attention on relational equilibria. In developing countries the circumstances under which a pure court-based system could effectively deter opportunistic breach of contract—low legal costs, predictable courts, large transactions, verifiability of contract terms, and wealthy defendants—are likely to be particularly problematic. The courts are typically underfunded and subject to political pressures, markets are thin and transactions small, illiteracy and lack of education preclude the widespread use of written contractual instruments, and many economic agents are poor. Consequently the threat of court action is unlikely to perfectly deter opportunistic breach, either because too many debtors are judgment-proof in the sense that they have insufficient assets to repay their debts, or because court action is too costly and unpredictable for a plaintiff to sue.

14. We postulate that economic agents can be unambiguously identified through group recognition, business registration, or identity card, and that the falsification of one's identity is prohibitively costly.

15. Behind this assumption is the idea that agents form informal and partially connected information-sharing networks (Raub and Weesie 1990). Lang and Nakamura (1990) argue that agents may not find it in their immediate interest to share information with others for fear of losing reliable partners to them. In the model presented here, this issue does not arise since, by assumption, unmatched agents do not choose their partners but are matched at random.

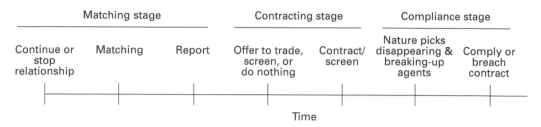

Figure 11.1
Sequence of events during a trading round

We assume that κ_i is exogenous and time invariant. Information circulates in both directions so that κ_i is also the proportion of agents who get a report on i. Agents who are new and have never traded are called untested.

The contracting stage begins with agents making one of three possible contracting offers: trade, screen, or do nothing.[16] If players choose to do nothing, they collect an instantaneous payoff of 0 and move to the next trading round. If they choose to screen each other, they incur a screening cost c, obtain information about the other player's type, and move to the next round.[17] If both choose to trade, they move to the compliance stage. Nature then first draws a proportion $1 - \theta$ $(0 < \theta \le 1)$ of competent agents who are replaced by new identical agents at the end of the round. The outcome of this random draw is privately revealed to agents at the beginning of the compliance stage; it is not verifiable and is purported to represent bankruptcy shocks. All incompetent agents are replaced at the end of the round.[18] Next, nature picks a proportion $1 - \hat{\tau}$ of agents who, for reasons outside the scope of the model, have to break up a relationship.[19] In both cases gains from trade for the concerned agent fall to zero—permanently for disappearing agents, until they find a new partner for breaking-up agents.[20] Agents discover that they must disappear or break up *after*

16. If offers differ, players continue to make offers until they are the same.

17. The screening cost is the minimum transaction that would induce an incompetent agent to reveal its type and is regarded as exogenous. We assume that agents cannot observe whether the other party has actually incurred the screening cost. Without this assumption, cheaters may be induced to reveal themselves by asking them to incur a screening cost, as is implicitly done in Milgrom et al. (1991). Here incompetent agents always agree to screen but never do.

18. Alternatively, B agents may be too numerous to be remembered or may easily conceal their identity.

19. For example, changes in economic conditions and trade patterns. See Greif (1993), Ghosh and Ray (1996), and section 4.2.1 for similar assumptions.

20. Since the number of agents is infinite, the probability that two agents are ever matched again is zero.

having incurred contractual obligations but *before* complying with them; they are able to complete the transaction but no longer make any profit from it.[21]

There are three states s in which a player can be at the end of the compliance stage: n, normal state, d, disappearing state, and b, breaking-up state.[22] The probabilities of being in the normal, breaking-up, and disappearing states are $\hat{\tau}\theta$, $(1 - \hat{\tau})\theta$, and $1 - \theta$, respectively. Knowing the state they are in—but not the state in which their partner is—agents take one of two actions: comply or breach. An agent's action may only depend on its own type and current state as well as on the known history of play. If both agents are competent and in the normal state, their payoffs take the familiar Prisoner Dilemma's form shown earlier and reproduced here:

Payoff matrix A		Comply	Breach
	Comply	$\hat{\alpha}, \hat{\alpha}$	$-1, 1$
	Breach	$1, -1$	$0, 0$

with $\hat{\alpha}$ representing agents' profit margin if both comply.[23] If a competent agent is in either the disappearing or breaking-up state, its payoff from compliance is 0 instead of $\hat{\alpha}$. Incompetent agents derive a negative payoff from compliance; for them, cheating is the only way to get a positive payoff.

11.3 Relational Strategies

Having characterized the economy, we now examine the conditions under which relational contracting enables agents to trade. We proceed, first, to define a set of relational strategies. Based on these strategies, we compute expected payoffs conditional upon the state agents are in. Next, we derive the laws of motion of the economy, given these strategies, and we derive the properties of the long-term steady

21. This situation is distinct from one where agents become unable to fulfill a contract due to temporary circumstances beyond their control (e.g., fire, riot, and flood). Such extraordinary circumstances may be ground for excusable default; they are ignored here. In other words, we abstract from efficient breaches (e.g., Craswell 1995; Cooter and Ulen 1988). If gains from trade fall to zero after the transaction is completed, agents may initiate an additional transaction with the intent of breaching the contract. In our model, premeditated and nonpremeditated breaches turn out to be formally equivalent and the distinction is ignored.

22. Consequently there are $2^3 = 8$ possible configurations of player pairs.

23. Gains from trade are divided equally among them so that payoffs are symmetrical. This assumption is not essential; similar results can be derived in a one-sided Prisoner's Dilemma game (see chapter 17). But it simplifies the analysis considerably by eliminating certain forms of strategic interaction, such as breaching a profitable contract to renegotiate its terms.

state. We then study the parameter configurations for which relational strategies are subgame perfect.

Let us define simple relational strategies as strategies in which two agents trade with each other until a breach of contract occurs, at which point they look for another partner. Within this broad class of strategies, we consider one specific set of strategies, which we denote SRS_a, and we show that for some parameter values, it constitutes a subgame perfect equilibrium and satisfies the bilateral rationality condition. Strategies SRS_a are as follows:

Matching stage. At time t, agents offer to continue trading with the agent with whom they were matched in the previous round unless, at $t - 1$, (1) screening revealed that the agent is incompetent, (2) a breach of contract has occurred, or (3) agents discover that they must break up the relationship. In all of these cases the agent seeks a new partner. New agents always seek a new partner.

Contractual stage. Competent agent offers to trade if they have chosen to continue trading with the same partner. In the case of a new match, they offer to trade if the credit report shows that the agent has complied at least once in the past; otherwise they offer to screen.

Compliance stage. Competent agents comply with their contractual obligations unless their payoff falls to 0 (i.e., they disappear or must break the relationship), in which case they breach the contract. Incompetent agents always breach.

No stigma is attached to breach of contract since, with probability 1, all competent eventually breach. Stigma is revised in chapter 12.

We now investigate the conditions under which these strategies form a sustainable, subgame perfect equilibrium, which we denote RE_a. Expected payoffs of incompetent agents are constant and are ignored from now on. Expected long-term payoffs for competent agents are derived as follows: At the beginning of each period, competent agents are in one of three possible states: matched (M), tested and unmatched (U), or untested and unmatched (K). Matched agents are those who are in a long-term relationship. Tested agent are those that have been screened as competent; untested agents are those who have never been screened. Dropping i subscripts for simplicity, we let V_t^M, V_t^K, and V_t^U denote the expected continuation payoff of a matched, unmatched but tested, and untested agent at the beginning of period t, respectively. We get

$$V_t^M = \hat{\alpha}\hat{\tau}^2\theta^2 + (1 - \hat{\tau}^2\theta)\theta\hat{\delta}V_{t+1}^K + \hat{\tau}^2\theta^2\hat{\delta}V_{t+1}^M. \tag{11.1}$$

The first part is the agent's instantaneous payoff times the probability that both agents comply. The second term is the expected continuation payoff if either of the two agents breaks up the relationship and they must each find a new partner. The third term is the continuation payoff if the relationship continues. Equation (11.1) incorporates the fact that disappearing agents have a continuation payoff of 0. To simplify the notation, we let $\tau^2 \equiv \hat{\tau}^2 \theta$, $\delta \equiv \hat{\delta} \theta$, and $\alpha \equiv \hat{\alpha} \theta$. Equation (11.1) can then be rewritten more succinctly as

$$V_t^M = \alpha \tau^2 + (1 - \tau^2) \delta V_{t+1}^K + \tau^2 \delta V_{t+1}^M. \tag{11.2}$$

To derive the expected payoff of unmatched agents, let I_t be the proportion of tested agents at time t, a fraction K_t of which are unmatched at the beginning of the period. Next, let U_t stand for the fraction of untested, and thus unmatched, agents. By construction, $G = I_t + U_t$ at all t. Let μ_t be the proportion of untested agents among the unmatched, and let p_t be the proportion of incompetent agents among the untested. By definition, we have

$$\mu_t \equiv \frac{B + U_t}{B + U_t + K_t}, \tag{11.3}$$

$$p_t \equiv \frac{B}{B + U_t}. \tag{11.4}$$

The expected payoff of a tested unmatched agent V_t^K can then be written

$$\begin{aligned} V_t^K = {} & (1 - \mu_t) \kappa (\alpha \tau^2 + (1 - \tau^2) \delta V_{t+1}^K + \tau^2 \delta V_{t+1}^M) \\ & + [(1 - \mu_t)(1 - \kappa) + \mu_t (1 - p_t)][(1 - \tau^2) \delta V_{t+1}^K + \tau^2 \delta V_{t+1}^M] \\ & + \mu_t p_t \delta V_{t+1}^K - [\mu_t + (1 - \mu_t)(1 - \kappa)] c. \end{aligned} \tag{11.5}$$

The first term represents the expected payoff from being matched with a known tested agent and trading from the start. This option is not open to untested agents because they are indistinguishable from incompetent agents and therefore never trade at their first encounter. The second and third terms are the expected payoff from being matched with an unknown but competent agent, and with an incompetent agent, respectively. The last term is the screening cost. A similar equation can be derived for untested agents:

$$V_t^U = (1 - \mu_t p_t)((1 - \tau^2) \delta V_{t+1}^U + \tau^2 \delta V_{t+1}^M) + \mu_t p_t \delta V_{t+1}^U - c. \tag{11.6}$$

If $\kappa = 0$, it is easy to verify that $V_t^K = V_t^U$ for all t.

Together, equations (11.2), (11.5), and (11.6) constitute a set of recursive equations that can be used to compute agents' payoffs provided that we know μ_t and p_t. Since the number of agents is infinite, the laws of motion of K_t and U_t are given by

$$K_{t+1} = \theta(1 - \tau^2)I_t + \theta\tau^2\mu_t p_t K_t, \tag{11.7}$$

$$U_{t+1} = (1 - \theta)G + \theta[1 - \tau^2(1 - \mu_t p_t)]U_t. \tag{11.8}$$

The economy's laws of motion do not depend on κ_i. This is because, unlike in Kranton (1996a), social networks are not used to speed up the search for reliable commercial partners. The economy starts with all agents in the untested, unmatched category, namely with $U_0 = G$, $I_0 = 0$, and $K_0 = 0$. The initial proportion μ_0 of untested agents in the population is equal to 1. Equations (11.7) and (11.8) constitute a self-contained system of difference equations that describes the law of motion of μ_t and p_t over time. Let p^* and μ^* denote the steady state of this system. Linearizing these equations around p^* and μ^*, it can be verified that the system is locally stable and that it is approached monotonically from below. Numerical simulations further suggest that the system is globally stable and that K_t increases monotonically over time.[24]

The properties of steady state expected payoffs are summarized in the following proposition. All proofs are given in appendix.

PROPOSITION 11.1   Steady state payoffs V^M, V^K, and V^U are increasing in α, κ, δ, and τ and decreasing in c, μ^*, and p^*.

Proposition 11.1 states that agents' payoffs are higher when gains from trade α are larger, when they have a dense network of relations κ, and when relationships last longer (τ large). They are lower when screening costs c are high, the proportion of untested agents μ^* is high, and the proportion of incompetent among the untested p^* is high. The reason is that the more incompetent agents there are in the economy, the more time competent agents waste (on average) trying to find a reliable trading partner. These results are comparable to propositions 4 and 5 in Ghosh and Ray (1996). Since the laws of motion of K_t and U_t do not depend on α, δ, c, or κ, if follows that:

PROPOSITION 11.2   For all t, V_t^M, V_t^K, and V_t^U increase with α, δ, and κ and decrease with c.

---

24. If $\theta = 1$ (competent agents are never renewed), the number of untested agents eventually tends to 0 and $p_* = 1$: in the long run, untested agents are all incompetent. If $\theta < 1$, the presence of newcomers among the unmatched ensures that p_* remains below 1: a certain proportion of unmatched agents remains competent even in the long run. It can also be verified that p^* and μ^* increase with θ. Moreover the proportion of competent agents among the unmatched falls with time and the product $\mu_t p_t \equiv B/(B + U_t + K_t)$ rises monotonically as initially untested agents progressively become known.

Proposition 11.2 generalizes the results of Ghosh and Ray (1996) by showing that important characteristics of the equilibrium around the steady state also hold during transitional dynamics. The proposition implies that returns to social network capital are unambiguously positive: agents with a high κ_i enjoy higher payoffs than those with low κ_i during all trading rounds.[25] They do so because they can save on screening costs and trade immediately. The sharing of information thus improves market efficiency, although reputation is not used to stigmatize cheaters. This kind of reputation effect has been ignored in much of the theoretical literature because agent heterogeneity is typically not considered (e.g., Raub and Weesie 1990; Milgrom et al. 1991; Kandori 1992; Greif 1993; Ellison 1994).

An immediate policy implication is that the welfare of market participants can be raised by favoring the circulation of market information among them. This can be accomplished in various ways, such as by creating a credit reference bureau, circulating information on potential workers, and fostering business associations and meetings. Identification of firms and agents, an essential ingredient of an information-sharing system, can be facilitated by setting up a business registration system. The circulation of inaccurate or ill-intended information can be punished as defamation or fraud. However, as we will demonstrate on the following pages, the circulation of information is not always beneficial.

11.4 Equilibrium Conditions

We now examine the conditions for which relational strategies RE_a form a self-enforcing, subgame perfect equilibrium. Although many individual rationality conditions need to be satisfied, only three types of conditions deserve to be investigated in detail:[26] continuation of relationship (CR) conditions that ensure that matched agents continue to trade with each other, breach deterrence (BD) conditions that ensure that contractual obligations are respected, and willingness to screen (WS) conditions that ensure that agents willingly screen each other.

For CR conditions to be satisfied, agents' payoffs must be higher when matched than unmatched:

$$V_t^M \geq V_t^K. \tag{CR}$$

25. Remember that i subscripts have been dropped from the notation to improve readability but are implicit in propositions 23.1 and 23.0 and all that follows.

26. The others are satisfied trivially and are left as an exercise for the reader.

This is always true since unmatched agents incur the cost of identifying a reliable agent while matched agents do not.[27] Next, consider breach deterrence. In a relational equilibrium, opportunistic breach is deterred by the prospect of having to incur the cost and risk of screening new potential partners. For agents in the "normal" state, the breach deterrence condition is

$$\tau(\alpha + \delta V_{t+1}^M) + (1 - \tau)(-1 + \delta V_{t+1}^K) \geq \tau + \delta V_{t+1}^K,$$

which can be rewritten more simply as

$$V_{t+1}^M - V_{t+1}^K \geq \frac{1 - \alpha\tau}{\tau\delta}. \tag{BD}$$

This condition cannot be satisfied unless V_{t+1}^M is strictly larger than V_{t+1}^K. For agents who have discover that they will disappear or that they must find a new partner deterrence is ineffective, however. To deter willful breach by breaking-up agents, it would have to be true that

$$\tau(1 + \delta V_{t+1}^K) + (1 - \tau)\delta V_{t+1}^K \leq \tau\delta V_{t+1}^K + (1 - \tau)(-1 + \delta V_{t+1}^K),$$

which boils down to $1 \leq 0$, an impossibility. A similar impossibility is found for disappearing agents since their have a zero continuation payoff. Breach by breaking-up agents cannot be fully deterred for two reasons. First, the economy does not stigmatize cheaters and cannot, therefore, penalize breaking-up agents above and beyond the loss that they already suffer from having to end a commercial relationship. This is true even though agents share information about each others through an informal reputation mechanism. Second, the economy is large enough that the chance that agents would be paired with the same agent again in the future is vanishingly small. If the number of agents was finite and sufficiently small, agents would worry that cheating some agents may seriously reduce their chances of finding a new commercial partner—a process that could support cooperation (e.g., Kandori 1992; Ellison 1994). This possibility is ignored here.

Let us now turn to willingness to screen conditions. First, it must be better for unmatched agents to screen unknown agents rather than withdraw from trade altogether:

$$V_t^K \geq 0 WS1K, \tag{11.9}$$

$$V_t^U \geq 0 WS1U. \tag{11.10}$$

27. This can easily be seen by comparing equation (11.3) to equation (11.6).

Second, untested agents must prefer to screen now instead of waiting for the next trading round:

$$V_t^U \geq \delta V_{t+1}^U. \tag{WS2U}$$

Finally, tested agents must prefer to screen now rather than wait until next period in the hope that they will be matched with a known agent and will not have to incur the screening cost:

$$[(1 - \mu_t)(1 - \kappa) + \mu_t(1 - p_t)][(1 - \tau^2)\delta V_{t+1}^K + \tau^2 \delta V_{t+1}^M]$$

$$+ \mu_t p_t \delta V_{t+1}^K - [\mu_t + (1 - \mu_t)(1 - \kappa)]c \geq [\mu_t + (1 - \mu_t)(1 - \kappa)]\delta V_{t+1}^K,$$

which can be rewritten as

$$V_{t+1}^M - V_{t+1}^K \geq \frac{c(\mu_t + (1 - \mu_t)(1 - \kappa))}{\delta \tau^2(\mu_t(1 - p_t) + (1 - \mu_t)(1 - \kappa))}. \tag{WS2K}$$

If either of these conditions is violated, agents refuse to screen unknown agents. If the breach deterrence condition (BD) and the four willingness to screen conditions are satisfied, it can be verified that other individual rationality constraints are satisfied as well. Together, these conditions therefore define the set of model parameters for which the relational equilibrium RE_a is self-enforcing. They can be used to derive the following propositions.

PROPOSITION 11.3   In a relational equilibrium RE_a,

i. Breach cannot be fully deterred and economic efficiency is not achieved.

ii. Breach deterrence is harder when κ is large.

iii. Gains from trade α must be strictly positive.

iv. If $c = 0$ and $\alpha > 0$, willingness to screen conditions are always satisfied.

Proposition 11.3.i is a consequence of the fact that breach by breaking-up agents cannot be deterred. Proposition 11.3.ii follows from the fact that the breach deterrence condition is harder to satisfy when information is shared widely. The reason is again due to the absence of stigma: tested agents trade more easily when unmatched and are thus less penalized if they breach. The larger κ is, the easier it is to trade, and the harder it is to prevent opportunistic breach. Proposition 11.3.iii is an immediate consequence of the breach deterrence condition: for a relational equilibrium to exist, agents must derive strictly positive expected gains from trade; otherwise, they have no incentive to preserve commercial relationships. In these circumstances agents may naturally interpret gains from trade as returns to their social capital in the form of commercial relationships and reputation (Coleman 1988). Proposition 11.3.iv implies that if screening is costless, it is always in an agent's interest to sample unknown firms in the hope of finding a suitable commercial partner. In this case the only equilibrium condition that is possibly binding is equation (BD). A contrario, if screening is costly, it may be better for agents to stop screening altogether or to wait until they are matched with a known firm. To illustrate what patterns of trade may emerge in relational equilibria, two special cases are examined more in detail.

11.5 Pure Relational Equilibria

We now investigate the conditions under which a pure relational equilibria may be self-emerging. Let $\kappa_i = 0$ for all i and modify SRS_a accordingly by instructing agents to screen all unknown agents. Call the result pure relational strategies or PRS_a, and denote the corresponding equilibrium a pure relational equilibrium PRE_a. In the steady state this equilibrium is very similar to that discussed in Ghosh and Ray (1996) and to what Greif (1993) call bilateral punishment strategies.

In PRS_a, equilibrium conditions boil down to $V_t^M - V_t^U \geq (1 - \alpha\tau)/\tau\delta$, equation (BD), and $V_t^U \geq 0$, equation (WS1U).[28] The set of α and c values for which equilibrium conditions in PRS_a are satisfied evolves over time in the manner illustrated in figure 11.2 (see proof of proposition 11.4). II_0 and JJ_0 depict the locus of α and c values such that equilibrium conditions are exactly satisfied at time t_0; II^* and JJ^* represent steady state equilibrium conditions.[29] Values of α and c above the II and JJ lines ensure that a PRE_a exists. It is easy to show that equilibrium conditions are more easily satisfied when relationships are stable (high τ) and agents are patient (high δ).

Two shaded areas, A and B, are of particular importance. For values of α and c in the B shaded area, equilibrium conditions are satisfied in the steady state but not at t_0. The reason is that at $p_0 = B/(B + G)$, unmatched agents find each other easily and the penalty for breach of contract is not strong enough to induce compliance.

---

28. Since $V_t^K = V_t^U$ for all t, conditions (WS1K) and (WS2K) drop out. It is easy to verify that V_t^U and V_t^M unambiguously fall over time. The reason is that the proportion of incompetent agents among the unmatched, $\mu_t p_t$, increases with t: $\mu_t = 1$ for all t and $p_t = B/(B + U_t)$ rises as agents, who initially are all unmatched, progressively identify commercial partners. Condition (WS2U) is thus always satisfied along the equilibrium path.

29. These can be derived algebraically by solving recursive equations (11.2), (11.5) and (11.6) for a fixed V^M and V^U, and replacing μ_t by its steady state value μ^*.

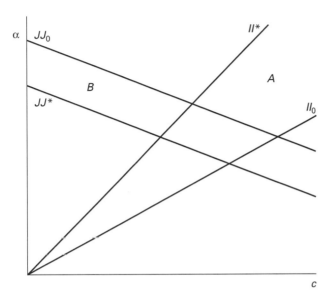

Figure 11.2
Existence of pure relational equilibria

The pure reputational equilibrium is sustainable and locally stable, but it cannot be reached from a no trade situation. A relation-based market fails to emerge even though, if it were there, it would be sustainable. Under these circumstances an unanticipated shock to the economy that would break existing relationships between agents could permanently eliminate trade.[30]

Shaded area A correspond to another scenario, one in which the development of commercial relationships initially satisfies equilibrium conditions, but eventually fails to satisfy $V_t^U \geq 0$: as the number of competent agents among the unmatched falls, unmatched agents eventually find it too costly to sample each other and withdraw from the market. The reason is that as p_t rises, the cost of sampling c is no longer compensated by the hope of finding a reliable long-term partner. This means that PRS_a are not sustainable in the long run; a pure relational equilibrium does not exist. It is possible, however, to find other relational strategies that support trade in the long run (see proof of proposition 11.4). These results are summarized in the following proposition:

---

30. For example, warfare, the expulsion of a merchant group from the country, or a brutal change in economic conditions that calls for a change in trade patterns.

PROPOSITION 11.4   When $\kappa_i = 0$ for all i,

i. A PRE_a is not sustainable if gains from trade α are small and screening costs c are high.

ii. A PRE_a is more likely to be sustainable when relationships are stable (high τ) and agents are patient (high δ).

iii. For α sufficiently high and c sufficiently low, there exists a sustainable, reachable pure relational equilibrium of the first kind PRE_a; market emergence is spontaneous.

iv. For certain values of α and a low enough c, PRE_a may be sustainable but not reachable from $U_0 = G$. Spontaneous market emergence does not occur; shocks may destroy markets.

v. For certain values of α and a high enough screening cost c, PRS_a are satisfied at $t = 0$ but not at the steady state. Alternative equilibrium relational strategies nevertheless exist, but at the steady state a fraction of competent agents are shut out from trade.

History abounds with examples of trading relationships that resemble pure relational strategies, such as the spice and silk trade of the pre-industrial world (Braudel 1986), long-distance cattle and kola trade in West Africa (Hopkins 1973), or gold trade along the Zambezi river (Shillington 1989). These ancient patterns of trade have in common to be highly profitable (high α) and, if undisturbed, extremely stable over time (high τ). Yet history suggests that they often are vulnerable to temporary trade disruptions in the sense that once trading routes are disturbed by warfare or political turmoil, these routes are difficult to reestablish.

It is still possible to find examples of similar trade patterns in contemporary Africa (e.g., Jones 1959; Meillassoux 1971; Amselle 1977; Staatz 1979). One of the reasons is that the semi-legal nature of much cross-border African trade precludes recourse to courts. In addition the small size of the transactions implies that suing is seldom an attractive option. The embryonic manufacturing sector of Ghana operates largely in the same manner (e.g., Cuevas et al. 1993; Fafchamps 1996). The reason appears to be that the Levantine businessmen who run much the country's manufacturing sector are prohibited by law to run trading businesses. As a result they find themselves sandwiched between suppliers and clients from other ethnic groups with whom socialization and thus the exchange of information is problematic. Trade in illegal drugs is another contemporary example of a pattern of exchange essentially based on relational contracting: the illegal nature of the trade prevents the use of courts to enforce contracts, while the fear of informants complicates the exchange of business information. Efforts by drug enforcement agencies to disrupt trade channels (e.g., by arresting dealers) in the hope of permanently stopping trade can be seen as an application of proposition 11.4.iv. As part i of proposition 11.4 suggests, however, these efforts are bound to fail if gains from trade are sufficiently large.

11.6   Closed-Shop Equilibria

Things are somewhat different if agents exchange information. To focus on an interesting special case, we assume that competent agents are renewed slowly or are not renewed at all. To keep the notation simple, we assume that $\kappa = 1$. In this case equilibrium conditions simplify to the following:

$$V_{t+1}^{M} - V_{t+1}^{K} \geq \frac{1 - \alpha\tau}{\tau\delta} BD', \tag{11.11}$$

$$V_{t+1}^{M} - V_{t+1}^{K} \geq \frac{c}{\delta\tau^2(1 - p_t)} WS2K', \tag{11.12}$$

plus (11.9), (WS2U), and (11.10).

From proposition 11.3.iv we know that willingness to screen conditions are automatically satisfied when $c = 0$. It is then easy to verify that parameter values exist such that breach of contract can be deterred by SRS_a strategies. When $c > 0$, however, condition (11.12) is impossible to satisfy for values of p_t close enough to 1. In this case SRS_a are unsustainable in the long run. The reason is that tested agents cannot be convinced to incur screening cost $c > 0$ in order to sample untested agents when the latter are, in their great majority, incompetent. Tested agents prefer to limit their dealings to tested agents whom they can immediately trust. Since $p_t \rightarrow 1$ as $t \rightarrow \infty$ when agents are not renewed (i.e., when $\theta = 1$), we get the following proposition:

PROPOSITION 11.5   If $\kappa = 1$, $\delta < 1$, $c > 0$, and $\theta = 1$, the RE_a is unsustainable in the long run.

By extension, RE_a is unsustainable for θ or κ close enough to 1. This, however, does not imply that no transaction can ever occur between tested and untested agents. In early periods the number of tested agents K_t is small and competent agents U_t constitute a large proportion of all untested agents. In this case, waiting to be matched with another tested agent would take too long; screening untested agents, even though it means incurring screening cost c, is likely to constitute a more profitable alternative. This leads to the following proposition:

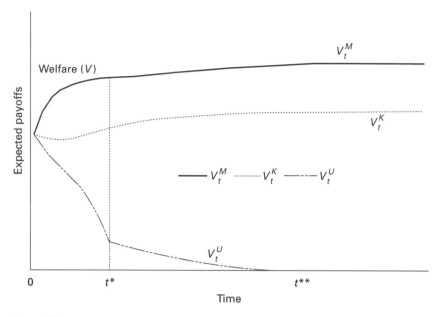

Figure 11.3
Closed-shop equilibrium

PROPOSITION 11.6   If $\kappa = 1$, $\theta = 1$, and $c > 0$,

i. There exist parameter values for which a relational equilibrium is sustainable. This equilibrium involves changes of strategies over time.

ii. There is a time $t^* \geq 0$ such that for all $t < t^*$, SRS_a satisfy equilibrium conditions, and for all $t \geq t^*$, tested agents refuse to transact with untested agents. After t^*, absorption of agents into the group of tested agents is slower than before t^*.

iii. There is a time $t^{**} \geq t^*$ such that for all $t \geq t^{**}$, untested agents refuse to screen each other. After t^{**}, untested agent are permanently excluded from trade.

The evolution of equilibrium payoffs implied by proposition 11.6 is illustrated in figure 11.3.[31] The proposition implies that, if screening is costly, firms are long lasting, and information circulates freely among them, then trade is likely to take a "closed-shop" form: established firms deal only with other established firms and refuse to even consider unknown agents as potential partners.[32] The reason is that

31. Figure 11.3 shows the result of a computer simulation using the following parameter values: $\theta = 1$, $\kappa = 1$, $\delta = 0.95$, $\tau = 0.95$, $\alpha = 0.3$, $c = 0.05$, $B = 2/3$, $G = 1/3$.

32. A similar result is derived by Taylor (2000) using different assumptions and a static setup.

there are too few competent agents among the unknown, untested agents, and it would be too costly to identify them. In such a world, agents with no payment history find it difficult if not impossible to be given a chance to prove themselves: the deck is stacked against newcomers. Possible real life examples of such equilibria include, for instance, the difficulties that young inexperienced workers often encounter getting their first job, and the problems that start-up companies face in qualifying for credit from banks and suppliers. Similar examples can be found in developing countries where a closely knit business community has a hold on a particular economic activity: for instance, the Chinese in Indonesia, the Asians in Kenya, or the whites in Zimbabwe. Proposition 11.6 suggests that this hold is strongest in societies where economic opportunities are unchanging over time (high τ) and firms are long lasting (high θ).

A corollary of proposition 11.6 is that setting up a mechanism to improve the circulation of business information among agents—such as a credit reference bureau—may result in excluding from the market those firms that have not yet established a name for themselves. Allowing established firms to better exchange information among themselves indeed makes it easier for them to identify each other—and thus to economize on screening costs by waiting to be matched with each other. Empirical work on Ghana, Kenya, and Zimbabwe manufacturing suggests that widespread circulation of information may indeed be detrimental to newcomers (e.g., Cuevas et al. 1993; Fafchamps et al. 1994, 1995; Fafchamps 1996). The three countries differ greatly in the extent to which manufacturing firms exchange information. For reasons discussed earlier, Ghanaian manufacturers share little information. In contrast, Kenyan manufacturers, who are predominantly of Asian origin, informally exchange information among themselves. In addition to informal information sharing, Zimbabwe has a credit reference bureau. Of these three countries, it is also the one where manufacturing appears the most closed to newcomers, especially blacks, while Kenya occupies an intermediate position and Ghana is the most open (e.g., Fafchamps 1996, 1997c). This evidence is only suggestive, given that it is based on a small number of case studies in three countries, but it is consistent with the idea that information sharing may hurt newcomers. This issue deserves further investigation.

11.7 Conclusion

This chapter has examined the conditions by which decentralized market exchange may emerge in the absence of external enforcement. We have seen that the presence of "bad" types in the economy can serve as disciplining device. Economic agents form long-term economic relationships to minimize screening costs—namely the costs associated with the building of trust that we discussed in part III.

Information sharing about agents' types improves efficiency because it enables connected agents to skip the trial period. But it reduces the penalty for breach and can thus undermine the decentralized market equilibrium. It can also result in closed-shop equilibria where certain agents are shut off from trade.

What this chapter does not elucidate is whether sharing information about agents' behavior can be used to better deter breach. To this we now turn.

11.8 Appendix: Proofs of Propositions

Proof of Proposition 11.1   First, solve equations (11.2), (11.5), and (11.6) for constant V^M, V^K, and V^U. Convoluted algebraic expressions result, one of which is shown below:

$$V^M = \frac{\alpha\tau^2(1 - \delta - \delta\kappa\mu + \delta\tau^2 + \delta\kappa\mu\tau^2 - \delta\mu p\tau^2) - c\delta(1 - \kappa + \kappa\mu)(1 - \tau^2)}{1 - \delta - \delta\kappa + \delta\kappa\tau^2 - \delta\mu p\tau^2 - \delta^2\mu p\tau^2}. \quad (11.13)$$

Differentiating V^M, V^K, and V^U with respect to various parameters yields complicated expressions like the one shown below:

$$\frac{\partial V^M}{\partial \alpha} = \frac{\tau^2(1 - \delta(1 - \mu p\tau^2(1 - \delta)) - \delta\kappa\mu(1 - \tau^2))}{1 - \delta(1 - \mu p\tau^2(1 - \delta)) - \delta\kappa(1 - \tau^2))} > 0. \quad (11.14)$$

Careful analysis such as the one illustrated above makes it possible to sign the various derivatives.   ∎

Proof of Proposition 11.2   Using equations (11.2), (11.5), and (11.6), apply backward induction to proposition 11.1, noting that μ_t and p_t are unaffected by changes in α, δ, κ, or c.   ∎

Proof of Proposition 11.3   The first part follows from the text and the fact that $\alpha + 0 > -1 + 1$: cheating at the end of a relationship is inefficient. To show the second part, we solve for steady state values V^M and V^K and compute the difference between the two. We get

$$V^M - V^K = \frac{(c + \alpha\tau^2)(1 - \kappa(1 - \mu))}{1 - \delta\mu p\tau^2}. \quad (11.15)$$

It clear that $V^M - V^K$ is a decreasing function of κ. This result can be extended to all periods using a recursive argument.

For the third part, combining all the willingness to screen conditions, we get that $V_t^K \geq 0$: since trade is voluntary, agents cannot be forced below their autarkic payoff. Consequently V_t^M must be strictly positive for (BD) to be satisfied. For this to be true, α must itself be strictly positive.

For the fourth part, if $c = 0$, V_t^U must be ≥ 0: the worst thing that could happen to an untested firm would be to be matched repeatedly with incompetent firms as then its expected discounted payoff would be 0. This takes care of condition (11.10). Since $\alpha > 0$, V_t^K and V_t^M are also ≥ 0. From this it follows that the other willingness to screen conditions are satisfied as well.   ∎

Proof of Proposition 11.4   Equilibrium conditions (BD) and (WS1U) define a locus of values of α and c below which a TBE is not sustainable. To investigate the long-term sustainability of a TBE, we evaluate these two conditions at the long-run steady state. Solving for the steady state values of V_t^M and V_t^U, we get

$$V^M = \frac{\alpha\tau^2(1 - \delta + \delta\tau^2 - \delta p\tau^2) - c\delta(1 - \tau^2)}{(1 - \delta)(1 - \delta p\tau^2)}, \tag{11.16}$$

$$V^U = \frac{\alpha\delta\tau^4(1 - p) - c(1 - \delta\tau^2)}{(1 - \delta)(1 - \delta p\tau^2)}. \tag{11.17}$$

Plugging the above into the two equilibrium conditions and solving for α and c, we get

$$\alpha = \frac{1 - \delta p\tau^2 - c\delta\tau}{\tau(1 + \delta\tau^2 - \delta p\tau^2)}, \tag{11.18}$$

$$\alpha = \frac{c(1 - \delta\tau^2)}{\delta\tau^4(1 - p)}. \tag{11.19}$$

The two lines intersect at $\alpha^* = (1 - \delta\tau^2)/\tau$ and $c^* = \delta(1 - p)\tau^3$. It is easy to verify that the shape of the sustainable set is as depicted in figure 11.2 where the JJ' and II' lines represent the two above equations. This proves part i.

To show part ii, note that $\partial\alpha/\partial\tau \leq 0$ and $\partial\alpha/\partial\delta \leq 0$ in both equations. Higher values of τ and δ thus shift both II' and JJ' downward, making it easier for a TBE to be sustainable.

To show part iii, it suffices to show that II and JJ shift over time as shown in figure 11.2. This can be demonstrated with the following recursive argument. Let T be the time at which V_t^M and V_t^U reach their steady state values. Then

$$V_{T-1}^U = (1 - p_{T-1})((1 - \tau^2)\delta V_T^U + \tau^2\delta V_{T-1}^M) + p_{T-1}\delta V_T^U - c, \tag{11.20}$$

which is above V_T^U since $p_{T-1} < p_T$. Since V_{T-1}^U is larger than V_T^U, the willingness to screen constraint $V_t^0 \geq 0$ is easier to satisfy and *JJ* shifts clockwise as one goes back in time (see figure 11.2). Using the fact that

$$V_T^M - V_T^U = (c + \alpha\tau^2)/(1 - \delta p_T \tau^2),$$

we also get

$$V_{T-1}^M - V_{T-1}^U = \frac{c + \alpha\tau^2}{1 - \delta p_T \tau^2}(1 - \delta\tau^2(p_T - p_{T-1})) > \frac{c + \alpha\tau^2}{1 - \delta p_T \tau^2}. \tag{11.21}$$

The breach deterrence constraint is thus harder to satisfy as one goes back in time and the *II* locus shifts down as shown in figure 11.2.

Part iv follows from the text. To show part v, we simply need to find other relational strategies that support trade in the long run. One such set of strategies, which we denote PRS_b, has two parts: the first part is exactly like PRS_a, and is played until the proportion p_t of incompetent agents among the unknown rises so much that V_t^U approaches zero. At that point agents are requested to switch to randomized screening whereby only a fraction of unknown agents are screened in any period. By choosing the proportion of screened agents just right, p_t can be maintained at a level such that V_t^U remains exactly zero forever. At that point unmatched agents are indifferent between screening and not screening, and the willingness to screen condition is satisfied exactly. For those who find this kind of coordinated randomization unlikely, we propose a set of pure strategies, denoted $PRS_{b'}$, that closely approximates PRS_b. In $PRS_{b'}$, agents are instructed to screen all unknown agents until V_t^U falls below zero, at which point all screening stops. When this happens, the law of motion of the system is temporarily replaced with

$$U_{t+1} = (1 - \tau^2)(G - U_t) + U_t. \tag{11.22}$$

As a result of the breakup of relationships and replacement of agents, the number of unmatched competent agents begins to rise, hence driving p_t down. After a while, V_t^U becomes positive again. At this point agents are again instructed to screen all unknown agents until V_t^U again falls below zero, at which point they again stop screening. The cycle is then repeated ad infinitum, and the economy oscillates around a value of p that satisfies $V^U = 0$. With either PRS_b or $PRS_{b'}$, relational markets emerge spontaneously, but in the long run not all unknown agents get instantly screened. Market participation is interrupted for some agents who are denied screening and cannot prove their worth. This completes the proof.   ∎

Proof of Proposition 11.5   All we need to show is that the left-hand side of (11.9) is bounded below ∞. It is easy to see that V_t^M is bounded from above by $\alpha/(1-\delta)$: agents cannot receive more than the equivalent of full gains from trade every period. From (11.9), $V_t^K \geq 0$. The difference $V_t^M - V_t^K$ is thus bounded by $\alpha/(1-\delta)$. As long as $\delta < 1$, there exists a p_t close enough to 1 such that (11.9) is violated. $\blacksquare$

Proof of Proposition 11.6   From the text we see that there exist a t^* such that, if agents follow SRS_a,

$$V_{t+1}^M - V_{t+1}^K \geq \frac{c}{\delta\tau^2(1-p_t)} \tag{11.23}$$

for $t \leq t^*$, and

$$V_{t+1}^M - V_{t+1}^K < \frac{c}{\delta\tau^2(1-p_t)} \tag{11.24}$$

for $t > t^*$. Tested agents K_t initially find it profitable to sample untested agents U_t, but they stop doing so beyond t^* when K_t gets too large and U_t too small. At this point the economy must switch to another set of strategies in which tested agents no longer trade with untested agents. Call this set of strategies SRS_c. In SRS_c, tested agents are instructed not to screen untested agents but to wait for a match with another tested agent instead. As long as $V_t^U \geq 0$, untested agents continue to sample other untested agents. By screening each other, untested agents may still join the ranks of tested agents K_t. In a SRS_c, agents' payoff are defined as follows:

$$V_t^M = \alpha\tau + (1-\tau^2)\delta V_{t+1}^K + \tau^2\delta V_{t+1}^M, \tag{11.25}$$

$$V_t^K = (1-\mu_t)[\alpha\tau + (1-\tau^2)\delta V_{t+1}^K + \tau^2\delta V_{t+1}^M] + \mu_t\delta V_{t+1}^K, \tag{11.26}$$

$$V_t^U = (1-\mu_t+\mu_t p_t)\delta V_{t+1}^U + \mu_t(1-p_t)[(1-\tau^2)\delta V_{t+1}^U + \tau^2\delta V_{t+1}^M] - \mu_t c. \tag{11.27}$$

The corresponding law of motion for U_t is now

$$U_{t+1} = [1 - \mu_t\tau^2(1-p_t)]U_t, \tag{11.28}$$

which implies slower absorption into the ranks of tested agents. If the (WS2K$'$) condition is violated at time 0, but $V_t^U \geq 0$, then $t^* = 0$, and the economy begins with SRS_c from the start. Otherwise, SRS_a are followed until t^*, at which point agents spontaneously switch to SRS_b.

This is not the end of the story, however. If SRS_c strategies are followed indefinitely until all competent agents have been tested and $p = 1$, the steady state value of V^U will be

$$V_R^U = -\frac{c\mu}{(1-\delta)}, \tag{11.29}$$

which, for $c > 0$, violates the $V_t^U \geq 0$ equilibrium condition. This implies that there is yet another time, say t^{**}, beyond which V_t^U falls below 0. Beyond that point, untested agents find it too risky to screen each other, and the population of untested agents remains constant. The economy then operates in a closed-shop relational equilibrium: only tested agents trade with each other; untested agents remain excluded permanently. If $V_0^U < 0$, competent agents, who by assumption are all untested in period 0, never transact, never acquire reputation, and a relational equilibrium does not exist. This completes the proof.   ∎

12 Decentralized Reputational Penalties

In the previous chapter we observed that exchange can take place in the absence of formal institutions for the enforcement of contracts. Unlike much of the theoretical literature on informal contract enforcement, we did so without resorting to any coordinated punishment strategy. Instead, we showed that the value that agents attach to commercial relationships can be sufficient to deter breach of contract whenever agents are heterogeneous. Better deterrence could, however, be achieved if breach of contract resulted in permanent exclusion from trade. Indeed, we saw in section 11.1 that in an equilibrium where breach is not sanctioned by permanent exclusion from trade, a commercial relationship always ends with a breach of contract.

In this chapter we examine the conditions under which the threat of exclusion may be credible even without coordination among agents, that is, without meta-punishment. We show that reputational equilibria in which cheaters are permanently excluded from trade (e.g., Kandori 1992; Greif 1993) are not decentralizable unless breach of contract is interpreted as a sign of impending bankruptcy.

The basic intuition of our argument is as follows:[1] Agents who know they are leaving the business have no incentive to comply with their contractual obligations. Consequently they are willing to take on contractual obligations they cannot fulfill and go bankrupt.[2] We begin by showing that permanent exclusion of known cheaters serves as an additional deterrent to opportunistic breach. We then examine the conditions under which permanent exclusion is self-enforcing. We show that breach of contract may trigger permanent exclusion from trade if it is interpreted as a signal of impending bankruptcy. Self-enforcement then comes from what breachers reveal about themselves.[3]

12.1 Exclusion from Trade

We now investigate strategies in which agents who breach contracts are stigmatized and permanently excluded from trade. We keep the modeling apparatus developed in

---

1. An ingenious example of self-enforcing exclusion can be found in Greif (1993). Using a stylized model of merchant-agent relations, Greif shows that when other merchants punish deviant agents, it is not in any merchant's interest to trade with a cheater. The reason is that a cheater must receive a higher wage to be deterred from cheating again. Although formally appealing, Greif's approach requires that merchants extract all gains from trade, subject to the agents' participation constraint. If, in contrast, gains from trade are shared by both parties, as is implicitly assumed here, cheaters could presumably propose to take a lower share of the gains in order to resume trade. In this case the threat of exclusion would no longer be credible.

2. We abstract from legal penalties attached to fraudulent bankruptcy.

3. When agents receive credit from multiple sources, breach of contract can lead all sources of credit to withdraw their support simultaneously, thereby precipitating the firm's demise. This may serve as additional deterrent to breach of contract. A formalization of some of these arguments can be found in the literature on bank runs (Diamond and Dybvig 1983).

the previous chapter, and we continue to assume that agents do not observe the other party's gains from trade, even ex post. Since agents cannot verify the conditions of a breach, all breaches must be equally punished. Let us define stigma-augmented relational strategies (*SARS*) as strategies in which only agents who are incompetent or going out of business cheat. Other agents never cheat, even at the end of a relationship. Cheaters are stigmatized: if they are matched with a competent agent who knows them, the agent refuses to trade with them. When matched with unknown agents, cheaters follow simple relational strategies. For the surplus, strategies are identical to simple relational strategies.

Since there is less cheating, the following proposition obtains:

PROPOSITION 12.1   Expected payoffs, and thus market efficiency, are higher when agents follow stigma-augmented relational strategies instead of simple relational strategies.

Conditions for $SARS_a$ to form a subgame perfect equilibrium are largely unchanged, except for a new breach deterrence condition along the equilibrium path:

$$\delta V_{t+1}^K \geq \theta + \delta V_{t+1}^C, \qquad\qquad\qquad\qquad\qquad\qquad (\text{BD}'')$$

where V_{t+1}^C is the expected payoff to a one-time cheater. Manipulating equation (11.8) and combining it with payoff functions implied by the *SARS* yields the following proposition:

PROPOSITION 12.2

i. Stigma-augmented relational strategies become more easily sustainable over time.

ii. Stigma-augmented relational strategies are more likely to be sustainable if κ is large for all agents.

The reason for proposition 12.2.i is simply that the gap between the expected payoff of a cheater V_t^C and that of an established noncheater V_t^K increases over time, hence making equation (11.8) easier to satisfy. The gap increases because the proportion of tested agents among the competent agents rises over time, making it difficult for cheaters to establish relationships with untested competent firms. Proposition 12.2.ii follows from the fact that deterrence is more effective when the probability of punishment is higher.

An immediate corollary of proposition 12.2 is that stigmatization is ineffective with entirely unknown agents, that is, agents whose $\kappa_i = 0$. Trade with such agents is only feasible via simple relational strategies. If agents differ with respect to their κ_i, stigmatization may be feasible only within a closely knit group. This opens the door to more complicated strategies, whereby agents play stigma-augmented strategies with certain agents and relational strategies with others. For lack of space, we do not explore this possibility here, but it fits rather well the way Kenyan manufacturing firms interact: while Asian entrepreneurs share information with each other and refuse to deal with Asian cheaters, African entrepreneurs do not (Fafchamps et al. 1994). A similar contrast among various business groups could be observed in Zimbabwe (e.g., Fafchamps et al. 1995; Fafchamps 1997c). Further analysis is found in Fafchamps (2000).

Proposition 12.2 implies that changing one's identity must be sufficiently costly for an *SARS* to constitute a subgame perfect equilibrium. An *SARS* cannot exist if agents who opportunistically breach a contract can subsequently hide among unknown agents. Stigmatization requires a precise way of identifying agents. In the absence of a formal identification system—such as business registration or an identity card system—stigmatization must remain confined to face-to-face interaction. This may explain why the threat of stigmatization is largely ineffective against so-called informal sector firms which, as a rule, are not registered—and hence why transactions among informal sector firms remain quite unsophisticated. Interviews with entrepreneurs in Africa further suggest that running away to one's village—and resurfacing later with a different identity—is a widely used strategy to escape contractual obligations. Such strategies are typically not available to expatriate communities, a feature that may explain why stigmatization is easier among them and hence why breach is more easily deterred. This feature alone could explain why expatriate communities dominate business in many agrarian societies of the Third World.

Finally, we note that an *SARS* shares essentially the same willingness to screen conditions as the simple relational equilibria discussed in section 12.1. Consequently propositions 11.5 and 11.6 also apply. For instance, if $c > 0$, $\kappa = 1$, and $\theta = 1$, established agents eventually refuse to trade with untested agents. Stigmatization does not preclude closed-shop equilibria.

12.2 Self-enforcing Stigmatization

We now investigate the circumstances under which the stigmatization of cheaters is self-enforcing, that is, does not require that agents who trade with cheaters be themselves punished.[4] We begin by noting that cheaters lucky enough to find someone willing to trade with them cannot be deterred from breaching the contract at the

---

4. In this case stigmatization satisfies the bilateral rationality condition of Ghosh and Ray (1996) and is also renegotiation-proof.

end of the relationship: in their case (BD″) cannot be satisfied since δV_t^C cannot be greater than $\theta + \delta V_t^C$.[5] During the relationship, however, breach deterrence is easier (i.e., $V_t^N - V_t^C \geq V_t^M - V_t^K$). This is because a cheater has a harder time finding a new partner, making a commercial relationship more valuable to him or her than to a noncheater. Cheaters can therefore credibly promise that they will not cheat again[6] while at the same time proposing to split gains from trade differently, such as by offering a bribe b whereby the cheater gets a cooperation payoff of $\alpha - b$ and the stigmatization buster gets $\alpha + b$. Cheaters may therefore escape exclusion by credibly promising to amend their ways while at the same time anticipatively compensating the other agent for the fact that they will cheat at the end of the relationship. The threat of permanent exclusion from trade is thus not credible and a stigma-augmented relational strategy is unsustainable without meta-punishment.

There is, however, one possible mechanism by which stigmatization can be self-enforcing. So far we have postulated that with probability $1 - \theta$, competent agents leave business and are immediately replaced by new, untested competent agents. We now assume, instead, that these agents remain in the economy. Since these agents do not derive any gain from trade, they have no incentive to honor contracts. Like incompetent agents, they take advantage of every opportunity to cheat, but unlike them, they have been "tested" by the market and enjoy a long history of honored contracts. In a simple relational equilibrium they could offer to trade with the tested agent they are matched with—and profit by cheating them. All they would have to do is to claim that they cheated their previous commercial partner because they had discovered they needed to find a new partner, an event that affects all agents with probability $1 - \tau$. In a simple relational equilibrium therefore, agents going out of business would find it in their interest to remain in the economy only to cheat others.

Things are different with *SARS* because agents are instructed not to trade with known cheaters. The threat of exclusion deters cheating by all agents except those who have nothing to gain from any future trade. In equilibrium therefore, all cheaters are either incompetent or going out of business, and no competent agent should deal with them. Refusing to deal with cheaters is then self-enforcing and the threat of exclusion credible.[7]

That *SARS* are self-enforcing does not guarantee that a stigma-augmented relational equilibrium or *SARE* is the only possible equilibrium configuration. Consider

5. The expected loss from breach of contract at the end of a relationship may, theoretically, discourage agents to deal with cheaters, but in practice, the loss is not discovered until some (distant) time in the future.

6. Except at the end of the relationship.

7. Agents may even be willing to pay a credit reference bureau for the names of cheaters.

an agent who is matched with a known cheater. If all cheaters are incompetent or going out of business, refusing to trade is optimal. If, however, most cheaters are competent agents who follow simple relational strategies, trading is optimal. There will therefore be parameter configurations in which two rational expectations equilibria are possible, one in which agents believe cheaters to be incompetent or bankrupt, in which case competent agents never cheat, and one in which agents believe most cheaters are competent agents who reached the end of a relationship, in which case cheating at the end of a relationship is not deterred. The first equilibrium is an *SRE*, and the second an *SARE*.[8] These results can be summarized in the following proposition:

PROPOSITION 12.3

i. An *SARE* can be self-enforcing if agents going out of business remain in the economy.

ii. There exist parameter vectors for which both an *SRE* and an *SARE* exist and are self-enforcing; the *SARE* is Pareto superior to the *SRE*.

12.3 Spontaneous Market Emergence

We are now in a position to speculate as to how markets may spontaneously emerge in the absence of any formal institutions for the enforcement of private contracts.[9] We first discuss the conditions required for exchange to be initiated. We then examine how the sharing of information among agents leads to an increase in the role of information and generates returns to social connectedness. Finally, we demonstrate that given the right conditions such as a major economic downturn, agents may spontaneously switch to a higher level of breach deterrence in which all cheaters are permanently excluded from trade.

12.3.1 The Initiation of Exchange

What makes relational contracting a convincing working hypothesis about the way markets emerge is that unlike other equilibrium concepts discussed in the literature (Kandori 1992), it does not require any coordination. One could possibly argue that if all agents are cheating on all transactions, it is not in anyone's interest to contract, so markets may never emerge. No trade is thus always a possible equilibrium.

---

8. For another example of multiple signaling equilibria, see the model of criminal deterrence presented by Rasmusen (1996).

9. Formal institutions may nevertheless be required to define and protect property rights (North 1990).

If the conditions for a simple relational equilibrium are satisfied, however, no trade violates the bilateral rationality condition of Ghosh and Ray (1996). It is also not renegotiation-proof. All that is required to initiate market exchange is for two deviant players to take the risk of what Axelrod (1984) calls "brave reciprocity" with each other. Once trade is initiated between these two agents, breaches are even easier to deter than when all agents follow a simple relational strategies because the penalty for cheating in a no-trade equilibrium is a zero payoff forever. When *SRE* conditions are satisfied, a no-trade equilibrium is thus also not evolutionary stable.

The mere presence of gains from trade is not, however, sufficient for trade to take place if external breach deterrence is absent. Unless opportunistic breach of contract is deterred by market discipline, agents will optimally choose not to initiate exchange. It is thus quite possible to observe situations in which trade appears beneficial but fails to occur. For trade to be initiated, gains from trade must rise above a certain threshold sufficient to compensate agents for the cost of screening potential partners and incur some opportunistic breaches. As proposition 11.4 demonstrated, this threshold is higher before a market has emerged than after it is in place. Spontaneous market emergence thus requires that gains from trade be sufficiently high. Once trade has started, however, market exchange may continue even if gains from trade α subsequently fall. Market emergence is thus a path-dependent process: abnormally high arbitrage opportunities can induce agents to take the risk of trading. Once established, trade patterns become somewhat resilient to variations in returns to arbitrage and other gains from trade.

12.3.2 From Pure Relational Contracting to Reputation-Based Contracting

In the absence of any information about other agents, agents are likely to proceed with caution. Their first goal is to identify a reliable commercial partner. This may take some time, given the presence of incompetent agents in the economy. Having found one, they continue to trade with each other until one of them finds the relationship no longer profitable. At that point, breach of contract occurs and both agents look for another partner. Markets at the early stage of their development is thus characterized by pure relational contracting.

At times goes on, however, the population of tested agents grows. Circulating the names of tested agents reduces screening costs. Reputation becomes important. Agents may begin spending resources to expand their information network and raise κ_i, a form of social capital on which they can capitalize (proposition 11.2). If the rate at which economic agents are renewed is low (θ high) and if information circulates widely among agents, the economy eventually reaches a stage at which tested agents refuse to deal with untested agents. The reason is that over time most competent agents have been uncovered and remaining unmatched agents are mostly incompetent. For a while untested competent agents may continue to trade with each other, but eventually they find that the expected gain from identifying a reliable agent among the unmatched is more than outweighed by the cost of finding one. The economy then reaches a steady state in which established firms trade exclusively with each other and net new entry is zero. Prospective entrants must wait until one of the "in" agents retires and makes room for them.

By contrast, if agents are renewed fairly rapidly, as would be the case if new firms are regularly created and new entrepreneurs enter the market, screening of untested agents continues indefinitely. Established firms conserve sufficient hope of finding competent agents among the unmatched to induce them to incur the screening cost. In this case markets are somewhat less inimical to start-ups and newcomers, although the latter still have to be screened before joining the mainstream. This nevertheless supposes that a sufficiently large proportion of newcomers are competent. If many of them are not, a self-disciplining market may be quite inimical to newcomers, closing its doors to numerous promising agents because it would be too costly to screen them all.

12.3.3   The Emergence of Stigmatization

As is clear from the contrast between sections 12.1 and 12.2, information sharing is not a sufficient condition for exclusion from trade as a collective punishment to be implementable in a decentralized manner—that is, without meta-punishment. For exclusion to be self-enforcing, agents must interpret breach as a signal of impending bankruptcy—that is, of a change in type from competent to incompetent. We now investigate the conditions under which the economy may switch spontaneously from simple reputation-based contracting to stigma-augmented relational contracting or *SARE*.

We know from proposition 12.2 that an *SARE* is hard to get started: the presence of lots of untested firms in the economy makes it easy for cheaters to avoid immediate punishment. An emerging market is therefore unlikely to take the form of an *SARE* right from the start. The question then arises: Could an economy naturally evolve from an *SRE* into an *SARE*? We know that an *SARE* gets more easily sustainable as the proportion of established agents among the unmatched rises over time (proposition 12.2). Therefore, even if the conditions for an *SARE* are not initially be satisfied, they eventually may. This can be illustrated as follows: Suppose that *SARE* conditions are not satisfied at t_0 and that the economy follows simple reputation-based contracting—the SRE_a path. Assume further that as p_t rises, *SARE* conditions—and in particular, the breach deterrence condition (BD″)—become satisfied at t_1. It follows from proposition 12.2 that they are also satisfied for all $t \geq t_1$. By proposition 12.3.ii, however, we know that the economy may not automatically switch to the superior $SARE$ because multiple equilibria are possible.

How can the switch to the superior equilibrium take place then? One possibility is for agents to coordinate their actions. Once agents have agreed to refuse to trade with cheaters, breach of contract is prevented, and, by proposition 12.3.ii, the $SARE$ is self-enforcing. How such a coordinated change of strategy can be achieved is unclear, however. In their detailed study of a Moroccan market in the 1950s, Geertz et al. (1979) report that religious authorities and business leaders play an important role in defining norms of acceptable commercial conduct and in sanctioning deviations. Such institutions could possibly use their moral authority to promote the switch to higher standards of business ethics and favor the stigmatization of opportunistic breach of contract. Another possibility is that agents might get so aggravated at being cheated that they threaten all their business acquaintances with commercial and social retaliation if they deal with cheaters. Although such an action is not rational, it may be sufficient to trigger the switch to an $SARE$. The belief that opportunistic breach of contract results in ostracism is easier to generate if members of the group feel a sense of moral outrage toward breach of commercial contracts. This feature may help explain why social norms, in general—and religion, in particular—play an important role in market emergence (e.g., Geertz et al. 1979; Ensminger 1992; Platteau 1994a, 1994b; Greif 1993, 1994).

There exists another decentralized avenue through which an economy could spontaneously switch from an SRE to an $SARE$. In an SRE there are three types of cheaters among unmatched agents: incompetent agents, agents going out of business, and competent agents in search of a new partner. The latter should be contracted with, the first two should be avoided. It is intuitively clear that if the first two categories represent a high enough proportion of cheaters, agents will refuse to deal with all cheaters. To show this formally, let D_t be number of agents going out of business but still present in the economy, and let d_t denote their proportion among the unmatched:

$$d_t = \frac{D_t}{B + U_t + K_t + D_t}. \tag{12.1}$$

Define d_t^* as the value of d_t that would make agents indifferent between trading and not trading with cheaters. If, somewhere along the SRE equilibrium path, the actual proportion of agents going out of business, d_t, rises above d_t^*, agents refuse to deal with known cheaters. If this moment arises at $t \geq t_1$, the economy switches from the

SRE to the superior *SARE*. The change occurs suddenly but in a decentralized manner.

To demonstrate this possibility, suppose that bankrupt agents never leave the economy:

$$D_{t+1} = D_t + (1 - \theta)I_t. \tag{12.2}$$

This assumption is unrealistic, but it is made for the sake of illustration. It is then possible to show that the economy eventually switches from an *SRE* to an *SARE* equilibrium:

PROPOSITION 12.4

i. $0 < d_t^* < 1$.

ii. There exists a time t_2 after which agents refuse to trade with known cheaters.

iii. If $t_2 \geq t_1$, at t_2 the economy spontaneously switches from an *SRE* to an *SARE*.

An economy may also spontaneously switch from an *SRE* to an *SARE* if it is hit by an unexpected shock that suddenly drives a large proportion of competent agents out of business—such as a major recession or a structural adjustment. By abruptly raising d_t, such a shock may induce agents to revise their interpretation of breach of contract and now see it as a sign of impending bankruptcy, hence refusing to deal with known breachers. Once this change of inference is internalized by all agents, it yields a shift in what Greif (1994) calls cultural beliefs and Platteau (1994b) moral norms. Expectations about the market behavior of other agents can thus be interpreted as the result of an endogenous market formation process, not as the product of extra-economic social factors. This is another example of path dependence in market institutions.

12.4 Extensions

12.4.1 Incompetence and Social Learning

We have assumed that incompetent agents participate to trade only to defraud others. Some may find this assumption objectionable because it postulates that dishonesty is widespread among the population. A more benign assumption is that new agents do not know their type; they have to learn it through exchange. In this case trade also serves the role of social learning mechanism. Our propositions 11.4 and 11.5 then imply insufficient social learning. For an application of this principle to the screening of credit applicants by banks, see, for instance, Lang and Nakamura (1990).

12.4.2 Endogenizing Screening Costs

So far we have treated the screening cost c as exogenously given. It can, however, be endogenized as the minimum transaction size that induces incompetent agents to reveal themselves. We begin by noting that since incompetent agents never gain from trade, it is always in their interest to cheat now rather of later. Cheating on a maximum size transaction is thus always a dominant strategy for incompetent agents. Offering to trade in full right from the start thus induces incompetent agents to immediately reveal their type. In that case c is simply equal to 1, the loss from being cheated.

Offering a full transaction is sufficient but not necessary to induce immediate self-revelation. As long as incompetent agents have nothing to gain by imitating the behavior of competent firms for a while, they will reveal their type instantly. Self-revelation can be achieved more cheaply by offering a transaction of size $\delta - \lambda \leq 1$. Only if $\hat{\alpha}$ is larger than the odds of being matched with an incompetent agent is it optimal for competent agents to offer a full-fledged transaction anyway.[10]

Relational strategies can easily be extended to economies with multiple types. Say there are J types each with a different level of incompetence, that is, a different λ_j, and let types be ranked by decreasing size of λ. Agents with large λ's are the most incompetent. They can be induced to reveal themselves with a transaction of size $\delta - \lambda_1$. In the next period the second least incompetent types can then be weeded out with a transaction of size $\delta - \lambda_2$, and so on. The least incompetent reveal themselves last. It is clear that a trial period of length J is always sufficient to deal with J different types. It need not be necessary, however: inducing several types to reveal themselves simultaneously may be more efficient, depending on the proportion of these different types in the economy.

12.4.3 Formal Information Sharing

Information sharing may take place in an informal manner through business networks, community events, and family ties. The circulation of information is then constrained by the limited number of acquaintances people can maintain. The centralization and dissemination of business information through a formal mechanism such as a credit reference bureau is an effective way of ensuring that information circulates more widely—namely in setting $\kappa_i = 1$ for all i. The analysis presented here, however, suggests that doing so is not always beneficial: if agents follow simple

---

10. Since screening by offering a full-fledged transaction always induces self-revelation, c never exceeds the probability of being matched with an incompetent partner.

relational strategies, more information dissemination may actually dilute incentive to comply with contracts. On the other hand, more information is always beneficial if agents follow stigma-augmented strategies; setting κ to 1 may actually be a prerequisite for stigmatization to become self-enforcing. Whether it is optimal to introduce formal information sharing thus depends on the type of equilibrium being followed.

Our analysis also brings to light the fact that widespread circulation of information may hurt new agents: making it easier for tested agents to identify other tested agents reduces the incentive to screen untested ones. This is especially true if the rate of agent renewal is low and new entries are few. In this case, proposition 11.4 has shown that closed-shop equilibria is likely to arise in the steady state. Static economies with very little reshuffling of economic opportunities are thus more prone to closed business communities and the social stratification that accompanies them.

12.4.4 Anonymous Markets

We have shown that relational contracting is likely to dominate emerging markets. There are many economists, however, who would argue that relational contracting does not deserve the name of market exchange because it is too personalized. Anonymity is seen as a necessary condition for competition and thus a defining feature of markets. Relational exchange is viewed as restricting mobility and hindering economic forces and, hence, as an inefficient way of organizing exchange. Can our analysis throw some light on the process by which markets become anonymous?

We would like to argue that this is the wrong way to approach the problem. Markets can never be anonymous. If no information whatsoever was available on the identity of the agent one is trading with, anyone could claim to be a software giant and markets would be a paradise for con artists. Ultimately markets can only function if agents can be identified. They function best if competence is easily assessed. This requires that information about agents' competence and behavior to circulate widely. Only then can agents safely decide to switch from one supplier to another; only then can agents escape the grip of pure relational contracting. Contractual safety is not achieved by making agents anonymous but rather by making them better known by more people. Moreover, switching suppliers and clients frequently is very destructive if agents breach contract each time they switch partner. Full mobility is achievable only if such breaches are deterred, that is, in a stigma-augmented relational equilibrium. Our analysis has shown that this is only possible if information about breaches of contract and business competence circulates widely.

Consequently the wider circulation of information about agents' behavior and competence is a precondition for more mobile, more efficient markets. This can be achieved through various ways such as credit reference bureaus, business registration and licensing, an active press, external auditing procedures, and public oversight institutions. Formal information sharing may supersede informal business networks; they do not make markets anonymous. Brand recognition is also a powerful way of circulating business information. Agents invest considerable amounts of energy building up the reputation of their products.[11] This is again an illustration that markets are not anonymous. In fact brand recognition can be seen as information about a producer's competence that is perfectly represented by our model. Relational strategies may thus be a better characterization of most markets than textbook general equilibrium models.

12.5 Conclusion

Approaching market exchange from the angle of commitment failure, we have examined the conditions under which markets may emerge. We showed that when economic agents are differentiated, a fully decentralized market equilibrium can spontaneously emerge and discipline itself in the absence of formal market institutions, provided that gains from trade are large enough. Incompetent agents are screened away through a trial period, which also serves as sanction for breach of contract, as in Shapiro and Stiglitz (1984) and Ghosh and Ray (1996). Agents who have identified reliable partners continue to transact with each other until economic gains from the relationship vanish. Exchange is not anonymous but personalized and based on mutual trust. Agents collect rents from their business relationships; these rents cannot be competed away lest trade stops.

We investigated whether the circulation of information improves the efficiency of relational contracting. We showed that when agents are heterogeneous, two types of information must be distinguished: information about revealed types, and information about cheating. Sharing information about types resembles name recognition. In the presence of screening costs, agents might refuse to screen unknown agents, thereby leading to closed-shop equilibria in which newcomers are excluded from trade. We showed that such an outcome is more likely if agents are long-lived and opportunities to trade are stationary—as is often the case for agricultural and other primary products. We interpreted this result as throwing light on the well-documented existence of closely knit business communities the world over. Contrary to what one might expect, wider circulation of information—for instance, via a credit bureau—does not eliminate the problem; it only makes it worse. This might

---

11. In Western law, business reputation or "goodwill" has a well-defined commercial value, separate from that of the physical assets of a firm. Brand recognition, a distinct but related concept, is also recognized commercial value by laws and courts.

account for the virtual exclusion of Black firms from the business mainstream in Zimbabwe despite the existence of an active credit reference agency (e.g., Fafchamps 1997c, 2000).

We also investigated the conditions under which an economy might shun all cheaters. We demonstrated that strategies that condition on cheating behavior are not as easily enforceable as previously assumed in the literature (Kandori 1992). We also showed that exclusion from trade of all cheaters is unlikely to arise at early stages of market development. This finding may explain why Western firms dealing with developing countries for the first time are often surprised by different norms of contractual behavior and react very negatively to breach of contract (Biggs et al. 1994). For exclusion of cheaters to be self-enforcing and decentralizable without meta-punishment, breach of contract must be interpreted as a sign of impending bankruptcy. Multiple equilibria may arise. The switch from simple name recognition to exclusion of all cheaters is a path-dependent process sensitive to shocks.

Taken together, our results demonstrate that market exchange can emerge with minimal intervention by the state but that it is unlikely to be fully efficient, at least initially. This is in accordance with the pervasive use of personal recommendation and other reputation mechanisms in labor markets (e.g., Montgomery 1991 and the literature cited therein). It is also broadly consistent with observed characteristics of markets for manufacturing inputs and outputs in Africa. Less advanced economies such as Ghana are indeed characterized by less advanced market development, while in more industrialized economies such as Zimbabwe and, to a lesser extent, Kenya there is observed a stricter respect of contracts and wider circulation of information (e.g., Cuevas et al. 1993; Fafchamps et al. 1994, 1995; Fafchamps 1996, 1997c, 2000). The model presented here thus provides a realistic framework for studying emerging markets.

12.6   Appendix: Proofs of Propositions

Proof of Proposition 12.1   When all agents follow an *SARS*, payoffs are as follows:

$$V_t^M = \alpha\tau\theta^{-1/2} + (1 - \tau^2)\delta V_{t+1}^K + \tau^2\delta V_{t+1}^M, \tag{12.3}$$

$$V_t^K = (1 - \mu_t)\kappa[\alpha\tau\theta^{-1/2} + (1 - \tau^2)\delta V_{t+1}^K + \tau^2\delta V_{t+1}^M]$$
$$+ [(1 - \mu_t)(1 - \kappa) + \mu_t(1 - p_t)][(1 - \tau^2)\delta V_{t+1}^K + \tau^2\delta V_{t+1}^M]$$
$$+ \mu_t p_t\delta V_{t+1}^K - [\mu_t + (1 - \mu_t)(1 - \kappa)]c, \tag{12.4}$$

$$V_t^U = (1 - \mu_t p_t)[(1 - \tau^2)\delta V_{t+1}^U + \tau^2\delta V_{t+1}^M] + \mu_t p_t\delta V_{t+1}^U - c. \tag{12.5}$$

The laws of motion of U_t, K_t, μ_t, and p_t are unchanged. It is immediately apparent that less cheating leads to higher payoffs: $\tau\theta^{-1/2} \geq \tau^2$, with strict inequality if τ or $\theta < 1$. ∎

Proof of Proposition 12.2 We begin by noting that cheaters can continue to trade with agents who did not find out about their dishonest behavior. Their expected payoffs when unmatched V_t^C and matched V_t^N are thus

$$V_t^C = [(1 - \mu_t)(1 - \kappa) + \mu_t(1 - p_t)][(1 - \tau^2)\delta V_{t+1}^C + \tau^2 \delta V_{t+1}^N]$$
$$+ [(1 - \mu_t)\kappa + \mu_t p_t]\delta V_{t+1}^C$$
$$- [\mu_t + (1 - \mu_t)(1 - \kappa)]c, \tag{12.6}$$
$$V_t^N = \alpha\tau\theta^{-1/2} + (1 - \tau^2)\delta V_{t+1}^C + \tau^2 \delta V_{t+1}^N. \tag{12.7}$$

The equations above take into account the fact that one-time cheaters subsequently follow simple relational strategies. Because cheaters cannot trade with agents who know about their cheating, their expected payoff is lower than that of untested agents, namely $V_t^C \leq V_t^U$. The inequality is strict as long as tested agents accept to trade with untested agents.

Part i follows from the fact that the instantaneous difference between V_t^K and V_t^C (i.e., $(1 - \mu_t)\kappa\alpha\tau\theta^{-1/2}$) is increasing over time given that μ_t declines with t. As the instantaneous gap widens, so does the difference between the two expected payoffs. Part ii follows from the fact that V_t^C, and thus V_t^N, is decreasing in κ while V_t^K is increasing in κ. It is easy to verify that if $\kappa = 0$, cheating goes unnoticed and $V_{t+1}^C = V_{t+1}^K = V_{t+1}^U$, in which case condition (BD″) cannot be satisfied. ∎

Proof of Proposition 12.3 See text. ∎

Proof of Proposition 12.4 Note first that the laws of motion of K_t and U_t—and thus μ_t and p_t—are the same along *SRE*s and *SARE*s. Consider the choice of an *SRE* agent faced with a known agent. Since in an *SRE* cheating is not deterred at the end of a relationship, known agents tend to all have cheated at some moment in the past. (Strictly speaking, not all K_t agents have breached contracts. They may be in the pool of unmatched agents because they themselves were cheated by another agent. We skip this detail for the sake of clarity. This omission has no influence on the proof.) It is rational for the agent to trade with the known cheater iff

$$(1 - \mu_t)(1 - d_t)[\alpha\tau^2 + (1 - \tau)\delta V_{t+1}^K + \tau^2 \delta V_{t+1}^M] + d_t(-\tau^2 + \delta V_{t+1}^K)$$
$$\geq [(1 - \mu_t)(1 - d_t) + d_t]\delta V_{t+1}^K, \tag{12.8}$$

which can be rewritten

$$(1 - \mu_t)(1 - d_t)\tau^2\delta(V_{t+1}^M - V_{t+1}^K) \geq d_t - (1 - d_t)(1 - \mu_t). \tag{12.9}$$

Clearly, in an *SRE*, if $d_t = 0$, equation (12.9) is always satisfied. On the other hand, if $d_t = 1$, equation (12.9) boils down to $0 \geq 1$, an impossibility. As d_t rises, the right-hand side of equation (12.9) rises and the left-hand side falls: $1 - d_t$ decreases, and it can be shown that, other things being equal, V_{t+1}^K falls more rapidly with d_t than V_{t+1}^M. Finally, both sides of the equation are continuous in d_t. There exist therefore a level of d_t^* such that equation (12.9) is satisfied. This completes part i.

To show part ii, note that $D_0 = 0$ implies that $d_0 = 0$. Since D_t increases without bounds, $\lim_{t \to \infty} d_t = 1$. Over time, d_t thus increases monotonically from 0 to 1. Part ii then follows from part i. To show part iii, simply note that if $t_1 > t_2$, the *SRE* will collapse before conditions are satisfied for an *SARE* to take over. If, in contrast, $t_1 \leq t_2$, agents will stop dealing with known cheaters at a time when this refusal deters cheating without endangering trade. ∎

13 Information Sharing and Socialization

We saw in chapter 8 that some firms rely on information provided by other firms to screen new customers and suppliers. These findings are consistent with the referral model presented in chapter 10.

In this chapter we present additional evidence on information sharing and socialization by owners and managers of manufacturing firms in Kenya and Zimbabwe. We also present limited evidence on reputational penalties in an effort to test whether breach of contract is stigmatized in the way predicted in chapter 11.

13.1 Manufacturers in Kenya and Zimbabwe

We saw that Kenyan and Zimbabwean firms use recommendations by people they know as means of screening new clients. These recommendations come in various forms—from telephone calls and friendly visits to referrals by banks and credit reference bureaus. Most firms nevertheless rely on a trial period as the default screening procedure.

13.1.1 Socialization

Additional information on the extent of socialization among firms is presented in table 13.1. We find that most firms socialize to some extent with their suppliers. Arm's-length transactions are the exception, especially in more developed Zimbabwe. In Kenya one-third of case study firms pay business visits and take an occasional lunch or tea with their suppliers or their staff. Some 30 to 40 percent are even better acquainted as they meet socially outside business—at weddings, religious events, or sports events. Several respondents commented on the importance of a good relationship with suppliers, not just to have access to trade credit or flexibility in repayment but also to ensure that supplies are available, reliable, and of good quality. Relationships with clients follow a similar pattern in Zimbabwe where the information was collected, but firms socialize less with clients than with suppliers—a feature consistent with the fact that at the time of the survey Zimbabwe was still a supply-constrained economy.

For Kenyan firms, information was also collected on other indicators of acquaintance. They paint the same picture. Half of the firms meet their suppliers personally, either occasionally or frequently—on average, every five months. Half of the suppliers know the location of the respondent's residence. Suppliers of two-thirds of the firms would know of major events affecting their customers, often through the community or from other businesses.

Acquaintance with suppliers shows no clear relationship with firm size, except that large firms seem more likely to deal with each other in an anonymous fashion.

Table 13.1
Socialization with suppliers and clients

	Socialization with suppliers						Socialization with clients		
	Kenya			Zimbabwe			Zimbabwe		
	All firms	Blacks	Others	All firms	Blacks	Others	All firms	Blacks	Others
No socialization	33%	59%	13%	11%	23%	7%	29%	38%	26%
Business socialization only	37%	32%	40%	48%	62%	44%	50%	54%	49%
Socialization outside business	31%	9%	47%	41%	15%	49%	21%	8%	26%
Chi-square test between blacks and others	14.1855	0.001		5.7583	0.056		2.1205	0.346	
Number of observations	52	22	30	56	13	43	56	13	43

Source: RPED case study surveys.

Traders as a rule are better acquainted with their suppliers than manufacturers. There is, however, a sharp difference between firms managed by ethnic Africans and those managed by people of Asian or European descent: firms headed by blacks are less likely to socialize with suppliers. The difference is significant in both countries. There is not significant difference regarding clients, however. To verify that these univariate test results are not due to an omitted variable bias, we estimate ordered probit regressions controlling for various firm characteristics in addition to race. Results, presented in table 13.2, confirm that African firms have more superficial relationships with their suppliers but show no significant effect of firm size or age. This suggests that ethnic barriers may be more limiting to African firms than their young age and small size. Firm characteristics do not seem to explain whether firms have a social relationship with their clients.

A similar picture emerges from other indicators of acquaintance collected in Kenya. Two-thirds of Kenyan-African businesses, for instance, never meet their suppliers and do not know them other than by name, against only one-sixth of the non–Kenyan-African businesses. None of the Kenyan-African businesses meet their suppliers in the community, against two-fifths of the non–Kenyan-African businesses. Kenyan-African businesses also know less about their suppliers and their supplies, know less about them than their non–Kenyan-African counterparts. They are particularly mutually ignorant of details that are not directly observable through casual visits, like private residence, profit, and major events affecting each other's business.

Table 13.2
Ordered probit regression on socialization

| | Socialization with suppliers | | | | Socialization with clients | |
| | Kenya | | Zimbabwe | | Zimbabwe | |
	Coefficient	z-statistic	Coefficient	z-statistic	Coefficient	z-statistic
Firm characteristics						
Age of firm, in log (years since creation)	−0.587	−2.03	−0.074	−0.26	0.304	1.03
Number of employees, in log	−0.053	−0.25	0.055	0.40	0.099	0.72
Subsidiary dummy	2.011	1.31	−0.194	−0.43	−0.557	−1.22
Manufacturer dummy	−1.347	−2.60	−0.201	−0.48	0.912	2.10
Ethnicity (white is omitted category)						
African owner dummy	−3.040	−3.04	−0.934	−2.14	−0.584	−1.30
Other owner dummy	−0.516	−0.62	−0.183	−0.24	−0.449	−0.60
Sector (metal sector is omitted category)						
Food processing sector dummy	−0.550	−0.85	0.639	1.05	−0.285	−0.47
Textile and garments sector dummy	1.073	2.14	0.625	1.12	0.971	1.72
Wood sector dummy	0.467	0.79	−0.138	−0.21	0.206	0.31
Cut 1	−4.462		−1.423		1.385	
Cut 2	−2.778		0.242		3.043	
Number of observations	50		54		54	
Pseudo R-squared	0.362		0.111		0.187	

Source: RPED case study surveys.

As we saw in chapter 3, Kenya and Zimbabwe are peculiar in that business is largely in the hands of nonindigenous groups—Asians in Kenya and Europeans in Zimbabwe. What tables 13.1 and 13.2 suggest is that in these two countries, members of the dominant business group socialize more with suppliers than African businessmen and women. Better business contacts may help these firms enforce contracts and economize on screening costs. This issue is revisited in subsequent chapters.

13.1.2 Information Sharing and Reputational Penalties

As predicted by chapter 11, reputation plays a role in enforcing trade credit contracts. Some 45 percent of Kenyan respondents believe that suppliers exchange information about them. More detailed questions on reputational penalties were asked to Zimbabwean case study firms. Most respondents believe that defaulting on a particular supplier could result in losing credit from all suppliers. This perception is more common among larger firms. An implication is that larger firms have more "social capital" at stake, and so their reputation can be used as an enforcement mechanism.

Table 13.3
Probit regression on reputational penalties in Zimbabwe

	Lose trade credit from others if fail to pay supplier	
	Coefficient	p-value
Firm characteristics		
Age of firm, in years	0.00	0.797
Number of employees, in log	0.89	0.058
Manufacturer dummy	0.58	0.358
Ethnicity (white is omitted category)		
African owner dummy	−0.10	0.890
Other owner dummy	−0.39	0.515
Sector (metal sector is omitted category)		
Food processing sector dummy	−2.01	0.012
Textile and garments sector dummy	−0.85	0.213
Wood sector dummy	−0.74	0.373
Intercept	−1.09	0.325
Number of observations	44	

Source: Zimbabwe case study.

Most firms also indicate that delinquent customers may lose the ability to obtain credit from other suppliers.

Microenterprises constitute an exception: only one such firm indicated that it could face a reputational penalty. This is important because it may explain why microenterprises fail to get trade credit in the first place. Microenterprises also appear unable to impose a reputational sanction onto their own customers. Probit analysis indeed supports the conclusion that smaller firms are less likely to impose reputational penalties (table 13.3). This alone would explain their reluctance to grant trade credit.

In Zimbabwe the most common means by which reputational penalties are imposed are the information published in the Dun and Bradstreet gazette, and informal networks of suppliers who share information. Most firms indicate their reluctance to spread "bad press" about a problematic client as long as there's a chance they may get paid. But many respond to inquiries made about particular customers. Reputational penalties are thus strongest in case of clear-cut default.

The importance of formal credit ratings via Dun and Bradstreet suggests a degree of sophistication in the circulation of credit reference information not found in Ghana or Kenya, where firms rely exclusively on informal information networks, if at all (e.g., Fafchamps 1994; Fafchamps et al. 1994). Taken together, these results support the importance of both reputation and personal relationships in commercial transactions and particularly trade credit. Reputation is important in Zimbabwe because of the existence of several interconnected networks of credit reference information, at the center of which lies Dun and Bradstreet.

The existence of these networks is what enables firms to rely on formal screening procedures and to grant credit to many first-time buyers, as we saw in chapter 9. This system frees firms from exclusive reliance on personal relationships and past experiences. It does not benefit all firms in the same way, however. Large firms with well-established reputations are the major beneficiaries of the system. Many small firms eventually benefit from the system as well, once they have established a track record.

But the reputation system represents a formidable hurdle for new firms and generally fails to benefit microenterprises because they often fail to meet an essential prerequisite, registration with the Registrar of Companies. Registration is indeed costly as it requires the establishment of formal accounts and the payment of various fees. Firms without a publicly visible track record must fall back on more rudimentary practices for establishing trade credit relationships of the kind that we documented in chapter 9, namely personal recommendation and trust building.

Firms that have no public track record and fail formal screening often are given a chance to prove themselves via a trial period. They may also be able to drum support from a third party who will vouch for them or even, in some rare cases, guarantee the payment of their debts. At the bottom of the scale are clients who failed in the past, or who are too small for the supplier to bother.

At every step of the screening mechanism, suppliers must assess the information they collect in light of what they know of the general population of potential trade credit recipients. To do so, they are likely to use all the information available to them, including one piece of information that is difficult to hide: the ethnic origin of the firm's owner or manager. Because blacks as a group are poorer and black firms tend to be younger and less experienced, statistical discrimination probably affects how suppliers perceive them, particularly, but not necessarily, if it is reinforced by prejudice. We revisit this issue in part VI.

13.2 Agricultural Traders

To assess the presence of reputational penalties in agricultural trade, grain traders in Malawi and Benin were asked whether other suppliers would find out if a client had not paid the respondent (table 13.4). In Benin 45 percent of respondents said other suppliers would learn about it, against 70 percent in Malawi. In the latter country a similar question was asked if the respondent did not pay one of its suppliers. A similar answer was obtained. These proportions indicate that a fair amount of informa-

Table 13.4
Information sharing about bad payers in Malawi and Benin

	Benin	Malawi
Other suppliers would know if client does not pay respondent	45%	70%
Other suppliers would know if firm does not pay a supplier	na	74%
Number of observations	598	731

Source: Benin and Malawi trader surveys.

Table 13.5
Information sharing on nonpayment in Madagascar

	Small	Medium	Large	Total
Discuss bad paying clients with other traders[1]				
At least once a day	0%	1%	2%	1%
At least once a week	0%	3%	4%	3%
At least once a month	2%	18%	14%	13%
At least once a year	81%	71%	79%	77%
Never	100%	100%	100%	100%
Number of observations	339			

Source: Madagascar trader survey.
Notes: To facilitate comparison, cumulative percentages of answers are reported. (1) Asked to traders with regular clients only.

tion sharing about bad payers is taking place. But they do not state what action agents take on the basis of that information.

More detailed information was collected in Madagascar. Table 13.5 shows that the frequency with which Malagasy respondents actually share information on bad payers is low. Although three-quarters of Malagasy grain traders discuss bad payers with other traders, they do so rarely: the overwhelming majority of them do so less than once a month. This suggests that respondents do not actively share information about bad payers, although, as we have seen earlier in chapter 9, they share information about prospective clients' type. This is consistent with the model of market emergence presented in chapter 10: agents share information about type but not about behavior.

To investigate this issue further, reputational penalties are illustrated in table 13.6. To avoid selection bias, the question was asked only to respondents who receive or give trade credit. Results show that if a respondent did not pay a supplier, the credit of the respondent with other suppliers would not be affected very much: half of the respondents estimated that not paying would only reduce their chances of getting trade credit with none or at most some of their suppliers. Similar responses were

Table 13.6
Loss of trade credit in case of nonpayment in Madagascar

	Nonpayment	
	To supplier	By client
No loss of supplier credit	11%	21%
Loss of credit from some other suppliers	40%	59%
Loss of credit from most other suppliers	31%	15%
Loss of credit from all other suppliers	17%	5%
Number of observations[1]	194	344

Source: Madagascar trader survey.
Note: (1) Computed for the respondents with regular suppliers only.

Table 13.7
Difficulty of finding suppliers if lose one (Madagascar)

	Small	Medium	Large	Total
Very easy	6%	8%	10%	8%
Fairly easy	3%	18%	20%	16%
Fairly difficult	56%	43%	41%	44%
Very difficult	36%	31%	30%	31%
Number of observations	36	87	71	194

Source: Madagascar trader survey.
Note: Computed for the respondents with regular suppliers only.

obtained when the question was asked about the respondent's clients. Taken together, these findings suggest that the reputational sanctions for breach of contract are mild among Malagasy grain traders. Knowledge about breach of contract does not circulate widely and individual traders can easily evade group sanction. This again is consistent with the model presented in chapter 11.

The loss of the relationship, however, is valuable: as shown in table 13.7, the large majority of Malagasy respondents feel that it would be difficult for them to find a new supplier if they were to lose one—as would most probably be the case if they failed to pay. These results are consistent with theoretical models of trade that emphasize the self-disciplining role of relationships, as those presented in chapters 8 and 11.

13.3 Conclusion

The evidence on information sharing and reputational penalties is mixed. The surveys showed some evidence that firms and traders socialize and share information with each other. But we could find only moderate evidence that firms collude to exclude breachers from future trade, except perhaps within tightly knit communities or with the help of a credit reference bureau.

This finding is agreement with the model presented in chapter 10, but contradicts the approach of Greif (1994) based on cultural beliefs. The majority of respondents believe that cheating on a supplier would hurt their relationship with that particular supplier but would not make it impossible to trade with others. Suppliers, however, worry that their clients may leave the business or go bankrupt. The nonpayment of another supplier, if known, is often interpreted as a sign of financial difficulties that calls for increased scrutiny and reduced credit. There is therefore limited evidence of stigma-augmented relational strategies as discussed in chapter 11.

Field observations also emphasize significant differences between the three countries covered in the case studies. In Ghana first-time customers are virtually never offered trade credit from the date of their first purchase. The normal way of accessing supplier credit is to build up a relationship by buying cash for six to twelve months. In contrast, many Kenyan firms get trade credit from the date of their first purchase. One Nairobi respondent, for instance, was able, at start-up, to fill his shop with goods on credit because he was recommended to his new suppliers by friends and relatives. Only the members of the Kenyan-Asian community seem to benefit from this system, however. Other entrepreneurs, as in Ghana, initially have to pay with cash. Zimbabwe offers yet another picture. The presence of a credit reference bureau, combined with informal information sharing, enables suppliers to screen new clients more effectively than in Kenya or Ghana. As a result established firms find it easy to switch suppliers. New firms, however, especially those headed by blacks, appear to be left out of the system.

Two factors appear to contribute to differences between these three countries: the size of the manufacturing sector, and the circulation of information among firms. Of the three case study countries, Zimbabwe is the most industrialized, which could explain why it has a Credit Reference Bureau (CRB) while the other two have not. It is also the only country among the three where a universal identity card system is in place. Finally, courts seem more impartial and relatively more efficient than that of the two other countries. Despite these institutions the evidence suggests that established firms operate what could be described as a closed-shop equilibrium: new entrepreneurs find it difficult to gain a foothold in business. This is in agreement with our proposition 11.4, that wider circulation of information penalizes untested agents.

In contrast, formal market institutions appear equally weak in Kenya and Ghana. The two countries nevertheless differ in the strength of informal reputation mechanisms. In Kenya, Asians benefit from well-organized information-sharing institutions, although there is ample evidence of segmentation among various Asian subgroups. Efforts to develop a CRB have so far failed, due to a massive failure of coordination and the cost and risks involved in setting up a fully operational system.

The absence of widespread information sharing in Ghana is, at first glance, puzzling. It may be due to a government policy that prohibits people of Lebanese origin from operating a trading business in Ghana. This policy, in place since the 1970s, is an effort to break the dominant position that Lebanese businessmen had initially gained in the country. It has led them to concentrate in manufacturing, leaving trade to people of different ethnic origin. Since socialization across ethnic lines is rare, the diverse ethnic makeup of manufacturers and traders may prevent the establishment of an informal reputation network.[1] Ghanaian input markets can thus be approximately described as pure relational equilibrium. The use of personal recommendations for screening purposes by some entrepreneurs can be interpreted as the beginnings of information sharing. A similar equilibrium seems to characterize grain trade in Madagascar.

1. The relationship between ethnicity and markets is discussed in more detail in Fafchamps (2000, 2002a) and part VI.

V NETWORKS AND MARKETS

In previous chapters we saw that relational contracting is the primary contract enforcement mechanism in African markets. There is some evidence of information sharing to screen new clients but little evidence of reputational penalties.

These findings have far-reaching consequences regarding the structure of trade. Exchange is more difficult between strangers because of the lack of trust. As a result many potential transactions cannot take place because agents are not connected. Exchange takes place exclusively or primarily among agents who have formed long-lasting personalized relationships. In the words of Granovetter (1985), "market transactions become embedded in webs of social relations."

Intuitively, markets characterized by relational contracting are likely to differ from impersonal markets with perfect contract enforcement. This part of the book examines how.

We begin by noting that the density of relations between agents is likely to affect the proportion of potential trades that is possible, and thus the efficiency of the allocation process. An immediate implication is that agents that are better connected, in the sense that they occupy a more central position, can extract rents. These rents obtain because central agents have more bargaining power. These notions are formalized in chapter 14.

Using survey data on agricultural traders, we then test whether business contacts indeed yield returns to market participants. We also investigate what drives the returns to business contacts—oligopoly rents or transactions costs.

14 Market Formation

The existence of screening costs tends to lock economic agents into long-term trading relationships. These screening costs are but one possible example of nonconvex transactions cost. The purpose of this chapter is to suggest a consistent framework to study patterns of economic exchange with nonconvex transaction costs. The framework is particularly relevant to the study of villages, communities, or sectors of economic activity in which economic transactions tend to recur over time between the same individuals or firms. It is directly inspired by the evidence presented in earlier chapters.

This chapter starts from the following premises:

A1. Economic agents have access, at little or no cost, to local information, such as to information regarding their technology and preferences, their past and current performance, and their propensity and ability to meet deadlines and comply with contractual obligations.

A2. Because of the possibility of moral hazard, truthful self-revelation of local information is often not incentive compatible. Consequently self-revelation is suspect and needs to be independently verified.

A3. The collection, verification, and dissemination of economically relevant information is costly. Possible examples are the costs of searching for and identifying potential buyers or sellers, of screening untrustworthy or incompetent partners, of monitoring compliance with contractual obligations, of processing information so that activities (e.g., deliveries) can be coordinated, and of verifying the quality and quantity of supplies and payments.

A4. There are fixed or sunk costs in information processing. Consequently information costs increase less than proportionally with the size of market transactions (at least up to a point).

The first three assumptions are entirely in the tradition of Hayek (1945). Assumption A4 generates nonconvexities in trade. As a result economic agents tend to capitalize on their individual market experience; when having to choose among possible partners for economic exchange, they tend to prefer partners they already trade with or have traded with in the past. In other words, trade flows tend to be concentrated along well-defined axes and to display a certain degree of persistence over time. In this case the trade flow structure of the economy can be described as a meshlike pattern, or *network*, and graph theory can be used to describe characteristics of various types of trade patterns.

In the presence of nonconvexities in trade, a multitude of equilibrium patterns of trade in general corresponds to any given information cost structure. Yet the outcome of economic exchange—that is, the allocation of consumption in the economy after trade has taken place—in general, depends on the shape of trade flows. In other words, multiplicity of equilibria is generic, and as we will see, some of these equilibria may even be Pareto ranked. Moreover the shape of trade flows is also a partial determinant of market power.

The emphasis of this chapter is on the general equilibrium features of an economy satisfying all four assumptions. Consequently informational issues are modeled in a stylized fashion and information costs are captured as transaction costs in the Coase (1937) and Williamson (1975) tradition. Formally, a model of economic exchange is constructed in which partners to economic transactions have to incur transaction costs. Elements of graph theory are introduced that help characterize the resulting general equilibrium. In particular, it is shown that social network based exchange naturally follows from the existence of nonconvex transaction costs. The relationship between the structure of such networks and market power is then partly characterized with the help of concepts such as the core of bargaining equilibria and the connectivity of graphs. In section 14.3 various general equilibrium concepts are briefly presented and discussed. It is suggested that patterns of economic exchange are likely to be fairly persistent over time. The possibility that parties to economic transactions may learn something about each other is introduced in section 14.4. Strategic behavior and resistance to change are then briefly discussed in economies characterized by strong learning effects.

14.1   General Equilibrium with Nonconvex Transaction Costs

Consider a stationary exchange economy with S nonstorable commodities. Each individual i is endowed with a constant vector of goods $[e_i^s]$, $s \in S$. For simplicity, assume that no monetary instrument is available and that all trade takes place through bilateral barter. This does not, however, preclude the use of a particular (perishable) commodity or commodities to play the role of money and facilitate transactions.

A transfer of good s from individual i to individual j in period t is denoted $g_{ij}^s(t)$. Only net transfers are considered; thus $g_{ij} = -g_{ji}$ always. What individual i consumes of good s is denoted by $y_i^s(t)$. Therefore

$$y_i^s(t) = e_i^s + \sum_j g_{ji}^s(t). \tag{14.1}$$

Each individual has a time-separable utility function defined over the consumption of all goods. In order for economic exchange to take place, transaction costs must be incurred. These costs, denoted c_{ij}, are given in utility terms; they are relation-specific in the sense that they are determined by the extent of the relation or exchange between individuals i and j. In general, they may increase with the size of current transactions between them, for instance, to reflect the fact that more intense monitoring is required in order to prevent cheating, although, by A4, they are assumed to increase less than proportionally with the size of the transaction. In most of this chapter, however, we will restrict our attention to a particularly simple form of transaction costs, and assume that (A5) the transaction cost between any two players is a constant (utility) cost c when some goods are exchanged between them, and 0 otherwise.[1]

In section 14.4 we will allow for the possible existence of relation-specific learning by doing in trade and monitoring. In that case transaction costs will be assumed to decrease with the accumulation of relation specific experience, or *trust* (Fafchamps 1992), denoted K_{ij}. In general, K_{ij} depends on the trade history between individuals i and j. For instance, it could be assumed proportional to past exchanges:

$$K_{ij}(t) = \overline{K}_{ij} + \sum_s \int_{\tau=0}^{t} \omega_{ij}^s g_{ij}^s(\tau) \, d\tau, \tag{14.2}$$

where the ω_{ij} are some constant aggregation weights and $\overline{K}_{ij} \geq 0$ is the initial level of trust players start with.

In their most general form, transaction costs are thus given by

$$c_{ij}(t) = c(g_{ij}^1(t), \ldots, g_{ij}^S(t), K_{ij}(t)), \tag{14.3}$$

where the first S derivatives of the $c(.)$ function are nonnegative and the last derivative is nonpositive. The welfare of each individual is

$$W_i = \int_{t=0}^{T} e^{-\rho t} \left[U(y_1(t), \ldots, y_S(t)) - \sum_j c_{ij}(t) \right] dt. \tag{14.4}$$

---

1. Alternatively, the transaction cost function could be regarded as an ad hoc way of eliminating trades that do not satisfy individual rationality constraints (IRC). Note that given the existence of learning in cross-monitoring, cheating on a long-time partner entails the loss of accumulated trust (Fafchamps 1992). Consequently, for any given vector of exchanged commodities between two players, IRCs become more easy to satisfy over time. Ignoring IRCs thus implicitly assumes (1) that crooks self-reveal themselves at $t = 0$ and are then weeded out for the remainder of the game and (2) that the volume of trade between two players does not grow faster than the value of trust. Given these assumptions, if an IRC is satisfied between two individuals when they trade for the first time, then it will be satisfied forever. For simplicity, however, in this chapter opportunistic behavior is assumed to be perfectly preventable through costly monitoring and verification.

The economy depicted in equations (14.1) through (14.4) can be treated as a dynamic coordination game. Note that since commodities are not storable and investment is ignored, the only dynamic element of the game concerns players' expectations, learning, and strategies. We analyze the game in three steps. In section 14.2 the game is reduced to a one-period economy, and the structure of the resulting exchange discussed in detail. A special emphasis is put on characterizing market power. Equilibrium in an intertemporal exchange economy without learning is examined in section 14.3. Finally, the effects of learning are discussed in section 14.4.

14.2   The One-Period Economy

In this section we focus our attention on a one-period version of the economy described in equations (14.1) through (14.4). We first clarify coordination issues and discuss the relationship between transaction costs and the perfect competitive allocation with the help of a simple symmetric economy. We then introduce elements of graph theory and use them to discuss the various facets of connectivity. Finally, we present some results regarding market power, bargaining, and exchange.

14.2.1   Coordination Problems and the Perfect Competitive Allocation

The one-period economy raises subtle coordination problems. To see why, notice that in the absence of transaction costs, it boils down to a simple exchange economy. As is well known (Arrow and Hahn 1971), even in this stylized economy a Nash equilibrium may be hard to achieve. Take the perfect competitive allocation (PCA), for instance. Certainly, in the absence of transaction costs, it is feasible. Yet, without the help of a Walrasian auctioneer, it may be difficult for individuals to coordinate their actions so that the PCA is achieved in practice.

An alternative approach in the absence of transaction costs is to look for a coalition-proof bargaining equilibrium, that is, for an allocation in the core (Hildenbrand 1974). Again, as is well known, the core typically contains more than one possible allocation vector. Which one gets picked requires some coordination mechanism, which may or may not, in this case, depend on the details of the bargaining process.

When transaction costs are present, coordination problems significantly increase in complexity. To make this clear, in the remainder of this subsection, we focus our attention on a simplified symmetric version of a one-period exchange economy. Say there are N players and a same number of commodities. Let e_{ij} stand for individual i's endowment of good j. All players are endowed with one unit of a different commodity, that is, $e_{ii} = 1$ and $e_{ij} = 0$ for $i \neq j$. They also have an identical utility function $U(.)$, which is defined symmetrically over all goods and is strictly quasi-concave. As a consequence all players wish to trade with each other.[2] Utility is nevertheless assumed to remain strictly greater than 0 even when the consumption of all goods except one is 0—that is, $U(0, \ldots, 0, 1, 0, \ldots, 0) > 0$ for all goods (A6). Assumption A5 also applies; in other words, the transaction cost between players i and j is a constant c if any amount of trade occurs between them, and zero if it does not.

Clearly, in this economy if $c = 0$, the perfect competitive equilibrium has all players consuming $1/N$ of each commodity. Call this allocation the perfect competitive allocation (PCA). Of course, the PCA belongs to the core (e.g., Arrow and Hahn 1971; Hildenbrand 1974). If transaction costs are high enough, however, the PCA may not be achievable by generalized barter.

PROPOSITION 14.1   Given the assumptions listed above, there exists a $\underline{c} > 0$ for which the perfect competitive allocation $(1/N, \ldots, 1/N)$ cannot be achieved by a generalized bilateral barter mechanism involving each possible pair of players.

Proof   Pick $\underline{c}$ just high enough such that each player, if faced with a choice between $U(1/N, \ldots, 1/N) - \underline{c}(N - 1)$ and $U(0, \ldots, 1, \ldots, 0)$, would prefer the second alternative. By assumption A6, such a $\underline{c}$ always exist.   ∎

Proposition 14.1 does not necessarily imply that the PCA cannot be supported. What it implies is that, at $\underline{c}$, players wish to lower the number of their partners to less than $N - 1$. But the PCA can still be achieved by using other players as *intermediaries*. All that is required is that all players be directly or indirectly *connected*.

Since, by assumption A5, transaction costs are not a function of the volume of trade, the most efficient symmetric equilibrium requires that each player be connected only to two others, who are themselves connected to two others, and so on, until all players are included. Graphically this can be illustrated by locating all players on an imaginary circle and connecting each of them to their two closest neighbors (figure 14.1). In this fashion goods can circulate among all players along the circle, and the PCA can be achieved at a much lower transaction cost of $2c$ for all players. This leads to the following proposition:

PROPOSITION 14.2   For $c < \underline{c}$, the PCA allocation can be supported by all symmetric equilibria in which each player is connected to $N - k$ other players, with $2 \leq k \leq N - 2$.

---

2. Many of these simplifying assumptions are not essential for the results presented on the following pages, but they have the merit of clarifying the presentation.

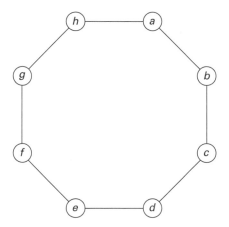

Figure 14.1
Wheel graph

Proof By definition, for $c < \underline{c}$, $U(1/N, \ldots, 1/N) - ck > U(0, \ldots, 1, \ldots, 0)$. Thus any player presented with the PCA and an implementation scheme requiring k partners would find in his or her best interest to accept it. ∎

DEFINITION 14.1 Let c_3 be defined as the smallest c for which $U(1/N, \ldots, 1/N) - 3c_3 < U(0, \ldots, 1, \ldots, 0)$. By assumption A6, c_3 always exist.

COROLLARY 14.1 For all $c < c_3$, there exist multiple Pareto ranked equilibria that implement the PCA.

Proof Use the symmetric equilibria of proposition 14.1. That they are Pareto ranked follows from the fact that they require a different number of connections and therefore of transaction costs. ∎

The PCA can also be implemented by a very large number of nonsymmetric equilibria, that is, of equilibria in which individuals are not all connected to the same number of other players. At this juncture we can no longer proceed without introducing some concepts from graph theory.[3]

---

3. Note that in graph theory, the term *network* is used exclusively to refer to a directed graph with a unique source and sink (Foulds 1992). Here, as in the geography (Tinkler 1977) and sociology literatures (e.g., Mitchell 1969; Burt 1980; Knobe 1990), we will continue to use it interchangeably with the term graph.

14.2.2 Elements of Graph Theory

Definitions

A *graph* (V, E) is an ordered pair, where V is a finite nonempty set whose elements are termed *vertices* or *nodes*, and where E is a set of unordered pairs of distinct vertices of V. Each element $\{p, q\} \in E$ (where $p, q \in V$) is called an *edge* or *link* and is said to *join* the vertices p and q (Foulds 1992, p. 9).

A graph $G = (V, E)$ is termed *weighted* if there exists a function $\omega : E \to R^N$ (where R is the set of real numbers) that assigns a real vector, called a *weight*, to each edge of E. (generalized from Foulds 1992, p. 11).

A *path* is a sequence of distinct vertices and edges of a graph G of the form:

$$\langle v_1, \{v_1, v_2\}, v_2, \{v_2, v_3\}, v_3, \ldots, v_n \rangle$$

(arranged from Foulds 1992, p. 17).

A graph G is termed *connected* if every pair of vertices in G are joined by a path, and is termed *disconnected* if it is not connected (Foulds 1992, p. 18).

A *spanning tree* of a connected graph G is a path that includes all its N vertices. Consequently it also contains $N - 1$ edges.

A graph in which every pair of its N vertices is connected by an edge is termed *complete* and is denoted by K_N (Foulds 1992, p. 18).

A graph in which each of its N vertices is incident to the same number e of edges is termed *regular* and is denoted by $K_{(N, e)}$. It corresponds to what we have earlier called a *symmetric equilibrium*.

These definitions allow us to represent any equilibrium of the one-period economy as a graph in which each individual is a node, each exchange relationship is an edge, and the weights are the vectors of goods being exchanged. Given the structure of the stylized economy, the PCA can only be achieved in a connected graph.

PROPOSITION 14.3   For $c < c_3$, the Pareto-efficient way of implementing the PCA requires $N - 1$ barter trades.

Proof   By definition, the PCA can only be implemented in a connected graph. For a given allocation, Pareto efficiency can be increased by minimizing the number of transactions required to implement it and thus the number of edges. For $c < c_3$, the minimum is achieved by any spanning tree of the complete graph.   ■

Note that the Pareto-efficient way of implementing the PCA does not lead to a symmetric equilibrium: indeed, the players at both ends of the spanning tree only incur transaction costs once, while all other players incur them twice. There are, of course, a large number of other nonsymmetric ways of implementing the PCA, as well as many other allocations that can be achieved depending on the graph of the economy.

We now turn to an analysis of economic power in economies characterized by nonconvex transaction costs. We do so in three steps: first, we discuss ways of characterizing the connectivity in the economy. Second, we characterize power in its relation to connectivity. Finally, we focus our attention on a certain class of bargaining processes that satisfy regularity properties and derive further results regarding the relationship between connectivity and economic power.

14.2.3 Connectivity in Graphs and Economies

Graph theory provides us with various ways of describing connectivity. Here are some useful definitions (Foulds 1992):

The *valency* or *degree* d_i of a vertex v_i is the number of edges incident to it.

The *distance* between two vertices is the shortest path between them.

A *component* is a maximal connected subgraph of a graph G. In other words, it is a connected subgraph of G that is disconnected from the rest of G. An isolated vertex is by definition a component.

If N and L are the number of vertices and edges, respectively, of a graph G, then the *density* of the graph is $2N/L = \sum_i d_i/N$.

The *adjacency* matrix A of a graph is an $N \times N$ symmetric matrix in which each element a_{ij} is one if vertices i and j are adjacent to each other, that is, incident to the same edge, and zero otherwise. (Diagonal elements are usually set to zero, but Tinkler 1977 has shown that for some applications, setting them to one is useful.)

The *incidence* matrix B of a graph is an $N \times L$ matrix in which each element b_{ij} is one if vertex v_i and edge e_j are incident, and zero otherwise.

Given these basic definitions, we get the following simple results, taken from Foulds (1992, pp. 77–78), and Temperley (1981):

PROPOSITION 14.4

i. A graph G is connected if and only if its adjacency matrix can be transformed into a block diagonal matrix by relabeling some or all of its vertices.

ii. The valency of a vertex v_i is equal to the sum of elements of the ith row or ith column of A.

iii. For $i \neq j$, the (i, j) element of A^2 is equal to the number of paths containing exactly two edges from v_i to v_j; the (i, i) entry of A^2 is the valency of v_i.

iv. If G is connected, the distance between two vertices v_i and v_j is the least integer m for which the (i, j) element of A^m is nonzero.

v. The rank of the incidence matrix is $N - k$, where k is the number of components of the corresponding graph.

The definitions above together with proposition 14.3 allow us to characterize connectivity in a graph.[4] The first and most important facet of connectivity is the degree of *fragmentation* or *segmentation* of the economy, which is captured by the number of components of the corresponding graph. For instance, only if the graph is fully connected can the PCA be achieved. Therefore the number of components constitutes a rough indicator of efficiency losses. Fragmentation, however, only imperfectly characterizes connectivity. To get a better picture, other measures are necessary.

The valency of the graph's vertices is one of them. For any vertex, it gives the number of direct connections that link it to the rest of the graph. In symmetric (i.e., regular) graphs, all nodes have the same valency, which is also equal to the density of the graph. In nonregular graphs, valency provides a rough measure of centrality: better connected nodes have higher valency, while peripheral nodes have a lower valency. Highly centralized or polarized graphs, like the star, for instance, are characterized by a highly skewed valency distribution. The distribution of valency across nodes is thus a way of representing polarization, that is, the extent to which some economic agents occupy a central position in the economy. As we will see in the next subsection, polarization is likely to affect the *power* that certain players have to influence the final allocation of commodities.

Valency alone, however, fails to capture another important facet of connectivity that, following Mitchell (1969) and Knobe (1990), we will call *reach*. To see why, consider the graph presented in figure 14.2. It has two components: a star with five branches and a regular $K_{(8,2)}$ circle.[5] For the moment, ignore the dashed line connecting them. The valency of the star center c is 5; that of each of its adjacent nodes

---

4. The reader may wonder if the eigenvalues and eigenvectors of the adjacency matrix convey useful information about the connectivity of the corresponding graph. Unfortunately, they do not, except for special categories of graphs (e.g., Tinkler 1972b; Biggs 1974; Cvetkovic et al. 1980).

5. On stars, wheels, and other radial structures, see, for instance, Tinkler (1972a).

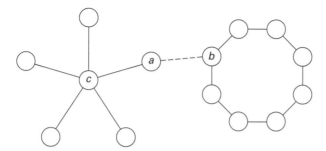

Figure 14.2
Valency and connectivity

is 1. The valency of each of the nodes on the circle is 2. If one were to characterize connectivity by valency alone, one would miss the fact that nodes on the circle are indirectly connected to and can thus ultimately reach a larger number of nodes than the center of the star. That reach is important can immediately be seen by considering figure 14.2 as a representation of an equilibrium of our exchange economy. In that equilibrium, players on the circle can get access to more consumption variety and possibly achieve a higher utility than players on the star, including its center. To measure indirect connectivity or reach, the definition of valency can usefully be expanded as follows:[6]

DEFINITION 14.2   The valency of order m of a vertex v_i is the number of vertices v_j $(i \neq j)$ such that the distance between v_i and v_j is less or equal to m.

Connectivity in figure 14.2 can now be described better by considering valencies of various orders. That the center of the star enjoys better direct connections is evident from the high value of its first-order valency. But valencies of higher orders confirm that nodes of the circle enjoy better indirect connections: indeed, the second and higher order valency of all nodes of the star remains 5, while the second and higher order valencies of the nodes of the circle grow to 4, 6, and 8, respectively.

First and higher order valencies are useful devices to describe important aspects of connectivity. Unfortunately, they fail to emphasize the possible existence of key links or vertices, that is, of links or vertices whose removal would make a connected graph or subgraph disconnected.

6. See Mitchell (1969), Haggett and Chorley (1969), and Tinkler (1977) for similar concepts.

Definitions (adapted from Foulds 1992)

A *cut-vertex set* v of a graph G is a minimal set of vertices whose removal from G increases the number of its components.

A *bridge* is a cut-vertex set with a single vertex.[7]

A *cut-(edge) set* of a graph G is a minimal set of edges whose removal from G increases the number of its components.

The *edge (vertex) redundancy* of a connected graph or subgraph is the number of elements of its smallest cut-edge set (cut-vertex set).

In figure 14.2 any edge of the star or pair of edges of the circle constitutes a cut-edge set. The star has a bridge; its vertex-redundancy is thus one. The vertex and edge redundancy of the circle are both two. To understand the usefulness of the above concepts, again interpret figure 14.2 as portraying one possible equilibrium of an exchange economy, and assume that the set of possible links among players is restricted to those shown in the figure. Then, clearly, being a bridge confers a considerable amount of power to a player. Consider the star center. The nodes adjacent to it have no way of exchanging commodities other than by trading directly with the center. This in all probability should confer a good deal of bargaining power to the star center.

On the other hand, none of the nodes on the circle is a bridge. If any of them was to put pressure on one of his or her neighbors and threaten to refuse trading unless advantageous terms are complied with, the neighbor could literally circumvent that pressure and secure commodities indirectly. In order to be effective, pressure would have to be coordinated among a number of players equal to the vertex redundancy of the connected subgraph, in this case two otherwise unconnected players.

The importance of cut-sets can be further illustrated if we add a single edge to figure 14.2, say between a and b (dashed line). This new link suddenly connects the entire graph and allows trade to take place indirectly between players on the circle and the star. Since all players value diversity in consumption, this new link enables the economy to capture gains from trade and increases allocative efficiency. But the new link also dramatically modifies the economic power of players a, b, and, to less extent, c, the old star center. Indeed, all of them are now bridges. Furthermore they are adjacent. Consequently, as a group, they have a lot of power over other players in the sense that if they are able to coordinate their efforts, they should

7. Biggs (1974), however, reserves the term *bridge* for a single cut-edge set.

extract a significant share of the potential gains from economic exchange as payment for their trade services. Among themselves, however, they constitute a rather complex monopoly triad since each of them in isolation can block all trade to and from the star and the circle.

Edge and vertex redundancy also convey important information about the fragility of a system of economic exchange. Indeed, they give the minimum number of existing edges or vertices that would have to disappear before the graph becomes disconnected. If, for some reason or another, relationships among individuals (edges) or individuals themselves (vertices) are subject to exogenous shocks and may vanish unexpectedly, then redundancy is a rough measure of the extent of the damage that such disappearances can cause to the economy. Of course, to figure out the actual extent of the loss, one would also have to know the welfare value of the mutual gains from trade between the two disconnected parts.

There is yet another important dimension of connectivity that depends not only on the existence or absence of links between nodes but also on the capacity of these links. To see why, suppose for an instant that the exchange economy is modified so that the amount of commodities that can be transferred between any two single individuals is now constrained by some capacity limit. In these circumstances, knowing that all players are connected is no longer a guarantee that the PCA can be implemented: one also has to worry about being able to transfer commodities within the economy while ensuring that capacity constraints are satisfied.

To verify that this is the case is far from trivial. Efficient algorithms have been developed that check whether a certain flow can be accommodated between any two nodes of a graph (see the maximum-flow, minimum-cut theorem; Foulds 1992, p. 248). But economic exchange raises significantly more complex issues, since it requires that capacity not be exceeded jointly for all flows between agents. It is unclear at this point whether efficient algorithms can be developed to deal with these issues, even for economies of fairly small size (e.g., 20 nodes and 60 edges). Examination of the capacity of cut-edge sets, however, may still help identify some of the important bottlenecks.

14.2.4 Power, Bargaining, and Exchange

In this section we examine how the exchange of commodities among players are determined, taking links among them as given. The emphasis is put on the relationship between connectivity, power and commodity flows. To do so, we formalize the bargaining process between players as follows. The *core* of an economy is the set of its feasible coalition-proof allocations (e.g., Arrow and Hahn 1971; Hildenbrand

1974; Friedman 1990). The *graph* of an economy with N agents is the graph whose $N \times N$ adjacency matrix has elements a_{ij} equal to 1 if individuals i and j directly exchange commodities, and 0 otherwise.

PROPOSITION 14.5   Consider the economy presented in equations (14.1) to (14.4) and assumption A5, together with one of its possible graphs.

i. The core of this economy is nonempty.

ii. The core depends on the graph of the economy.

iii. When the graph of the economy is complete, the core is identical to that of an equivalent exchange economy without transaction costs.

iv. The core is smallest when the graph is complete, in the sense that it is included in the core corresponding to any other graph.

v. When capacity constraints are absent, the core of a complete economy converges to the perfect competitive allocation as the number of players goes to infinity.

Elements of proof   Denote an allocation by an $N \times S$ matrix M in which each element m_{ij} represents the consumption of good j by individual i. Since, by assumption A5, transaction costs are independent of commodity flows, the graph of the economy fully determines transaction costs. Taking the graph of the economy, and therefore the structure of transaction costs as given, we find that an allocation matrix M is individually rational, that is, is not opposed by any individual player i provided that

$$U(m_{i1}, \ldots, m_{iS}) \geq U(e_{i1}, \ldots, e_{iS}). \tag{14.5}$$

Note that the graph of the economy does not influence equation (14.5).

Now consider an individual player i. Denote the connected subgraph of which he or she is a element by C_i. Since there are no capacity constraint, an allocation is feasible if

$$\sum_{i \in C_i} m_{ij} \leq \sum_{i \in C_i} e_{ij} \qquad \forall j, \forall i \tag{14.6}$$

We restrict our attention to nonwasteful allocations, namely such that equation (14.6) holds with equality.

Proving the proposition hinges on showing that coalitions of unconnected players are redundant in the sense that they cannot credibly claim for more than what each of their connected subgraphs can ask for its members. To see why, consider an unconnected set of players, and suppose that they threaten to refuse any allocation that does not provide them with whatever utility they could theoretically achieve by pooling their endowments together. But since these players are not directly connected, their threat, in order to be carried out, requires the tacit cooperation of players that are not members of their coalition. Such threat therefore could not be enforced by the coalition and therefore is not credible.

The core of an economy is essentially the set of feasible and individually rational allocations that also satisfy a series of coalition-proofness constraints. Whenever some coalitions are ineffective in the sense that they cannot achieve jointly more than their connected components, then the corresponding coalition-proofness constraints can be dropped. Thus the size of the core depends on how many of these coalition-proofness constraints must be satisfied. When the economy is complete, all possible coalitions are effective and the core corresponds to that of a pure exchange economy without transaction costs. Since any departure from completeness removes some coalition-proofness constraints, the core of a complete economy is thus contained in the core of an economy with any other graph (though not strictly in case where the added coalition-proofness constraint is not binding). The same holds a fortiori for unconnected economies. That the core is not empty follows from the above and from the fact that the core of a pure exchange economy is never empty (Hildenbrand 1974). That the core of complete economies converges to the PCA is a direct extension of proposition 14.5.iii and well-known theorems on the core of pure exchange economies (e.g., Arrow and Hahn 1971; Hildenbrand 1974).   ∎

The usefulness of proposition 14.5 comes from the fact that once two players have made the transaction cost investment required to trade with each other, they will end up in a form of bilateral monopoly. The terms of the exchange that take place between them must be the result of implicit or explicit bargaining (Geertz et al. 1979). The limits within which each player is willing to bargain are likely to depend on the alternatives open to them. If players have many other valid options, one expects much tighter limits on the terms they are willing to accept. On the other hand, if players have few other options, they are likely to be more willing to negotiate and more amenable to pressure by stronger players. So, for instance, one would expect a seller to be able to extract more advantageous conditions from a captive customer than from someone who has other options open.

Proposition 14.5.v establishes the fact that as the options open to players increase, the core converges to the PCA. In other words, the range of possible negotiated terms of exchange shrinks and lies closer and closer to the relative prices corresponding to the perfect competitive equilibrium. The converse of this proposition is that when players have few options, the range of possible negotiated outcomes is

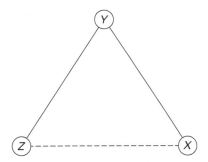

Figure 14.3
Connectivity and power

large and terms of exchange may vary significantly across transactions.[8] This is true not only when the number of players in the economy is small but also when the links between them are few.

Proposition 14.5 also suggests a framework in which to model the kind of economic power that individuals derive from being better connected than others. In the previous subsection we intuitively argued that a bridge player should enjoy more power than a pendant player (i.e., a player incident to a single link). This intuition can now be formalized by elaborating on the concept of core. The basic intuition is that someone who belongs to many possible coalitions has more opportunities of promoting his or her interests than players who are relatively isolated.

To see why, consider an economy with three players, X, Y, and Z. Suppose that the only links that exist are XY and YZ (figure 14.3). Take these links as exogenously given. Clearly, Y is better connected than the other two players; Y is in fact a bridge. Let $\underline{U}_x$, $\underline{U}_y$, and $\underline{U}_z$ stand for the autarchy utility levels of the three players. Similarly let $\{U_x^{xy}, U_y^{yx}\}$ and $\{U_z^{zy}, U_y^{yz}\}$ stand for the set of joint utility levels achievable by two-person coalitions between X and Y, and Z and Y respectively. Denote the maximum achievable utility for Y under each two-person coalitions as $\overline{U}_y^{yx}$ and $\overline{U}_y^{yz}$ respectively—for instance, $\overline{U}_y^{yx} \equiv \sup_{U_x^{yx}}\{U_x^{xy}, U_y^{yx}\}$.

Now suppose that Y and Z strike a two-person deal that gives Y a utility $\hat{U}_y^{yz}$. If $\hat{U}_y^{yz} < \overline{U}_y^{yx}$, then X could possibly bribe Y out of the deal with Z by proposing him or her an alternative, more attractive two-person deal. Similarly, if Y were to strike a deal with X that gives Y a utility $\hat{U}_y^{yx} < \overline{U}_y^{yz}$, Z could possibly bribe Y out of that

---

8. This may help explain, for instance, why price data for individual transactions in African villages display a lot of variability, even within the same period of the year.

deal too. Call $\min\{\overline{U}_y^{yx}, \overline{U}_y^{yz}\}$ Y's reference payoff. X and Y, on the other hand, cannot bribe each other out of a deal with Y. Therefore their autarchy payoffs $\underline{U}_x$ and $\underline{U}_z$ are their reference payoffs.

Y cannot guarantee himself his reference payoff, however. To see this, consider allocation a in the economy represented by figure 14.3. This allocation provides all players more utility than they can get in two-person coalitions; it therefore cannot be defeated by any coalition of two players and is coalition-proof. But it fails to provide Y a utility at least equal to his reference payoff. Although a perfect case cannot be easily made against a as a possible bargaining equilibrium of this particular economy, Y is likely to be able to extract some leverage from his key position, particularly given the fact that X and Z are not even interacting with each other. Since Y's leverage is captured by his reference payoff, we now make the following assumptions: (1) the bargaining power of a player is positively related to his or her reference payoff and (2) the payoff that each player gets as an outcome of the bargaining process is positively related to that players' bargaining power. In the three player game between X, Y, and Z, any bargaining mechanism that satisfies assumptions A7 and A8 will then confer the better connected player Y a higher level of utility.

Now add a link to the economy above so that X and Z are also connected. The graph of the economy has become a circle. Because of the new connection, X and Z also become able to bribe each other out of unsatisfactory deals with Y. Consequently their reference payoffs are now $\min\{\overline{U}_x^{xy}, \overline{U}_x^{xz}\}$ and $\min\{\overline{U}_z^{zy}, \overline{U}_z^{zy}\}$ respectively. Their bargaining power has thus increased, and they should be able to obtain a higher level of utility for themselves.[9]

This simple example has demonstrated that the graph of the economy influences how resources get allocated. We now generalize it to more complex situations.

14.2.5   Economies with Regular Bargaining Processes

Definitions

An *admissible coalition* is any set of connected players; it is denoted $C(i_1, i_2, \ldots, i_k)$, where k is the number of players in that coalition and $i_1, i_2, \ldots, i_k$ are their indexes $\in N$.

The *complement* of a coalition is the set of all other members of the economy.

The set of *feasible payoffs* for an admissible coalition is defined as the set of payoff vectors that can be achieved by that coalition on its own resources.

---

9. Note that the core of the star economy is larger than the core of the circle economy. However, it is not larger in all directions equally. It is this lack of symmetry that tips the balance of power in favor of the better connected player.

The set of *coalition-proof payoff vectors* of an admissible coalition C, denoted $V(C)$, is the set of feasible payoffs that confers to members of C payoffs that are superior or equal to what (1) any admissible subcoalitions of the members of C could achieve jointly and (2) any admissible coalition of members of C and of its complement could achieve jointly.

Define a *multiple set* as a set with strictly more than one element.

Consider the collection of all possible multiple sets of admissible coalitions that have player i as their a unique intersection. Denote that collection by O_i and each of its constitutive set by S_l^i. The *reference payoff* of player i is then defined as

$$R_i \equiv \sup_{S_l^i \in O_i} \ \inf_{C_k \in S_l^i} \ \sup_{U_i} V(C_k).$$

A *bargaining process* B is an N-dimensional mapping from players' reference payoffs $\{R_1, \ldots, R_N\}$ to their realized payoffs $\{U_1, \ldots, U_N\}$ in the core.

A *regular bargaining process* is a bargaining process that also satisfies A8, (i.e., $\partial U_i / \partial R_i > 0$ for all i, as well as $\partial U_i / \partial R_j \leq 0$ for $i \neq j$).

PROPOSITION 14.6

i. There exists at least one regular bargaining process.

ii. Consider a complete economy with a regular bargaining process. Let the number of players go to infinity. Then the regular bargaining process supports the PCA.

Proof (i) The conditions for a regular bargaining process are satisfied, for instance, by the following equilibrium concepts for cooperative games: cooperative Nash, Shapley value (Friedman 1990), and Rubinstein alternating offers (Rubinstein 1987). (ii) This is obvious since, by definition, any regular bargaining process maps into the core and the core converges to the PCA. ∎

Connectedness plays a critical role in determining the reference payoff of players because it limits the number of admissible coalitions to which a player can belong. The following propositions capture some of the relationships between power and connectedness:

PROPOSITION 14.7 Let R_i and R_j be the reference payoffs of two unconnected players. Add a link between them, and let their new reference payoff be R_i' and R_j'. Then $R_i' \geq R_i$ and $R_j' \geq R_j$.

Proof Adding a link between two players increases the collection of all possible multiple sets of admissible coalitions that have either of these two players as their a unique intersection. Then the proposition follows by applying Le Chatelier principle and the definition of reference payoff. ∎

Proposition 14.7 suggests that establishing a new link between previously unconnected players should benefit them. Whether or not it does, however, depends on what happens to other players' reference payoff. This is, in general, hard to establish. To see why, consider a connected economy. In this case the set of feasible allocation is not affected by the addition of the new link. The new link between i and j, however, now allows them to form a coalition among themselves. As a consequence any coalition, admissible or not, that contains both of them must, in order to be coalition-proof, grant them a joint payoff that lies above what they could achieve together as a pair. Similarly any coalition, admissible or not, that contains either of them, but not both, may now be vulnerable to bribes by the other, and therefore may have to guarantee the former a higher payoff. This means that the set of coalition-proof payoffs for all other players has shrunk.

Now consider the initial collection of admissible coalitions for an arbitrary other player, O_k, $k \neq i, j$. Clearly, the new link between i and j cannot have increased the maximum reference payoffs player k can get within that initial set; if anything, it has decreased it. There are, however, new collections of admissible coalitions that now need to be examined. In general, one cannot tell whether these new sets of admissible coalitions may improve other players' reference payoff. When the bargaining process is regular, however, proposition 14.8 shows that the realized payoffs of the newly connected players must increase.

PROPOSITION 14.8   Consider a connected economy with a regular bargaining process. Adding a link between two players i and j can only increase their realized payoff.

Proof   First of all, the new possible two-person coalition between i and j imposes new constraints on all previously admissible coalitions that include one of them. This tends to reduce other players reference payoffs and thus to increase i and j's realized payoffs since the bargaining process is regular. Second, all the coalitions that have become admissible thanks to the new link, by definition, include both i and j. The realized payoffs of either i or j cannot therefore decrease as a result of these new coalitions because, if they did, i and/or j simply would find it in their interest not to participate to them. ∎

COROLLARY 14.2   Consider an economy with three players, two of which are initially unconnected, and add a link between them. Then the reference payoff of the third cannot increase. If the economy has a regular bargaining process, then the realized payoff of the newly connected players can only increase, while the realized payoff of the other player can only decrease.

In a perfectly symmetric economy, corollary 14.2 can be extended to circles of any length but not so in general. To understand why, consider a list of players initially joined by a single line. Then join the two ends of that line. Clearly, by proposition 14.8, the two connected players are now better off. But some of their adjacent players may be better off too.

For instance, consider a situation where one player has a monopoly on a highly valued commodity, and players are arranged in a line with the monopolist at one end. Also, for simplicity, assume that all other players have identical endowments and thus no prospect for mutually beneficial trade. Coalitions not containing the monopolist can thus be ignored. Consider the smallest possible coalition, that between the monopolist m and the first player next to him. The maximum that player 1 could bargain for is the efficiency gain that she is able to procure to m. Then consider the second player next to m. Clearly, player 2 cannot bribe player 1 away from her coalition with m since 1 and 2 have identical endowments. Again, the maximum that player 2 could bargain for is the efficiency gain that she is able to procure to m. If the highly valued commodity and other commodities are substitutes, the maximum marginal utility gain that player 2 can procure to m is smaller than that procured by player 1, and similarly for all other players. Consequently, if the economy has a regular bargaining process, players close to the monopolist will achieve a higher realized payoff than players far away from him.

Now suppose that a new link is created between the monopolist and the last player on the line. This undoubtedly complicates the pattern of possible coalitions, but it should be intuitively clear that the situation of players at the end of the line has significantly improved. The symmetry of the game implies that the worst off player will now be the one (or pair) farthest away from m on the newly formed circle.

COROLLARY 14.3   If a new link is added between two branches of a star, the star center's realized payoff decreases while the realized payoff to the newly connected players increases.

Proof   Apply corollary 14.2.   ∎

COROLLARY 14.4   Consider an economy and two of its feasible graphs, one being a star, and the other a wheel, both with the same center. Then the realized payoff of the star center is higher than that of the wheel center.

Proof   Apply corollary 14.3.   ∎

Definition

An *extended star* is a graph constructed as follows:

1. Take any finite vector of positive integers $H = (h_1, h_2, \ldots, h_k)$.

2. Start to build with h_1 branches, each with a pendant node.

3. To each of the pendant nodes, attach h_2 incident edges whose ends are h_2 corresponding nodes.

4. Continue the process until the vector H is exhausted.

COROLLARY 14.5   Consider an economy with any extended star graph. Then connecting the pendant nodes together can only decrease the realized payoff of the star center.

Proof   By recursion on corollary 14.4.   ∎

The corollaries above have some interesting applications to simple hierarchies, which can be thought of as simple or extended stars whose center is the hierarchical superior. What corollary 14.5 says is that the superior's power is diminished if his subordinates can form credible coalitions among themselves. This intuitively leads to the conclusion that it is in the interest of the management to oppose unionization of workers—unless, of course, other gains can be identified that result from workers being connected to each other (teams, circulation of information, etc.); see, for instance, Itoh (1991), Holmstrom and Milgrom (1990), and Bolton and Dewatripont (1994).

14.3   Equilibrium and Repeated Interaction

In the previous subsection it should be clear that for any given connected graph of the economy, any regular bargaining process results in a well-defined allocation of resources among players. Consequently, given a regular bargaining process, players can, in principle, compute their payoff for any graph of the economy. If this information is combined with the transaction costs of trade, the normal form of the game can, in principle, be computed.

The normal form one-period game is characterized by complex coordination problems, however. To see why, consider the following example: Suppose that there are two sets with an equal number of players. Endowments are identical within sets but differ across sets. Then one possible Nash equilibrium of this game has each player in one set paired with one player in the other. How players are paired is largely irrelevant, but the pairing may be difficult to coordinate. Consequently this game also has an equilibrium in mixed strategies.

Ultimately we are interested in modeling how people interact over extended periods of time. Given the highly complex coordination problems raised by the game, the number of possible subgame perfect equilibria is extremely large and increases exponentially with time. Many of these equilibria, however, are counterintuitive. To see why, denote the set of possible Nash equilibria of the one-period normal form game as Z. Then any sequence of elements of Z is a subgame perfect equilibrium of the dynamic game. In other words, there are many equilibria in which players switch partners in a chaotic and inexplicable fashion. Such equilibria are not very appealing as positive descriptions of reality.

Providing a complete characterization of the plausible intertemporal equilibria of this game is beyond the scope of this chapter. We nevertheless propose the following promising lines of enquiry as to how the matching of players takes place.

14.3.1 Evolutionary Game

One way of describing the matching process is to model the intertemporal economy as an evolutionary game. Players start with an arbitrary set of initial moves, and then conduct random or targeted searches. From time to time players meet other players who are willing to trade with them. When that happens, they conduct mutually beneficial trade using the regular bargaining process of the one-period game. Once two players have identified each other as mutually beneficial partners, they should continue trading together in the future if only because, in the class of coordination games considered here, randomized equilibria always yield lower expected payoffs than equilibria in pure strategy. They may nevertheless continue searching randomly for other possible partners. Eventually, when all possibilities for mutually beneficial trade have been found, one would expect the game to stabilize in a certain pattern of exchange.

In order to be evolutionary stable, this pattern would have to be a Nash equilibrium in pure strategies; otherwise, players would find it in their interest to continue moving (e.g., van Damme 1987; Swinkels 1992). In principle, the strong coordination nature of the game analyzed here should guarantee that Nash equilibria in pure strategy do exist, and thus that the evolutionary game converges to a single graph. If, however, the game were to have only Nash equilibria in mixed strategy, we speculate that the evolutionary process sketched above would converge to a limit cycle. Furthermore, if we were to compute the relative amounts of time spend in the various graphs of the cycle, we should recover the probability weights of one of the mixed strategy equilibria of the normal form one-period game (Kreps and Fudenberg 1993).

14.3.2   Strategic Interaction

There is another, less benign way of looking at how the coordination game may be played over time, one that involves strategy. Analyzing the coordination game in terms of strategy is beyond the scope of this chapter, but the reader should be aware that the type of connections that players manage to form determines their long-run realized payoff. In particular, other things being equal, better connected players—in the sense of being at the center of a symmetric game, or closer to a valuable player, or bridging large components of the economy (i.e., being a trader)—have better payoffs. Consequently players may try to manipulate the process by which connections are made. For instance, they may present themselves as naturally superior beings that deserve to be in the center of an extended star (feudal nobility, charismatic leader, etc.). They may aggressively seek the direct companionship of people with special endowments or connections, either to use that friendship/relationship exclusively for their own benefit (e.g., clientelism), or to use it in their relations with others (e.g., political peddlers and exclusive car dealers). Or they may resort to various forms of signals in order to attract potential partners (e.g., advertising).

Another approach that players may take is to let their bargaining strategy within each period be influenced by the global structure of the game. For instance, what contracts some players may have already secured within a single period may affect their bargaining position in subsequent negotiation rounds within that same period. Alternatively, players may opt for time-dependent bargaining strategies whereby they propose a good deal today in exchange for increased exchange and/or higher (barter) prices tomorrow. Failure to comply then triggers retaliation (e.g., tit for tat; see Axelrod 1984).

The examples above have a real life quality about them, for some people do attempt to manipulate the matching process to their advantage. Given the complexity of the game, and the difficulty of predicting how other players' future randomization will affect the final outcome, we should not be too surprised if these manipulation strategies are more an art than a science. This art, however, is what enables simple traders to subsist and even, if they are smart and lucky enough, to prosper beyond reason.

14.3.3   Overlapping Generations

Researchers interested in social mobility and class structure may find yet another way of modeling the matching process particularly attractive. This approach relies on an overlapping generations version of the model. In this version one starts with some arbitrary graph, and then lets new, long-lived generations be born every period. The members of these new generations build, during the course of their childhood, a series of relations with their parents, relatives, and kin. When they reach maturity, they start their independent life as "players" in the game and may decide to build new economic links on their own. Childhood, however, largely determines the kind of links they have already weaved with other players, many of which have also come of age, as well as the links that connect these players themselves to others. As a result of this process, some players will undoubtedly start in life with much better connections than others—some of these connections being direct family links, others being the result of attending better schools and universities, and so on.

In primitive pre-industrial societies in which prospects for exchange are limited to rudimentary forms of mutual insurance, links with relatives and kin may actually exhaust most of the opportunities for economic exchange. In these cases virtually all exchange takes place among family and friends (Ben-Porath 1980).

As economies increase in sophistication and specialization, the number of opportunities for economic exchange increases as well, and links with relatives and friends may no longer be sufficient. They may, however, subsist for a long time and continue to provide certain types of specialized services even in industrialized societies (e.g., home care for the elderly, the disabled, or the sick; provision of advice and information, particularly about jobs and business opportunities; access to jobs and business opportunities, directly or via personal network; and provision of political support). Examining these kinds of links would be a promising starting point for studying social mobility and social stratification in general.

14.3.4 Inefficient and Unconnected Equilibria

Any of the three mechanisms briefly sketched in the previous subsections should, with time, eventually lead to a situation in which no more opportunities for mutually beneficial trade remain. Nothing guarantees, however, that the resulting equilibria be Pareto efficient, or even connected. Given the path-dependent and haphazard order in which connections are made, it is quite possible for the resulting graph to be inefficient, and for individual players to remain unconnected. There is therefore room for coordinating the process of link formation itself! A discussion of this topic is beyond the scope this chapter, but three remarks come to mind.

The first is that most, if not all, so-called primitive societies have a well-defined and well-controlled matching mechanism, namely the rule governing how marriages are formed and lineages are defined. Exogamy, matrilocal marriages, and the like, can all be seen as organized ways of ensuring an optimal "mix" of connections, possibly with an eye on redundancy, or the sharing of risk.

The second remark is a consequence of the very complexity of the meta-coordination process. As is the case for other complex, nonlinear processes (e.g., Guckenheimer and Holmes 1983; Grandmont 1988; Arthur 1988), the outcome of meta-coordination may not be predictable, even if we were able to entirely specify its underlying deterministic process. This implies that a falsifiable theory of meta-coordination may be particularly difficult to construct.

The preceding remark leads to a third one, namely that the complexity/nonlinearity of the meta-coordination process potentially allows small causes to have big effects. In particular, it leaves room for charismatic leaders to influence the course of events. For instance, someone who has a clear vision of a better arrangement of economic or social life and who is able to communicate his or her convictions to others may in fact help the community achieve a more efficient outcome, and achieve it more rapidly. A similar role could be played by external actors, like the government, development projects, religious groups, and NGOs.

14.4   Learning Effects

In the previous section it was suggested that if the intertemporal economy can be modeled as an evolutionary game of random matching, then the simple fact that two players have found in each other opportunities for mutually beneficial trade favors continued interaction in the future. This feature tends to lock economic partners into a given structure of exchange. As a result a certain permanence of exchange is achieved in which trade flows largely reproduce themselves over time.

Permanence in trade flows is likely to be further reinforced if the process of exchange itself allows economic partners to progressively gain relevant information about each other. For instance, the user of a particular product may progressively learn something about the ability and willingness of its supplier to satisfy consistent quality standard, to meet deadlines, to show flexibility in dealing with unexpected events, or to meet other relevant contractual obligations. More generally, close business partners probably learn about each other's technology and preferences after repeated business interactions.

In some cases the information gained will not be flattering for one of the parties (or even both). When this happens, the unsatisfied party is likely to resume his or her search for reliable partners, and as a result economic exchange with the unsatisfactory partner is likely to dwindle or even disappear, provided of course that other sources of demand or supply are available. On the other hand, if economic interaction reveals flattering information about each parties, business relations are likely to get strengthened over time. In this case successful economic exchange will to result in long-term business partnerships.

Learning thus tends to reinforce lock-in and to crystallize patterns of economic exchange around existing trade flows. As a consequence it progressively isolates long-term trading partners (and here trade extents to any form of economic exchange, e.g., labor, capital, credit, and management) from competing sources of demand and supply. Their situation eventually resembles that of a bilateral monopoly, in the sense that the terms of economic exchange among them become dominated by intense bilateral negotiations. At the same time, however, long-term interaction favors the emergence of implicit cooperation or "gentleman's agreements" whose main purpose is to share the benefits of reduced transaction costs. This form of cooperation between otherwise competing business partners is best exemplified by their ability to place large orders or borrow large sums of money on a simple telephone call. The terms of the deal (price, quality, delivery, etc.) may be avidly negotiated between the two parties, but the form of communication (e.g., telephone) and the contract enforcement and monitoring procedures (e.g., absence of written contract, own accounting used as proof in court) are kept to the strictest minimum.

As exogenous conditions change over time (e.g., new products and technologies, emerging new business partners), prospects for mutually beneficial trade evolve and deals are struck with new partners. As a result trade flow patterns will be progressively modified, cards will be reshuffled, and economic opportunities will be revised. An immediate corollary is that the existence of learning effects generates novel opportunities for strategic behavior. As we just saw, learning strengthens the natural tendency of economies with nonconvex transaction costs to lock into a relatively permanent trade pattern. Furthermore learning generates cooperative gains by reducing information costs. Therefore, whenever new unexploited opportunities for mutually beneficial trade emerge in an economy with learning, rapidity of action determines along which lines trade flows are likely to crystallize. In other words, the degree of alertness and flexibility of various economic agents determines who secures key positions in new trade flows, and who is able to extract economic rents from market power and transaction cost reduction. Some economic agents may therefore position themselves in order to be better prepared to take advantage of new economic opportunities. Consequently they may actively seek possible new trading opportunities and adopt a flexible posture in anticipation of promising ventures (liquid assets, geographical mobility, etc.).

Economic agents who specialize in this kind of activity are typically traders and businessmen. The arguments presented in this chapter suggest that success in their endeavors requires a mix of human qualities that combines competitiveness with reliability, caution with audacity, and that is hard to achieve in the right proportions. Consequently, though success in trade or business may be very unequally distributed, the reward may remain so great that it keeps attracting new adventurous spirits.

There is also a darker side to learning effects. The advantage that existing business partnerships derive from experience may slow down the reshuffling of economic opportunities and preserve, at least temporarily, the existing structure of trade flows and economic power. In some circumstances the slowing down may give enough time to established businesses to copy new products, or to remodel their production methods and take advantage of new technologies. In other words, the old boys network of corporate executives, or the religious fraternity of Sefrou traders (Geertz et al. 1979), may work in such a way as to slow down entry and reduce social mobility. When the slow down is too strong and the "establishment" too well entrenched, incentives for innovation by new entrants are likely to be seriously stifled and economic progress suffers.

There is thus an Hegelian tension that inhabits economies characterized by nonconvex transaction costs and learning effects: new economic opportunities induce innovators to challenge the existing economic order, but only to put in place their own. As a consequence the process of economic transformation is more likely to resemble a Schumpeterian locomotive (with pressure building up, explosion, and release) than a neoclassical clock (with a smooth, continuous, and gentle movement).

14.5   Conclusion

In this chapter we showed how nonconvex transaction costs result in economic exchange that is based on relatively permanent networks of business or trade partnerships. We also showed how economic power is influenced by trade patterns and suggested a characterization of such power with the help of graph theory and the definition of regular bargaining processes. Next we proposed various ways by which economies with nonconvex transaction costs reach one of their multiple equilibria. Finally we discussed how learning effects strengthens lock-in and influences social mobility and economic transformation.

The framework presented here, although obviously stylized and barely sketched at places, generates insights that are relevant for a wide variety of situations. It generates patterns of economic exchange that are largely in agreement with available evidence regarding trade networks in pre-industrial societies (e.g., Mitchell 1969; Meillassoux 1971; Amselle 1977; Geertz et al. 1979; Greif 1993). It is applicable to nonmarket exchange among primitive societies and rural communities of the Third World (e.g., Posner 1980; Fafchamps 1992; Platteau 1994a). But it is also relevant for analyzing business networks and other long-term informal partnerships in developed countries (e.g., Dore 1987; Aoki 1988). It also has the advantages of building bridges with some of the sociology literature on networks in economic and other contexts (e.g., Mitchell 1969; Laumann and Pappi 1976; Burt 1980; Raub and Weesie 1990).

Much of what the model implies about strategic behavior, market power, evolution of trade flows, social mobility, or intergenerational effects is consistent with casual observation and the limited scientific evidence available (e.g., Mitchell 1969; Laumann and Pappi 1976; Knobe 1990). It also leaves the door open for theoretical refinements and empirical verification of its predictions. Finally the methodology proposed here offers a promising avenue for studying trade per se, a branch of economic activity that, paradoxically, has been largely ignored in economic theory, whether in general equilibrium, international trade, or industrial organizations. A number of economists have now begun tackling these difficult theoretical issues in some detail (e.g., Bala and Goyal 1998, 2000; Kranton and Minehart 2000a, b; Kranton and Minehart 2001). Much remains to be done.

15 Business Networks in Africa

In this chapter we investigate the connection between business networks and community. We do so for markets that are at the early stages of their development, as is the case in much of sub-Saharan Africa. We have shown that for firms above a minimum size, relational contracting is the rule in markets for agricultural products as well as for manufacturing inputs and outputs. Many markets in sub-Saharan Africa can best be thought of as composed of core networks of trade relationships that are fairly stable over time. This core is surrounded by a fringe of atomistic competitive firms that operate with high transactions costs because they lack trust in each other.

We have documented the many important roles that relationships play in facilitating market exchange, such as information sharing and the informal enforcement of contracts. These sets of trade and information-sharing relationships can be thought of as business networks and we discuss the implications of this idea for our understanding of African markets. We then explore the role that community affiliation plays in the membership of business networks. We examine observed patterns of ethnic concentration and conclude that at least in some African countries, these patterns are very unlikely to have been generated from a firm entry and growth process that grants equal access to business opportunities for all—even if we account for colonial heritage.

From this observation we conclude that entry into existing networks is biased. We discuss the possible sources and mechanism behind this bias. Based on the limited existing evidence, we argue that referral by family and friends is the most likely channel through which ethnic concentration arises. We also discuss the effect that business networks have on community formation.

15.1 Relationships and Networks

Before proceeding further, we must specify what we mean by network—the term not yet having found its way into economic jargon. The theory of networks was first proposed by sociologists to transcend the concept of community which was thought too vague and no longer adequate (e.g., Mitchell 1969; Landa 1994). Borrowing notation and concepts from the mathematical theory of graphs, individuals came to be regarded as nodes and relationships between them as links. The combination of nodes (individuals) and links (relationships) constitutes a graph or network.[1] Links

---

1. Mathematicians give the term "network" a more specific sense than that used in sociology (Foulds 1992). In this chapter we follow sociologists (and standard English) and use the term to refer to what mathematicians call "graphs." Sociologists also distinguish between subjective networks (the graph of all links emanating or leading to a specific individual) and objective networks (the graph of all the links between a set of nodes or individuals). While subjective networks are always well defined, objective networks often are open in the sense that links exist between members of the set and outsiders, such as between businessmen in Africa and Europe. Here we use one meaning or the other, depending on the context.

can be of various kind (e.g., trade, family, and information sharing) and of various strength (e.g., trade amount, and closeness of family relationship). Links can be unidirectional, as when one individual knows another but the reverse is not true (e.g., a movie star). They can be superposed, in which case sociologists speak of multiplex societies Gluckman (1955; see also Basu 1986). They can also vary over time.

Laid out in these general terms, the concept of network is nothing but a way of visualizing social relations of any kind. To give it life, one must specify a population of individuals or nodes, a particular kind of link, and a time frame. One could, for instance, construct the graph of all the trades that occurred among a set of economic agents during a particular time period, and call it a market or trade network. Alternatively, one may consider only certain types of transactions, such as repeated transactions, to generate the relational contracting network. In either case the resulting networks will just be a graphical depiction of the market itself, perhaps useful to study interindustry linkages but not substantively different.

The concept of network comes to full fruition when the definition of a link is broadened to include other useful economic functions such as informal contract enforcement and information sharing. Abundant evidence indeed exists that such links are central to the functioning of labor, credit, and insurance markets (e.g., Udry 1990; Fafchamps 1992; Udry 1994). In the words of Granovetter (1985), economic transactions are embedded in a social context. Mutual insurance among villagers, for instance, is now believed to revert primarily around long-term self-enforcing arrangements (e.g., Coate and Ravallion 1993; Fafchamps 1992, 1999a; Ligon et al. 2001; Fafchamps and Lund 2002).

15.2 Business Networks and Contract Enforcement

We have seen that relationships play a key role in facilitating exchange in sub-Saharan Africa. These relationship differ from pure market exchange in that they perform economic functions other than trade itself, such as information sharing, informal enforcement of contracts, and interlinking. To discuss the role that these relationships play in market development, let us define a business network as the set of such relationships with the agents they involve. Armed with this definition, we now examine in more detail the market configurations that naturally arise from the interaction between markets and business networks. To focus the discussion, we organize the presentation around one particular function that has recently received a lot of attention in the literature, namely contract enforcement.

In the preceding chapters we argued that networks can facilitate the establishment of trust by circulating essentially two distinct pieces of information: whether an agent has ever successfully completed a contract and whether an agent has ever breached a contract. Both types of information refer to the transaction history of an agent and they have generally been treated interchangeably in the literature. But the latter is, in general, more demanding than the former: it is fairly easy to ascertain whether a carpenter has ever manufactured a chair, but it is harder to ascertain whether he or she has ever failed to complete an order for a chair. Similarly it is easy to ascertain whether someone has ever paid a supplier; it is harder to assess whether the same person has ever paid a supplier late or not at all. Chapter 11 has shown that the characteristics of decentralized market exchange vary dramatically depending on whether the first or the latter type of information are circulated. Information sharing can play a positive role in facilitating exchange because the circulation of information about past contractual performances helps agents screen each other more cheaply.[2]

These theoretical results demonstrate that networks can facilitate market exchange in a purely decentralized manner, that is, without any collective action. It is clear, however, that networks sufficiently compact to form identifiable communities of common interest or "clubs" may mobilize to achieve better outcomes for themselves. Clubs can, for instance, organize the joint punishment of cheaters through ridicule, ostracism, or worse. To the extent that economic agents socialize and intermarry with members of their business community, rejection by business partners may impose an additional personal burden as well (e.g., Aoki et al. 1995; Spagnolo 1999): exclusion from social interaction such as marriage within a prosperous group is likely to be detrimental to the long term prosperity of cheaters.

Although these ideas have received much attention in the theoretical literature, evidence of collective punishments for opportunistic breach of contract is weak at best. In chapter 12 we showed that nonpayment of a supplier does not automatically lead to a loss of credit from other suppliers. This does not mean that ostracism is never used: in the course of a manufacturing sector survey in Kenya, the author met an Asian businessman who was shunned by his peers following a fraudulent bankruptcy. But such cases are very rare.[3] Furthermore, in countless interviews with African manufacturers and traders of all ethnic origins, never did respondents articulate the implicit obligation to participate to a collective punishment. One Ghanaian

---

2. Provided the information circulated within the community is reliable. In contrast to what is assumed by some theorists (Kandori 1992), gossip is a notoriously unreliable source of information. Not only is information distorted and imprecise, gossip can also be manipulated to hurt competitors. Gossip can be a channel of information or disinformation alike. This is why businessmen and women insist that they must know and trust the source of the information before giving it any credence.

3. Shunning may be more frequent for other social transgressions such as an adulterous wife.

trader in the Accra lumber market—a market known for its tight ethnic-based trading community—was asked whether he would oppose neighboring traders dealing with cheaters. His answer was: "If they want to deal with cheaters, it is their problem, not mine"—hardly the kind of answer one would expect if an explicit collective punishment strategy were in effect. Further discussions with respondents suggest that nonpayment of a supplier triggers loss of credit only when it is interpreted as a signal of financial difficulty and possible bankruptcy. This idea was formalized in chapters 11 and 12, where we show that collective punishment can arise in a fully decentralized manner without any explicit collective strategy, provided there is sufficient "churning" of firms.

Communities may also develop norms of behavior—a "business culture"—that are deemed suitable for the conduct of business (Hayami and Kikuchi 1981). Adherence to these norms of behavior may be further publicized through participation to religious rituals and membership in religious groups that reinforce respect of these norms. The role of these cultural norms is, for instance, documented for medieval trade in Greif (1993) and Greif (1994). In their detailed analysis of the Sefrou market in Morocco, Geertz et al. (1979) illustrate the role that Muslim brotherhoods play in helping market communities join forces for a common purpose. In her study of market emergence in pre-colonial Kenya, Ensminger (1992) documents the fact, historically, that traders who wanted to do business with coastal Arab traders and their descendants found it easier if they converted to Islam. Similar processes have been documented elsewhere in Africa (e.g., Cohen 1969; Shillington 1989). Poewe (1989) reports comparable motivations behind the spread of evangelical churches in present-day Zambia.

Although there is some evidence that business communities often pride themselves of having superior ethics, there is also an inordinate amount of circumstantial and anecdotal evidence that demonstrate that morality is an elastic concept. The truth is that few, if any, human societies are free from the temptations of greed and instant gratification. Although a moral code can probably discourage outright fraud and treachery, social and economic pressures are a more effective deterrent against opportunistic breach of contract than ethics alone.[4]

Another possibility is that business communities or "clubs" strive to build a reputation as a group with respect to other business communities with whom they are trading. This idea has been formalized by Kandori (1992) and Ellison (1994). This way trade takes place across communities and the benefits from repeated interaction are captured not through individual relationships but through community rela-

---

4. See, however, Platteau (1994b) who argues that during childhood individuals acquire, through what psychologists call "secondary socialization," what will constitute the moral fabric of their lives.

tionships. The reputation of the group becomes an asset that serves as collateral to guarantee good behavior. Each community may then choose to punish its own members for opportunistic breach of contract. Such situations have been described for ancient trade across ethnic boundaries—such as between Europeans and Africans along the Zambezi river (Shillington 1989).

Although such processes may have been at work in ancient times (Greif 2001), recent work on manufacturers and traders in Africa has found no recent evidence that communities punish their members for cheating individuals in other communities (e.g., Fafchamps et al. 1994, 1995; Fafchamps 1996; Fafchamps and Minten 2001a). If anything, cheating is perceived to be more prevalent across ethnic or religious boundaries as trust between communities is often low. Irrespective of whether culture and ethics should be considered an important contribution to business acumen, it remains that much social capital that is immediately relevant for market development and industrialization/modernization in poor countries is embedded within business networks and communities.

15.3 Business Networks, Competition, and Firm Entry

The existence of business networks also has some less desirable consequences. First of all, thanks to information sharing and joint punishment of deviant behavior, members of important and prosperous communities have a comparative advantage relative to others in the conduct of business. Evidence to this effect is provided by Barr (2000), Fafchamps (2000), and Fafchamps and Minten (2002b). Moreover, the more help and information agents receive from their community in their effort to screen each other, the less willing they become to screen individuals from outside their community. Economic agents in general prefer to deal with members of their own community (Macharia 1988). This process may explain why established Zimbabwean manufacturers, who for historical reasons are mostly of European and Asian origin, appear reluctant to deal with African firms despite good courts and widespread information sharing (e.g., Hoogeveen and Tekere 1994; Mumbengegwi 1994; Risseeuw 1994; Fafchamps et al. 1995; Fafchamps 2000). As a result prosperous communities have a tendency to reproduce themselves over time and to reinforce their grip on business—at least as long as they maintain their cohesion (Himbara 1994).

To the extent that membership to these communities is restricted and that members intermarry, social mobility is likely to be impaired as well. This reduces efficiency because entrepreneurs end up being selected from a small percentage of the population. Kenyan Asians, for instance, constitute 1 to 2 percent of the Kenyan population, yet they own the majority of light industries (Fafchamps et al. 1994).

Table 15.1 shows that similar patterns are present in other African countries (Bigsten et al. 2000a). The reader may wonder whether these patterns simply result from colonial heritage. While there is little doubt that colonial policies[5] favored non-African firms, it is fairly clear that the ethnic concentrations shown in table 15.1 could not have arisen from unbiased sampling since these policies were removed.

To see why this is the case, let the share of firms owned at time t by members of previously favored ethnic group be denoted η_t. Assuming, for simplicity, that the number of firms is constant[6] and that firms get replaced at a constant rate θ, the law of motion of η_t can be written

$$\eta_{t+1} = (1 - \theta)\eta_t + \theta\rho, \tag{15.1}$$

where ρ is the proportion of the favored ethnic group in new firms. If members of all ethnic groups are equally likely to start a new firm, then ρ should be equal to the proportion of the previously favored ethnic in the total population. Given our assumption that the number of firms is constant, an approximation for θ is obtained as one over the average age of firms. Table 15.2 reports the value of ρ implied by the current ethnic composition of manufacturing in Africa, assuming that at independence all firms were owned by non-Africans. The results are inescapable: in all nine countries except one (Ghana), the implied sampling rate for non-Africans exceeds their proportion in the total population—which in all cases is not larger than 1 or 2 percent. According to these simple calculations the inbreeding bias is largest in Côte d'Ivoire, Kenya, Zambia, and Zimbabwe.

Despite their crude character these findings makes us suspect that the average entrepreneurial talent is below what it could be if all agents had an equal chance. This outcome is also inequitable in the Jeffersonian sense of equal opportunity for all. Lack of social mobility is likely to be reinforced by social stratification through ethnicity, language, caste, education, and the like. For all these reasons the existence of strong business communities often creates social tensions, whose outcome can be the elimination of these communities and the dilapidation of the social capital they represent. History indeed abounds with examples of business groups earmarked for public retribution with or without the participation of the state.

Given the importance of these issues, it is worth investigating in more detail the process by which business networks reinforce themselves over time and end up

5. Including policies conducted during the Unilateral Declaration of Independence era in Zimbabwe.

6. This assumption is not too much of an oversimplification given that very little growth has taken place in African manufacturing since independence. Moreover, if the number of firms is increasing, one should observe even less ethnic concentration, hence reinforcing our conclusion.

Table 15.1
Ethnic composition of the ownership of African manufacturing firms

	Burundi	Cameroon	Côte d'Ivoire	Ethiopia	Ghana	Kenya	Tanzania	Zambia	Zimbabwe
African	82%	81%	60%	83%	91%	42%	73%	59%	33%
Asian	3%	2%	0%	0%	0%	51%	24%	26%	13%
European	6%	14%	23%	1%	1%	4%	0%	13%	47%
Mideastern	0%	1%	7%	0%	8%	2%	2%	2%	0%
Other	1%	3%	10%	15%	0%	2%	1%	0%	7%

Source: RPED panel surveys.

Table 15.2
Lower bound on ethnic bias in manufacturing entry

	Burundi	Cameroon	Côte d'Ivoire	Ethiopia	Ghana	Kenya	Tanzania	Zambia	Zimbabwe
Time between independence and survey	34	34	34	42	35	30	30	31	15
Average age of firms	11	12	16	17	15	19	16	18	24
Proportion of non-African owners at survey	10.0%	19.6%	39.4%	16.8%	8.7%	57.8%	27.1%	40.5%	67.1%
Implied minimum entry by non-Africans	6.4%	15.2%	31.8%	9.7%	0.0%	28.5%	14.8%	28.3%	30.3%

Source: RPED panel surveys.

excluding nonmembers from business exchanges. One point that has not been adequately recognized until now is that the circulation of information among agents is detrimental to entry. The reason is that when information on established agents is widely available, economic agents may rationally choose to wait until they meet an established agent on which they can obtain information rather than spending resources screening a new, unknown agent (see chapters 11 and 12). In fact the better information circulates, the harder it is for newcomers to be screened. Economies with well-established information-sharing networks are thus particularly inimical to new entrants as opposed to economies where information does not circulate and agents are forced to screen whoever shows up at their doorstep.

The contrast between Ghana, Kenya, and Zimbabwe manufacturing is, in this respect, quite telling. Ghana manufacturers form a diverse group without strong sense of community (e.g., Cuevas et al. 1993; Fafchamps 1996). This is, in part, the result of government efforts to curtail the economic and political influence of certain groups, such as Syro-Lebanese and Asante business communities. As a result information sharing is rudimentary and no single group is advantaged. This is not to say that networks of personal relationships are unimportant—Barr (2000) shows that they are—but the intersection of these personal networks does not constitute an ethnically homogeneous community.

In contrast, Kenyan manufacturing is dominated by entrepreneurs of South Asian origin—often second- or third-generation immigrants (e.g., Marris 1971; Himbara 1994; Fafchamps et al. 1994). Although in the 1960s the Kenyata government tried to prop up Kikuyu businesses, this policy failed to durably influence the ethnic composition of business (Himbara 1994). Kenyan Asians do not constitute a monolithic community, however. Survey respondents identified at least four distinct communities—"the Shahs, the Patels, the Sikhs, and the Ismaelians" as one respondent put it.[7] Within these communities, information circulates rather freely and client referral is a common practice. The survey uncovered little or no evidence of similar networks of information sharing among native entrepreneurs—at least in manufacturing.[8] As a result Asian businesses are at an advantage. Because informa-

7. The last two of these groupings are based on religious affiliation while the first two loosely correspond to Indian castes, despite the fact that Kenyan Asians do not, in general, follow caste distinctions. Respondents nevertheless pointed out that it is fairly easy for someone to change his or her name to Shah or Patel. The caste nature of the first two categories is thus quite blurred.

8. Why this is the case is unclear. Observations from the field suggest that African entrepreneurs commonly seek to establish personal relationships with existing businesses, which are predominantly Asian, instead of attempting to create a concurrent network. Granovetter (1995a), in contrast, provides examples of the development of separate business networks among immigrant minorities in the United States.

tion circulates only in an informal manner and networks are somewhat segmented, firms cannot rely purely on referral to identify reliable clients and suppliers; they must also screen agents from outside their network. Consequently it is possible for outsiders to gain acceptance in the business community. Entry then takes place through a lengthy probation process by which small amounts of credit are given to test the resolve and honesty of the prospective credit recipient (Fafchamps 1997c).

Zimbabwe presents yet another configuration. Except for very small businesses that are overwhelmingly in the hands of native entrepreneurs, most manufacturing firms are in the hands of people of European and Asian ascent (e.g., Daniels 1994; Bigsten et al. 2000a; table 15.2). Although this pattern of ethnic concentration was initiated by deliberate pro-white policies pursued during the colonial period and during the 1964 to 1979 Unilateral Declaration of Independence era, it is unclear why it has survived to this day. One contributing factor may, paradoxically, have been the presence of an active and widely used credit reference bureau which quickly developed in the 1980s. The existence of this bureau means that information on bad payers circulates widely in the economy   well beyond the confines of personal networks (Fafchamps et al. 1995). While this undoubtedly helps established businesses screen buyers and sellers, it also penalizes new businesses—especially those entrepreneurs unfortunate enough not to have been born within the existing business community. As a result information sharing may in fact have "frozen" the ethnic composition of Zimbabwean manufacturing. Fafchamps (2002b) investigates the theoretical conditions under which such outcome may arise and shows that it is most likely to arise when there is little firm renewal. This condition is by and large satisfied in Zimbabwe where manufacturing firms are, on average, much older than in other African countries (table 15.2). Setting up a credit reference bureau may thus have been detrimental to business entry.

If newcomers find it difficult to enter, one must then ask the question of how networks renew themselves over time. One possibility is no renewal: membership to the network is constant; the business community is a closed group. Such an outcome is more likely when opportunities for gains from trade are stable over time and the population of potential buyers and sellers does not change—as was more or less the case in Zimbabwe over the 15 years following independence. By the same token, markets dominated by closed groups are more likely to arise for trade flows driven by static comparative advantage—for instance, primary commodities, agricultural staples, and protected manufacturing goods. This may explain why long-distance trade in pre-industrial societies is often found in the hands of a tightly knit community (e.g., Braudel 1986; Greif 1993). In contrast, closed markets are unlikely for commodities that are subject to constant innovation and entry by Schumpeterian competitors, such as the Silicon valley. In these markets, constant reshuffling of firms and agents ensures that refusing to deal with unknown firms is uneconomical; free entry is more likely to arise in equilibrium. An immediate corollary of the above is that closed-shop markets are more likely in poor, stagnant economies where patterns of trade remain dominated by primary commodities. This is precisely what we observe in Africa.

There is also room for an intermediate solution which is for network members to co-opt new members. The advantage of this solution for the group is that new entry is reduced and competition minimized, thereby increasing the returns to the group's social capital while ensuring that sufficient entry takes place for the group to reproduce itself. Co-optation takes many different forms and raises a host of interesting issues. One possible form is for an established agent to screen a newcomer and then share the result of this test with others. A newcomer who successfully passes the test is then allowed to join the group—although he or she may not necessarily gain full access to information sharing. The client referral system described above for Kenya and, to a lesser extent, for Ghana essentially falls into this category (e.g., Fafchamps et al. 1995; Fafchamps 1996).

One difficulty of this kind of arrangement, which has been discussed in the finance literature (Lang and Nakamura 1990), is that sharing the result of the screening test may generate free riding: efforts by the testing agent to recoup screening costs from subsequent transactions may fail if the tested agent can immediately switch to another partner. In response, agents who perform the screening may seek to attach the tested agent for a minimum number of transactions. Examples of this strategy can be found in banks securing all the collateral of new borrowers to ensure they do not switch to another lender. Recourse to collateral is essentially unheard of in supplier credit, however (e.g., Bade and Chifamba 1994; Fafchamps et al. 1994; Fafchamps et al. 1995).

Co-optation may also take place before testing has occurred. Nepotism is one such form of co-optation whereby a member of the community with no prior experience is recommended for preferential treatment, such as credit without screening or a new job without trial period. Although nepotism is incompatible with the principle of equal opportunity for all—and is often stigmatized for this reason—it may represent an efficient way for a network to renew itself. The precise conditions under which nepotism is individually rational need to be ascertained, but intuitively nepotism is efficient for the group whenever, thanks to network externalities, an average person from within the community generates more returns for the group than an high-performance outsider. As to why this is the case may result from a variety of mechanisms, such as better exchange of information with other members of the group, easier monitoring of compliance with contractual obligations, and extra sanctions for deviant behavior. Anticipation that poor performance will be harshly punished ought to discourage below average community members to seek promotion through nepotism, thereby reducing adverse selection and false pretenses. Field observations suggest that nepotism is a reality, although it is unclear how important it is as a source of new entrepreneurs (e.g., Macharia 1988; Himbara 1994; Fafchamps et al. 1994, 1995). These issues deserve a more investigation.

It occasionally occurs that several distinct communities compete in the same markets. Bigsten et al. (2000a), for instance, reports that while ethnic concentration in manufacturing is strong in some African countries, in others several communities appear to be competing equally. Intuitively, in the absence of external intervention, the community whose social capital generates the largest private gains and cost reduction should grow at the expense of less efficient communities. Whether the long-term configuration of business involves one or several communities depends on whether the accumulation of social capital generates increasing or decreasing returns to scale. If returns to social capital are monotonically increasing with group size, then a single group should eventually dominate the market. If returns to social capital are monotonically decreasing in group size, exchange should remain atomistic, and communities should eventually disappear. If returns are initially increasing then decreasing, there is room for one or several communities depending on market size. Returns to group size might eventually drop because of the cost of information circulation increases exponentially with group size. It may also be that larger groups cannot impose social sanctions onto deviant members because they lack the capacity to set up meta-punishments, that is, punishments for those who refuse to ostracize past cheaters. Whatever the reason, if there are increasing returns to group size, one group should dominate.

Which group dominates, however, may be indeterminate. In this case, history matters: favoritism by governments and colonial administrations can give one group a head start, hence giving it an advantage that is subsequently difficult to shake (e.g., Shillington 1989; Himbara 1994). In other cases, historical accidents and relatively minor differences between groups can give one community a small initial advantage that gets reinforced over time. Expatriate communities seem to form a natural candidate for the formation of successful business communities, although there are many counterexamples as well. One possible explanation is that expatriate communities are, at least in part, the result of self-selection: only the most determined and the most ambitious migrate abroad in search of economic success. Expatriate communities are also often subject to residential and occupational restrictions that force them into certain neighborhoods and activities, thereby facilitating the circulation of information and raising the cost of exclusion from the group. Agriculture, for instance, is not a politically feasible option for Kenyan Asians (Himbara 1994). The same is probably true for Syro-Lebanese entrepreneurs in West Africa.

15.4   The Origin of Business Networks

In the preceding section we have remarked that business networks display a degree of ethnic concentration that is unlikely to have arisen from random matching of agents in the population at large. This raises the issue of the origin of business networks and the particular role that ethnicity plays in this respect. We begin by noting that although ethnic identity is a fluid and constantly evolving concept, no one would deny that identification with a particular ethnic group is a very strong emotion that can drive behavior that is otherwise irrational and destructive, such as civil war. Ethnicity is an important—and often ignored—issue in market development because unsupervised markets often develop a strong ethnic bias. It is nobody's secret, for instance, that many businessmen and women in Indonesia, Malaysia, and Singapore are ethnic Chinese. In much of East Africa, business is in the hands of ethnic South Asians, while in West Africa, individuals of Lebanese and Syrian origin dominate sectors of activity such as import-export trade.

Although it might be individually rational, ethnic bias is socially inefficient, in the Pareto sense; it is also inequitable and is an important source of political tension. The question then is: Where does ethnic bias come from? Fafchamps (2000) investigates the issue in Kenya and Zimbabwe manufacturing and concludes that the two most convincing sources of ethnic bias in market exchange are statistical discrimination and network effects. Ethnicity and community effects tend to reinforce each other whenever membership to the dominant business group is partly determined by one's ethnic origin.

The interface between ethnicity, communities, and economic exchange is perhaps the most explosive issue pertaining to markets. Government interventions in the functioning of markets have nearly always been motivated, implicitly if not explicitly, by resentment toward particular business communities and ethnic groups (e.g., Bauer 1954; Jones 1959). The restrictions on entry by noncommunity members that naturally derive from the development of dominant business groups nearly always generate suspicion of collusion, discrimination, and unfair business practices. When politicians become convinced that markets only serve the interests of a small prosperous minority, they are prompt to respond to economic and social crises by market repression and direct government intervention. The widespread use of roadblocks and other restrictions to the spatial movement of goods is perhaps the more vivid—

and most stupid—manifestation of governments' mistrust for the capacity of the market to serve the interests of producers and consumers. Whatever the cause for ethnic bias in market activity, failure to address the issue adequately is likely to result in policy reversal and the abandonment of market liberalization. Finding ways of ensuring nondiscriminatory markets is thus essential for sustained market-based economic development.[9]

To answer this question, we must understand the precise process that gives rise to ethnic bias. This raises the issue of whether business networks and communities organize around preexisting social constructs or create their own, new groupings. It is often believed that family and lineage play an important part in the formation of business networks. This belief is in part based on the observation that Third World autocrats often favor businesses owned by relatives.[10] Survey results from Africa paint a more nuanced picture. Family relationships are important in providing start-up capital and some initial business contacts (e.g., Hoogeveen and Tekere 1994; Bade and Chifamba 1994). They may also be a source of equity finance, possibly because information flows within the family facilitate monitoring (Fafchamps et al. 1995). For similar reasons partnerships and other forms of joint ownership are most commonly based on close family ties, except in very large firms. This situation is not peculiar to Africa but seems pervasive in developed economies as well.

There is, however, no evidence that family relations play a role in market exchange, contrary to what is often believed (Granovetter 1995a). Trade with relatives and friends is extremely rare (Bigsten et al. 2000a). Whenever it happens, it has a negative effect on firm performance, probably because trade with family members blurs the boundaries of the firm (Fafchamps and Minten 2002b). Discussion with survey respondents further indicate that entrepreneurs find it difficult to keep business with relatives within the confines of a sales transaction. Many respondents, for instance, emphasize that it is difficult to collect payment from relatives (Fafchamps and Minten 2001a). One Ghanaian carpenter put best when he stated that "dealing with relatives is the surest way to go out of business." This interpretation is reinforced by the work of Fafchamps and Lund (2002) on mutual insurance in rural Philippines: the authors show that risk sharing among close relatives is more likely to take the form of gifts rather than loans. Informal loans without interest and with no set repayment date are the dominant form of insurance with more distant friends and relatives. Platteau and Abraham (1987) report similar findings among Indian fishermen.

---

9. The same can be said of gender bias.

10. The last example to receive public attention is that of business interests held by Suharto's family in Indonesia.

Again, contrary to some commonly held views (Granovetter 1995a), kinship or place of origin appear to play little or no role in the formation of business networks. Individuals "from the same village" (an African aphorism often used to refer to close ethnic and kinship ties) constitute a minute portion of the suppliers and clients reported by African manufacturers (Bigsten et al. 2000a). Proportions might be somewhat higher among microenterprises (e.g., Macharia 1988; Fafchamps 1994), but this could be an outcome of the apprenticeship system: trade skills acquired through apprenticeship are likely to be concentrated by place of origin if apprentices are recruited principally among family and friends. Fafchamps (2002a) and Gabre-Madhin (1997) find no evidence of network formation by place of origin among grain traders in Madagascar and Ethiopia. These African findings are in contrast with those reported for Asia by Hayami (1996).

Religion and ethnicity play a complex role in the formation of business networks (e.g., Cohen 1969; Meillassoux 1971; Amselle 1977; Granovetter 1985; Poewe 1989; Granovetter 1995a). A thorough coverage of the extensive literature on this issue would take us too far, so we will limit it to a few observations. As we have discussed in previous sections, business networks often—though not always (e.g., Gabre-Madhin 1997; Bigsten et al. 2000a; Fafchamps 2002a)—display levels of religious and ethnic concentration that are extremely unlikely to result from random selection. What is often unclear is whether business networks arise from preexisting ethnic and religious networks or the opposite. Regarding religion, for instance, there is some evidence that religious conversion is sometimes motivated by the desire to join a particular business community (e.g., Shillington 1989; Ensminger 1992). The same is true of strict observance of religious principles, such as the adherence to a particular dress code or the obligation for devout Muslim to undertake a pilgrimage to Mecca if they can afford it (e.g., *hadji*[11] traders in the Sahel), and of membership in religious organizations (e.g., Muslim brotherhoods in Sudan, *marabouts* in Senegal). The upshot of this is that the relationship between religion and business networks is unlikely to be unidirectional. In their description of the Moroccan market of Sefrou, for instance, Geertz et al. (1979) show the close integration of business networks and religious festival committees. Their interpretation is that both types of social structures reinforce each other: involvement in religious activities provides meeting opportunities for businessmen, which is precisely why they participate in religious activities in the first place. In addition they argue that religious leaders use their moral authority to arbitrate certain disputes and to organize col-

---

11. A *hadji* is a person who has completed a pilgrimage to Mecca.

lective action (Platteau 1994b). Similar patterns are described for Chinese business-men in Southeast Asia in Geertz (1963).

At first glance ethnicity might appear more exogenous than religion, but reality is more complex. First, what constitutes an ethnic group is a fluid concept. This fluidity is perhaps best illustrated by the recent history of Somalia. In the 1976 Somalia launched a war against Ethiopia in an attempt to reunite all Somali people under the same flag. Fifteen years later the same Somalia collapsed into separate fiefdoms on the basis of ethnicity, now defined differently. Ethnicity and, more generally, community identity can be shaped by history to suit the social preferences of the time. Second, given a particular definition of ethnicity, the ethnic affiliation of a particular individual is not always clear because it depends on various factors such as one's place of birth, mother tongue, place of residence, religion, race, and ethnic affiliation of parents. Whenever these factors do not coincide, the ethnicity of an individual is subject to interpretation. Fulanis living in northern Nigeria are a good example: because they speak Hausa at home, they often can alternatively identify themselves as Hausas or Fulanis, depending on what suits them best (Cohen 1969). In many societies it is even possible to change one's ethnicity—at least superficially— by learning another language or by changing one's name. Intermarriage is another possible avenue into ethnic conversion. Many manifestations of these processes were apparent in surveys, although collecting quantitative data on these issues proved impossible due to the extreme sensitivity of ethnic issues in all societies studied.[12]

Assuming that ethnicity and ethnic affiliation were defined without any ambiguity, the relationship between ethnicity and business networks remains loose even when business networks are ethnically concentrated. The reason is that ethnic groups are, by definition, very large, often numbering in millions. Even ethnic minorities such as Asians in Kenya or whites in Zimbabwe still count over a hundred thousand individuals in each country, the overwhelming majority of which are not in business. Moreover those who are entrepreneurs often operate in unrelated sectors of activity. In contrast, business networks are small—a few hundred individuals at most, often much less (e.g., Mitchell 1969; Granovetter 1995a; Barr 2000)—and tightly knit. There is therefore no sense in which an ethnic "community" can serve as the only platform for the establishment of a business network. A Kenyan Asian cannot, for instance, walk into another Asian's shop and obtain supplier credit without referral. Unless the two individuals find a common acquaintance that can vouch for them and guarantee repayment, credit will not be offered (Fafchamps et al. 1994). Because

12. In some cases we had the distinct impression that raising the question of ethnic identification was sensitive precisely because respondents preferred to maintain some ambiguity as to their precise affiliation.

Kenyan Asians socialize principally with other Kenyan Asians, two Asians are more likely to find a common acquaintance than, say, an Asian and a Kikuyu. Consequently there is a high probability that a referral system will result in ethnically concentrated business networks. Fafchamps (2000) tests this proposition formally and shows that once networks are controlled for, the measured effect of ethnicity on access to supplier credit falls dramatically.

Although family, ethnicity, and religion play some role in the formation of business networks, the picture that emerges from numerous interviews with manufacturers and traders in Africa is one where business networks, for the most part, result from business interaction. Bigsten et al. (2000a), for instance, finds that more than 90 percent of African manufacturers describe their suppliers and clients as simple business acquaintances. In many cases commercial relationships are nurtured through business meetings and through socialization outside of work (e.g., Fafchamps 1994; Fafchamps et al. 1995). In this respect business is not very different from academe. Individuals who do not socialize with their clients and suppliers and who do not maintain regular business relationships are at a disadvantage (e.g., Fafchamps 2000; Fafchamps and Minten 2002b). Ethnic concentration therefore seems to result from nothing else than historical accident and socialization patterns that are reinforced by the practice of business itself.

15.5 Communities and Networks

Before concluding, it is worth spending a few pages discussing the various forms that networks can take so as to make the link with the main theme of this book, which is communities and markets. Empirical evidence collected in Africa indicates that there are many business networks that do not constitute communities. Malagasy traders and Ghanaian manufacturers, for instance, are embedded in various networks of interpersonal relationships, but they do not, as a rule, belong to an homogeneous business community. There may be identifiable communities regrouping subsets of traders or manufacturers, such as Malian traders in Accra's lumber market or Pakistani businessmen in Antananarivo, but these communities are small relative to the total size of the market. These simple observations raise the issue of when networks can be said to form communities.

This is not an easy question. It has been argued that it takes six people or less to connect any two people in America. In this sense the whole population of the United States—and even of the world—can be described as a single large network. While individuals must be connected to qualify as members of a community, the concept of network is clearly much larger than that of community as we normally understand it. What then defines a community? The approach adopted by sociologists seems to have been to regard relationships as the building block of social constructs and to visualize society as a network of relationships (e.g., Mitchell 1969; Coleman 1988). Some of these relationships may be stronger than others—strong links versus weak links, in the parlance of Granovetter (1995b); relationships may also be multifaceted, that is, may take place at multiple levels—economic, social, symbolical (Basu 1986).

Moving from the fuzzy concept of community to the more general notion of networks presents other advantages. Consider the issue of network capital, for instance. In general, someone who has more links has more options and, other things being equal, is likely to be better off. The number of one's connections can thus be taken as one measure of one's social capital: the more links, the more social capital (e.g., Barr 2000; Fafchamps and Minten 2002b). In contrast, measures of social capital built on the notion of communities are unable to make such fine distinctions (e.g., Coleman 1988; Putnam et al. 1993). The concept of network also throws new light on the definition of dominant market position. Consider a situation in which individuals with very few links command a key position in the economy. To see how, suppose that N producers and M consumers of a particular product do not deal with each other directly but use intermediaries—let's say traders. Further suppose that products are assembled from producers by one individual that we will call the assembler, and that they are sold to consumers by another individual that we call the retailer. Assembler and retailer deal with each other via a wholesaler. In this simplified example, the wholesaler has the least number of links—two—but the most market power: without the wholesaler, goods cannot move from producers to consumers. Unlike in a production monopoly, the wholesaler must buy what he or she sells. If transacting was costless, the wholesaler could not extract any monopoly rent: the threat of entry would prevent that. If transactions costs are nonconvex, however, as is the case in the presence of screening costs, trade concentration naturally arises as a way to economize on transactions costs (see chapter 14). This simple example illustrates that the network structure of the market can confer market power to some agents in a way that is not adequately captured by the concept of business community.

Within a network view of the world, communities or cliques can be defined as sets of agents or "nodes" that are linked to each other in multiple and strong ways (Mitchell 1969). Examples of such communities include the set of businessmen and women who regularly go to the same church or temple, members of the same golf club, and individuals affiliated to the same professional organization.[13] Some of

---

13. In contrast, family does not, in general, define a community in this sense. This is because individuals by definition belong to partially overlapping networks of family relations.

these communities may restrict or condition entry, in which case one may want to call them clubs (e.g., a golf club). Others are open to all (e.g., churchgoers). Some communities are formal and have a legal status with an internal constitution and rules of procedure (e.g., a business association). Others remain informal (e.g., the individuals who meet in a particular bar or restaurant).

The available empirical evidence suggests that it would be perilous to restrict the definition of communities to only some of these categories. For instance, Hendley et al. (1998) shows that, in Russia business communities can largely be identified with professional associations. Narayan and Pritchett (1999) similarly use membership in community associations as their concept of network capital. In contrast, discussions with African manufacturers indicate that Kenyan Asians meet at weddings and funerals and Zimbabwean whites meet at sport events and business conferences. Studying which form of organization is optimal is beyond the scope of this chapter, but intuitively, open communities should be better than closed ones and formal organizations with clear rules and procedures should be better than informal organizations. Communities are not always free to choose their internal organization, however: the form they take is partly influenced by the state's attitude toward business. Discussions with survey respondents, for instance, revealed that Ghanaian lumber mill owners used to meet at their professional association in Kumasi. In the late 1980s several of them found themselves indicted by the government in front of tribunals of exception. Although the exact reasons for these events are unclear, respondents expressed a strong suspicion that they were politically motivated and aimed at curbing the power of the association. In these circumstances it is not too surprising if Ghanaian manufacturers now prefer to meet informally.

15.6   Conclusion

The legal system alone cannot develop fully fledged markets. Personal trust and relationships are important, especially in early stages of development when firms—and therefore transactions—are small, product quality is not standardized, and economic agents have no forecloseable assets. In these circumstances business networks help reducing transactions costs by circulating information on contractual performance and by coordinating the punishment of cheaters. Networks thus play a important positive role in market development. The early development of markets cannot be understood without investigating the role played by business networks. In presence of nonconvex transactions costs, we also showed that we must worry about the market power that business networks confer to certain individuals who occupy key positions in an exchange system.

Regarding market development policy, we argued that the emergence of business networks can generate various forms of discrimination and exclusion that operate to the disadvantage of nonnetwork members. These effects get compounded by statistical discrimination when business networks are built around particular religious, ethnic, or racial groups. Efforts to develop markets should be take into account the potential for a political backlash when resentment against successful business networks reaches a breaking point.

Having spent time and effort investigating the role of business networks in market development, is it possible to imagine markets without them? The answer is a guarded yes. There are indeed ways by which institutions or technology can substitute for networks. Brand recognition is a good example. In a world where production is undertaken by a myriad of small producers and products are highly heterogeneous, such as agricultural products and crafts in poor countries, assessment of product quality is costly. In contrast, developed economies are characterized by the presence of a small number of producers offering products that are highly standardized and homogeneous over time. This enables consumers to economize on quality assessment by relying on brand name instead. Knowing this, producers may invest in the reputation of their products, which then becomes an additional guarantee of quality. A similar process takes place when traditional seeds, which often result from centuries of informal breeding by farmers and are extremely variable across space, are replaced by standardized modern varieties (Hayami and Ruttan 1985). Even in the absence of returns to scale in production, quality control can be simplified through standardization. Franchising is a good illustration of such a process. It is unclear why franchising is absent from poor countries while the need for quality control is so patent. One possible explanation is that franchise contracts are difficult to enforce.

Institutional innovations can also be found that facilitate credit checks. Credit reference bureaus exist that disseminate information about opportunistic breaches of contract. Organized exchanges can also be instituted that force market participants to post a bond before engaging in exchange. This bond ensures that contracts are honored, thereby eliminating the need for credit screening and speeding up transactions. The applicability of these innovations to poor countries deserves more research.

16 Returns to Network Capital in Agricultural Trade

The model presented in chapter 14 suggests that economic agents derive some advantages from the position they occupy in a network of business relations. In particular, agents at the center of a dense network are expected to collect rents. Let the number of links an agent has be called his network capital. The models presented in chapters 11 and 12 also generate returns to network capital because better connected agents can screen more cheaply. The discussion and evidence presented in chapter 15 suggests that network effects might be powerful enough to shape firm entry.

This chapter investigates the role played by network capital in the performance of agricultural traders. By network capital, we mean the network of business contacts that traders have. Using original survey data from three African countries, we establish that individual traders with more contacts have higher output. We investigate whether these returns should be interpreted as oligopoly or monopoly rents, as suggested in chapter 13, or whether they help firms increase traded quantities, probably because they economize on transactions costs. We also investigate the origin of network capital and other productive resources. The evidence suggests that start-up conditions and business experience have a paramount influence on social and physical capital. Family background is relatively unimportant after the creation of the firm, but it matters at start-up.

African trade in food products offers the perfect testing ground for an inquiry into the role of network capital: food is produced by millions of small farmers who typically sell a few bags of their surplus production (e.g., Barrett 1997a). These small quantities have to be assembled into truck-size loads and transported over poor quality roads to towns and cities, only to be broken down into smaller quantities for poor urban consumers. The small size of transactions at either ends of the marketing chain implies unusually high search costs. Transportation difficulties and delays dissociate price movement across space, so arbitrage opportunities are hard to predict. Finally, the small size of individual transactions and rapid turn-around time make it difficult to rely on courts and lawyers to enforce contracts. These conditions thus create an environment where transactions costs are expected to be high—and returns to network capital should be high as well.

Supposing that network capital raises the productivity of individual traders, the next question is: Where does network capital come from? Much of the sociology literature emphasizes the role of family and kinship. Network capital, it is argued, is inherited from parents and relatives in the form of business contacts, inherited attitudes, and identification with a group (e.g., Ben-Porath 1980; Granovetter 1995a). According to this approach, network capital is essentially vested in a group or community, which then tends to reproduce itself over time (e.g., Himbara 1994; Narayan and Pritchett 1999). A more individualistic approach to network capital is also conceivable. In this approach, individual entrepreneurs build up business contacts on their own. These contacts may be acquired prior to setting up a business—for instance, in school, as employee or apprentice in another firm—or they may be accumulated in the process of business itself. We test these various ideas and compare the accumulation of network capital with that of working capital and manpower.

16.1   Concepts and Testing Strategy

Economists normally think of production as depending on a series of resources under the control of the producing firm. These resources typically include physical and human capital as well as the management capabilities of the firm's owner or board of directors. Production efficiency depends on what takes place within the firm: combining factors of production in ways that maximize output, purchasing inputs in proportions to their relative prices, and so on. The way in which the firm relates to the market is supposed not to affect production efficiency. When firms buy and sell in perfect markets, this is the correct approach because the relationships that economic agents have with each other are then irrelevant: with full information and perfect enforcement of contracts, agents can change suppliers and clients costlessly in response to minute variations in publicly known prices. Relationships confer no advantage over the market; they have no value.

Ignoring network capital, however, is no longer valid when markets are imperfect. In that case relationships may convey information that minimizes search costs, as in Kranton (1996b), or they may facilitate the enforcement of contracts, as in chapter 10. Thanks to better enforcement of contracts, agents may be able to conduct business in a more efficient manner. Whenever trust is present, agents can lower their guard and economize on transactions costs such as the need to inspect quality before buying or the need to organize payment in cash at the time of delivery. As we saw in earlier chapters, relationships and social networks enable agents to economize on transactions costs, although they may fail to achieve the same level of aggregate efficiency as perfect markets. Network capital should be viewed as an imperfect response to the absence of perfect market.

Having clarified the reasons why network capital may affect efficiency, we now discuss how its effect on firm performance can be tested. Consider a firm with physical, human, and network (social) capital denoted K, H, and S, respectively. Let its production function be denoted

$$Q = F(L, K, H, S), \tag{16.1}$$

where Q and L stand for output and labor, respectively. If network capital is irrelevant for the firm's performance—for instance, because markets are nearly perfect—S

should have no effect on output once we control for L, K, and H. The effect of S on firm efficiency can thus be tested in the usual way (Chambers 1988), that is, by regressing output Q on labor and physical, human, and network capital: if S is shown to have a significant positive effect on Q, this constitutes evidence that firms with more network capital get more return from their labor and physical and human capital. A similar approach is used by Barr (2000).

For the estimation of equation (16.1) to yield consistent parameter estimates, however, the estimation must be devoid of simultaneity bias. It is possible, for instance, that traders would respond to good market opportunities by raising more working capital and hiring more workers. We deal with this possibility by instrumenting all potentially endogenous regressors.

16.2   Returns to Network Capital among Agricultural Traders

Returns to network capital are thus investigated by regressing value added on network capital as well as conventional factors of production such working capital, manpower, and the human capital of the entrepreneur. The data come from the three surveys of agricultural traders in Benin, Madagascar, and Malawi. The functional form used for regression analysis is basically a Cobb-Douglas production function and is estimated in log form. Given the Cobb-Douglas functional form, variables such as network capital that potentially raise the efficiency of labor and capital factor out as a Hicksian neutral multiplicative term; that is, we have

$$Q = (g(S)L)^{\alpha}(h(S)K)^{\beta} = g(S)^{\alpha}h(S)^{\beta}L^{\alpha}K^{\beta} = f(S)L^{\alpha}K^{\beta}, \tag{16.2}$$

where $g(S)$, $h(s)$, and $f(S)$ are functions that express the effect of network capital S on the efficiency of labor L and capital K. Network capital is measured as the number of traders known. The variable is entered in log form to account for the possibility that marginal returns to network capital are decreasing. If network capital raises the productivity of conventional factors of production, it should have a positive and significant coefficient. For Benin and Malawi, we also include membership in a local trader association as an alternative measure of network capital. This information was not collected in Madagascar. Associations are much more prevalent in Benin where they result from a deliberate promotion policy pursued by the Beninese government.

Since surveyed firms are traders, total sales is the relevant measure of production. Value added Q is measured as the difference between total sales and total purchases in US\$; it represents the total returns to labor, management, and capital. Ordinary least squares estimation of equation (16.2)—after taking logs—is reported in

Table 16.1
Determinants of value added

Regressors	Madagascar OLS		Benin OLS	
	Coefficient	t-statistic	Coefficient	t-statistic
Regressors				
Number of traders known	0.460	5.74	0.328	6.19
Member of trader association	na		1.000	6.44
Working capital	0.298	8.38	0.628	10.21
Manpower, in man-months	0.840	8.14	−0.200	−1.93
Female trader	−0.245	−2.18	−0.189	−1.01
Years of education	0.040	2.01	−0.034	−1.52
Years of experience in trade	0.143	1.56	0.066	0.60
Number of languages spoken	−0.248	−2.17	0.089	1.65
Regional dummies				
Intercept	3.052	4.25	0.882	1.88
Joint significant tests				
Labor and capital jointly significant	124.87		54.11	
p-value	0.0000		0.0000	
CRS in labor and capital	2.21		33.45	
p-value	0.1380		0.0000	
R-squared	0.446		0.425	
Number of observations	636		535	

Notes: Traders known, working capital, manpower, and experience are in logs. (1) Instrumented variables are traders known, membership in trader association, working capital, and manpower. Instruments listed in tables 16.4 to 16.6.

table 16.1. Results show that the number of traders known has a strong and significant effect on value added. The magnitude of the effect is large: a doubling in the number of traders known is associated with a 30 to 46 percent increase in value added. Membership in a trader association is also significantly positive in Benin and its effect is large—membership results in a doubling of value added.

Working capital is strongly significant in all three countries. Employment, measured in person-months, is significant in two of the three countries. In Benin collinearity with working capital yields a negative coefficient on labor.[1] Women are less productive than men in Madagascar and Malawi—a likely reflection of the many

1. In Benin, labor is not significant whether or not network capital—or other regressors—are included in the regression. One likely explanation is that Beninese traders—the overwhelming majority of which are women—often combine trade with childcare. To the extent that childcare distracts women for the trading activity itself, recording a child as a "family helper" may result in a negative or nonsignificant coefficient on labor. Another possibility is that when business is bad and there is little to do, some traders invite relatives to join them in the business to fight boredom. This issue deserves further investigation, but since it does not affect our main result—returns to social capital—we ignore it for now.

Malawi OLS		Madagascar IV[1]		Benin IV[1]		Malawi IV[1]	
Coefficient	t-statistic	Coefficient	t-statistic	Coefficient	t-statistic	Coefficient	t-statistic
0.301	5.42	0.961	2.72	0.484	4.66	0.551	4.04
−0.018	−0.06	na		2.730	3.44	−0.438	−0.27
0.591	12.56	0.306	1.35	0.848	4.50	0.663	3.64
0.361	3.06	0.972	1.75	−1.559	−3.10	−0.466	−0.78
−0.353	−2.85	−0.140	−0.98	0.305	1.08	−0.471	−3.00
−0.026	−1.39	0.028	1.09	−0.060	−1.88	−0.020	−0.95
0.065	0.80	−0.033	−0.25	−0.074	−0.46	0.061	0.69
−0.044	−0.70	−0.180	−1.32	0.204	2.46	−0.039	−0.56
		Included but not shown					
3.695	10.97	1.958	2.11	−2.052	1.94	2.782	3.15
137.31		27.98		10.58		22.87	
0.0000		0.0000		0.0000		0.0000	
0.22		0.60		15.25		3.31	
0.6425		0.4398		0.0001		0.0693	
0.438		0.406		0.132		0.360	
585		635		505		584	

demands on their time imposed by housework and on the resulting restrictions on their movements across markets. Education is positive and significant in Madagascar but negative and nonsignificant elsewhere. Agricultural trade may thus not be the best way to get a return on one's education. Experience in trade is positive but never significant once the number of traders known is included in the regression. Constant returns to scale in working capital and labor cannot be rejected in two of the three countries.

Because working capital, manpower, membership in associations, and the number of traders known are potentially subject to endogeneity bias, we reestimate the regressions using instrumental variables. Results are presented in the second part of table 16.1. Instruments include family background, personal characteristics, and start-up conditions; they are listed in tables 16.4 to 16.6 and are discussed below. Results confirm the overwhelming importance of network capital: coefficients remain large and significantly positive in all cases. If anything, instrumenting nearly doubles the size of estimated returns to network capital. The return to membership in trader association more than doubles in Benin. Multicollinearity between instrumented working capital and manpower (coefficients of correlation of 0.81, 0.91, and 0.80

Table 16.2
Quantities traded

| | Madagascar: Rice | | | |
| | OLS | | IV[1] | |
	Coefficient	t-statistic	Coefficient	t-statistic
Regressors				
Number of traders known	0.472	5.87	1.143	2.15
Member of trader association	na		na	
Working capital	0.253	6.79	0.280	1.77
Manpower, in man-months	0.685	6.57	0.513	0.97
Female trader	−0.344	−3.01	−0.254	−1.85
Years of education	0.073	3.47	0.063	2.58
Years of experience in trade	0.154	1.70	−0.028	−0.18
Number of languages spoken	−0.296	−2.81	−0.224	−1.62
Regional dummies				
Intercept	4.700	9.84	4.036	5.54
Joint significant tests				
Labor and capital jointly significant	100.88		13.06	
p-value	0.0000		0.0000	
CRS in labor and capital	0.48		0.27	
p-value	0.4868		0.6047	
R-squared	0.531		0.451	
Number of observations	429		428	

Notes: Traders known, working capital, manpower, and experience are in logs. (1) Instrumented variables are traders known, membership in trader association, working capital, and manpower. Instruments listed in tables 16.4 to 16.6.

in Madagascar, Malawi, and Benin respectively) precludes an identification of their individual effect on output. But their joint effect remains strong in all cases. Constant returns to scale in labor and working capital continues to be strongly rejected in Benin.

16.3   Testing for Network Rents

We have established that better connected traders have larger value added. We now investigate whether the effect operates through prices or quantities. Evidence that better connected traders obtain better prices—and thus have a higher unit margin—would be consistent with the network rents discussed in chapter 14. Evidence that they have similar unit margins but larger quantities traded would, in contrast, suggest that the effect of network capital operates through a reduction of transactions costs and a faster turn-around on working capital.

Benin: Maize				Malawi: Maize			
OLS		IV[1]		OLS		IV[1]	
Coefficient	t-statistic	Coefficient	t-statistic	Coefficient	t-statistic	Coefficient	t-statistic
0.236	4.40	0.375	4.25	0.175	2.14	0.318	1.49
0.995	5.96	1.754	1.81	−0.122	−0.28	−0.393	−0.17
0.561	9.04	0.702	4.22	0.712	10.11	0.958	3.79
−0.281	−2.71	−0.763	−1.64	0.465	2.89	−0.543	−0.69
−0.346	−1.84	−0.039	−0.15	0.135	0.67	0.101	0.35
−0.027	−1.17	−0.034	−1.22	−0.038	−1.44	−0.052	−1.60
0.123	1.05	0.034	0.21	0.155	1.32	0.228	1.67
0.080	1.49	0.081	1.11	−0.037	−0.41	0.024	0.21
		Included but not shown					
4.229	8.50	2.492	2.28	6.179	11.94	4.666	3.45
41.15		9.27		101.36		27.43	
0.0000		0.0001		0.0000		0.0000	
53.58		7.15		1.70		1.07	
0.0000		0.0078		0.1935		0.3017	
0.418		0.354		0.527		0.451	
436		414		283		283	

To test these ideas, we split value added into unit margin and quantity sold. This decomposition can only be done for homogeneous products. Consequently, for the purpose of testing, we focus on the most widely traded agricultural commodity in each sample—rice in Madagascar, and maize (corn) in Benin and Malawi. Ordinary least squares and instrumental variable results are summarized in table 16.2 for quantities and table 16.3 for unit margin. Instruments are as before.

In all three countries, network capital is shown to have a very strong and significant effect on quantities traded. In Benin, membership in a trader association also raises quantities sold. In contrast, in two of the three countries, network capital has no significant effect on unit margin. Only in Benin does unit margin show a significant relationship with network capital. This is true with and without instrumentation. In the other two countries, we appear unable to explain much of the variation in unit margin, which is dominated by regional differences.

To summarize, only in Benin do we find evidence that network capital generates network rents by raising the unit margin while limiting sales. This is also the country where trader associations are most widespread and active. We find, however, no

Table 16.3
Unit margin (sales price − purchase price)

	Madagascar			
	OLS		IV[1]	
	Coefficient	t-statistic	Coefficient	t-statistic
Regressors				
Number of traders known	−0.018	−1.15	−0.047	−0.61
Member of trader association	na		na	
Working capital	0.003	0.46	0.019	0.85
Manpower, in man-months	0.033	1.58	0.002	0.03
Female trader	−0.004	−0.20	−0.009	−0.38
Years of education	0.002	0.46	0.002	0.43
Years of experience in trade	−0.007	−0.41	0.008	0.34
Number of languages spoken	−0.027	−1.38	−0.032	−1.34
Regional dummies				
Intercept	0.004	0.03	0.002	0.01
Joint significant tests				
Labor and capital jointly significant	2.36		0.95	
p-value	0.0963		0.3887	
CRS in labor and capital	2811		228	
p-value	0.0000		0.0000	
R-squared	0.274		0.253	
Number of observations	378		377	

Notes: Traders known, working capital, manpower, and experience are in logs. (1) Instrumented variables are traders known, membership in trader association, working capital, and manpower. Instruments listed in tables 16.4 to 16.6.

evidence that these associations per se help traders raise unit margins. This suggests that network rents do not result from collusion to fix prices but from traders' ability to extract a intermediation monopoly rent. In the other two countries, we find no such evidence. These results suggest that contrary to commonly held beliefs, the primary effect of network capital on firm performance is through sales volume. Only in some cases does network capital seem to affect traders' ability to modify prices to their advantage.

16.4 Accumulation of Social and Physical Capital

Next we examine the origin of network and physical capital as well as employment. We focus on two possible accumulation processes: before and after the creation of the trading enterprise. We also control for personal characteristics, family background, and geographical location. We estimate regressions of the form:

Benin				Malawi			
OLS		IV[1]		OLS		IV[1]	
Coefficient	t-statistic	Coefficient	t-statistic	Coefficient	t-statistic	Coefficient	t-statistic
0.003	2.38	0.004	2.13	0.003	1.09	−0.002	−0.28
−0.005	−1.34	0.015	0.68	−0.002	−0.19	0.029	0.44
0.005	3.32	0.007	1.83	0.003	1.34	0.011	1.58
−0.005	−2.25	−0.016	−1.54	−0.011	−2.42	−0.032	−1.44
0.005	1.08	0.011	1.90	0.015	2.64	0.021	2.63
−0.001	−1.20	−0.001	−1.13	−0.001	−0.86	−0.001	−1.15
−0.003	−0.99	−0.006	−1.49	−0.001	−0.45	−0.001	−0.27
0.001	1.08	0.002	1.29	−0.000	−0.02	0.002	0.69
0.009	0.80	0.023	−0.92	0.020	1.36	−0.010	−0.26
6.07		1.87		2.94		1.26	
0.0025		0.1551		0.0545		0.2865	
205629		12530		67644		4153	
0.0000		0.0000		0.0000		0.0000	
0.062				0.080			
436		414		283		283	

$$\log S_{it} = \alpha \log S_{i0} + \beta \log K_{i0} + \gamma \log t + \mu Z_i + \theta F_i + \lambda D_i + u_i,$$

$$\log K_{it} = \alpha \log S_{i0} + \beta \log K_{i0} + \gamma \log t + \mu Z_i + \theta F_i + \lambda D_i + u_i,$$

$$\log L_{it} = \alpha \log S_{i0} + \beta \log K_{i0} + \gamma \log t + \mu Z_i + \theta F_i + \lambda D_i + u_i,$$

where S_{it}, K_{it}, and L_{it} stand for network capital, working capital, and manpower of agent i at the time of the survey, S_{i0} and K_{i0} are social and working capital at the time of enterprise creation, t is the time elapsed since creation, Z_i and F_i are vectors of personal and family characteristics, respectively, and D_i is a vector of location dummies. Information on S_{i0} was not collected in Madagascar; the variable is replaced by determinants of network capital at start-up. The number of sons, daughters, brothers, and sisters is included to control for family size effect.

Results are presented in tables 16.4 to 16.6. They show that network capital at start-up has a determinant effect on subsequent network capital. Since better connected traders are more productive, this implies that traders who start with more contacts have a strong initial advantage. The same is true for working capital. The two accumulation processes, however, are partially disconnected: initial network

Table 16.4
Determinants of social capital

	Madagascar		Benin		Malawi	
	Coefficient	t-statistic	Coefficient	t-statistic	Coefficient	t-statistic
Status at start-up						
Start-up capital	0.029	2.05	0.036	1.42	0.025	1.06
Number of traders known at startup	na		0.732	25.06	0.372	9.84
Trader association present in district	na		na		−0.035	−0.49
Time elapsed since start-up	0.321	7.23	0.191	2.85	0.094	1.73
Personal characteristics						
Born in capital city	0.009	0.07	na		na	
Born in another town	−0.002	−0.03	na		na	
Born in the location of trade	−0.086	−1.45	na		na	
Age of trader	0.032	2.01	−0.016	−0.68	0.015	0.71
Age squared	−0.000	−2.13	0.000	0.35	−0.000	−0.12
Female trader	−0.109	−1.95	−0.306	−2.87	−0.137	−1.76
Years of education	0.017	1.64	−0.013	−1.00	0.016	1.39
Number of languages spoken	−0.165	−2.90	0.069	2.44	0.028	0.74
Muslim dummy	0.166	1.48	−0.342	−2.98	0.133	1.46
Animist dummy			−0.034	−0.31		
Family background						
Number of close relatives in trade	−0.139	−2.37	−0.008	−0.14	0.203	3.24
Father was a farmer	−0.208	−2.23	−0.032	−0.35	−0.273	−3.38
Mother was a farmer	0.111	1.19	−0.005	−0.05	0.108	1.22
Father's experience in trade	0.012	0.31	−0.000	−0.01	−0.085	−2.92
Mother's experience in trade	−0.022	−0.58	0.020	0.83	−0.006	−0.21
Number of brothers over 15	−0.077	−1.35	−0.191	−3.09	−0.047	−0.73
Number of sisters over 15	−0.062	−1.07	−0.021	−0.31	0.004	0.07
Number of sons over 15	0.168	2.62	0.087	1.07	0.068	0.63
Number of daughters over 15	−0.023	−0.35	−0.029	−0.36	−0.242	−2.20
Regional dummies			Included but not shown			
Intercept	1.089	2.87	1.764	3.42	2.111	4.90
Number of observations	704		593		728	
R-squared	0.245		0.622		0.199	

Note: Dependent variable is the log of one plus the number of traders known. Start-up capital and traders known in log + 1. Years since start-up in log. Age and education in years. All family background variables in log + 1. Trader association present in all districts in Benin. Information not collected in Madagascar.

Table 16.5
Determinants of working capital

	Madagascar		Benin		Malawi	
	Coefficient	*t*-statistic	Coefficient	*t*-statistic	Coefficient	*t*-statistic
Status at start-up						
Start-up capital	0.244	7.27	0.369	11.19	0.505	16.71
Number of traders known at startup	na		0.027	0.73	−0.015	−0.32
Trader association present in district	na		na		0.024	0.26
Time elapsed since start-up	0.046	0.43	0.427	4.97	0.387	5.57
Personal characteristics						
Born in capital city	0.344	1.15	na		na	
Born in another town	−0.041	−0.22	na		na	
Born in the location of trade	0.124	0.90	na		na	
Age of trader	0.084	2.28	0.018	0.58	0.018	0.64
Age squared	−0.001	−1.70	−0.000	−0.51	−0.000	−0.33
Female trader	−0.477	−3.66	−0.618	−4.55	−0.757	−7.55
Years of education	0.070	2.93	0.057	3.45	0.097	6.63
Number of languages spoken	0.197	1.49	0.078	2.14	−0.082	−1.69
Christian dummy	−0.096	−0.36	−0.004	−0.02	0.066	0.56
Animist dummy			−0.151	−1.07		
Family background						
Number of close relatives in trade	0.200	1.46	−0.115	−1.56	0.108	1.34
Father was a farmer	−0.940	−4.34	−0.086	−0.72	−0.026	−0.25
Mother was a farmer	0.512	2.36	−0.066	−0.51	0.163	1.43
Father's experience in trade	−0.082	−0.92	0.058	1.22	−0.013	−0.34
Mother's experience in trade	0.102	1.14	0.054	1.73	−0.030	−0.78
Number of brothers over 15	−0.006	−0.05	0.005	0.07	0.145	1.75
Number of sisters over 15	0.127	0.93	0.237	2.77	0.008	0.11
Number of sons over 15	0.081	0.54	0.165	1.57	0.273	1.96
Number of daughters over 15	0.172	1.10	0.316	3.03	−0.142	−1.00
Regional dummies			Included but not shown			
Intercept	3.880	4.35	2.471	3.74	2.182	3.94
Number of observations	691		573		728	
R-squared	0.371		0.470		0.469	

Note: Dependent variable is the log of working capital, measured in US$. Start-up capital and traders known in log + 1. Years since start-up in log. Age and education in years. All family background variables in log + 1. Trader association present in all districts in Benin. Information not collected in Madagascar.

Table 16.6
The Determinants of employment

	Madagascar		Benin		Malawi	
	Coefficient	t-statistic	Coefficient	t-statistic	Coefficient	t-statistic
Status at start-up						
Start-up capital	0.097	8.63	0.054	2.67	0.143	11.20
Number of traders known at startup	na		0.074	3.18	0.053	2.58
Trader association present in district	na		na		0.029	0.75
Time elapsed since start-up	0.136	3.82	0.089	1.68	0.103	3.49
Personal characteristics						
Born in capital city	−0.183	−1.78	na		na	
Born in another town	−0.123	−1.99	na		na	
Born in the location of trade	−0.025	−0.52	na		na	
Age of trader	0.027	2.16	0.026	1.35	−0.027	−2.26
Age squared	−0.000	−1.31	−0.000	−1.72	0.000	2.42
Female trader	−0.082	−1.84	−0.192	−2.28	−0.143	−3.37
Years of education	0.013	1.61	−0.001	−0.05	0.015	2.45
Number of languages spoken	0.103	2.26	0.093	4.16	0.004	0.20
Christian dummy	−0.109	−1.21	−0.070	−0.77	−0.036	−0.73
Animist dummy			−0.042	−0.48		
Family background						
Number of close relatives in trade	−0.018	−0.39	−0.052	−1.15	0.012	0.36
Father was a farmer	−0.273	−3.66	−0.070	−0.96	0.020	0.46
Mother was a farmer	0.047	0.63	0.063	0.80	0.043	0.89
Father's experience in trade	−0.034	−1.12	0.011	0.38	0.037	2.32
Mother's experience in trade	0.041	1.33	0.097	5.07	−0.004	−0.23
Number of brothers over 15	−0.050	−1.11	−0.041	−0.83	0.010	0.30
Number of sisters over 15	0.063	1.36	0.002	0.04	−0.022	−0.67
Number of sons over 15	0.137	2.68	0.116	1.80	0.058	0.98
Number of daughters over 15	0.034	0.63	0.130	2.05	−0.017	−0.29
Regional dummies			Included but not shown			
Intercept	1.672	5.50	−0.874	−2.14	−0.136	−0.58
Number of observations	704		585		719	
R-squared	0.455		0.236		0.285	

Note: Dependent variable is the log of manpower employed in trading business, measured in months. Start-up capital and traders known in log + 1. Years since start-up in log. Age and education in years. All family background variables in log + 1. Trader association present in all districts in Benin. Information not collected in Madagascar. The omitted religion category is Muslim.

capital does not favor working capital accumulation; start-up capital helps the accumulation of network capital in Madagascar (where information on initial network capital is missing) but not in the other two countries. Employment, in contrast, responds to both initial network and working capital.

All three variables accumulate over time. Rates differ between Madagascar, on the one hand, and Malawi and Benin, on the other. The difference is probably due to the absence of information on S_{i0} in Madagascar. If we focus on Malawi and Benin, working capital is predicted to accumulate at the rate of 3.3 to 3.4 percent per annum, with a lot of variation around the average. In contrast, network capital accumulates more slowly at roughly 0.7 to 1.1 percent per year. This implies that start-up network capital has a lasting effect on firm productivity. Employment accumulates also at a slow 0.8 to 0.9 percent per year on average.

Women accumulate systematically fewer business contacts and less working capital and manpower over time. The effect is particularly strong for working capital. It is significant even in Benin where the majority of agricultural traders are women. This probably reflects the precarious financial status of female entrepreneurs in general and their tendency to invest in the education and nutrition of their children. Other regressors have less systematic influence on accumulation, once we control for initial conditions and time since creation. Better educated traders tend to accumulate working capital faster, suggesting that they are more ambitious than other traders (table 16.1 indicates that they are not systematically more productive). Other regressors have effects that vary across countries. Being Muslim, for instance, has no effect except in the network capital regression in Benin, where Muslims are shown to have less network capital; this result is possibly a reflection of the fact that Islam is practiced only by a minority of the population. The result, however, is different from Ensminger's (1992) finding that Islam penetrated East Africa along livestock trade routes because converted traders enjoyed better networks.

Family background has less effect on social and working capital accumulation after firm creation than commonly believed (Granovetter 1995a). Familiarity with agricultural trade is measured by the trading experience of parents. Family contacts in trade is measured by the number of relatives in trade. Relatives are limited to father and mother, sons and daughters, and brothers and sisters. Results show that these variables have no systematic effect on accumulation, suggesting that once an enterprise is created, family experience and contacts have little effect on firm performance.

Regressions of start-up network and working capital on family background and personal characteristics (not shown here) nevertheless indicate that family background has some systematic effect on start-up conditions. The number of relatives in trade is associated with more start-up network capital in Malawi and Benin (data missing for Madagascar). The trade experience of the mother and father is associated with more start-up network capital in Benin. Family background, however, has little effect on start-up working capital, in contrast with education, which has a strong positive effect. Being a woman is associated with significantly lower levels of start-up social and working capital in all three countries.

16.5 Conclusion

In this chapter we showed that knowing other traders boosts the productivity of agricultural traders. This result is not due to endogeneity; if anything, it is stronger after instrumentation. Close investigation further reveals that returns to network capital are primarily due to increased volume of activity. Only in Benin do we find possible evidence of network rents, that is, that better connected traders have higher unit margins. This latter finding constitutes limited evidence in support of the model presented in chapter 14.

We also studied the accumulation of social and working capital. Results suggest that start-up conditions have a long-lasting effect on the productive resources of agricultural traders. Working capital accumulates at 3.3 to 3.4 percent per annum, on average, in contrast to 0.7 to 1.1 percent for network capital and 0.8 to 0.9 percent for employment. Initial contacts play a determinant role in trader performance.

Family networks and parental experience have no systematic effect on factor accumulation after enterprise creation, but they help determine the initial level of network capital. Female entrepreneurs appear systematically disadvantaged despite the fact that they represent the majority of surveyed agricultural traders. They have lower productivity, accumulate productive assets more slowly, and start their trading business with less social and working capital.

Much work remains to be done to investigate other predictions made by the conceptual framework of chapter 14. For instance, the model presented there argued that centrally positioned traders may extract rents. In this chapter, we have investigated this possibility by testing whether the number of persons known raises productivity. This test implicitly assumes that networks are star shaped and that traders are of equivalent size. In chapter 14, however, we showed examples of networks in which economic power comes not from the number of links but from the location in the marketing chain. Bauer (1954) and Jones (1959) make a similar observation, and Fafchamps et al. (2002) peripherally touch on the issue. But more research is needed.

VI ETHNICITY AND DISCRIMINATION

In part V we saw that networks play an important role in the way markets operate. We also observed that networks often organize around race and ethnicity. In this part, we revisit these issues in more detail.

We begin with a model of market interaction that allows for statistical discrimination and network effects. The model is an extension of the model presented in chapters 10 and 11. We show that statistical discrimination and networks can have similar consequences on exclusion from trade and on differentiated treatment. They nevertheless differ in their predictions regarding discrimination by agents who are themselves discriminated against. In chapter 17 we test whether statistical discrimination or networks best account for observed trading patterns. Although we cannot reject the presence of discrimination, we conclude that at least part of observed discrimination is due to network effects.

17 Discrimination and Networks

We saw in earlier chapters that the ethnic makeup of local business communities is quite different from that of the population at large. It is not uncommon for members of a particular ethnic or religious group, or even for residents of foreign origin, to account for an overwhelming proportion of entrepreneurs. The historical record too is replete with examples of a particular ethnic group dominating commerce for extended periods of time (e.g., Braudel 1986; Greif 1993, 1994). Accounts by historians, anthropologists, and sociologists also demonstrate that the ethnic and religious background of dominant business groups varies considerably from place to place (e.g., Bauer 1954; Geertz 1963; Cohen 1969; Meillassoux 1971; Jones 1972; Amselle 1977; Geertz et al. 1979; Staatz 1979; Landa 1994). It even varies across economic activities within the same country.[1] Lack of business diversity is a priori inefficient: drawing entrepreneurs from a small talent pool reduces the average quality of local entrepreneurship. It is also inequitable as it leads to income disparities between groups that inevitably fuel political tension (e.g., Marris 1971; Himbara 1994). Animosity toward prosperous ethnic or religious groups may, in turn, serve as investment disincentive if members of the group fear being subsequently expropriated. Such fears are not baseless, as the historical record demonstrates.[2]

Colonial policies and other historical and political factors[3] have often favored particular ethnic groups and communities, enabling them to gain a dominant position in a particular segment of economic activity. These factors, however, do not explain why ethnic concentration persists long after favorable factors and policies have been removed. The postindependence experience of many African countries, as discussed in chapter 14, suggests that once a group has established a dominant position in an activity, it can retain its advantage long after initially favorable conditions have been eliminated—and even after having been actively combatted by postcolonial governments.[4] Similar questions have been raised in the United States regarding the survival of ethnic disparities between blacks and whites after the removal of explicit discrimination (e.g., Yinger 1998; Loury 1998). Ethnic concentration appears to be self-sustaining, at least under certain conditions. The objective

1. The fish trade in Kenya, for instance, is dominated by the Luos, while textile manufacturing is largely in the hands of Kenyan-Asians.

2. For example, the expulsion of Asians from Uganda in the 1970s and, more recently, the looting of ethnic Chinese shops in Indonesia.

3. Including those of the white-dominated government of the Unilateral Declaration of Independence era in Zimbabwe.

4. In the late 1960s the Kenyata government actively favored the transfer of Asians businesses to ethnic Kenyans, particularly Kikuyus, with very little success (Himbara 1994). Similar policies have been pursued, although less forcefully, by the Mugabe administration in Zimbabwe.

of this chapter is to investigate whether market interaction can alone perpetuate a lack of ethnic diversity in business.

17.1 The Various Sources of Discrimination

The interplay between trust, trade, and ethnicity or religion has long been recognized. It has, for instance, been argued that Islam penetrated the East African interior due to coastal merchants' preference to deal with Muslims (e.g., Shillington 1989; Ensminger 1992). Sociologists have similarly emphasized that African entrepreneurs prefer to do business with members of their own ethnic group (e.g., Marris 1971; Macharia 1988; Himbara 1994). Together with a number of economists, they have emphasized the role that trust and reputation among individuals and communities play in creating an enabling environment for trade (e.g., Mitchell 1969; Granovetter 1985; Coleman 1988; Hart 1988; Milgrom et al. 1991; Greif 1993, 1994; Platteau 1994b). There is a growing consensus that sharing the same ethnicity and religion are elements that favor the establishment of trust (e.g., Gambetta 1988; Fukuyama 1995; Cornell and Welch 1996; Barr and Oduro 2002).

Conceptually there are several ways by which ethnicity may influence the allocation of credit, for instance, through taste for discrimination (e.g., Becker 1971; Akerlof 1985), erroneous expectations or "prejudice" (e.g., Yinger 1998; Loury 2002), difficulties of communication across cultural boundaries (e.g., Cornell and Welch 1996; Loury 1998), statistical discrimination (Arrow 1972), and network effects (e.g., Saloner 1985; Montgomery 1991; Taylor 2000). There is widespread disagreement as to the relative empirical contributions these mechanisms make to ethnic and gender bias in labor and credit markets.[5] Becker (1971), for instance, has argued that prejudice and taste for discrimination are costly and should result in lower profits. In a competitive environment, he argues, firms that discriminate on the basis of taste or maintain erroneous expectations should, in the long run, be competed out by more open-minded, better informed businesses. Becker's view has not gone unchallenged, however.[6]

---

5. See Donohue (1998), Darity (1998), and the spring 1998 issue of the *Journal of Economic Perspectives* for recent surveys of the literature in the United States.

6. As pointed out by many (e.g., Donohue 1998; Darity and Mason 1998), the idea that market forces should eliminate discrimination and prejudice relies critically on the assumption that markets are competitive. In the US South during the Jim Crow era, Donohue emphasizes that employers who hired blacks were ostracized by the white-dominated establishment and feared being targeted by the Ku Klux Klan. In such circumstances, the author argues, market forces could not operate, and without external intervention, discrimination could have perdured indefinitely. Becker's view has been used to oppose affirmative action in the United States.

Unlike prejudice and tastes, statistical discrimination is perfectly compatible with the profit-seeking motive and cannot therefore be competed out. Whenever firms cannot assess clients and suppliers directly, it is rational for them to screen on the basis of whatever observable information they can collect. If groups of different race or gender differ in unobservable attributes, statistical discrimination will arise. The role that it plays in explaining actual ethnic bias has, however, been the object of much debate. In addition the presence of statistical discrimination is extremely difficult to prove, since it requires the econometrician to have as much, if not more, information about applicants than employers themselves (Darity 1998).[7]

Network effects have received somewhat less attention in the discrimination literature, but they have long been studied in labor markets Granovetter (1995b). The basic idea is that information about opportunities for exchange and agents' types circulates along interpersonal networks. People talk with their friends and professional acquaintances about jobs, bad payers, and arbitrage opportunities, and they refer job and credit applicants to each other. In such an environment individuals with better networks collect more accurate information, which enables them to seek out market opportunities more aggressively and to better screen prospective employees and credit recipients. As we saw in chapters 10 and 11, in a world of imperfect information, they provide an economic advantage to better connected agents (e.g., Kranton 1996b; Taylor 2000).

To the extent that members of a particular group cultivate close links with each other, be it for historical or cultural reasons,[8] the group will be seen to perform better than others in market exchange. If this group recruits its members primarily along ethnic or gender lines, ethnic or gender bias will occur although, strictly speaking, agents need not have a taste for discrimination and they need not rely on statistical discrimination.[9] Network effects thus puts the emphasis on patterns of socialization as an alternative explanation for ethnic or gender bias.[10] The primary

7. To see why, suppose that we have information on wages and gender. To test for statistical discrimination against women, we regress wages on gender. The problem with this test is that statistical discrimination assumes that gender is correlated with a worker characteristic unobserved by the econometrician. If this characteristic is observed by the employer, however, statistical discrimination does not arise, though gender is correlated with wages, because of the omitted variable bias.

8. Such as persecution.

9. In statistical discrimination models, ethnic bias arises when two populations have different hidden characteristics. In network effects, ethnic bias may arise even when they have the same hidden characteristics, provided that members of one group can more easily screen members of their own group *and* one group has acquired a dominant position, perhaps for historical reasons.

10. The concept of network effects bears some ressemblance with another explanation for ethnic bias based on the existence of a dominant group seeking to protect its supremacy. The difference is that network effects can arise in a completely decentralized manner, that is, even in the absence of any collusion

objective of this chapter is to assess how much of the observed ethnic and gender bias in African enterprise credit can be attributed to network effects.

Our analysis focuses on supplier credit which has been shown to play an important part in firm finance (Fafchamps 1997c). At the core of our argument lies the recognition that normal commercial transactions require a temporal dissociation between delivery and payment; otherwise, the conduct of business would be too unwieldy. Market transactions thus normally encompass an element of credit.[11] Because recourse to formal collateral is impractical for most business transactions, trade credit gets allocated essentially on the basis of trust (e.g., Fafchamps 1996, 1997c). Trade credit is thus typically offered on a selective basis; those who do not qualify must buy cash.[12] Since only very small firms can operate on a cash-only basis, how trust is established and with whom dictates not only how trade takes place but also which firms are able to operate in a businesslike fashion and which must remain micro-enterprises. In addition credit from suppliers is also an important source of finance for small and medium-size firms (e.g., Cuevas et al. 1993; Bade and Chifamba 1994; Fafchamps et al. 1994, 1995).[13] An examination of the process by which trade and bank credit are attributed is therefore expected to throw light on the ethnic composition of business communities.

17.2   A Model of Trust-Based Exchange

To formally illustrate how statistical discrimination and network effects influences trust, we begin by constructing a stylized market economy in which economic agents screen potential commercial partners, grant trade credit to clients, and pay suppliers.

among members of the dominant group and without need for metapunishment (e.g., see the discussion in Donohue 1998). Of course, the presence of discrimination or of collusion to exclude members of other groups can coexist with network effects, and the existence of ethnic-based networks can facilitate collusion. The point is that the coexistence of ethnic bias and interpersonal networks does not alone imply collusion.

11. The duration of trade credit is normally defined as the time elapsed between invoicing and payment. In developed countries this delay typically ranges from 30 to 60 days (e.g., Schwartz 1974; Schwartz and Whitcomb 1979). Similar delays were found among African manufacturers (e.g., Cuevas et al. 1993; Bade and Chifamba 1994; Fafchamps et al. 1994; Fafchamps et al. 1995).

12. In this chapter we use the phrase "cash payment" to designate payment in currency or by certified check at the time of delivery. Accepting a payment by check is about as risky as granting credit and is considered as such here. In the business world, payment for materials and inputs out of petty cash is extremely rare, except for very small infrequent purchases. One of the reasons is that large movements of cash are unsafe. Among businesses the word "cash" is often given a meaning different from the one used here; it refers to early payment.

13. Although trade credit is formally considered short-term financing, it is normally renewed with each order so that, in practice, it provides firms with a long-term source of working capital.

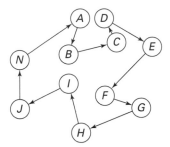

Figure 17.1
Trade flows among matched agents

The model, which is inspired of the works of Grossman and Van Huyck (1988), Milgrom et al. (1991), Greif (1993, 1994), and chapters 11 and 12, integrates screening and strategic default considerations. There is no external mechanism for the enforcement of contracts other than the discipline imposed by the market itself.[14]

Consider an economy composed of a large number of firms $2N$ living indefinitely and discounting the future with factor δ. Time is divided into rounds within which firms trade with each other. Since each transaction involves a buyer and a seller, each firm assumes two distinct roles, that of supplier and client. To keep things simple, we assume that each firm buys from one supplier and sells to one client at a time. With these assumptions, a particular trading round can be visualized as directed graph in which each firm, say A, B, and C, is a node and each sales transaction is an arrow (figure 17.1).

There are two types of firms, competent and incompetent. Their proportion in the economy is constant and common knowledge, but firm type is private information. Competent firms gain from trade. Incompetent firms, in contrast, cannot make a profit by processing or reselling goods purchased from suppliers. They can, however, profit from cheating suppliers by taking goods on credit and failing to pay.[15] Many—though not all—African microenterprises satisfy this definition of incompetence: the inadequacy of their equipment and technical expertise and the fragility of their financial base make it difficult for them to complete large commercial transactions.

14. In small transactions, the threat of court action is not credible because the cost of court proceedings exceeds the expected gain from suing. Furthermore in poor countries many defendants are judgment-proof because they have no assets to serve a judgment against them. As long as the external enforcement of contracts is imperfect, most of the qualitative results presented here carry through.

15. In our model, it is irrelevant whether incompetent firms know their own type and thus are dishonest, or ignore their type and discover subsequently that they cannot repay. See chapter 11.

Firms decide whether or not to grant trade credit to their client.[16] Those who do not receive credit must pay in cash. Payment in cash is risky (e.g., theft) and costly to administer. The use of trade credit among competent firms is thus efficient. Payoffs are normalized so that the profit of competent firms is 0 without trade credit. The main concerns of suppliers is to get clients to pay back the trade credit they received and thus to avoid granting trade credit to incompetent clients. To do so, suppliers spend resources screening potential customers. For the sake of brevity, we take c to be the cost of the optimally chosen screening method, and we assume that it is sufficient to identify incompetent firms after one period.[17]

The game played between firms is depicted in extensive form in figures 17.2, 17.3, and 17.4. Realized payoffs, which are the sum of instantaneous and continuation payoffs, are shown at the extreme right of each figure. The payoff to client C is shown on top, the payoff to supplier S below. The expected continuation payoff of a matched supplier is denoted V^S; that of an unmatched supplier is written V^N. The corresponding continuation payoffs for clients are written V^C and V^U. The value of continuation payoffs depend on the strategies pursued by firms, to be discussed below. Parameters α and β are the supplier's and client's net profit margins, respectively. In case of nonpayment, a client's instantaneous payoff is $1 > \beta$: clients always have a short-term incentive to default. Suppliers make a profit of α in case of repayment; otherwise they make a loss of -1. Since the profit margin of the supplier can be increased and that of the client reduced by raising the sales price (or, equivalently, the interest rate on trade credit), α can be increased by lowering β, and vice versa. The combined gains from trade $\alpha + \beta$ is denoted κ and assumed to be exogenously determined by market conditions. By negotiating over the price, supplier and client bargain over the share of $\kappa = \alpha + \beta$ that goes to each of them. We are not interested here in this bargaining process but rather on the constraints that incentive conditions put on the choice of α and β. To ensure that trade patterns change over time, we assume that, with probability $1 - \tau$, clients discover that gains from trade

16. For simplicity we assume that the purchasing and buying sides of each firm can be analyzed separately. In practice, a firm that does not receive trade credit from its supplier may not be able to offer it to its clients. This possibility is ignored here.

17. The screening cost c depends on whether the reliability of the client can be assessed directly—for instance, by inspecting the client's business premises—or indirectly—for instance, by selling small amounts on credit and observing whether the client repays. For indirect screening to be effective, the supplier must grant an amount of credit that is sufficient to induce an incompetent firm to reveal its type: if too little credit is given, incompetent clients will repay only to cheat the supplier more later. For evidence on the screening methods used by African suppliers, see Fafchamps (1996, 1997c), Fafchamps et al. (1994), and section 17.4. Indirect screening is the most commonly used method.

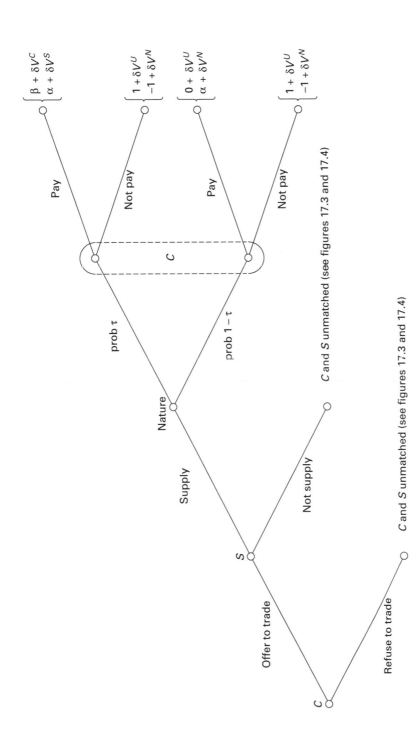

Figure 17.2
Game between matched agents

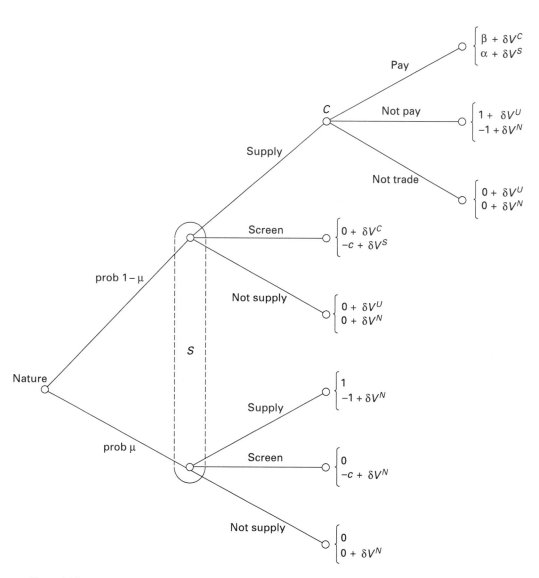

Figure 17.3
Game between unmatched agents: A supplier's perspective

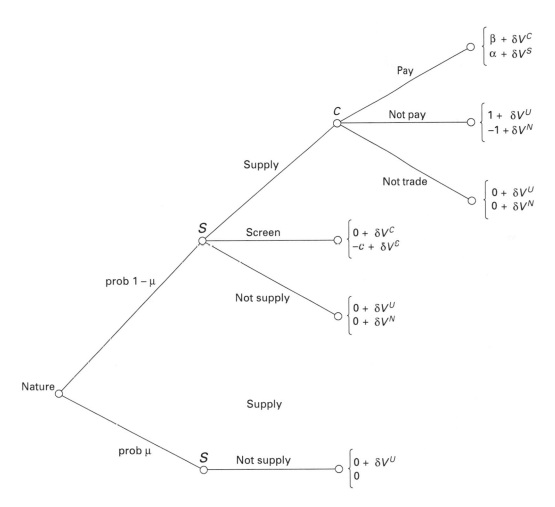

Figure 17.4
Game between unmatched agents: Client's perspective

with their current supplier permanently fall to 0 and that they need to change supplier (see Greif 1993 for a similar assumption).

Since trade is voluntary, supplier and client can both stop the relationship at the beginning of the trading period, in which case they both must seek a new commercial partner. Nature randomly pairs unmatched firms with each other so that, with probabilities μ and $1 - \mu$, suppliers are matched with an incompetent or a competent client, respectively (figure 17.2).[18] Suppliers do not observe the client's type. Neither do they know whether the client has ever failed to pay other suppliers.[19] Suppliers must decide whether to refuse to trade, to screen the new client at cost c, or to offer trade credit. Incompetent clients invariably cheat suppliers who offer credit from the start (lower branches in figure 17.2).[20] It is never in a client's interest to refuse credit when offered. Unmatched clients must similarly seek a new supplier (figure 17.3). With probabilities μ and $1 - \mu$, nature matches them with an incompetent or competent supplier, respectively. Incompetent suppliers cannot provide trade credit. Clients then get an instantaneous payoff of 0 and search for another supplier in the next period.

If the economy lasts only one period (i.e., $\delta = 0$), clients always refuse to pay. Anticipating this, suppliers do not offer trade credit. The economy resembles a one-sided Prisoner's Dilemma game: the unique subgame perfect equilibrium is one in which all payments are made in cash and Pareto efficiency is not achieved. If agents live long enough, however, they may be able to deter opportunistic breach of contract by forming long-term relationships. To show this formally, we focus on a class of trust-based strategies in which suppliers and clients form business relationships that last until one party breaches its promise.[21] Clients pay suppliers to avoid having to search for another supplier who will grant them trade credit. The market disciplines itself in a way that is reminiscent of unemployment as a disciplining device in

18. The proportion of competent and incompetent firms among the unmatched depends not only on the proportion of incompetent firms in the economy but also on the number of competent firms that are unmatched. Here we ignore transitional dynamics and treat μ as an exogenously determined constant. See chapters 11 and 12 for a precise treatment.

19. This assumption is lifted in section 17.3.

20. Since incompetent firms never behave strategically, their continuation payoff can be ignored from figure 17.2.

21. Formally, the strategies are as follows: Unmatched suppliers screen new clients. If the client is identified as incompetent, suppliers screen another firm in the subsequent period and continue to do so until a competent client is found. Once one is found, suppliers offer trade credit and the parties engage into a long-term commercial relationship. As long as the client's gains from trade remain positive, the client pays and the relationship continues. When a client discovers that gains from trade have fallen to 0 and that the time has come to change supplier, default occurs and the relationship ends. The supplier then starts screening new clients, and the client starts being screened by new suppliers.

Shapiro and Stiglitz (1984; see also Ghosh and Ray 1996). Transitional dynamics are ignored, and we focus exclusively on the long-term equilibrium of the economy.[22]

When all agents follow trust-based strategies, expected continuation payoffs to matched and unmatched suppliers are, respectively,

$$V^S = \tau(\alpha + \delta V^S) + (1 - \tau)(-1 + \delta V^N), \tag{17.1}$$

$$V^N = \mu \delta V^N + (1 - \mu)\delta V^S - c. \tag{17.2}$$

The corresponding payoffs to matched and unmatched clients are

$$V^C = \tau(\beta + \delta V^C) + (1 - \tau)(1 + \delta V^U), \tag{17.3}$$

$$V^U = \mu \delta V^U + (1 - \mu)\delta V^C. \tag{17.4}$$

Since, by construction, incompetent firms always get screened away, their payoff is zero and can be ignored.

For trust-based strategies to be subgame perfect, seven equilibrium conditions must be satisfied: it must be beneficial for matched supplier and client to continue a commercial relationship (EC1 and EC2), it must beneficial for a client to pay a supplier (EC3), it should not be in a client's interest to respect the contract once the relationship ends (EC4), it pays for unmatched clients and suppliers to screen and be screened by other firms (EC5 and EC6), and it does not pay to grant instant trade credit to all applicants (EC7). Formally, we need

$$V^S \geq V^N \qquad\qquad EC1, \tag{17.5}$$

$$V^C \geq V^U \qquad\qquad EC2, \tag{17.6}$$

$$\beta + \delta V^C \geq 1 + \delta V^U \qquad\qquad EC3, \tag{17.7}$$

$$0 + \delta V^U \leq 1 + \delta V^U \qquad\qquad EC4, \tag{17.8}$$

$$V^N \geq 0 \qquad\qquad EC5, \tag{17.9}$$

$$V^U \geq 0 \qquad\qquad EC6, \tag{17.10}$$

$$V^N \geq \mu(-1 + \delta V^N) + (1 - \mu)(\alpha + \delta V^S) \qquad EC7. \tag{17.11}$$

Let us denote the client's trade margin that is just sufficient to ensure voluntary payment, denoted β^*, and the supplier's trade margin that is just sufficient to induce screening, denoted α^*. By manipulating equations (17.1) to (17.4) and (EC1) to

22. Dynamics are examined in detail in chapters 11 and 12.

(EC7), we obtain

$$\alpha^* \equiv \frac{1 - \tau}{\tau} + \frac{c(1 - \delta\tau)}{\tau\delta(1 - \mu)}, \qquad (17.12)$$

$$\beta^* \equiv \frac{1 - \delta\mu}{1 + \delta - \delta\mu}. \qquad (17.13)$$

This yields the following proposition:

PROPOSITION 17.1

i. If $\alpha^* \leq (\mu - c)/(1 - \mu)$ and if the combined gain from trade κ is greater than $\alpha^* + \beta^*$, then there exist a division of the gains from trade $\{\alpha, \beta\}$ such that the provision of trade credit is self-enforcing by trust-based strategies.

ii. A self-enforcing division of gains from trade $\{\alpha, \beta\}$ must satisfy $(\mu - c)/(1 - \mu) \geq \alpha \geq \alpha^*$ and $\beta \geq \beta^*$.

(Proof in appendix)

Proposition 17.1.ii shows that it is not in the interest of the supplier to raise the sale price beyond the point at which β falls below β^*: the client must make money from the transaction for repayment to be in his or her interest. This is true irrespective of the bargaining power of both parties: when the repayment constraint is binding, the selling price is entirely determined by β^*. The same holds on the supplier side: unless suppliers make a profit of at least α^*, they will refuse to screen clients for trade credit.

A immediate corollary of proposition 17.1 is that β must be strictly positive: a trust-based equilibrium cannot exist if clients never gain anything from trade. This is in sharp contrast with the standard competitive equilibrium in which free entry guarantees that pure profits are 0. Here clients collect a payment that can be interpreted as the return to their relationship—what Coleman (1988) calls "social capital." It is the fear of losing this return that guarantees repayment of trade credit. For most parameter values, β^* is nontrivial. If $\delta = 0.9$ and $\mu = 0.5$, for instance, then $\beta^* = 0.38$: transactions with a client's margin lower than 38 percent are not self-enforceable.

It is easy to verify that α^* rises with μ: suppliers are more willing to screen if the proportion of incompetent firms among in the unmatched is low and thus the chances of finding a reliable client are high. In contrast, β^* decreases with μ: commercial contracts are easier to enforce if there are many incompetent firms. The reason is that the more incompetent suppliers there are, the longer it takes for an unmatched client to find a new reliable supplier. The presence of incompetent suppliers thus helps discipline clients.[23] Proposition 17.1 further shows that even if the screening cost c is 0, there must be some incompetent firms in the economy for screening to be worthwhile. The more costly screening is, the more tempting it is for suppliers to take a chance and grant instant credit, and the larger μ must be for screening to be in suppliers' self-interest. In the absence of incompetent firms, it is individually optimal for suppliers to grant credit without screening; in this case clients incur no punishment for breach of contract and the equilibrium unravels (see below).[24] Although α^* increases with μ, it is possible to show that as long as c is small and μ is not too close to 1, $\alpha^* + \beta^*$ falls with μ. In general, therefore, the presence of incompetent firms makes it easier for a trust-based system of trade credit to be self-enforcing.

If $\kappa < \alpha^* + \beta^*$, there exists no allocation of the gains from trade among supplier and client that provides sufficient incentives for both the supplier to screen and the client to pay. It is then rational for suppliers to refuse trade credit to their clients. This is because a client could not convince a supplier to provide trade credit by offering a higher price because doing so would only reinforce the client's incentive to default.[25] Circumstances that make both constraints $\alpha > \alpha^*$ and $\beta > \beta^*$ more binding—short horizon (low δ), high firm turnover (low τ), and high screening costs (high c)—are likely to result in the absence of trade credit. Markets then take the form of a flea market economy in which all transactions are on a cash-and-carry basis and gains from trade are dissipated through inefficient business practices.

---

23. Since $\lim_{\mu \to 0} \beta^* = 1/(1-\delta)$, even in the absence of incompetent suppliers there exists a sufficiently high trade margin such that the repayment condition is satisfied. The reason is that in a trust-based equilibrium, unmatched clients first get screened before receiving trade credit and thus lose at least one trade round. It is not, however, optimal for suppliers to wait before granting trade credit if there are no incompetent clients in the economy. Of course, one could imagine a tit-for-tat punishment strategy whereby cheaters must wait for one (or more) periods before being granted trade credit. For such punishment to be credible, however, suppliers would have to be punished for granting credit to cheaters. The informational requirements for such punishments to be implemented are daunting and there is little or no evidence that they occur in practice. Dun and Bradstreet, for instance, circulates information about bad payers but not about firms who deal with bad payers. See chapters 11 and 12 for further discussion.

24. In the case where (EC7) is violated but $\mu > 0$, a market equilibrium with instant trade credit may still be sustainable provided that clients who fail to pay their supplier are not instantly matched with an another competent supplier. Provided that μ is large enough, and thus that the expected waiting time is long enough, this punishment may be sufficient to deter breach. Demonstrating that such an equilibrium exists is left as an exercise for the reader. Other equilibria, such as reputational equilibria (e.g., Milgrom et al. 1991; Kandori 1992; Greif 1993) or contagious equilibria (e.g., Kandori 1992; Ellison 1994), may nevertheless be sustainable. Reputational equilibria require the sharing of information and the existence of metapunishment; they are discussed in chapter 12. Contagious equilibria are susceptible to external shocks (see, however, Ellison 1994) and to the presence of incompetent firms; for that reason they are not very plausible.

25. Stiglitz and Weiss (1981) derive a similar result in a model of adverse selection.

17.3 Statistical Discrimination in Trade Credit

We now investigate the conditions under which statistical discrimination arises. Economic agents typically differ in characteristics that are relevant for contractual performance (Arrow 1972): some entrepreneurs, for instance, are more competent and financially secure and thus a better trade credit risk than others. Most individual characteristics are private information, but some, like gender or ethnicity, are not. These observable traits typically have no effect on contractual performance, but they may be correlated with underlying characteristics, such as size and financial security, that they help predict. It is then rational to treat agents with different observable traits differently, not because these observable traits indicate inherent inferiority, but because they are correlated with hidden characteristics of interest (e.g., Foster and Rosenzweig 1993; Foster and Rosenzweig 1994). Zimbabwean firms headed by blacks, for example, are on average much smaller than those headed by whites (e.g., Hoogeveen and Tekere 1994; Risseeuw 1994; Fafchamps et al. 1995). They also appear to be less financially secure, judging by the high proportion of business failure among them (Daniels 1994). When reviewing applications for trade credit, a Zimbabwean supplier may thus consider that white applicants are better risks and give them a preferential treatment. This state of affairs is quite unfortunate since it penalizes many promising black businesses, but to the extent that it is based on statistical discrimination, it is individually rational.[26]

A compounding feature of statistical discrimination is that it can be self-fulfilling. Coate and Loury (1993), for instance, study the allocation of black and white workers between demanding and nondemanding tasks (see also Milgrom and Oster 1987; Borjas and Bronars 1989). Using a theoretical model, they show that an equilibrium exists in which the belief that black workers are inferior is self-fulfilling: because blacks expect to be discriminated against by employers, they invest less in their own education and work ethics, which makes them less suitable for demanding tasks. Similar forces may be at work concerning trade credit.

To apply these ideas to trust-based markets, we now assume that the firm population is made of two separate ethnic groups, denoted A and B, with $A + B = 2N$. Firm ethnicity is publicly observable through the entrepreneur's language, name, attire, race, and so on.[27] The proportion of A firms in the total population is denoted

26. In case where ethnicity perfectly predicts competence and hence contractual performance, discrimination is not only individually rational; it is also socially optimal—unless, of course, incompetence is itself a result of discrimination Milgrom and Oster (1987) and Coate and Loury (1993). This case is ignored here.

27. Identical results obtain if what differentiates firms is not ethnicity but gender, religion, and the like, as long as it is externally observable.

θ, and the proportion of incompetent firms among unmatched firms in each group is written μ_i, $i \in \{A, B\}$. For statistical discrimination to arise, ethnicity must help "predict" competence. Without loss of generality, we assume that the proportion of incompetent firms in larger in group B than in group A, that is, $\mu_B > \mu_A$.[28] This may be because entrepreneurs in group B are less educated, have less technical and commercial experience, or have a weaker financial base.

Several types of discriminatory equilibria can obtain when firms apply trust-based strategies: price discrimination, in which B clients are asked to pay more than A clients; discriminatory exclusion, in which B firms are denied any access to trade credit; and discriminatory rationing, in which only a fraction of B firms gain access to trade credit. To see this formally, let β_A^* and β_B^* denote the minimum trade margin that an A- and B-type clients, respectively, must receive in order not to breach the contract. Similarly let α_A^* and α_B^* denote the minimum trade margin suppliers must make in order to screen A and B clients, respectively. Whenever suppliers refuse to screen B clients, we have

$$\beta_A^* \equiv \frac{1 - \delta\theta\mu_A - \delta(1 - \theta)\mu_B}{1 + \delta - \delta\theta\mu_A - \delta(1 - \theta)\mu_B}, \tag{17.14}$$

$$\alpha_A^* \equiv \frac{1 - \tau}{\tau} + \frac{c(1 - \delta\tau)}{\delta\tau(1 - \mu_A)}, \tag{17.15}$$

$$\alpha_B^* \equiv \frac{1 - \tau}{\tau} + \frac{c(1 - \delta\tau + \delta\theta(\mu_B - \mu_A))}{\delta\tau(1 - \mu_B)}, \tag{17.16}$$

$$\beta_B^* \equiv 1 - \delta. \tag{17.17}$$

This leads to the following proposition:

PROPOSITION 17.2

i. If $\alpha_A^* + \beta_A^* < \kappa < \alpha_B^* + \beta_B^*$, the only self-enforcing trust-based equilibria that exist are equilibria in which suppliers provide trade credit only to competent A firms.

ii. If $\kappa > \alpha_A^* + \beta_A^*$ and κ is sufficiently larger than $\alpha_B^* + \beta_B^*$, the only self-enforcing trust-based equilibria that exist are equilibria in which suppliers provide trade credit to competent A and B firms but require a higher minimum profit rate before screening B firms.

---

28. Discrimination can also be obtained if firm populations differ in the probability τ of continuing a commercial relationship; or if screening costs vary by firm type, for instance, if $c_A < c_B$ for A firms, as assumed in Cornell and Welch (1996).

iii. For intermediate values of κ, a third, the only self-enforcing trust-based equilibria that exist are hybrid equilibria in which price discrimination and discriminatory rationing coexist.

(Proof in appendix)

Proposition 17.2 demonstrates that five types of trade credit equilibria are theoretically possible in the presence of statistically different firm populations: equal treatment for all, price discrimination, price discrimination with discriminatory rationing, discriminatory exclusion, and no exchange.[29] How severe statistical discrimination is depends principally on the level of screening costs c and the difference between firm populations $\mu_B - \mu_A$: the higher the screening costs are and the larger the gap between the two populations, the more likely discrimination occurs. When discriminatory exclusion is an equilibrium, it constitutes a best response for all suppliers: even those who belong to the B group discriminate against their own kind. This is in contrast with a situation where discrimination is due to prejudice, in which case B suppliers would presumably not refuse trade credit to B clients. Here what induces suppliers to discriminate is their desire to save on screening costs by refusing to consider B clients because they come from a worse population.

Of the five possible equilibria, discriminatory exclusion is potentially the most damaging for B firms because it can be self-fulfilling and even self-reinforcing over time. To see why, suppose that entrepreneurs learn from experience. For instance, say that firms get to know the tricks of the trade and become more efficient producers and better payers through contact with established businesses (see Borjas and Bronars 1989 and Coate and Loury 1993 for other examples of self-reinforcing discrimination). Formally, let the proportion of incompetent firms μ_i, $i \in \{A, B\}$ fall with exposure to established businesses. It is then easy to show that if an easily identifiable group gains prominence in business, it may keep it forever. Suppose that thanks to luck, historical conditions, or government support, a group of A firms manage to establish themselves.[30] Further assume that thanks to learning among A firms, μ_A falls sufficiently that granting trade credit to A firms becomes individually rational. Trade credit then begins to flow among A firms. Inexperienced A firms are screened by established A businesses. Through this process they progressively learn and adopt more sophisticated business practices, which make them more reliable

---

29. This list should not be considered as exhaustive. Other possible equilibria include no screening for all and screening of B clients only.

30. For instance, colonial authorities and white-dominated governments supported various nonindigenous business groups across Africa—Asians in Kenya, and Europeans in Zimbabwe (e.g., Marris 1971; Himbara 1994; Bade and Gunning 1994).

commercial partners. Learning among A firms brings μ_A further down, making it *less* likely that the screening equilibrium condition will be violated. Learning through screening thus makes discriminatory exclusion a self-reinforcing process. In these circumstances the development of a prosperous business community, once started, ends up marginalizing less experienced groups.

The model can thus, in principle, account for some of the difficulties black-owned African firms face to graduate into the mainstream business establishment. It also may explain why the overwhelming majority of black-owned African firms remain confined to the microenterprise sector (e.g., Daniels 1994; Fafchamps 1994). Discrimination need not be the sole possible explanation for this state of affairs, however. Network effects can also theoretically account for the prominence of ethnically homogeneous business groups. They are examined in the next section.

17.4 Reputation and Network Effects

Network effects may affect the allocation trade credit through the circulation of information and the use of social sanctions. The circulation of business-relevant information within a closely knit, ethnically or religiously homogeneous community benefits its members. In particular, the dissemination of information about reliable clients and suppliers helps members of the community identify trustworthy commercial partners. Such network effects have been studied in other markets—in particular, labor (see Montgomery 1991 and the references cited therein). The circulation of information within a business network also makes group sanctions possible: the community can punish breach of contract by jointly refusing to deal with bad payers (e.g., Kandori 1992; Greif 1993; Greif 1994).[31] Exclusion from other forms of economic and social interactions may also be used to punish deviance (e.g., Basu 1986; Spagnolo 1999; Ligon et al. 2001). Group punishment makes firms more confident that they will not be cheated by group members. As a result they may prefer to trade within their community. Whenever business communities are built along ethnic, religious, or gender lines, network effects result in apparent discrimination.

We now investigate the possibility that network effects influence the allocation of trade credit. For the sake of generality, we adopt minimalist assumptions regarding

---

31. For a discussion on how joint punishment can be enforced, see also Ellison (1994) and chapters 11 and 12. A shared sense of moral outrage may help ensure widespread participation even if the punishment imposes a cost on the punishing party and is not otherwise individually rational. Platteau (1994b) discusses the relationship between ethics and markets. Raub and Weesie (1990) illustrate how the contract enforcement advantage of closed groups ("cliques" in the language of sociology; Mitchell 1969) extends to interconnected networks.

the role that networks play in economic exchange: we simply assume that firms in a particular group share information about each other. Behind this assumption is the idea that clients come recommended by members of their community. Provided that the source of information is known to the supplier, recommendations can be used to screen trade credit applicants. It may even enable them to receive instant credit (see Fafchamps 1996, 1997c, and Fafchamps et al. 1994 for examples). Unknown prospective customers can, as before, be screened at a cost c. The possibility of group punishment—exclusion from trade and social ostracism—is ignored from the formal presentation;[32] including it would only magnify network effects.

We focus on one situation of interest: that in which one group has established a dominant position upon a particular activity. We call them the "in-group," indexed with subscript I.[33] Other competent agents—the "out-group," indexed with subscript O—belong to the population at large and are assumed not to benefit from network effects. This situation is the most relevant for the study African manufacturing where a close-knit business community operates among a mass of informal sector firms (e.g., Bade and Chifamba 1994; Fafchamps 1996, 1997c). Extending the model to competing networks is left for future research. We now show that networking can yield patterns of discrimination that are difficult to distinguish from statistical discrimination. To show this formally, let β_I^* and β_O^* be the trade margins that are just sufficient to deter breach of contract among the in- and out-firms, respectively. Define α_I^* and α_O^* as the trade margins required for the in- and out-suppliers to screen unknown prospective customers, respectively. When the in-suppliers refuse to screen the out-clients, simple algebra yields

$$\beta_I^* = \frac{1 - \delta\mu}{1 + \delta\theta - \delta\mu\theta},$$
(17.18)

$$\beta_O^* = \frac{1 - \delta\mu}{1 + \delta - \delta\mu},$$
(17.19)

$$\alpha_I^* = \frac{1 - \tau}{\tau - (1 - \theta)(1 - \mu)} + \frac{c(1 - \delta(\tau - (1 - \theta)(1 - \mu)))}{\delta(1 - \mu)(\tau - (1 - \theta)(1 - \mu))},$$
(17.20)

32. Information sharing makes it theoretically possible to construct reputational equilibria in which breach of contract is punished by exclusion from future trade credit with all members of the group (e.g., Kandori 1992; Greif 1993; Greif 1994). Voluntary participation to collective punishment raises complex enforcement issues that are discussed in chapters 11 and 12.

33. Since "in" agents are established firms, they are, by definition, competent. One could, of course, conceive a more general model in which all the network does is provide a signal that is more precise than ethnicity but does not predict competence perfectly. It should be intuitively clear that as long as the signal transmitted by the network is sufficiently precise, the results derived here carry through (e.g., Taylor 2000; chapter 11).

$$\alpha_O^* = \frac{1-\tau}{\tau} + \frac{c(1-\delta\tau)}{\delta\tau(1-\mu)}.$$ (17.21)

Armed with these expressions, we can now state the following proposition:

PROPOSITION 17.3

i. If $\alpha_I^* + \beta_O^* \leq \kappa$ and $\beta_I^* \leq \kappa$, the only self-enforcing trust-based equilibria that exist are equilibria in which the out-clients are all screened but the in-clients receive instant credit from the in suppliers. If in addition $\beta_I^* + \alpha_I^* > \kappa$, the in-suppliers charge a higher price to the out- than the in-clients.

ii. Let $\beta_O^{**} = \tau - (1-\mu)(1-\theta)$. If $\beta_I^{**} < \kappa$, $\beta_O^{**} + \alpha_I^* > \kappa$, and $\beta_O^{**} + \alpha_O^* < \kappa$, the only self-enforcing trust-based equilibria that exist are equilibria in which in-suppliers refuse to screen out-clients, but out-suppliers accept to screen them. These conditions are more likely to be satisfied when θ is small, that is, when the proportion of insiders in the economy is large. Discriminatory rationing (in which in-suppliers randomize) may also arise.

iii. For high enough screening costs, the only self-enforcing trust-based equilibria that exist are equilibria in which out clients are never screened and thus never receive trade credit; the latter form a flea market economy that operates at the margin of a closely knit business community where trade credit is the norm.

(Proof in appendix)

Proposition 17.3 shows that network effects are theoretically capable of generating equilibrium configurations that resemble those resulting from statistical discrimination. The reason is that if members of a particular ethnic group manage to establish an information-sharing network among themselves, they will trade with each other more easily than with outsiders. The higher payoffs of well-connected firms can be understood as returns to "social capital" (Coleman 1988). Clients outside the group may then find themselves discriminated against, through prices, rationing, or exclusion. This occurs even though, strictly speaking, they are not the victim of discrimination. Rather, they are disadvantaged because they do not belong to an information diffusion network.[34] The absence of a general information-sharing

34. This begs the question of why outsiders do not respond by creating their own information-sharing group. One possible explanation is that ethnic heterogeneity hinders outsiders' effort to construct an independent network. Outsiders may also find it more attractive to individually join the existing network, for instance, through marriage, conversion, or friendship, instead of forming a competing network that would, initially at least, be very small. The tension between an integration strategy and a self-segregation strategy may thus undermine outsiders' efforts. These issues deserve further research.

mechanism that includes members of all ethnic groups makes deals across ethnic boundaries difficult.[35]

17.5 Conclusion

The model presented in this chapter has illustrated that statistical discrimination and network effects have superficially similar effects on rationing and exclusion from trade. The presence of statistical discrimination explains why members of a disadvantaged group can be treated in a less desirable fashion—namely by being excluded from trade or treated in a less trusting manner. Network effects can have similar consequences.

Social networks often are organized around ethnicity for a variety of reasons such as intermarriage, spatially segregated residence, language, and culturally determined interest in particular activities (e.g., going to church) or sports (e.g., golf). If business networks develop around ethnicity, the arguments presented in this chapter demonstrate under what circumstances ethnic bias will subsist.

In the following chapter we examine whether the African evidence supports the idea that ethnic bias in market exchange is due to network effects.

17.6 Appendix: Proofs of the Propositions

Proof of Proposition 17.1   Steady state payoffs are

$$V^S = \frac{(1 - \delta\mu)(\alpha\tau - 1 + \tau) - c\delta(1 - \tau)}{(1 - \delta)(1 + \delta - \delta\mu - \delta\tau)}, \tag{17.22}$$

$$V^N = \frac{\delta(1 - \mu)(\alpha\tau - 1 + \tau) - c(1 - \delta\tau)}{(1 - \delta)(1 + \delta - \delta\mu - \delta\tau)}, \tag{17.23}$$

$$V^C = \frac{(1 - \delta\mu)(\beta\tau + 1 - \tau)}{(1 - \delta)(1 + \delta - \delta\mu - \delta\tau)}, \tag{17.24}$$

$$V^U = \frac{\delta(1 - \mu)(\beta\tau + 1 - \tau)}{(1 - \delta)(1 + \delta - \delta\mu - \delta\tau)}. \tag{17.25}$$

---

35. To the extent that *B* firms are unreliable because of their lack of experience, setting up a credit reference system may actually make it harder for them to join the mainstream (chapter 12). Indeed, their initial incompetence gets widely advertised, making it potentially difficult for them to be granted a second chance.

Let us now turn to the seven equilibrium conditions (EC1) through (EC7). Equilibrium condition (EC4) is always satisfied, implying that trust-based strategies cannot prevent breach of contract at the end of a relationship. It is easy to verify from equations (A3) and (A4) that (EC2) and (EC6) are always satisfied. Condition (EC1) holds as long as (EC5) does. Conditions (EC3), (EC5), and (EC7) are thus the only constraints to consider.

By plugging equations (A3) and (A4) into (EC3) and simplifying, we obtain

$$\beta \geq \frac{1 - \delta\mu}{1 + \delta - \delta\mu} = \beta^*. \tag{RC}$$

Using equation (A2), we can similarly simplify screening condition (EC6) as

$$\alpha \geq \frac{1 - \tau}{\tau} + \frac{c(1 - \delta\tau)}{\tau\delta(1 - \mu)}. \tag{SC}$$

For (EC7) to be satisfied, the proportion μ of incompetent firms in the economy must such that

$$\mu \geq \frac{c + \alpha}{1 + \alpha}. \tag{EC7'}$$

Rearranging (RC), (SC), and (EC7'), we prove both part 1 and part 2. ∎

Proof of Proposition 17.2 (i) Define a discriminatory exclusion equilibrium (DEE) as one in which suppliers screen A firms but not B firms; as a result B firms never receive trade credit. With probability $1 - \theta$, unmatched suppliers meet B clients; in a DEE they refuse to screen them and choose instead to wait until the next trading round. With probability θ, they are matched with A firms which they screen. A μ_A proportion of them turn out to be reliable and become long-term clients; the others cheat and are discarded. Screening costs θc are lower than if all trade credit applicants are screened. In such an equilibrium, suppliers' expected payoffs are

$$V^S = \tau(\alpha + \delta V^S) + (1 - \tau)(-1 + \delta V^N), \tag{17.26}$$

$$V^N = \delta V^N(\theta\mu_A + 1 - \theta) + \delta V^S\theta(1 - \mu_A) - \theta c. \tag{17.27}$$

Since in a DEE all suppliers behave in the same way, A clients receive trade credit from competent A and B suppliers alike. The expected payoffs of matched and unmatched A firms are, respectively,

$$V_A^C = \tau(\beta + \delta V_A^C) + (1 - \tau)(1 + \delta V_A^U), \tag{17.28}$$

$$V_A^U = (\theta\mu_A + (1 - \theta)\mu_B)\delta V_A^U + (\theta(1 - \mu_A) + (1 - \theta)(1 - \mu_B))\delta V_A^C. \tag{17.29}$$

By construction, all B clients remain forever unmatched, and their expected payoff V_B^U is 0. If, by chance, a B client is able to establish a trade credit relationship with a supplier, its expected payoff will be

$$V_B^C = \tau(\beta + \delta V_B^C) + (1 - \tau). \tag{17.30}$$

Steady state equilibrium values for V^S, V^N, V_A^C, V_A^N, and V_B^C can be derived from the equations above; they are similar to equations (A1) to (A4) and are skipped for the sake of brevity.

For a DEE to be self-enforcing, several equilibrium conditions must be satisfied, four of which deserve consideration: A clients must pay their suppliers (EC8), suppliers must screen A clients (EC9), they must not screen B clients (EC10), and B cannot credibly induce suppliers to screen them by offering to pay a higher price. We begin with the first three conditions:

$$\beta + \delta V_A^C \geq 1 + \delta V_A^U \qquad (EC8), \tag{17.31}$$

$$V^N \geq 0 \qquad (EC9), \tag{17.32}$$

$$V^N \geq (\theta\mu_A + (1 - \theta)\mu_B)\delta V^N$$
$$+ (\theta(1 - \mu_A) + (1 - \theta)(1 - \mu_B))\delta V^S - c \qquad (EC10). \tag{17.33}$$

Replacing by equilibrium values and solving for β and α, we get

$$\beta \geq \beta_A^* \equiv \frac{1 - \delta\theta\mu_A - \delta(1 - \theta)\mu_B}{1 + \delta - \delta\theta\mu_A - \delta(1 - \theta)\mu_B} \qquad (EC8'), \tag{17.34}$$

$$\alpha \geq \alpha_A^* \equiv \frac{1 - \tau}{\tau} + \frac{c(1 - \delta\tau)}{\delta\tau(1 - \mu_A)} \qquad (EC9'), \tag{17.35}$$

$$\alpha \leq \alpha_B^* \equiv \frac{1 - \tau}{\tau} + \frac{c(1 - \delta\tau + \delta\theta(\mu_B - \mu_A))}{\delta\tau(1 - \mu_B)} \qquad (EC10'). \tag{17.36}$$

The repayment condition (EC8′) is essentially the same as that derived in section 17.2, except that the matching probabilities are slightly different. For the two screening conditions (EC9′) and (EC10′) to hold simultaneously, α_B^* must be greater than α_A^*. If $c = 0$, this requirement cannot be satisfied. Suppose that $c > 0$. Since, by assumption, $\mu_B > \mu_A$, the denominator of the c term is lower and the numerator larger in (EC10′) than in (EC9′). Consequently, whenever $\mu_B > \mu_A$, then $\alpha_B^* > \alpha_A^*$ regardless of the values of δ, τ, θ, c, μ_A, and μ_B, and there exist values of α that satisfy both screening conditions (EC9′) and (EC10′). The larger the gap between μ_B and μ_A, the larger is the set of values of α for which both conditions hold. For conditions (EC8′) to (EC10′) to be satisfied simultaneously, the combined gains from trade κ must be large enough to ensure that there exist values α and β such that $\beta > \beta_A^*$, $\alpha \geq \alpha_A^*$, and $\alpha + \beta = \kappa$. If this requirement does not hold, suppliers will refuse to screen anyone and trade credit will not be offered.

So far we have implicitly assumed that suppliers charge the same price to all clients regardless of their ethnic background. Could B clients induce suppliers to screen them by offering to pay a price higher than that charged to A firms? To verify that the DEE is robust to such offers, we examine whether a supplier could improve its lot by departing from discriminatory exclusion in exchange for a higher sale price—and thus a higher α. Since we are considering a single deviation from the equilibrium path, we assume that other suppliers continue to exclude B firms from trade credit. If a B client can credibly offer to split gains from trade κ in such a way that $\alpha > \alpha_B^*$, then discriminatory exclusion is not self-enforcing.[36] Such an offer is credible only if repayment by the B firm is self-enforcing, if

$$\beta + \delta V_B^C \geq 1 + V_B^N. \tag{EC11}$$

Replacing V_B^C and V_B^N by their equilibrium value, we get

$$\beta \geq \beta_B^* \equiv 1 - \delta, \tag{EC11′}$$

where β_B^* is the profit margin that is just sufficient to induce an otherwise excluded B firm to repay trade credit. As is apparent from comparing (EC8′) to (EC11′), $\beta_B^* < \beta_A^*$: B firms who are lucky enough to receive credit from one supplier in a DEE are more reliable than A firms. The reason is that they value the relationship more than A firms since, unlike A firms, they would not receive trade credit from another supplier if they cheat.

If $\beta_B^* + \alpha_B^* > \kappa$, there exist no distribution of the gains from trade such that the supplier can be induced to screen a B firm and the B firm can be induced to pay the supplier. A DEE is thus self-enforcing if the value of κ is such that

---

36. More precisely, it is not sustainable without a metapunishment that deters suppliers from accepting higher prices from B clients. Since both supplier and client have an incentive to conceal that a higher price was charged, enforcing such a metapunishment is problematic. We prefer to focus here on decentralizable punishment mechanisms.

$$\alpha_A^* + \beta_A^* < \kappa < \alpha_B^* + \beta_B^*. \tag{EC12}$$

For such a κ to exist, $\alpha_A^* + \beta_A^* - \alpha_B^* - \beta_B^*$ must be negative, meaning that we must have

$$\frac{\delta^2(1 - \theta\mu_A - (1 - \theta)\mu_B)}{1 + \delta - \delta\theta\mu_A - \delta(1 - \theta)\mu_B} - \frac{c(\mu_B - \mu_A)(1 - \delta\tau + \delta\theta(1 - \mu_A))}{\delta\tau(1 - \mu_A)(1 - \mu_B)} < 0. \tag{EC13}$$

The first term corresponds to $\beta_A^* - \beta_B^*$; it is positive. The second term corresponds to $\alpha_A^* - \alpha_B^*$; it is negative whenever $c > 0$ and $\mu_B > \mu_A$. It is also decreasing (more negative) in c and $\mu_B - \mu_A$. Since (EC13) is linear in c, it is obvious that for any set of parameter values, there exists a screening cost c, say c^*, such that, for all $c > c^*$, (EC13) is negative. Then, for any $c > c^*$, there exist values of κ that satisfy equation (EC12) and for which the DEE is self-enforcing. This completes part (i).

(ii) When discriminatory exclusion is not self-enforcing, price discrimination may nevertheless arise. To see why, consider an equilibrium in which all agents, regardless of their type, are screened by suppliers. The minimum level of β that deters breach of contract is thus the same for all. It is equal to β_A^* from (EC8). The minimum level of α that is needed to induce suppliers to screen, however, depends on the client's ethnicity. The difference between the two can be computed to be[37]

$$\alpha_B^{**} - \alpha_A^{**} = \frac{c(\mu_B - \mu_A)(1 + \delta(1 - \tau) - \delta\theta\mu_A - \delta(1 - \theta)\mu_B)}{\delta\tau(1 - \mu_A)(1 - \mu_B)}. \tag{17.37}$$

The sign of $\alpha_B^{**} - \alpha_A^{**}$ is the same as the sign of $\mu_B - \mu_A$: suppliers require a higher minimum profit rate before screening client populations with a higher proportion of incompetent firms. Since the buyer's profit rate is equal to $\kappa - \alpha$, a higher α means that β must be lower. This does not, however, imply that price discrimination arises whenever observable characteristics such as ethnicity help predict competence; as long as $\alpha_B^{**} + \beta_A^* < \kappa$, suppliers can charge the same price to all. In that case there exists a supplier margin $\alpha > \alpha_B^{**}$ that satisfies both screening conditions and deters breach (i.e., $\beta = \kappa - \alpha \geq \beta_A^*$). Whether or not suppliers can set such a price depends on their bargaining power. Powerful buyers may try to force the price below α_B^{**}. Only suppliers dealing with A buyers may agree to do so, in which case A and B buyers will pay a different price. Price discrimination is thus more likely when suppliers' market power is weak.

---

37. Equation (17.37) is derived as follows: Equilibrium values for V^S and V^N are computed assuming that all firms are screened as in section 17.2. α_A^{**} and α_B^{**} can then be computed from the screening conditions $\mu_i \delta V^N + (1 - \mu_i)\delta V^S \geq \delta V^N$, for $i \in \{A, B\}$.

(iii) A third, hybrid equilibrium is also possible in which price discrimination and discriminatory rationing coexist. To see how such an equilibrium may arise, let us go back to our discussion of discriminatory exclusion. Consider what happens when c is just below c^*, that is, when

$$\kappa = \alpha_A^* + \beta_A^* = \alpha_B^* + \beta_B^* + \varepsilon \tag{17.38}$$

with ε small. Discriminatory exclusion is not self-enforcing, but this cannot imply that all B firms suddenly get access to trade credit, even at a higher price. The reason is that if they did, the level of profit required for them to respect contracts would jump from β_B^* to the much higher β_A^*: the profit rates required to deter breach and guarantee the screening of B firms would exceed total gains from trade κ. Consequently, when c falls just below c^*, only a fraction of the B firms, say γ, can gain access to trade credit. Let β_B^o be the minimum profit level that ensures trade credit repayment when the likelihood of being screened by a supplier is γ:

$$\beta_B^o = \frac{1 - \delta + \delta\gamma - \delta\gamma\mu_A\theta - \delta\gamma\mu_B(1 - \theta)}{1 + \delta\gamma - \delta\gamma\mu_A\theta - \delta\gamma\mu_B(1 - \theta)}. \tag{17.39}$$

Clearly, β_B^o is an increasing function of γ: the more likely B are to receive trade credit after cheating on a supplier, the harder it is to deter breach. By keeping γ low enough, it can be ensured that $\alpha_B^* + \beta_B^o \leq \kappa$.

For a particular level of discriminatory rationing γ to be an equilibrium, suppliers must randomize. For randomization to constitute a best response, suppliers must be indifferent between screening and not screening B firms. This condition is satisfied only when their margin on B sales is equal to α_B^*. Furthermore, it must not be possible for B firms to credibly offer a buying price higher than α_B^*; otherwise, suppliers would not be indifferent between screening and not screening, and randomization would not be optimal. Consequently, for discriminatory rationing to be self-enforcing, it must be that

$$\alpha_B^* + \beta_B^o = \kappa. \tag{17.40}$$

Equation (17.40) thus implicitly determines the equilibrium value of γ and thus the fraction of B clients that suffer from discriminatory rationing. It also indicates that discriminatory rationing must coexist with price discrimination: since $\gamma < 1$ only when $\beta_A^* > \kappa - \alpha_B^* = \beta_B^o$, it follows that the price charged to B firms must exceed that charged to A firms. As μ_B falls relative to μ_A, discriminatory rationing becomes less severe: α_B^* falls, leading to an increase in β_B^o, and thus to a rise in γ. When γ reaches 1, discriminatory rationing disappears, and $\beta_B^o = \beta_A^*$: A firms and B firms have the same breach deterrence condition. Price discrimination may persist, although it is no longer necessary for the equilibrium to be sustainable. This completes the proof. ∎

Proof of Proposition 17.3   (i) We begin by showing that network effects can support steady state equilibria in which out-clients are all screened but in-clients receive instant credit from in-suppliers. We call such equilibria preferential treatment equilibria (PTE). Let θ be the proportion of out-firms among unmatched firms.[38] Payoffs to matched suppliers and clients in a PTE are given by, respectively,

$$V_k^S = \tau(\alpha + \delta V_k^S) + (1 - \tau)(-1 + \delta V_k^N)k \in \{I, O\}, \tag{17.41}$$

$$V_k^C = \tau(\beta + \delta V_k^C) + (1 - \tau)(1 + \delta V_k^U)k \in \{I, O\}. \tag{17.42}$$

Payoffs to unmatched suppliers are

$$V_I^N = \theta(\mu\delta V_I^N + (1 - \mu)\delta V_I^S - c) + (1 - \theta)(\mu\delta V_I^N + (1 - \mu)(\alpha + \delta V_I^S)), \tag{17.43}$$

$$V_O^N = \mu\delta V_O^N + (1 - \mu)\delta V_O^S - c. \tag{17.44}$$

Payoffs to unmatched clients can be similarly derived as

$$V_I^U = \theta(\mu\delta V_I^U + (1 - \mu)\delta V_I^C) + (1 - \theta)(\mu\delta V_I^U + (1 - \mu)(\beta + \delta V_I^C)), \tag{17.45}$$

$$V_O^U = \mu\delta V_O^U + (1 - \mu)\delta V_O^C - c. \tag{17.46}$$

In a PTE, expected discounted payoffs of in-suppliers and clients are higher than those of out-firms: in-suppliers save on screening and establish full business relationships faster; in-clients receive trade credit more rapidly. For a PTE to be self-enforcing, breach deterrence and screening conditions must be satisfied as in sections 17.1 and 17.2.

It is easy to verify that $\beta_I^* > \beta_O^*$ always: it is easier to deter breach of contract among out-firms because they face a higher penalty. Similarly it is straightforward to verify that $\alpha_I^* > \alpha_O^*$ always: in-suppliers are more tempted than out-suppliers to stop screening unknown firms because they can hope to be matched with a known firm in a subsequent period. In contrast, it is never in insiders' interest to refuse instant credit to recommended clients (as long as $\beta_I > \beta_I^*$, of course). For a PTE to be sustainable, total gains from trade κ must be sufficient to ensure that trade margins exist that satisfy the equilibrium conditions above; that is, it must be that $\alpha_I^* + \beta_O^* \le \kappa$ and $\beta_I^* \le \kappa$. If in addition $\beta_I^* + \alpha_I^* > \kappa$, in-suppliers have to charge a higher price to out-

---

38. As in the previous two sections, we abstract from the fact that the proportion of unmatched firms depends on strategies. See chapter 11 for a thorough treatment.

than in-clients. The reason is that in-clients have to be cajoled into repaying suppliers (i.e., $\beta_I^* > \beta_O^*$), while in-suppliers have to be bribed into screening out-clients (i.e., $\alpha_I^* > 0$). Price discrimination may thus arise in a PTE.

(ii) To see why network effects can lead to discriminatory exclusion, note that for trade between in-suppliers and out-clients to be possible, it must be that $\alpha_I^* + \beta_O^* \leq \kappa$: in-suppliers must be compensated for the risk they take in screening unknown firms, and out-clients must be motivated to pay suppliers. If total gains from trade κ are not sufficient to ensure that both conditions are satisfied, in-suppliers cannot be convinced to screen outsiders. They may continue to offer instant credit to insiders, however. This can be shown formally by considering an equilibrium in which in-suppliers offer instant trade credit to in-clients but refuse to deal with outsiders. Depending on parameter values, out-suppliers may find it optimal to screen clients or to refuse credit to all.

Let us first consider the case in which out-suppliers screen clients. Call this equilibrium an outsider exclusion equilibrium (OEE). In an OEE, in-clients face the same payoffs as in a PTE and the breach deterrence condition is satisfied for $\beta_I \geq \beta_I^*$. For outsiders the breach deterrence conditions is now satisfied for

$$\beta \geq \beta_O^{**} \equiv \frac{1 - \delta\mu - \delta\theta + \delta\theta\mu}{\tau - (1 - \mu)(1 - \theta)}. \tag{17.47}$$

Threshold trade margins for suppliers are the same as in the PTE; in-suppliers refuse to screen out-clients as long as $\alpha_I < \alpha_I^*$; out-suppliers screen all clients whenever $\alpha_O > \alpha_O^*$.

An OEE is sustainable provided that $\beta_I^* < \kappa$, $\beta_O^{**} + \alpha_I^* > \kappa$, and $\beta_O^{**} + \alpha_O^* < \kappa$. Since $\alpha_O^* < \alpha_I^*$ always (see above), it is possible to satisfy the second and third conditions simultaneously. That the three conditions are satisfied for some parameter values is straightforward to verify numerically. It is also easy to check that these conditions are more likely to be satisfied when θ is small, that is, when the proportion of insiders in the economy is large. Discriminatory exclusion can thus result from network effects. Discriminatory rationing may also arise. This can be shown using the same approach as in section 17.2.[39]

(iii) If out-suppliers find screening too costly, network effects lead to what we may call a closed-shop equilibrium (CSE): only members of the network receive trade

---

39. The need for randomization can be seen by noting that $\beta_O^{**} < \beta_O^*$: if, in the vicinity of $\beta_O = \beta_O^{**}$, all out clients were to be suddenly screened by in-suppliers, there would be a jump in the breach deterrence condition from β_O^{**} to the higher β_O^*. This jump may violate the requirement that $\alpha_I^* + \beta_O^* < \kappa$, therefore requiring that in-suppliers randomize.

credit; outsiders are excluded from receiving any trade credit. To show that a CSE is possible, we must demonstrate that the breach deterrence condition can be satisfied for in-clients while at the same time the screening condition is not satisfied for out-clients. It is easy to verify that the former holds whenever $\beta_I \geq 1 - \delta\mu - \delta\theta + \delta\theta\mu$. The latter is satisfied if $\alpha_O < \alpha_O^*$. Provided therefore that

$$\alpha_O^* > 1 - \delta\mu - \delta\theta + \delta\theta\mu, \qquad\qquad (17.48)$$

there exist values of κ such that a CSE is sustainable. Since α_O^* is an increasing function of c, it is clear that there always exists a high enough level of screening costs such that equation (17.48) is satisfied. A CSE is thus more likely to arise when screening is very costly, as intuition would suggest.   ∎

18 Supplier Credit and Ethnicity

This chapter investigates the presence of ethnic bias in market transactions among African manufacturing firms. We examine trade (supplier) credit because it offers a perfect vantage point into the functioning of decentralized markets involving a large—though not infinite—number of participants: supplier credit will be offered only if sufficient trust exists between the parties. An additional reason for investigating supplier credit is that it represents a nonnegligible source of firm finance for the overwhelming majority of African manufacturers. It is particularly important for small firms with limited access to bank finance. It is true that the credit firms receive from their suppliers is short term: each credit is due within a month or so. But supplier credit is constantly renewed as firms place new orders. As a result it provides a more stable source of external funds than a bank loan that typically has to be paid back within a couple of years.

As we have discussed in the previous chapter, ethnic bias can originate from a wide variety of source. Finding evidence that market outcomes are correlated with ethnic origin does not, by itself, constitute evidence of discrimination or prejudice. In fact, in the next chapter we will argue that at least part of the observed bias can be attributed to network effects. In this chapter our purpose is simply to investigate whether market outcomes depend on the ethnicity of agents.

To keep things as simple and straightforward as possible, we use very broad categories based on race alone. In the work that follows, we identify at most five ethnicity categories, based on descent and not citizenship: African (black), European (white), Asian (primarily from South Asia), Mideastern (primarily from Syria and Lebanon), and other (primarily individuals of mixed ancestry). This very broad categorization offers three advantages. First, race is most of the time readily identifiable via physical features and name. Race information is therefore straightforward to collect. As we have seen in earlier chapters, there is quite a bit of racial diversity among African entrepreneurs so that it is a meaningful categorization as well.

Second, race is a fairly objective dimension of ethnicity. There is a lot of ethnic differentiation within the population of African ancestry which constitutes the majority of surveyed entrepreneurs. But ethnic identity is often a matter of subjective assessment, especially among urban entrepreneurs who over the years have loosened their ties with rural relatives. Even in rural areas, ethnic identity is seldom clear-cut because people move and intermarry. As a result ethnicity is often open to interpretation and personal appreciation. In a number of cases language could be used as a marker for ethnicity. But there are plenty of situations where this does not work. In Burundi, for instance, one of the countries in our sample, Tutsis and Hutus consider themselves as separate ethnic groups, yet they speak the same language. Most

Table 18.1
Supplier credit and ethnic composition

	Burundi		Cameroon		Côte d'Ivoire		Ethiopia	
	Number of observations	Mean	Number of observations	Mean	Number of observations	Mean	Number of observations	Mean
Annual sales	117	389,694	225	3,952,165	213	4,886,052	174	4,857
Firm age	120	11	237	12	230	16	208	17
Account payables	111	50,076	199	149,271	179	348,712	149	462
Account receivables	110	22,971	190	169,983	183	411,668	129	261
Payables/annual sales		13%		4%		7%		10%
Receivables/ annual sales		6%		4%		8%		5%
African descent	110	89%	239	81%	234	57%	209	83%
European descent	110	6%	239	13%	234	25%	209	1%
Asian descent	110	4%	239	2%	234	0%	209	0%
Other non-African descent	110	1%	239	4%	233	18%	209	15%
Some foreign ownership	120	30%	210	32%	234	47%	209	3%
Limited liability status	120	38%	207	62%	234	58%	209	19%
% imported inputs	115	42%	225	46%	220	20%	189	47%
% exported output	119	4%	242	10%	232	21%	209	1%

Note: All figures are given for wave 1, except for Ghana where wave 2 figures are given (no account payable and receivable information was collected for wave 1 in Ghana).

entrepreneurs in the sample speak several languages, if only because it is a business necessity. Language is thus not a useful distinction either.

Third, there often is quite a bit of tension around the issue of ethnic identification in Africa. The 1994 genocide in Rwanda is one extreme example, but there are plenty of others. Ethnic identity has a political dimension in every single country in the sample. In this context it was difficult—and often counterproductive—to ask respondents to define their own ethnicity publicly, beyond what cannot be denied such as race. This is why race is the focus of our empirical analysis.

18.1   The Data

The data used in our analysis come from the RPED manufacturing surveys described in chapter 3. The basic features of the data are summarized in table 18.1. We only show figures for wave 1; figures for the other waves are qualitatively similar.

Ghana		Kenya		Tanzania		Zambia		Zimbabwe	
Number of observations	Mean	Number of observations	Mean	Number of observations	Mean	Number of observations	Mean	Number of observations	Mean
194	209,186	215	41,275	201	274,354	205	304,309	202	25,556
200	16	223	19	217	16	215	18	202	24
181	13,935	190	3,721	197	21,225	199	9,758	182	2,350
181	10,750	193	2,772	191	18,985	197	26,585	189	3,849
	7%		9%		8%		3%		9%
	5%		7%		7%		9%		15%
126	91%	222	42%	177	71%	185	59%	173	33%
126	1%	222	4%	177	0%	185	13%	173	47%
126	0%	222	50%	177	28%	185	26%	173	13%
126	8%	222	4%	177	1%	185	2%	173	7%
212	17%	223	18%	217	12%	215	13%	203	23%
200	45%	223	51%	217	66%	215	72%	202	74%
171	15%	222	19%	211	11%	214	24%	199	17%
209	4%	223	7%	216	4%	214	2%	199	11%

As can be seen, firms receive credit from their suppliers and give credit to their clients.[1] On average, at the time of the survey, firms owed to their suppliers the equivalent of 8 percent of their annual sales. This is equivalent to one month of sales on average. Credit from suppliers is smallest in Zambia (3 percent) and highest in Burundi (13 percent). There is some variation between years, possibly because of changes in interest rates and macroeconomic conditions. Trade credit to clients is of the same order of magnitude—8.2 percent of annual sales on average, with a low of 4 percent in Cameroon and a high of 15 percent in Zimbabwe. In some countries trade credit is a net source of funds for firms—they receive more than they give (Burundi, Ethiopia, and Ghana). In others, it is a net drain on the firm's financial resources (Zimbabwe and Zambia).

---

1. In a very small number of cases, firms receive credit from clients (advances) or give credit to suppliers (downpayment). The amounts involved are usually quite small and these cases are ignored here. We repeated our analysis using combined credit figures (e.g., credit received from suppliers and clients, and credit given to suppliers and clients). Qualitative results are unaffected.

No matter what the net contribution of trade credit is on average, what is clear from discussions with entrepreneurs is that firms that do not receive credit from their suppliers are at a disadvantage relative to others. In virtually all cases, firms that are offered supplier credit make use of it because it is cheaper than bank credit, it is flexible, and it simplifies the conduct of business. By the same token, firms that cannot offer credit to their clients find it more difficult to compete for market shares. The ability to receive and offer trade credit is thus one factor in the success of a firm.

As is clear from table 18.1, the ethnic makeup of manufacturing samples differs quite significantly across countries.[2] In countries such as Cameroon, Côte d'Ivoire, Zambia, and especially Zimbabwe, a significant minority of surveyed entrepreneurs is of European ascent. Asian entrepreneurs are found throughout Eastern and Southern Africa, for example, in Kenya, Tanzania, Zambia, and Zimbawe. A number of entrepreneurs of Mideastern origin are found in Côte d'Ivoire and Ghana while Ethiopia counts a number of entrepreneurs of mixed origin (primarily European and Ethiopian or Eritrean).

Surveyed firms also differ in other dimensions that are likely to be correlated with supplier credit usage, such as foreign ownership or limited liability status. Firms that import much of their inputs or export much of their output may also deal differently from other firms. Average characteristics are given on table 18.1 for RPED sample firms.

18.2 Multivariate Analysis

We are interested in finding out whether ethnicity explains part of the variation in trade credit usage. In other words, we wish to estimate the relationship between credit received $C^r_{i,s,c,t}$ and given $C^g_{i,s,c,t}$ and the ethnicity $E_{i,s,c}$ of a firm (entrepreneur/ manager) i in sector s in country c at time t. In other words, we want to estimate

$$C^r_{i,s,c,t} = f_r(E_{i,s,c}),$$

$$C^g_{i,s,c,t} = f_g(E_{i,s,c}).$$

Ethnicity is measured by a series of dummies defining the race of the entrepreneur. It does not change over time.[3]

---

2. What is measured is the ethnicity of the entrepreneur, that is, of the manager of the firm. In most cases this is also the main if not sole owner of the firm.

3. In very few cases the ethnicity of a firm appears to have changed over time. This may be due to a change in ownership or management, or be the result of measurement error. These cases are ignored in the analysis presented here.

To estimate this relationship in a meaningful manner, we need to control for other factors likely to influence trade credit usage. The first of these is simply firm size: other things being equal, enterprises that sell more, receive and give more trade credit as well. We also need to control for firm age: older firms might have built a reputation that enables them to access supplier credit, as well as a stronger financial base that makes it possible to offer credit to clients. Foreign ownership may affect trade credit usage as alternative sources and uses of funds exist for these firms. Once we control for other firm characteristics, limited liability status should, in principle, discourage supplier credit since creditors cannot recover their debt on the personal assets of the owner(s). The percentage of imported inputs or exported output may also affect trade credit usage because international transactions often rely on the letter of credit which, by construction, dissociates supplier credit from the sale. The estimated equations are thus of the form

$$\log C^r_{i,s,c,t} = \alpha_0 + \alpha_s \log S_{i,s,c,t} + \alpha_r E_{i,s,c} + \alpha_i I_{i,s,c} + \alpha_z Z_{i,s,c} + u_{s,c,t} + \varepsilon_{i,s,c,t}, \quad (18.1)$$

$$\log C^g_{i,s,c,t} = \alpha_0 + \alpha_s \log S_{i,s,c,t} + \alpha_r E_{i,s,c} + \alpha_x X_{i,s,c} + \alpha_z Z_{i,s,c} + u_{s,c,t} + \varepsilon_{i,s,c,t}, \quad (18.2)$$

where $S_{i,s,c,t}$ denotes total sales, $E_{i,s,c}$ is a vector of ethnicity dummies, $I_{i,s,c}$ is the share of imported inputs, $X_{i,s,c}$ is the share of exported output, $Z_{i,s,c}$ is a vector of firm characteristics thought to influence trade credit usage, and $u_{s,c,t}$ is a sector–country–wave specific fixed effect. African ancestry is the omitted dummy.

Equations (18.1) and (18.2) are estimated using the data summarized in table 18.1. Estimation results are presented in table 18.2 for equation (18.1) and table 18.3 for equation (18.2), individually for each country and for the combined sample. Results are extremely variable from one country to another. Entrepreneurs of European ancestry tend to receive more supplier credit in the countries in which they constitute a significant minority (Cameroon, Côte d'Ivoire, Zambia, and Zimbabwe). In other countries they do not differ significantly from entrepreneurs of African descent. Asian entrepreneurs constitute significant minorities in Kenya, Tanzania, Zambia, and Zimbabwe, but being Asian does not appear to have a consistent effect on credit from suppliers. In Zambia and Zimbabwe, Asian entrepreneurs receive more trade credit (only significantly so in Zimbabwe), but they receive less in Tanzania. In Kenya where they constitute the bulk of the business class, they do not appear to receive more credit from suppliers than entrepreneurs of African descent. Regarding entrepreneurs of other or mixed ancestry, they appear to receive more supplier credit than Africans in Ethiopia and Zimbabwe. In other countries, their dummy is not significant.

Turning to credit given to clients (table 18.3), we again see that entrepreneurs of European descent are, on average, more likely to give trade credit. The effect

Table 18.2
Supplier credit received

	All		Burundi		Cameroon		Côte d'Ivoire		Ethiopia		Ghana	
	Coefficient	t-statistic	Coefficient	t-statistic	Coefficient	t-statistic	Coefficient	t-statistic	Coefficient	t-statistic	Coefficient	t-statistic
Annual sales (log)	0.895	26.22	0.426	1.58	1.044	10.46	1.112	9.78	0.180	1.92	0.489	2.72
Age of firm (log)	0.433	5.29	1.164	2.88	0.895	3.42	0.658	2.28	0.125	0.68	-0.137	-0.43
Foreign ownership (yes = 1)	0.594	3.43	0.870	1.10	-0.035	-0.06	1.127	2.43	-0.242	-0.26	0.919	0.91
Limited liability status (yes = 1)	0.616	4.06	3.778	3.43	1.288	2.88	0.791	1.23	0.428	0.68	0.979	1.34
% imported inputs	0.352	1.58	-0.338	-0.39	-0.090	-0.16	2.152	2.87	-0.688	-1.54	0.751	0.59
European descent (yes = 1)	0.988	4.45	0.192	0.11	2.035	3.05	0.766	1.15			-3.052	-1.22
Asian descent (yes = 1)	-0.159	-0.80	1.429	0.71	0.418	0.32						
Other non-African descent (yes = 1)	0.010	0.03	2.709	0.80	0.790	0.67	-0.415	-0.57	1.357	1.80	-0.232	-0.20
Intercept	-6.765	-22.17	-4.642	-2.15	-10.16	-8.87	-10.41	-9.42	-0.807	-1.33	-2.237	-1.28
Number of observations	3,052		97		509		334		143		202	
Number of groups	84		4		12		8		4		8	
R-squared:												
Within	0.408		0.485		0.413		0.590		0.277		0.156	
Between	0.477		0.818		0.523		0.763		0.453		0.630	
Overall	0.419		0.502		0.416		0.607		0.280		0.179	
Fraction of variance due to fixed effects	0.170		0.025		0.034		0.096		0.023		0.026	

Note: The dependent variable is the (log of) the value of account payables (due to suppliers) at the time of the survey. The "other non-African descent" category includes mideasteners and people of mixed ancestry. In Tanzania and Zambia the very few observations in the "other" category were combined with the "Asian" and "European" category, respectively (mideastern in Tanzania; mixed ancestry in Zambia).

	Kenya Coefficient	Kenya t-statistic	Tanzania Coefficient	Tanzania t-statistic	Zambia Coefficient	Zambia t-statistic	Zimbabwe Coefficient	Zimbabwe t-statistic	Wave 1 Coefficient	Wave 1 t-statistic	Wave 2 Coefficient	Wave 2 t-statistic	Wave 3 Coefficient	Wave 3 t-statistic
	0.863	9.94	0.695	6.69	0.763	7.83	0.963	21.45	0.818	15.86	1.012	17.15	0.875	12.34
	0.199	0.93	0.456	2.01	0.487	2.25	0.201	1.92	0.440	3.80	0.437	3.03	0.473	2.51
	0.700	1.79	0.491	0.70	0.369	0.51	-0.055	-0.27	1.173	4.55	0.127	0.45	0.199	0.50
	0.695	1.78	-0.363	-0.96	0.444	1.09	0.358	2.18	0.582	2.47	0.739	2.82	0.566	1.87
	-0.277	-0.45	0.865	1.13	1.265	1.98	0.355	1.08	0.332	1.06	0.410	1.02	0.307	0.62
	-0.063	-0.09			0.752	1.42	0.834	3.70	0.661	1.92	1.279	3.46	1.010	2.19
	0.027	0.07	-1.307	-2.88	0.615	1.37	0.561	2.31	-0.600	-1.99	-0.474	-1.37	0.811	1.96
	0.811	1.03					0.765	2.17	-0.428	-1.00	0.837	1.69	-0.268	-0.38
	-4.828	-6.51	-5.562	-5.22	-7.485	-8.12	-4.426	-14.94	-6.274	-14.58	-7.537	-14.00	-6.867	-9.74
	503		343		453		468		1,273		992		787	
	12		12		12		12		32		28		24	
	0.424		0.154		0.315		0.811		0.391		0.482		0.362	
	0.259		0.308		0.365		0.824		0.573		0.556		0.163	
	0.405		0.165		0.306		0.811		0.429		0.490		0.321	
	0.093		0.116		0.050		0.040		0.157		0.170		0.168	

Table 18.3
Supplier credit given

	All		Burundi		Cameroon		Côte d'Ivoire		Ethiopia		Ghana	
	Coefficient	t-statistic	Coefficient	t-statistic	Coefficient	t-statistic	Coefficient	t-statistic	Coefficient	t-statistic	Coefficient	t-statistic
Annual sales (log)	0.868	25.31	0.805	2.92	0.487	4.95	1.227	11.03	0.237	2.21	0.366	2.33
Age of firm (log)	0.304	3.73	0.614	1.64	0.936	3.80	0.032	0.12	-0.011	-0.05	-0.080	-0.29
Foreign ownership (yes = 1)	0.111	0.65	-0.013	-0.02	-1.245	-2.42	0.286	0.64	0.875	0.80	1.545	1.72
Limited liability status (yes = 1)	1.175	7.89	3.203	2.96	2.334	5.52	0.563	0.93	1.212	1.68	2.711	4.46
% exported output	-0.701	-2.16	-5.297	-1.74	-0.070	-0.08	-2.779	-3.64	0.366	0.21	-2.789	-1.36
European descent (yes = 1)	0.786	3.60	-1.806	-1.17	1.657	2.59	1.254	2.00	0.523	0.61	1.438	0.65
Asian descent (yes = 1)	0.211	1.07	-1.937	-0.99	-1.441	-1.16						
Other non-African descent (yes = 1)	-0.278	-0.96	0.550	0.17	0.701	0.65	0.479	0.70			-1.913	-1.82
Intercept	-4.796	-15.41	-5.403	-2.34	-1.944	-1.71	-7.641	-7.16	-0.523	-0.73	0.224	0.15
Number of observations	3,021		99		506		342		129		216	
Number of groups	84		4		12		8		4		8	
R-squared:												
Within	0.396		0.511		0.255		0.529		0.295		0.250	
Between	0.542		0.402		0.084		0.613		0.660		0.808	
Overall	0.427		0.498		0.213		0.533		0.238		0.280	
Fraction of variance due to fixed effects	0.144		0.050		0.104		0.124		0.121		0.058	

Note: The dependent variable is the (log of) the value of account receivables (due by clients) at the time of the survey. The "other non-African descent" category includes mideasteners and people of mixed ancestry. In Tanzania and Zambia the very few observations in the "other" category were combined with the "Asian" and "European" category, respectively (mideastern in Tanzania; mixed ancestry in Tanzania; mixed ancestry in Zambia).

	Kenya		Tanzania		Zambia		Zimbabwe		Wave 1		Wave 2		Wave 3	
	Coefficient	t-statistic	Coefficient	t-statistic	Coefficient	t-statistic	Coefficient	t-statistic	Coefficient	t-statistic	Coefficient	t-statistic	Coefficient	t-statistic
	0.885	11.01	1.018	8.29	1.092	11.42	0.956	20.00	0.824	15.88	0.937	15.72	0.851	11.95
	−0.013	−0.07	0.420	1.51	0.235	1.00	0.299	2.67	0.238	2.08	0.382	2.65	0.354	1.86
	0.753	2.13	0.281	0.33	1.372	1.98	0.047	0.21	0.324	1.27	−0.016	−0.06	−0.038	−0.10
	0.957	2.67	−0.189	−0.42	1.345	3.26	0.741	4.27	1.426	6.15	1.086	4.23	0.923	3.12
	−0.316	−0.50	−2.473	−1.45	3.156	1.98	0.319	0.78	−1.601	−3.27	0.474	0.89	−1.051	−1.42
	0.755	1.13			−0.904	−1.75	0.738	3.09	0.879	2.62	0.404	1.11	1.049	2.29
	0.565	1.66	0.074	0.14	0.024	0.05	0.391	1.50	0.226	0.75	−0.320	−0.94	0.786	1.96
	0.860	1.19					0.590	1.59	−0.265	−0.64	−0.635	−1.31	0.237	0.33
	−3.881	−5.62	−7.031	−5.54	−7.398	−7.75	−4.254	−13.48	−4.508	−10.31	−5.209	−9.39	−4.884	−6.74
	502		346		406		475		1,272		967		782	
	12		12		12		12		32		28		24	
	0.519		0.221		0.440		0.798		0.401		0.444		0.344	
	0.352		0.125		0.024		0.038		0.608		0.549		0.330	
	0.500		0.216		0.363		0.770		0.458		0.458		0.332	
	0.083		0.089		0.171		0.166		0.171		0.140		0.109	

is positive and significant in three of the four sample countries where European entrepreneurs form a significant minority—Cameroon, Côte d'Ivoire, and Zimbawe. In the fourth one, Zambia, the European dummy is significant but with the wrong sign. This particular result, however, is not robust; it disappears with a small change in the list of regressors. Entrepreneurs of Asian descent give more trade credit in Kenya, where they represent the bulk of entrepreneurs. In other countries, being Asian is not significant. In Ghana, entrepreneurs of Mideastern ancestry who constitute a small proportion of the sample appear to receive less credit, but again this effect is not robust and may be due to the small number of observations.

To check for robustness, we also reestimated equations (18.1) and (18.2) with annual sales $S_{i,s,c,t}$ and ethnicity $E_{i,s,c}$ only. The purpose of this procedure is to examine whether a stronger ethnic bias is present in the data but is correlated with other regressors—imported inputs $I_{i,s,c}$, exported outputs $X_{i,s,c}$, and firm characteristics $Z_{i,s,c}$—and goes away when they are included in the regression. If true, this could generate strong perceptions of ethnic bias among the population even though the bias is probably due to other firm features. Results show that the elimination of extra regressors has no noticeable effect on ethnic bias: the qualitative results shown in tables 18.2 and 18.3 are essentially unaffected. If, however, we simply regress log $C^r_{i,s,c,t}$ and log $C^g_{i,s,c,t}$ on ethnicity $E_{i,s,c}$ alone, not controlling for size $S_{i,s,c,t}$, we obtain very strong and highly significant ethnicity effects in all countries except Burundi and Tanzania. This suggests that much of the observed ethnic bias is related to firm size: African entrepreneurs tend to operate smaller enterprises that receive and give less trade credit. Of course, it remains unclear why enterprises run by African entrepreneurs are smaller. It could be because they receive less trade credit in the first place.

18.3   Conclusion

Taken together, our results suggest the presence of an ethnic bias in trade credit usage among manufacturing firms in sub-Saharan Africa. The direction of the bias is, in general, detrimental to entrepreneurs of African descent and favorable to entrepreneurs originating from outside Africa. Much of this bias disappears when we control for firm size, a reminder of the fact that African entrepreneurs run smaller businesses. But some bias remains even after we do. Ethnic bias is stronger and more favorable for entrepreneurs of European descent, who both receive and give more trade credit. For other non-Africans, the effect is not strong and it is not present in all countries once we control for firm size. But when it is there, it is usually positive, and when it is negative, it is usually not robust.

These findings are a priori paradoxical since, in all the studied countries, African entrepreneurs are surrounded by African entrepreneurs like them and they operate in countries run by African politicians. One would therefore expect them to do better than people who originate from outside the continent and are minorities in Africa— often very small minorities. Moreover, after independence, many African governments have taken a pro-active stance on these issues and have tried to favor the emergence of an indigenous business class. In these circumstances it would be politically difficult for nonindigenous businessmen and women to collude to discriminate against Africans. Of course, it would be naive, simply on this basis, to dismiss prejudice and discrimination as possible explanations for our results. They nevertheless suggest another possible explanation, namely the presence of business networks that favor members of particular minorities. Examining this possibility is the purpose of the next chapter.

19 Discrimination and Networks in African Manufacturing

In the last chapter we saw that trade credit usage varies systematically with ethnicity in African manufacturing. In this chapter we continue our investigation of the attribution of supplier credit for evidence of ethnic bias. In chapter 17 it was suggested that ethnic bias can result from discrimination or network effects. Our objective in this chapter is to disentangle the two. To this effect, we focus on two countries—Kenya and Zimbabwe—where discrimination is easier to study because non-indigenous business groups—Asians in Kenya, Europeans in Zimbabwe—represent a large proportion of the entrepreneurs.

To the extent that networks are based on ethnicity, both grant one particular ethnic group an economic advantage. Their testable implications differ in two important dimensions, however. First, if networks do not matter, possible access to business information through socialization and screening methods should not affect how firms get and give credit. In contrast, if network effects are present, better access to information should help predict which firms get and give credit.

Second, if bias is the result of statistical discrimination, firms that are discriminated against will themselves discriminate among their clients. To the extent that all firms face the same pool of potential clients, the ethnicity of a firm's owner or manager should then help determine whether the firm gets credit but not whether it gives credit to its clients.[1] In contrast, if ethnicity is correlated with network affiliation, and if bias is the result of network effects, then insider firms should find it easier not only to be recognized by suppliers but also to identify reliable clients. In this case ethnicity should explain not only whether firms get credit but also whether they grant credit to clients.[2] The same holds for gender bias. These testable implications form the basis of our empirical analysis.

19.1 Descriptive Analysis

The data used for this analysis come from the Kenya and Zimbabwe case study samples. Descriptive statistics are given in table 19.1 for all firms and by ethnic

---

1. In contrast, if discrimination is due to taste, firms should favor members of their own ethnicity and one should observe the reverse effect (Darity and Mason 1998). By comparing the provision and attribution of credit, this test is less subject to the criticism that affects so-called standard tests of discrimination that regress, say, wages or credit received on observable characteristics and race (e.g., Heckman 1998; Darity 1998).

2. The validity of the test rests on the assumption that credit reliability is not itself a determinant of the willingness to grant trade credit to clients. If this were the case, being discriminated against would be correlated with customer credit through unreliability. Given that all clients ask for credit, it is hard to believe that firms would fail to realize that granting credit to their clients helps their sales.

Table 19.1
Descriptive statistics

	Number of valid obser- vations	All firms	Black (1)	Other (2)	Dominance (3)
Firm characteristics					
Number of employees (median)	111	48	4	65	73
Year the firm was created (median)	113	1975	1975	1970	1973
% of firms that are formally registered/ incorporated	113	65%	41%	88%	73%
% of firms that are a subsidiary	113	14%	14%	6%	17%
% of firms headed by a woman	114	12%	30%	13%	2%
% of firms reporting severe cash-flow problems in recent past	103	35%	45%	38%	29%
Bank finance					
% of firms with overdraft facility	113	69%	40%	69%	85%
% of firms who ever got a loan from financial institution	92	43%	27%	54%	50%
Credit from suppliers					
Share of credit purchases in total purchases (median)	111	75%	17%	85%	90%
Duration of supplier credit in days (median)	110	30	10	30	30
Cash discount on supplier credit (median)	57	3.75%	2.50%	3.75%	3.25%
Implicit monthly interest rate (median)	53	2.50%	5.00%	3.75%	2.50%
% of firms that ever purchase on credit	113	85%	62%	94%	97%
% of firms who are offered credit on first purchase	92	68%	35%	60%	84%
Credit to clients					
Share of credit sales in total sales (median)	81	50%	0%	33%	75%
% of firms that ever sell on credit	114	79%	57%	88%	90%
% of firms who ever offer credit from first purchase[a]	54	63%	42%	50%	74%
Socialization					
% of firms that do not socialize with suppliers at all	109	46%	46%	7%	10%
% of firms that socialize with suppliers outside business[b]	109	36%	11%	64%	44%
% of firms that do not socialize with clients at all[a]	56	29%	38%	22%	26%
% of firms that socialize with clients outside business[a,b]	56	21%	8%	44%	21%
% of firms that do not socialize with bank staff at all	102	41%	72%	20%	32%
% of firms that socialize with bank staff outside business[b]	102	15%	3%	33%	16%

Table 19.1
(continued)

	Number of valid obser- vations	All firms	Black (1)	Other (2)	Dominance (3)
Screening of customers (multiple answeres allowed)					
% of firms that ask clients to fill forms	98	51%	30%	71%	56%
% of firms that rely on trial period to screen clients	98	56%	48%	64%	58%
% of firms that rely on reputation to screen clients	98	73%	59%	93%	75%
% of firms that rely on direct investigation to screen clients	98	37%	59%	50%	23%

Notes: Group (1) = owner/manager is a native African. Group (2) = owner/manager is neither a native African nor member of the ethnic group that dominates business. Group (3) − owner/manager belongs to the ethnic group that dominates business in the country (South Asians in Kenya; whites in Zimbabwe). The exact number of nonmissing observations varies across questions.
a. Data were collected in Zimbabwe only.
b. Other firms socialize during business hours.

group. Only 12 percent of sample firms are headed by women. There appears to be a strong correlation between ethnicity and firm size. Similar—if not stronger—correlations have been found in other studies (e.g., Daniels 1994; Bade and Gunning 1994; Himbara 1994). Ethnicity is also correlated with the amount of trade credit the firm receives and gives and, to less extent, with availability of bank finance. Black firms are less likely to socialize with their clients and suppliers than other firms, an indication that black entrepreneurs largely remain outside the main business network. Probably for this reason, mainstream firms are more likely than black firms to screen customers using some sort of information sharing, and less likely to investigate clients directly. Black firms are also less likely to be "formal": fewer of them are registered, and they are less likely to request clients to fill forms.

In Kenya the case study firms have, on average, 15 regular suppliers, two-thirds of whom extend trade credit. One-sixth of the case study firms pay occasional advances to suppliers. The absolute number of regular suppliers to Kenyan-African firms is considerably smaller than that for other firms. Although the number of regular suppliers increases with firm size, black entrepreneurs have, on average, fewer regular suppliers than even small firms. The proportion of suppliers who extend trade credit also varies dramatically with the ethnicity of the firm's owner: 39 percent of the regular suppliers to Kenyan-African entrepreneurs provided credit, against 74 percent for other entrepreneurs. The two results are related: Kenyan-African firms, because they are less likely to qualify for trade credit, are also less likely to rely on regular suppliers. Instead, they shop around for the lowest cash price.

In Zimbabwe, supplier credit is well developed. On average, purchases on credit account for 81 percent of all purchases. Again, there are sharp differences across ethnic groups or firm sizes. White entrepreneurs in the case study sample purchase virtually all of their inputs on credit; black entrepreneurs, on the other hand, only buy a little more than half on credit. The pattern of supplier credit use is similar to that of overdraft facility: usage is high in all firm size categories except microenterprises. It appears therefore that suppliers are not significantly better than banks in their ability to reach microenterprises. This result somewhat contradicts expectations from the theory: since suppliers gather information on their clients as a by-product of the sale, one would have expected them to use that information to screen trade credit applicants more effectively than banks do—and thus to grant credit to clients with no access to banks. If this result is confirmed, it implies that there is little hope of channeling more credit to microenterprises by granting more credit to their suppliers. Similar patterns emerge with regard to credit sales, with African firms and microenterprises less likely to sell on credit than other firms. Large enterprises sell a smaller fraction of their output on credit than do medium size firms. A possible explanation for this is that large firms have market power and can impose their payment terms onto customers (see Fafchamps et al. 1994 and Fafchamps 1996 for similar conclusions).

19.2 The Role of Trade Credit

In this chapter we have implicitly assumed that receiving and giving trade credit is good for business. Do we have evidence to back our claim? The answer is yes. Case study firms in Kenya were asked why they give credit to certain customers. The major reason they gave is that clients cannot pay cash and ask for credit. A few respondents gave a more sophisticated answer, however. Some use credit to retain big customers and maintain good relationships with them. In a world where trade credit is only given to a few trustworthy customers, firms find it difficult to buy supplies on credit from suppliers they have never dealt with. Firms therefore become somewhat "captive" of suppliers who give them credit. Captivity is what makes trade credit possible through the establishment of relation-specific social capital, but it may also have some efficiency costs. One-fifth of the firms cite competition with others as a reason for offering credit. Offering advantageous credit terms is one way by which firms compete for goods customers. The chief reason for not giving credit to customers is the risk of nonpayment. In other words, the inability to costlessly and perfectly enforce contracts is what limits firms' willingness to extend credit to their customers. Lack of funds is also cited, but less frequently.

To pursue this point further, case study respondent were quizzed about repayment guarantees. These discussions reveal an implicit hierarchy of available payment forms: all customers may purchase on a cash basis, a more select group is allowed to pay by check, and an even more select group receives trade credit. Within the trade credit category itself, a hierarchy of instruments is used. Bills of exchange are used to signal minimum flexibility and indicate a relative lack of trust. Few firms like to sign bills. Postdated checks perform a function similar to that of bills. More privileged customers are only asked to sign the supplier's invoice. At the top of the hierarchy trade credit is unmediated by any written or legally binding instrument. Firms that have the capacity to grant credit to their clients with a reasonable expectation of repayment are clearly at a market advantage.

To throw additional light on the use of trade credit, Zimbabwean case study firms were asked why they buy on credit. By far the most common response, cited by firms of all sizes and ethnic group, is that credit improves a firm's ability to manage its cash flow. White firms, however, are more likely to cite other reasons as well. Some, for instance, said that buying on credit is more convenient than cash from an accounting standpoint, and that it is safer than using cash for transactions because of concerns about theft. This can be taken as circumstantial evidence that liquidity considerations might be less important and security considerations more important for white firms. Some respondents also said that they buy on credit because the supplier does not offer a cash discount, or because the implicit cost of trade credit is cheaper than alternative sources of finance. Only large firms stated that credit is automatically offered, suggesting that reputation and market power facilitate the provision of trade credit.

Firms were also asked why, if at all, they buy cash. The most common reason cited is that the supplier doesn't offer credit. African firms are more likely to cite the supplier's unwillingness to grant credit as the only reason for paying cash. Other firms often volunteered other reasons as well. Some said they prefer to take the cash discount, others that cash purchases are for small, occasional purchases not worth the hassle of applying to the supplier for a line of credit. One large firm saw cash purchases as a way to attract suppliers of timber from the countryside. A handful of firms, all microenterprises or small firms, stated they don't like to incur debt and prefer to pay cash. Self-rationing is consistent with the models of demand for credit developed by Zeldes (1989), Carroll (1992), and Zame (1993): these firms probably shy away from credit because they fear that a cash flow shock may reduce their ability to pay, lead to default, and have disastrous consequences on their personal assets. Consistent with this interpretation, most of the self-rationed firms keep precautionary savings to deal with emergencies, and only one indicated it had other sources of income it could draw upon in a crisis.

Asked why they sell on credit, most firms answered that it is an important dimension of their ability to compete. Customers don't like to pay cash, they say, competitors offer credit, and the firm can sell more by providing credit. Several firms, none of them a microenterprise, cited accounting convenience as another reason for selling on credit. One firm explained it was using factoring and thus could sell on credit and get cash right away from the factor. From the point of view of the firms, the sales promotion motive is therefore the most important motive from providing credit to customers (Schwartz and Whitcomb 1979). Firms were finally asked why, if at all, they sell cash. Enforcement considerations dominate respondents' answers. In most cases the firm sells cash because it believes it may not be paid and cannot enforce repayment. In fact the client's failure to repay in the past is often cited as a reason for selling cash. As predicted in section 19.1, rationing of credit thus takes place whenever firms do not believe they can trust their clients to pay them. Other reasons for selling cash mirror those cited for buying cash: small, infrequent sales are mostly on a cash basis; some buyers prefer to pay cash; and the respondent may be unable to provide credit to its customers. There are no strong differences across firm sizes and ethnicity. Microenterprises are more likely to have customers who prefer to pay cash, a possible reflection of self-rationing on the part of buyers. Buyers may also prefer to pay cash simply for convenience reasons. Indeed, microenterprises sell mostly to final consumers, who may prefer to pay on the spot to avoid coming back to pay and having to keep track of debt obligations. To summarize, evidence of rationing in trade credit is pervasive in the sense that certain buyers do not receive credit from their suppliers. The purpose of the next section is thus to examine what determines access to trade credit.

19.3   Access to Supplier Credit

Table 19.1 indicates that ethnicity and credit are related, but a number of other factors—firm size, sector of activity, and susceptibility to liquidity problems—may account for this relationship. To test for ethnic bias, we must rely on a multivariate analysis. To this effect, we begin by regressing the surveyed firms' proportion of purchases and sales made on credit on a series of firm characteristics thought to influence the supply and demand of trade credit, plus dummy variables measuring ethnicity and network effects. We also use the limited information available on whether firms ever purchase from or sell on credit to first-time commercial partners, and on credit terms and implicit interest in credit purchases. If statistical discrimination and network effects are absent, the latter variable should be nonsignificant.[3] The accuracy of the test for discrimination rests critically on the absence of omitted variable bias (e.g., Yinger 1998; Heckman 1998). If suppliers observe certain characteristics of prospective clients that are not recorded in the data but are correlated with ethnicity, we may erroneously conclude that ethnicity matters.[4] To minimize this bias, we include as regressors most of firms' easily observable characteristics, such as sector of activity, registered status, and subsidiary status, plus characteristics for which the econometrician probably has better data than creditors, namely the actual number of employees of the firm and its cash-flow history. Still the possibility of omitted variable bias should be kept in mind before a significant coefficient on ethnicity or gender is taken as evidence of discrimination, as the work of Neal and Johnson (1996) reminds us.

The estimated regression for credit purchases is

$$P_i = \gamma_0 + \gamma_1 X_i + \gamma_2 D_i + \gamma_3 N_i^S + e_i. \tag{19.1}$$

The dependent variable P_i is the proportion of purchases made on credit; it can take any value between and including 0 and 1. The vector X_i contains firm characteristics such as country, sector, legal status, and size. Vector D_i stands for ethnicity and gender, while vector N_i^S captures available information on network effects with suppliers. The error term e_i is assumed to be iid. Equation (19.1) is estimated as a two-sided censored tobit on the pooled data and on each country sample separately. Firm size is measured as the log of the number of employees (plus one). Given that firms with better access to trade credit may grow faster, we control for simultaneity bias by replacing firm size W_i by its predicted values from the following equation:

$$W_i = \lambda_0 + \lambda_1 X_i + \lambda_2 D_i + \lambda_3 N_i^S + \lambda_4 A_i + \lambda_5 A_i^2 + e_i. \tag{19.2}$$

Equation (19.2) is run on each country sample separately. The age and age squared of the firm (A_i and A_i^2) serve as identifying restrictions;[5] they are jointly significant

3. As Heckman (1998) pointed out, such a test can only show whether discrimination has no effect on market outcomes. Discrimination by certain (but not all) individuals is quite compatible with the absence of market discrimination if individuals who are discriminated against can always choose to deal with nondiscriminating firms.

4. It would have been useful to obtain the information about surveyed firms that is publicized by the credit reference bureau operating in Zimbabwe. Similarly it would useful to get access to the information banks have on surveyed firms. Unfortunately, this information was not collected.

5. Although the age of the firm may have a small effect on access to credit for very young firm, the effect is likely to be much smaller than the effect of firm age on size (e.g., Hoogeveen and Tekere 1994; Risseeuw 1994). When regressing access to trade credit on uninstrumented firm size and firm age (not shown), age is not significant.

Table 19.2
Prediction equation for firm size

	Kenya		Zimbabwe	
	Coefficient	t-ratio	Coefficient	t-ratio
Intercept	−4,381.7	−2.27	−1,468.5	−1.02
Manufacturing dummy	0.96	2.95	0.48	0.96
Food sector dummy	0.06	0.12	0.14	0.27
Wood sector dummy	−0.40	−0.91	0.09	0.14
Metal sector dummy	−0.20	−0.47	−1.50	−2.55
Year firm was created	4.50	2.28	1.53	1.03
Year squared	−11.55	−2.30	−3.98	−1.05
Registered business dummy	0.95	2.69	1.02	1.92
Owner/manager is a woman	−0.96	−1.73	−1.55	−1.99
Owner/manager is black	−1.07	−1.73	−0.63	−0.96
Owner/manager belongs to the dominant ethnic business group	−0.56	−1.06	0.07	0.12
Number of observations	55		55	
R-squared	0.64		0.47	

Note: Dependent variable = log (number of employees + 1).

and explain a large portion of the variation in firm size. Estimation results for equation (19.2) are given in table 19.2.

Given that Zimbabwe enjoys the presence of a formal credit reference bureau while Kenya does not, we expect the country dummy to be positive, reflecting the relative ease with which Zimbabwean firms screen trade credit applicants. Food products are typically perishable and turnover is fast, so that less trade credit may be offered in that sector (e.g., Nadiri 1969; Schwartz 1974; Schwartz and Whitcomb 1979; Ferris 1981; Emery 1984). Larger firms are expected to purchase a larger share of their inputs on credit, since it would be inconvenient for them to operate on a cash basis. Firms that are registered and incorporated, and subsidiaries of large holding corporations, are more likely to elicit suppliers' confidence than informal partnerships. A dummy variable is also included that takes the value of one if the respondent experienced severe cash-flow problems in the past. Presumably incompetent firms are more likely to run into problems, not only because they are incompetent but also because they receive less credit, which makes them more vulnerable to shocks (e.g., Fafchamps et al. 1994; Fafchamps et al. 1995). Having faced serious cash-flow problems in the past is thus a signal of incompetence; if information on such occurrences circulates, one should observe a negative relationship between past problems and current credit.

The regression of P_i on firm characteristics is shown in the first two columns of table 19.3 for the pooled sample. Separate results for the Kenya and the Zimbabwe

Table 19.3
Tobit regressions on the share of credit purchases: Pooled data

	Coefficient	t-statistic	Coefficient	t-statistic	Coefficient	t-statistic	Coefficient	t-statistic
Zimbabwe dummy	0.13	1.11	0.36	2.99	0.04	0.41	0.25	2.04
Manufacturing dummy	-0.08	-0.81	-0.05	-0.53	0.00	0.01	-0.01	-0.06
Food sector dummy	-0.56	-4.69	-0.52	-4.78	-0.48	-4.13	-0.51	-4.57
Wood sector dummy	-0.36	-3.07	-0.41	-3.70	-0.27	-2.26	-0.37	-3.11
Metal sector dummy	-0.11	-0.93	-0.33	-2.66	-0.08	-0.70	-0.29	-2.25
Log (number of workers), instrumented	0.16	3.32	-0.03	-0.44	0.14	3.02	0.01	0.09
Registered business dummy	0.20	1.68	0.39	3.01	0.14	1.28	0.30	2.35
Subsidiary dummy	0.39	2.36	0.41	2.70	0.44	2.80	0.44	2.94
Past cash-flow problem dummy	-0.23	-2.52	-0.15	-1.81	-0.21	-2.50	-0.16	-2.03
O/M is a woman			-0.36	-2.26			-0.30	-1.92
O/M is black			-0.35	-3.43			-0.29	-2.63
O/M does not socialize with suppliers					-0.18	-1.60	-0.08	-0.75
O/M socializes with suppliers outside business					0.16	1.85	0.07	0.84
Intercept	0.15	1.20	0.76	4.16	0.17	1.36	0.67	3.42
Selection term	0.36		0.32		0.33		0.31	
Number of observations	97		97		93		93	
Log-likelihood	-51.74		-43.77		-43.66		-38.84	
Pseudo R-squared	0.41		0.50		0.48		0.54	

Note: Dependent variable is the share of credit purchases in total purchases from suppliers. The reported estimates are two-limit censored tobit. Standard errors are not corrected for the presence of predicted variables in the regression.

samples are discussed but not shown. Firms in the food and wood sectors receive significantly less credit than others. Large firms, registered firms, and subsidiaries receive more supplier credit, firms with cash-flow problems less. We then add ethnicity and gender dummies. Results are shown in the third and fourth columns of table 19.3. The coefficient on ethnicity is significantly negative in all three regressions; gender is significant in the pooled sample and in Kenya. Other things being equal, the share of credit purchases in total purchases is 27 to 35 percentage points lower for black firms, and 36 to 60 percentage points lower for female-headed firms. Although these results do not per se constitute evidence of discrimination, they nevertheless suggest that ethnicity and gender are obstacles to supplier credit regardless of firm size. In fact the effects of gender and ethnicity are so strong that the coefficient of firm size becomes nonsignificant in all regressions. The significant coefficient of firm size in column 1 thus appears entirely due its correlation with ethnicity and gender (see table 19.2). The country dummy also becomes significant: as anticipated, firms give out more trade credit in Zimbabwe than Kenya.

What remains unclear is why ethnicity and gender matter. To investigate this issue, we replace ethnicity and gender with network effects. Respondents were asked to describe their relationship with their suppliers and the extent to which they socialize during and outside business. From these responses two dummy variables were created. The first one identifies firms that deal with suppliers in an entirely anonymous fashion; the second takes the value of one when the respondent socializes with suppliers outside business (e.g., through sporting events, community gatherings, and religious celebrations). Respondents who socialize during business hours constitute the omitted category. Results show that entrepreneurs who socialize with suppliers receive significantly more trade credit in the pooled sample and in Kenya; in Zimbabwe the effect is not significant, however. Network effects thus appear stronger in Kenya than Zimbabwe, a result in line with the absence in Kenya of a credit reference bureau that circulates credit worthiness information widely. When gender, ethnicity, and network variables are combined, results are more mixed, probably because of multicollinearity in the data (last two columns of table 19.3): network effects are (jointly) significant in Kenya and Zimbabwe, but gender and ethnicity factors remain present. From this we conclude that gender and ethnicity influence access to supplier credit in ways that are at least partly accounted for by network effects.

To further investigate the determinants of access to trade credit, we examine whether respondents ever receive instant credit from first-time suppliers. To do so, we run a probit regression similar to equation (19.1) on whether or not the respondent is usually offered credit by first-time suppliers. Results are shown in table 19.4.

Table 19.4
Probit regressions on supplier credit at first purchase: Pooled data

	Coefficient	t-statistic	Coefficient	t-statistic	Coefficient	t-statistic	Coefficient	t-statistic
Zimbabwe dummy	-0.77	-1.89	-0.40	-0.90	-0.79	-1.82	-0.47	-1.02
Manufacturing dummy	-0.39	-1.07	-0.39	-1.03	-0.43	-1.06	-0.50	-1.20
Food sector dummy	0.39	0.79	0.26	0.49	0.64	1.17	0.39	0.69
Wood sector dummy	-0.75	-1.73	-1.08	-2.30	-0.46	-0.95	-0.96	-1.77
Metal sector dummy	-0.06	-0.15	-0.57	-1.19	0.11	0.25	-0.49	-0.92
Log (number of workers), instrumented	0.45	2.98	0.16	0.84	0.45	2.75	0.18	0.92
Past cash-flow problem dummy	-0.22	-0.62	-0.14	-0.39	-0.07	-0.18	-0.01	-0.02
O/M is a woman			-0.98	-1.49			-0.99	-1.47
O/M is black			-1.12	-2.47			-0.94	-1.79
O/M does not socialize with suppliers					0.19	0.36	0.53	0.91
O/M socializes with suppliers outside business					0.92	2.38	0.67	1.62
Intercept	-0.48	-0.95	1.02	1.32	-0.96	-1.71	0.58	0.66
Number of observations	82		82		79		79	
Log-likelihood	-43.34		-38.60		-38.36		-35.38	
Pseudo R-squared	0.17		0.26		0.23		0.29	

Note: Dependent variable is one if supplier credit is usually offered from first purchase, zero otherwise. Standard errors are not corrected for the presence of predicted variables in the regression.

Although less significant, they confirm that ethnicity and socialization play a role in accessing supplier credit.

19.4 Payment Terms

Next we examine whether payment terms vary with ethnicity. Based on responses by RPED panel firms in Zimbawe, credit terms appear relatively standardized and do not differ substantially from those observed in developed economies (e.g., Dun and Bradstreet 1970; Duns information Services 1993): 41 percent of all firms reported that they pay suppliers in full 30 days after delivery, 13 percent pay after 45 days, and 11 percent only after 60 days. The 45-day average delay is very similar to the average delay between delivery and payment observed in the four sectors of enquiry in the United States (see Fafchamps et al. 1995, p. 11). This delay results from the combination of two elements: the time elapsed between delivery and statement, and the time between statement and payment. In Zimbabwe, suppliers normally establish monthly statements. The statement is sent toward the end of the calendar month— either on the 25th or on the last day of the month, depending on the sector and firm. The statement specifies a term for the client to pay, but we found that not everyone interprets the terms of the statement in the same way. Furthermore actual payment may fall short of what is written in the statement.

With these caveats in mind, three-fourths of the Zimbabwe case study firms stated that they are given 30 days from the date of statement to pay their supplier. Many of them, however, also indicated that credit terms vary across suppliers. Fewer of the small firms receive credit for over 30 days. Thus, not only are larger firms more likely to qualify for supplier credit, they also receive longer-term credit. Discussions with respondents suggest that this is due to the better reputations or relationship that these firms maintain with their suppliers, thereby reducing suppliers' fears about eventually getting paid. Credit duration is also affected by market power because monopsonistic firms (which tend to be larger) often are able to dictate credit terms to their suppliers. Firms in the food sector tend to buy on standard 30-day credit terms or less, presumably because inventory time is shorter.

Zimbabwean panel firms were also asked about credit to their customers. Credit terms are similar to those given by suppliers: in more than one-third of the cases, firms report that clients paid their accounts in full 30 days after delivery. Large firms allow their private trading customers longer to pay, on average, than other clients. Small firms give long credit terms because they are more likely to deal directly with private end users who take longer to pay.

Combining both case study data, results reported in table 19.5 confirm that size, sector of activity, and past cash-flow problems influence the duration of supplier credit. Gender is not significant, but being black translates into shorter credit terms in the pooled data and in the Zimbabwe subsample. Network effects are significant and have the expected sign in the pooled sample and in Kenya, but they have the wrong sign in Zimbabwe. There, firms that deal anonymously with suppliers receive longer credit terms. One possible interpretation is that the presence of a credit reference bureau makes it possible for firms to deal at arm's length.

19.5 Cash Discounts and Implicit Interest

Although explicit interest charges are rare, in half of the supplier credit transactions panel firms report they could have obtained a cash discount for early payment. A little less than half of the panel firms also offer cash discounts to (some of) their clients. We asked case study firms whether credit terms vary across suppliers and customers. Most firms reported that they do. In the discussion that followed, some respondents indicated that they indeed they use cash discounts to entice early payment by problematic customers. Others, in contrast, said that when they need cash, they give a big discount to their cash-rich customers to raise fresh money. Still others do not mention cash discount with problematic clients in the fear that it would undermine their price. All these findings suggest that trade credit terms are not set unilaterally by the selling firm but often are subject to negotiation. This is consistent with Bade and Chifamba (1994), who found that firms that negotiate prices with their customers are more likely to provide trade credit.

Next we examine the implicit interest rate that corresponds to the observed cash discounts. The discount rate reported in the Zimbabwe panel survey is 6 percent, on average; the median is 3.3 percent. Similarly case study firms report that discounts for early payment average between 3 and 6 percent. One possible reason why many firms continue to use trade credit is that the implicit interest rate is lower than alternative sources of credit. To see why, consider the average case in which the supplier must, in principle, be paid within 30 days of the date of statement. In practice, as the panel survey has shown, this means that the client has, on average, 45 days to pay from the date of delivery, assuming that deliveries are distributed randomly over the month—more if buyers concentrate their purchases early in the month. In addition penalties are typically charged only if payment has not been received by the next monthly statement. The buyer thus de facto has an additional 15 to 20 days to pay (taking into account postal and administrative delays). Thus we reckon that on

Table 19.5
Tobit regressions on payment terms made by suppliers: Pooled data

	Coefficient	t-statistic	Coefficient	t-statistic	Coefficient	t-statistic	Coefficient	t-statistic
Zimbabwe dummy	0.09	0.24	0.38	0.86	−0.12	−0.32	0.13	0.28
Manufacturing dummy	−0.12	−0.36	−0.04	−0.11	0.12	0.35	0.13	0.39
Food sector dummy	−1.04	−2.68	−0.99	−2.57	−1.02	−2.61	−1.05	−2.70
Wood sector dummy	0.09	0.24	0.00	0.00	0.03	0.08	−0.12	−0.29
Metal sector dummy	0.59	1.45	0.25	0.54	0.58	1.51	0.30	0.64
Log (number of workers), instrumented	0.61	3.54	0.36	1.51	0.61	3.48	0.43	1.82
Registered business dummy	0.26	0.63	0.44	0.94	0.13	0.31	0.27	0.57
Subsidiary dummy	−0.29	−0.66	−0.11	−0.23	−0.13	−0.30	−0.03	−0.06
Past cash-flow problem dummy	−0.52	−1.76	−0.38	−1.26	−0.58	−2.01	−0.49	−1.67
O/M is a woman			−0.38	−0.62			−0.32	−0.52
O/M is black			−0.69	−1.81			−0.53	−1.28
O/M does not socialize with suppliers					−0.78	−1.99	−0.62	−1.52
O/M socializes with suppliers outside business					0.02	0.06	−0.12	−0.37
Intercept	0.57	1.29	1.46	2.20	0.83	1.79	1.53	2.11
Selection term	1.30		1.28		1.24		1.23	
Number of observations	97		97		93		93	
Log-likelihood	−154.2		−152.4		−143.7		−142.8	
Pseudo R-squared	0.13		0.14		0.15		0.15	

Note: Dependent variable is the log of the number of days + 1 that separate delivery and payment; it is equal to 0 for firms that do not receive supplier credit. Standard errors are not corrected for the presence of predicted variables in the regression.

average, a client has 30 days more to pay (15 days before, 15 days after) than the explicit payment term written on the statement.

On this basis, for Zimbabwe, the annualized interest rate that correspond to cash discounts of, say, 3 and 6 percent are 18 and 36 percent respectively. For comparison purposes, lending rates of commercial banks in June 1993 ranged between 29.5 and 47.5 percent per year (e.g., Reserve Bank of Zimbabwe 1993, p. S23). At the time of the case study the normal interest rate charged on overdrafts was around 30 to 35 percent per annum. For many firms, then, trade credit is an attractive source of finance. Additional support for this interpretation is provided by the fact that 15 percent of the firms gave as a reason for using trade credit that it is cheaper than alternative sources of credit. On the other hand, one-third of the firms who buy cash said they do so to get the cash discount. Is there a contradiction? Not necessarily. If the cash discount is 6 percent or more, the return on early payment is equivalent to that of a money market financial investment, but without the transaction costs. A buyer with ample excess cash may thus choose to take the 6 percent cash discount. Furthermore not everyone has access to the money market. The highest return small investors can catch is 18 to 20 percent on a savings account. The 18 percent annual return implied by a 3 percent cash discount is thus sufficient to attract payment from a buyer who has enough excess cash to want to use it but not enough to consider investing it in the money market. There is evidence thus that market forces are at work in determining the level of cash discounts.

Regarding clients, explicit interest charges are again rare, but panel firms offer cash discounts in just over half of the transactions. The average cash discount is 3.2 percent. This cash discount is another measure of firms' subjective discount rates. We computed annualized interest rates for customer credit as we did for supplier credit. Results suggest that the minimum implicit rates are comparable to those charged by suppliers, although the maximum rates are a bit lower. There is little variation across firm size or ethnicity. In Zimbabwe we also have data from five firms that provide credit from invoice date. The estimated interest rates for these firms are higher: the average minimum and maximum rates is 50 percent and 65 percent respectively. Firms that grant credit from the date of invoice thus appear more cash constrained than those that grant credit from the date of statement.

To investigate these issues further, we conducted a regression analysis on the implicit monthly interest rate charged by suppliers. Sectoral dummies control for various factors including the effect of the market power of suppliers on the likelihood of price discrimination.[6] To control for selectivity bias—interest payments being

6. Unfortunately, we do not have data on the actual market power of suppliers in various sectors of activity.

observed only for firms receiving supplier credit—we run a two-step Heckman procedure. The regressors that appear in equation (19.1) are used for the selection equation.[7] Due to the possible presence of omitted variable bias, the results, presented in table 19.6, must be interpreted with caution. But they suggest that female-headed firms pay a higher implicit interest rate. Other variables are not significant.[8] We find therefore little evidence of discrimination in credit terms. This concludes our analysis of supplier credit received by surveyed firms.

19.6 Bank Credit

Next we examine the determinants of bank credit in the form of both overdraft facilities and bank loans. Most Kenyan case study firms deal with their bank in an anonymous way. Some, however, cultivate good relations with their branch manager and staff, occasionally meeting them outside business. Kenyan-African businesses are much less likely to consider bank staff as business acquaintances than other entrepreneurs, but a quarter of them actually met bank staff outside business. Discussions with respondents indicate that these Kenyan-African businesses, a minority to be sure, happen to be well connected with their bank staff. The relationship is seldom based on past business acquaintance. Rather, the branch manager happens to be a family friend, a former schoolmate, a neighbor. As a result of their fortunate personal connection, these businesses were able to secure easy access to bank credit, small sums being disbursed virtually instantly, often bypassing bank procedures regarding collateral. The amounts lent, however, remain small because branch managers must report to headquarters all loans above a certain limit. The benefits firms can derive from such acquaintances is also short-lived, as branch managers are rotated among various branches—probably to limit this kind of behavior. One should add that in all cases we encountered, the loans were repaid promptly.

None of the Kenyan-Asian businesses we spoke to were personally acquainted with bank staff, but several felt they could rely for emergency loans on members of their community who staff nonbank finance companies. One went even as far as

7. Since we do not dispose of truly convincing instruments—a common problem in sample selection correction models—identifying restrictions must be imposed somewhat ad hoc. We simply omit from the interest rate equation the variables that we think are less directly related to interest charges and focus on variables of interest such as size, ethnicity, and network effects.

8. Discussions with respondents indicate that firms explicitly mention cash discounts only to clients who may take advantage of them. They usuallly refrain from mentioning cash discounts to those who are very unlikely to pay early. Respondents argue that doing otherwise would weaken their position in price negotiations with the client (e.g., Fafchamps et al. 1994, 1995; Fafchamps 1997c). If true, this attitude generates another form of sample selection bias that could explain why ethnicity and socialization are not significant.

Table 19.6
Heckman regression on implicit interest rate for supplier credit

	Coefficient	t-statistic	Coefficient	t-statistic
Intercept	1.59	3.04	1.65	3.18
Zimbabwe dummy	0.76	2.12	0.80	2.08
Log (number of workers), instrumented	−0.14	−1.07	−0.16	−1.13
Past cash-flow problem dummy	0.04	0.18	0.05	0.18
O/M is a woman	0.81	1.84	0.81	1.81
O/M is black	−0.23	−0.67	−0.28	−0.82
O/M does not socialize with suppliers			0.10	0.27
O/M socializes with suppliers outside business			−0.02	−0.09
Selection equation				
Intercept	−0.32	−0.14	−0.32	−0.17
Zimbabwe dummy	−0.04	−0.03	−0.04	−0.03
Manufacturing dummy	−2.88	−1.48	−2.88	−1.58
Food sector dummy	−3.42	−2.30	−3.42	−2.43
Wood sector dummy	−1.72	−1.23	−1.72	−1.36
Metal sector dummy	−0.82	−0.41	−0.82	−0.61
Log (number of workers), instrumented	1.47	1.80	1.47	1.86
Registered business dummy	0.91	0.86	0.91	0.91
Past cash-flow problem dummy	−0.21	−0.19	−0.21	−0.19
O/M is a woman	−1.90	−1.24	−1.90	−1.31
O/M is black	0.45	0.33	0.45	0.40
O/M does not socialize with suppliers	−1.03	−1.06	−1.03	−1.24
O/M socializes with suppliers outside business	−0.60	−0.37	−0.60	−0.37
Correlation between errors	−0.36		−0.42	
Number of observations	59		59	
Log-likelihood	−56.04		−56.59	

Note: Dependent variable is the log of the implicit monthly interest rate + 1, computed as cash discount × 30 divided by the delay between delivery and payment; one-step estimator using Mills ratio correction. Standard errors are not corrected for the presence of predicted variables in the regression.

explaining to us the workings of "black money," a secretive financial market in which the managers of banks and financial institutions and other well-connected individuals take private deposits and organize private loans for privileged customers. These loans are extremely flexible and are made without any security or collateral other than the knowledge of the lender's business that the lender has acquired through normal business transactions.

Case study firms in Zimbabwe were similarly quizzed about the extent of their socialization with bank staff. Social interaction takes a variety of forms, one of which is the attendance to the sport events (golf tournaments and rugby matches) that rhyme the life of Zimbabwe's corporate world. Given the nature of the social inter-action, it is not too surprising that only a small fraction of black entrepreneurs and owners of microenterprises have a social relationship with their banker, compared to other firms. They also are less likely to establish a social relationship with their bank.

Statistical analysis confirms the role played by ethnicity in social interactions: African-headed firms are less likely to have a significant relationship with a bank, even after controlling for firm size and other factors. Anecdotal evidence collected during the interviews tells the same story. One African entrepreneur, for instance, reported that her bank had repeatedly refused to even consider her application for a loan despite the fact that she had been successfully expanding her firm and had been banking with the same bank for many years. On the other hand, several of the larger white-owned firms commented on the usefulness of knowing the bank manager, not as a substitute for having a good financial record but because it improves the bank's responsiveness to the firm's problems and expedites credit availability when needed. These findings suggest that the lack of personal contact that most black entrepreneurs have with the world of finance probably reduces their ability to approach banks for credit and to discuss possible repayment difficulties with their banker on the basis of mutual trust.

To investigate these issues further, we proceed with regression analysis. We have information on whether firms have an overdraft facility—by far the most common form of bank finance—and whether they have ever received a bank loan. Probit regression results are summarized in table 19.7, using the same regressors as for supplier credit. Results show that in contrast to supplier credit, ethnicity and gender have essentially no effect on the use of bank loans and overdrafts once firm size is controlled for. Network effects are significant, however: not socializing with bank staff has a strong negative effect on access to bank finance. Socialization with bank staff *outside* business also has a negative effect on access to bank credit. What matters most for bank credit thus seems to be personal interaction of a businesslike character. Taken together, these findings provide little conclusive evidence of ethnic or community network bias in the attribution of bank credit in the two surveyed countries.

19.7   Credit to Clients

We now turn to the credit that respondent firms give to their clients. The estimated regression is

$$S_i = \omega_0 + \omega_1 X_i + \omega_2 D_i + \omega_3 \hat{P}_i + \omega_4 \hat{O}_i + \omega_5 C_i + e_i. \tag{19.3}$$

Independent variables X_i and D_i are as before, except that the legal status of the firm is dropped from X_i: there is no reason for it to influence firms' willingness to give

Discrimination and Networks in African Manufacturing

Table 19.7
Probit regressions on overdraft facility and bank loan: Pooled data

	Overdraft				Bank loan			
	Coefficient	t-statistic	Coefficient	t-statistic	Coefficient	t-statistic	Coefficient	t-statistic
Intercept	-2.01	-2.41	-0.97	-0.74	-0.91	-1.03	0.76	0.62
Zimbabwe dummy	-0.70	-1.27	-1.37	-1.77	-1.16	-2.04	-0.99	-1.59
Manufacturing dummy	-0.52	-1.23	0.06	0.11	0.32	0.83	0.75	1.63
Food sector dummy	0.14	0.30	0.29	0.48	0.55	1.21	0.62	1.26
Wood sector dummy	0.07	0.16	-0.12	-0.19	0.35	0.74	0.12	0.24
Metal sector dummy	1.65	2.70	1.82	2.30	-0.45	-0.71	-1.16	-1.45
Log (number of workers), instrumented	0.99	3.14	1.27	2.71	0.19	0.64	-0.14	-0.38
Registered business dummy	-0.63	-1.16	-1.49	-1.99	0.85	1.45	0.88	1.32
Subsidiary dummy	-1.60	-2.78	-1.85	-2.67	-0.86	-1.71	-0.67	-1.31
Past cash-flow problem dummy	-0.41	-1.12	-0.67	-1.42	-0.05	-0.15	-0.09	-0.23
O/M is a woman	0.49	0.72	0.60	0.62	0.41	0.56	-0.17	-0.20
O/M is black	0.03	0.07	0.37	0.69	-0.10	-0.21	0.06	0.11
O/M does not socialize with bank staff			-1.88	-2.98			-1.00	-1.95
O/M socializes with bank staff outside business			-2.39	-3.09			-0.34	-0.63
Number of observations	100		91		79		73	
Log-likelihood	-42.65		-28.05		-42.22		-37.63	
Pseudo R-squared	0.31		0.47		0.22		0.26	

Note: Dependent variable is one if the firm has a bank overdraft facility (first regression) or one if the firm has ever received a bank loan (second regression). Standard errors are not corrected for the presence of predicted variables in the regression.

credit. We expect Zimbabwean firms to sell more on credit because screening is facilitated by the presence of a credit reference bureau. Manufacturing firms in the sample seldom retail to final consumers; they are therefore expected to sell more on credit than trading firms. Firms in the food sector should offer less credit given that their output is perishable and turnover is fast. Large firms are anticipated to sell in larger quantities and thus to resort more to credit sales.

As was discussed earlier, ethnicity should have no effect on credit sales if ethnic bias is solely the result of statistical discrimination. If, in contrast, it is due to network effects, then it should have a significant negative effect on the share of sales firms made on credit. Finally, the effect of ethnicity should be positive if discrimination is due to taste. As emphasized before, these tests are vulnerable to omitted variable bias. In particular, lack of working capital among black firms could generate a spurious correlation between ethnicity and S_i if this is not properly controlled for. Three additional variables are therefore included in equation (19.3) to control for access to working capital: $\hat{P}_i$, the share of purchases on credit, $\hat{O}_i$, whether the firm has a bank overdraft facility or not, and C_i, whether the firm experienced a serious cash-flow problem in the past. Firms that faced cash-flow problems in the past or that have difficult access to working capital finance are expected to offer less credit to their clients. Because of potential endogeneity bias, $\hat{P}_i$ and $\hat{O}_i$ are instrumented.[9] For $\hat{P}_i$, the instrumenting regression is given in the last column of table 19.3. For $\hat{O}_i$, it is given in table 19.7. In both cases the identifying restrictions are the socialization variables, the registered business dummy, and the subsidiary dummy; the former are credit category specific, and the latter should have no direct effect on credit sales.

Coefficient estimates for equation (19.3) are reported in table 19.8. The first set of regressions use firm characteristics X_i, plus gender and ethnicity D_i. As expected, manufacturing firms and large firms sell more on credit, and firms in the food sector less. The Zimbabwe dummy has the correct sign but is nonsignificant. Gender appears to have no effect that is not already captured by other variables. Being black, however, has a significant and independent effect on credit sales. To test whether access to working capital influences credit sales, we reestimate equation (19.3) with $\hat{P}_i$, $\hat{O}_i$, and C_i but without gender and ethnicity. Results indicate that as expected, access to working capital—particularly supplier credit (overdraft finance is signifi-

---

9. C_i is relative to a past event and can thus be regarded as predetermined. Our identifying restrictions rest on the continued assumption that incompetence is not directly correlated with the willingness to grant credit to clients. This implies that where patterns of trade credit are dictated by statistical discrimination, indicators of competence affecting access to supplier credit should not affect the granting of credit to clients, *except* through their effect on the working capital of the firm.

Table 19.8
Tobit regressions on the share of credit sales: Pooled data

	Coefficient	t-statistic	Coefficient	t-statistic	Coefficient	t-statistic	Coefficient	t-statistic
Intercept	-0.02	-0.09	-0.76	-3.60	-0.43	-1.43	-0.36	-1.28
Zimbabwe dummy	0.18	1.36	0.15	1.31	0.19	1.53	0.11	1.10
Manufacturing dummy	0.27	2.74	0.49	4.79	0.45	4.40	0.33	4.04
Food sector dummy	-0.54	-4.41	-0.30	-1.93	-0.41	-2.43	-0.46	-3.21
Wood sector dummy	-0.14	-1.13	-0.14	-1.00	-0.23	-1.49	-0.15	-1.21
Metal sector dummy	-0.18	-1.29	-0.20	-1.50	-0.22	-1.64	-0.17	-1.49
Log (number of workers), instrumented	0.12	2.23	0.00	0.05	0.04	0.58	0.03	0.55
O/M is a woman	-0.10	-0.50			0.01	0.05	0.06	0.37
O/M is black	-0.30	-2.65			-0.24	-1.74	-0.11	-1.01
Share of credit purchases, instrumented			0.91	3.29	0.56	1.64	0.26	0.92
Probable overdraft, instrumented			0.41	2.12	0.24	1.14	0.36	2.08
Past cash-flow problem dummy			-0.07	-0.62	-0.10	-0.93	-0.13	-1.54
Client screening using forms							-0.05	-0.45
Client screening using reputation							0.39	3.25
Client screening using trial period							0.02	0.31
Client screening using pers. investigation							-0.19	-2.35
Selection term	0.37		0.32		0.31		0.23	
Number of observations	79		68		68		59	
Log-likelihood	-41.58		-27.88		-26.32		-6.83	
Pseudo R-squared	0.41		0.53		0.56		0.84	

Note: Dependent variable is the share of credit sales in total sales to clients. The reported estimates are two-limit censored tobit. Standard errors are not corrected for the presence of predicted variables in the regression cant only in the pooled sample)—influence customer credit: buying an additional 10 percentage points of one's inputs on credit translates into an additional 9.1 percentage points of credit sales. To control whether ethnicity is in fact capturing difference in access to working capital, we then re-estimate equation (19.3) with ethnicity and working capital variables. Pooled sample results suggest that both factors are at work: the coefficient on ethnicity is significantly negative, while the coefficient on supplier credit remains positive and is very close to being significant. Signs are correct but coefficients are not significant in the Zimbabwe only regression, possibly because of smaller sample size and multicollinearity problems.

We also have information about socialization with clients (Zimbabwe only) and about the screening practices followed by respondent firms.[10] This information is used to construct one network variable N_i^C and four dummy variables T_i. The first of these dummy variables takes the value of one if the respondent requires clients to fill forms before granting trade credit. The second is one if the respondent uses some sort of information-sharing mechanism to assess the reliability of prospective clients (e.g., credit reference bureau and references from members of the community). The third is one if the firm observes a client's purchase and payment behavior over a period of time before granting trade credit. The fourth takes the value of one if the respondent investigates clients directly, for instance, by visiting their home or place of work. The estimating equation becomes

$$S_i = \omega_0 + \omega_1 X_i + \omega_2 D_i + \omega_3 \hat{P}_i + \omega_4 \hat{O}_i + \omega_5 C_i + \omega_6 N_i^C + \omega_7 T_i + e_i. \qquad (19.4)$$

Variable N_i^C only exists for Zimbabwe. If information sharing truly helps screen reliable clients, firms that use reputation when screening should sell more on credit. In contrast, firms that must spend time and effort directly investigating clients, instead of relying on their reputation, should offer less credit to their customers. Formal procedures alone should make no difference unless they are used to directly assess the customer or to seek information from others.

Results, shown in the last columns of table 19.8, indicate that screening methods are a major determinant of credit sales. Individual coefficient estimates are largely consistent with expectations: firms that rely on information sharing to screen pro-

---

10. Because screening procedures are chosen by respondents, they are potentially subject to endogeneity bias. We do not, however, dispose of suitable instruments that would predict the choice of screening method. Regressing screening variables on X_i, D_i, and N_i^C indicates that very little of the variation in screening methods can be explained by observed firm characteristics. Qualitative information gathered in the field leads us to suspect that screening methods are largely dictated by the options available to individual respondents. Firms that are part of an information-sharing network rely on it to screen clients; those that are not must rely on trial period or personal inspection. The use of a particular screening method thus serves as a precious, even if potentially biased, indicator of its availability to the respondent.

spective credit recipients sell an additional 36 to 39 percent of their output on credit relative to others; firms that must investigate clients directly sell 19 to 40 percent less of their output on credit. The latter result is consistent with the impression gathered from interviews that firms rely on direct screening only when they do not have access to information sharing. Lack of socialization with clients and the reliance on trial periods are associated with lower credit sales in the Zimbabwe regression. Forms per se have no effect on credit sales, unless they are used in combination with an information-sharing network. All of these results conform with expectations and speak strongly of the importance of information sharing as a screening mechanism.

Finally, we run equation (19.4) on a dummy that takes the value one if respondents ever offer credit to first time customers (table 19.9). Data are available only for Zimbabwe and certain variables are dropped due to multicollinearity. Results confirm the paramount role that screening practices play in credit sales. They also confirm that firms that receive supplier credit are more likely to offer credit to their clients.

19.8 Conclusion

We have examined how African manufacturers gain access to supplier and bank credit, and how they grant credit to their customers. A proper understanding of these processes helps better assess not only barriers to enterprise development in Africa, but also how markets emerge. It is well known that statistical discrimination and network effects can exclude certain groups of firms from credit markets and, more generally, from normal commercial practices. Using data from Kenya and Zimbabwe, we provide preliminary evidence that network effects are present and deserve serious attention.

The two surveyed countries display high levels of ethnic and gender concentration in manufacturing. Black entrepreneurs and female-headed firms appear to have a harder time getting supplier credit, but ethnicity and gender plays no significant role in access to bank overdraft and formal loans. Variables measuring socialization and information sharing—what we called network effects—play a determinant role in access to trade and bank credit, and have an overwhelming effect on the granting of trade credit to clients. Although we cannot rule out the presence of discrimination, our results largely support the idea that network effects play an important role in explaining patterns of market interaction (Loury 1998). Based on discussions with respondents, our interpretation is that black and female entrepreneurs are penalized by their lack of connections with the business establishment, and by the difficulties

Table 19.9
Probit regressions on trade credit at first sale: Zimbabwe only

	Coefficient	t-statistic	Coefficient	t-statistic	Coefficient	t-statistic	Coefficient	t-statistic
Intercept	-0.67	-0.45	-1.84	-1.41	-4.00	-1.50	-3.26	-0.48
Manufacturing dummy	0.12	0.27	0.74	1.27	0.94	1.40	6.60	1.61
Food sector dummy	0.15	0.29	1.20	1.75	1.30	1.78	10.52	1.75
Wood sector dummy	0.03	0.05	1.34	1.53	1.71	1.75	-0.41	-0.21
Metal sector dummy	0.30	0.47	-0.64	-0.79	-0.59	-0.68	-7.57	-1.47
Log (number of workers), instrumented	0.19	0.73	-0.41	-1.05	-0.34	-0.79	-2.62	-1.49
O/M is a woman	0.63	0.75			1.41	1.28	a	
O/M is black	-0.60	-1.19			0.48	0.48	-2.92	-0.96
Share of credit purchases, instrumented			4.54	1.92	5.42	1.80	41.95	1.66
Probable overdraft, instrumented			-0.46	-0.33	0.31	0.19	7.44	1.08
Past cash-flow problem dummy			0.06	0.13	0.09	0.17	a	
O/M does not socialize with clients							17.38	1.74
Client screening using forms							-25.54	-1.67
Client screening using trial period							-10.50	-1.96
Client screening using pers. investigation							-4.69	-2.04
Number of observations	52		45		45		43	
Log-likelihood	-32.05		-23.75		-22.83		-7.83	
Pseudo R-squared	0.06		0.17		0.20		0.71	

Note: Dependent variable is one if respondent usually offers trade credit to first time clients, zero otherwise. The reported estimates are standard probit. Standard errors are not corrected for the presence of predicted variables in the regression.
a. Variables had to be dropped due to insufficient variation in the data.

they face distinguishing themselves from the mass of small, inexperienced micro-enterprises headed by blacks or women. These factors lead to the partial or complete exclusion of many black and female firms from trade credit practices.

Lack of access to supplier credit is likely to hinder firm growth and to prevent them from joining the mainstream. Moreover, to the extent that delaying payment to suppliers is a major avenue through which firms absorb cash flow variations, firms that are denied supplier credit are probably more fragile and are expected to fail more frequently (e.g., Daniels 1994; Fafchamps et al. 1994; Fafchamps et al. 1995). Exclusion may thus become a self-perpetuating process. The presence of these negative feedbacks could explain why small groups are able to dominate particular industries or activities.

Excluded firms are forced to resort to alternative and, generally, less efficient ways of contracting with each other. Together they create a flea market economy in which instantaneous transactions predominate and market institutions remain underdeveloped. Firms that operate in that market may invent ingenious, alternative ways of raising working capital—like *susu* collectors and rotating savings and credit associations (ROSCAs) (e.g., Besley et al. 1993; Aryeetey and Steel 1993). But they remain cut from mainstream institutions and cannot gain the experience required to compete in the global market place. Because large segments of the entrepreneurial population are prevented from reaching their potential, growth and development remain stunted.

The close ties that existing firms have weaved among themselves are themselves an efficient response to asymmetric information and contract enforcement problems. Networks constitute a valuable form of social capital (e.g., Fafchamps and Minten 1999; Fafchamps and Minten 2002b). Attempts by governments to alter the ethnic makeup of business through forceful removal of nonindigenous groups and other strong-arm approaches can result in a massive loss of network capital and in a significant deterioration in the level of market sophistication. The conceptual approach proposed here suggests another way out of the quandary. Nonindigenous groups in Kenya and Zimbabwe appear to owe at least part of their success to their ability to identify each other. One way to assist indigenous business could thus be to ensure that credit reference information circulates widely, so as to minimize the role of old-boy networks.[11] More research is needed on these important policy issues.

---

11. The experience of Zimbabwe suggests that such a move is, alone, insufficient to break the existing barriers that indigenous firms face. It may have to be combined with another approach adopted, for instance, by the Kenya Industrial Estates project. This approach consists in setting a small credit program that monitors repayment closely and keeps track of the credit history of its members. The information can then be disseminated and help reliable small businesses graduate into a larger firm pool and gain wider access to credit.

20 Discrimination and Networks in Agricultural Trade

In the preceding chapters we documented the presence of a strong ethnic bias in African manufacturing, at least in some countries. We also showed that much of this bias, though not all, can be explained by network effects. We now conduct a similar investigation in agricultural trade.

In this chapter we investigate the extent to which religion, ethnicity, and gender affects the functioning of markets through their effect on trust. As before, trade credit is our yardstick for trust. We also investigate the possible existence of location-invariant effects of religion, ethnicity, or gender that make members of a particular faith, ethnic group, or gender more or less trustworthy. The existence of such effects has been hypothesized in the literature under various guises. Since Max Weber, the economic success of the West has often been attributed to Protestant ethic. In the old literature on East Asia, for instance, Shintoism and Confucianism were seen as value systems antagonistic to development. Greif (1994) argues that in medieval Europe, certain communities of traders developed a "culture" that was better able to foster trust. Other, less presentable ideas about the superiority of one group over others have yielded similar predictions about race and gender.

Such generalizations are suspect both on philosophical grounds and on the grounds that they are regularly disproved by counterexamples and subsequent historical events. One possible exception concerns gender. In nearly all human societies, parenting responsibilities fall primarily on the shoulder of women.[1] This is also true in Africa. In such a context it is likely that men and women would differ systematically in the way in which they conduct business, particularly for women with children. We test for this possibility as well.

20.1 Descriptive Analysis

In table 20.1 we report the gender, ethnicity, and religion of surveyed traders. These characteristics are easily observable (e.g., name and attire) and are natural candidates for an investigation of discrimination. We see that agricultural trade is primarily a female occupation in Benin and Madagascar. For each sample we distinguish between six major ethnic groups, plus a residual category. The determinants of ethnicity vary between the three countries. In Benin, language is the main criterion for deciding someone's ethnic group. In contrast, ethnicity in Madagascar is determined partly by external appearance, and partly with reference to the region in which

---

1. Whether this is the result of women's choice or it is imposed on them by society is irrelevant for our analysis.

Table 20.1
Potential discrimination factors

	Benin	Malawi	Madagascar
Gender			
Female	80.8%	36.3%	61.4%
Ethnicity			
Ethnic group 1	18.9%	23.9%	45.5%
Ethnic group 2	8.1%	17.6%	26.9%
Ethnic group 3	22.5%	4.7%	4.7%
Ethnic group 4	14.3%	22.9%	3.5%
Ethnic group 5	3.5%	4.9%	8.6%
Ethnic group 6	12.7%	17.5%	2.3%
Other ethnic group	20.1%	8.4%	8.5%
Religion			
Muslim	40.9%	16.7%	2.4%
Christian	43.2%	82.1%	94.1%
Other	15.9%	1.2%	3.5%
Membership in locally dominant group			
Member of main gender group in district	78.0%	69.9%	63.8%
Member of main ethnic group in district	43.6%	43.1%	54.7%
Member of main religion in district	75.6%	89.2%	94.1%

someone's ancestors are buried. There is considerable ethnic diversity in each sample. Of the three surveyed countries, Benin has the highest level of religious diversity, with Muslims and Christians at par and a large minority of respondents who describe themselves as followers of traditional religions. In Malawi and Madagascar the overwhelming majority of traders are Christian.

Each country sample covers between 20 and 25 districts, each with a slightly different gender, ethnic, or religious makeup. Discrimination and group membership are thus likely to operate differently in different districts. What matters is whether a trader is part of the "mainstream," that is, is like the majority of traders in his or her immediate vicinity. To capture this idea, we construct a measure of membership in dominant local groups as follows. Within each district we compute the proportion of each gender, ethnic, and religious group in the sample. We then construct a variable that takes the value 1 if a trader has the same gender, ethnicity, or religion as the majority of other traders in the district. Districts where no group has more than 50 percent of surveyed traders are regarded as having no majority group. Averages are displayed at the bottom of table 20.1. We see, for instance, that in Benin some 44 percent of respondents are member of the locally dominant ethnic group albeit, in the sample as a whole, no group has more than 23 percent.

Table 20.2
Transaction technology

	Benin	Malawi	Madagascar
Whether credit is offered by suppliers	*Percentage of responses*		
No	38.2%	85.0%	44.9%
From some suppliers	56.8%	15.0%	43.6%
From all suppliers	5.0%	0.0%	11.5%
Whether respondent offers credit to clients			
No	23.7%	34.3%	31.9%
To some clients	73.9%	64.3%	67.5%
To all clients	2.4%	1.4%	0.7%
Information sharing with other suppliers			
No	54.6%	30.0%	70.8%
Some suppliers	37.3%	70.0%	27.0%
All suppliers	8.1%	0.0%	2.1%
Supplier credit	*Sample average*		
Percentage of purchases on credit	22.7%	3.2%	25.3%
Percentage of sales on credit	23.3%	10.9%	15.6%
Number of observations	662	738	885

The same is true for religion. This is because ethnicity and religion are geographically concentrated.

Our main dependent variables are summarized in table 20.2. Together they capture key dimensions of the transaction technology in each country. The first two variables are our measures of trust.[2] They are responses to questions "Does any of your suppliers let you buy on credit?" and "Do you let any of your client buy on credit?" These questions basically measure whether credit is offered. This is credit of very short duration—in three-quarter of the cases the duration of the credit is equal or less than seven days. Trade credit is much more likely to be offered in Benin and Madagascar than in Malawi. The next variable is a response to the question "If your client does not pay, will his or her other suppliers know it?" This is our measure of information sharing. In all three countries roughly two-thirds of the respondents claimed that some suppliers would get to know about it, representing a moderate level of information sharing. Our final two variables measure actual trade credit usage. The average percentage of purchases and sales on credit is small, especially in Malawi.

---

2. Payment by check, another indicator of trust, represents only a minute proportion of all payments, thereby precluding any statistical analysis.

20.2   Econometric Analysis

20.2.1   Testing for Ethnicity, Gender, and Religion

Having familiarized ourselves with the data, we begin by testing whether gender, religion, and ethnicity affect the transaction technology in a way that is common across locations. To this effect we regress our five measures of transaction technology on gender, ethnicity, and religion. To avoid omitted variable bias, we control for personal characteristics of the trader such as age and age squared, education, number of languages spoken, experience, and working capital.[3] Because our three variables of interest vary systematically across districts, we include district dummies to control for location-specific effects that are not due to gender, ethnicity, or religion. This means that our regression coefficients are only identified by variation across traders within districts. Each regression is estimated for each of the three countries separately. For each regression we conduct a joint significance test for ethnicity and for religion dummies. We also examine the sign of the coefficients. We expect women to be at an advantage in Benin and Madagascar since they represent the majority of traders. We also expect ethnic and religious groups that represent a smaller proportion of traders to receive and give less supplier credit.

An example of the kind of regression we estimate is given in table 20.3 for our first transaction technology variable. To save space, results are simply summarized here. We find that once we control for personal characteristics and district dummies, gender is seldom significant. For the only regression in which gender is significant (percentage of purchases on credit in Benin), the coefficient is negative, contrary to expectations. Ethnicity seldom plays a significant role in trade credit. When it occasionally tests significant, individual coefficients do not have the expected sign (i.e., a small ethnic group is shown to have better access to credit). The only exception is information sharing, for which ethnicity is jointly significant in all three countries. In Benin one coefficient has the expected sign: the Nago, which represent close to one-fourth of the Beninese sample, have a strong positive coefficient. But so do the Dendi, who are a small group. In the other countries no clear pattern can be seen since none of the ethnicity coefficient is individually significant and many signs for minor groups are positive.

Religion is a different story. Muslim traders in Malawi and non-Christian traders in Madagascar more often report being offered credit by suppliers. Purchases on credit also represent a significantly larger share of their total purchases. In contrast,

---

3. Because of possible endogeneity bias, working capital is instrumented using conditions at start-up.

Table 20.3
Whether credit is offered by supplier

	Unit	Benin Coefficient	Benin t-statistic	Malawi Coefficient	Malawi t-statistic	Madagascar Coefficient	Madagascar t-statistic
Number observed		607		730		879	
Pseudo R-squared		0.171		0.125		0.254	
Possible discrimination factors							
Gender	female = 1	−0.227	−1.25	−0.238	−1.38	0.017	0.17
Ethnic group 2	yes = 1	−0.236	−0.64	0.376	0.96	0.420	1.51
Ethnic group 3	yes = 1	−0.344	−1.60	0.293	0.74	0.515	1.81
Ethnic group 4	yes = 1	−0.065	−0.20	0.037	0.07	0.221	0.66
Ethnic group 5	yes = 1	0.329	0.75	−0.022	−0.06	0.108	0.32
Ethnic group 6	yes = 1	−0.136	−0.45	−0.500	−1.09	0.253	0.51
Other ethnicity	yes = 1	−0.311	−1.17	−0.316	−0.67	0.686	2.24
Christian (Muslim is omitted category)	yes = 1	−0.106	−0.56	−0.710	−2.71	−0.895	−3.00
Other religion	yes = 1	−0.282	−1.25			−0.744	−1.94
Personal characteristics							
Age of trader	log	0.003	0.09	−0.107	−2.31	0.096	3.82
Age of trader, squared	log*log	0.000	0.13	0.001	1.59	−0.001	−3.88
Number of languages spoken	log	0.245	1.96	0.120	0.66	−0.183	−1.18
Number of years of schooling	level	0.013	0.60	0.062	2.39	0.013	0.87
Years of experience	log + 1	0.209	2.23	0.441	4.19	0.175	2.85
Working capital (instrumented)	log	−0.359	−3.81	−0.299	−3.12	−0.115	−2.74
District dummies (20–25)				Included but not shown			
_cut1		−3.863		−3.314		2.150	
_cut2		−1.523				4.106	
Joint test of ethnicity variables							
chi-square		5.42		9.71		8.54	
p-value		0.4908		0.1373		0.2014	
Joint test of religion variables							
chi-square		1.69		7.36		9.13	
p-value		0.4305		0.0067		0.0104	

Note: The estimator is ordered probit.

non-Christian Beninese traders do not receive more credit but offer more credit to clients. While these results are not fully consistent (credit from suppliers in Malawi and Madagascar, credit to clients in Benin) and the sample of non-Christians in Madagascar is very small, they appear to suggest that Christian traders are less inclined toward trade credit and, by implication, less trusting and less trusted. These findings are in agreement, for instance, with the work of Ensminger (1992) who reports that Islam penetrated cattle trade in Kenya because it fostered trust. Greif (1994) emphasizes the role of religion in trade, but in his work on Genoese merchants, comes to a different conclusion regarding which "culture" is more sympathetic to trade.

20.2.2 Testing for Locally Dominant Groups

The lack of strong gender and ethnicity effect and the ambiguity of the reported religion effect may be due to an inappropriate aggregation scale. For dummies to be significant, a particular group—based on gender, ethnicity, or religion—would have to be better trusted over a very large geographical area. This need not be the case if the effect of trust and discrimination operate only at the local level. If this is true, what matters is not ethnicity per se but whether a trader is member of whichever group is locally dominant.

To investigate this possibility, we construct an indicator variable that takes the value one if the respondent has the same ethnicity as at least half of the other traders in the district. In districts where no group dominates, the indicator variable is zero. By this definition, members of even small ethnic group may have a local advantage. Similar indicator variables are constructed for gender and religion. Mean values of the variable were reported in table 20.1.

We add these variables to our regressions. Results, not shown here for lack of space, are mixed. While local group dummies are jointly significant in five cases out of fifteen, they do not always have the expected sign. Whenever the local ethnicity dummy is significant, it has the wrong sign. The national ethnicity dummies themselves become mostly nonsignificant. The local gender group variable is individually significant three times with the correct sign. But in Benin, when it is significant the gender dummy itself has a negative coefficient. The local religion group dummy is individually significant four times, always with the expected (positive) sign. Its presence does not subtract from the significance of the religion dummies, with Muslims more likely to offer and be offered trade credit.

20.2.3 Testing for Network Effects

So far our results provide mild evidence that religion matters. But they are in contradiction with the many sociological studies that insist on the importance of ethnicity in African trade. In an attempt to resolve this contradiction, we investigate the possible existence of network effects. Ethnicity may matter not because of general trust within ethnic communities and possible discrimination along ethnic lines, but because it is a determinant of membership in trade networks (e.g., Cohen 1969; Meillassoux 1971; Amselle 1977).

To investigate network effects, we add four new variables to the regressions: the number of suppliers known, the number of clients known, the number of relatives in trade, and membership in a trader association. The four variables are instrumented using start-up working capital, numbers of suppliers and clients known, the number of relatives, and the average association membership in each district. Results are much more encouraging: network variables are jointly significant in 12 regressions out of 15, albeit in three cases with the wrong sign. Religion effects again remain unchanged.

The conclusion we draw from this exercise is that networks matter. To be offered and to offer trade credit, knowing people seems more important than being of the "correct" ethnicity or gender. These results confirm our findings from chapter 19. In turn they raise the issue of how family background and ethnicity affect the formation of networks. To this issue we now turn.

20.3 Endogenous Networks

We investigate endogenous network formation in two steps. We first examine the determinants of networks at start-up. We then study the factors that affect the growth rate of networks over time. We also examine the role of working capital, in case ethnicity operates not through trade networks but through equity financing networks, for example, parents and kin investing in the respondent's business.

Start-up network variables are the number of suppliers and clients known at start-up as well as start-up working capital. Regressors include gender, ethnicity, and religion dummies as before. We also include personal characteristics such as age at start-up (and age squared), number of languages spoken, and years of schooling. Family background variables, such as profession of the parents and experience in trade, are added to control for possible financial effects and prior exposure to trade.

We estimate the regressions without and with local group effects. Regressions without local group variables show no effect of ethnicity or religion, except an occasional significant coefficient, always with the wrong sign. Results with local group effects are reported in tables 20.4, 20.5, and 20.6. We see that ethnicity variables are never jointly significant, except in one case with the wrong sign: members of ethnic groups marginally represented in trade appear advantaged in start-up conditions, a

Table 20.4
Number of suppliers known at start-up

	Unit	Benin Coefficient	Benin t-statistic	Malawi Coefficient	Malawi t-statistic	Madagascar Coefficient	Madagascar t-statistic
Number observed		547		717		869	
Pseudo R-squared		0.142		0.062		0.092	
Possible discrimination factors							
Gender	female = 1	-1.643	-3.80	-0.166	-0.98	-0.112	-1.44
Ethnic group 2	yes = 1	0.085	0.21	-0.148	-0.45	0.644	2.68
Ethnic group 3	yes = 1	0.056	0.24	0.149	0.45	0.595	2.47
Ethnic group 4	yes = 1	0.472	1.23	-0.073	-0.22	0.599	2.18
Ethnic group 5	yes = 1	0.605	1.16	0.264	0.62	0.501	1.71
Ethnic group 6	yes = 1	0.484	1.31	-0.123	-0.34	0.933	3.33
Other ethnicity	yes = 1	-0.141	-0.44	0.310	1.06	0.375	1.52
Christian (Muslim is omitted category)	yes = 1	0.024	0.11	-0.067	-0.24	-0.141	-0.68
Other religion	yes = 1	-0.043	-0.16			-0.275	-1.06
Personal characteristics							
Age at start-up	level	-0.021	-0.74	-0.005	-0.21	0.010	0.80
Age at start-up, squared	level ^{2}	0.000	0.59	0.000	0.10	-0.000	-0.90
Number of languages spoken	log	-0.203	-1.49	-0.160	-1.12	-0.299	-2.93
Number of years of schooling	level	0.008	0.38	0.035	2.03	-0.004	-0.41
Family background							
Father was a trader	yes = 1	0.251	1.21	-0.072	-0.47	0.110	0.67
Father was an employee	yes = 1	0.050	0.22	0.309	2.12	0.062	0.64
Mother was a trader	yes = 1	0.157	0.64	0.157	0.84	-0.339	-2.07
Mother was an employee	yes = 1	1.072	1.34	0.435	1.28	-0.095	-0.48
Father's years of experience as trader	log + 1	0.029	0.42	0.090	1.77	0.015	0.25
Mother's years of experience as trader	log + 1	0.034	0.50	0.025	0.48	0.163	2.72

Membership in local majority group							
Member of main gender group in district	yes = 1	1 257	2.69	−0.120	−0.73	−0.102	−1.33
Member of main ethnic group in district	yes = 1	−0.142	−0.46	−0.050	−0.29	−0.001	−0.01
Member of main religion in district	yes = 1	−0.174	−0.97	−0.153	−0.65		
District dummies (20–25)				Included but not shown			
Intercept		2 293	3.35	1.105	1.80	1.602	1.78
Selection-term		1 229		1.184		0.787	
Number of observations censored at 0		156		237		96	
Number of uncensored observations		391		480		773	
Joint test of ethnicity variables							
F-test		0.97		1.01		2.59	
p-value		0.4443		0.4146		0.0171	
Joint test of religion variables							
F-test		0.04		0.06		0.58	
p-value		0.9568		0.8098		0.5584	
Joint test of membership in majority group variables							
F-test		2.81		0.40		0.88	
p-value		0.0389		0.7555		0.4148	

Table 20.5
Number of clients known at start-up

	Unit	Benin		Malawi		Madagascar	
		Coefficient	t-statistic	Coefficient	t-statistic	Coefficient	t-statistic
Number observed		548		717		869	
Pseudo R-squared		0.175		0.028		0.091	
Possible discrimination factors							
Gender	female = 1	−1.007	−2.54	−0.157	−1.19	−0.096	−1.29
Ethnic group 2	yes = 1	−0.058	−0.16	0.148	0.57	0.259	1.13
Ethnic group 3	yes = 1	−0.263	−1.21	0.220	0.84	0.262	1.14
Ethnic group 4	yes = 1	0.017	0.05	0.212	0.80	0.368	1.40
Ethnic group 5	yes = 1	0.133	0.26	0.230	0.68	0.282	1.01
Ethnic group 6	yes = 1	0.509	1.53	0.415	1.44	0.595	2.22
Other ethnicity	yes = 1	−0.026	−0.09	0.337	1.43	0.265	1.12
Christian (Muslim is omitted category)	yes = 1	−0.222	−1.13	0.101	0.47	0.004	0.02
Other religion	yes = 1	−0.006	−0.03			−0.106	−0.42
Personal characteristics							
Age at start-up	level	−0.009	−0.35	−0.010	−0.48	−0.003	−0.22
Age at start-up, squared	level ^ 2	0.000	0.62	0.000	0.55	0.000	0.20
Number of languages spoken	log	0.072	0.58	−0.102	−0.90	−0.340	−3.46
Number of years of schooling	level	0.012	0.64	0.011	0.83	−0.002	−0.18
Family background							
Father was a trader	yes = 1	0.311	1.62	0.245	2.00	0.057	0.36
Father was an employee	yes = 1	0.170	0.83	0.385	3.31	0.167	1.79
Mother was a trader	yes = 1	0.291	1.27	−0.090	−0.61	−0.283	−1.78
Mother was an employee	yes = 1	0.819	1.10	−0.192	−0.70	−0.412	−2.13
Father's years of experience as trader	log + 1	0.058	0.92	−0.028	−0.68	0.038	0.67
Mother's years of experience as trader	log + 1	−0.031	−0.49	0.044	1.06	0.126	2.18

Membership in local majority group						
Member of main gender group in district	yes = 1	0.807	1.88	−0.059	−0.46	−0.075	−1.01
Member of main ethnic group in district	yes = 1	0.253	0.90	0.125	0.89	−0.051	−0.47
Member of main religion in district	yes = 1	0.057	0.35	−0.118	−0.64		
District dummies (20–25)				Included but not shown			
Intercept		1.370	2.18	1.227	2.51	1.874	2.15
Selection-term		1.140		0.975		0.761	
Number of observations censored at 0		135		128		77	
Number of uncensored observations		413		589		792	
Joint test of ethnicity variables							
F-test		1.50		0.63		1.09	
p-value		0.1772		0.7072		0.3660	
Joint test of religion variables							
F-test		0.91		0.22		0.23	
p-value		0.4050		0.6390		0.7962	
Joint test of membership in majority group variables							
F-test		1.52		0.40		0.61	
p-value		0.2076		0.7509		0.5448	

Table 20.6
Start-up working capital

	Unit	Benin		Malawi		Madagascar	
		Coefficient	t-statistic	Coefficient	t-statistic	Coefficient	t-statistic
Number observed		531		717		869	
Pseudo R-squared		0.073		0.094		0.079	
Possible discrimination factors							
Gender	female = 1	-0.001	0.00	-0.204	-1.17	-0.292	-1.72
Ethnic group 2	yes = 1	0.008	0.02	0.365	1.07	0.268	0.52
Ethnic group 3	yes = 1	0.353	1.44	0.270	0.78	0.306	0.59
Ethnic group 4	yes = 1	-0.146	-0.37	0.235	0.68	0.322	0.54
Ethnic group 5	yes = 1	1.119	2.21	-0.050	-0.11	1.033	1.63
Ethnic group 6	yes = 1	-0.268	-0.73	0.245	0.65	1.033	1.70
Other ethnicity	yes = 1	0.104	0.32	0.633	2.05	0.405	0.76
Christian (Muslim is omitted category)	yes = 1	0.253	1.17	0.154	0.53	-0.478	-1.06
Other religion	yes = 1	-0.099	-0.37			-0.248	-0.45
Personal characteristics							
Age at start-up	level	0.016	0.50	0.027	1.00	0.037	1.28
Age at start-up, squared	level ^ 2	0.000	0.08	0.000	0.11	-0.000	-0.86
Number of languages spoken	log	-0.043	-0.31	0.232	1.55	0.214	0.97
Number of years of schooling	level	0.081	3.70	0.075	4.22	0.088	4.27
Family background							
Father was a trader	yes = 1	0.111	0.50	-0.143	-0.88	-0.557	-1.56
Father was an employee	yes = 1	-0.094	-0.40	-0.027	-0.17	-0.220	-1.05
Mother was a trader	yes = 1	0.309	1.24	0.280	1.42	0.095	0.27
Mother was an employee	yes = 1	-0.387	-0.47	0.043	0.12	0.585	1.36
Father's years of experience as trader	log + 1	-0.040	-0.54	0.114	2.09	0.081	0.62
Mother's years of experience as trader	log + 1	-0.020	-0.29	-0.049	-0.89	0.263	2.01

Membership in local majority group							
Member of main gender group in district	yes = 1	−0.671	−1.32	0.546	3.22	0.071	0.42
Member of main ethnic group in district	yes = 1	−0.114	−0.39	0.246	1.33	−0.688	−2.82
Member of main religion in district	yes = 1	−0.026	−0.14	−0.062	−0.25		
District dummies (20–25)				Included but not shown			
Intercept		3.938	5.36	0.133	0.21	0.462	0.23
Selection-term		1.309		1.310		1.723	
Number of observations censored at 0		17		0		68	
Number of uncensored observations		514		717		801	
Joint test of ethnicity variables							
F-test		1.58		1.12		1.38	
p-value		0.1496		0.3510		0.2211	
Joint test of religion variables							
F-test		1.42		0.29		0.72	
p-value		0.2429		0.5933		0.4859	
Joint test of membership in majority group variables							
F-test		0.65		3.98		4.09	
p-value		0.5829		0.0080		0.0171	

result that contradicts the presence of ethnic favoritism. Religion is never significant. In contrast, gender is often significant and always negative: female traders start their business with fewer contacts and less capital. This is consistent with the observation that for many African women, trade is a transient income generating activity in which they enter and exit depending on family circumstances (Spring and McDade 1998).

Being of the same ethnic group as the majority of traders in the district has a negative effect on start-up contacts and capital in six out of nine regressions—in one case this effect is significant. Being of the same religion has a negative coefficient in five out of nine regression and is never significant. In contrast, being of the same sex of the most local traders has a significant positive effect on trade contacts in Benin. Combined with the fact that being a women has a strong negative effect on start-up contacts, this suggests that Beninese male traders have more start-up contacts in districts where they represent the bulk of the traders.[4]

In contrast, family background is shown to have some effect on start-up conditions, especially trading experience. Better educated traders start with more working capital, possibly because they were able to save more money on an earlier, better paid wage job. To summarize, we fail to find strong evidence that ethnicity affects start-up networks and capital.

Let us now turn to growth of networks and working capital after start-up. If members of a particular gender, ethnic, or religious group are advantaged in business, they should accumulate contacts and capital faster. Results are summarized in tables 20.7, 20.8, and 20.9 for known suppliers, known clients, and working capital. As before, regressors include gender, ethnicity, and religion dummies together with district dummies. Personal characteristics include the age of trader at start-up (and age squared), number of languages, and years of schooling. Years of trading experience control for the time elapsed since start-up. Since both experience and the dependent variable are expressed in log, the (conditional) annual growth rate can be calculated as the coefficient of experience divided by years of experience.[5] Start-up conditions are included as well as the number of relatives. As before, local group effects are included to test for location specific favoritism.

Results show that the number of suppliers and clients known increases on average at 8 to 20 percent during the initial year, but rises slower in subsequent years.

---

4. If local group effects are not included in the regression, the female dummy has the same sign and remains significant, but with a much smaller coefficient in absolute value.

5. A constant growth rate of the number of traders known was strongly rejected by the data: growth is faster initially.

Working capital grows much faster, at 5 percent per year on average in Benin and Malawi, and 9 percent in Madagascar. Being a woman has a negative effect on the growth of working capital in all three countries; the effect is significant in two of them. The effect is also strongly negative and significant in Benin if either the district dummies or the local group dummies are omitted from the regression. Although we do not have information on why female traders accumulate capital more slowly, this finding is consistent with the often made observation that African women use their personal income to pay for school fees and better child nutrition. Women also accumulate business contacts more slowly in Malawi and Madagascar, perhaps because their freedom to move from market to market is hindered by parenting responsibilities.

Ethnicity and religion dummies are occasionally significant, but usually with the wrong sign—ethnic groups that represent a smaller proportion of traders being shown to accumulate contacts and capital faster. The only exception is the Christian dummy in Benin, which is positive and significant for number of suppliers known. The same effect is not, however, observed for clients known, suggesting that the finding is not robust. Membership in locally dominant groups is never jointly significant. Individual dummies are occasionally significant, but always with the wrong (negative) sign.

There are some other results of interest. Education has a strong positive effect on the accumulation of working capital in all three countries, suggesting that better educated traders not only start with more capital but also accumulate faster. Traders who speak more languages tend to accumulate working capital faster in Benin and Madagascar.

20.4   Conclusion

In this chapter we examined the role that gender, ethnicity, and religion play among agricultural traders. It is widely believed that these three factors play a paramount role in shaping African trade. It is common for African politicians and external observers alike to claim that trade is "in the hands" of a particular group and to call for policy interventions to curb what is often thought to result from favoritism and discrimination.

Using surveys conducted in three African countries (Benin in West Africa, Malawi in Southern Africa, and Madagascar in the Indian Ocean), we investigate these claims in detail. We begin with an examination of transactions practices, using the willingness to offer (very short-term) trade credit as a measure of trust. We also

Table 20.7
Growth in the number of suppliers known

	Unit	Benin		Malawi		Madagascar	
		Coefficient	t-statistic	Coefficient	t-statistic	Coefficient	t-statistic
Number observed		611		730		882	
Pseudo R-squared		0.323		0.109		0.411	
Possible discrimination factors							
Gender	female = 1	0.347	1.26	−0.205	−1.65	−0.124	−2.43
Ethnic group 2	yes = 1	0.068	0.29	0.157	0.66	0.213	1.76
Ethnic group 3	yes = 1	0.151	1.08	0.180	0.74	0.314	2.51
Ethnic group 4	yes = 1	0.354	1.58	0.127	0.41	0.418	2.92
Ethnic group 5	yes = 1	0.162	0.61	−0.006	−0.03	0.093	0.63
Ethnic group 6	yes = 1	0.345	1.68	0.049	0.19	0.297	1.56
Other ethnicity	yes = 1	0.349	2.07	0.275	1.00	0.257	1.93
Christian (Muslim is omitted category)	yes = 1	0.339	2.81	−0.084	−0.41		
Other religion	yes = 1	0.120	0.83			0.290	1.73
Personal characteristics							
Age at start-up	level	0.009	0.50	0.034	1.73	0.000	0.02
Age at start-up, squared	level ^ 2	−0.000	−0.63	−0.000	−1.49	0.000	0.31
Number of languages spoken	log	0.058	0.76	0.088	0.81	−0.131	−1.99
Number of years of schooling	level	0.016	1.27	0.008	0.59	0.008	1.23
Start-up conditions							
Years since start-up	log + 1	0.081	1.37	0.173	2.84	0.196	6.03
Number of suppliers known at start-up	log + 1	0.705	18.19	0.645	13.04	0.739	22.11
Number of buyers known at start-up	log + 1	−0.073	−1.89	−0.184	−3.58	−0.029	−0.88
Number of relatives	log + 1	0.136	1.64	−0.043	−0.45	−0.038	−0.84
Start-up working capital	log + 1	−0.042	−1.69	−0.012	−0.42	0.007	0.66

Membership in local majority group						
Member of main gender group in district	yes = 1	−0.558	−1.91	−0.015	−0.12	−0.024	−0.46
Member of main ethnic group in district	yes = 1	0.083	0.52	0.157	1.21	−0.002	−0.03
Member of main religion in district	yes = 1	−0.096	−0.96	−0.104	−0.60	0.047	0.35
District dummies (20–25)				Included but not shown			
Intercept		0.950	1.94	1.529	2.72	0.797	1.35
Selection-term		0.776		0.944		0.524	
Number of censored observations at 0		59		32		34	
Number of uncensored observations		552		698		848	
Joint test of ethnicity variables							
F-test		0.81		0.55		2.43	
p-value		0.5591		0.7664		0.0245	
Joint test of religion variables							
F-test		4.37		0.17		3.01	
p-value		0.0131		0.6812		0.0833	
Joint test of membership in majority group variables							
F-test		1.59		0.52		0.11	
p-value		0.1896		0.6669		0.9557	

Table 20.8
Growth in the number of clients known

	Unit	Benin		Malawi		Madagascar	
		Coefficient	t-statistic	Coefficient	t-statistic	Coefficient	t-statistic
Number observed		611		730		882	
Pseudo R-squared		0.331		0.100		0.394	
Possible discrimination factors							
Gender	female = 1	0.266	0.96	-0.147	-1.30	-0.116	-2.37
Ethnic group 2	yes = 1	0.044	0.19	-0.229	-1.05	0.241	2.09
Ethnic group 3	yes = 1	0.125	0.89	-0.278	-1.25	0.269	2.26
Ethnic group 4	yes = 1	0.174	0.78	-0.159	-0.56	0.381	2.79
Ethnic group 5	yes = 1	-0.077	-0.29	-0.173	-0.83	0.097	0.70
Ethnic group 6	yes = 1	0.084	0.41	-0.142	-0.58	0.328	1.81
Other ethnicity	yes = 1	-0.144	-0.85	0.083	0.33	0.263	2.07
Christian (Muslim is omitted category)	yes = 1	0.068	0.56	0.005	0.03		
Other religion	yes = 1	-0.020	-0.14			0.311	1.95
Personal characteristics							
Age at start-up	level	-0.017	-0.91	0.029	1.64	-0.001	-0.10
Age at start-up, squared	level^2	0.000	0.83	-0.000	-1.17	0.000	0.32
Number of languages spoken	log	0.094	1.23	0.167	1.69	-0.000	0.00
Number of years of schooling	level	-0.008	-0.68	-0.006	-0.52	-0.001	-0.25
Start-up conditions							
Years since start-up	log + 1	0.064	1.08	0.164	2.94	0.182	5.88
Number of suppliers known at start-up	log + 1	0.042	1.08	-0.036	-0.80	0.125	3.92
Number of buyers known at start-up	log + 1	0.613	15.86	0.489	10.38	0.493	15.49
Number of relatives	log + 1	0.263	3.16	0.104	1.19	-0.035	-0.81
Start-up working capital	log + 1	-0.029	-1.16	-0.033	-1.32	-0.007	-0.66

Membership in local majority group							
Member of main gender group in district	yes = 1	−0.431	−1.47	−0.089	−0.79	0.033	0.68
Member of main ethnic group in district	yes = 1	−0.060	−0.38	0.126	1.06	0.038	0.53
Member of main religion in district	yes = 1	−0.053	−0.53	−0.067	−0.42	0.071	0.56
District dummies (20–25)				Included but not shown			
Intercept		1.377	2.81	1.329	2.58	1.388	2.45
Selection-term		0.781		0.867		0.501	
Number of censored observations at 0		47		8		24	
Number of uncensored observations		564		722		858	
Joint test of ethnicity variables							
F-test		0.65		0.80		1.90	
p-value		0.6915		0.5665		0.0787	
Joint test of religion variables							
F-test		0.30		0.00		3.81	
p-value		0.7396		0.9800		0.0513	
Joint test of membership in majority group variables							
F-test		0.87		0.61		0.36	
p-value		0.4579		0.6073		0.7817	

Table 20.9
Growth in working capital

	Unit	Benin		Malawi		Madagascar	
		Coefficient	t-statistic	Coefficient	t-statistic	Coefficient	t-statistic
Number observed		592		730		828	
Pseudo R-squared		0.218		0.222		0.254	
Possible discrimination factors							
Gender	female = 1	−0.333	−0.88	−0.807	−6.09	−0.405	−3.77
Ethnic group 2	yes = 1	0.131	0.44	0.288	1.14	0.537	2.04
Ethnic group 3	yes = 1	−0.175	−0.98	0.279	1.08	0.632	2.33
Ethnic group 4	yes = 1	−0.079	−0.28	0.295	0.89	0.464	1.49
Ethnic group 5	yes = 1	−0.306	−0.87	0.409	1.69	0.553	1.75
Ethnic group 6	yes = 1	−0.104	−0.39	0.400	1.41	0.802	1.97
Other ethnicity	yes = 1	−0.234	−1.08	0.588	2.01	0.513	1.79
Christian (Muslim is omitted category)	yes = 1	0.122	0.80	0.020	0.09	−0.465	−1.57
Other religion	yes = 1	0.101	0.55			0.129	0.35
Personal characteristics							
Age at start-up	level	0.001	0.05	0.051	2.45	0.076	4.07
Age at start-up, squared	level ^ 2	0.000	0.41	−0.001	−2.08	−0.001	−3.30
Number of languages spoken	log	0.324	3.33	−0.066	−0.57	0.274	1.95
Number of years of schooling	level	0.046	2.93	0.077	5.50	0.023	1.76
Start-up conditions							
Years since start-up	log + 1	0.733	9.75	0.434	6.68	0.497	7.12
Number of suppliers known at start-up	log + 1	−0.005	−0.10	−0.026	−0.49	0.235	3.31
Number of buyers known at start-up	log + 1	0.104	2.13	−0.070	−1.28	−0.072	−1.02
Number of relatives	log + 1	0.223	2.08	0.213	2.08	−0.260	−2.67
Start-up working capital	log + 1	0.371	11.65	0.441	14.96	0.501	19.75

Membership in local majority group							
Member of main gender group in district	yes = 1	−0.529	−1.33	−0.295	−2.24	−0.040	−0.38
Member of main ethnic group in district	yes = 1	0.175	0.87	−0.101	−0.72	−0.038	−0.25
Member of main religion in district	yes = 1	0.050	0.40	−0.106	−0.58		0.18
District dummies (20–25)				Included but not shown			
Intercept		7.714	12.36	4.492	7.50	0.221	
Selection-term		0.981		1.010		1.089	
Number of uncensored observations		592		730		828	
Joint test of ethnicity variables							
F-test		0.47		0.97		1.02	
p-value		0.8273		0.4458		0.4107	
Joint test of religion variables							
F-test		0.33		0.01		4.17	
p-value		0.7196		0.9249		0.0158	
Joint test of membership in majority group variables							
F-test		0.88		2.03		0.10	
p-value		0.4512		0.1085		0.9052	

measure information sharing about breach of contract as the likelihood that other suppliers would learn about nonpayment. The effects of ethnicity, gender, and religion are tested both at the national level and at the local level, that is, relative to other traders in the same district.

Contrary to expectations, we find no conclusive evidence that members of a particular sex or ethnic group are more easily trusted by suppliers or that they trust clients more easily. Non-Christians—particularly Muslims—appear to trust and be trusted more, but the effect is apparent in only two of the three countries where Christians are an overwhelming majority. In Benin where Muslims represent 40 percent of the sample, no such effect is found. Perhaps it is being different from the rest (more devout?) that raises trust. This issue deserves more investigation.

In contrast, network effects have a stronger and more systematic effect on trust and information sharing—albeit occasionally with the wrong sign. These results are to be interpreted in the light of other work that has shown strong returns to network capital in African trade and business.

Finding network effects does not, however, eliminate the possibility of discrimination on the basis of ethnicity and the like. It is indeed conceivable that members of the dominant trading group start their business with better contacts and better access to equity finance. They may also accumulate contacts and funds faster over time, thanks to favoritism. To investigate this possibility, we examine whether ethnicity, gender, and religion affect start-up conditions and growth over time.

We find that women accumulate working capital much slower than men, but this appears to have little to do with their being marginalized: the effect is strong in two of the three countries, including in Madagascar where women represent 60 percent of surveyed traders. Women also start business with less capital. In contrast, better educated traders start with more capital and accumulate it faster. Ethnicity and religion appear to have little if any systematic effect on start-up conditions and accumulation of network and working capital. Whenever a relationship is found, it usually is contrary to what would occur if favoritism based on ethnicity and religion were present.

Taken together, these results suggest that ethnicity and religion only have limited effects on agricultural trade in the three countries studied. This suggests that if ethnicity and religion matter in other African countries, as is often claimed, these effects are probably country specific so that it would be hazardous to extrapolate them to Africa as a whole. Gender matters more, but at least part of the gender effect reflect the different role women play in the household—particularly the tendency to initiate smaller, more transient businesses and to siphon funds off the business, possibly to finance investment in children.

The result presented here do not rule out the existence of strong ethnic, gender, or religious bias in other African countries. But one should be cautious not to generalize these local situations to all of Africa. Our surveys suggest, instead, that in the three countries studied, agricultural trade is open to all, irrespective of gender, ethnicity, or religion. Networks matter, and better connected traders have larger and more prosperous businesses. But members of all groups start more or less from an equal footing to accumulate network and working capital. This ease of entry probably explain why scores of Africans, many of whom women, flock into agricultural trade as an income earning opportunity (Barrett 1997a).

21 Finance, Investment, and Networks

In the previous chapter we discussed firm growth among agricultural traders. Our coverage of African manufacturing, however, has been organized primarily around market exchange, not firm entry and investment. The two are closely linked, however. This chapter presents some preliminary thoughts about the effect networks are likely to have on firm entry and growth in African manufacturing. Since many of the issues discussed here are already well know, we cover the material rapidly.

We begin by discussing start-up capital. We then turn to investment finance and liquidity crises. How firms deal with either determines its path over time. We then briefly examine the role of networks in segmentation, competition, and international trade. These issues deserve more research.

21.1 Start-up Capital

It has long been known that personal wealth is the primary source of start-up capital for business. This is particularly true in Africa where the majority of surveyed firms are owner-established businesses—over three-quarters of surveyed manufacturing businesses and virtually all agricultural traders. For instance, in Kenya, 73 percent of RPED firms are owner-established businesses; only 23 firms were inherited and 19 businesses had been bought by the current owner(s).

Own savings constitute the most important source of start-up capital, followed by loans from local banks. The use of bank loans is correlated with firm size: larger firms have a higher proportion of start-up capital financed by bank debt. In Zimbabwe, bank loans were used at start-up by only 10 percent of firms; they constituted the exclusive source of start-up finance for two firms only. For many subsidiaries, start-up finance was provided by the parent company. Foreign banks, moneylenders, and supplier credit are negligible sources of start-up finance across all firm sizes. Loans from friends or family are significant sources of start-up capital for microenterprises and to a lesser extent for small firms. Discussions with respondents suggest that such loans share many of the features of venture capital investment in developed countries: repayment involves a grace period and is contingent on success. Lenders may also provide advice and other forms of support. There are significant differences among ethnic groups. For example, black Zimbabweans are less likely than other ethnic groups to have used a bank loan at start-up. These results are consistent with the evidence, reported earlier, that blacks are less well connected with banks.

Table 21.1
Equity financing in Zimbabwe

	All firms	Size				Ethnicity		
		Micro	Small	Medium	Large	African	White	Other
Has firm ever sought outside equity?	35%	0%	40%	56%	35%	40%	35%	29%
Has firm ever floated shares on the stock market?	7%	0%	0%	11%	11%	11%	7%	0%
Would firm consider going public?	26%	0%	0%	22%	53%	44%	23%	14%

Source: Case study survey in Zimbabwe.

21.2   Equity Financing

In addition to credit, firms can in principle finance their activities by seeking equity participation from partners or shareholders. To explore these issues, the case study firms in Zimbabwe were asked about the equity structure of their firm and their views of equity finance as a source of start-up and investment finance. Most of them turned out to have more than one equity holder. Only about one-third of the case study firms ever sought outside equity (table 21.1). Microenterprises, sole proprietors, and partnerships are much less likely to seek equity finance than larger, incorporated firms. Only four firms stated that they could not find equity finance because they did not know someone with money, all of them African-owned microenterprises. These results suggest that equity rationing is not generally a problem for sample firms, though it may be for African microenterprises.

Obtaining finance through the stock market is even more remote for the vast majority of firms. Only large firms view this as being a realistic possibility, given the fixed costs (auditing, etc.) and reputational requirements of going public. Sixty percent of the firms that stated they would not consider going public indicated that they are too small.

The slow pace at which new issues are allowed on the stock exchange may constrain some of the larger firms: over half of the large respondents would consider going public but only 11 percent have so far raised equity in the stock market. Discussions with respondents indicate that at the time of the survey (1995) large firms viewed the stock market with a renewed interest. For most firms, however, equity finance is not a strong option, primarily because of the intrusion it represents upon the autonomy of current firm owners. The most likely cases of equity rationing thus are large firms that want to raise capital through new issues on the stock market but

Table 21.2
Equity and management in Zimbabwe

	All firms	Size				Ethnicity		
		Micro	Small	Medium	Large	African	White	Other
Firms with multiple equity holders	58%	57%	67%	50%	57%	50%	55%	86%
Firms with shared management and control	86%	100%	100%	60%	83%	100%	78%	100%
Active partners								
Relatives/friends	55%	100%	78%	33%	27%	50%	47%	83%
Business acquaintance	7%	0%	11%	0%	7%	33%	0%	0%
Parent company	23%	0%	11%	33%	33%	0%	37%	0%
Other	23%	0%	0%	33%	40%	17%	26%	17%
Firms where partners participate in everyday management	59%	100%	89%	25%	40%	80%	45%	100%

Source: Case study survey in Zimbabwe.

have been prevented from doing so by the long queue of firms waiting for their issues to be allowed on the Zimbabwe Stock Exchange.

Asymmetric information between investors and managers about the quality of the firm's investments leads to adverse selection and incentive problems in equity markets. As a result investors are typically reluctant to put money in a firm without actively participating in its management. Moreover imperfect information may result in ownership shares being undervalued by investors, thus discouraging firms from seeking outside participation.

To explore these issues, we asked case study firms about who equity partners are and what they do. Most firms have more than one equity holder. Not surprisingly, the great majority of them turn out to be friends and relatives (table 21.2). Partners in virtually all cases are active in the firm. They participate in the daily management of the company rather than simply monitoring its progress periodically. Active partners are more likely to take part in the daily management of the firm in African and other ethnic firms than in white-owned firms; in micro and small-scale firms than medium and large firms; and in partnerships and corporations than in subsidiaries of holding companies. In most of the cases where the active partners do not participate in management, the firm is a subsidiary of a holding company and the partner is the parent company. In these cases the holding company may not directly manage the firm, but it always supervises its operations and monitors its progress. In the rest of the cases where partners do not participate in management, the firm is either a medium or large corporation. These findings suggest a dichotomy in terms of access to equity capital: large firms with well-established reputations can access equity capital without forfeiting a major degree of control over management decisions, while smaller and less well-known firms can only access equity by sharing management and control.

These results are in line with concerns about imperfect information and incentive problems that the active involvement of investors in the management of the firm attempt to correct. They also are consistent with the fact that only about one-third of the case study firms ever sought outside equity. Almost two-thirds of firms that have not sought outside equity stated they wanted to retain control of the firm or were worried about potential conflicts with new partners. For most entrepreneurs the main problem with equity finance is the loss of control of the firm this implies. Even for African microenterprises this is likely to be a concern, though they may not think of it because the possibility of obtaining outside finances is remote.

The implication is that for small- and medium-size businesses, equity financing is only conceivable with very close, trusted individuals—usually friends or relatives and occasionally former employees. For entrepreneurs whose family is poor, equity financing is not an option at start-up and it remains a remote option to finance subsequent investment.

21.3   Investment Finance

Once firms are created, they can grow by investing. Difficult access to start-up capital could be partly compensated by easy access to investment funding: good entrepreneurs with limited start-up capital could compensate their small beginnings by bringing in outside finance after creation. The speed and ease of access to investment finance therefore determines the extent to which the distribution of start-up capital among potential entrepreneurs is reflected in the distribution of firm sizes.

African manufacturing is not the best place to study investment finance because firms invest very little (Bigsten et al. 2000b). With trade liberalization continuing through the 1990s, subsequent manufacturing surveys indicated that the situation deteriorated further after the RPED surveys were done.

21.3.1   Source of Investment Finance

Having said this, most firms do incur occasional investment expenditures. In value terms, purchases of equipment account for most of investment expenditures (e.g., 82 percent in Zimbabwe). Investment in buildings accounts for only 16 percent and land for just 2 percent of investment expenditures in Zimbabwe. Investments in land and buildings are also infrequent.

Retained earnings are the dominant source of finance and the most frequently cited source of funds for investment. Bank loans come in second. Personal savings and informal loans are unusual sources of investment funding, except for very small firms. Hire-purchase is used by medium-size firms, primarily to finance the purchase of vehicles. Outside equity was little used, but when it was, it helped finance large investments. Other sources, like personal loans, were used only in a few cases.

There are sharp differences across firm sizes. Microenterprises did not use any external finance, while small firms depended to a significant extent on overdrafts and hire purchase. Larger firms have a more varied portfolio of financial sources, with bank loans playing a major role. These findings are consistent with the limited use of equity finance, hire purchase, and overdraft facilities by African firms and micro-enterprises. Overdrafts play a significant role in financing investments, particularly for small firms for whom the transactions costs of loan application and/or the delays and uncertainties associated with receiving a loan may be prohibitive. However, using an overdraft to finance investment may backlash if it creates a hard core of debt on the firm's bank account.

In terms of aggregate value, the picture is a bit different. This is because investment is distributed very unequally across firms, with a small number of enterprises making very large investments and most others investing in a small piece of equipment or not at all. How large investments are financed thus has a deep influence on how aggregate investment is financed. On average, in Kenya, for instance, 41 percent of the total investment value was financed from retained earnings and 44 percent from bank loans. In Zimbabwe, "other" sources of funding dominate the picture. A close look at the data reveals that these results are due to a small number of large investments financed through equity, advances from parent companies, and loans from development agencies. In terms of aggregate share, bank loans occupy in Zimbabwe an intermediate position between retained earnings and "other" sources: they finance very few purchases of buildings but about a third of all recorded purchases of equipment. As in the case of "other" sources of funding, investments in equipment financed by banks tend to be larger than those financed through retained earnings.

21.3.2 Kenya Case Study

These issues were examined in further detail in case study surveys in Kenya and Zimbabwe. Answering to specific questions about the financing of lumpy investments, case study firms in Kenya declare an average time between capital purchases of three and a half years. Half of the case study respondents are confident they could certainly find the money if they needed to, but the rest is less optimistic. Only one-sixth of the firms respond that they could not find the funds. These figures agree with Gunning and Mumbengegwi (1995) and Bigsten et al. (2002) who argue that credit constraints are not binding for most African manufacturers.

The expected length of time to secure the funds is four months. Eighty percent of the firms needed or wanted to borrow at least once. Manufacturing firms tend to require more credit than others, but otherwise there are few differences between firm categories in their desire to borrow. Virtually all firms know who they would approach if the need arose. But only 60 percent are always successful in securing the needed funds.

Entrepreneurs were quizzed about their strategies for securing funds. Answers confirm an overwhelming reliance on retained earnings and personal savings. Bank finance comes second, mostly in the form of a loan, occasionally in the form of an overdraft, and in several cases from a finance company. A fourth of the respondents also regard hire-purchase as an important source of credit. In Kenya, hire-purchase applies mostly to the financing of vehicles, usually with loans of up to three years at rates slightly above bank lending rates. Over time, hire-purchase companies may expand their activities to incorporate machinery and equipment. Loans from other sources are seldom cited by respondents as a source of investment finance they had considered seriously.

21.3.3 Zimbabwe Case Study

These issues were revisited in more detail in the Zimbabwe case study survey. Firms were asked whether they had considered sources of finance other than the ones they ended up using. Most firms had considered a loan from a bank or finance house and, in some cases, hire-purchase. The reasons for not using other sources of finance varied among firms. African firms and microenterprises most often stated that they could not get access to it. Medium and large firms, and firms owned or managed by whites and other ethnic groups, usually said either that they did not need the other finance or that the source they chose was cheaper and had a longer repayment period. Other reasons cited were that the application process required too much paperwork or was too slow, and that the firm was not sure it could repay the loan.

Firms that are a member of a group of companies were found to be in a more favorable position because holding companies play the role of an internal capital market. The parent company can better assess the viability of an investment by a subsidiary than any external lender. Consequently investment opportunities by subsidiaries are less likely to be forgone than if an external investor—lender or partner—had to be convinced of the profitability of the project.

To summarize, the picture that emerges is one in which internal financing and commercial bank loans constitute the most important sources of finance for the long-term credit needs of firms. Retained earnings are the dominant source of financing acquisition of equipment/machinery across all firm sizes. Established firms of a sufficient size find it easier to raise outside funds than start-ups and microenterprises. Medium and large firms have greater access to bank credit, especially if they belong to the dominant business community. This reflects the distribution of collateralizable assets, primarily land, across firms of different sizes, and the lower transaction costs to banks for evaluating creditworthiness of large firms. In a more sophisticated economy such as that of Zimbabwe, bank financing tends to be replaced with more specialized forms of investment finance for large investments.

The rationing of investment finance affects primarily microenterprises and small African firms. What remains unclear, however, is whether these firms are profitable enough to be able and willing to pay commercial interest rates. In Zimbabwe it was the opinion of some of the bank staff we spoke to that many firms cannot afford interest rates as high as those prevailing in the country at the time of the survey (36 percent nominal at a time when inflation was 20–25 percent per annum). To respond to these concerns, the government had made available to small African businesses a line of credit of several million Zimbabwe dollars at an interest rate of 5 percent per annum while the going rate on overdraft facilities was around 36 percent. Not surprisingly, there was excess demand for such loans and a few of the case study firms said they had unsuccessfully tried to get one of these loans.

To explore how financial constraints affect investment, we asked Zimbabwe case study firms whether they were forced to delay or downsize their most recent major investment due to lack of funds. Results are presented in table 21.3. About one-third of firms stated that they had to delay and about one-sixth that the investment was downsized due to lack of finance. African and microenterprises were, again, most

Table 21.3
Investment and finance

	All firms	Size				Ethnicity		
		Micro	Small	Medium	Large	African	White	Other
Firms delaying investment because of lack of funds	32%	57%	31%	18%	32%	64%	23%	25%
Firms that downsized investment because of lack of funds	17%	43%	15%	0%	16%	46%	4%	25%

Source: Case study survey in Zimbabwe.

likely to delay and downsize. Probit analysis (not shown) reveals that the effect of ethnicity on investment delay is statistically significant. Among the firms that were forced to delay their investment, more that three-fourths reported that the delay reduced the rate of return on the investment. These results suggest that timely access to finance is as important as the cost of finance. One respondent, for instance, told us that he had missed the purchase of a secondhand machine that he needed badly because he could not raise the funds on time. Others had similar stories. The importance of rapid access to credit also explains why many firms use overdraft facilities to finance investments.

As another indicator of whether firms face liquidity constraints, we then asked firms whether they have ever had excess funds that they could not invest profitably within the firm. These surplus funds are typically invested in financial assets or, in some cases, into raiding other firms. Subsidiaries typically revert all their excess funds to a centralized liquidity center with their parent company. Older firms and subsidiaries are more likely to be cash rich, an indication that they have come to a point where they have exploited all the profitable opportunities available to them.

In addition to questions about the firm's most recent investment, we asked whether firms had ever been prevented from investing because of lack of finance. Nearly half of the sample firms reported that this had occurred to them at least once. Again, African-headed firms and microenterprises were more likely to be affected. To understand better why the investment was not made, we asked why firms did not borrow and why they did not raise equity. Most African firms and microenterprises answered the first question by saying they were unable to obtain a loan, and the second by pointing out that they did not know people with money. Large firms and firms owned by whites and other ethnic groups also often cited the inability to obtain (more) credit as the reason for not borrowing, but many simply felt the interest rate was too high. When asked about why they did not raise more equity, none of non-black firms said they did not know people with money. Rather, these firms either didn't feel they needed the outside equity or didn't want it because of the loss of control and potential for conflicts that would result.

Results therefore indicate that except for microenterprises and African-headed firms, equity rationing in a strict sense is not the reason why firms rarely use outside equity to finance investments. As we saw in the previous section, loss of control and fear of conflicts are the main reasons for not bringing in equity finance. Regarding credit rationing, while it does not appear to be a regular problem for most firms, a substantial fraction of all firms feel that credit constraints have prevented them from investing at some time in the past. Taken together with the qualitative information collected during the interviews, these findings suggest that most firms, provided that they are above a certain size, can raise credit to finance equipment replacements and minor investments. But financing major expansions and reorganization of production are problematic for many, leading to frequent delays and downsizing of investments.

21.4 Liquidity Crises

Firm performance also depends on the way they handle liquidity crises. All firms find themselves short of cash at one point or another. The inability to deal with a crisis can be the firm's demise. In an environment characterized by little growth and large shocks, a firm's ability to survive liquidity crises might, in the long run, be the most important determinant of firm population.

21.4.1 Kenya Case Study

Kenyan case study firms were asked about the liquidity crises they face. Their responses are summarized in table 21.4. Most firms answered that they face liquidity constraints or cash-flow crises at one time or another. The average number of occurrences per year is two. Kenyan-African firms appear at a disadvantage, with about half of them frequently facing liquidity problems against one-fourth of the non–Kenyan-African firms.

Two-third of the firms are confident that they could find the funds to deal with the situation. Only a couple firms worried that they could not find the money at all. Two-thirds of the firms ever needed to borrow, and two-thirds of them could find a lender. Kenyan-African businesses are again at a disadvantage in terms of access to credit. Although a similar pattern exists across firm sizes, with small firms less likely to be able to borrow, it is not as marked as between ethnic groups. A probit regressions (not shown) indicates that ethnicity alone has a significant effect on the ability to borrow when faced with liquidity problems. Firm size has the expected sign but is not significant. Older firms are more likely to be able to borrow for liquidity crises.

The most often cited strategy to deal with liquidity crises is to delay payment to suppliers and to speed up payment from customers. Of course, only firms that receive credit from suppliers and offer credit to customers can use that strategy. This in itself penalizes Kenyan-African businesses because they receive trade credit less often. The second most important strategy is to request help from the bank, typically in the form of a temporary extension of the overdraft limit. A few respondents indicated that they could call up their bank and ask them to "sit" on one of their checks for a couple of days. In these cases the bank acts as the firm's accomplice in delaying payment to creditors. Borrowing from friends and relatives and other informal lenders comes next. It is the source of external funds most often cited by Kenyan-African

Table 21.4
Cash-flow management in Kenya

	All firms	African	Non-African
How often liquidity problems occur			
Frequently	33%	48%	24%
Occasionally	22%	19%	24%
Rarely	30%	24%	33%
Never	15%	10%	18%
Access to credit when facing financial difficulties			
% of firms that ever needed to borrow	69%	81%	62%
% of firms that were always able to borrow	68%	41%	91%
% of firms that were ever in a difficult position	30%	44%	23%
Possible sources of funds when facing financial difficulties			
Personal savings	30%	62%	23%
Banks and financial institutions	59%	33%	71%
Personal loan	46%	48%	46%
Delay payment/speed up recovery	63%	33%	80%
Sell faster, etc.	21%	29%	17%
Strategies to avoid or minimize liquidity problems			
Overlook liquidities carefully	31%	14%	41%
Limit production and purchases	65%	76%	59%
Limit credit to clients/insist on advances	45%	62%	35%
Use a buffer fund or open access to credit	18%	19%	18%
Reduce margin	22%	33%	15%
Other	7%	10%	6%
Buffer fund			
% firms with a buffer fund	67%	62%	70%
Buffer fund as proportion of liabilities	60%	61%	58%

Source: RPED case study.

businesses. Own funds in the forms of savings or alternative sources of income are the most often cited source of relief for Kenyan-African businesses. A third of them also mention reducing their margin to sell faster and stopping purchases of new goods, thereby hurting their business.

21.4.2 Zimbabwe Case Study

More detailed questions were posed to the Zimbabwe case study firms. Almost all of the firms declared having experienced cash-flow problems at one time or another (table 21.5). Respondents were asked whether they considered their cash flow as highly variable or not. Probit analysis (not shown) indicates that firms in the textile and garment sector were most likely to describe their cash flow as highly variable.

Table 21.5
Liquidy crises in Zimbabwe

	All firms	Size				Ethnicity		
		Micro	Small	Medium	Large	African	White	Other
Firms ever experiencing cash flow crises	91%	86%	100%	100%	82%	100%	88%	89%
Firms whose survival was ever threatened	40%	33%	53%	33%	35%	42%	38%	44%
Among those, firms forced to downsize	80%	100%	67%	100%	83%	100%	64%	100%

Source: Case study survey in Zimbabwe.

They indicated that variability is mostly due to seasonality in demand. All categories of firms are susceptible to liquidity problems, though a larger fraction of small firms and textile firms report having been through tough times. Forty percent of the case study firms at some point went through a major crisis in which the survival of the firm was threatened. In the great majority of crises, firms were forced to downsize their operations, but many respondents had since recovered. Of course, those who succumbed to a liquidity crisis were no longer around to be interviewed.

The causes of liquidity problems are both diverse and cumulative in the sense that problems typically result from a combination of negative shocks. The most commonly cited cause of cash-flow problems are lack of demand and seasonality in demand. The combination of a drastic drought in 1992 and of the liberalization of imports following ESAP in 1991 created difficulties for a number of firms. Several respondents said they were put in a critical situation when customers failed to pay them, suggesting that difficult conditions in one part of the economy ripple through the rest. These difficulties were compounded by rising interest rates and tightening finance.

To the extent that cases of failed commercial debts get publicized within the business community, a few cases of bad debt can create pessimistic expectations that get reflected in an unwillingness to grant trade credit. Many respondents, for instance, indicated that one of their responses to the 1992 drought was to "consolidate" their trade credit position by reducing their exposure and cutting off numerous marginal customers.

We then asked Zimbabwean case study firms how they respond to cash-flow problems. The most commonly cited response is to delay payments to suppliers (table 21.6). The flexibility of trade credit thus acts as an important source of cash-flow smoothing, helping firms to weather difficult times by shifting some of their liquidity

Table 21.6
Response to liquidity crises in Zimbabwe

	Firms
Delay payment and speed up revenues	
Delayed payment to suppliers	49%
Asked customers to pay early	8%
Delayed payments to government or workers	8%
Raise new funds	
Went over overdraft limit	20%
Got bank loan	6%
Borrowed from other sources	8%
Used personal savings	8%
Change business	
Stopped new purchases	24%
Reduced margins to sell faster	10%
Reduced production/employment	10%
Reduced credit to customers	2%

Source: Case study survey in Zimbabwe.
Note: Multiple responses were allowed.

problems onto their suppliers. It also provides strong support for the financial motive for trade credit. The next most often cited response was to rely on the overdraft facility. Over 20 percent of the firms experiencing problems borrowed above their overdraft limit. Slowing down purchases is much more common than reducing production when firms experience normal liquidity problems. This suggests that firms manage their inventories as a way of dealing with cash-flow problems, drawing down inventories of supplies and accumulating inventories of products when demand is low. It is only in times of serious crisis that they cut production and employment.

Other strategies for coping with cash-flow problems include reducing margins to speed up sales, securing a loan from a bank or parent company, asking customers to pay early (often using cash discounts as an incentive), and reducing the credit available to customers. A few respondents drew upon their own personal savings or managed to obtain a personal loan. A few firms confessed they had to delay payment to their workers. Though delaying payments to suppliers was often cited, reducing credit to customers was not, presumably because it undermines the ability of the firm to market its products precisely when demand is low. Reducing credit to customers may also signal that the firm is in difficulty and incite clients to search for new suppliers.

After having asked about specific problems and responses, we turned to prevention. We thus asked a series of specific questions about possible actions firms may

Table 21.7
Strategy to prevent liquidity crisis in Zimbabwe

	All firms	African	White
Financial buffer			
Keep a portion for overdraft as a reserve	50%	33%	63%
Keep savings as a reserve	32%	73%	16%
Have other income to use in an emergency	18%	27%	10%
Reduce exposure			
Refrain from expanding your business	40%	56%	39%
Refuse to give credit to customers	35%	58%	19%
Request advances from customers	15%	36%	9%
Delay purchases until money available	57%	58%	55%
Informal insurance			
Know someone to borrow from in an emergency	76%	64%	80%

Source: Case study survey in Zimbabwe.

take to prevent cash-flow problems, or make sure they can deal with them when they arise. Answers are summarized in table 21.7. About half of the respondents do keep a portion of their overdraft facility as a reserve; a third hold precautionary savings. This confirms our analysis in chapter 7. White-owned firms and firms other than microenterprises are more likely to have an overdraft reserve, presumably because they are more likely to have an overdraft facility. African and Asian firms and microenterprises and small firms are much more likely to hold precautionary savings, perhaps also because they are less likely to have an overdraft facility. Only a small proportion of firms have diversified sources of income that can be drawn upon in an emergency; more smaller firms and Asian firms are in this situation than other firms.

About 40 percent of firms claim that they have refrained from expanding their business because of concerns about cash flow; this is more of a concern for African and smaller firms. About one-third of the case study firms do not provide customer credit because of their concerns about cash flow—less among white-owned firms and medium-size firms. Few firms request advances from customers for cash-flow reasons, but most microenterprises and a substantial fraction of African and wood sector firms do. Delaying purchases is a commonly used strategy by all categories of firms, particularly textile firms. Three-fourths of the case study firms, without marked differences across firms of different ethnicity, size, or sector, stated that they know someone they could borrow from in the event of an emergency. Subsidiaries of a holding or parent company state that they could rely on their parent company to bail them out of most difficulties.

Taken together, these results show that the precautionary motive for saving is stronger among small and African firms, and for firms facing more cash-flow variability, a finding consistent with predictions made in chapter 7. They demonstrate the importance and flexibility of trade credit, and support the financial and sales promotion motives for trade credit. They again bring out the importance of overdraft facilities. They show that subsidiaries of holding companies have an important source of insurance against cash-flow problems as well as finance for investment. They indicate the minor role that other sources of credit (moneylenders, personal loans) and equity capital play in dealing with cash-flow problems.

These findings demonstrate the great importance of cash-flow management and the value that financial opportunities represent for preventing and coping with cash-flow problems. It is in their effort to deal with unexpected external shocks that firms find themselves most hurt by credit constraints like overdraft ceilings, which is why the presence and flexibility of trade credit are so important. It is therefore likely that financial constraints, even when they do not directly prevent firms from undertaking profitable expansionary investments, may indirectly retard them because firms worry about being able to deal with the increased risk associated with expansion. Because firms cannot find insurance against day to day liquidity problems and because overdraft facilities perform this task only imperfectly, long-term investment opportunities may be missed.

21.5 Enterprise Finance in Africa: A Typology of Firms

Based on the information summarized in previous sections and on the literature, the situation with respect to enterprise finance for African firms can be summarized as follows: At the bottom of the firm hierarchy are microenterprises who, for the most part, receive no credit from suppliers and financial institutions. Small African firms seem particularly disadvantaged. Some of them manage to collect advances from customers in order to cover the cost of raw materials, but the practice varies from country to country—less prevalent in Zimbabwe than in Ghana and Kenya (e.g., Cuevas et al. 1993; Fafchamps et al. 1994, 1995). The middle group of small- and medium-size firms have access to three, relatively simple sources of external finance: bank overdrafts, hire purchase, and supplier credit. The top half of this category may also have access to other forms of short-term domestic credit like bankers acceptances. In some countries such as Zimbabwe, the three systems—short-term credit from suppliers, line of credit from commercial banks, and medium-term credit from finance houses—are linked through a reputation mechanism whereby serious failure to comply with a particular lender affects one's ability to continue receiving credit from the others. In others, the three systems are not integrated and work much less effectively.

At the top of the hierarchy are not one but several, partly overlapping, categories of firms. Most of them are large by African standards, but they differ in their access to specialized, often cheaper sources of external finance. One type of finance is medium- and long-term loans. African commercial banks are reluctant to lend to manufacturing firms except on short term. To access medium- to long-term finance, firms must turn to other sources like finance houses, merchant banks, and development banks. Many of them typically economize on screening and monitoring costs by focusing on a few, large-scale investment projects. As a result medium- and long-term loans tend to disproportionately go to large firms that can justify large enough investments. Smaller long-term investments typically fall by the wayside and have to financed out of retained earnings or short-term credit. African countries with a small number of large firms do not have finance houses, merchant banks, and development banks. Another type of external finance that, in practice, is available only to a specific category of firms is offshore borrowing. It is not for the fainthearted given the frequent and abrupt devaluations that often affect African currencies.

Outside equity financing remains confined to a very small number of firms: for instance, in 1994 there were only 70 Zimbabwean manufacturing firms or so quoted on the Zimbabwe Stock Exchange at the time of the case study. At the same time the Kenyan Stock Exchange only had 35 listed companies, most of them not in manufacturing. All listed companies are large, well-known firms, many of them associated with popular products and brands. For those happy few who successfully floated stock, the amount of external finance that can be mobilized is substantial.

A special category of firms are those that belong to a group or a holding company. Because groups of firms and holding companies operate in effect like a mini capital market, members of a group find it easier to access finance for expansion projects or for crisis management. Such firms then can expand more easily if they so wish, or withstand shocks if they come under fire, even when on their own they would be too small to access project finance or equity investors. Holding companies are prominent in Zimbabwe, much less so in the rest of sub-Saharan Africa.

A small but promising category of firms are those promoted by venture capital firms. Here small- and medium-size firms have found access to outside equity through an institutional innovation that enables an outside investor to closely monitor start-up firms and prop them up until they are viable. The few firms we interviewed clearly benefited from the arrangement, and the availability of capital at critical periods of their development enabled them to survive growing pains. The downside of the arrangement is not negligible, however: loss of control and external interference. Managers who go for venture capital must be prepared to have a "big brother" constantly looking over their shoulder, patronizing them somewhat and scrutinizing their every little mistake. This is the price to pay to compensate for the lack of experience and reputation these firms begin with.

VII CONCLUSIONS AND POLICY IMPLICATIONS

We have covered a lot of ground in this book. This concluding part takes stock of what we have learned and draws lessons for policy. We also discuss issues for future research.

22 What Have We Learned?

22.1 Market Institutions

At the end of an already long book devoted to market institutions, it would be tedious to restate the conclusions of the various chapters. Instead, I propose to compare our findings with the initial conjectures I wrote in 1992 when I began working on market institutions in Africa. These conjectures are those that appeared in chapter 1. How many of these conjectures turned out to be correct? Let us examine each of them in turn.

CONJECTURE 22.1 Whenever contracts are not perfectly enforceable and therefore mutual trust is an essential condition for economic exchange, the probability for two parties to trade increases with previous economic exchange between them. Consequently a larger share of economic exchange takes place among acquaintances than predicted by random matching.

This conjecture was largely borne out by the facts. Relational contracting is the rule in African manufacturing, with firms buying from the same suppliers for many years on average. When relational contracting is not practiced, for instance, as among many agricultural traders, exchange takes a rudimentary form. Only when information is shared widely in the economy can firms easily secure alternative sources of finance or supply at similar conditions. Anonymous exchange is an oxymoron. Anonymity is not what market institutions should aim for: markets in which buyers and sellers do not know each other are the lowest possible form of market exchange. Rather, institutions should favor the circulation of reliable personal information, together with adequate forms of identification (e.g., business registration).

CONJECTURE 22.2 Whenever contracts are not perfectly enforceable and a reputation mechanism is nonexistent, no economic exchange can take place among unacquainted parties and all exchange is social network based.

Conjecture 22.2 was slightly overdramatic: exchange can take place when parties are unacquainted but it takes a rudimentary form—what we called the flea market economy. Breach of contract is avoided by insisting on cash-and-carry trade. Inspection of quality is done on the spot. There is no placement of orders, no invoicing, no trade credit, no brand name, and not even payment by check. More sophisticated form of exchange are limited to acquainted firms. Although the conjecture is correct to state that, in this case, exchange is based on social networks, it fails to recognize that network links can be created through repeated interaction—the trial period for trade credit documented in earlier chapters.

CONJECTURE 22.3   Economic exchange is more likely to be based on reputation in industrialized economies, and on social networks in pre-industrial societies.

Conjecture 22.3 was by and large verified by our observations, but with several important caveats. First of all, it is now recognized that social networks and personal relationships play a role in economic exchange even in developed economies (e.g., Bernstein 1992, 1996; Montgomery 1991; Granovetter 1995a).

Second, the form taken by social networks varies dramatically across countries. In Ghana, for instance, entrepreneurs typically know only a handful of clients and suppliers they deal with regularly. The density of business networks is low. Switching is difficult and costly. The same is true for agricultural trade in Malawi and Madagascar. In Kenya, business networks are more dense, at least among Asian entrepreneurs. This is also the case to some extent for Beninese agricultural traders. As a result information circulates more freely and efficiency is enhanced.

In Zimbabwe, where a credit reference system is in place, the situation resembles more closely the reputation-based exchange associated, in conjecture 22.3, with industrial development. It is true that Zimbabwe is more industrially developed than the other African countries in the sample, and so to some extent this finding supports the conjecture. But the Zimbabwe economy is still a long way from being a developed economy. This suggests that there is hope of approaching levels of market institution sophistication of advanced economies even at relatively low levels of development.

CONJECTURE 22.4   In social network based exchange, prices are established through mutual bargaining.

Although field observations are by and large consistent with conjecture 22.4, the price formation mechanism was not studied in detail in this volume, so we cannot say much about this conjecture. But the models presented in chapters 2, 11, and 12 make it clear that transactions must yield net positive benefits for relationships to be valuable. How the benefit from a transaction is shared between the two parties is limited by voluntary participation constraints: trying to squeeze too much out of a client may be counterproductive if it lowers the value of the relationship so much that the client no longer has an incentive to pay. But there typically remains a surplus after satisfying both participation constraints. This surplus must be allocated via bargaining. Conjecture 22.4 thus agrees with our preferred model constructed on the basis of the evidence presented here.

CONJECTURE 22.5   The number of intermediaries between consumer and producer is larger in social network based exchange than in reputation-based exchange.

No attempt was made to verify conjecture 22.5 directly, so we cannot provide hard evidence for or against. Field observations of agricultural traders in Benin, Malawi, and Madagascar, however, were by and large consistent with it. Traders are not vertically integrated and tend to cover only a small portion of the marketing chain. This issue deserves more research.

CONJECTURE 22.6   In social network based exchange, a large share of gains from trade is appropriated by trade intermediaries.

Our analysis of returns to network capital in chapters 16 and part VI and our study of networks and investment in chapter 21 suggest that better connected traders and firms do indeed appropriate a large share of the gains from trade. However, our results also indicate that network capital is not used by African traders to raise prices but rather to increase volume. To the extent that better connected traders have lower unit marketing costs, however, they reap larger gains from trade. The evidence suggests that competition among productive, well-connected traders is not sufficient to eliminate the competitive fringe. The presence of a fringe flea market economy seems to cap the surplus better connected traders can extract, without eliminating it totally.

CONJECTURE 22.7   In social network based exchange, trade relationships tend to remain nonspecialized, unless the development of commodity or activity specific skills are important and the volume of trade in a particular commodity is large, in which case traders may specialize in a particular commodity and/or activity.

Although we did not emphasize it here, the evidence on agricultural traders over-whelmingly confirms conjecture 22.7: specialization in a single crop is rare; many traders deal in nonagricultural products or farm inputs as well as crops. Traders operate in an opportunistic manner, using their contacts to identify arbitrage possi-bilities irrespective of the crop or product involved.

The same is obviously not true of manufacturing firms that specialize in a narrow range of items they produce. But they make use of unspecialized traders or import/export firms to secure inputs and distribute their products.

CONJECTURE 22.8   In stable pre-industrial economies, exchange may be influenced by culturally inherited economic roles.

We found little evidence that culturally inherited roles matter in Africa. It is true that in some African countries, nonindigenous groups occupy a dominant position in business. At first glance this might suggest that they harbor cultural values that are more conducive to trade and business. But the origin of these groups varies tremen-dously from country to country without noticeable impact on business practices.

For instance, Asians in Kenya are the dominant group in manufacturing. They deal with each other in a more businesslike fashion than their Kenyan-African counterparts. In other countries, however, Asians are not the dominant group. In neighboring Tanzania, where they are a minority in business, they appear, if anything, to operate in a less businesslike fashion than other firms, while in Zimbabwe, where whites dominate industry, Asians appear, if anything, less sophisticated. It is also worth pointing out that countries such as Cameroon and Côte d'Ivoire where business is mostly in the hands of Africans do not necessarily perform less well in terms of trade credit or exports, quite the contrary.

To a professor who claimed that whites were more attuned to Western culture, Condolezza Rice (advisor of President Bush and former provost of Stanford) is said to have responded, "I speak French, you don't, and I play piano better than you. Culture is something that you learn, not something you are born with." The evidence suggests that given the chance, African businessmen and women can learn to play by new, more modern rules and that they can adopt more efficient market institutions. The challenge is to help them do that. This is what we do in the final chapter. Before doing so, we examine the implications of our findings for other important research issues.

22.2   Firm Dynamics

In the first chapter of this book, we noted the relationship between modes of exchange and the size distribution of firms. We pointed out that the large number of small firms in Africa grants the market an important resource allocation role—probably more so than in developed economies where large firms and government administrations organize much of exchange through command and control within hierarchies. Many see the process of development as one by which increasing returns are captured, either at the level of the firm or at the level of an entire industry (e.g., Rosenstein-Rodan 1943; Nurkse 1953; Myrdal 1957; Hirschman 1958; Romer 1986; Rodriguez-Clare 1996a, b; Fafchamps 1997b). There is therefore a close relationship between development and the size distribution of firms (e.g., Staley and Morse 1965; Fafchamps 1994; Liedholm and Mead 1999). We now briefly discuss the feedback effect between market institutions, firm dynamics, and the size distribution of firms.

Among other things, market institutions determine access to finance, in the form of bank loans, bank overdrafts, supplier credit, or equity. Access to funds at the right time and the right quantity affects firms' ability to grow and survive. The financial structure is thus an important determinant of industrial structure, namely of the size and vintage distribution of firms. The evidence presented here and elsewhere (e.g.,

Bigsten et al. 1999a, b, 2000a, b, 2002) depicts firm dynamics in Africa as varying with different levels in the firm hierarchy. In this section we briefly discuss some of the lessons we learned and the remaining gaps in knowledge.

22.2.1 Microenterprises

Without doubt the firms whose potential is most restricted by difficult access to external finance are microenterprises. Entry for microenterprises is often easy (for caveats, see, however, Daniels 1994; Liedholm and Mead 1999; McCormick 1999), but growth and survival are not. Most microenterprises live a precarious life, vulnerable as they are to liquidity shocks. In their case, bank overdrafts and contractual flexibility cannot be used to smooth temporary cash-flow problems. It is therefore not surprising to note that the survival rate among microenterprises is indeed low: according to Daniels (1994), one-third of microenterprises close down each year. Only the most fortunate ones accumulate some personal savings that can be used as buffer stock against temporary difficulties. In order to grow, microenterprise must graduate into the middle category, that of small- and medium-size firms, those that have a bank overdraft and supplier credit and that can use hire-purchase if they choose to.

The hurdle that microenterprises must pass in order to graduate is, however, so difficult that very few succeed (e.g., McCormick et al. 1997; Liedholm and Mead 1999). Only a very small proportion of small- and medium-size firms grew out of microenterprises. The hurdle is difficult to jump over because several conditions must be satisfied more or less at the same time for graduation to be realistic. Because it belongs to a group of risky borrowers, a microenterprise cannot typically obtain a bank overdraft without providing collateral.

Even if a microenterprise has collateral, banks may turn them down for an overdraft. In the days of regulated interest rates African banks used to argue that they could not cover the costs of screening and processing small borrowers because rates were not remunerative enough. Now that rates have been liberalized in many countries, the bank staff we interviewed argued that small borrowers could not afford high interest rates. It appears as if microenterprises can never win! It remains, of course, that as a group they are risky borrowers and that bankers' suspicions will for a long time to come take the form of statistical discrimination. To combat such discrimination, ambitious and promising microentrepreneurs must be able to distinguish themselves from the rest.

One way they can potentially do so is by building a good track record with the bank and with other lenders. By making regular withdrawals and deposits on their bank account and by not bouncing checks, borrowers demonstrate they ability to handle their personal finances. Banks may then use this information as signal of good character. Ironically many Africans prefer to put their personal savings either with one of the building societies or on a post office savings account. These financial institutions do not open lines of credit to their clients. This is particularly damaging because microentrepreneurs are more likely to have a savings account than a checking account.

Another way microenterprise can potentially raise finance and at the same time establish a track record is through supplier credit. We saw that many suppliers are willing to grant limited credit to customers who have satisfied a trial period of several months of regular purchases. What suppliers do then is typically to set the customer's line of credit to his or her level of purchases over the preceding months. By paying regularly and progressively increasing purchases, a client can then gradually increase the line of credit. The process is very gradual and can take several years, but it enables the firm to establish a track record that is publicly available through credit reference and credit information services. A firm that has behaved in a satisfactory manner with one supplier can then secure credit from others, and so on. A good reputation with suppliers also helps the bank decide in favor of a bank overdraft and the finance house to decide in favor of a hire-purchase loan.

An essential element of the reputation mechanism, however, is firm registration with the Registrar of Companies. Although registration is not a prerequisite for any form of lending, it often facilitates the operation of the reputation mechanism because registration makes public crucial information on the firm, like the address of its owner(s) and the level of its capital. It also makes it easier to trace other relevant information like the number of its employees and involvement in court cases. Although registration per se does not provide immediate access to finance, in the long run it is probably beneficial. There are significant costs to registering one's business (e.g., fees and preparation of balance sheet), however, and the benefits are uncertain and only materialize in the distant future. This probably explains why most small firms never bother to register.

To sum things up, the path that leads from the microenterprise category to the small and medium firm category is narrow and treacherous. What compounds the difficulty is that without bank overdraft and credit from numerous suppliers, a firm is a worse debtor. This is because contractual flexibility is, as we have seen, a major way that firms smooth their cash flow. When the firm has a single creditor, that creditor alone has to bear the burden of whatever shock affects the debtor. This tends to make the debtor a worse payer and consequently makes it more difficult for a debtor with a small number of creditors to establish a good reputation. One should therefore not be surprised that so few microenterprises succeed to graduate into the small- and medium-size category.

These realities help understand the prevailing ethnic mix in African entrepreneurship. If a particular group, for historical reasons, establishes itself in business, it becomes easier for other members of that group to succeed in business as well: information about how lenders make credit assessments circulates more freely within the group so that candidate entrepreneurs can adapt their behavior accordingly; reputation spreads within a group that comprises other businesses, and thus potential suppliers and trade creditors; and the wealth accumulated by members of the group can be used, through inheritance or personal guarantees, to serve as start-up capital and to ease newcomers' access to bank credit. For all these reasons it is easier for members of that group to jump over the initial hurdle that slows down the growth of so many microenterprises and to immediately—or at least rapidly—join the ranks of small- and medium-size firms.

22.2.2   Small and Medium Firms

Let us now turn to the second category of firms, the small- and medium-size firms with access to bank overdrafts, trade credit, and hire-purchase finance. Although their situation is much better than that of microenterprises, it is not without flaws of its own. Firms in this category typically find it much easier to survive for the reasons we already talked about—bank overdraft and contractual flexibility. But those that perceive expansion opportunities often find it difficult to grow: many projects are deferred or downsized due to lack of funds; many investments are not undertaken because firms are reluctant to assume fixed debt obligations in order to finance them, and refuse to endanger their control and peace of mind by bringing in equity partners.

Shifting from one line of business to another is also difficult as it means establishing trade credit relationships with new suppliers. How easy this can be varies from country to country. We have seen, for instance, that Zimbabwean firms are at an advantage compared to Ghanaian or Kenyan firms because they are assisted by the existence of a sophisticated reputation mechanism (e.g., Cuevas et al. 1993; Fafchamps 1996; Fafchamps et al. 1994, 1995). The formal reputation mechanism through credit reference bureaus and information sharing among financial institutions, however, is largely tailored to the needs of existing firms; it benefits less the firms that, under any circumstance, have a harder time, namely new entrants. Word of mouth, personal contacts, and the backing of friends and relatives are what determines the success or demise of new entrants at the small- and medium-size level.

With luck and effort, small and medium firms can graduate into higher categories, for instance, by accessing cheaper offshore financing. To do so, they must be big enough to become customer of a merchant bank, and they need to export if they wish protection against foreign exchange risk. Exporting, however, is not without its own hurdles. Project loans are another option open to entrepreneurs who dedicated and patient enough to convince one of the few sources of long-term finance to invest in their project. The delays involved are significant and the administrative costs non-negligible, so the investment opportunity must be one that nobody else can jump on before the loan application goes through.

22.2.3 Large Firms

At the top of the industrial hierarchy, a few fortunate firms face few financial constraints. They can access external equity by floating shares on local stock exchanges, in case one is present. They can pool resources with other firms to form holding companies that can then raise credit and equity more easily.

For this category of firms, what are constraining is not their inability to raise external finance but the thinness of the market they can tap into and the paucity of financial instruments they can use. In the absence of corporate bonds, for instance, there is no secondary market through which institutional investors could invest in long-term corporate financing. Without mutual funds, small private investors find it difficult and risky to buy into equity. There is no market for derivatives, for futures on commodities or foreign exchange. There is no secondary market for mortgages.

One could argue that these markets do not exist because there is no demand, because Africa has not reached a sufficient degree of sophistication for these financial markets and instruments to emerge on their own. Whether or not this is the case is beyond the scope of this volume. What is clear is that operating in Africa is not easy even for large firms.

22.3 Networks, Specialization, and Segmentation

The evidence reported in this volume suggests that business networks (of which ethnicity is a strong predictor) influence firm entry, survival, and investment. As we discussed in the previous section, entry and investment require funds to purchase equipment and hire workers. Firm growth also requires information on which technology to adopt, which managers to hire, and the like. Better connected entrepreneurs have better access to factors of production and to the information required to package them into productive investments. Barr (2000), for instance, argues that better connected Ghanaian entrepreneurs are better able to identify profitable technologies. They may also identify and attract better technicians and workers.

Entry in a particular line of business also implies entry into a particular market. For instance, one cannot set up a grain trading business without buying and selling from other traders.[1] Potential investors who already know people in a particular line of business—or who can be introduced by relatives and friends—are therefore at an advantage. During survey work, for instance, we heard several similar stories in which traders set up an entirely new shop in a new location and immediately received credit from suppliers because they were well connected, while their less connected competitors were struggling to self-finance the expansion of their business. Potential entrepreneurs are thus most likely to enter a line of business in which they have relatives or friends, not because they can more easily buy from them or sell to them but because relatives and friends can provide them with much needed references and background information.

Once patterns of specialization are established, they are likely to get reinforced over time due to network externalities. For instance, if there are many Luos in fish trade, Luos who wish to start their own business are more likely to enter fish trade than any other trade, simply because they are more likely to already have contacts with fish traders. Segmentation reproduces itself.[2] Segmentation has several problems, however. First of all, not all segments of economic activity are equally profitable. This means that certain groups will be better off because the segment of activity in which they have an advantage happens to be more profitable. This is an important equity concern, but by itself it need not have an efficiency cost: as long as all profitable business opportunities are seized, investment is efficient. The political risk associated with segmentation may nevertheless be a disincentive to invest and a driving force behind capital flight.

Second, segmentation is likely to distort the aggregate allocation of investment. To see why, suppose again that Luos dominate fish trade. Since new Luo investors have an advantage in fish trade thanks to the contacts they have with other traders, they are likely to invest in fish trade as well. If there are many Luos who wish to enter business, there will be an oversupply of fish trading services, that is, excess entry. At the same time, another line of business, say software programming, may be undersupplied because the group of people who know about software is too small to grow. The end result is too many fish traders and too few software programmers.

Third, segmentation has implications for the kind of careers people plan for themselves. Consider again the choices open to an ambitious Luo. One option is to follow in his kinmen's footsteps and prepare for the fish trade; another option is to

---

1. Possible exceptions are rural markets where producers sell their products to local consumers, and urban fish and produce markets where smoked fish and vegetables are sold by producers directly. But these examples hardly constitute trading businesses.

2. One could hypothesize that the Indian caste system is the formalized end result of such segmentation process in an economy where patterns of activity specialization are very static over time.

study software programming. In addition to the fact that studying is costly, segmentation lowers the anticipated returns from learning programming relative to those generated by learning the fish trade. Of course, if our young man had lots of friends in Bangalore, India, software programming may begin to look more attractive. Short of this, fish trade is likely to be the optimal choice.

This reasoning therefore suggests that the aggregate efficiency cost of network segmentation might be quite high once its distorting effects on investment and choice of career is properly taken into account. More research is necessary to quantify the magnitude of these effects.

22.4 Networks and Competition

The existence of network segmentation also has deep implications about market competition. For lack of space, we will limit ourselves to a few observations. It is commonly believed that the number of firms operating in a particular market is a good indication of the extent of competition. This need not be the case in the presence of network effects, however. First of all, relationships are not in general tradable.[3] Although contacts are an accumulable assets (see Fafchamps and Minten 2001b, and chapter 20 for evidence), the absence of a market for individual contacts preclude that returns to contacts are arbitraged out. Consequently firms and individuals with better contacts will collect a rent and make more profit (e.g., Barr 2000, 2002b; Fafchamps and Minten 2002b).

This may explain why certain sectors of activity witness free entry and yet remain uncompetitive. Barrett (1997a), for instance, reports massive entry into grain trade following market liberalization in Madagascar, but points out that certain market functions such as grain assembly and large-scale wholesale remain more profitable and are more concentrated. This kind of result is usually interpreted as evidence of imperfect capital markets. Fafchamps and Minten (2001b, 2002b), however, suggest another possible explanation, namely social capital: better connected traders make more profit and hence invest more and expand their business. To put it differently, what appears to be happening is that a small group of well-connected traders captures the more lucrative portion of the business. Competition among them is insufficiently fierce so that smaller, less efficient traders are able to compete. In other words, the mere presence of small, inefficient traders together with large, well connected

3. More impersonal aspects of relationships, such as reputation in the population at large, may nevertheless be traded. The goodwill of firms, their brand name, and their trademarked products, for instance, are all subject to intellectual property rights and can be traded as such (Tadelis 1999).

traders is a sign that competition among large traders is insufficient—otherwise, they could drive the smaller traders out of business by cutting their margin. In this case the abundance of small firms coupled with a high concentration of activity in the hands of larger firms indicates less competition, not more as is usually assumed. If large traders were competing with each other more forcefully, small traders would disappear because they do not have the adequate social capital and operate in an inefficient manner (no invoicing, no credit, etc.).

At the same time the presence of a single seller or buyer in a market need not indicate insufficient competition. The reason is that the establishment of trust is a costly process. The same is true for the search process itself. Trust building, screening, and search costs are all examples of sunk transactions costs: they need be incurred only once. Once these costs have been incurred, it is in the interest of the parties to continue trading with each other. Other transactions costs have to be incurred repeatedly but may also have a nonconvex nature, such as transportation and negotiation costs. All are examples of nonconvex transactions costs.

To see how nonconvex transactions costs may naturally result in monopoly or monopsony, consider a remote village somewhere in Africa. Suppose that the cost of accessing this village by truck is C. Further assume that what villagers have to sell can represented by an inverse supply curve $P(Q) = a + bQ$, where $Q = \sum_i q_i$ is total quantity, with q_i being the quantity purchased by trucker i. Truckers charge Cournot prices; if a single trucker shows up in the village, he or she charges the monopsony price. Variable cost is ignored to simplify notation. The first-order condition for profit maximization is the usual

$$P + q_i P' = 0, \tag{22.1}$$

which, assuming a linear supply function, yields the usual

$$q_i^* = \frac{P^s - a}{b(n+1)}, \tag{22.2}$$

where P^s stands for selling price and n is the number of truckers. Free entry implies that truckers enter until they just break even. The break-even or zero profit condition is

$$\frac{(P^s - a)^2}{b(n+1)^2} \geq C. \tag{22.3}$$

Equation (22.3) determines the free entry equilibrium number of truckers n^*. It is clear from equation (22.3) that n^* is a decreasing function of C: the higher transactions costs are, the fewer truckers make the trip to the village. For sufficiently high C, a single trucker shows up, to whom villagers sell at the monopsony price. This examples illustrates that in the presence of nonconvex transactions costs, free entry need not result in competitive pricing. In fact, if the lone trucker was forced to pay a higher than monopsony price, he or she would not undertake the trip and villagers would be worse off. Yet, short of eliminating transactions cost C, monopsonistic or oligopsonistic competition naturally arise from free entry, without assuming any factor market imperfection (chapter 14). The implication of these tentative conclusions is that, in the presence of nonconvex transactions costs such as those incurred in the formation of relationships, contestability is a better measure of competition than industry or sector concentration.

In addition, when transactions costs are sunk, not only will oligopoly or monopsony arise, it will subsist over time. This pattern is quite apparent in manufacturing input markets. Bigsten et al. (2000a), for instance, report that most African manufacturers purchase their inputs from a handful of suppliers to whom they are extraordinarily loyal, even when alternative suppliers are available. This finding is consistent with the irreversible nature of screening and search costs and with the establishment of relationships based on mutual trust. Although theoretical and empirical work has begun on the structure and efficiency of trade in the presence of networks (for recent theoretical work, see, e.g., Bala and Goyal 1998, 2000; Kranton and Minehart 2000a, 2001), much work remains to be done.

22.5 Application to International Trade

Before we present our final conclusion, it is useful to briefly explore how the concepts developed here apply to international trade. The example of the Luo fish trader and Bangalore software programmer illustrates that the concepts of trade networks and market segmentation, which we developed to describe how domestic African markets function, may actually help us understand Africa's place in the world economy: if African entrepreneurs are more familiar with primary commodities such as coffee or vanilla than with manufacturing or software programming, chances are they will invest in coffee and vanilla.[4]

Although economists actually have very little hard evidence on what makes a country a successful exporters, casual observation suggests that network and segmentation effects are worth investigating (e.g., Casella and Rauch 1998; Rauch and Casella 1998; Banerjee and Munshi 1999; Banerjee and Duflo 2000; McCormick

---

4. In several African countries, market liberalization has resulted in new entry, but much of it seems to be in primary production and exports (Akiyama et al. 1999). On the theoretical side, Young (1991)'s model provides a formal description of lock-in into specialization patterns that perpetuate themselves over time.

1999). It has long been recognized that it is difficult for a country to break into export markets. Traditional explanations for international patterns of trade, such as labor costs and comparative advantage, fail to explain why some cheap labor countries manage to export manufactures while others do not. Could it be that network and segmentation effects could explain them better?

Biggs et al. (1994), for instance, documents efforts by US retail corporations to source products in Africa. What is immediately apparent from the description of these efforts is that the search and screening process is extremely costly for US corporations. Sourcing from Africa is complicated by the fact that US firms lack reliable contacts in the continent that can assist them in screening out undesirable firms—or even countries. If US retail corporations with all the resources and finance they can muster find it hard to source products in Africa, it must be extremely difficult for African firms to investigate and penetrate Western markets, except in sectors where they already have some contacts.

Circumstantial evidence suggests that contacts among expatriate communities across international boundaries may play a crucial role in the international location of industries (e.g., Casella and Rauch 1998; Rauch and Casella 1998). The relocation of textile and garment industries from Taiwan to Mauritius has, for instance, been attributed to links with the local Chinese community. Similar international links and the particularly important role played by expatriate Chinese have been noted in East Asian economies such as Singapore, Malaysia, Indonesia, and Thailand. Interpersonal relationships with businessmen and women in Hong-Kong and Taiwan have similarly been credited for the rapid development of the coastal areas of mainland China (Rauch and Casella 1998).

What remains to be seen is whether expatriate communities present in sub-Saharan Africa (e.g., Asians, Syro-Lebanese, and Europeans) can play a comparable role of bridge between Africa and more developed economies,[5] and whether newly established expatriate African communities in Europe and North America can serve as a beachhead for African manufacturing exports. Empirical work on international networks involving African and foreign entrepreneurs is much needed to get a more accurate picture of the prospects for export-driven growth in sub-Saharan Africa.

---

5. If the East Asia experience is representative, it is disappointing to note that unlike Taiwan and Hong-Kong, the parts of the world where Africa's expatriate communities primarily come from are not faring much better than Africa itself (e.g., South Asia, Middle East). This simple fact may explain why sub-Saharan Africa has so far remained by the wayside in the industrial globalization process. Of course, not so long ago Taiwan and Hong-Kong had incomes per head comparable to those of Africa today. If this experience can be extrapolated to Africa, all that is needed is for one or two African economies—not necessarily large ones—to take off and establish themselves as manufacturing export platforms. Contagion to neighboring countries could then follow the East Asia example, for instance, through African expatriate communities within Africa.

22.6   Conclusion

We have seen that allocation of resources can be organized in essentially three different ways: via gift exchange, through markets, and using command and control.[6] Gift exchange continues to play a major role in the allocation of subsistence goods among individuals and households in much of sub-Saharan Africa. Unlike developed economies where command and control allocation dominates within large corporations and public agencies, in Africa markets are the primary allocation mechanism outside of gift exchange. These markets, however, are different from those portrayed in economic textbooks: they involve individuals who form relationships and networks to economize on transactions costs. In the words of (Granovetter 1985), markets are embedded in webs of social relationships that help shape them.

We have discussed in detail the different types of market imperfections that give value to relationships and we have documented the formation of networks. Contrary to what is often believed, buying and selling to family members is rare. Relatives appear to play a role principally in terms of business exposure, training, equity financing, and referral. Evidence suggests that communities form around business activities, be it through wedding and funerals or sports events, rather than the contrary. Ethnic concentration probably reinforces itself over time as a result of the referral process, possibly compounded by statistical discrimination once business populations become sharply differentiated.

These principles apply to product as well as factor markets. We provided evidence regarding equity and labor markets in particular. Much work remains to be done to ascertain how much of an impediment to growth moral hazard in factor markets actually represents, once preventive measures adopted by economic agents are taken into account. Network segmentation was shown to have allocation costs that affect firm entry and investment in a perverse manner. Thanks to the referral process, familiarity with a particular type of business tends to reproduce itself over time, thereby locking particular groups or countries into a specific production pattern.

We then applied these insights to international trade issues. Although the data on international networks is still in its infancy, circumstantial evidence, particularly from East Asia, suggests that network externalities might be quite large. Research is urgently needed on the relationship between network segmentation and the international division of labor.

---

6. These three institutional arrangements largely overlap with what Braudel (1986) calls the subsistence, market, and capitalist spheres.

23 Policy Implications

In this final chapter we speculate on the possible policy implications of our work. Drawing policy prescriptions from economic analysis is a hazardous endeavour. The reason is that while the analysis itself is based on rigorous scientific principles, policy prescriptions are not. Neither could they be since, by definition, they are about changing the current state of affairs and thus about something that does not exist— and cannot be studied.

The following example illustrates perfectly the dangers of drawing policy prescriptions from analysis. When we finished the Ghana study in early 1993, we were struck by the virtual absence of any information-sharing mechanism on bad payers, let alone of a coordinated process to punish breach of contract. Even courts appeared unwilling to punish opportunistic breach. An interview with a lumber trader on the Accra market perfectly summarized the situation. When asked what he would do if he saw a client in arrears trying to buy from a neighboring trader, he responded he would simply relish the thought of having a competitor deal with a bad customer. What a perfect example of coordination failure. The only form of information sharing was not on bad payers but on good types. This took the form of an information referral system by which people would recommend others to suppliers.

Combined with ample evidence of breach of contract and risk avoidance practices, these findings suggested a highly inefficient form of market exchange. We speculated that sharing information more widely could only deter breach, reduce the need for risk avoidance, and thereby improve efficiency. We also expected it to favor equity as it would punish bad payers and reward good types. Our policy recommendation for Ghana was thus to favor networks and business associations while at the same time reinforcing courts.

The next case study took place in Kenya in September 1993. It became immediately apparent that information sharing was much more prevalent than in Ghana but that it was primarily practiced among Asian businesses. Several informal networks seemed to coexist and partially overlap. As a result well-connected entrepreneurs could more easily initiate trade and even, in some cases, set up a business. Information sharing was thus delivering the improvement in market performance that we had anticipated. The downside was that the system benefited predominantly Asian entrepreneurs and seemed to preclude entry by African businesses. As a result the population of Kenyan businesses was unrepresentative of the population, a source of political and economic tension in the country. Consequently capital flight was rampant and investment low.

On the basis of these findings, we concluded that information sharing was too confined. The problem, we argued, was that only network members benefited from it. Networks were organized around socialization, and socialization was driven by things like religion and ethnicity. As we hypothesized, informal networks were too restrictive in their composition and, by their very nature, could never grow to encompass all segments of society. The solution, we speculated, was to spread information more broadly so as to encompass all entrepreneurs. We therefore advocated the establishment of a formal information-sharing mechanism, such as a credit reference bureau.

One year later we conducted the Zimbabwe case study. To our delight, Zimbabwe had a well-organized formal credit reference agency with, according to the manager, no less than 75,000 business entries in its database. The services of the agency were widely used by businesses of all sizes except microenterprises. Banks also had a formal information-sharing arrangement on bad credit risks. To our amazement, however, this sophisticated system did not yield the outcome we had anticipated.

Granted, it made it much easier for established businesses to deal with each other in an impersonal manner. Business networks remained important, albeit their role was more subtle—access to technology and market opportunities—than simply deterring breach of contract. But sharing information widely made it extremely difficult for starting firms to be accepted in the system. The reason was that unlike in Kenya and Ghana, established firms could afford to refuse dealing with an unknown client or supplier: information sharing ensured that a known firm would show up sooner or later. The end result was that unknown firms found it difficult, if not impossible, to establish a track record because they were never given an opportunity to prove themselves. Given that established businesses were in their overwhelming majority in the hands of entrepreneurs of European and Asian descent, the outcome was hardly equitable. Nor was it efficient because it de facto excluded from business the majority of the population. These observations were formalized in the models presented in chapters 11, 12, and 17.

Although we learned a lot from this sequence of events, it also made it clear that recommending policy in the absence of counterfactual evidence is dangerous. While our recommendations in Ghana and Kenya were not entirely misguided, judging from the experience of the other countries, they would not have yielded the outcomes we had predicted. To the extent that informal networks have a tendency to generate ethnically biased business communities, and to the extent that ethnic bias fuels political tension and depresses investment, it is not even clear that our recommendation for Ghana to favor informal networks would have yielded a superior outcome. While it would most likely have improved the operation of markets in the short run, it might have generated a situation that, in the long run, would have been more detrimental to the country.

Having made this clear, we nevertheless venture to propose a number of policy implications from the work presented here. These suggestions should be taken with a grain of salt. Hopefully they are better informed than alternative recommendations. But policy makers should be prepared to adjust their policies as they learn more about how these policies work in practice.

23.1   The Scope for Policy Intervention

We now turn our attention to potential remedies to inefficient market institutions. Markets are imperfect because of information asymmetries and enforcement problems. No policy action can remove the roots of market imperfection. If anything, the implementation of government policies suffers from information and enforcement problems of its own. What policy action can nevertheless do is to seek to mitigate some of the problems and redress the most glaring consequences of market imperfections. The macroeconomic environment must also be such that finance is available to manufacturing firms at the aggregate level, and that they have adequate incentives to invest and expand into socially desirable activities.

Incremental institutional change can help reduce enforcement problems and improve access to markets and credit. To identify what set of policy interventions may be appropriate, one has to specify the reasons why efficient institutional responses have not emerged in practice. To this task we turn first.

23.1.1   Why Institutions Do Not Emerge

The economic literature on institutions is basically split into two camps: the neo-classical institutional economists who believe that efficient institutions arise naturally to respond to any transaction cost or information asymmetry, and the others who believe that efficient institutions do not always arise spontaneously.

Neoclassical institutional economics point out that individuals are typically aware of where their best interest lies. As a result they are quick to exploit ways to improve their lot, whether in production and consumption activities or in contractual relations with others. Parties to a negotiated contract have a mutual interest in identifying the most efficient way of organizing their relationship. Even if, on their own, they may not be imaginative enough to find out what the optimal contract is, they promptly copy ideas concocted by the smartest among them. Firms and patterns of behavior that are inefficient are less profitable and quickly disappear as a result of economic competition. By this logic, economic systems and institutions are expected to quickly converge toward their evolutionary stable equilibrium.

Those who disagree with the neoclassical view give essentially three sets of reasons why institutions may fail to emerge that efficiently take care of transaction costs and information asymmetries: coordination failure, innovation failure, and authority failure. Coordination failure refers to the fact that in many cases an efficient institutional solution requires that economic agents coordinate their actions. Although coordination may arise naturally, in many cases it does not. Innovation failure treats institutions like technology: just like medieval man did not discover the nuclear bomb, he did not invent credit-rating systems. Institutional innovations invented in some places can be usefully transferred to others—such as, contract law, the credit card, and the credit reference agency. Of course, when attempting to introduce an institutional innovation elsewhere, one should be careful not to create havoc in whatever indigenous institutional setup is already in place.

Authority failure follows from the fact that decentralized self-enforcing mechanisms cannot rely on the coordinated use of force. Coercion requires the intervention of a central authority, typically the government. By putting the government's authority at the service of contracts, the government can achieve a level of contract enforcement that is out of the reach of informal mechanisms built upon the idea of reciprocity and repeated interaction (Benson 1990). Furthermore, unlike medieval states under which the law merchant blossomed (Milgrom et al. 1991), modern states oppose themselves to groups who build coercive forces to police the behavior of their members or to influence others. Private militias and vigilante groups are illegal in most countries, and groups that try to enforce their own separate law through violence (e.g., the Mafia) are a threat to the state (Gambetta 1993). Under these conditions groups of merchants and entrepreneurs typically find it impossible to separately organize the use of force to sanction contracts.

23.1.2   Coordination Failure, Innovation, and Coercion: Examples

Several examples of coordination failure have been given in previous chapters. When certain categories of firms do not qualify for supplier credit as a result of statistical discrimination, there is coordination failure. When firms fail to share information about bad payers even though they would all collectively benefit from doing so, there is coordination failure. When certain financial instruments are not provided because the market for them is too small to justify the required investment, and this results in an inferior business environment and depressed investment, there is coordination failure.

Innovation failure provides another possible explanation for the nonexistence of specialized markets and financial instruments. Before Milken thought of it, there was no market for junk bonds. Before someone thought of setting up the required financial infrastructure, there was no such thing as a stock exchange or a futures market. Before someone thought of credit reference, it did not exist. Before Black-Scholes, there was no market for derivatives. In all these cases new institutions emerged as the result of an innovation process, much like new technologies are invented over time. One should not assume, like the neoclassical school does, that institutions and contracts automatically and instantaneously emerge in response to relative price changes. There is scope for improving Africa's institutions by borrowing ideas from other countries and cultures.

The role of state imposed coercion in supporting contract enforcement is central to most of the writing of North and his followers. Better courts and tribunals are needed to protect property rights and enforce private contracts (e.g., Benson 1990; Milgrom et al. 1991; Cooter 1997; Messick 1999). Registration and titling increase the collaterizability of land and vehicles and help enforcing credit contracts. External auditing increases the verifiability of a firm's situation, thereby enlarging the range of enforceable contingent contracts including participation to a stock market. Reputation mechanisms are improved when disinformation is punished by the law. External verification and publication of critical events, like failing to pay a bill of exchange on time, favors the circulation of accurate information and encourages firms to pay promptly in order to preserve their reputation. In all these cases state intervention is able to achieve results that private parties cannot achieve on their own. The state, by putting its monopoly of the use of coercion to the service of private contracts, enables private parties to go beyond purely self-enforcing agreements and to expand the enforcement mechanisms they rely on.

How do these general principles apply to African market institutions? To this we now turn.

23.2   Policy Implications for Countries with Undeveloped Market Institutions

The level of market development in Ghana is representative of much of sub-Saharan Africa, with an embryonic manufacturing sector and a plethora of small firms. The example of SGS (Société Générale de Surveillance) and the letter of credit suggest that even in such an unappealing environment, appropriate institutions for the enforcement of international commercial contracts were able to expand the economic reach of Ghanaian firms. Other institutional innovations may be relevant for Ghana and similar countries. The recommendations we make are, of course, purely tentative.

Before we begin, three caveats must be kept in mind. First, even if contract enforcement institutions are dramatically reformed, firms in Ghana as elsewhere will continue to conduct most of their business on the basis of interpersonal relations and trust (e.g., Williamson 1985; Stone et al. 1992). The objective of policy intervention should not be to undermine existing institutions but to add new options to existing ones. Second, contractual flexibility is necessary and will continue to be. New institutions should not aim at the rigid enforcement of all contracts, thereby closing the door to risk sharing and excusable default. Third, collecting payment from insolvent firms and individuals is always problematic, regardless of contract enforcement institutions. Since many Africans are poor and many firms are small and undercapitalized, insolvency is likely to continue creating payment problems. No new institution can—or should try to—eliminate noncompliance altogether.

In our view, the focus of policy intervention for countries at low levels of market development such as Ghana should be to enable firms to conduct at least a portion of their business with other reliable firms and individuals with whom they have no or little prior acquaintance. By extending the economic reach of firms, policy intervention should improve economic efficiency and foster the development of a dynamic business community. Success in this endeavor requires that opportunistic behavior be discouraged in contractual matters, either by attaching a higher penalty to opportunistic breach of contract or by helping firms assess the reliability of potential clients and suppliers.

The fact that a couple of respondents to the Ghana case study are ready to extend credit on the sole basis of a bank credit report suggests that establishing a system of credit rating for Ghanaian enterprises could open access to trade credit for reliable firms.[1] Disseminating information about credit repayment performance should assist firms in screening out unreliable business partners and enable good payers to access credit by differentiating themselves from bad payers. Once credit rating is commonly used, trustworthy firms would probably find it in their interest to signal their reliability by establishing an excellent track record. Firms with a good record would therefore be good credit risks not only because they have demonstrated their ability to comply with strict payment schedules but also because they want to preserve their reputation.[2] Credit rating could similarly be used by banks and financial institutions to assess the credit worthiness of their clients. Thanks to credit rating, firms that cannot offer sufficient real security as collateral may still qualify for bank credit through the discounting of bills and postdated checks.

The court system in Ghana, although not particularly expensive nor inefficient by African standards, remains too costly for most commercial cases. The value of com-

1. Stone et al. (1992) come to a similar conclusion regarding Brazil and Chile.

2. Kreps et al. (1982) apply the same principle to a very different situation, that of a chainstore facing potential entrants.

mercial transactions rarely justifies the cost and time involved in a legal suit in front of Ghana's regular court system. Setting up small claims courts tailored, for instance, on the American example may reduce the cost of legal proceedings and help bring the court system closer to small Ghanaian businesses. An alternative and perhaps complementary option would be to favor private arbitration, particularly for small cases. One could also envisage specialized commercial courts with simplified judicial and asset recovery procedures.

When faced with the breakdown of a relationship, a few firms in the sample sought help by bribing members of the police or paramilitary groups. The police, however, has no authority to seize property. All it can do is to threaten to detain or, perhaps, mistreat bad payers. Alternative options should be made available that put state coercion at the service of expeditious debt recovery without infringing on the debtor's human rights. A more liberal use by judges of the impounding of accounts and movable assets at the outset of court proceedings, for instance, would discourage delaying tactics by recalcitrant debtors. Ghanaian judges' concern for a certain conception of fairness seems to currently stand in the way, but this issue deserves more investigation. The same idea could be taken one step further by instituting a rapid, nonadversarial procedure to assist commercial creditors. A special judge or legal officer could be instituted whose duty would be to impound assets and accounts to serve clearly identifiable commercial debt instruments, such as postdated checks, bills of exchange, and signed invoices. The ultimate objective of these measures, however, should neither be the replacement of face-to-face negotiations nor the reduction of contractual flexibility, but rather deterrence of opportunistic behavior and the prevention of unnecessary delays. Since all these measures ultimately remain at the discretion of the creditor and since it is not in the interest of a creditor to jeopardize a valuable relationship, they are unlikely to be used in cases of excusable default. We therefore expect most contractual disputes to continue being handled through direct negotiations.

The system of international payments generally works well but it could be improved in a important areas. Without third-party inspection of their exports, Ghanaian exporters face the risk of foreign firms disputing shipment on arrival, thereby delaying payment and forcing them into granting discounts. To reduce this problem, third-party inspection could be extended to Ghanaian exports.[3] Another area of possible improvement concerns trade between Ghana and its neighbors. Discussions with respondents suggest that it is much safer for a Ghanaian firm to trade

---

3. Ghanaian firms may, however, object to SGS inspection on exports because it reduces opportunities for underinvoicing.

with Europe than with a neighboring African country. Effort by the Ghanaian government and the international community to ease inter-African border procedures, reduce rent seeking, and assist the enforcement of regional import and export contracts could only boost trade between African neighbors. Increased trade in turn should help manufacturing firms gain access to a larger market and capture returns to scale.

23.3 Policy Implications for Countries with Intermediate Market Institutions

Kenya is an example of an African country with intermediate market institutions. Strong business networks exist and operate well. But they are too limited and only partially overlap. Policies to address these problems fall under two broad categories: those that seek to remove barriers to trade directly, and those that seek to redress unwanted consequences of barriers to trade. We first consider ways of shifting credit boundaries through policy action and projects. Through various types of institutional reform and legal improvements, policy can help reduce coordination failure, promote institutional innovation, and put state coercion at the service of private contracts.

23.3.1 Coordination Failure

Perhaps the best example of coordination failure uncovered in Kenya during empirical work is the absence of a credit reference bureau. Information about bad payers is not shared among firms. As a result firms are less able to identify bad payers from good payers and less inclined to give supplier credit and accept payment by check. The absence of an information-sharing mechanism makes it particularly difficult for new firms to secure supplies at normal conditions. Indeed, they must establish a credit repayment history with each potential source of supply individually. Established firms also find it difficult to shift their activities in response to changes in relative prices because, in the absence of information sharing, dealing with new suppliers requires establishing a new credit history with them directly.

Subsets of the Kenyan-Asian business community have managed to overcome these limitations by establishing reputation mechanisms among themselves. Information about business behavior and debt repayment is exchanged between businessmen. One should be careful, however, not to assume that all of Kenya's 80,000 strong Asian population shares business information. Reputation remains largely confined within small business communities—"the Patels, the Shahs, the Sikhs, and the Ismaelians," as one respondent to the case study survey put it. These communities distrust each other about as much as they distrust non-Asians. There is therefore considerable scope for improving the circulation of information even among Kenyan-Asian businesses.

To our surprise information sharing does not appear to take place among the Kenyan-African business community, along ethnic lines or otherwise. We may have missed it because the four sectors of economic activity on which we focused happen to be dominated by Kenyan-Asians. At any rate, Kenyan-African firms in these four sectors at least are at a clear disadvantage in terms of access to supplier credit because information about their credit repayment history does not currently cross ethnic boundaries. Because good Kenyan-African businesses cannot rapidly and costlessly differentiate themselves from bad ones, they are statistically discriminated against in terms of access to credit. There is a coordination failure in information dissemination.

At the time of the survey, a private firm was attempting to overcome this coordination failure by pooling business credit histories from various sources onto a computer data bank, and making the information available to its customers in convenient form. The firm was experiencing serious difficulties as Kenyan businesses reluctantly relinquish information that can help their competitors without knowing if they will receive similar information from them (the Ghana lumber market syndrome). Banks, in particular, are unwilling to share information about bounced checks and bills of exchange.

The same is true for credit card companies and hire-purchase firms. All have their own credit history data bank that they will not give away without assurances that others will do the same. Indeed, in a world of imperfect information, credit histories constitute an important asset on which credit suppliers of all kinds base their business. Unless all agree to share information, no one will, at least until the credit reference data bank is large enough that the participation of a single major player would not give a competitive edge to its competitors. There is therefore a role for policy to help coordinate action and favor the establishment of a critical mass of credit information. This could perhaps be achieved if the efforts of a small enterprise promotion project to establish a database on the credit history of its own customers is coordinated with private efforts to establish a credit reference service in Kenya.

23.3.2 Institutional Innovations

Just as one does not expect African firms to know how to make computer chips simply because they are manufactured elsewhere, one should not assume that institutional innovations introduced elsewhere are instantaneously transferred to Africa. The establishment of computerized credit reference services is one example of an institutional innovation that is not immediately transferable because of coordination problems. There are many examples of policy interventions whose success, hypothetical or real, rests on institutional innovation. We focus on a few.

A number of development projects distribute credit to small businesses. In Kenya at the time of the survey, the Kenya Industrial Estates was such a project. A computerized credit history for firms that have received credit from project lenders to micro and small enterprises could be developed. Regardless of whether that information is shared with other lenders, as has been suggested, computerization is an innovation that enables a lender to keep track of thousands of credit histories and therefore to use more effectively the information at its disposal. By enabling small firms to establish a credit repayment history, computerization helps good payers get access to more credit (Onyango and Tomecko 1995).

Group lending is a relatively recent addition to the panoply of credit instruments promoted in Africa and elsewhere in the Third World. Its success as an effective way of channeling credit to firms that otherwise would not get it relies on the ability of the group to help enforce repayment by one of its members. Group lending is thus an contract enforcement innovation. Viewed in this light, group lending is most effective if it generates incentives on the group to put pressure on delinquent members, if group members have some leverage on other members, and if it is not in the interest of the group to defect collectively (e.g., Ghatak and Guinnane 1999; Morduch 1999; Ghatak 2000; Laffont and N'Guessan 2000; Armendariz de Aghion and Morduch 2000).

From the conversations we had with various organizations (banks, NGOs, and projects) involved in group lending, it appears that the most successful programs are those that stagger credit to members over time. As a result those members who are becoming eligible for credit have an incentive to put pressure on delinquent members, and the group as a whole finds it difficult to collude to default. The ability of group members to put pressure on others, however, is problematic, especially in groups that were formed exclusively to receive credit. The cost of keeping the group together is high. This is hardly surprising given that in order to provide incentives for repayment, one has to create antagonistic relations between group members. The disbursement of large amounts of money through group lending therefore requires large investments in group formation and maintenance. For this reason group lending is costly if attempted on a large scale. It may not even be possible as many potential recipients of credit refuse to join groups and to get embroiled in other people's affairs and problems.

Credit guarantee is another recent institutional innovation in Africa. The idea is for an outside party (donor or government agency) to partially guarantee a supplier of credit against default. A special fund is usually created whose purpose is to compensate a creditor who faces default. The success of such programs depends on whether lenders prefer to collect the insurance premium without spending much effort collecting from their delinquent clients, or prefer to bear the full cost of screening, monitoring, and recovery. If the cost of recovery is higher than the risk borne by the lender, no effort to recover will take place, and the guarantee fund will be rapidly depleted. Credit guarantee does nothing to increase debtors' willingness to repay. It only reduces the lender's risk in trying out new borrowers. It constitutes a possible avenue out of statistical discrimination by providing good borrowers an opportunity to prove themselves that is denied when the lender has to assume all the risk.

Hire-purchase can be considered an institutional innovation as well. According to our observations, hire-purchase is a rapidly growing form of credit in Africa, especially for vehicles, and to some extent for consumer durables. Hopefully it will expand to include equipment and machinery as well. What is innovative about hire-purchase is that it relies on the collaterizability of movable assets. Because the lender remains owner of the good until full payment, the good can be repossessed from the delinquent debtor without having to resort to court action. A new avenue for credit is thus created through the establishment of an alternative enforcement procedure.

A similar idea is behind the resuscitation of chattel mortgages. The idea behind the chattel mortgage is similar to that behind hire-purchase, namely to make a piece of movable property directly responsible for servicing a debt. The difference with hire-purchase is that in a chattel mortgage the lender is not the owner of the property. Repossession of a chattel in case of loan delinquency involves simplified procedures that are less costly than for unsecured loans. Chattel mortgages have enabled many micro and small firms to receive credit from Kenya Industrial Estates using their equipment as collateral (Onyango and Tomecko 1995).

The collateral value of equipment and machinery currently suffers from thin, unorganized markets for used capital. The absence of registration for items other than vehicles also introduces an element of uncertainty in equipment transactions. A dishonest debtor may be tempted to evade contractual obligations by liquidating the firm's equipment. If buyers cannot easily verify if a piece of property is free of lien, the market for secondhand equipment may suffer. The solution is to set up a registry of industrial machinery and equipment and to develop a market for auctioned equipment. These actions would increase the collateral value of equipment and improve access to credit for small and medium manufacturing firms in Kenya.

23.3.3   State Coercion at the Service of Private Contracts

The key feature that differentiates the state from private agents is its monopoly on the use of public force. The state can help decrease barriers to credit by putting public force at the service of contract enforcement. To do so effectively, public force must be harnessed at reasonable cost to private agents. Currently the use of courts and tribunals in many African countries is too costly for most commercial contractual disputes. The attractiveness of hire-purchase and chattel mortgage is precisely that they bypass the need for full-fledged court proceedings. The usefulness of African courts could be increased by setting up small claims courts in which lawyers are not admitted. Specialized courts for business disputes could also be envisaged.

The state can also help contract enforcement by assisting informal mechanisms. The sharing of information on credit repayment, for instance, is an essential ingredient of any reputation mechanism. The state can favor the circulation of information by assisting the establishment of private or public credit reference services. The state should encourage collaboration, in whatever form, between private credit reference companies, lending organizations, the Kenyan Firm Registration Office, private and public banks, credit card agencies, and hire-purchase companies. By pooling their information together, the coordination failure can be overcome. The official registration of chattel mortgages and hire-purchase contracts on equipment and machinery could also be envisaged. This would be far cheaper than registering all equipment and machinery. Finally, the government could help set up an auction market for used equipment through which all repossessed items could be liquidated.

23.3.4   Directed Credit

Although highly desirable, policies striving to eliminate barriers to credit are unlikely to be fully successful. Directed credit may remain necessary. The difficulty, however, is that any credit program, directed or not, is bound to run out of funds if sufficient care is not given to contract enforcement issues. Many targeted credit programs turn out to operate as welfare transfers: when loans become due, default rates rise, and funds are no longer replenished. As a result many directed credit programs are short-lived. Moreover they constitute an ineffective form of welfare transfer since they fail to reach the neediest. Because these programs often hesitate to seek loan repayment from their target population, they favor the emergence of dishonesty and cynicism among those who would most benefit from establishing their credit worthiness.

Directed credit must therefore rely on innovative contract enforcement mechanisms, whether they be group lending, credit guarantee schemes, hire-purchase, computerization of credit histories, or chattel mortgages. Credit programs that entertain a naive attitude toward credit repayment should be discouraged. Political interventions to protect delinquent debtors beyond reason should be avoided.

23.4   Policy Implications for Countries with Developed Market Institutions

We have seen that market institutions in Zimbabwe are sophisticated by African standards. There nevertheless remain a number of problems in financing investment and cash-flow management. The emphasis is thus on finance. There are also many areas in which improvements can be made, in particular, regarding the ethnic selection of entrepreneurs through the workings of the market institutions. In this section we draw a series of policy implications for countries at the level of sophistication of Zimbabwe. The first subsection is devoted to institutional solutions for small, medium, and large firms. The second subsection examines in detail the predicament of microenterprises and African-headed firms.

23.4.1   Institutional Policy for Small, Medium, and Large Firms

In the previous chapter it was argued that firms in different categories face different kinds of difficulties accessing markets. The situation of microenterprises and African-headed firms, in particular, was sharply contrasted with that of other small, medium, and large firms. There also were significant differences within the latter category. Even though more fortunate than microenterprises from an enterprise finance point of view, small manufacturing firms were shown to have less access to certain types of financial services and markets than large firms. Large corporations themselves were not exempt of problems, particularly regarding the limited sophistication of available financial instruments. Finally, expanding firms were often limited in the pace and size of their investments by financial considerations. Although there is considerable overlap among these various issues, we address the needs of each of these categories in turn. We begin with small- and medium-size firms, continue with large corporations, and finish with rapidly expanding and contracting firms. The plight of microenterprises and African-headed firms is reviewed in the next section.

Institutions for Small- and Medium-Size Firms

Small- and medium-size firms raise most of their finances in the form of overdraft facility, trade credit, and, to less extent, hire-purchase. How can the finances of these firms be improved? For a number of firms, access to bank overdrafts can be facilitated by enlarging the stock of titled urban property. This seems to be true, in particular, in Harare townships, secondary towns, and so-called growth points. One of the main bottlenecks appears to be the small number of qualified surveyors available and the resulting high cost of securing a title. These difficulties should be amenable provided that new surveyors are trained and facilities expanded. One may also wish to examine whether the use of satellite imaging could reduce the costs of land surveying.

Another often used form of contractual security, notarial bonds, could also be improved. Zimbabwe and South Africa follow Dutch Roman Law and thus do not allow liens and other contractual obligations to follow movables into the hands of a new owner. This tends to weaken the security value of a notarial bond. Short of revising one of the major tenets of Dutch Roman Law, however, this weakness cannot be accommodated within the existing system. What can nevertheless be done is to enforce the seniority of notarial bonds, that is, to prevent a debtor from pledging his movables to several creditors. A way to achieve this is to institute the registration of notarial bonds. With this system a debtor would find it harder to issue a second notarial bond against the will of the first creditor. It may seem paradoxical to restrict debtors' freedom of movement to improve their financial situation. But the reason why access to finance may be restricted is precisely that in the current system, creditors cannot prevent opportunistic behavior by some. Because lenders are unable to discriminate between honest and opportunistic borrowers, the security value of the notarial bond fails to achieve its potential. As a result good borrowers are penalized even though they do not feel the need or inclination to pledge the same collateral twice. The registration of notarial bond should enable good borrowers to distinguish themselves from potentially opportunistic borrowers and thus enhance efficiency in the delivery of credit.

Hire-purchase is important in Zimbabwe and could become more important in other African countries as well. The success of hire-purchase derives from the fact that the good being financed is its own collateral. The legal form the security takes is a simple one: the lender is or becomes the owner of the good. As such, the lender can repossess the good from the borrower or from anyone who may have fraudulently purchased it from the borrower. The security value of hire-purchase is highest when two conditions are satisfied: the ownership of the good used as security is officially registered, and the good can easily be liquidated by the lender with little loss of value. Registration makes it difficult for the borrower to dispose of the item without falsifying ownership documents and thus incurring criminal penalties. This explains why hire-purchase is most popular for the movable item par excellence, motor vehicles. Ease of liquidation depends on the existence of a strong secondary market for used equipment. In Zimbabwe this is achieved through well-attended public auctions. Specialized equipment and large pieces of machinery are not good candidates for hire-purchase because the secondary market is too thin and their resale value is highly uncertain. Hire-purchase works best for small standardized equipment and machinery—cars, trucks, farm equipment, simple textile looms, industrial sewing machines, and so on.

Hire-purchase is also a popular way of financing consumer durables. In view of protecting Zimbabwean consumers against their own lack of foresight, the government has instituted certain restrictions on hire-purchase contracts. In particular, the duration of the contract must be three years and the down payment must be 40 percent of the value of the sale. These restrictions, although sensible for consumer durables, often are too constraining for productive equipment. Certain financial institutions have sought to circumvent these restrictions by using sui generis lease agreements. The widespread use of such contracts is currently held back by taxation issues. We recommend that these taxation issues be resolved so that more flexible lease agreements can be used.

The third main type of credit small and medium firms have access to is trade credit. This form of credit, however, is largely decoupled from financial credit and the collateral value of receivables is little used. Trade bills have fallen in disfavor, partly, we were told, because of past abuses. Furthermore bill discounting facilities offered by banks typically deduct discounted bills from the client's overdraft ceiling. Consequently the discounting of trade bills does not serve as an independent route to external finance. Postdated checks, which elsewhere constitute the basis of an active curb market (Biggs 1991), are not commonly used in Zimbabwe. Debtors in arrears typically offer postdated checks to their creditors as a sign of good faith when asking for further delay, and as a form of commitment that they will pay by the due date. Indeed, a bounced check constitutes a convenient legal basis to secure an expeditious judgment. The only form of financial arrangement in which receivables are used as stand-alone security is factoring. What distinguishes factoring from bill discounting is that all the receivables of the firm are discounted, independent of the firm's need for funds, for a set period of time, typically three to four years. The borrower also loses the ability to pick and choose which debtor to discount. Factoring is not widespread, but it was used by several of the firms we spoke to. All said that it improved their ability to manage their cash flow and that the backing of the factor had significantly reduced payment delays by their customers. Factoring is particularly appealing for small and medium firms, which have little bargaining power to enforce prompt repayment by large monopsonistic customers. One can only surmise, however, that the burden of late payment is then passed onto firms that do not use factors. There do not seem to be institutional impediments to the use of factoring in Zimbabwe. The practice could be encouraged, however.

Orders are occasionally used to raise external finance, particularly when they are large and come from well known, established buyers. Tenders from the Central Purchasing Agency can also be used as security. Orders, however, constitute an imperfect form of collateral because the recipient of the order may be unable or unwilling to complete it. If the order is not completed to the satisfaction of the buyer, the borrower will not be paid, and the lender will not recover his or her money. Lenders are therefore reluctant to finance firms solely on the basis of an external order. They usually require other forms of security and assess the borrower's ability to complete a large order on time and to the satisfaction of the buyer. The most widespread use of orders as security is in pre-shipment export financing. In Zimbabwe this form of finance can, for the most part, only be accessed through merchant banks. Since merchant banks cater only to the needs of large corporate clients, this means that small- and medium-size firms typically have no access to pre-shipment financing. Filling this lacuna is essential before small- and medium-size firms can actively take advantage of new export opportunities opened by structural adjustment.

Other forms of government interventions are also required in foreign trade finance. Since the Reserve Bank of Zimbabwe discontinued its foreign exchange guarantee scheme, exporters who wish to import raw materials and equipment on offshore credit currently must pay extremely high premia to insure themselves against foreign exchange risk. While large firms and firms that are already exporting may be able to withstand such risk, this is not typically the case for small and medium candidate exporters. The establishment of a foreign exchange guarantee fund for businesses willing to expand into manufacturing and other nontraditional exports could only enhance small and medium firms' desire to take on exporting. Postshipment finance could also be made more readily available, particularly if it is coupled with export credit insurance. Finally, the Zimbabwean government and financial institutions may investigate the possibility and desirability of making offshore finance available in Rand. In the long run the economies of Zimbabwe and South Africa are destined to become more integrated. Yet exporters to South Africa can currently secure offshore financing only in hard currencies, although their exports receipts will be in Rand. This forces them to shoulder a significant currency risk. One of our respondents, for instance, was put into a difficult predicament as a result of the depreciation of the South African currency.

Institutions for Large Corporations
The difficulties large corporations face in accessing external finance are different in nature from those faced by small- and medium-size firms. The existence of an active stock market in Zimbabwe makes it possible to envisage extending the existing sys-

tem in several directions. These extensions will undoubtedly require that the physical infrastructure on which the stock exchange currently rests be upgraded and modernized and that the number of authorized traders be expanded. The first step is to float some interesting shares on the market as to increase the stock of securities available for trade. Some people we spoke to, for instance, suggested that the government put some of its shares in Delta onto the market. These are, no doubt, sensitive political issues with which we do not wish to interfere, but what is clear is that more interesting stuff on the stock market would raise the level of activity and make participation to the stock market easier to corporations wishing to expand.

The time may also have come to consider creating new financial instruments. Derivatives were on the lips of many of the people we spoke to. The idea is that by adding to a standard debt contract the option to participate in the debtor's future benefits, one may increase the profitability of lending and thus make more credit available. We do not have any strong disagreement with this view, but derivatives may prove to be too delicate to leave the rarefied confines of high Zimbabwean finance. To open the market for long-term credit, there may be a simpler, more promising instrument: the corporate bond. There is currently no secondary market for long-term private credit in Zimbabwe. Financial institutions who lend to corporations cannot, as they do with government bonds, resell their claims to other investors. As a result pension funds and insurance companies end up putting their money into government securities and, more recently, into the stock market; none of it goes to finance medium-term credit to the corporate sector. Yet creating a market for corporate bonds should not, given the level of financial sophistication achieved by Zimbabwe, present major difficulties. Merchant banks, which already operate as underwriters for many stock market flotations and as intermediaries for institutional investors in the case of long-term mortgages, could easily take on the additional function of underwriting and circulating corporate bonds. This would enable institutional investors to diversify their portfolio into medium-term instruments. These instruments, unlike mortgages but like government bonds, would be liquid and could be traded in a secondary market, a feature that should greatly increase their attractiveness.

Another institutional innovation for which the time may have come is the mutual fund. To our knowledge, there is currently no mutual fund in which private Zimbabweans can invest their savings. This lacuna increases the risk and effort investors must incur in order to participate in the stock market. As a result investing in the stock market probably remains confined to a small number of private individuals. Mutual funds seriously reduce the risk of stock market operations through portfolio diversification. They also lower transaction costs as many investors delegate the management of their finances is to a single specialist. Mutual funds would of course not limit themselves to securities quoted on the stock market. They could include money market funds, corporate bonds funds, government and AMA bonds funds, and combinations of the above. Before mutual funds can become a reality, however, a Mutual Funds Act is needed that sets up some guidelines as to the operations and capitalization of such funds, and protect private investors against abuse.

Institutions for Start-ups and Rapidly Expanding Firms

The institutional innovations suggested above should help all firms gain better access to external finance. They may, however, be insufficient for start-ups and rapidly expanding firms. As should be clear from the analysis presented in chapters 3 to 6, start-up firms have the hardest time getting access to external finance. This is why so many firms begin on the sole financial resources of the initial investor, and why therefore in a country like Zimbabwe where many people have little personal wealth, so many firms also are microenterprises. It would be naive to advocate the free distribution of credit to whoever wishes to establish a new enterprise. The potential for abuse would indeed be enormous and few loans would probably be repaid. What then are the alternatives? We discuss several of them in the next section devoted to microenterprises. Here we wish to address two of them that are suitable for larger firms, namely venture capital and project loans.

Venture capital is a reality in Zimbabwe. As mentioned at the outset of chapter 4, we made an effort to meet with some of the entrepreneurs who got started thanks to venture capital. Their experiences were all positive in the sense that venture capital allowed them to survive initial miscalculations and mishaps and to grow to become viable small- and medium-size enterprises. The price to pay, however, is fairly high in terms of loss of independence and pride. Venture capital works because the venture capitalists is intimately involved in the everyday conduct of the business. Close-range monitoring is what substitutes for collateral and social capital. Firms that receive venture capital are kept on a short financial leash, but they also receive fatherly advice and support in bad times. The venture capitalist is also involved in directing the course of the firm toward profitable activities, for instance, by intimating that the firm abandon a project or take on another. Because monitoring is time-consuming, there is a limit to the number of firms a single venture capitalist can optimally oversee. There is thus plenty of room in Zimbabwe for other venture capital firms to step in. In due course venture capitalists may be able to raise funds from institutional investors and thus serve as intermediaries to channel external finance toward start-ups. The success of venture capital in Zimbabwe ultimately lies in the rapid growth of some sectors of manufacturing and services, and in turn on Zimbabwe's ability to export manufactured goods and other nontraditional products. In other words, if a few people get rich overnight through venture capital, more venture capital will be forthcoming.

Project lending is another area for possible expansion. We saw in chapter 3 that commercial banks do not see it as their business to help their clients expand. Merchant banks are more pro-active in helping their customers secure project financing, but they only cater to large corporations. Moreover they are reluctant to tie up their own money in long-term lending and typically act as intermediary for other long-term investors. Although there are a number of development banks operating in Zimbabwe, they seem to be difficult to reach and appear to have had a minimal impact. One respondent even got into serious financial difficulties as a result of a development bank's delays in disbursing funds. Although an in-depth analysis of development banking in Zimbabwe is beyond the scope of this book, we can safely say that should many new investment opportunities arise in manufacturing, Zimbabwe would be ill prepared to respond to the demand for project financing.

Institutions for Contracting Firms
Just as some firms expand, others contract. What happens when a firm must abruptly reduce its activities affects lenders' expectations regarding debt recovery, and thus their willingness to lend. Following ESAP and the 1992 drought, Zimbabwe has an unprecedented series of failures among major companies. Banks have responded by taking a closer interest in the running of distressed companies. Because bankers are not in the business of managing large corporations, however, they seldom feel qualified to do so well. As a result some voices have asked for a formal receivership status akin to chapter 11 in the United States. This would allow judges to nominate an external manager with the power to reorganize the company and change the management. There was no consensus on this issue among the people we spoke to and we had no time to investigate it in detail. But it is possible that a modification to bankruptcy law could help firms, especially medium and large companies, to access external finance. This issue deserves more investigation.

23.4.2 Microenterprises and African-Headed Firms

In the preceding section we examined what institutional innovations can facilitate the flow of external finance to small, medium, and large manufacturing firms. Our recommendations were all directed at helping the existing system work better by removing impediments erected by information asymmetries and enforcement problems. These recommendations, if implemented, would nevertheless be largely ineffective in assisting microenterprises. Moreover they fail to address the specific difficulties African-headed firms face in Zimbabwe today. In this section we propose a series of measures tailored especially for these two groups of firms.

Institutions for Microenterprises

Information asymmetries, enforcement problems, and transaction costs combine to make extremely difficult the delivery of credit to microenterprises whenever one is serious about debt recovery. We do not believe that doling out funds to micro-enterprises without concern for recovery is justifiable for reason of either equity, as only a few fortunate microenterprise benefit, or efficiency, as it fosters the wrong kind of mentality and attitude toward business. Poverty alleviation is better served by welfare programs and the delivery of social infrastructures than by lax credit to a handful of microenterprises. What then should be the objective of a credit program to microenterprises? One possibility is to foster the extension of the microenterprise sector by the multiplication of the number of microenterprises. Achieving this objec-tive requires helping individuals set up their own microenterprises. Although laud-able, such effort can only be undertaken at the grassroots and is bound to be onerous per unit of credit disbursed. Another possibility is to help existing microenterprises grow and graduate into the pool of small- and medium-size firms that we discussed in the preceding section. Both objectives, although often confused in practice, are quite different as to their assumptions regarding the ultimate usefulness of microenterprises (see Fafchamps 1994 for a discussion). The first approach sees nothing wrong with assisting the proliferation of extremely small production units. The second assumes that production by microenterprises is suboptimal, but that for a variety of reasons, one of which being lack of funds, microenterprises are prevented from reaping returns to scale and reaching their full potential. The first approach makes sense in sectors where returns to scale in production, organization, and marketing are entirely absent, as may be the case in vegetable farming or micro-retail, for instance. The second is more appropriate when returns to even a minimal scale are present, as is typically in manufacturing. Since this report is concerned with manufacturing firms, we focus on the second approach.

To be successful, the second approach must identify promising microentrepreneurs and help them graduate into the regular pool of small-scale businesses. In Zimbabwe the financial institution that has most effectively followed this line is SEDCO (see chapter 3). Because its ultimate objective is to graduate firms, SEDCO puts a lot of emphasis on screening and monitoring. It is not easy to get SEDCO funding. One has to demonstrate commitment and endurance. But these are precisely the qualities one expects from a successful business person. We therefore recommend that as long as SEDCO's objective is to identify promising entrepreneurs, it should not lower its standards. More funds, however, could be piped through SEDCO. The queue of loan applicants is way beyond what SEDCO can accommodate on the basis of its limited capital. As a result credit rationing is extreme, and the level of endurance that is requested from loan applicants is probably so high that it eliminates a good number of perfectly good candidates. We feel that government special lines of credit would be better disbursed through programs like SEDCO than via highly subsidized loans, like the 5 percent interest CGC loans that were being allocated while we were in Zimbabwe.

In line with its objective of helping selected microenterprises grow, SEDCO puts a lot of emphasis on training. In our interviews, we developed the feeling that, among microenterprises, a dominant mental attitude is to try to "beat the system." Entrepreneurs with such a mind-set cannot survive long among small- to medium-size firms that share a much different business ethic of mutual trust and reliability. We thus feel that part of the SEDCO training should be to make entrepreneurs aware of the importance of establishing a good track record for their long-run success. Entrepreneurs should be introduced to the mysteries of credit reference and told that business reliability is essential. They should also be told what payment delays are typically considered acceptable and what delays are not. They should be made aware that business registration and operating a checking account are ways by which they can upgrade their credit standing. They should be encouraged to seek title on their property so that they can get a band overdraft facility. In other words, they should be told the rules of enterprise finance that prevail among small and medium Zimbabwean enterprises.

There are other forms of institutional innovations that could help promising microenterprises grow. One is to follow UDC's model but for smaller enterprises, that is, to facilitate the hire purchase of secondhand equipment for microenterprises and small firms. In practice, this means setting up or expanding the existing market for secondhand equipment to encompass smaller and older pieces of equipment. It may also require more flexibility in contractual terms than currently possible under the Hire-Purchase Act. As the market develop, the collateral value of the equipment should increase and the lender's risk decrease. Through the regular repayment of hire-purchase agreements, microentrepreneurs could also accumulate a track record that helps them qualify for other sources of credit later on.

We mentioned titling in section 23.1. It appears that some microentrepreneurs have real property, in Harare townships, for instance, that can serve as security for a bank overdraft. But they often do not have sufficient funds to cover the costs of securing a formal title. The government may wish to consider simplifying procedures for the acquisition of title in residential areas where the bulk of microentrepreneurs live. One cannot overemphasize the importance of securing a bank overdraft as a first step into establishing one's reputation as a bona fide business.

Regarding the first objective listed at the start of this section, namely the promotion of the microenterprise sector as a whole, a number of potential institutional innovations have received increased attention in the recent past. Two categories are particularly promising: group loans relying on peer monitoring, and the use of rotating savings and credit associations or savings collectors to channel credit to microenterprises. In part because sample design eliminated the smallest of firms, we collected no evidence on either of these credit delivery systems during the case study survey. We thus have little to contribute to the debate regarding their possible effectiveness. Some of the people we spoke to, however, expressed concern that group loans are costly to administer because group cohesion is hard to sustain when some borrowers fall into arrears. For that reason channeling funds through savings associations or collectors is probably more cost effective. As far as we can judge from the limited evidence we collected, savings associations seem unimportant in Zimbabwe. There also appears to be no statute for savings and loans associations. Small depositors often put their savings in building societies or the post office, but these institutions do not make small loans to individuals.

The Zimbabwean government may want to consider encouraging the emergence of financial institutions that channel at least part of the savings of small depositors back to them in the form of consumption and small investment loans. There are several ways of achieving this. The Kenyan system of SACCOs (Savings Associations and Credit Cooperatives) is one possibility. In this system, small depositors can withdraw up to three or four times their savings provided that two other depositors give their guarantees. Others have also suggested that a flexible legal status for rotating savings and credit associations (ROSCAs) and savings collectors be defined so that they can be used to channel and deliver credit to small investors (Aryeetey and Steel 1993).

Institutions for African-Headed Firms

We have seen that African-headed firms experience problems in accessing external finance that cannot solely be attributed to their smaller size and young firm age. These difficulties are due to two partly overlapping factors: network effects and statistical discrimination. Network effects tend to penalize African-headed firms because blacks are largely outside the old-boy network, that is, the web of social interactions that link wealthy whites and Asians with the corporate and financial world. As several respondents emphasized, a "new-boy network" linking black businessmen and people of influence is gradually being formed, but it has not reached the clout that the old-boy network still commands. Until the time that the new-boy network becomes as powerful as the old-boy network, black businessmen and women will be at a disadvantage. Statistical discrimination is a distinct phenomenon, one that has little to do with contacts and a lot to do with relying on visible characteristics to infer someone's type. Statistical discrimination in financial and trade credit plays against blacks because they belong to a group of entrepreneurs that, on average, is smaller and thus more fragile financially. As a result rational lenders are more reticent to grant credit to black entrepreneurs than to whites or Asians. In addition to all the difficulties inherent to any credit contract, promising black entrepreneurs must thus also differentiate themselves from the mass of microenterprises headed by blacks. Statistical discrimination tends to perpetuate itself because it breeds prejudice and, by hindering certain firms' access credit, makes it harder for them to handle liquidity shocks and thus de facto turns them into less reliable debtors.

It is not easy to devise forms of policy intervention that correct these inequalities. Yet, without intervention, they may persist for an unacceptable length of time. The first form of intervention consists in fostering and strengthening the new-boy network. Many respondents hinted that this is indeed taking place through political connections. We were told, for instance, that certain sectors of activity, like public transports in Harare, were earmarked to particular political interests. There is no doubt that a black bourgeoisie has rapidly emerged since independence and that its wealth has initially been acquired, as elsewhere in Africa, thanks to political contacts. Members of this bourgeoisie are now moving into business at large and manufacturing in particular. With time one therefore should witness an Africanization of business in Zimbabwe. Such development may, however, fail to benefit the mass of black entrepreneurs who, for the most part, are not politically connected. Furthermore it is not known whether newcomers will continue to be co-opted in the new-boy network, or whether, once a certain size achieved, the club will close its ranks.

To help the mass of black entrepreneurs, one must then fight statistical discrimination. Given Zimbabwe's history, it is unlikely that the problem can be eliminated without some form of affirmative action. The Zimbabwe government has experimented with targeting certain lines of credit to blacks—"indigenous entrepreneurs" as the politically correct jargon of the moment calls them. According to certain people we spoke to, there has been considerable resistance to such practices by the established business community: "we are all indigenous entrepreneurs" has been the war cry of many of its members. It is, of course, beyond the scope of this report to comment on these highly sensitive political issues. What we can do, however, is to comment on the conditions for the success of a targeted credit program. As Coate and Loury (1993) emphasized, affirmative action can backlash whenever it results in a patronizing equilibrium in which the target population is assisted but prejudice remains. Applied to enterprise credit, this principle suggests that targeted credit programs should avoid generating an "assisted" mentality. Rather, they should strive to help black enterprises to join the ranks of existing firms and be able to compete with them on the same terms. As far as we can judge, the 5 percent CGC loans are precisely an example of counterproductive targeting because they convey the idea that blacks deserve special conditions. In addition, because the loans have a heavily subsidized interest rate, their allocation suffers from all the usual problems associated with rationing. Loan applicants attempt to manipulate the outcome of the rationing process, for instance, it is argued, by bribing CGC officials, splitting large firms into smaller ones in order to qualify, or using token blacks as the front men. In the long run SEDCO and Venture Capital of Zimbabwe serve black entrepreneurs better than highly visible, politically motivated loans.

Another approach that has been tried and should be continued is the credit guarantee program. In this program a special line of credit, or credit guarantee, is earmarked for small projects. The funds are made available to all financial institutions who take care of retailing them according to program guidelines. The funds are allocated in pro rata to the financial institution's past success in reaching small businesses. To make participation in the program attractive for financial institutions, the funds are typically lent to them at a low interest rate and the loans are partially insured by CGC. All financial institutions seem to have responded positively to the program by setting up Small Business Units and emulating some of SEDCO's practices. Recently, however, interest in the program has faltered as many financial institutions feel small borrowers cannot afford the high interest rates currently prevailing in Zimbabwe. Once interest rates return to more reasonable levels, the continuation of this program should help small businesses gain better access to credit and thus benefit small African entrepreneurs. What the program can probably not achieve is the delivery of credit to microenterprises. To do this, alternative credit delivery systems are required. We discussed some of them in the preceding subsection.

23.5 Special Policies for Agricultural Markets

In earlier sections the discussion of policy issues was general. There are besides specific policy interventions that are necessary for agricultural markets to perform better. We discuss them here.

23.5.1 Distance, Isolation, and the Rule of Law

The first problem raised by agricultural markets in Africa is geography. Africa is a very large continent—the contiguous United States alone can fit into the Sahara desert. Distances are enormous. The ultimate purpose of agricultural trade is to reach all parts of the continent to enable rural dwellers to buy and sell their products. Doing so is a formidable logistical undertaking that critically depends on the availability of roads, trucks, fuel, and spare parts. The importance of transport in Africa is commonly accepted among policy makers so there is no need to revisit the issue here.

Distance has other, less commonly recognized implications. One of them is the reach of the law. Villages isolated by distance and high transport costs largely escape formal law and remain ruled by local norms. The existence of laws and courts operating in urban areas does not guarantee that similar legal principles govern rural transactions. The contradiction between formal law and local practices is most visible in patrimonial issues, such as land tenure practices and family law (e.g., Andre and Platteau 1998; Platteau 2000a, b; Fafchamps and Quisumbing 2002a). It also affects markets. The reach of formal law may be broaden in various ways. One original innovation is that of itinerant judges who tour the country side using simple procedures and equipment (Ministère de la Justice 1999).

Contract farming and outgrower schemes illustrate the difficulties of enforcing contracts in rural Africa. With the elimination of state marketing boards across much of Africa, input delivery to farmers has become problematic. One issue is that of credit and insurance for expenditures on fertilizer by small farmers. An institutional solution that has been proposed is to rely on credit by traders. How problematic this solution can be is well illustrated by contract farming schemes. In such schemes farmers typically receive inputs and advice on credit but commit to sell their output. Although there are many issues affecting the success of such schemes (e.g., Glover 1990; Little and Watts 1994; Jaffee and Morton 1995; Porter and Phillips-Howard 1997; Warning and Key 2002), one is particularly relevant to our study of market institutions: contract enforcement.

One difficulty that often plagues contract farming schemes is leakage, that is, sales of output outside the scheme. This difficulty originates in the design of the scheme itself: credit (or subsidy) on inputs is factored in the output price paid by the scheme. If an alternative market exists for the produce, growers have an incentive to sell outside the scheme to avoid repaying the inputs. If this problem cannot be solved, the scheme collapses. This explains why schemes involving produce that has a local market often fail, especially if they are close to an urban market.

A similar problem used to plague marketing boards as well. In many cases the board's monopsony on an agricultural output was used to recover credit on inputs. In such a system it was in the farmers' interest to sell to private traders in order to abscond repayment (Fafchamps 1999b). Countries with a long porous border like Senegal or Ghana suffered massive leakages of peanuts and cocoa, for instance. Contract farming must solve the same problem but with less powerful tools, for it cannot enlists the authority of the state to set up roadblocks to prevent movements of agricultural produce. To the extent that rural communities follow different legal principles, such as sharing norms (Platteau 1996), they are likely to oppose the enforcement of contracts, especially if this entails seizing the growers' land. This inability or unwillingness to enforce contracts on farmers is, in my view, a major hindrance to the development of input markets and interlinked input-output contracts.

Distance and isolation generate other problems. Data from Madagascar, Fafchamps, and Moser (2002) show that crime is highest in isolated and less populated areas. Cattle theft is the dominant problem, with likely spillovers in homicides and rape. As we speculated in this earlier study, the relationship between crime and isolation may be related to conflicts between communities over the control of land and water. Fafchamps and Minten (2002a) further illustrate the importance of crop theft in rural areas. As this work demonstrates, contrary to what is often believed, rural areas need not be safer. The rule of law fails to extend everywhere, an observation that may be related to the widespread prevalence of crime-linked guerilla activity in remote areas of Sierra Leone, Columbia, Burma, Nepal, and the like. If confirmed by further work, the inescapable conclusion is the need for better law enforcement in rural areas to promote markets and market-related activities.

23.5.2 Institutional Support

Empirical work has brought to light other aspects of agricultural markets that can benefit from improvement. Much trade in farm products takes place in market towns. By nature, towns usually have better road connections and transportation facilities than villages, but they suffer from a number of other shortcomings.

Space is a case in point. In many agricultural markets, space is at a premium. This is particularly true in large urban retail markets, which are nearly always congested and unhygienic, with negative repercussions on public health. From an urban planning point of view, allocating more space to food retail may not seem to be a priority as it is the plethora of traders that creates the need for more space. Food retail could potentially be organized with fewer traders and much less space. This view, however, ignores the difficulties of organizing food distribution to thousands of consumers via a large hierarchical organization, whether public or private. The unhappy fate of public efforts at food distribution in Africa serves as a stark reminder of the difficulties involved. This outcome is usually interpreted as an indictment of government intervention. Fafchamps et al. (2002) show that there are no increasing returns in African agricultural trade, thereby suggesting that the nature of the problem may be more with large organizations than with state intervention per se.

Whatever the cause, it remains that space is a constraint to agricultural trade in many African towns. Initial results from the 2001 Madagascar trader survey, for instance, indicates that between 1997 and 2001 many traders lost their business due to relocation and forcible removal of their place of work.

Other institutional issues deserve attention as well. For instance, payment by check is virtually unknown in agricultural trade, even when supplier credit is provided. This stands in sharp contrast to manufacturing where payment by check is the norm whenever invoicing takes place. The reason for the difference probably lies in the very short duration of supplier credit in agricultural trade: 7 days compared to 30 to 60 days in manufacturing. The slow speed with which African banks transfer funds from one account to another probably explains why traders refrain from using banks. A by-product of this state of affairs is that banks do not observe flows of funds and hence cannot use this information to grant overdraft facilities. As of now, agricultural traders receive virtually no bank credit of any kind. Speeding up bank transfers may encourage traders to channel more of their funds through banks, thereby reducing the risk of theft. We expect that in due course this would also increase bank credit to agricultural trade.

Telephones are another burning issue. Empirical work indicates that agricultural traders have access to phones for personal use but make virtually no use of them for business purposes. This is in part a reflection on the lack of trust between traders, but also of the absence of land line telephone services in agricultural markets. Consequently traders constantly have to travel to supply markets, raising transport and search costs. It would be much cheaper if traders could operate over the phone from their offices. The spread of mobile phones may ease this constraint. Time will tell.

Storage is another difficult issue. In Benin the government has encouraged the creation of trader associations in each market town. These associations solve various coordination failure problems, such as common storage and market calendars. Ayouz et al. (2002) provide some evidence that the effect on trader performance is positive. This example could be emulated elsewhere.

Grading and quality control are other important issues where the intervention of the state could help. Currently traders spend a lot of time verifying the quality of the agricultural goods they purchase. This task requires experience and is seldom delegated to junior members of the trading business (e.g., Fafchamps and Minten 1999;

Fafchamps and Minten 2001a; Fafchamps and Gabre-Madhin 2001). As a result it takes much of the trader's time. The need to inspect quality also makes it difficult to trade over the phone.

A commonly accepted set of grades would simplify trade to a large extent. The experience of the United States suggests that the shift to standard grades requires that farmers use common seeds and that handling practices (e.g., drying) be relatively uniform (Cronon 1991). African farmers still plant predominantly land races (or improved varieties mixed or interbred with land races). As a result grade standardization is difficult to implement, given the enormous diversity of seed material and the related differences in taste and quality. As improved seeds are introduced, however, a consistent effort should be made to encourage the adoption of a common grade classification.

A similar effort should be done to standardize weights and measures. The overwhelming majority of agricultural trade takes place using "traditional" measures. These measures vary from one trader to another, generating noisy price signals and necessitating transfers from bag to bag at each transaction. A standardization of measures would undoubtedly reduce noise, discourage dishonest practices (e.g., half-filled bags), and reduce transactions costs (e.g., transfers from bag to bag). For grain, the key to success is shifting from weight-based to volume-based measures: weight-based measures encourage improper drying of grain (or even wetting the grain on purpose) and wet grain tends to rot. Moreover the caloric content of grain basically depends on volume, not weight, since moisture can be added back at the cooking stage. Quality control for export crops is also a critical issue that requires policy attention.

As agricultural markets increase in sophistication, other institutional improvements will become necessary. Price insurance is a good example. Recently a consortium of funding agencies led by the European Union and the World Bank has initiated a program offering price insurance to coffee traders—whether corporate traders or farmer cooperatives. The idea behind this program is to insure traders against a fall in price so that they can more easily announce and commit to a given price level. Although it is still at an early stage of development, this approach may over time facilitate input credit and contract farming.

23.6   Conclusion

The main objective of market institution policy is to facilitate trade. As we have shown here, trade can take place even in the crudest institutional environment. Such trade revolves around long-term personal relationships, around personal exchange. The institutional challenge is to move from personal to impersonal exchange (North 2001).

The classical approach to this challenge is a modernization of the laws and an improvement in the court system (e.g., Cooter 1997; Messick 1999). Several of the suggestions made in the preceding pages go along the same lines, namely small claims court, itinerant judges, laws regarding slander, and the like.

Many of the policy examples given here, however, go well beyond contract law and court. Most have a hybrid nature in that they combine government intervention with private or collective action. Their purpose is not to substitute court enforcement to private screening but rather to facilitate and broaden trade opportunities. They work by strengthening civil society, not replacing it with formal institutions.

This is a significant departure from the standard approach because, as we have clearly demonstrated in this book, laws and courts alone are never sufficient to achieve the transition from personal to impersonal exchange. As Hayek (1945) argued and as we discussed in chapter 2, asymmetric information is an endemic problem that cannot simply be resolved through courts. Screening and monitoring by private agents will always be essential. What market institutions must strive to accomplish is to facilitate screening and monitoring.

Having said this, nearly all the policies advocated here require a change in the law, taken in its broad sense to include regulations, decrees, and administrative action. For instance, a grading system for grain typically requires creating an organization responsible for setting the standard. This organization may be a government agency, a private association, or a hybrid organization. But the concept of standard must be recognized in law for a grading system to be implementable.

How much of a change in law is required will vary from country to country, depending on existing laws and on the capacity of civil society to self-organize. Yet a change in law will nearly always be necessary. In this sense it is correct to state that better market institutions require better laws. But then any government policy is implemented through a change in the law, broadly defined. This is not specific to market institutions. The key about market institutions is that improvements require subtle modifications in the legal environment that help economic agents better perform their market exchange function.

Postscript

As I was putting the final touchs to this volume, I attended a conference organized by Douglas North and the Mercatur Center at George Mason University. The meeting on From Personal to Impersonal Exchange took place in Charlottesville in June 2002. It brought together a small number of individual researchers working on similar issues in the fields of economics, history, anthropology, law, and psychology.

I learned many things from this fascinating mix of people, but the one thing that struck me most was the idea, put forward by Kevin McKabe and Pascal Boyer, that the human brain is fine-tuned for personalized exchange. Socializing and interacting with others is something that, as a species, we are very good at. As a result we have a tendency to experience, and therefore express, many situations as personalized exchange. In contrast, impersonal exchange based on following simple rules, such as paying an invoice on time, does not evoke in the brain quite as much activity and emotional involvement.

This observation led me to notice that individuals often implicitly personalize their interaction with large organizations, as when they say they "trust" Mercedes to produce quality cars. At the meeting, Larry Neal reported on the early development of stock markets in Europe, a form of impersonal exchange par excellence. Interestingly his story had much to do with the actions of a small group of individuals who knew each other well. He also emphasized the importance of the personal relationships early brokers had with their aristocrat and merchant clients. Avner Greif made similar observations in his commentary on the rise and fall of the community responsibility system, pointing out the critical role that a small number of large traders played in the transition, thanks to the personal relationships they entertained with merchants in other cities. In both examples the transition from personal to impersonal exchange involved a small number of individuals who bridged the gap between organizations—cities and stock markets—and other individuals or organizations.

This observation suggests that a transition path from personal to impersonal exchange involves various forms of interface between the two types of exchange, without necessarily eliminating personalized exchange entirely. There are many possible illustrations of this idea. Stock market brokers, for instance, link their clients—many of whom they know personally—to a large organization, the stock market, based on impersonal rules. Marketing agents of large corporations often build personalized relationships with their clients while the relationship with their employer is largely rule based. Many marketing ploys can be seen in the same light, as when firms seek to foster customer loyalty by personalizing brands and products and by favoring an emotional attachment to a trademark. It is as if individuals were easy to trick back into a personalized exchange mode even when it is obvious that the exchange is not.

Perhaps the gap between personal and impersonal exchange is not as wide as one may think. If so, the transition from one to the other may be facilitated. The historical examples cited above further suggest that the transition from one mode to the other can be gradual and need not affect all transactions simultaneously. The transition can be staggered. This is good news for Africa because it means that moving to a higher plane of economic exchange need not be insurmountable.

My earlier observation about bridging individuals suggests one further avenue through which the transition could be implemented. The idea of bridging agents is one that I already put forward in Fafchamps (1994). Applied to Africa, it means that what the continent most need to penetrate export markets is personal links that bridge different regions of the world. Similar views are expressed in Casella and Rauch (1998) and Rauch and Casella (1998). These issues deserve more research.

Bibliography

Abel, A. B. 1985. Inventories, stock-outs and production smoothing. *Review of Economic Studies* 52 (2): 283–93.

Abreu, D. 1988. On the theory of infinitely repeated games with discounting. *Econometrica* 56: 383–96.

Akerlof, G. A. 1985. Discriminatory, status-based wages among tradition-oriented, stochastically trading coconut producers. *J. Political Economy* 93 (2): 265–76.

Akiyama, T., Larson, D., Varangis, P., and Baffes, J. 1999. Market liberalization: Lessons across country and commodity experiences. Mimeo.

Amselle, J.-L. 1977. *Les Négociants de la Savanne*. Editions Anthropos, Paris.

Andre, C., and Platteau, J.-P. 1998. Land relations under unbearable stress: Rwanda caught in the Malthusian trap. *Journal of Economic Behavior and Organization* 34 (1): 1–47.

Aoki, M. 1988. *Information, Incentives and Bargaining in the Japanese Economy*. Cambridge University Press, New York.

Aoki, M., Murdoch, K., and Okuno-Fujiwara, M. 1995. *Beyond the East Asian Miracle: Introducing the Market Enhancing View*. CEPR Publication 442. Stanford University, Stanford.

Armendariz de Aghion, B., and Morduch, J. 2000. Microfinance beyond group lending. *Economics of Transition* 8 (2): 401–20.

Arrow, K. J. 1971. *Essays in the Theory of Risk Bearing*. Markham, Chicago.

Arrow, K. J. 1972. Models of job discrimination. In *Racial Discrimination in Economic Life*, Anthony H. Pascal (ed.). Heath, Lexington, MA.

Arrow, K. J. 1974. *The Limits of Organization*. Norton, New York.

Arrow, K. J., and Hahn, F. 1971. *General Competitive Analysis*. Holden-Day, San Francisco.

Arthur, W. B. 1988. Self-reinforcing mechanisms in economics. In *The Economy as an Evolving Complex System*, P. W. Anderson, K. J. Arrow, and D. Pines (eds.). Addison-Wesley, Redwood City, CA, pp. 9–31.

Arthur, W. B., and Lane, D. A. 1991. Information constriction and information contagion. Mimeo.

Aryeetey, E., and Steel, W. F. 1993. Individual savings collectors in Ghana: Future financial intemediators? Mimeo.

Axelrod, R. 1984. *The Evolution of Cooperation*. Basic Books, New York.

Ayouz, M. K., Fares, M., and Tassou, Z. 2002. Association des commer cants, capital social et compétitivité: Tests économétriques sur les données des commerc cants des produits vivriers du Bénin. Mimeo.

Bade, J., and Chifamba, R. 1994. Transaction costs and institutional environment. *The Manufacturing Sector in Zimbabwe: Dynamics and Constraints*. World Bank, Amsterdam.

Bade, J., and Gunning, J. W. 1994. The Survey: *The Manufacturing Sector in Zimbabwe: Dynamics and Constraints*. World Bank, Amsterdam.

Baer, H. L., and Gray, C. W. 1995. Debt as a control device in transitional economies: The experiences of Hungary and Poland. Policy research working paper 1480. World Bank, Washington, DC.

Bala, V., and Goyal, S. 1998. Learning from neighbors. *Review of Economic Studies* 65 (3): 595–621.

Bala, V., and Goyal, S. 2000. A non-cooperative model of network formation. *Econometrica* 68 (5): 1181–1229.

Banerjee, A., and Munshi, K. 1999. Market imperfections, communities, and the organization of production: An empirical analysis of Tirupur's garment-export network. Mimeo.

Banerjee, A. V., and Duflo, E. 2000. Reputation effects and the limits of contracting: A study of the Indian software industry. *Quarterly Journal of Economics* 115 (3): 989–1017.

Bardhan, P. 1995. Analytics of the institution of informal cooperation in rural development. In *State, Markets and Civil Organizations: New Theories, New Practices, and Their Implications for Rural Development*, A. de Janvry, S. Radwan, E. Sadoulet, and E. Thorbecke (eds.). Macmillan, London.

Barr, A. 2000. Social capital and technical information flows in the Ghanaian manufacturing sector. *Oxford Economic Papers* 52 (3): 539–59.

Barr, A. 2002a. Cooperation and shame. Mimeo.

Barr, A. 2002b. Enterprise performance and the functional diversity of social capital. *Journal of African Economies* 11 (1): 90–113.

Barr, A., and Oduro, A. 2002. Ethnic fractionalization in an African labour market. *Journal of Development Economics* 68 (2): 355–79.

Barrett, C. B. 1997a. Food marketing liberalization and trader entry: Evidence from Madagascar. *World Development* 25 (5): 763–77.

Barrett, C. B. 1997b. Liberalization and food price distributions: ARCH-M evidence from Madagascar. *Food Policy* 22 (2): 155–73.

Basu, K. 1986. One kind of power. *Oxford Economic Papers* 38: 259–82.

Bates, R. H. 1983. *Essays on the Political Economy of Rural Africa*. University of California Press, Berkeley.

Bauer, P. T. 1954. *West African Trade: A Study of Competition, Oligopoly and Monopoly in a Changing Economy*. Cambridge University Press, Cambridge.

Bayart, J.-F. 1989. *L'Etat en Afrique: La Politique du ventre*. Fayard, Paris.

Becker, G. S. 1968. Crime and punishment: An economic approach. *Journal of Political Economy* 76: 169–217.

Becker, G. S. 1971. *The Economics of Discrimination*. University of Chicago Press, Chicago.

Becker, G. S. 1981. *A Treatise on the Family*. Harvard University Press, Cambridge.

Becker, G. S., and Madrigal, V. 1994. The formation of values with habitual behavior. Mimeo.

Becker, G., and Stigler, G. 1974. Law enforcement, malfeasance, and compensation of enforcers. *Journal of Legal Studies* 3 (1): 1–18.

Ben-Porath, Y. 1980. The F-connection: Families, friends, and firms and the organization of exchange. *Population and Development Review* 6 (1): 1–30.

Benson, B. L. 1990. *The Enterprise of Law*. Pacific Research Institute for Public Policy, San Francisco.

Bental, B., and Eden, B. 1993. Inventories in a competitive environment. *Journal of Political Economy* 101 (5): 863–86.

Berg, E. 1989. The Liberalization of Rice Marketing in Madagascar. *World Development* 17 (5): 719–28.

Bernheim, B. D., Peleg, B., and Whinston, M. D. 1987. Coalition-proof Nash equilibria: I. Concepts. *Journal of Economic Theory* 42: 1–12.

Bernstein, L. 1992. Opting out of the legal system: Extralegal contractual relations in the diamond industry. *Journal of Legal Studies* 21: 115–57.

Bernstein, L. 1996. Merchant law in a merchant court: Rethinking the code's search for immanent business norms. *University of Pennsylvania Law Review* 144 (5): 1765–1821.

Besley, T., Coate, S., and Loury, G. 1993. The economics of rotating savings and credit associations. *American Economic Review* 83 (4): 792–810.

Bhagwati, J. N., and Srinivasan, T. N. 1983. *Lectures on International Trade*. MIT Press, Cambridge.

Biggs, N. 1974. *Algebraic Graph Theory*. Cambridge University Press, New York.

Biggs, T., Moody, G., von Leewen, J., and White, E. 1994. Africa can compete! Export opportunities and challenges in garments and home products in the U.S. market. RPED Discussion Paper. World Bank, Washington, DC.

Biggs, T. S. 1991. Heterogenous firms and efficient financial intermediation in Taiwan. In *Markets in Developing Countries: Parallel, Fragmented, and Black*, Michael Roemer and Christine Jones (eds.), ICS Press, San Francisco, pp. 167–97.

Bigsten, A., Collier, P., Dercon, S., Fafchamps, M., Gauthier, B., Gunning, J. W., Isaksson, A., Oduro, A., Oostendorp, R., Patillo, C., Soderbom, M., Teal, F., and Zeufack, A. 2000a. Contract Flexibility and Dispute Resolution in African Manufacturing. *Journal of Development Studies* 36 (4): 1–37.

Bigsten, A., Collier, P., Dercon, S., Fafchamps, M., Gauthier, B., Gunning, J.-W., Isaksson, A., Oduro, A., Oostendorp, R., Patillo, C., Soderbom, M., Teal, F., Zeufack, A., and Appleton, S. 2000b. Rates of return on physical and human capital in Africa's manufacturing sector. *Economic Development and Cultural Change* 48 (4): 801–27.

Bigsten, A., Collier, P., Dercon, S., Fafchamps, M., Gauthier, B., Gunning, J. W., Oduro, A., Oostendorp, R., Patillo, C., Soderbom, M., Teal, F., and Zeufack, A. 2002. Credit constraints in manufacturing enterprises in Africa. Mimeo.

Bigsten, A., Collier, P., Dercon, S., Fafchamps, M., Gauthier, B., Gunning, J. W., Oduro, A., Oostendorp, R., Patillo, C., Soderbom, M., Teal, F., and Zeufack, A. 1999a. Exports of African manufactures: Macro policy and firm behaviour. *Journal of International Trade and Economic Development* 8 (1): 53–71.

Bigsten, A., Collier, P., Dercon, S., Fafchamps, M., Gauthier, B., Gunning, J. W., Oduro, A., Oostendorp, R., Patillo, C., Soderbom, M., Teal, F., and Zeufack, A. 2000. Exports and firm level efficiency in the African manufacturing sector. Mimeo.

Bigsten, A., Collier, P., Dercon, S., Fafchamps, M., Gauthier, B., Gunning, J. W., Oduro, A., Oostendorp, R., Patillo, C., Soderbom, M., Teal, F., and Zeufack, A. 1999b. Rent and risk sharing in African manufacturing. Mimeo.

Bigsten, A., Collier, P., Dercon, S., Gauthier, B., Gunning, J. W., Isaksson, A., Oduro, A., Oostendorp, R., Patillo, C., Soderbom, M., and Teal, F. 1999. Investment in Africa's manufacturing sector: A four country panel data analysis. *Oxford Bulletin of Economics and Statistics* 61 (4): 489–512.

Blanchy, S. 1995. *Karana and Banians: Les Communautés commercantes d'origine Indienne à Madagascar.* L'Harmattan, Paris.

Blinder, A. S. 1982. Inventories and sticky prices: More on the microfoundations of macroeconomics. *American Economic Review* 72 (3): 334–48.

Blinder, A. S. 1986. Can the production smoothing model of inventories be saved? *Quarterly Journal of Economics* 101: 431–53.

Blinder, A. S., and Maccini, L. J. 1991. Taking stock: A critical assessment of recent research on inventories. *Journal of Economic Perspectives* 5 (1): 73–96.

Bolton, P., and Dewatripont, M. 1994. The firm as a communication network. *Quarterly Journal of Economics* 109 (4): 809–39.

Borjas, G. J., and Bronars, S. G. 1989. Consumer discrimination and self-employment. *Journal of Political Economy* 97 (3): 581–605.

Braguinsky, S. 1999. Enforcement of property rights during the Russian transition: Problems and some approaches to a new liberal solution. *Journal of Legal Studies* 28: 515–44.

Braudel, F. 1986. *Civilization and Capitalism.* Harper and Row, New York.

Braverman, A., and Stiglitz, J. 1982. Sharecropping and the interlinking of the agrarian markets. *American Economic Review* 72: 695–715.

Brown, L., and Haddad, L. 1995. *Time Allocation Patterns and Time Burdens: A Gendered Analysis of Seven Countries.* International Food Policy Research Institute, Washington, DC.

Burt, R. S. 1980. Models of network structure. *Annual Review of Sociology* 6: 79–141.

Carroll, C. D. 1992. The buffer-stock theory of saving: Some macroeconomic evidence. *Brookings Papers on Economic Activity* 2: 61–156.

Casella, A., and Rauch, J. 1998. Anonymous market and group ties in international trade. Working paper 132. Russell Sage Foundation, New York.

Chambers, R. E. 1988. *Applied Production Analysis.* Cambridge University Press, New York.

Charny, D. 1990. Nonlegal sanctions in commercial relationships. *Harvard Law Review* 373: 391–446.

Chew, D. C. 1990. Internal adjustments to falling civil service salaries: Insights from Uganda. *World Development* 18 (7): 1003–14.

Coase, R. 1937. The nature of the firm. *Economica* 4: 386–405.

Coate, S., and Loury, G. C. 1993. Will affirmative action policies eliminate negative stereotypes? *American Economic Review* 83 (5): 1220–40.

Coate, S., and Ravallion, M. 1993. Reciprocity without commitment: Characterization and performance of informal insurance arrangements. *Journal of Developmental Economics* 40: 1–24.

Cohen, A. 1969. *Custom and Politics in Urban Africa: A Study of Hausa Migrants in Yoruba Towns.* University of California Press, Berkeley.

Coleman, J. S. 1988. Social capital in the creation of human capital. *American Journal of Sociology* 94 (suppl.): S95–S120.

Collier, P., and Gunning, J. W. 1999. Explaining African economic performance. *Journal of Economic Literature* 37 (1): 64–111.

Cooter, R. D. 1997. The rule of state law and the rule-of-law state: Economic analysis of the legal foundations of development. *Annual World Bank Conference on Developement Economics 1996.* World Bank, Washington, DC, pp. 191–217.

Cooter, R., and Ulen, T. 1988. *Law and Economics.* Scott, Foresman, Glenview, IL.

Cornell, B., and Welch, I. 1996. Culture, information and screening discrimination. *Journal of Political Economy* 104 (3): 542–71.

Cortes, M., Berry, A., and Ishaq, A. 1987. *Success in Small and Medium-Scale Enterprises: The Evidence from Columbia.* World Bank, Washington, DC.

Craswell, R. 1995. When is a willful breach "willful"? General vs. specific deterrence in contract remedies. Mimeo.

Cronon, W. 1991. *Nature's Metropolis.* Norton, New York.

Cuevas, C., Hanson, R., Fafchamps, M., Moll, P., and Srivastava, P. 1993. *Case Studies of Enterprise Finance in Ghana.* RPED. World Bank, Washington, DC.

Cvetkovic, D., Doob, M., and Sachs, H. 1980. *Spectra of Graphs: Theory and Applications.* Academic Press, New York.

Daniels, L. 1994. *Changes in the Small-Scale Enterprise Sector from 1991 to 1993: Results from a Second Nationwide Survey in Zimbabwe.* Gemini technical report 71. Gemini, Bethesda, MD.

Darity, W. A. 1998. Intergroup disparity: Economic theory and social science evidence. *Southern Economic Journal* 64 (4): 806–26.

Darity, W. A., and Mason, P. L. 1998. Evidence on discrimination in employment: Codes of color, codes of gender. *Journal of Economic Perspectives* 12 (2): 63–90.

Datta, S. 1996. *Building Trust.* Discussion paper series TE/96/305. London School of Economics, STICERD, London.

Deaton, A. 1991. Saving and liquidity constraints. *Econometrica* 59 (5): 1221–48.

Dercon, S., and Krishnan, P. 2000. Risk-sharing within households in rural Ethiopia. *Journal of Political Economy* 108 (4): 688–727.

Diamond, D. W., and Dybvig, P. H. 1983. Bank runs, deposit insurance, and liquidity. *Journal of Political Economy* 91 (3): 401–19.

Donohue, J. J. 1998. Discrimination in employment. *The New Palgrave Dictionary of Economics and the Law*, Vol. 1. Macmillan Reference, London, pp. 615–23.

Dore, R. 1987. *Taking Japan Seriously: A Confucian Perspective on Leading Economic Issues.* Stanford University Press, Stanford.

Dorosh, P., and Bernier, R. 1994. Staggered reforms and limited success: Structural adjustment in Madagascar. In *Adjusting to Policy Failure in African Economies*, David Sahn (ed.). Cornell University Press, Ithaca, pp. 332–65.

Dun and Bradstreet. 1970. *Handbook of Credit and Collection*. Dun and Bradstreet Credit Services, New York.

Durlauf, S., and Fafchamps, M. 2002. Empirical studies of social capital: A critical survey. Mimeo.

Eaton, J., and Gersovitz, M. 1981. Debt with potential repudiation: Theoretical and empirical analysis. *Review Economic Studies* 48: 289–309.

Eaton, J., Gersovitz, M., and Stiglitz, J. E. 1986. The pure theory of country risk. *European Economic Review* 30: 481–513.

Eddy, E. 1979. *Labor and Land Use on Mixed Farms in the Pastoral Zone of Niger*. Livestock Production and Marketing in the Entente States of West Africa, Monograph 3. University of Michigan, Ann Arbor.

Eggertsson, T. 1990. *Economic Behavior and Institutions*. Cambridge University Press, Cambridge.

Eichenbaum, M. 1989. Some empirical evidence on the production level and production cost smoothing models of inventory investment. *American Economic Review* 79 (4): 853–64

Ellickson, R. 1991. *Order without Law: How Neighbors Settle Disputes*. Harvard University Press, Cambridge.

Ellison, G. 1994. Cooperation in the Prisoner's Dilemma with anonymous random matching. *Review of Economic Studies* 61: 567–88.

Emery, G. W. 1984. A pure financial explanation for trade credit. *Journal of Financial and Quantitative Analysis* 19 (3): 271–85.

Ensminger, J. 1992. *Making a Market: The Institutional Transformation of an African Society*. Cambridge University Press, New York.

Fafchamps, M. 1992. Solidarity networks in pre-industrial societies: Rational peasants with a moral economy. *Economic Development and Cultural Change* 41 (1): 147–74.

Fafchamps, M. 1994. Industrial structure and microenterprises in Africa. *Journal of Developing Areas* 29 (1): 1–30.

Fafchamps, M. 1996. The enforcement of commercial contracts in Ghana. *World Development* 24 (3): 427–48.

Fafchamps, M. 1997a. Introduction: Markets in sub-Saharan Africa. *World Development* 25 (5): 733–34.

Fafchamps, M. 1997b. Mobile capital, location externalities, and industrialization. *Journal of Comparative Economics* 25: 345–65.

Fafchamps, M. 1997c. Trade credit in Zimbabwean manufacturing. *World Development* 25 (3): 795–815.

Fafchamps, M. 1999a. Risk sharing and quasi-credit. *Journal of International Trade and Economic Development* 8 (3): 257–78.

Fafchamps, M. 1999b. *Rural Poverty, Risk, and Development*. Economic and Social Development paper 144. FAO, Rome.

Fafchamps, M. 2000. Ethnicity and credit in African manufacturing. *Journal of Development Economics* 61 (1): 205–35.

Fafchamps, M. 2001. Intrahousehold Access to Land and Sources of Inefficiency: Theory and Concepts. In *Access to Land, Rural Poverty, and Public Action*, Alain de Janvry, Gustavo Gordillo, Jean-Philippe Platteau, and Elisabeth Sadoulet (eds.). Oxford University Press, Oxford.

Fafchamps, M. 2002a. Ethnicity and networks in African trade. Mimeo.

Fafchamps, M. 2002b. Spontaneous market emergence. In *Topics in Theoretical Economics*, vol. 2 (1), art. 2, Berkeley Electronic Press at *www.bepress.com*.

Fafchamps, M., Biggs, T., Conning, J., and Srivastava, P. 1994. *Enterprise Finance in Kenya*. World Bank, Washington, DC.

Fafchamps, M., and Gabre-Madhin, E. 2001. Agricultural markets in Benin and Malawi: Operation and performance of traders. Working paper. DECRG, World Bank, Washington, DC.

Fafchamps, M., Gabre-Madhin, E., and Minten, B. 2002. Increasing returns and market efficiency in agricultural trade. Mimeo.

Fafchamps, M., and Gubert, F. 2002. Contingent loan repayment in the philippines. Mimeo.

Fafchamps, M., Gunning, J. W., and Oostendorp, R. 2000. Inventory and Risk in African Manufacturing. *Economic Journal* 110 (466): 861–93.

Fafchamps, M., and Lund, S. 2003. Risk sharing networks in rural Philippines. *Journal of Development Economics*, forthcoming.

Fafchamps, M., and Minten, B. 1999. Relationships and traders in Madagascar. *Journal of Development Studies* 35 (6): 1–35.

Fafchamps, M., and Minten, B. 2001a. Property rights in a flea market economy. *Economic Development and Cultural Change* 49 (2): 229–68.

Fafchamps, M., and Minten, B. 2001b. Social capital and agricultural trade. *American Journal of Agricultural Economics* 83 (3): 680–85.

Fafchamps, M., and Minten, B. 2002a. Crime and poverty: Evidence from a natural experiment. Mimeo.

Fafchamps, M., and Minten, B. 2002b. Returns to social network capital among traders. *Oxford Economic Papers* 54: 173–206.

Fafchamps, M., and Minten, B. 2002c. Social capital and the firm: Evidence from agricultural trade. In *The Role of Social Capital in Development: An Empirical Assessment*, Christiaan Grootaert and Thierry van Bastelaer (eds.). Cambridge University Press, Cambridge.

Fafchamps, M., and Moser, C. 2002. Crime, isolation, and the rule of law. Mimeo.

Fafchamps, M., and Oostendorp, R. 2002. Investment. In *Industrial Change in Africa: Zimbabwean Firms under Structural Adjustment*, Jan Willem Gunning and Remco Oostendorp (eds.). Palgrave, New York.

Fafchamps, M., Pender, J., and Robinson, E. 1995. *Enterprise Finance in Zimbabwe*. World Bank, Washington, DC.

Fafchamps, M., and Quisumbing, A. 2002a. Control and ownership of assets within rural ethiopian households. *Journal of Development Studies* 38 (2): 47–82.

Fafchamps, M., and Quisumbing, A. R. 2003. Social roles, human capital, and the intrahousehold division of labor: Evidence from Pakistan. *Oxford Economic Papers* 55 (1): 36–80.

Fafchamps, M., and Soderbom, M. 2002. Wages and Worker Supervision in African Manufacturing. Mimeo.

Ferris, S. J. 1981. A transaction theory of trade credit use. *Journal of Political Economy* 96 (2): 243–70.

Fisman, R. 2001. Trade credit and productive efficiency in developing economies. *World Development* 29 (2): 311–21.

Fisman, R. 2002. Ethnic ties and the provision of credit: Relationship-level evidence from African firms. Mimeo.

Foster, A. D., and Rosenzweig, M. R. 1993. Information, learning, and wage rates in low-income rural areas. *Journal of Human Resources* 28 (4): 759–90.

Foster, A. D., and Rosenzweig, M. R. 1994. A test for moral hazard in the labor market: Contractual arrangements, effort, and health. *Review of Economics and Statistics* 76 (2): 213–27.

Foulds, L. R. 1992. *Graph Theory Applications*. Springer-Verlag, New York.

Free University of Amsterdam. 1995. *Regional Program on Enterprise Development: Report on Round III (1995) of the Zimbabwe Survey*. Economic and Social Institute, Free University of Amsterdam, Amsterdam.

Friedman, J. W. 1990. *Game Theory with Applications to Economics*. Oxford University Press, Oxford.

Fudenberg, D., and Maskin, E. 1986. The folk theorem in repeated games with discounting or with incomplete information. *Econometrica* 54: 533–54.

Fudenberg, D., and Tirole, J. 1991. *Game Theory*. MIT Press, Cambridge.

Fukuyama, F. 1995. *Trust: The Social Virtues and the Creation of Prosperity*. Free Press, New York.

Gabre-Madhin, E. 1997. Grain markets in Ethiopia. Mimeo.

Gale, D., and Hellwig, M. 1985. Incentive-compatible debt contracts: The one-period problem. *Review of Economic Studies* 52: 647–63.

Gambetta, D. 1988. *Trust: Making and Breaking Cooperative Relations*. Basil Blackwell, New York.

Gambetta, D. 1993. *The Sicilian Mafia: The Business of Private Protection*. Harvard University Press, Cambridge.

Geertz, C. 1963. *Peddlers and Princes: Social Change and Economic Modernization in Two IndonesIndonesian Towns*. University of Chicago Press, Chicago.

Geertz, C., Geertz, H., and Rosen, L. 1979. *Meaning and Order in Moroccan Society*. Cambridge University Press, Cambridge.

Genicot, G. 2002. Bonded labor and serfdom: A paradox of voluntary choice. *Journal of Development Economics* 67 (1): 101–27.

Ghatak, M. 2000. Screening by the company you keep: Joint liability lending and the peer selection effect. *Economic Journal* 110 (465): 601–31.

Ghatak, M., and Guinnane, T. W. 1999. The economics of lending with joint liability: Theory and practice. *Journal of Development Economics* 60 (1): 195–228.

Ghosh, P., and Ray, D. 1996. Cooperation in community interaction without information flows. *Review of Economic Studies* 63: 491–519.

Glover, D. 1990. Contract farming and outgrower schemes in East and Southern Africa. *Journal of Agricultural Economics* 41 (3): 303–15.

Gluckman, M. 1955. *Custom and Conflict in Africa*. Basil Blackwell, Oxford.

Goyal, S., and Vega-Redondo, F. 2000. *Learning, Network Formation and Coordination*. Econometric Institute, Erasmus University, Rotterdam.

Grandmont, J.-M. 1988. Nonlinear difference equations, bifurcations and chaos: An introduction. Discussion paper 8811. CEPREMAP, Paris.

Granovetter, M. 1985. Economic action and social structure: The problem of embeddedness. *American Journal of Sociology* 91 (3): 481–510.

Granovetter, M. 1995a. The economic sociology of firms and entrepreneurs. In *The Economic Sociology of Immigration: Essays on Networks, Ethnicity, and Entrepreneurship*, Alejandro Portes (ed.). Russell Sage Foundation, New York, pp. 128–65.

Granovetter, M. S. 1995b. *Getting a Job: A Study of Contacts and Carreers*, 2nd edition. University of Chicago Press, Chicago.

Greif, A. 1993. Contract enforceability and economic institutions in early trade: The Maghribi traders' coalition. *American Economic Review* 83 (3): 525–48.

Greif, A. 1994. Cultural beliefs and the organization of society: A historical and theoretical reflection on collectivist and individualist societies. *Journal of Political Economy* 102 (5): 912–50.

Greif, A. 2000. The fundamental problem of exchange: A research agenda in historical institutional analysis. *European Review of Economic History* 4 (3): 251–84.

Greif, A. 2001. Impersonal exchange and the origin of markets: From the community responsibility system to individual legal responsibility in pre-modern Europe. In *Communities and Markets in Economic Development*, Masahiko Aoki and Yujiro Hayami (eds.). Oxford University Press, Oxford, pp. 1–41.

Grossman, H. I., and Van Huyck, J. B. 1988. Sovereign debt as a contingent claim: Excusable default, repudiation, and reputation. *American Economic Review* 78 (5): 1088–97.

Guckenheimer, J., and Holmes, P. 1983. *Nonlinear Oscillations, Dynamical Systems, and Bifurcations of Vector Fields.* Springer-Verlag, New York.

Gunning, J. W., and Mumbengegwi, C. 1995. *The Manufacturing Sector in Zimbabwe: Industrial Change under Structural Adjustment.* Free University of Amsterdam and University of Zimbabwe, Amsterdam.

Haddad, L., Hoddinott, J., and Alderman, H. 1997. *Intrahousehold Resource Allocation in Developing Countries: Models, Methods, and Policy.* Johns Hopkins University Press, Baltimore.

Haddad, L., and Kanbur, R. 1990. How serious is the neglect of intra-household inequality? *Economic Journal* 100: 866–81.

Haggett, P., and Chorley, R. J. 1969. *Network Analysis in Geography.* St. Martin's Press, New York.

Hart, K. 1988. Kinship, contract, and trust: The economic organization of migrants in an African city slum. In *Trust: Making and Breaking Cooperative Relations,* D. Gambetta (ed.). Basil Blackwell, New York.

Hart, O. 1995. *Firms, Contracts, and Financial Structure.* Clarendon Press, Oxford.

Hart, O., and Holmstrom, B. 1987. The Theory of Contracts. In *Advances in Economic Theory,* Truman F. Bewley (ed.). Cambridge University Press, Cambridge.

Hayami, Y. 1996. Peasant in economic modernization. *American Journal of Agricultural Economics* 5: 1157–67.

Hayami, Y., and Kikuchi, M. 1981. *Asian Village Economy at the Crossroads: An Economic Approach to Institutional Change.* University of Tokyo Press, Tokyo, and Johns Hopkins University Press, Baltimore.

Hayami, Y., and Ruttan, V. 1985. *Agricultural Development: An International Perspective,* rev. edition. John Hopkins University Press, Baltimore.

Hayek, F. A. 1945. The Use of Knowledge in Society. *American Economic Review* 35 (4): 519–30.

Heckman, J. J. 1998. Detecting discrimination. *Journal of Economic Perspectives* 12 (2): 101–16.

Hendley, K. 1999. Beyond the tip of the iceberg: Business disputes in Russia. Mimeo.

Hendley, K., Murrell, P., and Ryterman, R. 1998. Law, relationships, and private enforcement: Transactional strategies of Russian enterprises. Mimeo.

Hildenbrand, W. 1974. *Core and Equilibria of a Large Economy.* Princeton University Press, Princeton.

Himbara, D. 1994. The failed Africanization of commerce and industry in Kenya. *World Development* 22 (3): 469–82.

Hirschman, A. O. 1958. *The Strategy of Economic Development.* Yale University Press, New Haven.

Holmstrom, B., and Milgrom, P. 1990. Regulating trade among agents. *Journal of Institutional and Theoretical Economics* 146: 85–105.

Holt, C. C., Modigliani, F., Muth, J. F., and Simon, H. 1960. *Planning Production, Inventories, and the Work Force.* Prentice Hall, Englewood Cliffs, NJ.

Hoogeveen, H., and Tekere, M. 1994. *Entrepreneurship: Who Is a Successful Entrepreneur?* Zimbabwe. World Bank, Amsterdam.

Hopkins, A. G. 1973. *An Economic History of West Africa.* Longman Group, London.

Horner, J. 2002. Reputation and competition. *American Economic Review* 92 (3): 644–63.

IFPRI. 1998. Une Analyse descriptive du marché des intrants et des produits agricoles et du comportement des ménages ruraux à Madagascar. Special Report 2, Submitted to USAID/Madagascar. Ministère de la Recherche Scientifique de Madagascar and International Food Policy Research Institute, Washington, DC.

Itoh, H. 1991. Incentives to help in multi-agent situations. *Econometrica* 59 (3): 611–36.

Jaffee, S., and Morton, J. 1995. *Marketing Africa's High-Value Foods: Comparative Experiences of an Emergent Private Sector.* Kendall-Hunt, Dubuque, IA.

Jerome, A., and Ogunkola, O. 1999. Characteristics and behaviour of African commodity/product markets and market institutions and their consequences for economic growth. Mimeo.

Johnson, S., McMillan, J., and Woodruff, C. 2000. Entrepreneurs and the ordering of institutional reform: Poland, Slovakia, Romania, Russia and Ukraine Compared. *Economics of Transition* 8 (1): 1–36.

Johnson, S., McMillan, J., and Woodruff, C. 2002. Courts and relational contracts. *Journal of Law, Economics, and Organization* 18 (1): 221–77.

Jones, W. O. 1959. *Manioc in Africa*. Stanford University Press, Stanford.

Jones, W. O. 1972. *Marketing Staple Food Crops in Tropical Africa*. Cornell University Press, Ithaca.

Kahn, J. A. 1987. Inventories and the volatility of production. *American Economic Review* 77 (4): 667–79.

Kali, R. 1999. Endogenous business networks. *Journal of Law and Economic Organization* 15 (3): 615–36.

Kandori, M. 1992. Social norms and community enforcement. *Review of Economic Studies* 59: 63–80.

Kimball, M. S. 1988. Farmers' cooperatives as behavior toward risk. *American Economic Review* 78 (1): 224–32.

Kletzer, K. M. 1984. Asymmetries of information and LDC borrowing with sovereign risk. *Economic Journal* 94: 287–307.

Knobe, D. 1990. *Political Networks: The Structural Perspective*. Cambridge University Press, Cambridge.

Kocherlakota, N. R. 1996. Implications of efficient risk sharing without commitment. *Review of Economic Studies* 63 (4): 595–609.

Krane, S. D. 1994. The distinction between inventory holding and stockout costs: Implications for target inventories, asymmetric adjustment, and the effect of aggregation on production smoothing. *International Economic Review* 35 (1): 117–36.

Kranton, R. E. 1996a. The formation of cooperative relationships. *Journal of Law, Economics, and Organizations* 12 (1): 214–33.

Kranton, R. E. 1996b. Reciprocal exchange: A self-sustaining system. *American Economic Review* 86 (4): 830–51.

Kranton, R. E., and Minehart, D. F. 2000a. Networks versus vertical integration. *RAND Journal of Economics* 31 (3): 570–601.

Kranton, R., and Minehart, D. 2000b. Competition for goods in buyer-seller networks. *Review of Economic Design* 5 (3): 301–31.

Kranton, R., and Minehart, D. 2001. A theory of buyer-seller networks. *American Economic Review* 91 (3): 485–508.

Kreps, D. M. 1990. *A Course in Microeconomic Theory*. Princeton University Press, Princeton.

Kreps, D. M., and Fudenberg, D. 1993. Learning mixed equilibria. *Games and Economic Behavior* 5 (3): 320–67.

Kreps, D., Milgrom, P., Roberts, J., and Wilson, R. 1982. Rational cooperation in the finitely repeated Prisoner's Dilemma. *Journal of Economic Theory* 27: 245–52.

Krueger, A. O. 1974. The political economy of the rent-seeking society. *American Economic Review* 64 (3): 291–303.

Krugman, P. R. 1990. *Rethinking International Trade*. MIT Press, Cambridge.

La Ferrara, E. 1997. Ethnicity and reciprocity: An analysis of credit transactions in Ghana. Mimeo.

La Lettre de l'Ocean Indien. 31/07/1999. Le Prix des Juges. In *La Lettre de l'Ocean Indien*, vol. 868, Indigo Publications, Paris. Publication on the Web: *http://www.africaintelligence.Fr/unes/p_une_LOI.asp*.

Laffont, J.-J., and N'Guessan, T. 2000. Group lending with adverse selection. *European Economic Review* 44 (4–6): 773–84.

Laffont, J., and Tirole, J. 1988. The dynamics of incentive contracts. *Econometrica* 56 (5): 1153–75.

Landa, J. 1994. *Trust, Ethnicity, and Identity: Beyond the New Institutional Economics of Ethnic Trading Networks, Contract Law, and Gift-Exchange.* University of Michigan Press, Ann Arbor.

Lang, W. W., and Nakamura, L. I. 1990. The dynamics of credit markets in a model with learning. *Journal of Monetary Economics* 26: 305–18.

Laumann, E., and Pappi, F. U. 1976. *Networks of Collective Action: A Perspective on Community Influence Systems.* Academic Press, New York.

Liedholm, C., and Mead, D. C. 1999. *Small Enterprises and Economic Development: The Dynamics of Small and Micro Enterprises.* Routledge, London.

Ligon, E., Thomas, J. P., and Worrall, T. 2001. Informal insurance arrangements in village economies. *Review of Economic Studies* 69 (1): 209–44.

Little, I., Mazumdar, D., and Page, J. M. 1987. *Small Manufacturing Enterprises: A Comparative Study of India and Other Economies.* World Bank and Oxford University Press, New York.

Little, P. D., and Watts, M. J. 1994. *Living under Contract: Contract Farming and Agrarian Transformation in sub-Saharan Africa.* University of Wisconsin Press, Madison.

Lonely Planet. 1994. *Madagascar and Comoros.* Lonely Planet Puliblications, New York.

Lorenz, E. H. 1988. Neither friends nor strangers: Informal networks of subcontracting in French industry. In *Trust: Making and Breaking Cooperative Relations*, D. Gambetta (ed.). Basil Blackwell, New York.

Loury, G. C. 1998. Discrimination in the post–civil rights era: Beyond market interactions. *Journal of Economic Perspectives* 12 (2): 117–26.

Loury, G. C. 2002. *The Anatomy of Racial Inequality.* Harvard University Press, Cambridge.

Macharia, K. 1988. Social networks: Ethnicity and the informal sector in Nairobi. Working paper 463. Institute for Development Studies, University of Nairobi, Nairobi.

Marris, P. 1971. African businessmen in a dual economy. *Journal of Industrial Economics* 19: 231–45.

McCormick, D. 1999. African enterprise clusters and industrialization: Theory and reality. *World Development* 27 (9): 1531–51.

McCormick, D., Kinyanjui, M. N., and Ongile, G. 1997. Growth and barriers to growth among Nairobi's small and medium-sized garment producers. *World Development* 25 (7): 1095–1110.

McKinnon, R. I. 1973. *Money and Capital in Economic Development.* Brookings Institution, Washington, DC.

McMillan, J. 1996. Markets in transition. In *Advances in Economics and Econometrics: Theory and Applications*, David M. Kreps and Kenneth Wallis (eds.). Cambridge University Press, Cambridge.

McMillan, J., and Naughton, B. 1996. *Reforming Asian Socialism: The Growth of Market Institutions.* University of Michigan Press, Ann Arbor.

McMillan, J., and Woodruff, C. 1999a. Dispute prevention without courts in Vietnam. *Journal of Law, Economics, and Organization* 15 (3): 637–58.

McMillan, J., and Woodruff, C. 1999b. Interfirm relationships and informal credit in Vietnam. *Quarterly Journal of Economics* 114 (4): 1285–1320.

McMillan, J., and Woodruff, C. 2000. Private order under dysfunctional public order. *Michigan Law Review* 98 (8): 2421–58.

McMillan, J., and Woodruff, C. 2001. Entrepreneurs in Economic Reform. Working paper 102. Center for Research on Economic Development and Policy Reform, Stanford University, Stanford.

Meillassoux, C. 1971. *The Development of Indigenous Trade and Markets in West Africa.* Oxford University Press, Oxford.

Merryman, J. 1977. Comparative Law and Social Change: On the Origins, Style, Decline and Revival of the Law and Development Movement. *American Journal of Comparative Law* 25: 457–83.

Messick, R. E. 1999. Judicial reform and economic development: A survey of the issues. *World Bank Research Observer* 14 (1): 117–36.

Milgrom, P., and Oster, S. 1987. Job discrimination, market forces, and the invisibility hypothesis. *Quarterly Journal of Economics* 102 (3): 453–76.

Milgrom, P. R., North, D. C., and Weingast, B. 1991. The role of institutions in the revival of trade: The law merchant, private judges, and the Champagne fairs. *Economics and Politics* 2 (19): 1–23.

Ministère de la Justice. 1999. *Justice selon les justiciables: Une enquête auprès des usagers du système judiciaire.* (Justice according to citizens: A survey among users of the judicial system). Gouvernement de Madagascar, Antananarivo.

Minten, B. 1995. Price transmission and transaction cost in a liberalized food marketing system: The case of Zaire. PhD dissertation. Department of Agricultural Economics, Cornell University, Ithaca.

Minten, B., and Kyle, S. 1999. The effect of distance and road quality on food collection, marketing margins, and traders' wages: Evidence from the former Zaire. *Journal of Development Economics* 60: 467–95.

Minten, B., Randrianarisoa, C., and Zeller, M. 1998. Niveau, evolution, et facteurs déterminants du riz à Madagascar. *Cahier de la Recherche sur les Politiques Alimentaires 8.* IFPRI-FOFIFA, Antananarivo.

Mitchell, J. C. 1969. *Social Networks in Urban Situations: Analyses of Personal Relationships in Central African Towns.* Manchester University Press, Manchester.

Montgomery, J. D. 1991. Social networks and labor-market outcomes: Toward an economic analysis. *American Economic Review* 81 (5): 1408–18.

Morduch, J. 1999. The microfinance promise. *Journal of Economic Literature* 37 (4): 1569–1614.

Morris, M. L., and Newman, M. D. 1989. Official and parallel cereals markets in Senegal: Empirical evidence. *World Development* 17 (12): 1895–1906.

Mumbengegwi, C. 1994. Indigenous and small scale enterprises. In *The Manufacturing Sector in Zimbabwe: Dynamics and Constraints.* World Bank, Amsterdam.

Murphy, K. M., Shleifer, A., and Vishny, R. W. 1991. The allocation of talent: Implications for growth. *Quarterly Journal of Economics* 106: 503–30.

Myrdal, G. 1957. *Economic Theory and Under-developed Regions.* Gerald Duckworth, London.

Nadiri, M. I. 1969. The determinants of trade credit in the U.S. total manufacturing sector. *Econometrica* 37 (3): 408–23.

Narayan, D., and Pritchett, L. 1999. Cents and sociability: Household income and social capital in rural Tanzania. *Economic Development and Cultural Change* 47 (4): 871–97.

Neal, D. A., and Johnson, W. R. 1996. The role of premarket factors in black-white wage differences. *Journal of Political Economy* 104 (5): 869–95.

North, D. 2001. Comments. In *Communities and Markets in Economic Development*, Masahiko Aoki and Yujiro Hayami (eds.). Oxford University Press, Oxford, pp. 403–408.

North, D. C. 1973. *The Rise of the Western World.* Cambridge University Press, Cambridge.

North, D. C. 1990. *Institutions, Institutional Change, and Economic Performance.* Cambridge University Press, Cambridge.

Nurkse, R. 1953. *Problems of Capital Formation in Underdeveloped Countries.* Oxford University Press, New York.

Onyango, I. A., and Tomecko, J. 1995. Formulating a national policy for small enterprises: The Kenyan experience. In *Agents of Change: Studies on the Policy Environment for Small Enterprises in Africa*, Philip English and Georges Henault (eds.). International Development Research Centre, Ottawa, pp. 25–44.

Platteau, J.-P. 1991. Traditional Systems of Social Security and Hunger Insurance: Past Achievements and Modern Challenges. In *Social Security in Developing Countries*, E. Ahmad, J. Dreze, J. Hills, and A. Sen (eds.). Clarendon Press, Oxford.

Platteau, J.-P. 1994a. Behind the market stage where real societies exist: Part I—The role of public and private order institutions. *Journal of Development Studies* 30 (3): 533–77.

Platteau, J.-P. 1994b. Behind the market stage where real societies exist: Part II—The role of moral norms. *Journal of Development Studies* 30 (4): 753–815.

Platteau, J.-P. 1995. An Indian model of aristocratic patronage. *Oxford Economic Papers* 47 (4): 636–62.

Platteau, J.-P. 1996. Traditional sharing norms as an obstacle to economic growth in tribal societies. Cahiers 173. CRED, Facultés Universitaires Note-Dame de la Paix, Namur, Belgium.

Platteau, J.-P. 2000a. Allocating and enforcing property rights in land: Informal versus formal mechanisms in Subsaharan Africa. *Nordic Journal of Political Economy* 26 (1): 55–81.

Platteau, J.-P., and Baland, J.-M. 2001. Impartible inheritance versus equal division: A comparative perspective centered on Europe and sub-Saharan Africa. In *Access to Land, Rural Poverty, and Public Action*, Alain de Janvry, Gustavo Gordills, Jean-Philippe Platteau, and Elisabeth Sadoulet (eds.). Oxford University Press, Oxford, pp. 27–67.

Platteau, J.-P., and Abraham, A. 1987. An inquiry into quasi-credit contracts: The role of reciprocal credit and interlinked deals in small-scale fishing communities. *Journal of Developmental Studies* 23 (4): 461–90.

Poewe, K. 1989. *Religion, Kinship, and Economy in Luapula, Zambia*. Edwin Mellen Press, Lewinston, ME.

Porter, G., and Phillips-Howard, K. 1997. Comparing contracts: An evaluation of contract farming schemes in Africa. *World Development* 25 (2): 227–38.

Posner, E. A. 1996. The regulation of groups: The influence of legal and nonlegal sanctions on collective action. *University of Chicago Law Review* 63: 133–97.

Posner, R. A. 1980. A theory of primitive society, with special reference to law. *Journal of Law and Economics* 23: 1–53.

Posner, R. A. 1998. Creating a legal framework for economic development. *World Bank Research Observer* 13 (1): 1–11.

Putnam, R. D., Leonardi, R., and Nanetti, R. Y. 1993. *Making Democracy Work: Civic Institutions in Modern Italy*. Princeton University Press, Princeton.

Radner, R. 1985. Repeated principal-agent games with discounting. *Econometrica* 53: 1173–98.

Ramey, G., and Watson, J. 1999. Conditioning institutions and renegotiation. Discussion paper 1225. Yales Cowles Foundation New Haven.

Ramey, V. A. 1991. Nonconvex costs and the behavior of inventories. *Journal of Political Economy* 99 (2): 306–34.

Rasmusen, E. 1996. Stigma and Self-Fulfilling Expectations of Criminality. *Journal of Law and Economics* 39 (2): 519–43.

Raturi, M., and Swamy, A. V. 1999. Explaining ethnic differentials in credit market outcomes in Zimbabwe. *Economic Development and Cultural Change* 47 (3): 585–604.

Raub, W., and Weesie, J. 1990. Reputation and efficiency in social interactions: An example of network effects. *American Journal of Sociology* 96 (3): 626–54.

Rauch, J. E., and Casella, A. 1998. Overcoming Informational Barriers to International Resource Allocation: Prices and Group Ties. Discussion paper 1978. Center for Economic Policy Research, London.

Rauch, J. E., and Watson, J. 1999. Starting small in an unfamiliar environment. Working paper 7053. NBER, Cambridge, MA.

Reserve Bank of Zimbabwe 1993. *Quarterly Economic and Statistical Review* 14 (3).

Risseeuw, P. 1994. Firm growth in Zimbabwe 1981–1993. *The Manufacturing Sector in Zimbabwe: Dynamics and Constraints*. World Bank, Amsterdam.

Rodriguez-Clare, A. 1996a. The Division of Labor and Economic Development. *Journal of Development Economics* 49: 3–32.

Rodriguez-Clare, A. 1996b. Multinationals, linkages, and economic development. *American Economic Review* 86 (4): 852–73.

Romer, P. M. 1986. Increasing returns and long-run growth. *Journal of Political Economy* 94 (5): 1002–37.

Root, H. 1993. *Environment for Investment in Madagascar: Institutional Reform for Market Economy.* Country report 11. Center for Institutional Reform and the Informal Sector, University of Maryland, College Park.

Rosenstein-Rodan, P. 1943. Problems of industrialization in Eastern and South-Eastern Europe. *Economic Journal* 53: 202–11.

Rubinstein, A. 1987. A sequential strategic theory of bargaining. *Advances in Economic Theory, Fifth World Congress, Econometric Society*, Truman F. Bewley (ed.). Oxford University Press, Oxford.

Sahlins, M. 1972. *Stone Age Economics.* Aldine-Atherton, Chicago.

Saloner, G. 1985. Old boy networks as screening mechanisms. *Journal of Labor Economics* 3 (3): 255–67.

Schwartz, R. A. 1974. An economic model of trade credit. *Journal of Financial and Quantitative Analysis* 9 (3): 643–57.

Schwartz, R., and Whitcomb, D. 1979. The trade credit decision. *Handbook of Financial Economics*, J. Bicksler (ed.). North-Holland, Amsterdam.

Shapiro, C., and Stiglitz, J. E. 1984. Equilibrium unemployment as a worker discipline device. *American Economic Review* 74 (3): 433–44.

Shillington, K. 1989. *History of Africa.* St. Martin's Press, New York.

Singh, N. 1989. Theories of Sharecropping. *The Economic Theory of Agrarian Institutions*, P. Bardhan (ed.). Clarendon Press, Oxford.

Smith, A. 1975. *The Wealth of Nations.* Modern Library, New York.

Spagnolo, G. 1999. Social relations and cooperation in organizations. *Journal of Economic Behavior and Organization* 38 (1): 1–25.

Spring, A., and McDade, B. E. 1998. *African Entrepreneurship: Theory and Reality.* University Press of Florida, Gainesville.

Staatz, J. M. 1979. *The Economics of Cattle and Meat Marketing in the Ivory Coast.* Livestock Production and Marketing in the Entente States of West Africa. University of Michigan, Ann Arbor.

Staatz, J. M., Dione, J., and Dembele, N. N. 1989. Cereals market liberalization in Mali. *World Development* 17 (5): 703–18.

Staley, E., and Morse, R. 1965. *Modern Small Industry for Developing Countries.* McGraw-Hill, New York.

Steel, W. F., and Webster, L. M. 1991. *Small Enterprises under Adjustment in Ghana.* Technical paper 138. World Bank, Washington, DC.

Stiglitz, J. E. 1974. Incentives and risk sharing in sharecropping. *Review of Economic Studies* 41 (2): 219–55.

Stiglitz, J. E., and Weiss, A. 1981. Credit rationing in markets with imperfect information. *American Economic Review* 71 (3): 393–410.

Stone, A., Levy, B., and Paredes, R. 1992. Public Institutions and Private Transactions: The Legal and Regulatory Environment for Business Transactions in Brazil and Chile. Policy research working paper 891. World Bank, Washington, DC.

Swinkels, J. 1992. Evolutionary stability with equilibrium entrants. *Journal of Economic Theory* 57 (2): 306–32.

Tadelis, S. 1999. What's in a name? Reputation as a tradable asset. *American Economic Review* 89 (3): 548–63.

Taylor, C. R. 2000. The old-boy network and the young-gun effect. *International Economic Review* 41 (4): 871–91.

Temperley, H. N. 1981. *Graph Theory and Applications*. Ellis Horwood, Chichester.

Tinkler, K. J. 1972a. Bounded planar networks: A theory of radial structures. *Geographical Analysis* 4 (1): 5–33.

Tinkler, K. J. 1972b. The physical interpretation of eigen-functions of dichotomous matrices. *Transactions of the Institute of British Geographers* 55: 17–46.

Tinkler, K. J. 1977. *An Introduction to Graph Theoretical Methods in Geography*. Concepts and Techniques in Modern Geography 14. Institute of British Geographers. Geo Abstract Ltd., University of East Anglia, Norwich.

Townsend, R. M. 1979. Optimal contracts and competitive markets with costly state verification. *Journal of Economic Theory* 21: 265–93.

Tsiang, S. C. 1969. The precautionary demand for money: An inventory theoretical analysis. *Journal of Political Economy* 77 (1): 99–117.

Udry, C. 1990. Credit markets in northern Nigeria: Credit as insurance in a rural economy. *World Bank Economic Review* 4 (3): 251–69.

Udry, C. 1994. Risk and insurance in a rural credit market: An empirical investigation in northern Nigeria. *Review of Economic Studies* 61 (3): 495–526.

van Damme, E. 1987. *Stability and Perfection of Nash Equilibria*. Springer-Verlag, Berlin.

Velenchik, A. D. 1995. Apprenticeship contracts, small enterprises, and credit market in Ghana. *World Bank Economic Review* 9 (3): 451–75.

Warning, M., and Key, N. 2002. The social performance and distributional consequences of contract farming: An equilibrium analysis of the Arachide de Bouche Program in Senegal. *World Development* 30 (2): 255–63.

Watson, J. 1999. Starting small and renegotiation. *Journal of Economic Theory* 85 (1): 52–90.

Williamson, O. E. 1975. *Markets and Hierarchies: Analysis and Antitrust Implications*. Free Press/ Macmillan, New York.

Williamson, O. E. 1985. *The Economic Institutions of Capitalism*. Free Press/Macmillan, New York.

Winn, J. K. 1994. Relational practices and the marginalization of law: Informal financial practices of small businesses in Taiwan. *Law and Society Review* 28 (2): 193–230.

World Bank. 1981. *Accelerated Development in sub-Saharan Africa: An Agenda for Action*. World Bank, Washington, DC (also known as the Berg report).

World Bank. 1995. Madagascar: New horizons—Building a strategy for private sector, export-led growth: A private sector assessment. Report 14385-MAG. World Bank, Washington DC.

World Bank. 1999. Madagascar: Overview of the coffee sector. Mimeo.

Yinger, J. 1998. Evidence on discrimination in consumer markets. *Journal of Economic Perspectives* 12 (2): 23–40.

Young, A. 1991. Learning by doing and the dynamic effects of international trade. *Quarterly Journal of Economics* 106 (2): 369–405.

Zame, W. R. 1993. Efficiency and the role of default when security markets are incomplete. *American Economic Review* 83 (5): 1142–64.

Zeldes, S. P. 1989. Optimal consumption with stochastic income: Deviations from certainty equivalence. *Quarterly Journal of Economics* 104 (2): 275–98.

Index

Accra, Malian traders in, 308
Admissible coalition, 280
Adverse selection, 31n
  and contracting, 31–32
  in equity markets, 423
  from information asymmetries, 14
Affirmative action, for Zimbabwe, 477–78
Africa. *See also individual countries*
  business shocks in, 34 (*see also* Shocks)
  food products trade in, 313
  gift exchange in, 8–9
  indigenous business class encouraged in, 369
  institutional arrangements and transaction costs
    in, 3–4
  and institutional innovations, 463
  and Islam, 32
    in Benin, 325
    and business culture, 296
    in East Africa, 325, 332, 402
    and Muslim brotherhoods, 200n, 296
  legal institutions in, 30 (*see also* Legal
    institutions)
  long distances in, 479
  manufacturing in (close-knit), 348
  and market, 4
  and movement from personal to impersonal
    exchange, 486
African businessmen and women, 444
African-headed firms. *See also* Ethnicity and
    ethnic groups
  in Cameroon, 444
  in case study samples, 44
  and cash-flow concerns, 433
  and contract enforcement, 90, 92, 93, 97, 101,
    103, 104, 106, 107, 108
    and complaints of deficient quality, 92
    and conflict resolution method, 102
    and suppliers, 94, 98
  in Côte d'Ivoire, 444
  and credit, 184–85
  and information sharing (Kenya), 463
  institutions for, 476–78
  among manufacturers, 41
  microenterprises of (Kenya and Zimbabwe), 45
  in RPED samples, 40
  as smaller, 368
  and socialization, 252
  and statistical discrimination, 347
  in Zimbabwe, 258
African manufacturers. *See* Manufacturers
African markets. *See* Market(s) in Africa
Agricultural markets (food sector)
  delivery and quality problems in, 90
  special policies for, 478–82

Agricultural traders (Malawi, Benin, and
    Madagascar)
  and information sharing, 255–56, 259, 399
  and network capital, 313, 315–26
  religion, ethnicity and gender as factors in trust
    among, 397–402 (*see also* under Trust)
  and social networks, 442
Agricultural trader surveys, 45–47, 51, 111–12
  legal institutions and deterrence in, 121, 123,
    126–33
  and personal relationships (Madagascar), 187–88,
    189, 199–200
  emergency financial assistance from, 202
  information sharing from, 191–92
  regularity of supply and demand from, 192–94,
    199
  risk sharing in, 198–99
  and trade credit, 194, 195, 197–98
  training and start-up support from, 188, 190
  and relocations (Madagascar), 481
  and theft or breach of contract, 111, 112–17,
    118–21, 122, 124–26, 128, 134, 135
Allocation
  and graph of economy, 280
  mechanisms for
    barter, 168
    gift exchange, 5–6, 7, 9, 168, 454
    hierarchy (command and control), 5, 7–8, 9, 20,
      284, 454
    hybrid, 8n
    market exchange, 5, 6–7, 9–12, 454 (*see also* at
      Market)
    perfect competitive allocation (PCA), 268–70,
      272
    and core of complete economies, 278
    and graph theory, 271–72
    power to influence, 273
Allocation in Africa, markets in, 4, 5, 444, 454
Alternative contract enforcement institutions, 30
Ancient patterns of trade, 226
  across ethnic boundaries, 297
Anonymous markets or exchange, 245–46, 441
  and legal institutions, 38
Antananarivo, Pakistan businessmen in, 308
Aoki, Masa, xvi
Arbitration, 85n
  in case study surveys, 67, 73
  as Ghana recommendation, 461
  in manufacturing panel surveys, 85, 86
Asian traders or entrepreneurs, 299, 362
  in case study samples, 44, 45
  in Kenya
    and agriculture, 304
    and business networks, 307–308